More praise for *Ticket to the Opera*

"[Goulding] deploys an arsenal of definitions alongside useful biographical sketches of leading singers, and dreams up offbeat features such as a summary of criminal-law findings related to the deaths that occur in thirty well-known operas. . . . In his introduction, he says *Ticket to the Opera* is 'for the opera Unwashed . . . or the minimally Washed,' but a lot of squeaky-clean experts are probably wishing they had done something as fine."

—*The Washington Post*

"[*Ticket to the Opera*] will make it easier for those seeking operatic knowledge to not only understand it better, but offer the best performances for those interested in the best the genre has to offer. Featuring capsule reviews and story plots and even a bit of history about each operatic work, Goulding weaves a wonderful narrative throughout. . . . His humor is dry, his research extensive, and he keeps the read light enough to entice even the most jaded neophyte to risk being busted by his/her rock-and-roll buddies while scouring the bargain bin for Mozart's *Don Giovanni*."

—*Music Monthly*

For Brent, Joshua, Elizabeth, Adam, Jeremy,
Katherine, and Megan
And for the children and grandchildren of Bob Goulding

ALSO BY PHIL G. GOULDING

CLASSICAL MUSIC:
The 50 Greatest Composers
and Their 1,000 Greatest Works

CONFIRM OR DENY

Ticket to the Opera

DISCOVERING AND EXPLORING
100 FAMOUS WORKS,
HISTORY, LORE, AND SINGERS,
WITH RECOMMENDED RECORDINGS

Phil G. Goulding

FAWCETT BOOKS
THE BALLANTINE PUBLISHING GROUP
NEW YORK

A Fawcett Book
Published by The Ballantine Publishing Group

Copyright © 1996 by Phil G. Goulding

All rights reserved under International and Pan-American Copyright Conventions. Published in the United States by The Ballantine Publishing Group, a division of Random House, Inc., New York, and simultaneously in Canada by Random House of Canada Limited, Toronto.

Fawcett is a registered trademark and the Fawcett colophon is a trademark of Random House, Inc.

http://www. randomhouse.com/BB/

Grateful acknowledgment is made to the following for permission to reprint previously published material:

Bantam Books: Excerpts from *Beverly: An Autobiography* by Beverly Sills Lawrence Linderman. Copyright © 1987 by Beverly Sills. Reprinted by permission of Bantam Books, a division of Random House, Inc.

Columbia University Press: Excerpts from *A Short History of the Opera*, 3rd edition, by Donald Jay Grout. Copyright © 1988 by Columbia University Press. Republished with permission of Columbia University Press, 562 W. 113th St., New York, NY 10025. Reproduced by permission of the publisher via Copyright Clearance Center, Inc.

Robert B. Ewen: Excerpt from *Music for the Millions* by David Ewen. Reprinted by written permission of Robert B. Ewen.

Henry Holt and Company, Inc.: Excerpts from *20th Century Composers* by H. H. Stuckenschmidt. Reprinted by permission of the publisher.

Alfred A. Knopf, Inc.: Excerpt from *A Short History of Music* by Albert Einstein, translated by Eric Blom, Marianne Brooke, Richard Capell, Beryl de Zoete. Translation copyright © 1937 and renewed 1965 by Alfred A. Knopf, Inc. Copyright © 1938 by Alfred A. Knopf, Inc., and renewed 1966 by Rhoda Hellman. Reprinted by permission of the publisher.

W.W. Norton & Company, Inc.: Excerpts from *The Lives of the Great Composers*, revised edition by Harold C. Schonberg. Copyright © 1981, 1970 by Harold C. Schonberg. Excerpts from *The Experience of Opera: An Informal Introduction to Operative History and Literature* by Paul Henry Lang. Copyright © 1971 by W. W. Norton & Company, Inc. Reprinted by permission of W. W. Norton & Company, Inc.

Viking Penguin and Georges Borchardt, Inc.: Excerpt from *The Viking Opera Guide* by Amanda Holden, with Stephen Walsh and Nicholas Kenyon. Copyright © 1993 by Amanda Holden. Reprinted by permission of Viking Penguin, a division of Penguin Books USA Inc., and Georges Borchardt, Inc.

The Virgil Thomson Foundation, Ltd.: Excerpts from the writings of Virgil Thomson in the *New York Herald Tribune, New York Review of Books,* and *Modern Music.* Reprinted by permission of the Virgil Thomson Foundation, Ltd., copyright owner.

Library of Congress Catalog Card Number: 99-90446

ISBN: 0-449-00566-6

Cover illustration by John Stephens
Text design by Holly Johnson

Manufactured in the United States of America

First Hardcover Edition: November 1996
First Trade Paperback Edition: September 1999

10 9 8 7 6 5 4 3 2 1

mation by mail, fax, and an 800 number. Videos are available for nearly all of the eighty-five central operas in the book, and in some cases there are several to choose from.

Outside the music world, I'm indebted primarily to my two closest lifetime friends. One is the late Bob Goulding, who decided at age five that his kid brother could do anything, and in his awesome love persisted in that preposterous, flawed belief for seventy more years. The second is my wife, Miriam, attorney and coauthor, who strengthens my writing adventures with love and understanding. Without her strong counsel, writing skills, analytical help, and total backing, I wouldn't consider these retirement ventures into new worlds.

Dick Fryklund, friend for forty years, edited much of the manuscript as a representative of the wholly Unwashed, while Honey and Bob Hager worked with us as surrogates of amateur season ticket holders. Four attorneys joined me in a game of returning 1990s indictments for long-ago opera homicides and other crimes: my fine brother-in-law Paul Bower and his friend Roger Diamond of Los Angeles, former prosecutor Joseph Ryan of Chateaugay, NY, and my friend Joe Russo of Washington, D.C.

Everyone over seventy, and some fortunate younger folk, know that those we love are what life is about. I am blessed with my own five children and their spouses, my seven grandchildren, and my brother's brood, whom I regard as my own. Several cheerleaders are among them, and all are tolerant of my late-in-life preoccupation with music, even if bemused both by my choice of a field so foreign to my experience and my ineptitude at the computer.

This book was suggested and commissioned by Joëlle Delbourgo, former editor-in-chief of Ballantine Hardcovers. In midstream she moved upward to new challenges, and I have missed her dreadfully. I want to thank the first of my two editors at Ballantine, the skilled, resourceful, intelligent, and cooperative Lesley Malin Helm, who also edited my book on classical music. Lesley also left Ballantine for a new career when this book was half finished. Her replacement has done a remarkable job of managing it to completion, and I would like to name her, but she believes it is inappropriate and unprofessional for editors to be acknowledged, so I will honor that strange position and not comment on her dedication and important contribution.

If she chooses to remain anonymous, others welcome the spotlight, and I must keep a solemn commitment to three whom I promised to acknowledge by name. They are our furry four-footed children who shared writing space with me: a bearded collie called Angus, and his two sibling 100-pound Bernese mountain dogs, the lovely late Grindel and her successor, who, at-her-will, responds to Holly. By their presence, they have supported and encouraged my writing projects, which keep us home together to spoil one another, a good thing for us all.

Unquestionably I have sometimes unwittingly misinterpreted expert counsel. The fault for inaccuracies and blemished findings is mine alone. If you wish to voice harsh objections, please knock before encountering Holly.

INTRODUCTION

Τhis book is for the opera Unwashed . . . or the minimally Washed.

The Unwashed may never have seen an opera live, or even on television. The minimally Washed may go to the opera occasionally and/or may own a few recorded excerpts. Basically, however, Unwashed and minimally Washed are amateurs, novices, neophytes, beginners. They're people who feel equally uncomfortable with opera as with the sport of cricket.

Yes, that's the best analogy. This book is primarily for those in the United States who know little more about opera than they do about cricket.

Leopold Mozart, father of Wolfgang Amadeus, would have understood my approach. Son Wolfgang was opera's greatest spontaneous genius, who made music when George Washington was president. While he was working in Vienna in the late 1700s, Leopold sent him this written counsel:

"I advise you when composing to consider not only the musical, but also the unmusical public. You must remember that for every ten real connoisseurs there are a hundred ignoramuses. So do not neglect the so-called popular style."

Leopold recognized what every big city ward leader knows: There are more amateurs out there than there are experts. Certainly I'm not inclined to characterize readers of this book as "ignoramuses," but in writing it I've tried to follow the thrust of the senior Mozart's advice.

Superstar Beverly Sills once wrote that opera was not only for hothouse plants. Easy for her to say, but, in fact, she was right on target. My objective is to bring opera closer to more people, and my main message is that anyone can become modestly washed in opera in a reasonably short period of time. Nothing is scary about it. With radio, television, and today's recording technology, it doesn't even have to cost very much. Opera is sitting out there for everyone. In many cities, there is even smaller-scale live opera in theaters and auditoriums that are not formal opera houses.

Sadly—in part because of high ticket prices in the major houses, rich patrons, highbrow critics, wealthy board members, and indifferent public relations—opera in this country has an elitist history. The regrettable truth is that here in the mid-1990s it still intimidates or bores a lot of people.

The happy reality is that it shouldn't. Opera is theater, designed to entertain. It is about magic, mystery, mayhem, mistresses, and murder. And, above all, about love. In Europe, pasta-eating and sausage-munching lowbrows who drink cheap wine and cheaper beer have enjoyed it for centuries.

So can millions of Americans today, whether they're into Chablis, Brie, and the new-rage coffee bars or into hot dogs, a Budweiser, and a stop at the Dairy Queen.

Much of opera combines superb spectacle with marvelous tunes. Someone has said it is better than a circus because it can include a circus. It is drama and melodrama, sparked by passion, sex, sentiment, and suspense and heightened by lovely music. Unfortunately, a few well-meaning experts talk about "demystifying" opera, a psychological turnoff from the start for the Unwashed. Professional football is a whole lot more complex and harder to understand than opera, and no one expounds about "demystifying" it.

Common sense shows several advantages of opera over straight drama, for the Washed or the Unwashed. Song is more compelling than mere speech. Vocal duets, trios, and quartets offer an incomparable way of communicating different emotions simultaneously, impossible to achieve in a spoken play. Background orchestral music, as every moviegoer knows, intensifies dramatic color for comedy or tragedy.

Sure it's different from straight drama, concert, or Stephen Sondheim's latest hit Broadway musical—but, if you can speak the language, not all that different.

Don't be put off by these nice folk who declare that opera is a "sublime life-enriching art form whose poetry transcends mere narrative." Maybe so, but I prefer a sunset for life enrichment. Better yet, a third dog. Forget about art form. Think of opera as something that's entertainment, that's fun.

How to tell the Washed from the Unwashed? Several quick tests can help you distinguish them.

1. The Washed historically have opposed translations in lights above the opera stage or printed at the bottom of the television screen. They have argued that these encourage the audiences to pay less attention to the singers, action, and drama.

The Unwashed, neither fluent in foreign languages nor familiar with opera plots, find these on-the-spot translations enormously valuable.

"Just listen," the Washed say. "You don't need to know the words. You can hear the expression of love."

Yeah, right. That's okay for music alone, if you're in front of the fire with a lover listening to a tape, but it doesn't do much for the drama.

2. The Washed say: "No Norma seems able to encompass all aspects of the role, although Callas comes closest—closer than Sutherland, Caballé, Verrett, Bumbry, Scotto, and Olivia Stapp."

The Unwashed probably know a Norma but may not identify *Norma* as an opera by a fellow named Vincenzo Bellini. They almost certainly have heard of Maria Callas, in part because Jackie Kennedy later married Callas's boyfriend, Aristotle Onassis. And maybe they recognize Joan Sutherland as a great singer, but quite likely they consider Verrett, Bumbry, and Stapp to be a law firm in Beverly Hills.

3. The Washed write that "Sills 'made' the Tudor trilogy." The Unwashed, not ignorant and doubtless aware that the Tudors once ruled England, picture the trilogy as three London houses in a row with stucco and dark brown wood—not as three operas in which Beverly Sills played English queens.

The Washed include all professionals who have to do with opera—from critics to composers and conductors, from singers to scenery movers and set designers, from management to musicologists and musicians. The Washed also include academicians, lecturers, authors, a lot of experts heard on classical radio, and countless true opera buffs out in the civilian world.

The Washed would score an A on the following quiz, and the Unwashed would do poorly. But here's a promise to the Unwashed: After reading the book, you'll be able to answer at least ten of the seventeen questions without referring back to the text. That won't make you a professional, but it will impress your dinner guests.

BEFORE AND AFTER TEST

1. What French opera is the partial counterpart of Richard Wagner's German *Ring*?

2. Who or what is a *Cav-Pag*?

3. How many operas, if any, did Ludwig van Beethoven write?

4. How many operas, if any, did Johann Sebastian Bach write?

5. What German-born opera composer is buried in London's Westminster Abbey?

6. Who are the three major bel canto opera composers?

7. Which American opera is the best known overseas?

8. Name five other American operas and/or opera composers.

9. Who or what is a Bayreuth?

10. Give two classic examples of a trouser role.

11. When Richard Strauss was a little boy, why did he dislike Richard Wagner?

12. Why is French *opéra comique* sometimes pure tragedy?

13. What is the opera connection of the famous astronomer Galileo?

14. What do these three men have in common: Lorenzo da Ponte, Arrigo Boito, and Hugo von Hoffmannsthal?

15. Name one opera by Claudio Monteverdi.

16. Who is the Spectacle King of opera?

17. Which composers and operas are more oriented toward the orchestra than the voice? Which use the plot chiefly as a backdrop for the singers?

If you can answer most of these already, return the book and ask for a refund. You're excessively Washed, you can comprehend opera reviews in *The New Yorker* and *The New York Times*, and you own (or aspire to own) a condominium on New York's Upper East Side or a house in Old Greenwich, Connecticut.

AMATEUR AUTHOR

I'm a nonmusician who, eleven years ago at age sixty-four, was a musical know-nothing. Then, chiefly as a self-education project, I spent seven years researching, interviewing professionals, and writing a book on classical music. Published in late 1992, it is entitled *Classical Music: The 50 Greatest Composers and Their 1,000 Greatest Works*. I wanted to call it *Classical Music for Dummies Like Me*, but Ballantine wouldn't do it. That book worked pretty well, and the publishers asked me to do the same thing on opera. This one has been nearly four years in the making.

I'm now retired, but my career was wholly unrelated to music, as a Washington journalist covering politics, presidents, and the Pentagon; assistant secretary of defense; author of a book on the Pentagon, the press, and the public; and executive with the American Petroleum Institute. Today, I'm a sometime judge of the Rooster Crowing Contest at the annual Franklin County Fair in New York's upstate Adirondacks.

Oh, and a soda jerk, grill cook, and Cleveland taxi driver before college graduation and World War II naval service. Nothing in this nontechnical operatic road map will be over the head of any other taxi driver, including those in Washington who tried to surrender to their fares during the Gulf War.

Since several composers in my classical music book wrote operas, when this project began I was opera-neutral and blandly bathed. But I remain an amateur, a onetime journalist looking in from the outside and here reporting my findings back to other amateurs.

INSIDE THE BOOK

The first step is to narrow the field.

More than 25,000 opera scores are in the Library of Congress. A thousand or more operas are produced internationally with reasonable regularity. That's far more than any nonconnoisseur can handle. This book reduces the number of players and the size of the playing field, in part by identifying great operas and herding them into three separate groups:

The Collection
The Twentieth-century European Package
American Opera

The Collection

The guts of the book is The Collection, which consists of eighty-five operas that have dominated the seasons of major opera houses in the United States and abroad. Most of them have been eclipsing their competition for scores of years, some for hundreds of years. They are listed from one to eighty-five, in order of popularity. Giuseppe Verdi's *Aida* and Wolfgang Amadeus Mozart's *Marriage of Figaro* are examples. To highlight the most popular and successful, I've called the first twenty-five the "Warhorses."

Toward the end of The Collection are works that were the smash hits of their day and now are performed much less often, but neither they nor their music has totally disappeared. The Three Tenors might be singing one of their arias on television one day, a workshop producing the complete work on another. Ambroise Thomas's *Mignon* and Friedrich von Flotow's *Martha* are examples.

The Collection also includes a small cluster of Golden Oldies written centuries ago by the founding fathers of opera. Claudio Monteverdi's *Orfeo* and George Frideric Handel's *Julius Caesar* are examples. No American operas and only a few twentieth-century operas are in The Collection.

The Twentieth-century European Package

Beyond The Collection, the book explores a group of some thirty additional European operas, all from the twentieth century.

Some of these endure actively but haven't been staged frequently enough to qualify for the flagship Collection, some have earned great critical acclaim but haven't won the hearts of operagoers, and some have achieved their greatest success relatively recently. An example of the first type is Erich Wolfgang Korngold's *Die Tote Stadt*, an example of the second is Arnold Schoenberg's *Moses und Aron*, and an example of a fast-rising star is Francis Poulenc's *Dialogues des Carmélites*.

American Opera

Finally, the American operas. Opera is alive and well in the United States, some of it engaging, some intriguing, some passionate, and some powerful. Some of these operas are everyone's favorites, some are popular with the public and downgraded by the Establishment, some are praised by the critics and bypassed by the public. And some live on a borderline between conventional opera and forms unique to the American twentieth century. George Gershwin's magnificent *Porgy and Bess* is one example, Philip Glass's *Einstein on the Beach* another, and Stephen Sondheim's *Sweeney Todd* a third.

No reader is going to pursue all the operas discussed here, but at least the quantity is reasonably manageable. Opera the public loves best—the twenty-five Warhorses and most others in The Collection—begins with Mozart and ends with Giacomo Puccini, who died in 1924. It includes magnificent melodrama from Giuseppe Verdi, passionate drama from Richard Wagner, and lyric French opera like Léo Delibes's *Lakmé*, a work that is delicate, charming, and graceful.

It's not a sin to be delicate, charming, and graceful. Delicate, charming, and graceful is not as dramatic as murder of mother and stepfather, but it's a joy to see and hear. The important point is that there's opera here for any interest.

NO TECHNICAL OR EXPERT DOUBLE-TALK

Do not look here for technical expertise. This is a guidebook, one in which you'll not find a comment such as the following, stolen from a fine music book written for a different audience by a close friend of mine: "In one piece, in the course of 32 measures, through a series of subtle modulations, the key changes from D to G." Or this: "This composition has been cast in the key of E flat with a time signature of $^3/_4$ utilizing a three-part form."

This book is for those who wouldn't recognize a subtle modulation if it came to dinner escorting the statue of the Commendatore. (If the Commendatore in *Don Giovanni* is not now familiar, he will be if you stick with us.)

Professionals enjoy talking about how opera is a hybrid, a mishmash of different arts and skills. Patently true. Some experts then add that it is, therefore, exceedingly difficult to comprehend and/or enjoy.

Balderdash. It doesn't take a degree in musical composition or a graduate course in tragic drama to comprehend and find pleasure in opera. No musical or theatrical background is required. A review in front of me of the Metropolitan Opera's 1995–96 season opener advises that the tenor's voice is harsh and surprisingly unimpressive in a particular aria and that the soprano in this production has proved that her rich, empathetic voice is just right for her character's baffled protestations of innocence. That's nice, and doubtless accurate, but you don't need to worry about it right now.

Ignore all who would intimidate you because you don't know enough. You know a lot of things they don't know.

The connoisseurs tell us we should look for unity of all the elements, for variety of contrasting characters, and for truth in human nature.

No, not yet. Maybe later. This year let's not concern ourselves about unified elements. Let's just get a little more familiar with the composers, with their best-known operas, with some of the humor, romance, and drama in those operas, and with some of that wonderful music.

HOW MUCH WORK?

The question most asked by the Unwashed is this: Do I have to work to really get into opera?

No . . . and yes.

No, if you mean opera music. Yes, although not all that hard, if you mean opera proper. There's a big difference.

Opera isn't just a concert. It's a drama, a play. And it's not a play *with* music but a play *in* music.

If the drama isn't *in* music, it's not opera. If you sprinkle a few great songs through a dramatic version of William Shakespeare's *Hamlet*, you might have a wonderful play coupled with beautiful music, but you don't have an opera. If you turn Shakespeare's *Othello* into a full drama-in-music as Giuseppe Verdi did, the music itself defining the characters, the music providing the dramatic essence, now you have opera.

If you just want to enjoy glorious opera music, you don't have to study anything, you don't have to read a libretto (text), you don't need to know a sotto voce from a soubrette, and you don't have to care about differences between a Verdi and a Wagner. Just listen to some assorted songs over a beer in the rec room, a cup of herb tea in the living room, or on your car tape deck. It doesn't have to be a big deal. You never need to see a live opera. You don't need a tuxedo, or $120 for a ticket, or those little pearly binoculars my great-aunt Maude had.

Given radio, television, audiocassettes, and compact discs, VCRs, and tape decks, and the CD-Rom computer things my grandchildren understand, today's opera resources are unequaled in history. Fortunately, almost from the first days of sound recordings, the great singing stars have been anxious to leave a recorded legacy of their voices on cylinder or disc. Modern technology has made all but the very earliest of these recordings delightfully listenable. In the late 1940s came the LP format, which was followed by stereo sound, when most of the Warhorses were recorded again.

NEVER ON SKIS

In the record stores you can choose among assorted opera arias, or highlights from an individual opera, or a complete opera CD set.

Beginners at a ski resort are herded to a sign reading NEVER ON SKIS. My recommendation for people NEVER INTO OPERA is to start with assorted arias.

On my desk are several compact-disc examples, plucked from the shelves of a local record store. One features Plácido Domingo and other opera stars presenting *The World's Best-Loved Opera*, with arias from several Warhorses. Another has Monserrat Caballé singing the best-known Puccini arias, a third stars Kiri Te Kanawa and Luciano Pavarotti offering *Great Italian Love Arias*, and a fourth offers twelve choruses from five Wagner operas.

Each CD is about an hour long. In a few days, with the expenditure of maybe thirty dollars for three CDs (or less for cassette tapes) the most Unwashed beginner can begin to become familiar with opera music. Just sample a few of these hit tunes from Collection operas:

The Elixir of Love—"Una furtiva lagrima"
Aida—"Celeste Aida"
Pagliacci—"Vesti la giubba"
Rigoletto—"La donna è mobile" and "Caro nome"
Tosca—"Vissi d'arte" and "Recondita armonia"
La Bohème—"Che gelida manina" and "Mi chiamano Mimi"
Madama Butterfly—"Un bel dì, vedremo"
Faust—the "Jewel Song"
Orfeo ed Euridice—"Che farò senza Euridice"
Carmen—the "Toreador Song" and the "Flower Song"
Tristan und Isolde—the "Liebestod"
La traviata—"Ah! fors' è lui . . . and Sempre libera"

Other highlight arias are cited in the book for each Collection opera. One hundred standard hits are singled out in chapter nine. They're all available in the record stores or by mail order. Many will sound familiar, even for the totally Unwashed. After only a few weeks of listening you'll be saying to yourself, "That's 'Donna Whatsis' from *Rigoletto*." I hope that will give you a warm and fuzzy feeling.

If you never go beyond twenty or thirty hit opera tunes, you're way ahead. There's no need to press on. Just drink in the beautiful music at your leisure. Life will be more fun with Plácido Domingo than without him.

BITING THE BULLET

Now, if you *do* want to make the move from opera music to opera proper, you need to get more specific and start thinking a little. After trial and error, the route I chose was to pick a single opera and buy a CD recording of highlights from it alone. I'd recommend any Warhorse because the tunes might be more familiar.

Some CDs supply English texts of the individual arias, and your local public library is apt to have several books with titles like *The Great Operas of Mozart* or *A Treasury of Opera Librettos*. It doesn't take long to match the music with the text, which opens the door into opera itself.

The obvious next leap is to a complete opera. What worked better for me than listening to a CD set was to watch and hear a videotape with English subtitles, sometimes supplemented by a full text, bought for a few dollars or borrowed from the library. Although the range of available operas on videotape is nowhere near as wide as it is for CDs, it's getting there. Almost every Collection opera is available on video. In addition to record stores, there are fine mail-order businesses.

Some purist connoisseurs argue that the video does too much for viewers, that it hampers them from using their imaginations and makes it harder for them to hear and appreciate the inherent drama in the music. Viewers obviously must accept the director's idea of what is important at any one time and submit themselves to his sense of timing, which may not be that of the conductor or the composer. Furthermore, it's difficult to relate each individual detail to the larger picture when the camera rarely shows the larger picture.

Although those are valid criticisms, don't let anyone shame you out of opera on videotape. Every opera has a drama in it (even if sometimes a weak one), and that drama comes across in the video. You'll see real people, loving, quarreling, joking, and killing. You'll be drawn into their lives and feelings before you can say "Days of Our Lives." And—in the good operas—you'll often find that their feelings are surprisingly like your own. (If you stick to Wolfgang Amadeus Mozart, you'll almost always find that their feelings are surprisingly like your own, which is part of his genius.)

Once you're familiar with the drama, you'll be listening for clues about the people, their actions, and the emotions that impel them to do what they do. It's exciting to recognize what has brought on this storm-cloud music, this passionate scene, or this orchestral suspense.

Not all videotapes have English subtitles. My recommendation is to look for those that do. At some sacrifice in quality, you can also record the videotape sound on an audiocassette and listen to the full work on a long car trip or while stuck in commuting traffic.

Meanwhile, keep open your radio ears and television eyes. Without spending a penny, in most parts of the country you can tune in Saturday afternoons during the opera season for the Texaco broadcasts of the Metropolitan. In many areas there are other radio possibilities during the year—broadcasts of the Lyric Opera of Chicago, as just one example, or weekly programs such as Peter Fox Smith's excellent "Saturday Afternoon at the Opera" on Vermont Public Radio. His expert commentary is infectious.

If you have a tape deck, you can buy blank cassette tapes for a couple of dollars each and record radio broadcasts, doing an entire opera season for under one hundred dollars. Now you have opera at home and in your car. More important, you also have your Saturday afternoons free to rake leaves or watch Michigan play Ohio State.

One way to listen is with a text in hand, but I don't consider that essential.

IN THE OPERA HOUSE

What about live opera? Sure, anytime. If money is an issue, buy the cheapest seats you can. If you live near Prague in the Czech Republic, the upper balcony is, perhaps, $3.50, American money. Unfortunately, the opera house nearest you runs a little higher, although nearly all companies in the United States charge much less than the Metropolitan in New York. But, hey, it costs fifty dollars to take the family to the movies, with popcorn. Nothing equals the live experience.

In a good-sized city, there's a lot of opera in addition to the main event downtown—and at a cheaper price. In 1995, for example, my wife and I saw a production of Mozart's *Don Giovanni* at Mount Vernon College in Washington, D.C., staged by an organization called "the In Series." It was performed in English, in modern dress, with an orchestra of a string quintet, keyboard, and mandolin. There was no chorus. Don Giovanni's valet was changed to an accountant who devoured junk food. In a famous aria that summarizes the sexual conquests of the hero, a long printout from a laptop computer came down from the balcony. At twenty dollars a ticket, on an arena-type stage in the college chapel, it was superb entertainment.

Along the way, you're apt to find fascinating variety. There's a major difference between a production of opera and, say, a great classical movie. The movie is the same every time. But whether you see an opera onstage, watch it on a new videotape, enjoy a new film of it, or hear a new compact disc, you always get a particular interpretation. This is one reason why the reasonably Washed come back year after year to see the same Warhorse operas over and over again.

Different singers obviously make a big difference. Most have a distinct personality, which comes across in the sound and color of their voices. Some go for clarity of diction, others for purity of the vocal line, still others for the inherent drama in everything they sing. Some sing the music relatively straight; others play around with the rhythms, almost like a jazz performer.

Then there's the personality of the conductor—the King, the Emperor, the Grand Pooh-Bah. The great conductors place their indelible stamp on a performance. The same opera, even sung by many of the same singers, can sound entirely different in the hands of two different conductors.

Another key figure is the stage director, the man or woman in charge of everything except the music. Occasionally, this is a bigger fish even than the conductor. (Opera people talk of "Zeffirelli's *Bohème*," a reference to Franco Zeffirelli, famous Italian producer and designer.) He or she is in charge of interpreting the opera dramatically, discussing the concept with the singers, and leading them into the way they fill their characters.

Those who do not now know him soon will meet Count Almaviva in Mozart's *Marriage of Figaro*. The stage director can influence the singer to play him in a dozen ways, ranging from stupid buffoon to arrogant cad to lonely weakling, and the portrayal can make the opera a farce, a lightweight comedy, or a balanced masterpiece of human relationships.

The conductor wants dramatic input also, and, in case of conflict with the stage director, he usually gets the last word—in part because he's more apt to have a bigger name and in part because he's still got the baton during the performance, long after the director has packed his bags and gone home.

In my own exploration, I picked up scads of interesting tricks of the trade that I've tried to share with other nonexperts. For example, in Mozart's day court music, such as a minuet, was for the nobility. Peasants didn't dance to minuets; they had their own music. So if a peasant or servant in a Mozart opera is given a minuet, that's a signal that he or she is about to upend the noble. Not essential to know, but it makes watching Mozart opera more fun.

HAIL TO THE IGNORAMUSES

As I'm now addicted, my declared objective is to addict others. Episcopalian missionary blood that hasn't surfaced in my family for centuries is flowing strongly.

Opera *is* fun, it *isn't* only for the rich-in-purse, it *can* easily be comprehended—and it *isn't* boring. Once you get into it, even the boring parts aren't boring. Well, there are exceptions. Some of the boring parts stay boring.

But have you never been to a boring ball game or seen a boring movie or read a boring book or watched a boring TV sitcom or had a boring date or spent a boring evening with your beloved or listened to a boring office colleague? Come on; boring is part of the culture. Sometimes you eat the bear, sometimes the bear eats you. Why should opera be an exception?

Claude Debussy wrote a magnificent opera called *Pelléas et Mélisande*. When you know it, you can't not like it. Some of it is boring. Richard Wagner is superb. Yes he is, don't run. But anyone who denies some Wagner scenes are boring is playing with a fifty-one-card deck.

Give opera a fair chance.

THE SOON FUTURE

Let's set the scene eighteen months from now, after you've read the book and listened a little. By this time, you no longer are Unwashed. Assume that you are invited to a black-tie dinner on one weekend and on the next to an outdoor family neighborhood picnic with volleyball before hamburgers. Opera is on your mind, and, indeed, the dinner party hostess has advised you that opera is on the agenda.

The Black-tie Dinner Group

The guests include a retired music critic from the local newspaper and some dedicated operagoers who have held season tickets for decades.

You will show urbanity, refinement . . . and a sense of history. You will exhibit your knowledge about the founders and reformers of opera, the major developers, the men who contributed something to music. Your dinner partner will exclaim: "Oh yes. He made a splendid contribution. How right you are."

For this dinner with the Terribly, Terribly Washed, you'll consciously avoid the top public favorites, though you recognize one never avoids Mozart in any company. Not now, but then, you'll be comfortable discussing the following list of composers, with one opera for each.

1. Claudio Monteverdi—*Orfeo*
2. Christoph Willibald Gluck—*Orfeo ed Euridice*
3. Wolfgang Amadeus Mozart—*Don Giovanni*
4. George Frideric Handel—*Julius Caesar*
5. Richard Wagner—*Parsifal*
6. Giuseppe Verdi—*Otello*
7. Benjamin Britten—*Peter Grimes*
8. Modest Mussorgsky—*Boris Godunov*
9. Claude Debussy—*Pelléas et Mélisande*
10. Alban Berg—*Wozzeck*
First Alternate: Leoš Janáček—*Jenůfa*

You'll do beautifully. "How learned you are," someone will say. Or: "I'm astounded, but so delightfully astounded, that you included *Wozzeck*."

You can't miss.

The Volleyball Picnic

Sensitive and informed, you know that the black-tie list has too much couth for this group. In all probability they will not have heard of Monteverdi, Gluck, and Berg. Chances are only a little better on Mussorgsky. And while the name of Debussy may be familiar, the fact that he wrote an opera will be less so.

Wisely, you will steer the conversation to the Warhorses with which the volleyball players may be familiar. Otherwise, relatives and friends will look at you strangely and talk behind your back about how snobby you've become. Your new list is all Warhorses except for one well-known operetta:

1. Verdi—*La traviata*
2. Giacomo Puccini—*La Bohème*
3. Bizet—*Carmen*
4. Johann Strauss—*Die Fledermaus*
5. Charles Gounod—*Faust*
6. Wagner—*Lohengrin*
7. Gaetano Donizetti—*Lucia de Lammermoor*
8. Gioacchino Rossini—*The Barber of Seville*
9. Mozart—*The Marriage of Figaro*
10. Richard Strauss—*Der Rosenkavalier*
First Alternate: Ruggerio Leoncavallo—*Pagliacci*

Someone at the picnic is apt to say, "What about *Aida?*" You'll be wholly at ease: "Oh my yes, but it costs so much to stage these days, doesn't it?" And, Uncle Kent, a Wagnerian, will get apoplectic because you haven't included the *Ring* cycle. With a Washed shrug and a gulp of beer, you'll nod: "Yeah, right. There's always *The Ring,* isn't there?"

P.S. At the picnic, you'll say good things about Aaron Copland, Leonard Bernstein, Victor Herbert, Jerome Kern, and *Oklahoma!* At the black-tie dinner, you'll volunteer that opera is far from dead and that there are many fine contemporary composers.

It's a no-brainer guarantee. Your spouse will be envious but proud. The jealous faces of your in-laws will darken. You'll be the opera guru of the neighborhood.

Enjoy.

Ticket to the Opera

Chapter One

THE COLLECTION:
WHAT IT IS AND
WHAT IT ISN'T

❧

Q: How did you choose the operas in your book?

A: The core of the book is The Collection of eighty-five operas. Except for a handful of Golden Oldies included for historical purposes, these are the operas that have been performed most frequently in the world's major opera houses. My solid statistical base is from the Metropolitan Opera in New York, which provided exact data beginning with its first production in 1883. This base is modified by less precise input from major houses in Milan, Paris, Prague, Moscow, and other cities. It isn't feasible to survey every commercial opera house in the world, of any size, nor are complete records available, so any "most-performed" list must be a weighted approximation. Also, operas are performed in workshops, music conservatories, and universities.

Q: Would The Collection results differ if you could have surveyed all the smaller houses?

A: Yes. Because of financing, casting, and other reasons, the large companies tend to be less imaginative and to go with the old standbys, even though today they are experimenting more than they used to. Their audiences also prefer bigger, more spectacular opera rather than the chamber operas that are becoming increasingly more important today in smaller houses. For example, several Mozart works beyond those in The Collection provide the staple fare of many of these smaller houses.

Q: So you can't say unequivocally that your eighty-five have been the world's most frequently performed operas?

A: Certainly not. Can't and don't. But the statistical base from the

Metropolitan is precise, and when it's modified The Collection constitutes a sound representation of the ones that have been staged most often in the major houses.

Q: Is there a big difference in the repertories of Paris, London, Milan, and the Metropolitan?

A: For those major cities, not as much as you might expect. The French, English, Italian, and German houses have their own national favorites, but the similarities in the international repertories over the years is remarkable. The same few international works are the big favorites. This is somewhat less so in Russia and perhaps even less in Central Europe, where more time is given the home folks. But there, too, the best-known international works are performed frequently. For example, in three days in Prague in the spring of 1993 my wife and I saw two German operas and one French. A year earlier we saw one Italian, one French, and one Czech. All are in The Collection.

Q: What about those few older operas in The Collection? If they aren't performed often, why include them?

A: Because they're classics from the founding fathers of opera in Italy, Germany, France, and England.

Q: Does eighty-five Collection operas mean eighty-five different composers?

A: No. Several of the Big-Time composers have several operas each.

Q: Am I to assume that your Collection operas are the all-time greatest eighty-five operas?

A: Definitely not. Common sense indicates that most of music's "greatest" operas are here, but public preference and greatness clearly aren't synonymous.

Q: Examples, please.

A: Many musicologists consider Arnold Schoenberg's unfinished *Moses und Aron* to be a great opera. One school holds that Schoenberg was the top classical instrumental composer of the twentieth century. Because *Moses und Aron* is complex, because the music is different, and because of the tastes of general operagoers, it's never been a big public hit. So it doesn't make The Collection, even though its partisans rush for tickets when it *is* produced. On the other hand, I didn't want to ignore it. It's an example of operas in The Twentieth-century European Package that were chosen subjectively after research and strong guidance from opera professionals I interviewed.

Q: Why didn't you provide us with the eighty-five greatest instead of basing your Collection on long-term success and popularity with the public?

A: I don't know how to pick the eighty-five "greatest." That's why I've given the operagoing public the controlling vote for The Collection. Opera is made up of different parts, including voice, orchestral music, balance between voice and orchestra, plot, dramatic tension, poetry, portrayal of the human condition, character depiction through music, finales, ballet, theater, scenic effects, and much more. Who's to say which operas shape these into the "greatest" whole? Some composers are more clever than others, some more creative. Some are more poetic, others more musical; some more serious, others more trivial and sentimental. Back at the turn of the century, George Bernard Shaw, then an esteemed music critic in London, wrote about greatness in music: "The greatest [classical] composer is he who, by the rarest of chances, is at once a great musician and a great poet—who has Brahms's wonderful ear without his commonplace mind, and Molière's insight and imagination without his musical sterility. Thus it is that you get your Mozart or your Wagner." I'm not a trained musicologist, and every professional would have a different mix in a Top 10 or Top 20.

Q: Spare me George Bernard Shaw. Just answer the questions. Which fine operas are left out of The Collection now?

A: I mentioned *Moses und Aron.* Sixty-odd more are identified and discussed in the separate European and American twentieth-century chapters. Francis Poulenc's *Dialogues of the Carmelites* is a European example; George Gershwin's *Porgy and Bess* is an American example. Space permitting, I'd add others from Collection composers plus many from other composers in earlier centuries.

Q: Examples, please.

A: For chamber operas, some of Franz Joseph Haydn's. Among others, perhaps Luigi Cherubini's *Médée,* 1797, and Russian Mikhail Glinka's *A Life for the Tsar,* 1836. There's Spanish opera, South American opera, Polish opera, Scandinavian opera, other English opera, and much American opera. We could include another one hundred works and not run out of good opera.

Q: Even so, some operas must be judged "superior" to others.

A: Of course. But it isn't reasonable to compare comic operas like Donizetti's *Elixir of Love* or *Don Pasquale* with grand operas like Verdi's *Aida,* or a spectacle like *Aida* with a short shock-you work like Richard Strauss's erotic *Salome,* just as it's not reasonable to compare *My Cousin Vinny* or *When Sally Met Harry* with *Gone With the Wind* or *Gone With the Wind* with *Schindler's List.* Mozart's *Marriage of Figaro* is no more like Wagner's *Tristan und Isolde* than Jimmy Stewart's classic *Harvey* is like Steven Spielberg's *Jurassic Park.* They are different kinds of creatures.

Q: This Collection is unfair to an opera that premiered last year or even twenty years ago. Those don't have a statistical chance, no matter how good they are.

A: Correct. It also excludes wonderful works like *Porgy and Bess,* which not only came 150 years later than some Warhorse operas but also was for decades performed chiefly in theaters rather than opera houses. That's why I've added the two safety-net chapters to help handle the twentieth century.

Q: Why do you number The Collection from one to eighty-five instead of using alphabetical or chronological order?

A: Because the popularity ranking is sound, even if not exact, and it offers information that's helpful for beginners. The works at the top of The Collection are the big Warhorses the public likes best. The ones toward the bottom of the list, while still public favorites, are no longer the same household names.

This gives readers the option of concentrating on the most famous if they choose. But the opera police won't come and take you away if you start viewing at Number 85 and work backward.

Q: We've been talking mostly about operas. Let's talk composers. Are the composers in The Collection history's finest?

A: That's the same kind of question, and it gets fairly much the same answer, although it's more reasonable to weigh the total production of one composer against another than to "rate" individual operas. The greatest opera composers are here, but The Collection also represents several second-level composers who wrote very popular operas and bypasses some first-level composers who wrote less popular ones.

Q: Were most of The Collection operas written by opera specialists or the great masters of classical music?

A. Good question. Both. Not all the geniuses and giants of classical music have produced great opera—and not all great opera has come from the top masters of classical music. Among all-time classical masters who were not into opera are Johann Sebastian Bach, Johannes Brahms, Robert Schumann, Felix Mendelssohn, Frédéric Chopin, Franz Liszt, and Gustav Mahler. Classical Hall-of-Famers Franz Schubert and Haydn did write operas—Haydn as many as Mozart—but Schubert's have never really worked and Haydn's are chamber works that are of an astonishing standard musically although not as strong dramatically. On the other hand, classical masters who *are* in The Collection include Mozart, Ludwig van Beethoven, Peter Il'yich Tchaikovsky, Hector Berlioz, Claude Debussy, Camille Saint-Saëns, Béla Bartók, Leoš Janáček, and Richard Strauss. Some of these classical masters wrote only one opera and some wrote many.

Q: How many women are among your composers?

A: None. One highly acclaimed woman in opera is Sarah Caldwell (b. 1924), U.S. producer and conductor, founder of the Opera Company of Boston. While still a student, she produced Ralph Vaughan Williams' *Riders to the Sea* (see The Twentieth-century European Package). Later she produced the first full version of *Moses und Aron*, and in 1976 she became the first woman conductor at the Met. A respected twentieth-century opera composer is Thea Musgrave, born in Edinburgh, Scotland, in 1928, whose *Simón Bolívar* premiered in January 1995 in Norfolk, Virginia, with Virginia Opera. The general director and conductor of the company is Peter Mark, Musgrave's husband. The European premiere was in the following March in Regensburg, Germany. Another of her major works is *Mary, Queen of Scots*, 1977. Although her works don't yet qualify statistically for The Collection, Musgrave is cited in the chapter on opera in America. She studied in Paris with *the* woman in classical music, Nadia Boulanger, 1887–1979, the twentieth century's most famous teacher of composition.

Q: Who are the most important opera composers in the book? The three all-time greats. No waffling.

A: Try Mozart, Verdi, and Wagner.

Q: Yick. Some of Wagner goes on forever.

A: Sure it does. But some of it doesn't. Anyhow, the goal isn't to tell people what they'll like. It's to provide a road map that I hope will help beginners sort out the whole opera picture. Then they're on their own.

Q: I know. But here at the beginning, you can tell me, confidentially. Like the TV people say, just between ourselves. Who are the three next greatest?

A: So long as it's just between ourselves. Pick from Monteverdi, Richard Strauss, Rossini, Bizet, and Puccini. For this century, there's Britten, Janáček, and Berg. If you're French, add Debussy and Berlioz, if English Purcell, if German Handel, and if Russian Mussorgsky.

Q: Why are you being so Politically Correct? I hate Politically Correct. Just spit it out.

A: We're dealing with apples, oranges, and bananas. How do we compare great classical composers like Beethoven who wrote one opera with specialists like Rossini and Donizetti who spent their lives writing dozens of successful operas? Composers who contributed something original and lasting in opera could be put in one group. Composers whose total works make up the bulk of the international repertoire could be placed in another. Mozart, Verdi, and Wagner would lead both groups, which makes them special.

Q: Not helpful. You're weaseling.

A: Yes I am. Check chapter nine for the findings of a panel that tried to identify history's Top 10 operas.

Q: Can you promise me anything about your Collection?

A: I can promise you that these represent the operas that the Western world has most enjoyed over 150 to 200 years.

Q: Am I supposed to thank you for that?

A: I don't know.

Q: I'm not sure I've enjoyed this conversation.

A: So go listen to the first acts of *La traviata* and *La Bohème*. Try the "Pilgrims' Chorus" from *Tannhäuser* and some orchestral music from *Die Meistersinger von Nürnberg*. Maybe you'll feel better.

Chapter 2

A TREASURY OF
OPERA

∾

THE COLLECTION
The Twenty-five Warhorses

1. *Aida*, 1871. Giuseppe Verdi (1813–1901). Italian. (p. 82)
2. *La Bohème*, 1896. Giacomo Puccini (1858–1924). Italian. (p. 99)
3. *Carmen*, 1875. Georges Bizet (1838–75). French. (p. 111)
4. *La traviata* (*The Erring One*), 1853. Verdi. (p. 85)
5. *Tosca*, 1900. Puccini. (p. 101)
6. *Faust*. 1859. Charles François Gounod (1818–93). French. (p. 119)
7. *Madama Butterfly*, 1904. Puccini. (p. 105)
8. *Pagliacci* (*The Players*), 1892. Ruggerio Leoncavallo (1857–1919). Italian. (p. 127)
9. *Rigoletto*, 1851. Verdi. (p. 87)
10. *Lohengrin*, 1850. Richard Wagner (1813–83). German. (p. 141)
11. *Cavalleria rusticana* (*Rustic Chivalry*), 1890. Pietro Mascagni (1863–1945). Italian. (p. 177)
12. *Tristan und Isolde*, 1865. Wagner. (p. 143)
13. *Die Walküre*, 1870. Wagner. (p. 164)
14. *Il trovatore* (*The Troubadour*), 1853. Verdi. (p. 90)
15. *Lucia di Lammermoor*, 1835. Gaetano Donizetti (1797–1848). Italian. (p. 186)
16. *Die Meistersinger von Nürnberg* (*The Mastersingers of Nuremberg*), 1868. Wagner. (p. 147)
17. *Tannhäuser*, 1845. Wagner. (p. 152)

18. *Don Giovanni*, 1787. Wolfgang Amadeus Mozart (1756–91). German. (p. 197)
19. *Il barbiere di Siviglia* (*The Barber of Seville*), 1816. Gioacchino Rossini (1792–1868). Italian. (p. 215)
20. *Der Rosenkavalier* (*The Knight of the Rose*), 1911. Richard Strauss (1864–1949). German. (p. 224)
21. *Le nozze di Figaro* (*The Marriage of Figaro*), 1786. Mozart. (p. 201)
22. *Parsifal*, 1882. Wagner. (p. 155)
23. *Die Zauberflöte* (*The Magic Flute*), 1791. Mozart. (p. 205)
24. *Siegfried*, 1876. Wagner. (p. 167)
25. *Roméo et Juliette* (*Romeo and Juliet*), 1867. Gounod. (p. 123)

More Great and Popular Operas

26. *Götterdämmerung* (*Twilight of the Gods*), 1876. Wagner. (p. 169)
27. *Boris Godunov*, 1874. Modest Mussorgsky (1839–81). Russian.
28. *Otello*, 1887. Verdi. (p. 235)
29. *Manon*, 1884. Jules Massenet (1842–1912). French. (p. 239)
30. *La forza del destino* (*The Force of Destiny*), 1862. Verdi. (p. 245)
31. *Hänsel und Gretel*, 1893. Engelbert Humperdinck (1854–1921). German. (p. 250)
32. *Un ballo in maschera* (*A Masked Ball*), 1859. Verdi. (p. 254)
33. *Manon Lescaut*, 1893. Puccini. (p. 258)
34. *Fidelio*, 1805. Ludwig van Beethoven (1770–1827). German. (p. 262)
35. *L'elisir d'amore* (*The Elixir of Love*), 1832. Donizetti. (p. 269)
36. *Andrea Chénier*, 1896. Umberto Giordano (1867–1948). Italian. (p. 273)
37. *Samson et Dalila*, 1877. Camille Saint-Saëns (1835–1921). French. (p. 277)
38. *Pelléas et Mélisande*, 1902. Claude Debussy (1862–1918). French. (p. 283)
39. *Les contes d'Hoffmann* (*The Tales of Hoffmann*), 1881. Jacques Offenbach (1819–80). German-born Parisian. (p. 289)
40. *La Gioconda* (*The Ballad Singer*), 1876. Amilcare Ponchielli (1834–86). Italian. (p. 297)
41. *Turandot*, 1926. Puccini. (p. 301)
42. *Salome*, 1905. Richard Strauss. (p. 305)
43. *Das Rheingold*, 1869. Wagner. (p. 162)
44. *Falstaff*, 1893. Verdi. (p. 310)
45. *Der fliegende Holländer* (*The Flying Dutchman*), 1843. Wagner. (p. 314)
46. *Gianni Schicchi*, 1918. Puccini. (p. 316)
47. *Don Carlos*, 1867. Verdi. (p. 319)
48. *Norma*, 1831. Vincenzo Bellini (1801–35). Italian. (p. 323)
49. *Die Fledermaus* (*The Bat*), 1874. Johann Strauss (1825–99). German. (p. 329)
50. *Così fan tutte* (*Women Are Like That*), 1790. Mozart. (p. 335)
51. *Les Troyens* (*The Trojans*), 1856–63. Hector Berlioz (1803–1869). French. (p. 339)

52. *Orfeo ed Euridice* (*Orpheus and Eurydice*), 1762. Christoph Willibald von Gluck (1714–87). Bohemian-German. (p. 345)
53. *Les Huguenots*, 1836. Giacomo Meyerbeer (1791–1864). German-born Parisian. (p. 350)
54. *La fanciulla del West* (*The Girl of the Golden West*), 1910. Puccini. (p. 356)
55. *Simon Boccanegra*, 1857. Verdi. (p. 361)
56. *Don Pasquale*, 1843. Donizetti. (p. 364)
57. *Le coq d'or* (*The Golden Cockerel*), 1909. Nicolai Rimsky-Korsakov (1844–1908). Russian. (p. 369)
58. *La sonnambula* (*The Sleepwalker*), 1831. Bellini. (p. 373)
59. *Elektra*, 1909. Richard Strauss. (p. 376)
60. *Lakmé*, 1883. Léo Delibes (1836–91). French. (p. 379)
61. *La fille du régiment* (*The Daughter of the Regiment*), 1840. Donizetti. (p. 383)
62. *Ernani*, 1844. Verdi. (p. 386)
63. *The Bartered Bride*, 1866. Bedřich Smetana (1824–84). Bohemian. (p. 391)
64. *Macbeth*, 1847. Verdi. (p. 395)
65. *Eugene Onegin*, 1879. Peter Il'yich Tchaikovsky (1840–93). Russian. (p. 398)
66. *Pique Dame* (*The Queen of Spades*), 1890. Tchaikovsky. (p. 404)
67. *Peter Grimes*, 1945. Benjamin Britten (1913–76). English. (p. 408)
68. *Der Freischütz* (*The Free-shooter*), 1821. Carl Maria von Weber (1786–1826). German. (p. 413)
69. *L'Italiana in Algeri* (*The Italian Girl in Algiers*), 1813. Rossini. (p. 419)
70. *Ariadne auf Naxos* (*Ariadne on Naxos*), 1912. Richard Strauss. (p. 422)
71. *Martha*, 1847. Friedrich von Flotow (1812–83). German. (p. 425)
72. *Mignon*, 1866. Ambroise Thomas (1811–96). French. (p. 428)
73. *Mefistofele*, 1868. Arrigo Boito (1842–1918). Italian. (p. 431)
74. *Prince Igor*, 1890. Alexander Borodin (1833–87). Russian. (p. 435)
75. *Louise*, 1900. Gustave Charpentier (1860–1956). French. (p. 439)
76. *Wozzeck*, 1925. Alban Berg (1885–1935). German. (p. 443)
77. *Werther*, 1892. Massenet. (p. 453)
78. *Jenůfa*, 1904. Leoš Janáček (1854–1928). Czech. (p. 456)
79. *Die lustigen Weiber von Windsor* (*The Merry Wives of Windsor*), 1849. Otto Nicolai (1810–49). German. (p. 461)
80. *Duke Bluebeard's Castle*, 1918. Béla Bartók (1881–1945). Hungarian. (p. 464)

Five Golden Oldies from the Founding Fathers

(CHRONOLOGICALLY, BY OPERA PREMIERE DATE)

81. *Orfeo* (*Orpheus*), 1607. Claudio Monteverdi (1567–1643). Italian. (p. 468)
82. *Atys*, 1676. Jean-Baptiste Lully (1632–87). Italian-born Parisian. (p. 475)
83. *Dido and Aeneas*, 1689. Henry Purcell (1659–95). English. (p. 479)
84. *Giulio Cesare* (*Julius Caesar*), 1724. George Frideric Handel (1685–1759). German turned English. (p. 483)
85. *Castor et Pollux*, 1737. Jean-Philippe Rameau (1683–1764). French. (p. 489)

The Collection Operas by Centuries

Most of the operas come from the nineteenth century—and more than half from the second half of that century:

Seventeenth century—3
Eighteenth century—7
Nineteenth century, first half—18
Nineteenth century, second half—41
Twentieth century—16

1600s
Orfeo, 1607. Monteverdi. Italian.
Atys, 1676. Lully. Italian turned French.
Dido and Aeneas, 1689. Purcell. English.

1700s
Julius Caesar, 1724. Handel. German.*
Castor et Pollux, 1737. Rameau. French.
Orfeo ed Euridice, 1762. Gluck. German Parisian.
The Marriage of Figaro, 1786. Mozart. German.*
Don Giovanni, 1787. Mozart. German.
Così fan tutte, 1790. Mozart. German.
The Magic Flute, 1791. Mozart. German.

1800–1850
Fidelio, 1805. Beethoven. German.
The Italian Girl in Algiers, 1813. Rossini. Italian.
The Barber of Seville, 1816. Rossini. Italian.
Der Freischütz, 1821. Weber. German.
La sonnambula, 1831. Bellini. Italian.
Norma, 1831. Bellini. Italian.
The Elixir of Love, 1832. Donizetti. Italian.
Lucia di Lammermoor, 1835. Donizetti. Italian.
Les Huguenots, 1836. Meyerbeer. German Parisian.
The Daughter of the Regiment, 1840. Donizetti. Italian.
The Flying Dutchman, 1843. Wagner. German.
Don Pasquale, 1843. Donizetti. Italian.
Ernani, 1844. Verdi. Italian.
Tannhäuser, 1845. Wagner. German.
Macbeth, 1849. Verdi. Italian.

*Following the *Harvard Dictionary of Music* and other music encyclopedias, composers born in German states and Austria in past years are identified as German.

Martha, 1847. Flotow. German.
The Merry Wives of Windsor, 1849. Nicolai. German.
Lohengrin, 1850. Wagner. German.

1851–1899

Rigoletto, 1851. Verdi. Italian.
Il trovatore, 1853. Verdi. Italian.
La traviata, 1853. Verdi. Italian.
Les Troyens, 1856. Berlioz. French.
Simon Boccanegra, 1857. Verdi. Italian.
Faust, 1859. Gounod. French.
A Masked Ball, 1859. Verdi. Italian.
The Force of Destiny, 1862. Verdi. Italian.
Tristan und Isolde, 1865. Wagner. German.
The Bartered Bride, 1866. Smetana. Bohemian.
Mignon, 1866. Thomas. French.
Don Carlos, 1867. Verdi. Italian.
Mefistofele, 1868. Boito. Italian.
Die Meistersinger von Nürnberg, 1868. Wagner. German.
Das Rheingold, 1869. Wagner. German.
Roméo et Juliette, 1867. Gounod. French.
Die Walküre, 1870. Wagner. German.
Aida, 1871. Verdi. Italian.
Boris Godunov, 1874. Mussorgsky. Russian.
Die Fledermaus, 1874. Johann Strauss. German.
Carmen, 1875. Bizet. French.
La Gioconda, 1876. Ponchielli. Italian.
Siegfried, 1876. Wagner. German.
Götterdämmerung, 1876. Wagner. German.
Samson et Dalila, 1877. Saint-Saëns. French.
Eugene Onegin, 1879. Tchaikovsky. Russian.
The Tales of Hoffmann, 1881. Offenbach. German Parisian.
Parsifal, 1882. Wagner. German.
Lakmé, 1883. Delibes. French.
Manon, 1884. Massenet. French.
Otello, 1887. Verdi. Italian.
The Queen of Spades, 1890. Tchaikovsky. Russian.
Prince Igor, 1890. Borodin. Russian.
Cavalleria rusticana, 1890. Mascagni. Italian.
Werther, 1892. Massenet. French.
Pagliacci, 1892. Leoncavallo. Italian.
Manon Lescaut, 1893. Puccini. Italian.
Hänsel und Gretel, 1893. Humperdinck. German.
Falstaff, 1893. Verdi. Italian.

La Bohème, 1896. Puccini. Italian.
Andrea Chénier, 1896. Giordano. Italian.

1900s

Louise, 1900. Charpentier. French.
Tosca, 1900. Puccini. Italian.
Pelléas et Mélisande, 1902. Debussy. French.
Jenůfa, 1904. Janáček. Czech.
Madama Butterfly, 1904. Puccini. French.
Salome, 1905. Richard Strauss. German.
Elektra, 1909. Richard Strauss. German.
The Golden Cockerel, 1909. Rimsky-Korsakov. Russian.
The Girl of the Golden West, 1910. Puccini. Italian.
Der Rosenkavalier, 1911. Richard Strauss. German.
Ariadne auf Naxos, 1912. Richard Strauss. German.
Gianni Schicchi, 1918. Puccini. Italian.
Duke Bluebeard's Castle, 1918. Bartók. Hungarian.
Wozzeck, 1925. Berg. German.
Turandot, 1926. Puccini. Italian.
Peter Grimes, 1945. Britten. English.

THE TWENTIETH-CENTURY
EUROPEAN PACKAGE

Rusalka, 1901. Antonín Dvořák, 1841–1904. (p. 498)
Die lustige Witwe (*The Merry Widow*), 1905. Franz Lehár, 1870–1948. (p. 501)
Sàvitri, 1916. Gustav Holst, 1874–1934. (p. 502)
L'heure espagnole (*The Spanish Hour*), 1911. Also *L'enfant et les sortilèges* (*The Child and the Enchantments*), 1925. Maurice Ravel, 1875–1937. (p. 504)
Die Frau ohne Schatten, 1919. Richard Strauss, 1864–1949. (p. 506)
Die Tote Stadt, 1920. Erich Wolfgang Korngold, 1897–1957. (p. 508)
The Love for Three Oranges, 1921. Also *War and Peace*, 1946. Serge Prokofiev, 1891–1953. (p. 509)
The Cunning Little Vixen, 1924. Leoš Janáček, 1854–1928. (p. 511)
Cardillac, 1926. *Mathis der Maler* (*Mathias the Painter*), 1938. Paul Hindemith, 1895–1963. (p. 513)
Jonny spielt auf (*Johnny Strikes Up the Band*), 1927. Ernst Krenek, 1900–91. (p. 515)
Die Dreigroschenoper (*The Threepenny Opera*), 1928. Also *Aufstieg und Fall der Stadt Mahogonny* (*Rise and Fall of the City of Mahagonny*), 1930. Kurt Weill, 1900–50. (p. 518)
Moses und Aron, written 1932, premiere, 1957. Arnold Schoenberg, 1874–1951. (p. 520)
Lady Macbeth of the Mtsensk District, 1934. Dmitri Shostakovich, 1906–75. (p. 523)

Riders to the Sea, 1937. Ralph Vaughan Williams, 1872–1958. (p. 525)
Lulu, 1937. Alban Berg, 1885–1935. (p. 527)
The Rake's Progress, 1951. Igor Stravinsky, 1882–1971. (p. 529)
The Turn of the Screw, 1954. Benjamin Britten, 1913–76. (p. 532)
The Midsummer Marriage, 1955. Also *King Priam*, 1962. Michael Tippett, 1905–. (p. 534)
Dialogues des Carmélites, 1957. Francis Poulenc, 1899–1963. (p. 536)
Der Prinz von Homburg, 1960. Also *Der junge Lord* (*The Young Lord*), 1965. Hans Werner Henze, 1926–. (p. 538)
Die Soldaten, 1965. Bernd Alois Zimmermann, 1918–70. (p. 540)
The Devils of Loudun, 1969. Krzysztof Penderecki, 1933–. (p. 542)
Taverner, 1972. Peter Maxwell Davies, 1934–. (p. 543)

THE TWENTIETH-CENTURY: AN AMERICAN OPERA DREAM SEASON

(CHRONOLOGICALLY, BY OPERA PREMIERE DATE)
Show Boat, 1927. Jerome Kern, 1885–1945. (p. 557)
Four Saints in Three Acts, 1934. Virgil Thomson, 1896–1989. (p. 560)
Porgy and Bess, 1935. George Gershwin, 1898–1937. (p. 563)
Oklahoma!, 1943. Richard Rodgers, 1902–79, and Oscar Hammerstein II, 1895–1960. (p. 572)
Regina, 1949. Marc Blitzstein, 1905–1964. (p. 569)
Amahl and the Night Visitors, 1951. Gian Carlo Menotti, 1911–. (p. 570)
Trouble in Tahiti, 1952. Leonard Bernstein, 1918–90. (p. 580)
The Tender Land, 1954. Aaron Copland, 1900–90. (p. 576)
Susannah, 1955. Carlisle Floyd, 1926–. (p. 578)
The Ballad of Baby Doe, 1956. Douglas Moore, 1893–1969. (p. 578)
West Side Story, 1957. Bernstein. (p. 580)
Vanessa, 1958. Samuel Barber, 1910–81. (p. 582)
The Crucible, 1961. Robert Ward, 1917–. (p. 584)
Postcard from Morocco, 1971. Dominick Argento, 1927–. (p. 584)
A Little Night Music, 1973. Stephen Sondheim, 1930– (p. 591)
Satyagraha, 1981 (or *Akhnaten*, 1983). Philip Glass, 1937–. (p. 586)
Nixon in China, 1987. John Adams, 1938–. (p. 587)
The Ghosts of Versailles, 1991. John Corigliano, 1938–. (p. 588)

Chapter 3

ID BRACELETS FOR
THE COLLECTION

❧

A s a tool to help sort out the eighty-five operas in The Collection, here are one-line identification bracelets for each, listed by composer nationality and century.

ITALY
Nineteenth Century

ROSSINI
69. *The Italian Girl in Algiers*, 1813. A farcical comedy.
19. *The Barber of Seville*, 1816. Comedy. His most famous opera.

DONIZETTI
35. *The Elixir of Love*, 1832. Light, sentimental, romantic comedy.
15. *Lucia di Lammermoor*, 1835. Melodramatic. His best-known work.
61. *The Daughter of the Regiment*, 1840. Gay. His first opera in French.
56. *Don Pasquale*, 1843. A fun-filled masterpiece of comic opera.

BELLINI
48. *Norma*, 1831. His masterpiece, a tragic drama in Ancient Gaul.
58. *La sonnambula*, 1831. Sleepwalker. Rustic with happy ending.

VERDI (12 OPERAS)
62. *Ernani*, 1844. His fifth opera. Passionate melodrama.
64. *Macbeth*, 1847. His first from a Shakespeare play.
9. *Rigoletto*, 1851. Brutal melodrama. First of his Big Trio.
4. *La traviata*, 1853. Next of the Trio. Drawing-room tragedy.
14. *Il trovatore*, 1853. Last of the Trio. Love, hate, and revenge.
55. *Simon Boccanegra*, 1857. Serious drama. Genoa in the 1300s.
32. *A Masked Ball*, 1859. Politics, morality, and regicide.
30. *The Force of Destiny*, 1862. A deadly bloody family feud.
47. *Don Carlos*, 1867. Grand opera of Spanish Inquisition.
1. *Aida*, 1871. A masterpiece spectacle of the pharaohs' Egypt.
28. *Otello*, 1887. Italy's top tragic opera, from Shakespeare.
44. *Falstaff*, 1893. His masterly final work and only successful comedy.

VERDI CONTEMPORARIES: BOITO AND PONCHIELLI
73. *Mefistofele*, 1868. Boito. The bass Devil loses a soul.
40. *La Gioconda*, 1876. Ponchielli. An old-fashioned melodrama.

POST-VERDI VERISMO: MASCAGNI, LEONCAVALLO, GIORDANO (REALISM)
11. *Cavalleria rusticana*, 1890. Mascagni. Sicilan revenge.
8. *Pagliacci*, 1892. Leoncavallo. Infidelity and death.
36. *Andrea Chénier*, 1896. Giordano. More Italian realism.

PUCCINI (SEVEN OPERAS)
33. *Manon Lescaut*, 1893. His third, which began his fame.
2. *La Bohème*, 1896. First of his Big Three. Wet-eyed romance.
5. *Tosca*, 1900. Next of the Big Three. Sex, sadism, and murder.
7. *Madama Butterfly*, 1904. Last of the Big Three. Ugly American.
54. *The Girl of the Golden West*, 1910. California miners' romance and banditry.
46. *Gianni Schicchi*, 1918. Puccini's only comedy. A gem.
41. *Turandot*, 1926. His last and most ambitious opera.

GERMANY

Eighteenth Century

THE GENIUS OF MOZART (FOUR OPERAS)
21. *The Marriage of Figaro*, 1786. Comic opera and social message.
18. *Don Giovanni*, 1787. Perhaps the greatest opera ever written.
50. *Così fan tutte*, 1790. The incarnation of Italian comic opera.
23. *The Magic Flute*, 1791. His last opera and his top German one.

Nineteenth Century

WAGNER (TEN OPERAS)

Early Romantic

45. *The Flying Dutchman*, 1843. His first operatic success.
17. *Tannhäuser*, 1845. Man's redemption via woman's sacrifice.
10. *Lohengrin*, 1850. Knight rescues lady. Favorite of public.

The Ring of the Nibelung, **A Four-Opera Set**

43. *Das Rheingold*, 1869. One-act scene-setter under the Rhine.
13. *Die Walküre*, 1870. The public's favorite of the four.
24. *Siegfried*, 1876. The critics' least favorite of the four.
26. *Götterdämmerung*, 1876. Twilight for the *Ring* gods.

More Music Dramas

12. *Tristan und Isolde*. 1865. Erotic passion personified.
16. *Die Meistersinger von Nürnberg*. Wagner's only comedy.
22. *Parsifal*, 1882. His last opera. Rampant symbolism.

FIVE OTHER GERMAN WORKS

34. *Fidelio*, 1805. Beethoven. His only opera. Wife saves mate.
68. *Der Freischütz*, 1821. Weber. First important German Romantic opera.
71. *Martha*, 1847. Flotow. Gay, lighthearted, and tuneful.
79. *The Merry Wives of Windsor*, 1849. Nicolai. Light comedy from Shakespeare.
49. *Die Fledermaus*, 1874. Johann Strauss. Waltz King's superb operetta.
31. *Hänsel und Gretel*, 1893. Humperdinck. Fairy-tale opera.

FRANCE

Eighteenth Century

52. *Orfeo ed Euridice*, 1762, Gluck. Opera's great reformer.

Nineteenth Century

53. *Les Huguenots*, 1836. Meyerbeer. The spectacle of grand opera.
 6. *Faust*, 1859. Gounod. Europe's most popular opera for decades.
51. *Les Troyens*, 1863. Berlioz. Huge epic from Virgil's *Aeneid*.
72. *Mignon*, 1866. Thomas. Two thousand performances in Paris.
25. *Roméo et Juliette*, 1867. Gounod. Tracks Shakespeare's text.
 3. *Carmen*, 1875. Bizet. The all-time most popular French opera.
37. *Samson et Dalila*, 1877. Saint-Saëns. Opera from the Bible.
39. *The Tales of Hoffmann*, 1881. Offenbach. Mr. Operetta's one opera.

60. *Lakmé*, 1883. Delibes. His masterpiece in serious opera.
29. *Manon*, 1884. Massenet. Same source as Puccini's *Manon Lescaut*.
77. *Werther*, 1892. Massenet. Lyric drama from a Goethe novel.
75. *Louise*, 1900. Charpentier. Women's lib opera set in Paris.

RUSSIA AND CENTRAL EUROPE
Nineteenth Century

63. *The Bartered Bride*, 1866. Smetana. *The* Czech national opera.
27. *Boris Godunov*, 1874. Mussorgsky. Great Russian masterpiece.
65. *Eugene Onegin*, 1879. Tchaikovsky. Russia's top composer.
66. *The Queen of Spades*, 1890. Tchaikovsky. From Pushkin tragedy.
74. *Prince Igor*, 1890. Borodin. Melodic Russian nationalist opera.

ALL COUNTRIES
Twentieth Century

38. *Pelléas et Mélisande*, 1902. Debussy. French impressionist masterpiece.
78. *Jenůfa*, 1904. Janáček. An international Czech favorite.
57. *The Golden Cockerel*, 1909. Rimsky-Korsakov. Russian fantasy.
80. *Duke Bluebeard's Castle*, 1918. Bartók. Hungarian allegory.
76. *Wozzeck*, 1925. Berg. Powerful German work with antihero.
67. *Peter Grimes*, 1945. Britten. Top English opera of century.

RICHARD STRAUSS (FOUR OPERAS)
42. *Salome*, 1905. Dissonance and plot that shook the music world.
59. *Elektra*, 1909. Another shocker by the famous German composer.
20. *Der Rosenkavalier*, 1911. A cheerful change-of-pace romance.
70. *Ariadne auf Naxos*, 1912. Blend of comedy and myth.

FIVE GOLDEN OLDIES

81. *Orfeo*, 1607. Monteverdi. Opera founder's first opera.
82. *Atys*, 1676. Lully. Italian-born father of French opera.
83. *Dido and Aeneas*, 1689. Purcell. The first real English opera.
84. *Julius Caesar*, 1724. Handel. German-born English genius.
85. *Castor et Pollux*, 1737. Rameau. French Classical Hall of Famer.

Chapter 4

BASIC
DEFINITIONS

❧

The great Russian master Peter Il'yich Tchaikovsky once wrote that opera
was a serious composer's only means of reaching the masses.

In the process of creating his own ten operas, however, Tchaikovsky often
became depressed. Shortly after completing *Eugene Onegin*, an opera based on a
work by the Russian poet Alexander Pushkin, he wrote a friend:

"How Pushkin's charming picture will be vulgarized when transformed to
the stage with its routine, its stupid traditions, with veteran players taking the
part of sixteen-year-old girls and beardless youths. The moral is: Writing instrumental music is far more satisfactory, has fewer disappointments. How I
agonized over the production of my operas."

Tchaikovsky's "agony" came in part from the nature of the beast. He acknowledged that opera demands a suspension of disbelief on the part of composer, performer, and audience.

That's because opera isn't a concert, but a drama, a drama in which music
is the indispensable factor. Concerts wouldn't reach Tchaikovsky's masses.
Opera involves many different arts: a stage play, instrumental and vocal music,
poetry, acting, dance, stage design, costuming, often spectacle, and more.

All of these ingredients contribute to the whole, one reason why unseen
opera doesn't stand up to live productions, filmed opera, or opera viewed on
the television screen.

Composers with different interests from different countries and centuries
treated those various arts in different ways, especially the relationship between
the music and the poetry.

Although all operas have a story of some kind, some operas in The Collection focus on the solo human voice and how best to exhibit it. In the years when the public's yen was to hear the performer sing, successful composers were inclined to produce operas that provided the best showcase for the voice. When the public's tastes changed, composers would use the music—vocal or orchestral—chiefly to enchance the poetry and the drama.

Opinions of types of opera changed over the years, as opinions do. What was "naked brutality" in one period was viewed in another as "dramatic intensity." What contemporary audiences enjoyed as "magnificent spectacle" was assessed by later generations as "stilted showmanship."

Any amateur can distinguish one opera from another in some layman ways. One composer is more hooked on the human voice and another on the orchestra. One opera is frothy entertainment, and another is concerned with ambiguous symbolism. One is drawing-room comedy, and another features the John Wayne He-Man of the day, whether bandit, chief, or prince.

This chapter presents a few nontechnical definitions of various kinds of opera and some of their ingredients.

Some of the characteristics of opera are found in other forms of music. An "oratorio" (which often, but not always, deals with a religious subject) is one example of this. Like an opera, an oratorio is performed on a stage with orchestra, soloists, and choruses—but typically without action, costumes, or scenery. Several Collection composers wrote oratorios, the best known of which is Handel's *Messiah*, a work known to many of the supremely Unwashed.

The oratorio has a first cousin, the "passion," which also is without action, costumes, or scenery. A form that predated opera, it is a musical setting of the suffering of Christ between the Last Supper and his death, according to St. Matthew, St. Mark, St. Luke, or St. John. The best-known one is Johann Sebastian Bach's glorious *St. Matthew Passion*. Bach was not in the opera business at all, although Handel, his 1685 birth year contemporary, was a high-level opera master, and Bach's youngest son, Johann Christian, wrote several fine operas.

I've tried to limit the definitions here to the ones most useful for opera newcomers. Let's begin with one of the most important:

LIBRETTO   Webster says succinctly: "The text of a work (as an opera) for the musical theater."

Music professionals elaborate: Traditionally, the libretto was written to give the composer a theme for the set, stand-alone numbers that were part of opera—the arias, duets, ensembles, choruses, marches, and finales. (Later, Richard Wagner and some others walked away from the notion of these detachable set numbers.) A good librettist will create characters with depth and a plot with dramatic insight. But he's not writing a play. His task is to fashion situations that justify the use of music—and, indeed, demand music for full dramatic realization. That's the core of it all; that's what opera is all about; that's why listening to arias on a compact disc gives you beautiful opera music but doesn't give you opera.

For composers dedicated to unifying drama and music in their works, the librettist obviously is especially important, since his libretto deals with plot, action, and psychology. Some librettos include stage instructions, and some don't. Amateurs in the audience can ask themselves the pivotal questions: How lifelike are the characters? How clear is the plot? How straightforward or complex is the action? Individual operagoers may (or may not) be interested in whether the libretto is an original story created by the librettist or, if not, what its source is. Let's say the subject is the literary figure of Dr. Faust, who made a deal with the Devil. Does the librettist retell the drama written by the great Goethe or, using librettist license, does he take Dr. Faust and the Devil as a starting point and create a new story in which Dr. Faust is an Arkansas governor who wants to be president?

Has the librettist gone to myth, to last year's hit play, to a fairy tale, to the beating of Rodney King, to his own concept of social injustice, to President Nixon in China, to the guys who wrote the constitution or to a recent best-selling novel?

Are other operas out there based on the same story? In many cases, yes. What has been common throughout opera is also common in the movies today. How many Robin Hood films has Hollywood made, ranging from high drama to farce, from swift action to panting romance?

Some composers, including Mozart, Verdi, and Richard Strauss, had favorite librettists with whom they worked and who helped make them famous. A few composers, including Wagner and Berlioz, were their own librettists. (So are many contemporary composers.) If you care to spend time studying the plot, you can see what plot "devices" are used—how natural is it, how far-fetched, how contrived? For example, are there eavesdroppers, hiding from the other characters even though they're right there on the stage in front of the audience? Many operas have two separate eavesdroppers at the same time, presumably "hidden" not only from the central characters but also from each other. Mozart's *Marriage of Figaro* has fine eavesdroppers. So does Verdi's *Rigoletto*. (Don't knock the notion; so did William Shakespeare.) The stage makes its own rules, and if those rules distress you perhaps some kinds of opera aren't your thing. That's okay; there are many other kinds.

(In a Hamilton College Shakespeare course a century ago I wrote a term paper on all the means Shakespeare used to get a dead body off the stage. In opera, as in Shakespeare, it's a lot easier to kill someone at the end of an act so the body can walk off when the curtain falls.)

Warning: Don't be overly quick to reject an opera because it has a convoluted or even ridiculous plot. Sometimes when the story line is tangled beyond belief the work still offers magnificent characters who depict deep human emotions.

A second critical part of most opera is recitative, which is encountered first with the Camerata and soon thereafter with Monteverdi.

RECITATIVE   The dictionary, as usual, says it most simply: "A type of declamation, as for operatic dialogue, with the rhythm of speech, but in musical tones."

The operative words are declamation "in musical tones." Not plain, ordinary old dialogue, or *spoken* words, but words that are sung. Most of us don't go around singing sentences at one another. And thus many of us today—and many operagoers of the past—have yawned through the "recitative" while waiting for the superstar to belt out the next big song. Many of us don't understand the language, we haven't studied the plot before leaving home, the lights are too low for us to read a libretto during the performance, and the producers (until recently) have supplied no help in supertitles above the stage or on the backs of the seats in front of us. In this situation, we can neither appreciate the poetry nor follow the action. So we paw the floor, or doze off, awaiting the solo song or duet we hope is coming sometime down the road.

We've put ourselves in a hard-to-win position. By and large, our enjoyment under these circumstances must come from the voices of the players and the chorus, the orchestra in the pit, possibly some ballet or other dancing, and perhaps some spectacular costuming and scenic effects. That may give us more pleasure than the evening television schedule, but we aren't giving opera much of a break. It's sort of like going to a football game under the misconception that each team can keep the ball until it scores.

There are many kinds of recitative. It can be sing-speech intoned with no instrumental accompaniment, or sing-speech attended only by background chords from a lute or harpsichord, or strong recitative that nearly overrides a full orchestra.

The recitative in Monteverdi's *Orfeo* doesn't sound anything like the recitative in Puccini's *Tosca*. Wagner in *The Ring* and Debussy in *Pelléas et Mélisande* pretty much do away with both recitative and big vocal arias, substituting what is sometimes called "continuous song," something not very detachable that is sort of midway between the conventional recitative and aria.

Not all opera demands recitative. Many works in The Collection, including Bizet's *Carmen* in its original form, rely on "spoken dialogue"—plain unsung words, as in a play—to carry the plot line between the set singing numbers. We'll see that this never happens in Italy, unless the Italian composer is writing French opera for a French audience, such as Donizetti did in *The Daughter of the Regiment*.

Traditionally, recitative had a specific job to do. Again, opera is a play, a drama—a play in music, but always a play. If it's to be a successful play, the audience must understand what the people on the stage are saying and recognize the reality of what the people on the stage are doing. The words of the recitative moved the plot along. They were the guts of the action.

But then there's the music part. Music, by definition, is the arrangement of sounds in time. For music to succeed in doing what it does, it must take control of time, often to the point of utterly altering the "natural" flow. Any moviegoer knows that a sad mood generally calls for slow-time music; an excited mood for fast-time music. The alternation between "drama" and "music" is inherent to the medium itself.

What about different kinds of opera?

There are almost as many types as there are recipes for key lime pie. There is opera seria, opera semiseria, comic opera, opéra comique, number opera, lyric tragedy, opera buffa, opéra bouffe, grand opera, ballad opera, opera-ballet, bel canto opera, rescue opera, chamber opera, German Singspiel, German Romantic opera . . . and more.

Let's begin with the early forms before things got complicated: opera seria; its comedic opposite, opera buffa; and a middle-ground compromise, opera semiseria.

OPERA SERIA   For a long time this Italian term was used for "just plain opera"—serious opera. It referred initially to eighteenth-century Italian opera that was based on a serious plot and divided into three acts. There were set rules: The language was always Italian, the subject was usually mythological or historical, and the ending was happy. Italian opera was so dominant that composers of many nationalities wrote opera seria and stuck to the Italian rules. The truest example of old-time opera seria in The Collection is *Julius Caesar*, written by the German-born Handel when he was living in London in 1724. Even though he was writing for the English public, he followed the Italian style of the day. Variants of opera seria are Gluck's *Orfeo ed Euridice* (1762) and Mozart's *Idomeneo* (1781), his first operatic masterpiece. The opera seria form ended with Mozart in the latter years of the eighteenth century.

OPERA BUFFA   Comic opera, the opposite of opera seria, an opera written in Italian that was meant to be funny. Like opera seria, it was developed in Italy in the eighteenth century. And like opera seria, it used recitative to link the arias. Works as late as Donizetti's *Elixir of Love* and Rossini's *Barber of Seville* from the first half of the nineteenth century are examples of opera buffa. Before them, in the late 1770s, opera buffa had led the way in developing the use of ensembles (singing numbers involving more than one voice: duets, trios, act finales with many characters participating, and so on), all commonly taboo in opera seria. Operas composed by Rossini a little later have at least as much ensemble as aria. That wouldn't have been found in the old opera seria.

Opera buffa is just one type of comic opera. Let's look at comic opera in general and some other types.

Generally speaking, whatever the country or century, comic opera is more tuneful to the ear than "serious" opera. It's perhaps easier to perform (although not necessarily easier to perform well), demanding less from the orchestra, the cast, and the production engineers. It's less complicated for the audience to follow and comprehend. Its characters are more likely to come from everyday life than from myths and legends, and there is not apt to be great spectacle.

Here are two forms of comic opera, plus a third definition included to help prevent confusion:

OPÉRA BOUFFE   Not Italian "buffa," as above, but French *"bouffe."* A special form of Parisian opera of which the foremost proponent was Collection composer Jacques Offenbach. He arrived as a boy in Paris in 1833 and, in 1855, opened his own theater, called the Bouffes-Parisiens, where he produced short musical works that were humorous, frequently farcical, and sometimes satirical. They were lighter than other comic operas, close to what came to be called "operettas."

OPÉRA COMIQUE A French term, the counterpart to Italian opera buffa. The Italians said opera buffa for their comic opera, the French said opéra comique for theirs. But there was one major difference. Italian opera buffa was sung throughout—that is, it used recitative between the big songs—whereas French opéra comique had regular speech, spoken dialogue. (For now, we'll waive the exceptions, which include a revised *Carmen*.)

OPÉRA-COMIQUE Be careful. With the capital O, the hyphen, and the capital C, this is not opera at all but rather an opera company and its building in Paris. For many years (although not indefinitely), all opera produced there used spoken dialogue rather than recitative. Also, for some years (but not indefinitely), any opera staged at the Opéra-Comique was, in fact, a comic opera.

OPERA SEMISERIA An early Italian serious opera with some comedy thrown in. Some composers flirted more than others with comic elements, and some varied the amount of those elements in different operas, so the lines get blurry. Mozart's *Don Giovanni* technically is opera buffa but really is a hybrid and more logically might be called opera semiseria. (Mozart called it "dramma giocoso" or "jocular drama," but that gets a little technical for us). (The Austrian Mozart was writing Italian-style opera, in Italian, because that's what successful opera composers did at the time.) The great classical composer Franz Joseph Haydn wrote many semiseria operas.

Composers are creative folk. In different opera-producing countries over several centuries there were countless variations in what was seen on the stage. Among a few of the other terms and forms we encounter:

BALLAD OPERA An eighteenth-century form of English musical theater in which spoken dialogue alternated with songs. The music usually was secondhand; new verses were written for tunes the audience already knew. The most important one was John Gay's *Beggar's Opera*, famous but not in The Collection.

BEL CANTO OPERA "Bel canto" is Italian for "beautiful singing." The term, an imprecise one, also embraces a particular style of singing that emphasizes beautiful tone and brilliant technique rather than dramatic expression. It's associated with Italian opera of the late eighteenth and early nineteenth centuries, especially the works of Rossini, Donizetti, and Bellini. Bel canto composers placed more emphasis on singing than on plot development and story. Donizetti's *Lucia di Lammermoor* is an example.

CHAMBER OPERA An opera requiring a smaller cast and a smaller orchestra than other opera. Britten's *Turn of the Screw*, in the Twentieth-century European Package, is an example. Because of its smaller scale, chamber opera is less frequently performed by the major opera houses.

GRAND OPERA   Think BIG. Another imprecise term, initially used chiefly for the nineteenth-century French operas composed by Collection composer Meyerbeer (*Les Huguenots*) and a few predecessors, contemporaries, and followers. French grand opera had five acts, was based on a serious subject, and employed recitative. The lavish productions included large musical numbers, huge orchestras, big choruses, ballet, elaborate and impressive staging, much spectacle, and big crowd scenes. Later on, composers from other countries also wrote this kind of opera, in part for Parisian audiences. Verdi's *Aida* is an example of an Italian grand opera. Today the term is used more broadly, to describe serious opera that is sung throughout and is "grand" but perhaps less spectacular than the original "grand."

LYRIC OPERA   In the pure sense, all opera is lyrical since it's sung poetry. But in a narrower sense lyric opera is a type of nineteenth-century French opera that was more serious than comic opera but tended to be smaller, less spectacular, and more unified than grand opera. (Webster defines lyric: "suitable for singing to the lyre or for being set to music and sung," also "expressing direct usually intense personal emotion.") Gounod's *Faust* is cited as an example by some academicians, although productions of it at the old Paris Opéra house could be very grand indeed. Opera is art; it isn't wise to look for hard, definitive walls that separate one form from another. Many, but not all, late-nineteenth-century lyric operas were produced at the Opéra-Comique.

MUSIC DRAMA   A term Wagner used to distinguish his works from opera composed by mere mortals. Wagner believed that the term "opera" emphasized the aria and a platform for the singer, whereas his "music drama" was designed as a work that unified vocal and instrumental music with the poetry of the text, did away with special virtuoso songs, and offered his long melodic combination of voice and orchestra. The result is something that is more tuneful than recitative but less so than conventional arias. In fact, although many other composers clearly wrote "music dramas," some special term is needed for Wagner inasmuch as so much of what he did was completely new and his influence was so great. So the music people tend to reserve the term "music drama" for his works, as the sports people retire the jersey number of a superstar jock. *Parsifal* is a classic example of music drama.

NUMBER OPERA   Generally, a number opera emphasizes the separate vocal operatic numbers within it—the arias, duets, and ensembles. Some composers actually numbered the songs—1, 2, 3, and so on—and some operas had as many as twenty-five or thirty. Some did not. Some grand operas are put in the number opera category; some are not. Stravinsky's twentieth-century *Rake's Progress*, in which he went to the past for a model, qualifies as a number opera.

L'OPÉRA   Another institution, not a type of opera. The longer title is the Paris Opéra, although in New York that would be like saying the New York Yankees instead of simply the Yankees. Parisians tend to condense it to the O. Technically, it is the Académie Royale de Musique.

OPERA-ORATORIO   A work combining both forms. Although there's action, as in an opera, most of the story is told through words and music, as in an oratorio. Stravinsky's *Oedipus Rex* is one example; Saint-Saëns's Collection work, *Samson et Dalila*, is sort of one. A large number of Handel's operas fit into this category.

OPERETTA   Literally, a short opera. It's impossible to draw a steady line between all operetta and all lighter forms of the earlier opéra comique. Both have spoken dialogue, usually deal with pleasant subjects, traditionally include comic elements, and often ooze charm. Both are usually sentimental. "Good" operetta doesn't demand the development of a character; "good" lighter opera does. More later on the differences between the two.

RESCUE OPERA   Especially popular during the French Revolution, this is opera in which the hero or heroine is rescued at the last minute from death or a fate worse than death. Beethoven's *Fidelio* is a rescue opera.

SINGSPIEL   A type of early German comic opera in which spoken dialogue rather than recitative was used between folk-type songs and bigger opera-type arias. Mozart's *Magic Flute* would be an example, except that in it he took the form to its highest musical peak—and then soared beyond it. There's no news in this, inasmuch as Mozart did the same thing with everything he touched.

TRAGÉDIE LYRIQUE   (lyrical tragedy). A type of serious French opera established by Lully and his librettists in Paris in the 1670s and 1680s. Picked up later by Rameau and others, it combined elements of classical drama and ballet and gave bigger roles to instrumental and choral numbers. Rameau's Collection *Castor et Pollux* is an example.

VERISMO OPERA   *Verismo* is Italian for realism. A verismo movement developed in literature in Italy in the 1870s, influenced by the French naturalism movement that was led by Emile Zola. Both were dedicated to the depiction of real-life events. One of the major Italian veristic figures was Giovanni Verga in Sicily, among whose works was a story called *Cavalleria rusticana*. Verismo operas often dealt with contemporary people in lower economic circumstances. Not pretty. The two biggest operatic proponents were Collection composers Mascagni and Leoncavallo, with *Cavalleria rusticana* and *Pagliacci*. Some analysts include Puccini in the latter-day verismo school, and his *La Bohème* and *Tosca* have some veristic elements, but they aren't the real thing.

OTHER MUSICAL TERMS

Here are a handful of terms concerned with the singing and music in an opera.

ARIA   A composition for solo voice. A song, often of an emotional kind. Something to clap for. For years, different kinds of arias were built to rigid specifications, just as symphonies and sonatas in instrumental music or sonnets in literature were. As centuries passed, the rules changed and/or were ignored.

Now an aria is any operatic vocal solo. One of the best known is the "Laugh, Clown" number from *Pagliacci*.

ARIETTA   A diminutive aria, usually no longer than a minute or two.

ARIOSO   A style of recitative, not a thing, like an arietta, but a condition. It's closer to full-blown singing, usually more expressive than ordinary recitative.

BARCAROLLE   A song or instrumental piece in the style sung by Venetian gondoliers. The most famous is the Barcarolle in Offenbach's *Tales of Hoffmann*.

CABALETTA   One of several terms included here because newcomers to opera are apt to come across it in other reading or hear it on radio or television. In the eighteenth and early nineteenth centuries, a cabaletta was a short aria, an example of which is Rosina's "Una voce poco fa" in Act I of Rossini's *Barber of Seville*. Later in the nineteenth century, the term was used for the end section of a long aria or duet. It was quick and lively, the name having come from the Italian for cavallo, which suggested the galloping of a horse. The first section of that two-part piece, this one in slower tempo, was called a *cavatina*. The two combined constituted an aria—or a *scena*. An example of a cavatina/cabaletta combination is Violetta's aria-scena in Act I of Verdi's *La traviata*, in which she first sings the cavatina "Ah! fors' è lui," which is followed by recitative and then by the cabaletta, her "Sempre libera." If you listen to Metropolitan Opera broadcasts, you'll hear talk of cabalettas and cavatinas. Think of them simply as songs singers sing.

CANTATA   Not an opera term but one associated with music-and-drama. A vocal piece that's nearly always on a religious subject, performed without action or scenery. Bach was the master's master of cantatas. A long one is similar to a short oratorio. In Act I of *Tosca*, the people are pleased to learn that Tosca will sing a cantata offstage—and a bit of it is heard at the start of Act II.

CHORUS   A body of singers. In seventeenth-century operas, the chorus was used to reflect the action but not to participate in it. Gluck, the great reformer, made it a bigger part of the game.

COLORATURA   Italian for "coloring." The purpose of coloratura is to increase dramatic and emotional expressiveness. Coincidentally, it showed off the singing star. Many composers wrote for just that purpose. But in the hands of the great interpreters of the great composers—Maria Callas interpreting Bellini, for example—the main point is the drama that is produced, not the incidental vocal trills and other ornaments. A coloratura soprano is a soprano who specializes in coloratura.

CRESCENDO   Increasing loudness. Rossini used it so often as a structural device that he was called "Signor Crescendo." All compositions vary in loudness. Rossini, however, used crescendo as his main musical device for pages at a time.

DA CAPO   Literally, Italian for "from the head," a direction in a musical piece for the performer to start again, from the beginning. In a da capo aria, the third and last of three sections is a repetition of the first. This form controlled opera for years. Although it slowed down the pace of the action, inasmuch as the audience heard the same words twice, the virtuoso singers loved it since they could do a lot of improvising as they decorated the repetitive parts.

DUET   A composition for two performers of equal importance, with or without accompaniment. Purists say that two voices singing the same words and tune together do not necessarily make an *opera* duet. With few exceptions, opera until the nineteenth century consisted of recitative and arias. Big continuous scenes were comparatively rare before Mozart (and non-Collection Haydn). In the early days, when two people sang together they were simply blending. In a true opera "duet" the two are singing different words, supplementing one another or being in conflict. Rossini incorporated "confrontational" duets into *The Barber of Seville* (and a great one into *Semiramide*, which is not in The Collection). Verdi, supreme master of duets, then seized the idea. In addition to his lover-and-lover duets, his greatest ones include mother and son (*Il trovatore*), father and daughter (*Rigoletto*), and father and son (*Don Carlo*). The analysts tell us that virtually all of Verdi's great duets are confrontational, and nearly always move through a dramatic sequence toward a climax or resolution.

ENSEMBLE   Trios, quartets, quintets, sextets, septets, all useful for communicating several contrasting emotions at the same time. Experts cite three advantages an opera has over spoken drama. First, song is more expressive than speech. Second, the orchestra supports the drama. Third, the intensity of a drama or the tone of a comedy can be increased when several characters verbalize simultaneously. Assume that word is received that a fugitive has been killed. In one short scene there's instant and varied emotion from his wife, lover, jailer, and priest. In spoken drama, this would be babble.

FINALE   The final stage-filling scene before a curtain falls, developed in Italian comic opera during the late eighteenth century. Not all composers tried to tie up the whole situation as the curtain came down, with all main characters onstage, but many did. Mozart's comic operas, including The Collection's *Così fan tutte*, are famous for their finales, and so are Rossini's. A finale does not necessarily end the opera; often it is put at the end of an act in midopera. One fine example is the end of Act II of the four-act *Marriage of Figaro*.

LEITMOTIF   German for "leading motive," or "leading theme." These short patterns of music were used by Richard Wagner and many subsequent composers. Although not the first to adopt the idea of recurring patterns associated with particular characters, emotions, or things, Wagner used them much more frequently and skillfully than other composers. But it didn't stop there. Wagner's contemporary, Verdi was influenced by this leitmotif concept and so were virtually all other composers—including Puccini and Debussy.

ORCHESTRA   Provides the accompaniment (professionals advise me that conductors don't like that term, preferring to think of a singer-orchestra "partnership" rather than accompaniment) and plays independently for the overture and other nonvocal musical writing. Orchestral pieces that occur during the opera are called preludes and interludes, or intermezzi, according to whether they are before, during, or after an act. Richard Wagner and Richard Strauss featured the orchestra; Donizetti gave it a less important role.

OVERTURE   Orchestral music before an opera begins. An overture may or may not "quote" from the music of the opera. It is generally longer than a prelude, and usually the curtain doesn't open until the overture has ended. But the lines between an overture and a prelude are blurry. In many—but not all—cases, the overture introduces the entire opera, whereas the prelude is related more specifically to the opening scene.

PRELUDE   A short orchestral introduction to any act, leading directly into the act without a curtain or formal ending. Again, the terms are nebulous. Some composers called pieces preludes that others would have considered overtures. Wagner's Prelude to *Die Meistersinger* is an example.

RITORNELLO   Literally, "little return." A short instrumental passage that introduces a vocal piece and/or returns at several points, during the middle, or at the end.

VOICE CLASSIFICATIONS   In the simplest breakdown, for women, from high to low: soprano, mezzo-soprano, and contralto. For men: tenor, baritone, and bass. The coloratura soprano has the highest range and the greatest agility, the dramatic soprano does drama, the lyric soprano prefers gentler music. See chapter nine, on voices, for much greater detail.

WHYS AND WHEREFORES OF KEYS, SCALES, TONES, AND TONALITY

I open this can of worms reluctantly to help explain why some opera music sounds different from other opera music—particularly early twentieth-century compositions from music of previous centuries. Here we'll stick to the sounds of a Richard Strauss, a Wagner, a Debussy, a Stravinsky, or a Berg and not yet get into more recent things like minimalism or electronic music.

Virtually all compositions between 1700 and 1900 are called *tonal*. They are written in a set key, the key of C, for instance, with notes and chords returning to or resolving into that basic key. Beginning around 1900, many composers consciously avoided having such a tonal center or definite key and wrote music called atonal.

While avoiding Music Composition 101, let's pursue the idea of tone a little.

TONE   A sound of distinct pitch and duration. In our system—traditional Western European music—all tones are a half step apart. (That in-between space is called an interval.) This half-step distance between tones is not true everywhere. India, for example, has tones a quarter step apart. Indian music could not be played on our piano, although it could be played on a violin. On a piano, starting on the white key of C, and following each key in order, whether white or black, it goes C, black C sharp, D, black D sharp, E, F, black F sharp, G, black G sharp, A, black A sharp, B . . . and back to another C. These twelve notes, constituting an octave, represent all tones normally used in Western European music. Thus all A's on the piano have exactly the same tone, although the *pitch* of one is higher or lower than other A's. (Pitch is the highness or lowness of sound due to the difference in sound waves.) So no clashing sound is heard if all A's on the keyboard are hit simultaneously.

DIATONIC SCALE   A scale is a series of tones, rising or falling. The diatonic scale is the one we know best, the do-re-mi-fa-sol-la-ti-do scale of eight notes we learned in school (seven different ones, plus a repetition of the first). It was used almost exclusively in Western European music from before 1700 to the late 1800s. The beginning note, that first do, is called the key, or the tonic, note. *Tonality* is the relationship between the other six notes and chords on a diatonic scale and that central note on which a given passage is centered. The note that is five notes up the diatonic scale—the white G, in the key of C, the sol—is called the dominant because of its "dominating" position in harmony and melody. Try it. Singing up the scale, you don't emphasize the fa or the la; you hit the "sol." If you start on the C on a piano keyboard and go up the white keys, you hear the familiar do-re-mi sounds all the way through. Our ears are so accustomed to this scale that if we try to stop with ti, without repeating the initial do, we find ourselves hanging in midair. Something demands that we resound that initial do, this time an octave higher, and resolve the tension. If we begin on any note other than C, white or black, we still can pick out the familiar do-re-mi diatonic scale, although each time we will use different combinations of white and black notes to get there—and thus, in each case, we will have different notes as the tonic and the dominant. But our composition still will be tonal.

CHROMATIC SCALE   A scale made up of the twelve half steps in an octave—all of the seven white and five black piano notes identified above, as opposed to the total of seven that are in the do-re-mi diatonic scale.

CHROMATIC NOTES   For composers using the diatonic scale, the leftover five notes after employment of the other seven. These five don't have the plague; no law forbids the composer who is writing tonal music from taking advantage of them here and there as decorations. Old Mr. Bach, for example, did so freely, without significant loss of stability in his work.

CHROMATIC MUSIC   This is a different fish. The composer does not merely use the chromatic notes as occasional ornaments, he uses them consistently, as structural elements. He walks away from the conventional Western music of several centuries and from the foundations traditionally provided by the sense of remaining in one key for a period of time. His music sounds different from Bach, Mozart, Beethoven, and Brahms. Leading examples of opera composers who wrote chromatic music are Wagner and Richard Strauss. Their music is more restless than earlier music, less rigid, not as "resolved." But it is still tonal; there still are references to a tonal center.

Now consider *atonal* composition. Atonality, literally, is the absence of tonality—the organization of tones without relation to a key note. As noted, the breakdown of conventional tonality began in the work of Wagner, Strauss, and others and was taken much further by Berg. The reference to a tonal center that is found in music using the diatonic scale now is gone.

WHOLE-TONE SCALE   The smallest interval in Western European music is the half step, as noted. The next smallest is a whole step, consisting of two half steps. In our "traditional" diatonic scale, in two cases the notes are only a half tone apart. Check the piano keyboard. With the C major scale, the distance from E to F and from B to the second C is only half as large as the other distances. In the whole-tone scale, all the notes are a full step apart; the scale thus consists of only six notes to the octave. Impressionist Claude Debussy uses this approach. Unlike the diatonic scale, the whole-tone scale does not involve a tonic, or tonal, center. We don't have the familiar do-re-mi that resolves itself. This is why Debussy's *Pelléas et Mélisande* sounds hauntingly vague and indefinite.

TWELVE TONE MUSIC   Music based on all twelve notes of the chromatic scale, *each treated with equal importance*. The old traditional hierarchy of notes, the to-and-fro discussed above, is abandoned. The familiar do-re-mi progression no longer is heard. Unlike the music of Wagner and Richard Strauss, this is true atonality. The composition no longer is in any set key, and there is no center to which to return. The most successful opera using the twelve-tone scale is Alban Berg's *Lulu*, which is in the Twentieth-century European Package. (Berg's *Wozzeck* is in The Collection.)

SERIAL MUSIC   This is music based on a twelve-tone, chromatic scale, but with all twelve notes sounded in a specific order. Arnold Schoenberg, mentor of Berg and composer of *Moses und Aron*, devised this system. When Schoenberg's music first appeared, many critics and many music-loving amateurs protested that it shrieked, grunted, and growled. But that was eighty-five years ago. Still, while professional respect for Schoenberg—and for Berg—now is great, not many operas in serial music have shown strong staying power.

Finally:

Opera composers didn't work in a vacuum. The five major periods of music are the Renaissance, about 1450–1600; Baroque, 1600–1750; Classical, 1750–1825; Romantic, 1825–1910; and Twentieth Century, 1910–on. The dates are approximate and there is overlap in all of them. For background, here are a few of the major composers of classical music in those periods.

RENAISSANCE   Palestrina. Although the Renaissance is pre-opera, he was a classical giant of that period.

BAROQUE   Bach, Handel, Vivaldi, Gluck, Couperin, and Rameau.

CLASSICAL   Haydn, Mozart, and Beethoven.

BRIDGE TO ROMANTIC   Schubert.

ROMANTIC   Schumann, Mendelssohn, Liszt, Weber, Berlioz, Dvořák, Chopin, Brahms, Sibelius, Saint-Saëns, Franck, Mahler, Bruckner, Smetana, Tchaikovsky, and many, many more.

TWENTIETH CENTURY   Stravinsky, Prokofiev, Shostakovich, Hindemith, Bartok, and more.

Take a breath. The Unwashed and perhaps a few of the mildly Washed may want to come back to this chapter a time or two, but I hope most of the terms mentioned here will fall naturally into play.

Chapter 5

SETTING THE STAGE: A SHORT HISTORY OF OPERA

❧

This chapter is divided into two parts, The Beginnings of Opera and A Short History of Opera.

THE BEGINNINGS

Don Corleone, Liza Minnelli, Fiorello La Guardia, Joe Di Maggio, and Prego are known to most Americans.

Giulio Caccini, Vincenzo Galilei, Pietro Strozzi, Jacopo Peri, and Count Giovanni de' Bardi are not.

Actually, you *have* heard of Galilei's son, whose first name was Galileo and who got into astronomy.

But Vincenzo and his friends were part of the opera-inventing group called the Camerata.

"Camerata" is translated as a group that meets in a room. In the late sixteenth century in Florence such a group was formed to discuss music, literature, and the theater. Two noblemen led it, Count Bardi and Jacopo Corsi. Caccini, Galilei, Strozzi and Peri were musicians. A poet named Ottavio Rinuccini was there too. So was Emilio de' Cavalieri, musician and composer. Their mission, defined no doubt while consuming the wine of the province, was to restore the forms of ancient Greek drama, including drama with music. No one told them they were going to be an important part of music history.

Focusing on drama and the different ways in which it might be enhanced by music, they began to experiment by having the actors sing their lines instead of speaking them. Music was to be an integral part of the whole, assigned to help carry out the plot, not just appended onto the drama. Further, the song had to be clear song, which stood out and was understood by the audience—unencumbered by other voices singing other parts. Although the Camerata did not go so far as to create a single melody supported by the complex chords that were fashioned later, they did move away from the traditional multipart music that theretofore had been dominant.

In their studies they came across a Greek treatise by Aristoxenus, a fourth-century B.C. disciple of Aristotle and one of the earliest experts of classical music theory. He wrote that song should be patterned after speech. They also found some advice from Plato, the famed Greek philosopher, who said, "Let music be first of all language and rhythm, and secondly tone, and not vice versa." Guided by this counsel from the ancient past, the Camerata did utilize a speechlike single-voiced melody accompanied by very simple chords played by a harpsichord or an organ. They called it "stile rappresentativo," or "recitative." It was a dominant element of their new musical form.

"Recitative" often is called sing-speech, which is perhaps a misleading description. Although speechlike in rhythm, it is nonetheless definitely song, and it is sung. It is not talk; it is music—often highly expressive music, essential to the work. Even if there are no instruments, either playing by themselves or offering a soft accompaniment, a drama in which the actors sing all of their lines in recitative is not a play *with* music but a play *in* music. *This* was new. In time, it would be called *opera*.

The earliest operas consisted of a series of recitatives with minor instrumental accompaniment. To this day, recitative remains a critical building block of most operas.

It was not until a little later that the *aria*—a solo song, apart from the recitative, usually with instrumental accompaniment—appeared. Once that happened, there was a whole new ball game. Composers had to decide how many arias they would put in their works and who would sing them, and the audiences—at the prince's court or later in the public house—indicated what most appealed to them. Finally, Richard Wagner sort of did away with both recitative and arias in his operas, replacing them with what he called "unending melody," but that story comes later.

In fact, although it may be treasonous to put it this way, the aristocratic humanists who were the Camerata—I think of it as a Dead Poet's Society—failed in their primary mission, which was to resurrect Greek drama. In corporate employee performance evaluation terms, so far as that goal was concerned they did not even "achieve standards," let alone "exceed" them.

But, like the failure of Christopher Columbus one hundred years earlier, significant results came from their effort. Dedicated to the proposition that poetry could be enhanced emotionally by music and that the right combination of music and poetry could impact favorably on the quality of life of an audience, they took the text of a poem, turned it into sung recitative, and provided the singers with a simple instrumental accompaniment. And when that came off to their satisfaction, they took another step, using the same technique not only for a mere poem but for a full drama.

Unwittingly, they had then created opera. The details went something like this:

In 1590, Emilio de' Cavalieri wrote musical scenes in which he made use of the new recitative. A little later Galilei took some old Lamentations and put them into a musical setting (the Bible folk among readers know that Lamentations are about the fall of Jerusalem).

Peri married these approaches with an old Greek drama. In 1597 a work called *Dafne* was completed, with music by Peri to a text by Rinuccini. It was called a *drama for music*—the first stage work to be set to music from beginning to end and, as such, technically the first opera. Unfortunately, it has been lost.

Peri then took an ancient Greek myth about a lyre-playing chap named Orpheus who tried to rescue his true love, (English spelling) Eurydice, from Hades, converting its text into musical recitative. *Euridice* (Italian spelling) was performed on October 6, 1600, at the Pitti Palace in Florence. Given the loss of *Dafne*, it is accepted by many music historians as *the* first opera.

Another setting of the same Orpheus story was done by Caccini. Although completed at about the same time, it was not performed until two years later.

We can hope that the Camerata threw themselves a big party. They had done something unprecedented, even if it was not to reconstruct classic Greek drama. In the endgame, their operas were a continuous flow of recitative, accompanied by a small orchestra of lutes, gambas, and a harpsichord. (A viola da gamba, the bass of its family, was a stringed instrument held on or between the player's knees.)

Let's pause for a moment and go back to the development of the solo song that has such a key role in opera.

At the time of the Camerata, there was a big musical conflict in Italy involving *homophony* versus *polyphony*. It was related to opera development in that it was concerned with the solo song.

Music in the sixteenth century was mostly polyphonic—"poly" = many, "phonic" = voices. Each composition had two or more melodies going at the same time—sung or played on instruments. The challenge for the composer and the enjoyment for the listener came from the simultaneous interplay of the different melodic lines. Polyphonic music had been played for centuries, peaked some 150 years later under Johann Sebastian Bach, and still is with us today.

The musical term *counterpoint*, a word less known to most of us than needlepoint, is the art of weaving together melodic line against melodic line, this point against that point—and the musician doing this is creating polyphonic music. The term "contrapuntal" is not the formation used to try to block a kick in a football game but rather just the relevant adjective. Compose in a contrapuntal fashion and you have counterpoint.

When a chorus sings polyphonic music, different sections take different melodies. Let's say three. The listener hears three "voices" woven together into the whole. It sounds very nice, but there isn't much room there for a soloist.

As the art of singing developed, one early step was to lift out one of the simultaneous melodies (generally the top one) and give it to a solo singer. The other voices continued on their way as they had before. This did not make the soloist ecstatic. His (not hers on the public stage at that time) lone voice was competing against several choral melodies. Inevitably, the soloist began embellishing his part in order to capture a bigger share of the attention, but he still was hanging out there twisting in the wind.

Through experimentation, composers and musicians began to eliminate all melodies except one—and then to support that one with some instrumental chords in the background. This single-melody music is called "homophonic," from the Greek "homophonus," being in unison.

Most people know that a chord is three or more musical notes sounded at the same time. This gets us to *harmony*—musical harmony, not the harmony of some political nominating conventions. Harmony is the combination of the musical sounds in a chord and the progression of chords in a musical structure. With simultaneous melodies (polyphonic music, counterpoint), the music may be magnificent—but there is no "harmony." With a single melody, supported by chords, and with the chords themselves becoming less simple, changing, and progressing, the music sounds different—and now there is "harmony."

No one says it's "better" music. It's different music.

The composition with one melody-plus-chords clearly was a far better deal for a single human voice, and thus more appropriate for the onstage hero of the operatic form that was being invented. (As an aside of great importance to classical music, it also was more appropriate for a single instrument, pitted against other instruments. In polyphonic classical music, with different groups of instruments playing different melodies simultaneously, there was not much a single flute or violin could do for itself . . . unless it turned the volume way up while the rest of the group played very softly. That might work for a trumpet or tuba, but it doesn't do a lot for a flute. By contrast, in homophonic music the individual instrument could take the melody in the same way as the individual human voice. The result, in time, was the violin [or trumpet or piano] concerto—one instrument playing a star role, with the orchestra in the background.)

Most classical music before the 1600s and early 1700s was polyphonic. Most since 1750 has emphasized melody-plus-chords, although in the twentieth century there was something of a revival of polyphonic composition—a Back to Bach movement.

In talking about solo song, the music people like the word "monody"—not as in Monody, Tuesday, Wednesday but as in a melody sung with a single voice, with instrumental accompaniment. To musicologists, the evolution of monody constituted one of the greatest achievements of the Renaissance, and the "invention" of solo song was of critical importance to the development of opera.

To orient ourselves, let's check the timetable for 1600, when opera was beginning:

- It had been eighty-three years since Martin Luther had nailed ninety-five theses to the wall of a church in Wittenberg, Germany, starting the Protestant Reformation.
- In England, William Shakespeare had written *Romeo and Juliet* and was completing *Hamlet*.
- The first permanent English colony in America, in Jamestown, Virginia, was to be settled in another seven years. A year thereafter, the French would establish a colony in Quebec.

The point: We are scarcely in the Stone Age. Unlike instrumental "classical" music, opera is relatively new.

A SHORT OPERA HISTORY

I regard this as rather a dreary section, apologize for all the facts, dates, names, and detail in it, and am tempted to recommend that most readers skip it and move on to The Collection operas. But only tempted, since I hope it will be useful for the Unwashed in sorting out the players and their works. With eighty-five Collection operas by more than fifty composers, it helps me if I sort them out by century and nationality.

The Collection operas cover nearly four hundred years, beginning in 1607. These are described in chapter six, the major portion of this book. Other operas are identified and discussed in the Twentieth-century European Package and the American chapter.

This segment gives a fleeting look at opera's history, century by century and country by country. So it goes beyond The Collection and the other operas that come later to include a good many other fine composers who are part of opera development.

That's the rub. Although operas in The Collection are the more successful ones, we will return to them. The non-Collection works mentioned here, however, will not be cited again. Thus in these immediate pages sometimes those other operas and their composures receive more notice than The Collection works. The objective is to help orient the reader, fill in some of the blanks and illustrate that The Collection, the Twentieth-century European Package and the American chapter do not tell the whole opera story.

Some repetition between this overview and later chapters is inevitable, but that's not all bad. This is a road map, not a textbook; no tests will be given, and my recommendation is to just puff a little. No need to inhale.

Over-simplification is useful for those of us who are not connoisseurs. Historically, and overly simplified, countries and their operas came to be matched in the following fashion:

Italian opera—voice
French opera—spectacle, including ballet
German and Eastern European opera—orchestra

At the start of each section, The Collection composers will be listed, with their birth and death dates. Some of them will be discussed in that section and some dismissed until we meet them again later in the book.

The Seventeenth Century

Italy: The Seventeenth Century

> The genius of Monteverdi is dominant. The aria is emphasized and then overemphasized. Duets are developed. Public opera is born, and the public watching it demands more spectacle. Vocal music becomes more important than drama.

THE COLLECTION COMPOSERS
Claudio Monteverdi (1567–1643)

The Camerata predates The Collection, but two seventeenth-century Italians are in it: Monteverdi, father of all opera, and Jean-Baptiste Lully, founder of French opera. The latter, although Italian by birth (born Lulli in Florence in 1632), was so important to Parisian opera that he is discussed below under France.

Significant Italian composers not in The Collection include Francisco Cavalli (1602–76) and Antonio Cesti (1623–69).

As the century began, Monteverdi, born in Cremona in 1567 and not part of the Florentine Camerata, was in his early thirties. He had written motets (choral compositions on a sacred text) and madrigals (secular vocal pieces) and was both a string musician and a composition theorist. Seizing and developing the latest thing—opera—he composed his own music for the Orpheus story, a work first performed in 1607. Monteverdi was one of the giants of classical music, and his La Favola d'Orfeo, often shortened to L'Orfeo or Orfeo, was much more sophisticated than the Camerata versions, and it is the earliest opera that is performed today. Some musicologists call it the first "modern" opera, but that seems both strange and confusing so we won't.

Although opera began in Florence and Monteverdi worked first in the town

Claudio Monteverdi

of Mantua, during the century the cardinals' palace in Rome became the more important center of Italian opera. From there it spread gradually to Bologna, Parma,
and Venice, initially reserved chiefly for the courts of princes and other noble folk.

Then all hell broke loose or, more accurately, began to break loose. In
1637 the Teatro San Cassiano was opened in Venice, a public opera house that
plain, ordinary Italians could attend simply by paying a small admission fee.
Three more such public theaters quickly followed as sponsors competed with
one another. Soon sixteen Venetian houses were in business, an astonishing
number for entertainment presumed to be elitist. This was not patronage of the
arts designed to enrich the lives of the Venetian commoner but rather rampant

free-market capitalism, not unlike the spread of movie theaters in the United States earlier in this century. Nobles opened the houses and rented them out to entrepreneurs.

Opening opera to the public had the impact one might expect on composers and producers, the same one felt by television writers and producers today. Then, as now, there was motivation to give the public what it wanted. What it wanted, and received, was more realism flavored by some humor.

A standard type of overture was adopted for the orchestra, one with an introductory slow movement followed by a fast one. Although the orchestra also occasionally played other minor pieces, at this stage it was not particularly important. Even in the hands of the Master Monteverdi, its role was minimal.

After Monteverdi, the most important seventeenth-century figures in Italian opera were two Venetian residents, Cavalli and Cesti, who between them wrote more than one hundred works. Some of those crossed the borders for performance in Paris.

Recall that the poetry, and thus the recitative, had been a main thing for the Camerata. Important though the marriage of drama and music was to them, their chief interest was in the poetry itself, their major objective to enhance it through music. The music was a tool, a means to a greater poetic end. Monteverdi used solo arias, and Cesti gave them more emphasis, but even then at first only the lesser performers sang arias. The operatic duet was one of Cavalli's innovations. Two performers joined in an aria, such as shepherd and shepherdess lovers greeting the dawn after a night together.

Cesti, Cavalli, and others found that the accents and flow of the Italian language were ideal for this kind of vocal music and their tuneful songs.

In other ways, too, the works of both men reflected the influence of a ticket-buying public: elaborate staging, more characters, plot complexity—and some burlesque comedy.

Although there was no huge overnight explosion, the extra attention these composers paid to vocal music began a trend of enormous importance. It represented a move away from the Greek dramatic recitative, and thus away from the poet, and toward the aria and thus toward the composer—away from the dramatist and his text and toward the musician and his music.

This major trend endured in Italy. In time, the natural consequence of an increased emphasis on the song was the development of the virtuoso singer to sing that song. Once that happened in Italy, it was Katie Bar the Door. For the Italians, the virtuoso singer became the star of the show and everything else took second place—the poet and his text, the composer, the orchestra, and all other elements of the whole.

The main characteristic of most Italian opera was to be the human voice.

We have defined opera as a *play in music*, not a concert. For many years this out-of-proportion emphasis on the voice upset the balance between the drama and the music.

Despite the openings of public theaters in Venice and scattered other cities, Italian opera in the first half of the seventeenth century was geared chiefly to festive court occasions. As such, it began to make its way out of Italy to courts of other princes and nobles.

As the composers and producers paid more homage to the audience, Oscar-winning special effects people showed themselves. Demons and angels flew through the air, great storms came and went, gods and clouds descended from above—all of this a far cry from the concepts of the learned and humanist Camerata, even though this still was within one hundred years of their work.

On the music side, choral singing began to be accompanied by a few instruments—perhaps three violins, a harpsichord or two, a few lutes and other strings. The role of these small orchestras was not only to accompany choruses but also to play introductions, interludes, and epilogues.

Predictably, however, the audiences loved the spectacle and demanded more of it. Composers and librettists began to take the easy way out with the dramatic problems. When complex or disorganized plots met themselves coming around a corner, gods popped out of cloud machines to make everything right (a theatrical device the Greeks termed *deus ex machina*). Volcanoes erupted, battles raged, and ships sank with almost no relationship to the story. One opera in the 1680s advertised one hundred horsemen in armor, two lions, two elephants, chariots and cars drawn by several dozen horses, and a forest beset by wild deer and bear. Now *that* was opera, gobbled up by Giuseppe Six-Pack, easily understood without homework.

Still, this was Italy. Despite the audience clamor for the spectacular, in time the big singers gradually wore down the scenic designers just as they had worn down the poets. Some singers were not only uncontrolled but uncontrollable. They not only added their own notes to the written melodies but also occasionally threw in favorite arias from other operas, even those by different composers. There were no copyright laws. Consider Sidney Poitier, following his most dramatic scene in *Guess Who's Coming to Dinner*, interrupting the dialogue and, in a Rhett Butler–like tone, declaring: "Frankly, my dears, I don't give a damn. I didn't want this rotten dinner anyhow." It was something like that.

By the end of the seventeenth century, Italy and opera were well into an enduring marriage, even if the product had deteriorated significantly. Opera was Italy's musical pasta. Aside from religious music, from this century on opera was Italy's most important music.

The main memory to take from seventeenth-century Italy is this: Claudio Monteverdi was a genius. Not all Collection composers were geniuses, and not all produced true masterpieces. But Monteverdi was . . . and did. Get a copy of his *Orfeo*, preferably a videotape. Listen to the closing scenes. This is the first of a few road map musts. You'll find it interesting, soothing, and lovely. Less well known because *Orfeo* gets historic credit for being Monteverdi's first, but an even better opera is *L'incoronazione di Poppea* (*The Coronation of Poppea*). Composed in Monteverdi's last year, it was the first opera based on an actual historical event. It's not in The Collection but has Honorable Mention status, and today is performed more often than *Orfeo*.

After Monteverdi there was a marked deterioration in Italian opera during the 1600s. Perhaps the growing pains were too great. Too much was happening. The balance he had achieved between poetry and music was lost. Watching and hearing *Orfeo*, you will sense no need for erupting volcanoes and fierce battles.

For those who wonder whether they will enjoy an opera produced four hundred years ago, consider this: It was the middle of Shakespeare's life, and millions find him worth reading and hearing. Give *Orfeo* and *Poppea* a shot.

France: The Seventeenth Century

Lully comes from Italy to found French opera, geared to an audience of one man—the King. Italian recitative leaves the French cold, but they build into their opera their own traditions of tragic drama and ballet.

THE COLLECTION COMPOSERS
Jean-Baptiste Lully (1632–87)

One of the four statues in the foyer of Paris's beautiful Palais Garnier, the onetime home of L'Opéra, is Italian-born Lully, the only "French" Collection composer who worked in the seventeenth century and the first opera composer to be famous internationally. The first of three major figures of the first two centuries of French opera, he so dominated the scene that his years sometimes are called the Period of Lully.

But let's back up. There is little to report about French opera during the first part of the seventeenth century, before Lully. French musicians listened to Italian recitative, concluded that sort of sing-speech, or song, didn't fit well with the accent, rhythm, and flow of their language, shrugged their Gallic shoulders, and poured themselves a glass of wine. Inasmuch as recitative is the dialogue of Italian opera and the vehicle that moves the plot along, this decision had a chilling impact on French opera. The French, of course, always have been hung up on their own language, not partial to those who don't speak it and even less partial to the uncivilized intruders who try to speak it but fail. Was it Professor Henry Higgins who advised us that the French don't care what you say, so long as you pronounce it properly?

(In coastal Normandy in the weeks following D-day in 1944, the natives were remarkably friendly and not at all distraught by an American accent. Of course, bribery was rampant with cigarettes and candy bars, and compared with the occupying Germans our pluses presumably outweighed our ill-bred minuses).

What Parisians *were* partial to in the seventeenth century was drama, especially tragic drama, and ballet. Given French pride, this was understandable;

their drama and ballet were unsurpassed anywhere in Europe—or anywhere outside of Europe, for that matter.

Consider the native dramatic talent. Pierre Corneille, whose works included *Médée* and *Le Cid*, was alive for most of the seventeenth century. Both Jean-Baptiste Molière, the father of French comedy, and Jean Racine (author of *Phèdre*, *Mithridate*, and *Iphigénie en Aulide*) were alive for much of it. A nation with that kind of dramatic ability, serious and comic, is not driven to dilute it with music.

Ballet, performed chiefly at court festivities, had been France's favorite musical entertainment since the late 1500s. In one sense that tradition also dampened the early French reaction to Italian serious operas, inasmuch as the Italians were salting them with a little comic ballet. The French looked, listened ... and sniffed. They were quite satisfied, thank you, with their own superior ballet just as it was, pure and unattached to another form of entertainment.

Opera began officially in France when the Académie Royale de Musique was established in 1669. Enter Lully from Italy. He took control of the academy and over time, with the blessing of Louis XIV, created an opera form known as the "tragédie en musique," or "tragédie lyrique."

That a native-born Italian founded French opera is an example of the ascendancy of Italian opera at the time. For years, however, Lully *was* Parisian opera, his works first characterized chiefly by drama and ballet, and later by the roles of the chorus and the orchestra. But the emphasis was *not* on arias and vocal acrobatics.

Today Lully's operas are generally considered too formal and restrictive for modern ears. None has been performed at the Metropolitan and none will be coming soon to your neighborhood. But he was so important to the operatic scheme of things that you might consider trying a recording of any of his works, just for fun. Maybe you'll like it.

One major difference between Lully's French serious opera and Italian opera seria was that the French avoided the comic elements that Italy liked to inject. A second, which left Italy aghast, was that the French used spoken dialogue rather than recitative when the characters communicated with one another.

Musicologists today call early French opera "impressive and noble" on the one hand and "stereotyped and thin" on the other.

There was a good reason for the majestic ambience. Recall that in Venice the opera houses by this time were open to the public, a public that was voting with its tickets. In Rome, the opera basically was subject to the desires of the cumulative aristocracy. But in Paris, the Board of Elections counted only one vote—the one cast by the King, in this case Louis XIV. The new opera was for his pleasure.

When you write for the King, you are expected to show good taste. Kings, like United States presidents, get upset when they are startled. No shocking chords, for example, nor any violence or uncontrollable passion. Kings are a little antsy about violence and undue passion. Perhaps this Louis had visions of what lay ahead for the Louises who were to come.

French arias were different from Italian—shorter, narrower in range, more integrated into the text. And the French didn't share the Italian joy in high, high voices. The rational French, accustomed to good drama, insisted upon hearing the words in order to follow the plot. When a voice is too high the words become more difficult to understand. For the same reasons, both then and later, the French frowned on a lot of ornamentation and roodle-doodle in their opera.

Fifty years passed between Lully's death in 1687 and the first operas of the next important Parisian composer. In the interim, French opera marched in place.

Germany: The Seventeenth Century

> Little lasting operatic action. The opera form of choice is Singspiel, a comic opera with spoken dialogue. The Hamburg school tries but fails to make an impact.

Note: As the *Harvard Dictionary of Music* advises, musicologists customarily—and almost inevitably—include the development of opera in Austria with Germany because of the close political, cultural, and musical bonds between the two countries. Such outstanding "Austrian" composers as Beethoven were born in Germany, and such great "German" masters as Mozart were born in Salzburg. We'll stick to the custom of grouping them together, recognizing that in individual cases a Beethoven scarcely could be anything but German and a Mozart, so open to Italian influence, must be essentially Austrian.

No Collection composers worked in Germany in the seventeenth century. George Frideric Handel was born in 1685 and became famous in the early 1700s, but Germany let him get away—first to Italy and then to spend his life in England. In any case, all his work was in the next century.

Neither, of course, was there any "real" Germany at this time. What came to be Germany consisted then of more than 1,500 independent states and fifty-odd imperial cities. The early history of opera in German states and cities was mainly one of Italian composers working in local and regional German courts, following their own Italian style and most often writing in the Italian language. With rare exceptions, even native Germans used the same style and language.

The term of "Singspiel"—"song play"—for early German opera goes back to the preopera 1500s, when plays with songs were presented and that form goes back even earlier. It stuck to apply to German opera of the next three centuries. After the mid-1700s, all Singspiel was in spoken dialogue. In that sense,

Singspiel and French opéra comique were similar, Singspiel and Italian opera buffa different.

Two respected early German non-Collection opera composers were Johann Wolfgang Franck (1644–1710), who mixed together French, Italian, and German ingredients and is known best for his sacred songs, and Johann Kusser (1660–1727), son of Hungarian parents who was active in Germany, England, and Ireland. Having studied under Lully, he favored French dance forms in his operas, but of twenty-three known stage works nothing survives except some arias. For several years he gave considerable solidity to early German opera, but not enough to move it forward.

The only important seventeenth-century native German opera school was in Hamburg, which had a public opera for fifty years starting in 1678, the first one in Europe outside Italy. Its leading composer was Reinhard Keiser (1674–1739), a master of melody and color who wrote some 120 operas. History looks at him as perhaps the most important and original figure of German Baroque opera, committed to serious German texts and dramatic integrity and deeply respected by other musicians.

Despite his many gifts, Keiser was either not good enough—or maybe not strong enough or lucky enough—to stop Hamburg opera from deteriorating under the flood of foreign imports. No "German" style emerged to survive.

The Eighteenth Century

Italy: The Eighteenth Century

> Italian opera seria and Italian composers dominate European opera. The castrati do their thing. Arias and the superstars who sing them are all-important. Librettist Metastasio sets the rules that must be followed. Comic opera—opera buffa—arrives.

No Italian composers who were born and worked in the eighteenth century are in The Collection, which is not the same thing as saying there are no eighteenth-century Collection composers who wrote Italian-style opera.

European opera at this time basically was an Italian thing. Almost anyone involved composed in the Italian style, including three major Collection figures:

- Handel, born in Saxony in 1685, who wrote Italian opera seria in England.
- Christoph Willibald Gluck, born in Bavaria of Bohemian ancestry in 1714, who wrote Italian opera seria in Venice before reforming opera in Paris.
- Wolfgang Amadeus Mozart, born in Salzburg in 1756, who wrote both Italian opera seria and opera buffa as well as the first great German operas.

But even beyond those three masters, the eighteenth century was an active one for Italian opera. Six central non-Collection figures merit special mention. Four were important opera seria composers: Alessandro Scarlatti (1660–1725), Johann Adolph Hasse (1699–1783), Niccolò Jommelli (1714–74), and Tommaso Traetta (1727–79). A fifth was librettist Pietro Metastasio (1698–1782). And the last was Giovanni Pergolesi (1710–36), the most significant figure of the century in comic opera.

Among the highlights of Italian opera in the 1700s:

- One sign of Italian dominance: from the late 1600s to 1750 at least eighty Italian composers worked in London at one time or another, one hundred in Vienna, forty in Dresden, twenty-five far away in St. Petersburg—and as many as fifty traveling in and out of Paris. Not all composed opera, but many did.
- Even near the end of the century, opera in Europe was dominated by the Italian style. Italian castrato singers—men who had been castrated as boys to save the boyish quality of their voices—performed in different countries and were the equivalent of twentieth-century film stars. The more domineering these singers became, the less attention was paid to plot, poetry, dramatic integrity, and recitative.
- Opera seria continued to be the principal operatic form. Neither the chorus nor the orchestra was a *major* player. In general, each scene had two parts. The plot and action were carried by the recitative; without it there was no story line. Emotions and reactions of the characters were expressed in arias.
- A perfect opera seria would have had a relatively strong dramatic story, with plot-carrying recitative and crowd-pleasing arias carefully blended—a return to Monteverdi after the excesses that developed in his wake. The "number opera," which gave short shrift to the storytelling recitative, became popular. It was made up almost entirely of da capo arias, perhaps as many as twenty in one work. The number of arias was governed partly by competition between the stars, but mostly by the "doctrine of affections"—that is, each aria would illustrate a single mood: pathos, anger, heroic resolve, tender love, whatever. Since it took one aria to cover every emotion, a penetrating psychological portrayal of a complex character might demand a total of five or more. (It was Mozart's great genius to write arias that covered several emotions at once.) In some cases, opera seria was outstanding. In others, it was weak. What varied most was how logical and understandable the plot was and how well the arias were linked to the story line. When the story was relatively insignificant, often the recitative was as well. One French visitor to Rome said that the game of draughts was an ideal one to play in order to while away the tedium of the recitative. In such cases, dramatic principle was lost and most of what remained was a parcel of beautiful songs.

- With so much weight given the aria, strict rules and regulations were developed about how many arias an opera should have and how they should be divided among the various singer-actors.

One of the most talented individuals on the Italian scene was Alessandro Scarlatti, the most important master of opera seria in his generation, composer of sixty-six operas, who helped forge the da capo aria. Although his operas have not, as the wine folks say, "traveled well" over the centuries, he was also a talented composer of cantatas, so talented as to be considered second only to Mr. Bach himself. You could do much worse of an evening than sample recordings of Scarlatti cantatas, a treasury of melody. The Speaker of the House has not decreed that one cannot enjoy nonoperatic music while concentrating on opera.

After Scarlatti's death, a few other fine Neapolitan composers worked toward a better blend of dramatic truth and sound melody. Hasse, a German, writer of fifty-odd operas, lived so long in Italy that he was known as the "Beloved Saxon." For nearly fifty years his serious operas were performed in the most important Italian and German houses. A leading successor to him was Jommelli, who resisted the unfortunate trends of the time, paid more attention to the orchestra, and tried to return recitative in opera seria to a more important level. He wrote some one hundred stage works and, like Scarlatti, some wonderful cantatas, both sacred and secular. Our business is not to plug cantatas, but chances are you also would enjoy Jommelli's. Just think of a long cantata as being a mini miniopera.

Still another "reformer" with his mind on drama was Traetta, who worked in Italy, Germany, and Russia and whose work is still in the Venice repertory today.

Librettist Metastasio was the most prolific and influential artist in the text-writing field, famous beyond the boundaries of Italy. Seventy of his librettos were set to music more than eight hundred times by scads of composers. Among the biggies who liked and used them were Handel, Mozart, and Gluck, about as substantial an opera trio as a body can find. (In Vienna, Metastasio also lived in the same house with a young musician named Franz Joseph Haydn and helped him along.)

Metastasio was a rule setter who shaped opera in the eighteenth century. If you did business with him, you did it his way. Here are some of his rigid regulations about what an opera should be:

- Noble behavior is expected from the nobility.
- The aristocracy alone is to mingle with the gods.
- Inner personal conflict is good; outward show of excessive emotion is not.
- Reason and virtue are to triumph over inconsistency and evil.
- Endings are to be happy.
- And, of course, the language must be Italian.

Additionally, by Metastasian standards:

- Out were the irrelevant comic elements and the big theatrical scenes of the seventeenth century.
- In were three tightly written acts.
- Out was classic mythology.
- In were ancient history and legend.

The good news about Metastasio as a librettist is that he made order out of what had become near chaos after the post-Monteverdi seventeenth-century deterioration. The bad news is that the star system remained; plot, poetry, and action still were dominated by the virtuoso aria singers showing off their wares.

COMIC OPERA

Meanwhile, comic opera made a strong appearance in eighteenth-century Italy.

Early on, when serious opera inherited from the previous century was so artificial, entrepreneurs began introducing comic interludes between the acts of an opera seria. At first these were little intermission entertainments. Then some bright people began combining the first interlude and the second into a two-act whole. Inevitably, other alert entrepreneurs extracted the two-act whole from the parent opera seria and had it stand on its own feet as a separate comic opera. It was called "opera buffa," and it lasted in that basic form for a couple of hundred years.

Inasmuch as this was voice-happy Italy, with its long tradition of vocal religious music, opera buffa was sung throughout just as opera seria had been. Serious opera, comic opera, good opera, bad opera, any opera, it did not and does not matter. In Italy, between the set arias, comes sung recitative. One does not despoil one's Italian opera by stooping to spoken dialogue. That tradition never has changed.

The best-known work of early opera buffa is a 1733 work by Giovanni Pergolesi called *La serva padrona*, still sometimes performed in workshops (and available on videotape with the Rome Philharmonic Orchestra).

Given the disorganized state of opera seria when the eighteenth century began, and given the strict Metastasian rules imposed to clean it up, and given that it still was dominated by set arias, it is not surprising that some creative composers turned from serious works to opera buffa—nor is it surprising that opera buffa caught on fire. Its creators kept the crowd-pleasing arias or they would have been whistled and jeered out of business. But, not bound by opera seria rules, they were free to be more original and imaginative. Consequently, they wrote opera that was better than its serious counterpart. Further, the arias were generally shorter, more tuneful, less virtuosic, and more full of natural sound effects—like heartbeats and sneezes. And comic opera also experimented with duets, trios, and finales, the most fun parts of operas.

It is tempting for amateurs to fall into the trap of thinking that comic opera is somehow "less worthy" or "less artistic" than serious opera. But consider literature. Our time period now is the late 1700s. Classical comic drama had long been accepted as a valid art form, judged important as well as entertaining. William Shakespeare had written his world-famous comedies close to two hundred years earlier using many of the concepts that became part of opera buffa such as mistaken identities, disguises, confusion of characters, and social satire.

Although Italian opera buffa was not what we know as operetta, in important ways it was similar to it. It usually dealt with ordinary people rather than with the legends and gods of opera seria. The music was lighter and the melodies easier to pick up.

France — The Eighteenth Century

Rameau revitalizes Parisian opera with lyric dramatic tragedy, a different breed than Italian opera seria. The French still like ballet in their opera. These are the years of Gluck, the great reformer. A musical war is waged as Italian comic opera invades Paris. For comedy, the French choose spoken dialogue over sung recitative.

THE COLLECTION COMPOSERS
Jean-Philippe Rameau (1683–1764)

Lully was the first of three huge names in early French opera. The other two are Collection composers Rameau and Gluck, who moved from Vienna to Paris in 1773. The three covered 150 years. Let's pinpoint them before moving on:

- Lully, the seventeenth century, the father of French opera.
- Rameau, whose work all was in the eighteenth century, the next big Frenchman.
- Gluck, his successor, some 30 years younger, the great Parisian reformer of opera.

After Lully's death in the late 1600s, Paris swung to a melodramatic mishmash called opera-ballet. It was a peculiar sort of entertainment consisting of parts largely unconnected, like most Democratic administrations. (Republican administrations invariably are better organized, which is not necessarily a plus for the nation.) One opera-ballet, for example, presented four independent acts, one cast in Spain, one in France, one in Italy, and one in Turkey. But they were popular, in part because the composers threw into them a good amount of Italian melody.

They were not unlike Broadway musical revues in the 1920s before Jerome

Kern changed the mold with his magnificent *Show Boat*: light entertainment with a vague story line designed primarily as a platform on which performers could sing and dance.

Then, in 1733, Rameau, an all-purpose classical Baroque composer, produced a tragédie lyrique called *Hippolyte et Aricie*. Reactions were mixed. Conservatives found his work similar to the famed Lully in many ways: the same mythological or legendary subjects (unlike the Italians, who now preferred famous people out of history), the same pleasant scenes with choruses and ballets, and the same carefully drawn recitative. Liberals were upset less by what they saw than by what they heard—"old-fashioned" Baroque music. Rameau today is considered less of a dramatist than Lully but considerably more of a musician.

Rameau lived until 1764. In terms of classical *instrumental* music, the Baroque period had then ended and the Classical period was under way. The Land of the Giants was at hand: Franz Joseph Haydn was thirty-two, Mozart was a child prodigy, and Beethoven would be born in six years. Give me those three and you can have seventy-five percent of the Collection composers, an old Johnny Carson autograph, and a first-draft choice.

By the time Rameau died, the French lyric tragedy that had begun with Lully differed from Italian opera seria in these ways:

Jean-Philippe Rameau

- More emphasis on drama, drama still being the French thing.
- More instrumental music; the French had more of an instrumental tradition than the Italians, albeit less than the Germans.
- More ballets, choruses, and spectacular scenes; ballet continuing as a Parisian favorite.
- Shorter and simpler solo songs; light "airs" rather than elaborate "arias" since the individual singer was less important to the French.
- Smoother recitative, inasmuch as hearing and understanding the words was essential for the drama-orientated French.
- Different beginnings: A new two-part overture, known as the "French overture," in which a slow, pompous opener was followed by a fast-time movement.

Meanwhile, between Lully's death in 1687 and Rameau's work in the 1700s—and particularly after the death of Louis XIV in 1715—comic opera began to get a strong foothold in France. It began with something called "comédie mêlée d'ariettes," a farcelike creation, with songs added in a hit-or-miss way, and developed into forms akin to real opera.

Over time, every major country in Europe had some form of what the French came to call *opéra comique*. In Italy it was their opera buffa, in England ballad-opera, in Germany Singspiel.

Unburdened with the old-line conventions of serious opera, resourceful composers could swing out with imagination and creativity. Before long many comic operas were finer works of art than many "real" operas—better music, better drama, better acting (always essential for good comedy), and better singing. In comedy—then and now—the words *must* be heard. Therefore, except for Italian opera buffa—which was sung throughout just as Italian opera seria was sung throughout—comic opera in the various countries used spoken dialogue between the songs.

Like the Italian opera buffa, the French comedy passed up myths and legends in favor of stalwart peasants, blushing heroines, real-man heroes, and wicked nobles. "Tuneful" and "charming" were the words for its music—not "profound" or "dramatic." It is not a long way from these works to later American musicals.

Two major opera houses developed in Paris in the eighteenth century. The main one was the Académie Royale de Musique, known as L'Opera, from Louis XIV's day. This was *the* Paris Opéra. The other was L'Opéra-Comique, much later to be situated on the Rue Favart in Paris, established in 1715 in a deal with the Académie under which it would present only works with spoken dialogue. As suggested in chapter four's opera definitions, not only was that spoken dialogue policy dropped a century and a half later but by the beginning of the twentieth century many Opéra-Comique productions were not comedy at all.

But those changes were a long way off.

In the mid-1750s, a dozen Italian comic operas invaded the city. A musical battle ensued. The best known of these operas was Pergolesi's *La serva padrona*, put on by a company called the Bouffons. This influx from the south triggered the War of the Bouffoons. All wars are strange, but this was stranger than most since it was waged over the relative merits of French serious opera versus Italian opera buffa. Apples versus oranges. One happy result of all the fuss and debate was the development of opéra comique as a French national opera style.

One of its leading composers was a man who is not in The Collection, André Ernest Modeste Grétry (1741–1813), who wrote more than forty operas. Interestingly, his masterpiece was not a comic work but rather *Richard Coeur de Lion* (*Richard the Lion-hearted*), 1784, considered a landmark in early Romantic opera in that it anticipated the rescue opera that became popular during the French Revolution. As the name suggests, in this form the hero or heroine is rescued by his or her spouse or lover from a dreary situation—like lifelong confinement in a rat-infested prison dungeon or a sentence to be thrown into a pot of boiling water. The rescue opera is reminiscent for some of us—though there are not many of us left—of the Saturday-afternoon serials in the 1920s at movie theaters where melodramatic silent films were accompanied by an in-house piano player. You missed a lot if you missed *The Green Archer* in Baltimore in 1927 and the nearby house where a nice lady made red candied apples in her kitchen and sold them at the back door for a nickel if you were ten or your big brother was with you.

Gluck on Gluck

Gluck, the great reformer, on his reforms: "I sought to restrict music to its proper function, that of seconding the poetry by strengthening the expression and the interest of the situations without interrupting the action or weakening it by superfluous ornament. . . . I also thought that my chief endeavor should be to attain a grand simplicity, and consequently have avoided making a parade of difficulties at the cost of clearness."

Oriental settings were popular, often some untraveled Western European's idea of what Turkey should look like. Farces and fairy tales were presented. Often the good-guy peasants were oppressed by a bad-guy noble . . . but saved in the end by a good-guy noble.

Still, the rescue formula was truer to life than serious opera's reliance on gods or other external means of solving the characters' dramatic problems.

The Collection's Gluck, the great reformer of French opera, was born in 1714 and educated in Prague and Italy. His first operas were written for Milan and Venice. After competing for a while with Handel in London, he recognized that opera seria was becoming passé there and moved back to the Continent. In 1754 he was named musical director to the imperial court in Vienna and later worked his way to Paris.

Gluck was not impressed by Italian opera seria's stilted form, with all of its arias da capo in which the performer sang the first part, then a second contrasting one, followed by a repetition of the first, this time with ornamentation. It was a wonderful way for the performers to show off their stuff . . . but a poor way to sustain drama.

Although the voice-happy Italians were not apoplectic that the Camerata's "proper" drama had long since fallen by the wayside, this da capo approach distressed Gluck for several reasons. His German background was in instrumental music rather than in the vocal form. He also believed opera should present a simpler expression of human emotion. The philosophy of the day was naturalness. His goals were "noble simplicity" and "calm greatness," which he tried to show in several operas, including *Orfeo ed Euridice*, *Alceste*, and *Paride ed Elena*. France, with its background in drama, ate them up with a spoon.

Like the Italian Metastasio, he got rid of a lot of garbage.

Germany: The Eighteenth Century

The departure of the great Handel to Italy and England. Vienna becomes Europe's classical music center. Beethoven's instrumental music and the overpowering genius of Wolfgang Amadeus Mozart as he writes opera in both the Italian and German styles.

THE COLLECTION COMPOSERS
Ludwig van Beethoven (1770–1827)
Christoph Willibald Gluck (1714–87)
George Frideric Handel (1685–1759)
Wolfgang Amadeus Mozart (1756–91)

Handel, Mozart, and Gluck were all working in this century—plus Beethoven, although his only opera came in the early 1800s. This is as impressive a quartet of composers as one might find at a single watering hole. However, with Handel writing Italian-style opera in England and Gluck reforming French opera in Paris, it was Mozart, late in the eighteenth century, who first produced a "German-style" work that has endured until today.

What the incomparable Handel might have done to develop a serious

German form had he stayed home and worked at it with Keiser is an open question. Or what if Mr. Bach, born in 1685, had been a different type of fellow? His passions and cantatas show keen knowledge of the human voice, but opera never was his thing.

In the field of comic opera, the most important early German composer was non-Collection Johann Adam Hiller (1728–1804) of the Dresden-Leipzig part of North Germany. Using the Singspiel form, in 1770 he produced *Die Jagd* (*The Hunt*), the most popular German opera of its time.

Meanwhile, however, important things were happening in nonoperatic European music in the late eighteenth century. Vienna, in the "south," had become the center of the musical world. The Baroque period of classical music had ended; the Classical period had begun—the time of Haydn and Mozart, the former born in 1732 and the latter in 1756, and of Beethoven, only a generation away. The mighty traditions of classical music were of Vienna, not of Rome or Naples, where opera traditions were bred.

A classical orchestra was developing. Symphonies were being born. So were violin and piano concertos. Musicians were learning new things about string instruments and woodwinds. Mozart, classical music's greatest spontaneous genius, was an essential part of all this and his work in the form of opera influenced all opera of the future.

Details of the formidable Mozart and his magnificent Collection operas come later. It is enough now to note that *The Marriage of Figaro*, 1786, and *Don Giovanni*, 1787, although written in Italian and in an Italian style, are nonetheless viewed as the foundation of all subsequent comic opera, whether Italian, French, German, or English. Another Mozart Collection work in the same style is *Così fan tutte*, 1790.

It was not until *The Magic Flute* in 1791, completed only ten weeks before he died, written in German with a different format, that Mozart produced the first great German opera—and one that contained the seeds for German "Romantic opera," which was to flourish in the nineteenth century. (Some scholars argue that these seeds were planted almost a decade earlier with Mozart's *Abduction from the Seraglio*, more of a true Singspiel.)

The Nineteenth Century

Italy: The Nineteenth Century

Three great bel canto composers occupy the first half century. Verdi dominates nearly all the rest of it. Puccini is launched, and verismo opera explodes on the scene.

THE COLLECTION COMPOSERS
Vincenzo Bellini (1801–35)
Arrigo Boito (1842–1918)
Gaetano Donizetti (1797–1848)
Umberto Giordano (1867–1948)
Ruggerio Leoncavallo (1857–1919)
Pietro Mascagni (1863–1945)
Amilcare Ponchielli (1834–86)
Giacomo Puccini (1858–1924)
Gioacchino Rossini (1792–1868)
Giuseppe Verdi (1813–1901)

Having founded opera but lost its leadership, the Italians came home to it in strength in the nineteenth century. The first Italians in The Collection since Monteverdi (counting Lully as a French composer of Italian birth) now appeared. The list is long and formidable, consisting of familiar and less familiar names. If you feel at home with all ten, you're reading the wrong book.

In the first few years of the nineteenth century, the old Italian opera buffa faded to a close. But its germ had spread across Europe, contributing to the development of other comic works, including French opéra comique and certain forms of German Singspiel.

Back at home in Italy, nineteenth-century opera fits reasonably into three periods:

- The bel canto phase of Rossini, Donizetti, and Bellini.
- The Verdi years.
- The post-Verdi stark verismo time dominated by Mascagni, Leoncavallo, and Giordano, followed, at the turn of the century, by the early operas of Puccini, who sugarcoated verismo in some of his work.

BEL CANTO
The early period of bel canto ("beautiful singing") featured Rossini, Donizetti, and Bellini. As a group, their interests were in vocal melody and vocal acrobatics. A young genius, Rossini became famous in Europe with two operas in 1813, including an opera buffa, *The Italian Girl in Algiers*. The first performance of another opera buffa, *The Barber of Seville*, came three years later. A onetime extremely popular work that just misses The Collection is the grand opera *Guillaume Tell* (*William Tell*) from 1829. Despite grumpy gainsayers, Rossini is accepted today as a great opera composer, particularly of comic works. Many contemporary connoisseurs are taken especially by *Le Comte Ory*, 1828, his penultimate work, which is now drawing revived attention.

Donizetti was born next. His four operas in The Collection are *The Elixir of Love*, 1832, *Lucia di Lammermoor*, 1835, *The Daughter of the Regiment*, 1840, and *Don Pasquale*, 1843.

Bellini lived only to age thirty-three, but many musicologists consider him the most original of the three, although I'm wary of comparisons among them. His two famous Collection operas are *Norma*, 1831, and *La sonnambula*, 1831. Known chiefly for opera seria, he was the most poetic of the three and the one most concerned with unifying the text and the music.

Care must be taken in attempting to summarize bel canto opera, in part because two of the three major composers of the period, Rossini and Donizetti, wrote more than one hundred operas between them. That total production included the great, the good, the bad, and the ugly. Not much praiseworthy can be said about many bel canto *librettos*. "Humdrum" is an overstatement for many of them, but not all can be put down that way. Felice Romani (1788–1865), a lawyer by profession, librettist of *Norma*, *La sonnambula*, *The Elixir of Love*, and scores of others, was an original craftsman of the very first order. Some other librettists were hacks. In any event, the *music* was so fresh that a lot of operagoers over the years simply overlooked the librettos. Then Maria Callas, later followed by Joan Sutherland and Beverly Sills, showed that there was much more drama in some of the characters than had been suspected.

Thus today we have two schools of thought about bel canto works. One describes bel canto something like this:

- The solo voice—with vocal fireworks—is preeminent, and drama is secondary.
- Melody is essential.
- When the singer is singing, the orchestra is subdued, regardless of what is going on dramatically.

The other school gets quite upset about this "canary" view of bel canto. One of my favorite experts, who represents that second school, replies along these lines:

With Bellini, and at least the best of Donizetti, *drama is paramount*. But the drama is expressed chiefly through the inflection of the vocal line—through the coloratura passages. Coloratura is the technique by which that vocal line can be bent, stretched, speeded up, or slowed down, all to achieve better dramatic expressiveness. It was a difficult thing to do, and many of the public paid to hear the stars who could bring it off without always asking—or caring—*why* it was done. But it is ignorant—indeed, sinful—to describe this kind of singing as "nothing more than cheap vocal fireworks," to define the singers as "canaries," and to downgrade the dramatic intent of the composer.

On one central point, however, both sides agree: in bel canto opera the vocal line is the critical one. Listen for yourself and decide whether the result is chiefly vocal fireworks or chiefly dramatic poignancy and eloquence. Maybe both?

Bel canto opera dominated Italy in the first half of the century and into the second. It endured through Verdi but was torpedoed in the later 1800s—

first by Bizet's *Carmen* in France and then by the Italian verismo opera that followed *Carmen*.

THE VERDI ERA

Much of Italy's nineteenth century belongs to Verdi, the Master of Masters, an opera artist in a class by himself, the be-all and end-all of Italian opera music until his death at age eighty-seven. Donizetti's last important opera was *Don Pasquale* in 1843; from that point on the stage was dominated by Verdi.

It has been nearly 100 years since his death and 150 since his first successful works, but the opera public has not begun to enter a "post-Verdi" period. Indeed, just the opposite is true; today, in the 1990s, "lesser" Verdi operas are being produced more and more. His midcareer 1850s Collection works (*Rigoletto*, *La traviata*, and *Il trovatore*) were the high point of typical Italian opera—melodramatic plots, ultrasingable melodies geared precisely to the appropriate characters, human humans, and dazzling big vocal numbers. After perfecting that Italian style, he went far beyond it in his last three works—*Aida*, *Otello*, and *Falstaff*—blending music and drama as no Italian opera composer had done before him.

(That's what the experts say. I have a personal thing for Monteverdi, but that's another matter. The experts say I simply don't recognize the difference in scale.)

Verdi made opera into more realistic theater than the bel canto composers had produced, demanding more emotion and better acting ability from his singers and discouraging vocal acrobatics.

Wagner and the Germans were into the supernatural, mysticism, magic and mythology and symbolism—as well as the emotional side of opera. Verdi kept it simpler as he dealt with heroism and loyalty, jealousy and greed, love and hate, and devotion and patriotism.

His operas centered on the interaction of human beings in a structure that included vocal arias, duets, and ensembles connected by plot-carrying recitative, and with the orchestra in the background. For all of Verdi's genius, and even including his last advanced works, he was chiefly in the operatic mainstream. Indeed, he *was* the operatic mainstream.

The Collection includes two Italian composers who were younger contemporaries of Verdi, Ponchielli and the famed librettist Boito. Ponchielli, whose masterpiece is *La Gioconda*, 1876, was groomed by their joint publisher to be Verdi's successor, although this never came off. Boito collaborated with Verdi on two of his greatest works but also wrote both libretto and music for his own successful opera, *Mefistofele*, 1868.

POST-VERDI VERISMO

To set the stage for what happens next in Italy, we need to take a quick detour to France. There, in the later 1800s, Emile Zola led a literary movement

Pietro Mascagni

called *naturalism*. His writings were concerned with the rough-and-tough lives of regular working people. This movement spread from the printed page to opera, with Bizet's *Carmen*, 1875, emerging as the first famous French opera with some of its characteristics. When the naturalist school made its way to Italy, opera composers seized it and called it "verismo."

The two Italians who were most successful with this dark form were the verismo Bobbsey Twins, Mascagni, who wrote *Cavalleria rusticana*, 1890, and Leoncavallo, who wrote *Pagliacci*, 1892. For them, verismo came out something closer to "realism" than to "truth." Each work is so short that major repertory opera houses often put them together into a doubleheader. Some elitists say things like "only Italian barbers like them," which says more about the elitists than about the composers, their operas, or the barbers.

Verismo influenced Puccini, most of whose works are in the next century, but he is not regarded as a card-carrying member.

Verismo marked the end of the long century of Romantic music and pushed bel canto opera to a back burner (from which it was to return in the next century).

The verismo proponents examined life, saw ugliness, raw instincts, and violent passions and then romanticized the harshness in sweet-toned music. Verismo opera represented a drastic change from Romanticism's dreams, ideals, and beautiful thoughts of things beautiful. One critic wrote: "Whoever was conservative enough to believe in something—the soul, God or the here-after—beat a blushing retreat." Verismo was cold reality.

Although the verismo fad—and its "dark violence"—did not last long as an operatic movement, the individual operas that exploded on the operatic world in the 1890s have remained popular—not only *Cavalleria rusticana* and *Pagliacci* but Giordano's *Andrea Chénier*, 1896.

France: The Nineteenth Century

France's action and glory century. Paris becomes the focal point of European classical music, including opera: serious and comic opera, light and heavy opera, extravagant and lean opera, historic epic opera and social commentary opera. Paris has it all. The great Italians come, and so do many Germans, even including a younger Wagner.

THE COLLECTION COMPOSERS
Hector Berlioz (1803–69)
Georges Bizet (1838–75)
Gustave Charpentier (1860–1956)
Léo Delibes (1836–91)
Charles Gounod (1813–93)
Jules Massenet (1842–1912)
Giacomo Meyerbeer (1791–1864)
Jacques Offenbach (1819–80)
Camille Saint-Saëns (1835–1921)
Ambroise Thomas (1811–96)

During the nineteenth century, many opera composers from other European nations moved into Paris, some for short stays, others for life.

Of the ten Collection composers who were active in Paris over the century, eight were French and two came from Germany to settle in Paris. This does not count Italy's Rossini, who became the presiding genius of musical operatic life in Paris, or Bellini, Donizetti, and even Verdi and Wagner, who flitted in and out. Also, some other non-Collection Italians and Frenchmen made a big mark.

Among them were Etienne-Nicolas Méhul (1763–1817), Daniel-François-Esprit Auber (1782–1871), Jacques-François-Fromental-Elie Halévy (1799–1862), and Édouard Lalo (1823–1892).

Several Frenchmen are famous today for One Big Opera, regardless of how many they wrote. France has no Verdi, Wagner, Puccini, or Mozart—enduring superstars who still inundate opera houses with several works each. Massenet comes closest, with two great operas in The Collection and two or three more that just miss.

Among the century's highlights as Paris emerged as opera's hub are:

- Rescue opera, a serious dramatic work born of the Revolution, came and went.
- French grand opera, serious in subject matter, was born, ruled the opera world, and tumbled in excess . . . but left a large imprint.
- "Lyric opera" developed, a catchall term for works that were serious, sometimes tragic, sung throughout, and less grandiose than grand opera.
- Comic opera gained in stature and went through many transformations. Some composers wrote works wholly comical and frothy. Others focused on serious subjects, which they lightened with comic elements. And a new type of satirical comic opera surfaced called "opéra bouffe" (not Italian "buffa").

As the century began, a key Italian working in Paris was Luigi Cherubini (1760–1842). He and Méhul demonstrated that operas written in spoken dialogue rather than recitative could handle not only tuneful and picturesque works but also serious subject matters—and, especially in Cherubini's case, powerful drama. His *Médée*, 1797, is a tense psychological conflict, while *Les deux journées* (*The Two Days*, also called *The Water Carrier*), 1800, is the prototype rescue opera, with simple characters presented as normal human beings rather than comic figures.

A multifaceted composer, Cherubini also is known for comic opera and is one of the principal architects of Romantic opera. Beethoven, Haydn, and Weber all thought highly of him, Beethoven modeling the overture to his own *Fidelio* after the overture of *Les deux journées*. Although his operas had all but disappeared by the middle of his own century, *Médée* occasionally reappears and, even less frequently, in workshops, *Les deux journées*.

Méhul and Cherubini were followed in Paris by another Italian-born artist, Gaspare Spontini (1774–1851), the favorite composer of Napoleon—in part because Spontini knew how to butter his bread. His masterpiece was *La vestale* (*The Vestal Virgin*), 1807, a tragédie lyrique leading from the old Gluck mode toward the grand opera of Meyerbeer. Wise fellow that he was, he also wrote a huge spectacle-type opera, *Fernand Cortez*, 1809, a historical pageant designed specifically to glorify Napoleon.

La vestale helped set the style for the grand opera that for decades was the trademark of the institution called the Paris Opéra. (As noted earlier, Parisians call it just the O, but this chapter is being written in the North Country Adirondacks where "Oh!" means it was thirty-three degrees below zero last night. That's thirty-three real degrees; no chill factor involved.)

These French grand opera "spectacle" seeds planted by Spontini and others came into near full bloom in 1828 with the first performance of Auber's *La Muette de Portici* (also called *Masaniello*), 1828, a serious spectacle. Within a half dozen years it was followed by other works of the same ilk: Halévy's *La Juive*, 1835, and Rossini's *William Tell*, 1829.

Paris now was ready for the works of Meyerbeer, the Master of Grand Opera, whose operas include *Robert le Diable*, 1831, and then his Collection opera *Les Huguenots*, 1836, plus *Le Prophète* 1849, and *L'Africaine*, 1865. His spectacles had these characteristics:

- Serious drama, never comedy.
- Recitative, never spoken dialogue.
- Ballet virtually mandatory.
- Grandiose in all respects: singing, orchestra, and staging.

Audiences in the mid-1800s feasted on extravaganza, which in time got so out of hand that it overwhelmed both drama and music. The staging was so elaborate and the orchestras and choruses so large that the productions became operatic dinosaurs—in the words of musicologist Gerald Abraham, "foredoomed to extinction by their own nature."

Nonetheless, for two or three decades in the nineteenth century, grand opera was *the* focus of "serious" opera in France. After it had run its course, serious

Giacomo Meyerbeer

opera fared poorly in Paris for several years. The next boom came with the French "lyric opera," a less grand format that was more akin to Gluck's old tragédie lyrique. Its roots also were in what had been opéra comique, which had become more serious during the French Revolution, when most artists were moved by the spirit of the times to think serious thoughts, and which before the century ended was to stray even farther from sheer comedy.

Italian opera buffa had now been around a long time and was beset by its own conventions. Musicologists tell us French opéra comique was more imaginative than opera buffa, more open to pathos, and better fitted to serious subjects in general. The opéra comique also was more flexible than the spectacular French grand opera, now plagued by *its* own rules, and thus was a more attractive field for young creative composers.

The first Collection lyric operas are Gounod's remarkably popular *Faust*, 1859, and Thomas's *Mignon*, 1866, a *Faust* copycat in style if not quality. Both are halfway between serious opéra comique and true French grand opera.

These led to later nineteenth-century Collection operas such as Bizet's *Carmen*, 1875, Delibes's *Lakmé*, 1883, and Massenet's *Manon*, 1884—all produced at the opera house called the Opéra-Comique. Since grand opera had faded, the Opéra-Comique had replaced the Paris Opéra as the most important house in Paris and now was producing wholly serious works, some with recitative. As Paris visitors know, that magnificent Paris Opéra building is still standing, but the Paris Opéra now performs in the Bastille, a controversial modern structure that looks like an unhappy marriage between a stack of dominoes and a checkerboard. The fine old building, designed by a genius named Jean-Louis-Charles Garnier, houses drama, ballet, and—unlike the contentious administrators of the snobby Opéra—a warm and gracious staff.

A special type of grand opera was Collection composer Berlioz's *Les Troyens*, completed for the most part in 1858. An epic masterpiece about the Trojan War, it was so long that it was performed over two nights.

On a different front, several fine French classical music composers in the late nineteenth and early twentieth centuries became impressed by Richard Wagner and took what they wanted from him while remaining as independently French as ever. These included Emmanuel Chabrier (1841–94), Vincent d'Indy (1851–1931), and Ernest Chausson (1855–99).

While these men were reflecting Wagner, another group made up of good-ole-boy Frenchmen stuck to the traditional French line. Among them were Saint-Saëns and Massenet, who has been called the last French composer in the Main Highway French tradition.

The Catch of the Day for history, however, was Bizet's *Carmen*. Probably the world's most popular opera, it also is important as the first significant "realistic" opera in France—and as such is one source of Italian verismo opera. A later French true-to-life opera was Charpentier's *Louise*, 1900, the story of a dressmaker and her artist lover in the slums of Paris.

One leading non-Collection composer who held to comedy was Adolphe-

Charles Adam (1803–1856), famous creator of some eighty popular and frivolous works. These are similar to what came to be known as operetta and also what flourished in America one hundred years later as musical comedy. An operetta is usually light and sentimental in character, written in simple and popular style, with spoken dialogue, music, and dancing. An opera might share all of these characteristics, and differences between some operetta and some opera are slight. (But differences between operetta and Wagner's *Parsifal* or Verdi's *Otello* are substantial.)

The operetta czar in France was Offenbach, who wrote about ninety of them and originated the Paris strain of this kind of delightful musical entertainment. Another strain was conceived in Vienna by Franz von Suppé and Johann Strauss the Younger. Born in Germany, Offenbach conquered Paris with his musical talents, wit, and melodious works, some of which remain reasonably popular today. As we have seen, he also wrote one "true" opera, The Collection's *Tales of Hoffmann*.

The Offenbach form of opéra comique . . . or operetta . . . or lighter fare . . . spread to Germany, where it was picked up by people such as Collection composer Flotow, and to England, where it inspired a librettist named W. S. Gilbert and a composer called Arthur Sullivan.

Germany: The Nineteenth Century

Beethoven's only opera opens the new century after Mozart closed the previous one. German Romantic opera begins with Weber's masterpiece. The Waltz King and his great light operas appear. Above all, Richard Wagner dominates.

THE COLLECTION COMPOSERS
Ludwig van Beethoven (1770–1827)
Friedrich von Flotow (1812–83)
Otto Nicolai (1810–49)
Johann Strauss (1825–99)
Richard Wagner (1813–83)
Carl Maria von Weber (1786–1826)

When the nineteenth century began, little was known of *German* opera outside of Germany, given that all of Handel and nearly all of Mozart were in the Italian style. The classical demigod Franz Joseph Haydn had composed a good many small operas, but all but one were written at the Esterházy court for the Esterházy family. The largest of the theaters in which they were shown held four hundred people.

Beethoven's only complete opera, *Fidelio*, was produced between 1805 and

1814. Initially unsuccessful, it was withdrawn, revised, and restaged. Although technically a French Revolution grand-style rescue opera based on a French text, given Beethoven's stature it is reasonable to call it the second great German opera after Mozart's *Magic Flute*. Like *Flute*, it was in Singspiel form, with spoken dialogue.

Beethoven's death in 1827 began the long period of Romanticism in European music—the period of famous nineteenth-century classical composers, including Weber, Mendelssohn, Schubert, Chopin, Schumann, Berlioz, Brahms, Liszt, Mahler, Bruckner, Richard Strauss, and many others. Romanticism embraced self-expression, individual freedom, music-and-poetry, the poet's love story.

Most of the best-known Romantic classical music giants are Germans. The nineteenth century was the century of German ascendancy in classical music, due not to any specific school or movement but to the preeminence of this long string of individual German hot-shot composers.

But our business is opera, to which the contribution of most of the great classical composers of the nineteenth-century Romantic period was relatively meager. Brahms and Bruckner wrote no opera, Mahler completed none, and Mendelssohn only toyed a little with it in his youth. Schumann experimented with one work, and although Schubert started seventeen only one was produced in his lifetime.

Author Gerald Abraham points out that it was *Italian* opera that was court supported in Berlin until 1806 and in Dresden and Munich for another twenty-five years.

But in the climate of Romanticism, literary and musical, German opera at last began to flourish.

The late-eighteenth- and early-nineteenth-century French opera of Cherubini, Spontini, and Méhul influenced German composers and helped pave the way for what now came in Germany. One important non-Collection German composer was E.T.A. Hoffmann, a poet, painter, novelist, singer, composer, conductor, and critic, who is best known in opera for *Undine*; another was Ludwig (or Louis) Spohr, a composer, conductor, and violinist whose *Faust* was his own version of that legend. Both operas were performed in 1816.

And now arrived a more formidable figure, Carl Maria von Weber, often called "the first true Romantic composer of Europe" (following Schubert, who was the bridge between composers of the classical period and those of the Romantic period). Seeds planted by Mozart had been nourished by Beethoven, but the real beginning of nineteenth-century German Romantic opera came with Weber's *Der Freischütz*, performed first in Berlin in 1821. Chronologically, it was the third great German opera, after *The Magic Flute* and *Fidelio*, and in its time by far the most popular.

Weber himself was typical of Romanticism in many ways. The new piano was the big instrument of the Romantic period, and the four greatest European pianists were Chopin, Mendelssohn, Liszt . . . and Weber. The nineteenth century was the age of the virtuoso conductor—and the four greatest European composer-conductors were Berlioz, Mendelssohn, Wagner . . . and Weber.

German Romantic opera was characterized by:

- Melodies based on German folksong.
- Subjects based on German folklore.
- A portrayal of German lifestyle.
- A deep feeling for nature.
- The supernatural.

Der Freischütz contrasted evil magic with the good German life—and the good German life won in a walk, after enough supernatural things had happened in a forest.

Time check: When *Der Freischütz* was performed in 1821, Wagner and Verdi were eight years old, grand opera was beginning to surface in France, and James Monroe was serving his second term as president of the United States. The Greeks and Turks were fighting, but that could have been almost any year.

Two Collection composers who came between Weber and Wagner wrote light entertaining works that once were extremely popular and are still sometimes produced today especially although not exclusively in Germany: Flotow with *Martha*, 1847, and Nicolai with *The Merry Wives of Windsor*, 1849.

Wagner, who stood opera on its ear and joins Verdi as an all-time opera Super Master, first appears on the scene in Germany as a twenty-three-year-old in 1836. His last opera was first performed in 1882.

German Romantic opera reached its peak in Wagner's early works, which ended with *Lohengrin*, 1850. Then he turned to what he called "music dramas" with their "endless melody," which he insisted represented the "music of the future," a whole new thing, and which included his remarkable *Ring* cycle. Lengthy discussion of him is coming a little later. He was a giant in his field whose influence on artists of all kinds was unique. In music, it was pervasive, not only in Germany but in Italy, England, and Russia—and to a lesser degree in France, although some Frenchmen, including Collection composer Claude Debussy, didn't like to admit it.

Wagner was into something entirely different. His music dramas overflowed with symbolism and philosophy, with larger-than-life nonhuman characters, in a structure that used a more or less continuous vocal line—and with the orchestra solidly in the foreground.

As we have seen, he and Verdi dominate The Collection, with twenty-two operas between them.

If there were a final examination for German Opera 101, it would concentrate on six men: Handel, born and reared in Germany and German to his core, who cannot be excluded here even if his opera heyday came from Italian-style works composed during a long career in England, and Mozart, Weber, Wagner, and Richard Strauss. And inevitably Beethoven because he is Beethoven, even if he wrote only one opera. When we get to the twentieth century, the Washed would add Arnold Schoenberg, who is not in The Collection, and Alban Berg, who is. These two, and a half-dozen other Germans and Austrians, have works in chapter seven, The Twentieth-century European Package.

England: The Seventeenth through Nineteenth Centuries

> Henry Purcell founds British opera in the seventeenth century. The satirical *Beggar's Opera* represents Britain in the eighteenth. So does German-born Handel, who dominates the London scene. In the nineteenth came the wonderful works of Gilbert and Sullivan, demanding mention however they are labeled.

THE COLLECTION COMPOSERS
Henry Purcell (1659–95)

Only the two English-born opera composers are in The Collection—Purcell, who was at the beginning, and Benjamin Britten who is at the end in the twentieth century.

Opera in England developed from something called a "masque," an entertainment for upper-crust nobles involving instrumental music, poetry, singing, and dancing. Some scenes were humorous, and some were based on mythological subjects. Both costumes and scenery were ornate. By the late 1600s, when continental opera was well established—when Lully had come and gone—recitative began appearing in masques to replace spoken dialogue.

These shows presumably came to a dead stop during the Commonwealth period of 1649 to 1660, when the Puritans, who were running England, opposed all stage entertainment. (I would prefer "close to a dead stop" because of a sense that no government ever succeeds totally in anything it undertakes. Somewhere in musical speakeasys some musical folk doubtless kept entertaining, even if not out in the open where names could be taken and rumps kicked.)

A work entitled *Venus and Adonis*, although called a masque at its time, is accepted by some historians as the first opera in England. It was a drama written in 1685 by a gentleman named John Blow, an absolutely wonderful name for a British composer.

But the big early figure is Purcell, a Collection composer, universally hailed as the "father," or "founder," of English opera as a result of one work, *Dido and Aeneas*, staged in or about 1689. The music people tell us that French influence shows in its overture, rhythm, dancing, choruses, and instrumental pieces but that Purcell also stirred into these his own characteristically English melodies, rhythms, and harmonies.

No other great composer of serious English opera appeared until Benjamin Britten.

Comic opera in England was more successful. In the eighteenth century ballad opera flourished, a form that both ridiculed Italian opera seria—perhaps worth ridiculing at this time—and established an important British national concept. The best-known ballad opera, then and now, is John Gay's *Beggar's Opera*, first performed in London in 1728—possibly the only opera identified by the name of its librettist rather than its composer (although 199 years later entrepreneur Florenz Ziegfeld initially got more credit than Jerome Kern for *Show Boat*). More people may have heard of Gay, English poet and playwright, than of his musical arranger, John Christopher Pepusch (1667–1752). This is because the music for ballad opera came from secondhand tunes; Pepusch just did the arranging. Still, if Rodgers and Hammerstein and Lerner and Loewe, why not Gay and Pepusch? . . . although admittedly that doesn't go very trippingly on the tongue.

The Beggar's Opera is as far from Italian opera seria as an opera can be. It is alive with pickpockets, convicts, and prostitutes, not quite the stuff of legends and heroic figures. Using street language, it pokes fun at the Establishment— the established Whig government, the established Italian opera seria, any established operation that took itself too seriously.

The Beggar's Opera was not good news for the German-born Handel, who for most of his adult life earned a living in London writing classical music, oratorios, and opera. His Collection opera, *Julius Caesar*, had come shortly earlier, in 1724. The success of *The Beggar's Opera* caused the English not only to reject Italian opera seria in general but also in particular to turn away from Handel's London works, all of which were written in that Italian style.

England cannot be left without a few words about the apparently immortal operettas of W. S. Gilbert (1836–1911) and Arthur Sullivan (1842–1900), whose works were to London of the 1880s what Offenbach's had been to Paris of the 1860s. Librettist Gilbert produced wit, whimsy, topical satire, and parody, and composer Sullivan produced wonderful tunes that satisfied both the musical and dramatic tastes of the audience. In 1891 Sullivan attempted to break out of their highly successful format into a grand opera, *Ivanhoe*, but it was blasted by the reviewers and hasn't been successfully revived.

Russia and Central Europe: The Seventeenth, Eighteenth, and Nineteenth Centuries

Skip over the seventeenth and eighteenth. In the nineteenth, Russia enters the opera field with non-Collection Mikhail Glinka. Internationalist Tchaikovsky and nationalists Rimsky-Korsakov and Mussorgsky are soon to follow. The top work from Central Europe is Bedřich Smetana's *Bartered Bride*.

Peter Il'yich Tchaikovsky

THE COLLECTION COMPOSERS
Alexander Borodin (1833–87)
Leoš Janáček (1854–1928)
Modest Mussorgsky (1839–81)
Nicolai Rimsky-Korsakov (1844–1908)
Bedřich Smetana (1824–84)
Peter Il'yich Tchaikovsky (1840–93)

All Collection composers from "Russia" were born in the old Russia before the Soviet Union was established—or, later, disestablished. In this book, Hungary and the different sections of the old Czechoslovakia are included in "Central Europe."

A Russian national school of opera began with *A Life for the Czar* in 1836, composed by the father of Russian opera, Mikhail Glinka (1804–57). It was followed six years later by his *Russlan and Ludmilla*. Glinka was influenced not only by Western opera—by Weber in Germany, by French operas, and by Italian opera buffa—but also by the folk music of Poland and Eastern Asian Russia.

By the middle of the nineteenth century, two schools of Russian composers had developed. One was led by Anton Rubinstein (1829–94), who in some nineteen operas followed the techniques of French and German composers. The other consisted of the "Mighty Five," made up of César Cui, Mili Balakirëv and Collection composers Borodin, Rimsky-Korsakov, and Mussorgsky. Dedicated Russian nationalists, their goal was to create music that reflected Russia, not Paris—music on Russian themes, music that had its roots in Russian folk sounds.

Of the five, Mussorgsky was the power player, the Dostoyevsky of music. His *Boris Godunov*, 1874, was creative, original, forceful, and still the greatest music drama to come out of Eastern Europe. Rimsky-Korsakov, with *Le coq d'or* (*The Golden Cockerel*), 1907, showed more professionalism and musical training than the others, and Borodin, with *Prince Igor*, 1890, was the most melodious, exotic, and Oriental of them.

Russia's all-time leading classical music composer is Tchaikovsky. Professionally trained in the West, he was more influenced by Western music than the nationalist Five and much more international in nature. Still, all of his operas are based on Russian subjects.

In Central Europe, the founder of Czech national music was Collection composer Smetana, who also created the classical form of Czech serious opera in *The Bartered Bride*, 1866. A second Collection composer is Leoš Janáček, who is on something of a roll in the early 1990s, particularly with *Jenůfa*, 1904. The leading all-time Czech classical composer is Antonín Dvořák (1841–1904), whose best opera—not in The Collection but in the special Twentieth-century European Package—is *Rusalka*, which premiered in Prague in 1901. The most important person in the development of Polish opera is Stanislaus Moniuszko (1819–72), whose *Halka*, 1848, is still often performed in his country.

Hungary's talented Béla Bartók comes in the twentieth century with *Duke Bluebeard's Castle*, 1918. Another composer with Central European roots was Karl Goldmark (1830–1915), an Austro-Hungarian whose *Queen of Sheba* premiered in Vienna in 1875. It remained in the repertory until well into the twentieth century.

The Twentieth Century

All Countries

> Most twentieth-century Collection composers were born in the nine-
> teenth century. Two giant shadows loom as the century begins. Italian
> ascendancy fades with the death of Puccini. A century of incredible
> experimentation of music and themes, but at century's end the old
> Warhorses still prevail.

THE COLLECTION COMPOSERS
Béla Bartók (1881–1945)
Alban Berg (1885–1935)
Benjamin Britten (1913–76)
Gustave Charpentier (1860–1956)
Claude Debussy (1862–1918)
Leoš Janáček (1854–1928)
Giacomo Puccini
Nicolai Rimsky-Korsakov (1844–1908)
Richard Strauss (1864–1949)

Like most centuries, the twentieth is one hundred years long. Care must be
taken not to lump 1909 with 1990.

Sixteen twentieth-century operas by nine composers are in The Collection. Two of the composers, Charpentier and Debussy, are French, and two,
Berg and Richard Strauss, are German. Five countries are represented by one
composer each: Italy by Puccini, Russia by Rimsky-Korsakov, what then was
Czechoslovakia by Janáček, Hungary by Bartók, and England by Britten.

Major shift: Note that the only twentieth-century Italian here is Puccini,
whose works dominate opera for the first quarter of the century. After him, Italy
disappears from the Big Hit list.

Four twentieth-century Collection composers, Richard Strauss, Janáček,
Berg, and Britten, have contributed so much to opera that they have additional
works in the Twentieth-century European Package. Nineteen non-Collection
composers are also in that package, which consists of handpicked operas that
don't yet qualify statistically for The Collection—and some never will. American twentieth-century composers are discussed in their own, American, chapter.

The century began in a fairly straightforward way with general domination
by two giant shadows representing very different forms of opera:

- The shadow of Verdi, who had brought "traditional" opera to new heights.
- The newer, more controversial, shadow of Wagner and his vastly different
  music drama.

Except for overtures, you don't come across many recordings of orchestral excerpts of the more traditional Verdi-type opera. And you don't find many recordings of "vocal selections" of the newer, different Wagner type.

That's not to suggest that Verdi didn't care about the orchestra or that Wagner operas aren't jam-packed with the human voice. It isn't that Wagner deemphasized the voice, rather, that he changed the vocal line into what he called "endless melody," a form that bypassed big set arias and ensemble numbers.

Early twentieth-century opera went both ways. Some gravitated toward Wagner, consciously and subconsciously, and others deliberately or impulsively reacted against him. Puccini in Italy and the remnants of a faddish verismo school looked back to Verdi; Debussy in France and early Richard Strauss in Germany to Wagner, although Strauss changed in midstream and Debussy was wholly unlike Wagner in the sounds of his music.

And some twentieth-century composers went deeper into the past for the type of opera that was popular before Verdi or Wagner—back to Mozart and even earlier.

Not everything, of course, was either Verdi-like or Wagner-like. The French style, under the leadership of Massenet, depicted real people in real situations but accented charm more than passion. The Russians and Czechs concentrated either on nationalistic operas or grown-up fairy tales. The English, reentering the operatic picture after some three hundred years, did their own thing.

In France in 1902, Impressionist Debussy created *Pelléas et Mélisande*, the most important French opera of the twentieth century and one that also influenced many composers. Among them were Bartók with *Duke Bluebeard's Castle* in 1918 and non-Collection composer Paul Dukas (1865–1935) and his only opera, *Ariane et Barbe-Bleu*, in 1907. Both works were based on dramas by Belgian author Maurice Maeterlinck.

Opera throughout the century reflected the world around it, a world that included two world wars, the Great Depression, the horror of concentration camps, nations in which art was governed by dictatorial communism and fascism, and technology that included radio, television, cassette tapes and compact discs, VCRs, laser discs, moon landings, the atomic-bomb—and all things made possible by computers.

It has been a century in which 160 million people were killed by wars. And it is one that included the main writings of Sigmund Freud, his followers, and the noncouch psychiatrists who worked with the subconscious and the whole new sciences of psychoanalysis and therapy. Some twentieth-century operas by Collection composers concerned themselves with these more hidden recesses of the mind; for example, Strauss's *Salome*, 1905; Bartók's *Duke Bluebeard's Castle*; Janáček's *From the House of the Dead*, 1930; Britten's *Turn of the Screw*, 1954; and Berg's *Wozzeck*, 1925.

Musicologists make the case that even without those new sciences the perspective of a twentieth-century artist was changed by World War I alone.

With some exceptions (Mussorgsky's *Boris Godunov* is one), traditionally the individual had been the hero or heroine of the artist. His or her passion, or jealousy, or greed, or fate had been the focal point. When millions are killed, as in World War I alone, the approach of the sensitive artist inevitably is modified.

One solution for the twentieth-century opera composer was to create, or find in existing literature, a hero—or nonhero—representative of millions. The Collection's *Wozzeck* and *Peter Grimes* (1945) are two examples of ordinary men who simply couldn't cope.

It has been a century of unprecedented experimentation in every conceivable way, with opera drawn from all imaginable sources: folklore, legend, history, mythology, real people of today, imagined people of tomorrow, the subconscious, and so forth, and so forth, and so forth. It deals in comedy, tragedy, satire, high drama, farce, social commentary, propaganda, moral instruction . . . and any whim of the sometimes subsidized composer.

Opera in the 1900s doesn't lend itself to easy classification, nor is there any cause to expect that it would. Little in the twentieth century lends itself to easy classification, from yo-yos to Yeltsin.

The goal of some twentieth-century composers has been to entertain, and their works are written for a large public audience. The goal of others has been to make statements about social protest, or human frailty, and some of their works are aimed at a much narrower audience. And the goal of still others has been self-expression, with a remarkable absence of concern about whether anyone would come to see and hear their product.

Benjamin Britten has said he could see no reason for opera that wasn't written for *some* audience, even if only two or three persons. Not all twentieth-century composers believed that—which, of course, has been their privilege and right but also is one reason why people want to see and hear Britten's operas more than theirs. Another reason is that he's flat-out the better composer.

Still, we can't determine what will appeal to the next generation, or several generations hence. Fortunately, the Supreme Court doesn't prohibit egocentric composers from pleasing themselves musically any way they wish. Conversely, some composers—in the twentieth century or any other—have written opera specifically for the masses, with little reference to the content and with eyes only on the box office. This may be opera, but only in rare instances is it notable opera. Pleasing the public doesn't necessarily have redeeming social value, as television and the movies prove every day.

The two most interesting twentieth-century composers who are not in The Collection are Arnold Schoenberg, the man who devised a new method of composition, which uses in turn all twelve tones of the chromatic scale, and Igor Stravinsky, a Russian who became a naturalized American citizen and is a sound candidate to be the century's top composer of classical music. Both have been picked for the Twentieth-century European Package.

A case can be made that the basic theme of twentieth-century opera is tragedy, whether expressed in Impressionistic symbolism as in Debussy's *Pelléas et Mélisande*, expressionism as in Strauss's *Salome* and *Elektra*, 1909, or naturalism as in *Peter Grimes*, and other operas by Britten. But then, a case can be made for almost anything in the twentieth century.

One major point is that opera is not dead. By the end of World War I, opera companies had more to choose from than ever before in history—the old Warhorses, the other popular operas of the late nineteenth and early twentieth centuries, and a big field of experimental works.

Today, with the century virtually over, it is remarkable that the same standard operas prevail—despite a whole century of immense experimentation, despite the emergence of fine fresh talent, and despite a reasonable commitment by many opera companies, especially those off the main axis, to try something new. Nearly all the blockbusters not only hang on but continue to dominate. Pick almost any major opera house and look at the repertory. Gounod's *Faust* has slipped from its incredible peak (except for a 1990s centenary spurt), *Aida* is staged less frequently because it's so costly to produce, many highbrows have gone through (and most have emerged from) a period of dumping on Puccini, the bel canto composers have made a remarkable recovery after almost fading away, and Mozart is back where he belongs even after he had been put on the shelf for a while. So, despite everything, here in the late 1990s, the same operatic composers still are perched on the top of the charts: Verdi, Wagner, Puccini, Donizetti, Rossini, Richard Strauss, Mozart, and their ilk.

Twentieth-century operatic activity is different in Europe than in the United States. Overseas, where a long tradition of opera persists, the Warhorses are complemented in three ways. One is by lesser-known works by the Big Names—operas that have been popular at home but have traveled less well than the Warhorses. A second is by contributions from homegrown living composers. And a third is by old museum pieces from the country's own operatic history. Thus, Italy complements Verdi's *Aida* with his lesser-known *Stiffelio*, then adds twentieth-century Luigi Dallapiccola and reaches back to Giovanni Paisiello's 1782 *Barber of Seville*. Germany complements Wagner's *Parsifal* with his *Rienzi*, adds twentieth-century Hans Werner Henze's *Der Prinz von Homburg*, and restages old Carl Maria von Weber. The French stick solidly behind Bizet's *Carmen*, but also present his *Pearl Fishers*, add a work like twentieth-century Poulenc's *Dialogues des Carmélites*, and dust off old-timer Jean-Philippe Rameau from the early 1700s.

Today, the variety in Europe is somewhat greater than in the United States, in part because of government-subsidized experimentation abroad but more because Germany, France, and Italy possess such a treasure-house from the past. The United States—and Russia, Eastern Europe, and Britain—lack this opulence, although in recent years more attention has been paid here to the "other" operas of the Big Composers, such as *Stiffelio* and the *The Pearl Fishers*.

And we will see in the American chapter that there is an enormous amount of activity off the main U.S. axis of New York–Chicago–San Francisco.

This short rundown doesn't get to such works as electronic and rock opera. Some composers have combined traditional instruments with electronic music. Some have written operas specifically for television. There's no end to it. It's a long way from Mozart to the taped synthesized sounds of some twentieth-century composers. But tolerance is recommended. It also was a long way from Johann Sebastian Bach to the sounds of Claude Debussy.

No finer composer has lived than Mr. Bach. And one of his outstanding works, *The St. Matthew Passion*—among the most magnificent pieces of music ever written—was ignored for one hundred years before a young composer/conductor named Felix, son of a rich German banker named Mendelssohn, dusted it off and gave it to posterity.

Was it Mark Twain, Will Rogers, or both who said it is difficult to predict anything, especially the future?

Chapter 6

THE
COLLECTION

❧

THE TWENTY-FIVE WARHORSES

Four Warhorses by Giuseppe Verdi

October 10, 1813–January 27, 1901

AIDA *(Number 1)*
LA TRAVIATA *(Number 4)*
RIGOLETTO *(Number 9)*
IL TROVATORE *(Number 14)*

Giuseppe Verdi dominates The Collection proper and is second only to Richard Wagner in the Twenty-five Warhorses.

Italy was the operatic capital of the world as Verdi was growing up. In 1839, when he wrote his first opera, Bellini, Donizetti and Rossini were the big names, although Rossini had stopped composing after blowing everyone else off the stage.

In one sense, opera in Italy was where it had been for two centuries. It was a vehicle for singers; it was not great theater or drama. Singers carried with them their favorite arias reasonably appropriate to the plot: a "rage" aria, a "love" aria, or a "hate" aria. Few in the audience were upset by this practice. Unlike France and Germany, Italy had no strong dramatic tradition.

And the old opera buffa was in a state of decline, verging on death, absorbed by opera seria. Among other problems, most of the singers had no aptitude for

Giuseppe Verdi

comic opera. They were too busy showing off their voices to bother with acting or comic timing. Comedy demanded a delicacy, a touch, that they lacked.

Verdi's earliest operas were "formula works" that followed the system everyone understood. First, an overture. The tunes heard in it reappeared during the opera proper. Next, a chorus of townspeople, followed by the entrance of a major character, each of whom was given an entrance aria. If no entrance aria had been written, the top singers wouldn't perform. It was that simple. The formula called for the orchestra to play a little tune so that the audience could become familiar with it, and then the chorus sang it. The arias had sweeping lines and long melodic phrases. Verdi's early works obeyed the rules, and there was nothing especially remarkable about them.

Before too long, however, Verdi took opera from the bel canto style of Rossini, Bellini, and Donizetti and turned it into full-fledged Italian Romantic melodrama.

Once his career was launched, he moved away from "singer" shows and toward drama—or, at least, melodrama—set to music. This was not really a return to the Camerata, whose purpose was to use music to enhance the drama. Verdi undeniably considered the music more important—but he also wanted to tighten things up, to keep things moving, to make the drama more powerful and the entire undertaking more compelling.

Why is Verdi so popular? What did he have that made him so special? Why is he the most loved of all opera composers?

For openers, he was a musical genius. In opera composition, as in all-purpose classical music composition, that characterization applies only to a few of the world's artists. Johann Sebastian Bach was a genius of classical music; Jean Sibelius was a gifted composer. Verdi was a genius of opera; Jules Massenet was a gifted composer.

If your mission is to compose operas, an excellent starting point is to be a musical genius. But some geniuses, like many Rhodes scholars, lack balance and go awry. What else did Verdi have?

He had an ardent nature . . . passion and compassion . . . spontaneous melody . . . brains and wit . . . melody . . . sensuous beauty . . . melody . . . emotional power . . . melody.

He also had eighty-seven years of life. Mozart had thirty-five.

- Like William Shakespeare, he was fascinated by and acutely aware of the character of human beings. No composer (Mozart is an exception to everything) better understood the emotions within each of us. The story, the plot, the events were less important to him—not unimportant, but less important.
- He had a fierce desire to translate those human emotions into music and the discipline to do it.
- Because his genius was accompanied by supreme craftsmanship, he had the ability to fulfill this desire, to use music to portray these feelings: anger, envy, hate, joy, love, sorrow, zeal.
- As an *Italian* opera composer, inevitably he still was bound up in voice and melody. For him, melody for the human voice—not the sound of the orchestra—was the supreme vehicle for expression. (But toward the end, the analysts say, he also had become a pretty good orchestrator.)
- He had some very good librettists—and one supremely great one.
- Inevitably, as a successful composer of opera, he had a superb sense of the theater.
- Finally: He was a communicator. He wasn't trying to revolutionize music, to create a new style of opera, or to save the world. He used music to communicate the real-life strengths and weaknesses of men and women, not to explore in metaphysics. Basically, he was a K.I.S.S. composer—K.I.S.S., the byword of all great communicators: Keep It Simple, Stupid. Ronald Reagan the Great Communicator? He wasn't in Verdi's class. Abraham Lincoln, Franklin Roosevelt, and Winston Churchill were in Verdi's class. They employed no mysticism to reach their audience.

Verdi said it himself: "Art without spontaneity, naturalness, and simplicity is no art."

People hate. People love. People sometimes kill what they hate. And sometimes kill what they love. They die for love, prayerfully in their lover's arms. They are sometimes brutal. However tangled some Verdi plots, any audience can identify with hate, love, and death.

Safe in a Belfry

Verdi's parents kept a small inn and grocery store at Roncole, Italy. He was nearly killed as a small baby when his mother hid herself and him in a church belfry for twenty-four hours during a raid by Russian Cossack troops who slaughtered men, women, and children.

This was a rare man, one of history's greatest role models for the senior citizen. The American Association of Retired Persons would have paid him a fortune to lobby in the cause of the golden-agers (not that he needed the job; he achieved world fame, power, and a vast fortune on his own). But he was fifty-seven when he wrote *Aida*, seventy-three when he completed *Otello*, and on the edge of eighty when he composed *Falstaff*.

Verdi (unlike Wagner and Puccini) was not overly concerned about the authenticity of his plots and was apt to be casual about the staging details. And the *actions* of the hero interested him far less than the *passions* of the hero, and his fundamental weaknesses and self-deceptions. Any of us who isn't perfect can identify with Verdi characters.

Some say that Verdi was emotional heart, Wagner intellectual head. This is unfair to the German, who *was* intellectual and symbolic but also was capable of getting to the most basic emotions, often in such a way that the audience was unable to hide from them.

You Can't Win Them All

Don Pietro Seletti, an amateur violinist, was Verdi's boyhood Latin teacher in the town of Busetto. His reaction to the news that Verdi was interested in music:

"What do you want to study music for? You have a gift for Latin, and it will be much better for you to become a priest. What do you expect from your music? Do you fancy that some day you may become organist of Busetto? . . . Stuff and nonsense . . . That can never be."

Musicologist Paul Henry Lang notes that for Verdi the time and place are unimportant: "Verdi's men and women can be divested of their exterior, of their sixteenth-century ruffs, Egyptian tunics, Venetian armor, and gypsy robes, for Rigoletto's pathetic impotence, Aida's unflinching love, Iago's diabolic cunning [*Otello*], Otello's consuming, senseless jealousy, and Azucena's half-demented vengefulness [*Il trovatore*] will still remain. These constant elements in man Verdi has given us in music; in opera, which exemplifies the essence of the lyric drama: the transliteration of human emotions from a literary sketch into pure music."

"Pathetic impotence," "unflinching love," "diabolic cunning," "consuming jealousy," "half-demented vengefulness." No metaphysics here. This is gut-check music.

Across the Alps, in German Romantic opera of the same time period, nature painting was key. So were the supernatural, symbolism, and national legends. Verdi paid scant attention to any of them, although he was conscious of Herr Wagner, their primary creator.

Let's again place Verdi in the Italian scheme of things. Rossini's last stage work was *Guillaume Tell* in 1829; Donizetti's last hit was *Don Pasquale* in 1843. Puccini's first real success was *Manon Lescaut* in 1893. For those intervening fifty years between the end of Donizetti and the beginning of Puccini, Verdi *was* Italian opera.

With the exception of *Falstaff* (and one early failure), all of his operas are serious—and nearly all are gloomy and violent. Since the early 1970s in this country Congress has been asking (to little avail) the networks to cut back violence on television. TV's annual May sweeps fall far short of the violence standards set by Verdi.

For road-map purposes, Verdi's Collection work can be broken into four groups (the number in parentheses is the Collection number):

The early ones, which made his Italian reputation:

Ernani, 1844 (Number 62)
Macbeth, 1847 (Number 64)
Luisa Miller, 1849 (not in The Collection)

The Big Three, which brought him international fame and which, along with *Aida*, constitute the four Verdi Warhorses:

Rigoletto, 1851 (Number 9)
Il trovatore, 1853 (Number 14)
La traviata, 1853 (Number 4)

The later four of his middle period are not nearly as popular as the Big Three but are generally given higher marks by the professionals for having greater "dramatic unity." Author's counsel: Start with the Warhorses for Opera 101.

Simon Boccanegra, 1857 (Number 55)
A Masked Ball, 1859 (Number 32)

The Force of Destiny, 1862 (Number 30)
Don Carlos, 1867 (Number 47)

And the Final Three, which include *the* single most popular of all Verdi operas plus his last two—the "most mature" two, which most delight and intrigue the connoisseurs and academicians:

Aida, 1871 (Number 1), followed sixteen years later by
Otello, 1887 (Number 28), followed at age seventy-nine by
Falstaff, 1893 (Number 44)

And death in 1901, in Milan, as a national hero.

The Collection bypasses other good Verdi operas still being performed. These include four earlier operas, *Nabucco*, 1842; *I Lombardi*, 1843; *Attila*, 1846, and, especially, *Luisa Miller*, 1849, and one midcareer work, *Les vêspres siciliennes*, 1855.

Verdi was born in Roncole, Italy, in 1813. He tried to enter the Milan Conservatory at the age of nineteen but was rejected. "Privo di talento musicale," said the conservatory. "Lacking in musical talent."

Spin doctors for the institution found a number of valid reasons for the rejection, including the fact that he was overage for admission. But I'm glad I wasn't the dean of admissions who made the decision.

After studying with private teachers, his first opera, *Oberto*, was introduced at La Scala in Milan in 1839. The house commissioned him to write another and he attempted to do so, but his personal life was overflowing with tragedy. He lost a small daughter, then a baby boy, and within weeks his young wife. "My family had been destroyed, and in the midst of these trials I had to fulfill my engagement and write a comic opera!" he said later. Understandably, it was not a good work. In despair, he decided to give up opera, a decision that lasted only a few months, until an impresario connected with La Scala gave him the libretto of *Nabucco* (*Nebuchadnezzar, King of Babylon*). He liked it, set it to music, and, at age twenty-nine, in 1842, saw it open at La Scala with great success.

In its immediate wake came the first set of Collection operas and then the Big Three.

It is incomplete to write of Verdi—"the musical Garibaldi"—and not speak of his patriotism. (Garibaldi, another Giuseppe, was the military and nationalist leader who spent his life seeking freedom for Italy and a united Italian kingdom.) In the 1840s and 1850s, Verdi's operas—although unconnected with contemporary events—were an important spiritual part of the Italian revolutionary movements. Their sometimes complex plots sent the most simple messages: Liberty is worth fighting for, tyranny must be denounced, to die for your country is noble. In *The Force of Destiny*, for example, the gypsy girl Preziosilla spends much of her time singing of the glories of military life and the honor of fighting and dying for a cause. Verdi's clear commitment to independence was part and parcel of the immense popularity he enjoyed, a popularity that in Italy is nearly as strong now as it was more than a century ago.

Sinful Conduct

Even a Verdi couldn't always please everyone, even when he composed the world's most popular opera. After *Aida*'s premiere, some Italian critics thought it departed too much from conventional Italian methods and complained that he had turned to "Germanism" and "Wagnerism."

There even was a logo; by chance—or fate—the letters of Verdi's name coincided with the initials of the nationalist slogan for a united Italy under one monarch—Vittorio Emmanuele Re d'Italia (Victor Emmanuel, King of Italy). The cries of "Viva V-E-R-D-I" in Italian theaters both applauded the composer and voiced the national dream.

Music was Verdi's life. He bought an estate at Busseto, where he lived for fifty years with his second wife, Giuseppina Strepponi, a singer who had performed in his operas. She had lived with him for several years before they were married, and her past was on the shady side, including illegitimate children by different men. Her presence in Verdi's house caused massive problems with his own father, as well as the father of his first wife—a man important to him from a business standpoint—and, indeed, the whole village. Once Italy was free he ran for a seat in the first parliament, not because of political ambitions but rather to support the new government with his own prestige.

Comparisons are inevitable between Verdi and Richard Wagner, and long books are available on that topic alone.

In the public eye it is difficult to determine which is the favorite. More people see more Verdi operas than Wagner operas—but Verdi wrote more than twice as many. At the Deutsche Staatsoper in Berlin itself, available records show four Verdi operas to three by Wagner out of the twenty most frequently performed works. All that proves is that at the Staatsoper four Verdi operas are performed to three of Wagner's. Still, it *is* Berlin.

Yet all ten of Wagner's main operas make a Collection that is based on frequency-of-performance, so the impression shouldn't be left that he's somehow the darling of the connoisseurs but not of the general operagoing public.

The melodrama of Verdi perhaps stands alone in opera, but so does the orchestral mastery of Wagner. Though the beginner finds the emotion in Verdi more approachable, the emotion in Wagner becomes apparent when the second and third toes have been put into the opera water. Well, sometimes the fourth toe. But it will happen.

Sketch of the set for Act 1, Scene 2 of a 1963 Metropolitan Opera production of Aida

Extremist pro-Wagner German critics blast the "Italian tinsel" of Verdi and characterize his melodies as being only "half legitimate," but anyone who looks long enough can find some critic somewhere to condemn anything. The public, of course, sings those half-legitimate, tinsel tunes all the way home from the theater.

Wagner moved away from the conventional aria but substituted his "endless melody" to make up the whole. Verdi reveled in melodious arias but nearly always put them in the context of the whole.

Fortunately, we have both—both born in 1813, each the emperor of his own terrain, with two vastly different concepts. Some evidence exists that Verdi was influenced by elements of Wagner, although it is unclear if Wagner's ego would permit any mere Italian to influence him.

Number 1. *Aida*

Premiere at Cairo, 1871. Text by Antonio Ghislanzoni from the French prose of Camille du Locle, which was based on a scenario by the Egyptologist Auguste Mariette. Four acts.

KEYNOTE

Verdi's most popular opera. A masterpiece of art, blending Verdi's human passion, Italian melodrama, and French grand opera spectacle. Tragic love triangle, with the two who love one another dying together in a sealed tomb. A favorite for open-air festivals by companies with enough money to bring it off.

PLOT

Egypt, in the time of the pharaohs (no set century identified). Amneris (mezzo-soprano), daughter of the King of Egypt, loves Radames (tenor), the captain of the Egyptian guard. But he loves Amneris's slave, Aida (soprano), who also is in love with him. Unknown to the Egyptians, Aida is the daughter of Amonasro (baritone), the King of Ethiopia. As a reward for leading the Egyptian army to victory against Ethiopia, Radames is granted any wish by the King. Knowing one captive is the father of his beloved Aida, but unaware that he also is the King of Ethiopia, Radames asks for freedom for all prisoners. Aida's prisoner father persuades her to pry the secret battle line-of-march from Radames—information that would enable the Ethiopian army to defeat the Egyptians. Aida tricks Radames into disclosing the information, under the guise that they need it for a safe elopement. But he is heard by the Egyptians, refuses to defend himself, and is dishonored. For his treachery he is sentenced to be buried alive under the high altar of the god he has offended. Waiting there to die, Radames finds Aida hidden in the vault, sealed in with no chance of escape, preferring death with the man she loves to life without him.

HIGHLIGHTS

Act I: Radames's "Celeste Aida!" ("Radiant Aida!") in which he dreams of war heroism he will put before Aida: "If I were that chosen warrior! With my army of brave men . . . and victory . . . and the cheers of all Memphis, I'd return to you, my sweet Aida, covered with my laurels."*

Aida's "Ritorna vincitor." She has joined in prayers for his victory, although distressed that it would be over her own people: "Return victorious! My own lips spoke those treacherous words, though it means victorious over my father . . . I could see my beloved stained with my family's blood."

The solemn beauty of the closing section, inside the temple of Vulcan.

Act II: A cast-of-thousands finale, arguably Verdi's most grand, featuring the Triumphal Scene and the Triumphal March, as Radames returns, a conquering hero. Gladiators, chariots, ballet dancers, and prisoners. The Triumphal Scene and the Triumphal trumpet march: "Gloria all' Egitto" ("Glory to Egypt").

Act III: The entire Nile scene. Aida's "O patria mia," in which she longs for her native land: "O my homeland, never again shall I see you." The duet that follows between Aida and her father, "Pense che un popolo vinto, straziato," as he persuades her to pry battle secrets from Radames. It is one of Verdi's famous "family" (as opposed to lover) duets: "He loves you, he commands the

---

*Please note that the lyrics quoted throughout this book are intended as short recaps to give you a feel for the arias. They are not verbatim quotes from librettos. Thus you may see different translations or wordings in librettos, supertitles, or video captions.

Egyptians, we must know by which route they will come . . . I shall be true to my country." The subsequent Aida-Radames duet.

Act IV: The double-decker scene that ends the opera, with the priests who have ordered Radames's death chanting in the upper room while he, imprisoned in the vault, first mourns Aida and then finds her there to die with him. "La fatal pietra . . . ": "The fatal stone is closing now. Farewell to earth and to sorrow. Heaven is opening to us."

No Spin Doctors

Verdi was unhappy when Ricordi, his publisher, circulated copies of *Aida* before the opening night. He wrote them:

"You were wrong to show *Aida* to outsiders. Judgments made in advance are of no value at all and no good to anyone . . . Always mistrust these judgments, whether they come from friends or enemies. Also, I absolutely do not want *publicity*. Let the public judge on the first night, for better or for worse . . . I beg you in all seriousness, do not let anyone talk about *Aida* any more; let no one look at it; and let no one judge it. Be calm yourself: either *Aida* will succeed, then we will not need publicity, or it will go badly, and these premature views will just add to the fiasco."

COMMENTARY

Aida is the most successful nineteenth-century grand opera in the repertory, the most popular Verdi opera, the opera most performed by the Metropolitan, and, Bizet's *Carmen* aside, perhaps the most performed anywhere. Although it has an Italian libretto, it was written in the style of the French grand opera. The public loves it, and so do the singers. Musicologists say it's the first opera in which Verdi abandoned his technique of "great moments" in favor of a more integrated work. It is the first Verdi opera—indeed, the first Italian opera—to be "through-composed"—that is, to have songs in which the music changes throughout instead of being repeated for a series of verses. This approach becomes more common in the later "veristic" operas of the early twentieth century. The all-popular Big Three had musical ups and downs, but *Aida* is considered musically and dramatically level throughout—even if Verdi reached higher individual peaks in some of his other works.

Many operagoers regard it as the best evening's entertainment Verdi ever devised—flowing melodies, great pageantry, exciting, moving, and absorbing. It was successful from the start, with VIPs from all over the world attending the Egyptian premiere. After it came a sixteen-year gap, when Verdi spent his time as a working gentleman-farmer and wrote no opera.

MET PERFORMANCES

Nine hundred and eighty-six performances in ninety-three seasons, from 1886 to 1996. The Met's most frequently performed opera.*

RECORDING

CD—Decca/London 417 416–2 (3). Leontyne Price, Rita Gorr, Jon Vickers, Robert Merrill, Giorgio Tozzi, Plinio Clabassi. Rome Opera Chorus and Orchestra. Georg Solti. 1961.

VIDEO

Millo, Domingo, Zajick, Milnes. Metropolitan Opera. Italian; English subtitles. Levine, conductor. 1989. PGD (Polygram Group Distribution).

Number 4. *La traviata*

Premiere at Teatro la Fenice, Venice, 1853. Text by Francesco Maria Piave based on Alexander Dumas fils's 1852 play La Dame aux camélias. *Three acts.*

KEYNOTE

Refined drawing-room tragedy in contrast with the *Aida* spectacle. The love story of a tubercular courtesan who falls for a young man-about-town. His father, guarding the family reputation, will have none of it.

PLOT

Paris, 1850. Alfredo Germont (tenor) falls in love with the beautiful courtesan Violetta Valéry (soprano), known as the Lady of Camelias. Overcoming her doubts, he convinces her that a man can truly love a courtesan. Knowing she's dying of consumption, and in love for the first time, she goes to live with Alfredo in the country. There his family-oriented father, Giorgio Germont (baritone), persuades her she must give up Alfredo in order to protect the family's reputation and preserve the engagement of Alfredo's sister. Instead of telling him to shove it in his ear (my advice to my daughters and granddaughters), Violetta agrees and returns to her former protector, the Baron Douphol (baritone). Distressed at her departure, and unaware of his father's intervention, Alfredo humiliates her in public, is disowned by his father (who by now recognizes Violetta's merit and sacrifice), and is challenged by Douphol to a duel. When Alfredo later learns the truth about her selflessness, he returns to repent at her deathbed. She dies; he lives on.

HIGHLIGHTS

The Prelude, which includes lovely music from the opera.

*Metropolitan Opera data in the book begins in 1883 and is through the 1995–96 season. Scheduled performances for the 1996–97 season also are given.

Act I: The "Brindisi" (a drinking song). "Libiamo," by Alfredo, Violetta, and guests: "Friends find love and happiness in wine." Alfredo's "Un dì felice," singing of his love: "I loved you from the first day . . . Mysterious power of love," and Violetta's reply. When he has gone, Violetta's long scene ("scena" in opera talk), which includes a long double aria: "È strano . . . Ah! fors' è lui . . . Sempre libera." One moment she wonders whether Alfredo and his love can be for real; the next she tells herself that she'll not give up going from pleasure to pleasure.

In the midst of her scene, Alfredo's distant voice repeating the melody from their earlier duet, "Di quell'amor:" "Now at last, true happiness. Mysterious power."

Act II: Alfredo's "De' miei bollenti spiriti" as he sings of his joy and what Violetta has taught him of love: "Since she told me I was her love forever I have lived close to heaven."

The great baritone-tenor duet between the senior Germont and Violetta, which some analysts call *the* quintessential Verdi duet. And Germont senior's aria "Di Provenza il mar," begging Alfredo to leave Violetta for the family home in Provence: "I have never stopped praying that you would see your way to come home to us. God hear my plea."

Act III: Violetta's farewell scene in which she says good-bye to the world, "Addio del passato." Alfredo has returned, but too late. She cries out and dies.

Hasty Pudding

La traviata was written in less than two months in 1853, although it's uncertain just how much less. Verdi was working on *Il trovatore* at the same time.

COMMENTARY

Violetta is based on a real woman, Marie Duplessis, depicted in the Dumas play. Human and feminine, she's the dominant character in the opera, a worldly courtesan who ordinarily plays all the angles with men but here gives up the one man she truly loves because she does truly love him. The plot was considered immoral by some, especially by London critics, but London audiences, in droves, managed to overcome their shock. Some good P.R. man probably spread the word that it was zesty, immoral, and downright indecent, assuring long lines at the ticket window.

In the past, it had been acceptable for heroes to experience romantic dalliances, but not heroines. With Violetta, Verdi breaks new ground. Call her courtesan if you will; Violetta is a high-priced prostitute who, until Alfredo, has been in the game for money. It is a little icky that Alfredo is so naive, his father so selfish and so ready to guilt-trip his son, and Violetta so noble, but Verdi, as usual, has us right in his hands.

Verdi set the opera in contemporary Paris. But this caused problems. The women in the audience on opening night knew that many of their husbands kept girlfriends, though this wasn't discussed around the dinner table. They had come to the opera dressed in their finest, with their eighteen-year-old daughters dressed in *their* finest, and there on the stage were Violetta and her courtesan friends, making their living by selling sex and wearing the finest finery in the house. It was a little too much for the ladies to take. There were other opening-night difficulties: Violetta was coughing from the start, a clear signal that she would be dead before the opera ended, and that was a downer in itself. Additionally, the Violetta that night was a particularly full-figured lady who looked far too healthy to be dying of consumption or anything else. In order to soothe the ladies and start afresh, Verdi closed the show, pushed back the time period a couple of hundred years, and made a historical wig-and-costume piece of it.

Because of its vocal intensity and dramatic range, the role of Violetta is regarded as a tough test of a soprano voice.

MET PERFORMANCES

Eight hundred and seventy-four performances over ninety-one seasons, from 1883 to 1995. The Met's third most frequently performed work after *Aida* and Puccini's *La Bohème*. Fourteen performances are scheduled for the 1996–97 season.

RECORDINGS

CD—Angel/EMI CDMB 63628, (2) (mono). Maria Callas, Giuseppe Di Stefano, Ettore Bastianini. La Scala Chorus and Orchestra. Carlo Maria Giulini. 1955.

or

Deutsche Grammophon 415 132-2 (2). Ileana Cotrubas, Plácido Domingo, Sherrill Milnes. Bavarian State Opera Chorus and Orchestra. Carlos Kleiber. 1976.

VIDEO

Sills, Price, Fredericks. Wolf Trap Festival. Italian; English subtitles. Rudel, conductor. 1976. VAI.

Number 9. *Rigoletto*

Premiere at Teatro la Fenice, Venice, 1851. Text by Francesco Maria Piave from Victor Hugo's 1832 play Le Roi s'amuse. *Three acts.*

KEYNOTE

Brutal melodrama. Adoring father unwittingly causes the murder of his own daughter. "You who laugh at a father's anguish, the father's curse will be on your head." "La maledizione!" The curse that is the opera's core.

PLOT

Mantua, sixteenth century, at the decadent court of the lecherous Duke of Mantua (tenor). (Victor Hugo set his play at the court of the historical François I, but Italian opera censors wouldn't buy that setting.) Rigoletto (baritone), the hunchbacked court jester, has no family but his daughter, Gilda (soprano), loves only her, and lives for her alone. No saint, he's mean-spirited, unscrupulous, revels in mocking the courtiers, and willingly helps his lascivious master in his seductions. Needless to say, he has many enemies at court. Unwisely, he mocks Count Monterone (baritone), whose daughter had been one of the Duke's victims. Monterone, distraught over the dishonoring of his daughter is furious at Rigoletto's mockery and lays a curse on him. Meanwhile, unknown to Rigoletto, the Duke now is pursuing Gilda to bed her. Disguised as a student, he has convinced her that he loves her, and in her innocence she has actually fallen in love with him. The courtiers, believing Gilda is Rigoletto's mistress and weary of his mockery, trick him into helping them abduct her for the Duke's bed. The Duke seduces her, although he's unaware that she is Rigoletto's daughter. When Rigoletto discovers her in the Duke's chamber, dishonored, he hires the assassin Sparafucile (bass) to kill the Duke. Sparafucile later agrees to pleas from his sister (new woman friend of the Duke's) to spare the Duke, but he's been paid for a job and professional ethics demand that he substitute someone in order to carry out his contract. The substitute victim is thought to be a beggar, but actually it is Gilda in disguise. Having overheard the plan, she is sacrificing herself to save the Duke she loves. Rigoletto reappears and is given a sack that he thinks contains the Duke's body. Confident that he has his revenge, he carries it to the river, intending to dump it in. But he hears from the distance the voice of the Duke, obviously alive, singing his favorite song, "La donna è mobile" ("Women are fickle"). Rigoletto cuts open the sack, finds his beloved Gilda, dying, and realizes that he's been instrumental in murdering her. "Too much I loved him—now I die for him," she whispers, referring to the Duke. She dies in her father's arms as the music of Count Monterone's curse is heard.

HIGHLIGHTS

Act I: The Duke's "Questa o quella": "This woman or that. I pursue them all, whatever their name, rank and marital status. This one today, another tomorrow." The Gilda-Rigoletto duet, one of several Verdi father-daughter duets: "Daughter, you are my life. I am a poor cripple. Without you I have nothing . . . Father, I cannot bear to see you grieve and suffer. Why do you worry about me. An angel in heaven watches over us." Gilda's "Caro nome"

("Dearest Name"), her love dream of the Duke: "Dear name, I am yours until my last sigh."

Action

Critical assessment of Verdi at the time of his death: Not a great revolutionary or reformer. Not a man with a mission to open new paths. Not a man of theory. But a man of action, one who built magnificently with the materials bequeathed to him by earlier generations, and with a certain sense of knowing exactly where he was going and how to get there. No opera music could be more noble when it was time to be noble, nor more gay when it was time to be gay. And in his later works, no one came closer to Mozart in his power of character-drawing.

Act II: The Duke's "Ella mi fu rapita!" fearing that he has lost Gilda: "What villains dared steal you from me? The tears of my beloved demand vengeance." Rigoletto's dramatic aria, beginning "La rà, La rà" as he is searching the palace for Gilda. It is one of opera's most skillful scenes as he uses every emotion trying to learn from the courtiers what has become of his daughter: "Fiendish assassins, give her back or my revenge will be bloody . . . Noble lords, I implore you to have mercy . . . A father begs for pity." The subsequent father-daughter duet between Rigoletto and Gilda, one of Verdi's loveliest: "He swore his deepest love. Ruthless men brought me to this cruel ordeal . . . My blameless daughter, fate has been cruel. Let me console you."

Act III: The opera's Hit Parade tune, "La donna è mobile," sung by the Duke when he is disguised as an officer: "Woman's fidelity is a feather in the wind as she changes speech and thoughts. Never the same. Whether crying or laughing, her face may be lying. Yet men ignore the warnings and trust her." This is followed by one of Verdi's most famous quartets, "Bella figlia dell' amore," with the Duke, Maddalena, Gilda, and Rigoletto—tenor, contralto, soprano, and baritone—each expressing separate emotions as Rigoletto and his daughter hear the Duke trying to seduce another woman. Verdi designed this to be the high spot of the opera, but some famous tenors (including Caruso) have topped it with "La donna è mobile." Still, it ranks with the sextet from Donizetti's *Lucia di Lammermoor* as a leading operatic ensemble number.

COMMENTARY

"La maledizione!" The curse is the thing. Unlike the confusing plot of *Il trovatore*, the dramatic story here in Verdi's first great opera is easy for us to track. Gilda is pretty much an insipid character; Rigoletto is one of opera's most complex figures. Baritones love the role since, outside of Verdi, they are not often central characters who experience extreme emotional levels. (Tenors usually are the good guys who win the heroine, baritones the bad guys who foul things up. Basses often are kings or fill comic roles.) When Rigoletto finds that Gilda is probably in the Duke's chamber, he goes within moments from raging father to pleading sycophant to broken man. For emotional range in a single aria, this is one of the most dramatic scenes of opera.

Typically, Verdi handles the opera's emotions masterfully: Gilda's horror and despair; Rigoletto's rage, love, and despair; the Duke's shallowness. The final scene, in which Rigoletto finds his dying daughter in the sack, is one of the most chilling in all opera: the horror of a man losing the only thing in life that means anything to him.

Point of interest that we learn from the opera: It costs twice as much to kill a nobleman as it does to do in a commoner. Critics put down Donizetti because he turned out operas so rapidly, but Verdi wrote this masterpiece in six weeks.

MET PERFORMANCES

Six hundred and ninety-eight performances over eighty-four seasons, from 1883 to 1995. Fourteen performances are scheduled for the 1996–97 season.

RECORDING

CD—Decca/London 414 269–2 (2). Joan Sutherland, Huguette Tourangeau, Luciano Pavarotti, Sherrill Milnes, Martti Talvela. Ambrosian Opera Chorus. London Symphony Orchestra. Richard Bonynge. 1971.

VIDEO

Wixell, Pavarotti, Gruberová. A film by Jean-Pierre Ponnelle. Italian; English subtitles. Chailly, conductor. 1983. PGD.

Number 14. *Il trovatore (The Troubadour)*

Premiere at Teatro Apollo, Rome, 1853. Text by Salvatore Cammarano from Antonio García Gutierrez's 1836 Spanish play. Four acts.

KEYNOTE

Love, hate, revenge, and death. Gypsies, the evil eye, and burning at the stake. Only when the Count kills his own brother is the gypsy's mother avenged.

PLOT

Spain in the early fifteenth century. This is one of the most convoluted plots in opera. In reasonably simplified form it goes like this: Twenty-five years before the opera begins, Count di Luna burned to death a gypsy whom he thought had bewitched one of his sons. Azucena (mezzo-soprano), daughter of the gypsy, retaliated hysterically by throwing into the fire a baby she thought was the Count's. Mistakenly, she had killed her own child, so she kept and brought up the Count's. He's now known as a chieftain called Manrico (tenor), in the service of the Prince of Biscay, a warring foe of the Di Lunas.

At the time of the opera, a new Count (baritone), who is another son and the heir of the old di Luna, is in love with the Duchess Leonora (soprano), lady in waiting to the queen, and jealous of a troubadour (trovatore) she loves. The troubadour, who returns her love, is Manrico in disguise.

The dying words of the gypsy mother were "Avenge me," and Azucena has waited twenty-five years for the opportunity. She involves Manrico, who is unaware of his heritage, in a plot to kill the Count, but when it fails she is seized, brought before the Count, and condemned to die at the stake. Manrico is about to marry Leonora but leaves her to try to save his mother. He fails and is sentenced to be beheaded. Leonora offers to give herself to the Count if he'll free Manrico, although she plans to poison herself rather than live without her love. He will have me, but cold and dead, she sings to herself. When di Luna agrees, she goes to the prison to tell Manrico he's free to flee. Initially furious that she is selling herself to the Count, Manrico learns of the poison, which is acting too quickly, and she dies in his arms. The Count arrives, discovers her deceit, orders Manrico to the execution block, and forces Azucena to watch. Manrico dies. "He was your brother," Azucena shrieks at the Count. "You are avenged, mother." In some productions, she now is at a burning stake. The Count cries out in horror, having executed his long-lost brother.

HIGHLIGHTS

Act I: Leonora's "Tacea la notte," as she tells the story of her love. A passionate trio with the Count, Manrico, and Leonora, "Di geloso amor sprezzato," after the Count has learned Leonora loves another man—and then learns that the other man is Manrico, the enemy. "Jealousy burns in me like a fire . . . your words of love condemned him to death."

Act II: The Anvil Chorus at the gypsy campfire: "Gypsy maidens bring joy to the gypsy day and wine to give us courage." This is followed immediately by Azucena's memories of her mother being burned as a witch, "Stride la vampa!": "Upward the flames. The unruly crowd rushes to the fire, howling with joy as the flames crackle. The victim is ragged and barefoot. Her wild screams are heard through the hills: 'Avenge me.' "

Later, "Il balen del suo sorriso," in which the Count speaks of his great love for Leonora: "My burning love must make her mine."

The Act II finale, with the quartet of Leonora, Manrico, the Count, and his captain, and chorus, each character simultaneously expressing different emotions.

Act III: The Soldiers' Chorus, by the Count's soldiers. Now they are resting, but soon they will be ready to fight, find rich booty, and conquer the enemy.

Manrico's "Di quella pira," as he is about to marry Leonora but leaves her in order to try to rescue Azucena. There is a famous high C, a note not in the original score but reached by Caruso and since then by other superstar tenors. "The flames of the pyre set me on fire. I can't abandon my mother. I shall save you or die beside you."

Act IV: The entire act. Leonora, outside the prison, sends her love to Manrico to comfort him. "D'amor sull'ali rosee": "Let my love fly to him on rosy wings, carrying memories of our love." The Miserere, sung by Leonora outside the prison and Manrico and chorus offstage from within the prison—a prayer for the dead and once opera's most popular piece: "Have mercy on the soul so near to death. . . . Death comes slowly to those who want to die. I am giving my life for you." The duet between Azucena and Manrico in his cell, "Ai nostri monti" ("Home to our mountains"), as they face death together and dream of their happy mountain land.

COMMENTARY

Unless you like room-sized jigsaw puzzles, the details of this complex plot are a little formidable . . . but few care. For years *Trovatore* had more hit songs than any opera, except perhaps Bizet's *Carmen*. It was Europe's most successful nineteenth-century opera until replaced by *Faust* and *Carmen*, so popular that at one season in Venice three different companies were playing it at the same time. Analysts use words like "tragic power," "impetuous vigor," "poignant melancholy," "intense pathos," and "swift action." Some critics protest that there's not a smidgen of intellectual interest in it, although few deny the passion and the music. One 1853 reviewer called it a work of instinct that couldn't conceivably be taken seriously, but the public hasn't backed off for over 150 years. Now that several tunes are familiar even to nonoperagoers, it seems astonishing that a few early reviewers complained that too much attention had been paid to the characters and too little to the melody.

The music people say that Verdi paid more attention to the musical depiction of his characters in this opera than he had in any earlier works, and considerably more than Bellini, Donizetti, and Rossini in their bel canto operas.

Some analysts choose *Macbeth*, *Il trovatore*, and *Simon Boccanegra* as the three Verdi "dramatic" operas that signaled the route to *Otello*, his dramatic masterpiece.

Keep your eye on Azucena, one of opera's top mezzo-soprano roles. She's not only one of Verdi's most creative characters but one of opera's most vivid and human ones, dominated on the one hand by her great love for Manrico and on the other by her savage hatred for both Counts. She is part mother hen and part obsessed demon. Verdi wanted her to be the focal point of the opera—and she is.

That her role called for a mezzo-soprano voice was evidence of Verdi's major break with the bel canto opera of Rossini, Donizetti, and Bellini. To have a mezzo as the main female voice, as to have a baritone the main male voice

(Rigoletto), was something new. Other examples of big Verdi roles for mezzos are Eboli in *Don Carlos*, and Amneris in *Aida*.

For twenty-five years, the international Manrico of choice has been Plácido Domingo.

MET PERFORMANCES
Five hundred and thirty-seven performances in seventy-three seasons, from 1883 to 1993.

RECORDING
CD—RCA/BMG 6194-2-RC (2). Leontyne Price, Fiorenza Cossotto, Plácido Domingo, Sherrill Milnes, Bonaldo Giaiotti. Ambrosian Opera Chorus. New Philharmonia Orchestra. Zubin Mehta. (1969).

VIDEO
Pavarotti, Marton, Zajick, Milnes. Metropolitan Opera. Italian; English subtitles. Levine, conductor. 1988. PGD. DG.

∾

Three Warhorses by Giacomo Puccini
December 22, 1858–November 29, 1924

LA BOHÈME *(Number 2)*
TOSCA *(Number 5)*
MADAMA BUTTERFLY *(Number 7)*

When the heroine's music first sounded, it brought catcalls from the audience.

Then wisecracks from the balcony.

In the middle of the first act the hissing began.

At the end of that act, the jeering was heard above the applause and there was scornful laughter.

Throughout the second act came more derisive laughter and contemptuous shouting.

After the final curtain, the whole house responded to the performance with "an absolute glacial silence."

After that one black night, the composer withdrew the opera.

The time was February 17, 1904; the place was La Scala, Milan; the work was *Madama Butterfly*, which was to become one of the most popular operas of all time.

Six other operas by Giacomo Puccini are in The Collection; only Verdi and Wagner have more. Puccini has three here in the Warhorses; again, only Verdi and Wagner have more.

Giacomo Puccini

Still he has occupied a strange place on the spectrum. While the Higher-Brow elements of the Establishment have granted his rare ability to produce wondrously tuneful music, their position that he was far from a genius lasted seventy-five years—and has not wholly disappeared to this day.

Further, support for that view has come from some of the solid writers on opera, including Professor Donald Jay Grout, one of its most respected academics, no elitist, who writes in his excellent book, *A Short History of Opera*: "Puccini was not one of the great composers . . ."

Grout goes on to say that "within his limits—of which he was perfectly aware—he worked honorably and with mastery of his technique." Through most of the twentieth century, many other musicologists have declared that those limits were narrowly prescribed.

One music critic said in 1912 that Puccini was decadent, manipulative, and soon to be forgotten. I forget his name. And it's forbidden to manipulate an audience?

Nearly a half century later, another critic called *Tosca* a "shabby little shocker," described *Turandot* as "even more depraved" than *Tosca*, and declared that Puccini operas in general were "false through and through."

After the opening of *La Bohème* in Turin, one reviewer said it had left little impression on the minds of the audience and would leave no great trace on the history of lyric theater.

Puccini wrote little besides opera, but that really wasn't the problem. After all, it's also basically true of Verdi, Wagner, and many others in The Collection. A more serious charge leveled at Puccini for many years was that he was completely outside the intellectual trends of his times. (They said exactly the same thing about America's George Gershwin.)

Among the specific trends Puccini was accused of ignoring were these: polytonality, neoclassicism, impressionism, and dodecaphony.

In this road map those terms demand brief definitions:

- The polytonality of Stravinsky and Bartók, who composed in more than one key at the same time.
- The neoclassicism of Stravinsky and Paul Hindemith, who reverted back to the forms of Haydn and Mozart.
- The impressionism of Debussy and Maurice Ravel, who used new harmonies and scales to suggest a vagueness of form.
- The dodecaphony of Arnold Schoenberg, Anton Webern, and Alban Berg, who composed in twelve-tone (serial) technique, using all twelve notes of the scale in a particular order chosen by the composer.

Defenders of Puccini cry foul to these charges, arguing that several of these "intellectual trends" were either confined to relatively small regions of the composing world or were developing in Puccini's final years after he was well established. By then he was going his own way . . . and why not?

But poor Giacomo can't win for losing. Just when that argument is settled, a third set of critics charges that Puccini was not *original* enough, that he *copied* too much from Impressionist Debussy, from polytonal young Stravinsky, and from radical Arnold Schoenberg.

Clearly it's illogical to attack Puccini both for ignoring the intellectual trends of Debussy and Stravinsky and for being a Debussy-Stravinsky copycat.

In any case, for the last fifteen years or so the pendulum has been swinging steadfastly in his direction.

My recommendation is to nod wisely at each criticism and then go to as many Puccini operas as come into your neighborhood.

Here he is today, flanked in The Collection by the biggest names in music. On one side he is guarded by two accepted operatic immortals, Verdi and Wagner. On the other are music's most spontaneous musical genius, Wolfgang Amadeus Mozart, and another leading all-around classical music composer, Richard Strauss. What's a Giacomo Puccini doing in this company—an "honorable" fellow, "master of his own technique," acceptable within his narrow limits?

Prohibition of Silence

The life-loving Puccini and his cronies formed a club called La Bohème. Its constitution read, in part:

"The members swear to drink well and eat better . . . Grumblers,
pedants, weak stomachs, fools and puritans shall not be admitted . . .
The Treasurer is empowered to abscond with the cast . . . The President must hinder the Treasurer in the collection of monthly dues . . .
It is prohibited to play cards honestly, silence is strictly prohibited and
cleverness allowed only in exceptional cases . . . The lighting of the
clubroom shall be by means of an oil lamp. Should there be a shortage
of oil, it will be replaced by the brilliant wit of the members."

Who let him in? Who brought him to the party? What *does* he have?

What he has is *La Bohème, Madama Butterfly, Tosca, Manon Lescaut, Turandot, The Girl of the Golden West,* and *Gianni Schicchi.* What he has is three of
the top seven operas most frequently performed in the world and four more
that also fill the opera houses.

The public let him in . . . and kept him in . . . for one hundred years . . .
and today shows no signs of letting him out.

What is it that so appeals?

- Lovely, sensuous melody, melody that appeals to the least Washed.
- Easy-to-follow plots, no psychoanalysis required.
- Mastery of stagecraft.
- Dramatically, a sense of the surefire. Not with the insight of Verdi but with
  his own keen knowledge of his public.
- Sentimentality. Some of the elitists of the classical music Establishment
  also have peered down their nose at Peter Il'yich Tchaikovsky: too lush,
  too emotional, too sentimental. (But not for the people out there.)
- Skilled orchestration. One of my favorite experts says: "Puccini *was* influenced by Wagner in important respects, but he kept his own scale, his own
  subjects, his own sense of melody, his own humanity—in a word, his Ital-
  ianism. True, far more is carried by his orchestra than with any previous
  Italian composer; with Puccini, as with Wagner (but not with Verdi), you
  could play the vocal score on the piano, leaving out his vocal lines altogether, and still get most of the effect. But the 'manipulative' side of
  Puccini kept him from being too much of a symphonist for the singers or
  too far out harmonically for the ticket-buyer."
- Movement. Little in a Puccini opera is static. If the movement isn't forward, the analysts say, then it's swirling. Few composers do a better job of

holding the attention of the audience. Verdi and the bel canto trio liked long, sweeping huge arias. Puccini specialized in superb snippets here and there, punching across three or four ideas in just a few minutes, tightening the drama and keeping things in motion. Look for short vocal pieces with very compelling melodies.

Some Puccini operas, although not all, contain elements of the 1890s verismo tell-it-like-it-is cult rather than dealing with legend, myth, and ancient history. For the most part, the characters are real people, not kings and gods and their progeny. Puccini supporters say he goes beyond verismo and deals with wider subjects, trying to see farther and dig deeper. His critics acknowledge that he tried to do this—but assert that he couldn't quite make it because it was beyond his reach.

So it goes with Puccini. His defenders cite *La Bohème* and talk of the life he breathes into his characters. His critics—even those who support him generally—point out that *La Bohème* is different from the others in that it is the one opera that came from his own life. His other works, they say, have superficial characters, reflecting Puccini's own relative shallowness. Devotees of Mozart, Verdi, and Wagner ask this question: Has the composer developed the characters in *Tosca* and *Butterfly* (as opposed to *Bohème*) skillfully enough so that their actions and emotions are "in character"? Many professionals say no.

Although his supporters call him a legitimate successor to Verdi, experts such as musicologist Alfred Einstein argue that Verdi had foreshadowed everything Puccini did—that Puccini's *Tosca* had been anticipated by *Luisa Miller*, *La Bohème* by *La traviata*, and the oriental pomp of *Butterfly* and *Turandot* by *Aida*.

What this all tells us is that Puccini, like all other mortal composers, was imperfect. (Well, Mr. Bach was not into opera, and Mr. Mozart is an exception to everything.) The thing that makes opera so tantalizing is that there are so many facets to it. No matter how beautiful the music, for example, the work doesn't satisfy the professional judges as an "opera" if the characters are found shallow and/or unreal.

The operagoing public knows where it stands on Giacomo Puccini. And, indeed, even the expert Professor Grout, who always keeps two feet on the ground, never said he didn't love Puccini's operas. He just said Puccini was not one of the great composers.

In chronological order, The Puccini Collection works are:

Manon Lescaut, 1893 (Number 33)
La Bohème, 1896 (Number 2)
Tosca, 1900 (Number 5)
Madama Butterfly, 1904 (Number 7)
The Girl of the Golden West, 1910 (Number 54)

Gianni Schicchi, 1918 (Number 46)
Turandot, 1926 (Number 41)

Puccini was born in Lucca, Italy, on December 22, 1858. His great-great grandfather had ridden into Lucca to become the first of four generations to hold the post of choirmaster and organist of the Cathedral of San Martino. A Puccini biographer, Stanley Jackson, advises that the older Puccini received the same salary as the municipal hangman—until he got a raise of an extra small loaf of bread each month.

Giacomo's father was a musician highly regarded for his knowledge of counterpoint. Young Puccini was a performing organist at age fourteen. Before writing opera, he studied at the Milan Conservatory, thanks to a grant from the National Endowment for the Arts—well, a grant from the Queen of Italy—and help from a bachelor relative.

Lucca was a good birthplace for an opera composer. It had three theaters that presented opera and a strong tradition of spoken drama. Musicologists credit the relatively rich culture of Lucca for Puccini's talent of sniffing out opera possibilities from plays he read and watched.

While at the conservatory, his compositions included a string quartet and two orchestral pieces, one of which—the *Capricccio sinfonico*—became his opening theme in *La Bohème*.

He was soon into opera and a relationship with a strong publisher, Giulio Ricordi. Their friendship lasted until Ricordi died in 1912. Unlike most composers, Puccini's operas came at fairly long intervals. His first, *Le villi*, premiered in 1884, his second, *Edgar*, in 1889, and his third, *Manon Lescaut*, in 1893.

The French Massenet was a contemporary, and for many years some called Puccini an Italian Massenet. Both favored sensuous song, melody . . . and heroines. Mosco Carner, another of Puccini's biographers, is quoted by Harold Schoenberg: "While the ground bass of Verdi's operas is a battle cry; of Puccini's it's a mating call."

Although his heroines are more true to life than his heroes, it's not sexist to suggest that some aren't very bright. Mimi in *La Bohème* has no apparent sound reason for turning her back on Rodolfo, and no self-respecting geisha girl like Butterfly would really wait for that port-of-call sailor to come back—and even dump her religion for him.

In sum: Level-headed musicologists today seem to say this: Puccini was not Verdi. Nor was he Mozart or Wagner. He was an outstandingly good composer, while Verdi, Mozart, and Wagner were great ones. He was too picturesque to be truly tragic, to have real dramatic power. But, as George Bernard Shaw predicted, he has far outshone the other candidates as Verdi's successor: Mascagni, Leoncavallo, Giordano, and Ponchielli. And—genius or not—he was the last of the long line of Italian opera composers whose major strength was sensuous, magnificent melody.

Number 2. *La Bohème*

Premiere at Teatro Regio, Turin, 1896. Text by Giuseppe Giacosa and Luigi Illica from Henri Murger's 1847 Scènes de la vie de Bohème. Four acts.

KEYNOTE

Puccini's fourth opera, his first big hit, the first of the Big Three that made his worldwide reputation. Sentiment with tears, realism without violence. Supreme melodic voices. How to fall in love in twelve minutes.

PLOT

About 1830, Latin Quarter, Paris. Four Bohemians share a cheerless attic studio in Paris's Latin Quarter: the poet Rodolfo (tenor), the painter Marcello (baritone), the musician Schaunard (baritone), and the philosopher Colline (bass). After putting off the landlord, all but Rodolfo leave and Mimi (soprano), a neighbor, comes to the studio for a light for her candle. She is weak, ill, and out of breath. She and Rodolfo share life stories and fall in love during the opera's most glorious music. They leave, arm in arm, to join the others.

Meanwhile, Marcello recaptures the woman he loves, Musetta (soprano), who has been dallying with a wealthy sugar daddy named Alcindoro (bass). The friends and couples all go off together, leaving the cafe bill for Alcindoro to pay. Both relationships break down, Marcello-Musetta because she is a born flirt and Rodolfo-Mimi in part because of his jealousy and chiefly because he is worried about her constant coughing and feels he doesn't have enough money to care for her properly.

Rodolfo and Marcello return to their attic studio, both bewailing the fickleness of their women. Their two comrades join them for drinking, fun, and games, until Musetta bursts in to say that Mimi is below but too weak to climb the stairs. She's fragile and half frozen as the four men help her to the studio and into a chair.

Musetta leaves to sell her earrings in order to buy Mimi medicine and a muff to keep her warm in her last moments. Colline also leaves to pawn his overcoat. Mimi and Rodolfo sing of their love and of the happy days they once shared. When Musetta returns, Mimi loves the muff that will keep her hands warm and seems to fall asleep peacefully. Musetta and Marcello are reunited. But Schaunard finds that Mimi is dead, and Rodolfo, in despair, throws himself on her body.

HIGHLIGHTS

Act I: A continuous twelve minutes of pure melody, one of the richest scenes in all opera, beginning with Rodolfo's aria "Che gelida manina" ("Your tiny hand is frozen"), after Mimi has come into his room: "What an icy little hand, let me warm it. . . . Who am I? I am a poet . . . I have no worldly riches, but every poem is a treasure. So in poverty I am a millionaire." This is followed by Mimi's aria "Mi chiamano Mimi" ("They call me Mimi"): "Yes. They call me Mimi, but my name is Lucia. My story is short. I make my living by sewing and embroidering. I am quiet and cheerful . . . I live alone in a little garret room, overlooking the sky." The concluding section, a duet between Mimi and Rodolfo, "O soave fanciulla": "O lovely young girl in the moonlight. How sweet to be in love . . ." A big joint outpouring of love and a Pavarotti television favorite.

Act II: Musetta's famous attention-getting waltz song, "Quando me'n vo' soletta per la via": "When I walk alone in the street, people praise my beauty from head to toe. You must still love me; why don't you return?"

Act III: The closing scene after Mimi overhears Rodolfo saying she is dying. It includes her tearful farewell to him, a lyrical duet between them, and the quartet that ends the act, one of the better ones in all opera, with the delightful combination of the love music of Mimi and Rodolfo and the hammer-and-tongs quarrel of Marcello and Musetta.

Act IV: Rodolfo's tenor-baritone duet with Marcello, "Ah, Mimi, tu più non torni," as each mourns for his former sweetheart. Mimi's death scene.

COMMENTARY

By near unanimous agreement, this is Puccini's finest opera (a few hold out for the brilliant one-act comedy *Gianni Schicchi*). The life of the starving composer was one he had experienced briefly, and the analysts say the relationship of text to music is closer here than in any of his other works. "Play within yourself," my tennis coach used to advise, which at age eleven always confused me a little. In *La Bohème*, Puccini is said to have definitely played within himself, keeping totally within the borders of his art, his talent, and his powers—and thus producing a masterpiece.

Charming, lovely, poignant, lyrical, and sentimental, *La Bohème* caused an understandable explosion in the opera world, notwithstanding the contrary opening-night critic. The libretto is straightforward, the music and the drama match, and the popularity remains satellite high.

British musicologist Spike Hughes called it Puccini's "most nearly perfect opera . . . a work of consummate operatic craftsmanship, applied with a sureness of touch and exhilarating vigor." He praised its charm and warmth, its gaiety, and its genuine pathos. Although the characters may show little depth, they are real-life characters, drawn from a series of autobiographical vignettes that had appeared in the mid-1800s in a French periodical. There is little action or dramatic character development; some complain that *Bohème* is more a series of episodes than a work with a dramatic plot. Indeed, Puccini didn't please the contemporary critics, who wanted him to be more like Wagner and regarded *Bohème* as a step backward for opera, but it is uncertain that writing to please critics is the route to success and happiness.

Puccini on La Bohème

Puccini was understandably distressed at the early unfavorable reaction to his work.

"I, who put into *Bohème* all my soul and love it boundlessly and love its creatures more than I can say, returned to my hotel completely heartbroken. I passed a most miserable night. And in the morning I was greeted with the spiteful salute of the critics."

MET PERFORMANCES
One thousand and one hundred performances over eighty-nine seasons, from 1900 to 1996. Eleven performances are scheduled for the 1996–97 season.

RECORDINGS
CD—RCA/BMG. RCA 60288-2-RG; 60288-4-RG (mono). Licia Albanese, Anne McKnight, Jan Peerce, Francesco Valentino, George Cehanovsky, Nicola Moscona, Salvatore Baccaloni. NBC Chorus and Symphony Orchestra. Arturo Toscanini. 1946.

or

—Decca/London 421 049-2 (2). Mirella Freni, Elizabeth Harwood, Luciano Pavarotti, Rolando Panerai, Gianni Maffeo, Nicolai Ghiaurov, Michel Sénéchal. Deutsche Oper Chorus. Berlin Philharmonic Orchestra. Herbert von Karajan. 1973.

VIDEO
Stratas, Carreras, Stilwell. Metropolitan Opera. Italian; English subtitles. Levine, conductor. 1982. PAR. (Paramount Video).

Number 5. *Tosca*

Premiere at Teatro Costanzi, Rome, 1900. Text by Giuseppe Giacosa and Luigi Illica based on Victorien Sardou's 1837 play La Tosca. *Three acts.*

KEYNOTE
The second of Puccini's Big Three. Torture, murder, treachery, lust, execution, and suicide. Meet the evil Scarpia, one of opera's most villainous baritones. More melodious voices.

PLOT
Eighteen hundred. Rome. Cesare Angelotti (bass), the former consul of the Roman Republic, has escaped from prison and concealed himself in the

Tito Gobbi in Tosca

Attavanti chapel of the baroque church of Sant'Andrea della Valle. He is helped and sent to a hiding place by a republican sympathizer, Mario Cavaradossi (tenor), an artist who is painting the portrait of one of the worshipers. Cavaradossi is unaware that the subject of his painting is Angelotti's sister. Cavaradossi and Tosca (soprano), an opera singer who is the leading diva of Rome, are in love. When she comes to the church and sees Cavaradossi's work, she is jealous of the lady being painted.

Baron Scarpia (baritone) is a cruel, brutal, godless chief of police (sometimes called governor of Rome) who has two prizes in mind—the recapture and execution of Angelotti and the seduction of Tosca. "One for a noose; the other for my arms," he muses. He encourages Tosca to believe that Cavaradossi is having an affair with the woman of the portrait. After arresting Cavaradossi for harboring a fugitive, he plays on Tosca's love and jealousy to get her to reveal Angelotti's hiding place: "How can I reduce a jealous love to despair?"

Later he interviews her in the room adjacent to a chamber in which his men are torturing Cavaradossi, forcing her not only to hear his cries but also to see glimpses of him being physically abused. He is bound hand and foot; a spiked ring presses against his head. The pressure is too much; Tosca reveals that Angelotti is hiding in a well in Cavaradossi's nearby villa. A gleeful Scarpia tells her she can save Cavaradossi's life only by having sex with him. He will then arrange a mock execution, after which Cavaradossi will be able to escape.

Tosca at first refuses, fighting off his attempt to kiss her and begging for pity, a word that means nothing to Scarpia. A messenger reports to Scarpia that Angelotti has killed himself. When agents come to ask if it is time to hang Cavaradossi, Tosca, broken, nods, first singing of the life she has lived for art and love. But before the seduction begins she takes a fruit knife from the table, conceals it, stabs and kills Scarpia, and then puts candles at his head and a crucifix on his chest, in conformity with her religious upbringing. She rushes to tell Cavaradossi of the mock execution and the safe-conduct pass Scarpia wrote her before she killed him. The two start planning their future, "triumphant with new hope." But Scarpia has tricked her. Despite his promise, he had ordered that the execution should be real. Shots are heard, and Cavaradossi falls. Tosca rushes to him, horrified to find him dead. Shouts in the distance reveal that guards have found Scarpia's body. As they approach, Tosca, lover dead and a wanted murderess, throws herself from the battlements of Castel Sant'Angelo to her death.

The Customer Is Always Right

Puccini came in late for *La Tosca*, a play by Victorien Sardou (1831–1908), the rights for which already had been sold to another composer, Alberto Franchetti. Puccini's publisher, Ricordi, convinced him that it was too bloody and too violent, and it was released to Puccini.

Sarah Bernhardt, the most famous Tosca in Sardou's stage play, first performed it in Paris in 1889. After seeing her perform, Puccini decided that one day he would turn it into an opera—even though it was in French and he didn't understand the language.

Sardou was a blood-and-thunder, conflict-driven playwright who scoffed at criticism that his very popular works were not substantive enough.

"A play which has been given three thousand times is always right," he said.

HIGHLIGHTS

Act I: Cavaradossi's "Recondita armonia," as he compares the features of his painting with Tosca's face: "Strange is the harmony of different kinds of beauty! Tosca, a brunette, smiles in dark-eyed beauty and you, beautiful unknown woman, are blue-eyed with blond hair." A lovely in-church love duet between Tosca and Cavaradossi. Hear the music then change. Also the victory "Te Deum" as a procession comes into the church.

Act II: Tosca's "Vissi d'arte" in which she sings of how unfairly life has treated her even though she has devoted herself to art, love, prayer, and beauty: "I lived for art, I lived for love, I never harmed a living soul. In any misery I knew of, I gave help." This is the opera's most famous aria, sung just before she stabs Scarpia: "That is Tosca's kiss!"

Act III: Cavaradossi's aria as he writes farewell to Tosca, "E lucevan le stelle": "How the stars used to shine there . . . She'd come in smelling of flowers and fall into my arms." Also the final love duet, in prison, "O dolci manni mansuete e pure" ("Oh pitiful and tender hands" [that have killed Scarpia]).

Baron Scarpia's Lust Creed

Scarpia is not a fellow you want dating your daughter:

"I care nothing for sighs and milky moonlit dawns."
"I lust, and then I pursue the one I desire."
"I satisfy myself and throw her aside."
"Then I turn to new conquests."
"God created different beauties, different wines."
"I want to taste as many divine creatures as I can."
"All the hate you bear me only enhances my longing to possess you."
"How you despise me. But that is just how I want you."

COMMENTARY

A violent drama, all within eighteen hours and in one tiny Rome location. The choice is between *Otello*'s Iago and Scarpia as the most despicable baritone in opera—and they have a good bit in common: both suave, sophisticated, well dressed, and rank evil. (Barnaba, Inquisition spy in *La Giocanda*, is in the running.) What does Scarpia tell Tosca as her lover is being tortured by his orders? "When you cried out, despairing, passion inflamed me, and your glances almost drove my lust beyond bearing. How your hatred enhances my resolve to possess you." Scarpia, like Iago, is Satan himself.

Tosca is not an opera to see in a depressed state the day you've been thrown out by your wife and fired from your job. The immediate successor to *La Bohème*, it took Puccini three years to write—to create music to express love, jealousy, brutality, nobility, fear, and terror, not all in that order. With Scarpia stabbed, Cavaradossi executed, and Tosca a suicide, all three major characters are killed onstage. The happiest moment in the opera is the death-by-stabbing of the gruesome bad guy, who has said, "Tosca, you make me forget God." On second thought, maybe it *is* the thing that will cheer you up the day you have been thrown out by your wife and fired from your job.

Puccini, usually meticulous with detail, took the sound of the bell from the pitch of the great bell at St. Peter's—a familiar sound to all Romans and many other Italians. The premiere was an international media event, with one critic judging that it had "little or no chance of survival."

Unlike the librettos of *Bohème* and *Butterfly*, *Tosca*'s text is vulgar, brutal, and cruel. The onstage killing of Scarpia caused a fuss at the time. Musicologists say it works as a popular opera because Puccini's magic music smooths over all that.

The most famous of all Scarpias is the late Tito Gobbi, Italian baritone born in 1913, who performed the role 879 times. From his performances at Covent Garden, Sergei Leiferkus, Russian baritone, has been called the greatest since Gobbi. He played Iago at the Met in 1994.

MET PERFORMANCES

Seven hundred and sixty-four performances over 78 seasons, from 1901 to 1995. Eight performances are scheduled for the 1996–97 season.

RECORDING

CD—Angel/EMI CDCB 47174 (2) (mono). Maria Callas, Giuseppi Di Stefano, Tito Gobbi. La Scala Chorus and Orchestra. Victor De Sabata. 1953.

VIDEO

Behrens, Domingo, MacNeil. Metropolitan Opera. Italian; English subtitles. Sinopoli, conductor. 1985. PAR.

Number 7. *Madama Butterfly*

Premiere at La Scala, Milan, 1904. Text by Giuseppe Giacosa and Luigi Illica from American David Belasco's 1905 drama Madame Butterfly. *Three acts.*

KEYNOTE

The last of Puccini's Big Three. Meet the leading nominee for cad of all opera. Love, heartbreak, and warm tears in far-off Japan. Still more melodious Puccini voices. Butterfly's chosen fate: "To die with honor when one no longer can live with honor."

PLOT

Early twentieth century, Nagasaki. An American naval officer, Pinkerton (tenor), falls in love with a Japanese geisha girl, Cio-Cio-San, also known as Butterfly (soprano). Despite the warnings of Sharpless (baritone), the American consul, about the gravity of a relationship with a Japanese woman, Pinkerton goes through a marriage ceremony with her, and then returns to America with the navy. Butterfly bears their child, named Trouble, and waits for him to come back to her "one fine day," certain that he will. With her is her friend and servant, Suzuki (mezzo-soprano). When Pinkerton finally does return, he brings with him his legal American wife, Kate (mezzo-soprano), and learns that he has a son. After conversation and thought, Cio-Cio-San concludes that she must give up Trouble so he can go with Kate and be raised as a good Pinkerton back in the United States. She promises that Pinkerton can have him if he returns in a half hour. Finally (and far too late for any decent man), an anguished Pinkerton becomes sensitive to the misery he has brought. Overcome with grief, Cio-Cio-San says good-bye to her son, gives him an American flag to play with, blindfolds him, disappears behind a screen, and kills herself with her father's dagger. Pinkerton returns to find her dead, and Sharpless leads Trouble away. (The final scene changes in different productions.)

Critics and Confidence

After the opening-night failure of *Butterfly*, Puccini wrote a friend:

"It is I who am right. It is the finest opera I've written." And, to another friend: "You must have been dismayed at the vile remarks of an envious press. But never fear! *Madama Butterfly* is full of life and truth, and soon she will rise from the dead. I say it, and stick to it, with unwavering conviction."

HIGHLIGHTS

Act I: The famous long love duet at the end of Act I, hailed by Puccinians for its musical construction. It begins with "Viene la sera" ("Evening is falling") and ends with "Dolce notte! Quante stelle" ("Rapturous night; unnumbered stars"). Hear Jussi Bjoerling and Victoria de los Angeles sing it and there's no way to tell from its beauty that Pinkerton is such a miserable creep, especially when he assures her: "Don't be afraid; love doesn't kill."

Act II: One of the saddest of the famous arias in all opera, Butterfly's "Un bel dì vedremo": "One beautiful day we will see a thread of smoke rising on the horizon. And then the ship appears and enters the harbor and fires its salute . . . You see, he has come; I don't mind the long wait; I wait for him with absolute faith." Also the "Flower Duet" between Butterfly and Suzuki, "Scuoti quella fronda di ciliegio": "Shake the branches of the cherry tree and cover me with flowers."

Act III: Pinkerton's tearful farewell, "Addio, fiorito asil" (although fewer tears and more sensitive actions from this Ugly American might have been a nice thing). Butterfly's death.

COMMENTARY

After the horrendous opening night, Puccini withdrew *Butterfly* and began a series of revisions, recorded in detail in William Ashbrook's book *The Operas of Puccini*. Its next appearance was three months later in Brescia, where it had a big success. But it didn't reappear at La Scala until 1925, when Arturo Toscanini conducted it on the first anniversary of Puccini's death. A lot of things had gone wrong with the 1904 Milan premiere, including advance hostility from the spoiled press because rehearsals had been closed. Some of the early music was very similar to *La Bohème*. And it didn't help that the first Butterfly, Rosina Storchio, was having a well-publicized affair with Toscanini, already a famous conductor despite his youth. When she came on the Milan stage with Trouble in Act II, the audience let out hoots of "Il piccolo Toscanini" ("The little Toscanini"). This didn't enhance the cast's ability to throw itself into its work.

There is no real nationalist East-West conflict in *Butterfly*. Puccini dealt almost entirely in personalities and individuals, not in Verdi-like big canvases or Verdi-like messages of freedom and independence. In the early years, the Japanese-sounding background music was extremely popular, but today the oh-so-careful Politically Correct set considers it Politically Incorrect. One doubts that Puccini would see fit to change it if he were alive. The novelty also has worn off for parts of *The Star-Spangled Banner* being played as a mini–theme song for Pinkerton. Unsurprisingly, the opera wasn't shown in this country during World War II.

Analysts say Puccini made better use of the chorus in *Butterfly* than in any other of his operas, except for *Turandot*. The tenor role obviously must be sung, but the opera seems to succeed whenever it has just an outstanding soprano.

Because it portrays death by choice rather than by illness, fate, or the hand of others, some regard *Butterfly* as the most tragic of Puccini's operas. The harshest negative critics dismiss it condescendingly as a "sweet little opera," but that opinion has been ignored for nearly a century by the operagoing public.

MET PERFORMANCES

Seven hundred and ninety-five performances over seventy-one seasons, from 1907 to 1996. Nine performances are scheduled for the 1996–97 season.

RECORDINGS

CD—Angel/EMI CDCB 47959 (2) (mono). Maria Callas, Lucia Danieli, Nicolai Gedda, Mario Borriello. La Scala Chorus and Orchestra. Herbert von Karajan. 1955.

or

—Angel/EMI CMS7 69654-2 (2). Renata Scotto, Anna Di Stasio, Carlo Bergonzi, Rolando Panerai. Rome Opera Chorus and Orchestra. John Barbirolli. 1966.

VIDEO

Hayashi, Dvorsky, Kim. La Scala. Italian; English subtitles. Maazel, conductor, 1987. HOME VISION.

∾

One Warhorse by Georges Bizet
October 25, 1838–June 3, 1875
CARMEN *(Number 3)*

Georges Bizet and his *Carmen* constitute a rare breed. Here the musicologist and the public, the elitist and the guys in the balcony, the Washed and the Unwashed, ultimately agree.

Bizet was one jim-crack-dandy of an opera composer, and *Carmen* is a superior opera.

It also breaks down national barriers.

No one talks here of the delicate French with their powder and wigs in contrast to the lusty passion of the robust Italians. The most Germanic of the German

Grace Bumbry in the title role of a Metropolitan Opera production of Carmen

classical masters, Johannes Brahms, was irresistibly attracted to it. After seeing twenty performances, Friedrich Nietzsche proclaimed it one of the genuine masterpieces in operatic literature. Musicologist Alfred Einstein calls it the best thing in French opera after Meyerbeer. At its introduction in Russia, Tchaikovsky predicted that in ten years it would be the world's most popular opera.

One of Richard Wagner's many biographers, Ronald Taylor, acknowledges that Wagner "did not have the precocity of a Mozart, or a Mendelssohn, or a Bizet." No one was as precocious musically as Mozart and almost no one as precocious as Felix Mendelssohn. This is class company for the young Frenchman.

Maurice Ravel, one of France's greatest composers, found three things in music "paragons of perfection": the lyrical elegance of Franz Schubert, the Violin Concerto of Mendelssohn, and Bizet's *Carmen*.

Carmen is the most tragic of the opéras comique. It also is the most famous French opera. In 1904, nearly one hundred years ago, the one thousandth performance was given at the Paris Opéra.

Of course, some critics still find fault. Analysts have complained about the unequal quality of the music, protesting that masterly scoring on one page alternates with sentimental musical platitudes on another.

It is set in and near Seville. Bizet never saw Spain, and the music is more French than Spanish, but nobody seems to care.

And no one is turned off by the fact that Bizet departs from the custom of sopranos getting the best female roles. The role of the gypsy Carmen is one of the greatest that has been written for the mezzo-soprano voice. (Other favorite mezzo-soprano parts include characters in three Verdi Collection operas, Amneris in *Aida*, Azucena in *Il travatore*, and Eboli in *Don Carlos*, and Rosina in Rossini's *Barber of Seville* [although Rosina also is often stolen by sopranos]).

A New Ending

The relationship between singer and conductor is not always a happy one. At the New York City Opera Company's performance in the Chicago Civic Opera House on November 19, 1953, the Don José was a young singer who, during the opera, became increasingly displeased with the conductor. At the critical last scene, critic Irving Kolodin recalls, he "threw down his knife and marched offstage, bellowing at the conductor, 'Finish it yourself!' It was the only time in history that Carmen died of a heart attack."

Carmen was Bizet's first work for the Opéra-Comique on the Rue Favart in Paris and initially it was in French, with lines spoken, in the tradition of that opera house. But later the first performance in Vienna was conditional upon the spoken parts being changed to recitative. Since Bizet died only three months after the Paris opening, we don't know how he would have reacted to this demand.

The spoken dialogue was changed to recitative (in German, for that Vienna performance), by Ernest Guiraud, a close friend of Bizet's. Until the middle of this century that version was the most popular one, although from the start some musicians such as the French classical master Camille Saint-Saëns strongly opposed the change. More recently European productions have gone back to the spoken dialogue, but houses in the United States stage it both ways.

At the Paris premiere, the audience gave a good reception to the first act but gradually cooled off and was icy by the end. The Opéra-Comique at this time basically was a family theater, where middle-class parents took their sons and daughters. Even though the opera had been toned down during rehearsals, the sexy Carmen and her exploits still were a little much for them.

Certain that this would be his first real success, Bizet was disconsolate at the weak audience reaction and wandered half the night in Paris. Three months later, on June 3, 1875, before the start of his opera's great popularity, he died at age thirty-six from a throat infection that had plagued him for years. Evidence does not support earlier musicologist reports that he died of a broken heart.

Performances continued in Paris, with fifty at the Opéra-Comique by the end of the first year. It wasn't repeated there for seven years, but meanwhile it had become known all over the world. In the mid-1900s it was second in popularity to Gounod's *Faust* among French operas and probably is the most frequently performed of all operas today, although I know of no worldwide computer count to prove it.

Bizet is commonly considered a "one-opera composer" but without sound cause. One of his others, *La jolie fille de Perth* (*The Fair Maid of Perth*), 1867, has some fine orchestral music but an extremely weak libretto and is rarely staged. Much more successful is a fine work, *Les pêcheurs de perles* (*The Pearl Fishers*), 1863, which has done very well even though blanketed by *Carmen*'s extraordinary success. Written when Bizet was only twenty-five, it deals with two pearl fishers in Ceylon and their involvement with a priestess whom they both love. It includes a famous French tenor aria, Nadir's "Je crois entendre encore" and also a great tenor/baritone duet.

A lifelong Parisian, Bizet was born in 1838—eleven years after the death of Beethoven, when both Verdi and Wagner were twenty-five; at the beginning of the French grand opera period. His mother was a fine pianist, his father taught singing, he himself studied at the Paris Conservatory and won the Prix de Rome in 1857. In 1872 he married Geneviève Halévy, daughter of his former teacher, Jacques-Fromental Halévy, the uncle of Ludovic Halévy, one of *Carmen*'s librettists.

His best-known instrumental work is the incidental music to Alphonse Daudet's play *L'Arlésienne*. Although the play didn't succeed, the music endured and was arranged into two orchestral suites as part of Bizet's modest nonopera activity. Both are often heard on classical radio stations. Other instrumental works include a symphony in C Major.

The first opera music ever broadcast over the radio was an aria from *Carmen* from the stage of the Manhattan Opera House in the early 1900s.

Number 3. *Carmen*

Premiere at the Opéra-Comique, Paris, 1875. Text by Henri Meilhac and Ludovic Halévy based on Prosper Mérimée's 1852 novel Carmen. *Originally an opéra comique. Four acts.*

KEYNOTE

Gypsies, thieves, smugglers, cigarette girls, jealousy, and murder. A love triangle between a beautiful sexy gypsy woman, an army corporal who is in over his head, and a famous matador. A tragic story with a tragic and violent ending.

PLOT

About 1820 in Seville, Spain. Micaëla (soprano), a country girl who is engaged to young Don José (tenor), a corporal in the dragoons, arrives at the square in Seville to look for him. Carmen (mezzo-soprano), a gypsy who works in a cigarette factory, leaves work and is surrounded by José and other soldiers. She flirts boldly with José, singing to the rhythm of a habanera, a Spanish dance. With a shrug, she takes a red flower from her bodice and throws it at José, initiating the relationship that will end in tragedy. (In Oscar Hammerstein's 1943 Broadway musical, *Carmen Jones*, the "Habanera" goes something like: "You go for me, and I'm taboo, but if you're hard to get, I go for you.") When Micaëla delivers a letter to José from his mother, he appears to recover from Carmen's spell. Meanwhile, inside the factory, Carmen has quarreled with another girl, wounded her with a knife, and is arrested. José is left to guard her.

Waiting to be led off to jail, she sings the "Séguedille," saying that her heart is still waiting to be taken, and continuing her flirtation with José until she has persuaded him to loosen the ropes tying her. When she escapes, he is thrown into jail for letting her get away.

Act II opens at Lillas Pastia's inn, where Carmen and her friends are mingling with some officers. The famous bullfighter Escamillo (baritone) appears and, with chorus, sings one of opera's best-known arias, about the rewards of the life of a victorious toreador. He is struck by Carmen, and she is impressed by him, though she doesn't for a moment forget José. She and her lady friends also agree to help a band of smugglers.

After serving a two-month sentence, José still is bewitched by Carmen, despite his (formal and chaste) relationship with Micaëla. He and a fellow soldier quarrel after he ignores a trumpet calling him to duty. Having failed to report, his military career now over, he and Carmen join the smugglers.

In a mountain hideaway, he tells Carmen how passionately he loves her. Carmen being Carmen, she listens but is unmoved. Escamillo arrives looking for Carmen and José draws his knife on him, but she intervenes. Micaëla comes to the hideaway to tell José his mother is dying. Although at first he refuses to leave Carmen, he changes his mind and agrees to go to his mother, but vows he'll return.

Carmen now joins Escamillo back in the village square in a procession in his honor. As he enters the ring, they exchange vows of undying love. José appears, an outcast because of his love for Carmen, his life shattered, and his honorable career gone. He begs Carmen to treat him kindly, but she is listening to the cheers from the bullring for Escamillo and is indifferent to him. In torment, as he hears the crowd shouting Escamillo's name, José stabs her. When Escamillo leads his cheering supporters from the arena and moves toward Carmen, José gives himself up, sometimes throwing himself on her dead body.

HIGHLIGHTS

The Prelude: One of opera's best known, which includes the "Toreador Song" and the "Fate" theme.

Act I: Carmen's "Habanera," "L'amour est un oiseau rebelle," as she warns of the dangers of love: "Love is a rebellious bird that nobody can tame, a thing no force can hold. You call it in vain if it chooses not to come. If you don't love me, I love you, and if I love you, watch out for yourself." Her seductive "Séguedille," "Près des ramparts de Séville," as she captures José's heart and promises to be with him at the inn of her friend: "Near the ramparts of Sevilla, at my friend Lillas Pastia's, I shall go dance the Séguedilla and drink Manzanilla." Also the "Children's Chorus."

Act II: The wild gypsy song at Pastia's inn, led by Carmen, "Les tringles des sistres tintaient:" "The quiet at the end of the day is broken as the gypsy dance gets underway." The "Toreador Song" sung by Escamillo and chorus: "Toreador, be on your guard, Toreador, and remember while fighting that a dark eye is watching you and that love is waiting for you." Don José's "Flower Song," "La fleur que tu m'avais jetée," as he brings out the flower she had given him: "The flower that you had thrown at me was left with me in my prison . . . You had only to throw one glance at me to take my heart. I turned into a thing belonging to you."

Act III: The "Card Trio" by Carmen and her two gypsy friends, as she turns up the ace of spades, the card of death, and laments that fate cannot be escaped. Micaëla's prayer, "Je dis que rien ne m'épouvante": "I thought I could handle my terror, but now, too late, I see my error."

Act IV: The stirring music as the act opens, music that perfectly captures the vivacious atmosphere outside the bullring. And the closing scene of stark suffering.

COMMENTARY

What does *Carmen* have?

- Marvelous melody
- Brilliant orchestration
- Superb atmospheric color
- Fine dramatic instinct
- Skillful characterization

The dramatic finale, with Carmen screaming for her life against joyous sounds from the bullring, is tough to beat. As one writer points out, Wagner was a master of symphonic structure, Verdi a genius at melody, and Richard Strauss a dedicated craftsman, but one doesn't need any of those qualities to produce a great finale. What is needed is good judgment and great theatrical instinct.

Carmen is a good example of how individual producers alter the original— for better or for worse. In a 1967 production at the Metropolitan, all the action took place in a bullring. Carmen became a matador instead of a cigarette girl. The men with whom she was involved became her victims in the ring. The next time the Met produced it, in 1972, that idea was junked for a new one. A 1984 televised production by the New York City Opera was set in 1936 war-time Spain.

Although Carmen is a mezzo-soprano, the role is written for a voice too high for some mezzos and too low for some sopranos. (France never has been as dedicated as Italy to the high-voiced soprano.) A big voice is needed in part because the orchestral accompaniment in *Carmen* is much greater than it was a generation earlier when Verdi was writing his Big Three. Orchestral textures in 1875 were thicker and orchestras were larger—and still growing. Not many light lyric voices can handle this music.

Although not a verismo opera, *Carmen* has a good many of the verismo elements that were to come. Instead of princes we have a cigarette girl of doubtful virtue who is in the habit of making a little money on the side. The military involved is not the military of nobility but more like a Foreign Legion. Don José is not a duke but a good young soldier gone wrong.

The Carmen role is played in many ways. In the most common, she is a take-no-prisoners, live-for-the-moment, in-charge-of-her-own-life seductress, whereas José is the simple soldier, in over his head from start to end. But she also has been played as an innocent waif who doesn't begin to understand what love means to others.

One of the most famous Carmens was Emma Calvé (1858–1942), the first to interpret her as the sexy gypsy in a simple black dress and old shawl. Among relatively recent ones are Greek mezzo-soprano Agnes Baltsa, American mezzos Marilyn Horne and Tatiana Troyanos, Spanish mezzo Teresa Berganza, Spanish soprano Victoria de los Angeles, Greek-American soprano Maria Callas, and American soprano Jessye Norman.

Just a few of the many other stars who have sung Carmen are American soprano Geraldine Farrar, American mezzo Regina Resnik, Scottish-American soprano Mary Garden, American soprano Rosa Ponselle, American mezzo Risë Stevens, American mezzo Gladys Swarthout, American mezzo Grace Bumbry, and American mezzo Shirley Verrett.

MET PERFORMANCES

Nine hundred and fifteen performances in seventy-six seasons, from 1884 to 1996. Fourteen performances are scheduled for the 1996–97 season.

RECORDING

CD—Deutsche Grammophon Dig. 410 088-2 (3). Agnes Baltsa, Katia Ricciarelli, José Carreras, José van Dam. Paris Opera Chorus. Berlin Philharmonic Orchestra. Herbert von Karajan. 1982.

VIDEO

Migenes-Johnson, Domingo, Raimondi. A film by Francesco Rosi. French; English subtitles. Maazel, conductor. 1984. Columbia Tri-Star.

Two Warhorses by Charles Gounod
June 17, 1818–October 18, 1893

FAUST *(Number 6)*
ROMÉO ET JULIETTE *(Number 25)*

In Germany, when one of the world's most popular operas is performed it's advertised under the alias of *Margarethe*. In nearly all other opera houses it is called *Faust*.

So what's with the Germans?

Well, as even most opera amateurs know, *Faust* is based on the dramatic poem of the same name by Germany's greatest man of literature, Johann Wolfgang von Goethe (1749–1832).

But the opera was written by Charles François Gounod, born in Paris, died in Paris, as French as the Left Bank and Charles de Gaulle. It is not seemly for a *Frenchman*, of all persons, to be credited with a famous *Faust*, especially a Frenchman who was composing during the Franco-Prussian War. So the Germans call it *Margarethe* instead, the name of the woman Faust admires, seduces, impregnates, and abandons. The German rationale is that *Margarethe* is the title of the stage play associated with Goethe's work.

A Perfect Opera Season

A quarter of a century ago, in *The Opera Omnibus*, Irving Kolodin, past opera critic of *The Saturday Review*, included Bizet's *Les Pêcheurs* with his suggestions for "a perfect opera season." Leaning away from the normal Warhorses, Kolodin chose the following (the thumbnail descriptions are his):

Mozart's *Die Entführung aus dem Serail*, gaiety and sublimity in the same package
Beethoven's *Fidelio*, indispensable
Berg's *Lulu*, inimitable
Berlioz' *Benvenuto Cellini*, ignored
Bizet's *Pearl Fishers*, unknown
Britten's *Turn of the Screw*, unique
Charpentier's *Louise*, time for a revival
Debussy's *Pelléas et Mélisande*, full of unrevealed values
Delibes' *Lakmé*, Gallic, delightful, neglected
Donizetti's *La fille du régiment*, unregimented
Dvořák's *Rusalka*, unjustly slighted
Granados's *Goyescas*, time for reconsideration
Handel's *Giulio Cesare*, self-identifying
Humperdinck's *Hänsel und Gretel*, the ideal "first opera"
Massenet's *Manon*, the quintessence of "l'amour française"
Mussorgsky's *Boris Godunov*, one of a kind
Paisiello's *Il barbiere di Siviglia*, dawn of Beaumarchais
Puccini's *Manon Lescaut*, the most of the promise, with the least cost of the fulfillment
Rossini's *Le Comte Ory*, genius with a difference
Smetana's *Bartered Bride*, diversion supreme
Johann Strauss's *Die Zigeunerbaron*, rarely given its due
Richard Strauss's *Capriccio*, the summation of a great composer's experience
Verdi's *Don Carlos*, the opera complete, as rarely heard
Verdi's *Falstaff*, no season complete without it
Wagner's *Die Meistersinger*, the best of his best

It is an interesting list. Kolodin, a Metropolitan Opera expert, consciously combines some also-ran operas of the greatest opera composers, the greatest operas of some also-ran composers, the only operas of a few classical music giants, and a handful of others just because he likes them. All composers but three, Enrique Granados, Antonin Dvořák and Giovanni Paisiello, are in The Collection, as are fifteen of the twenty-five operas. All twenty-five are performed today.

Gounod was a gifted and highly trained composer who wrote pleasant symphonies, outstanding songs, much sacred music, and twelve operas. Although his other works have been overshadowed by the incredible popularity of *Faust*, he wasn't a one-hit composer. His *Roméo et Juliette* also is a Collection Warhorse, and a third work, *Mireille*, still is sometimes produced.

Faust alone, however, gives him special status. Along with Bizet's *Carmen*, it has been the most popular French opera over the decades. Gounod and Bizet, both in the Top Ten, are the only Frenchmen represented in the twenty-five Warhorse operas.

Because of *Faust*, Gounod was a major figure on the French operatic stage. By means of *Faust*, he helped open the door to a whole new kind of French opera, away from the grand opera spectacle of Giacomo Meyerbeer.

On opening night, one critic wrote that *Faust* was an experiment that had failed. At first, not a single publisher risked issuing it.

They erred. Before long it was everywhere. Its two thousandth Parisian performance was back in 1934. It has been produced in nearly fifty countries and scads of languages, earning it a top spot in The Collection even though its popularity has dimmed in recent years.

The Tannhäuser *Disaster*

Richard Wagner says in his autobiography, *Mein Leben*:

"I was told that Gounod has enthusiastically taken my part at all social gatherings, and that on one occasion he had cried, 'If only God would grant me a disaster like *Tannhäuser*!' I valued his attitude all the more since no obligation of friendship had been able to persuade me to go and see his *Faust*."

The first performance was in 1859, when Gounod was forty years old. It was his fourth opera, after three failures.

The serious spectacular grand opera of Auber (*La muete de Portici*), Halévy (*La Juive*), and chief of grand opera Meyerbeer (The Collection's *Les Huguenots* plus *Le prophète*, *L'Africaine*, and others) had dominated Parisian opera in the 1830s, 1840s, and 1850s. On the other extreme was the lighter, sophisticated opéra comique. *Faust*, called a "lyric opera," represented a middle ground between the two.

All opera is "lyric"—singable—but "lyric opera" is a general term sometimes used to describe works in which singing rather than drama is prominent. Another (lesser) Collection opera of the same type, Ambroise Thomas's

Mignon, was soon to follow. And still others of a similar genre such as Delibes's *Lakmé* and Massenet's *Manon* came later in the century.

Faust, like grand opera, is in five acts. Like opéra comique, the original had spoken dialogue, although Gounod quickly replaced this with recitative. It emphasized drama less than grand opera, but more than the opéra comique of the day. It was more delicate and sensuous than big grand opera.

When *Faust* was produced, Bizet's *Carmen* loomed ahead, although the musicologists tend to elevate it into another category. Bizet was a notch or two more gifted than Gounod, not only in harmony, melody, and orchestral color, but especially in characterization—in putting on the musical stage living people, not actors.

Some of the words used by the musicologists for *Faust* and *Roméo et Juliette* are "tuneful," "graceful," "unadventurous harmonically," "French chic," "sensitive harmony and orchestration," "refined and expressive lyricism," "ingratiating melody," and "supreme melody."

There we are. "Ingratiating melody." "Supreme melody." That's the major answer. But, relatively, it is dramatically weak, lacking Bizet's sense of theater.

Beethoven Slandered

Fanny Mendelssohn, talented older sister of the great German classical composer Felix, disclosed other news about a young Gounod that did little to increase his popularity with the German people. In *Some Composers of Opera,* author Dyneley Hussey tells this story:

While studying in Italy, Ms. Mendelssohn wrote in her diary about Gounod and two other French students who called themselves the three Caprices. On one occasion, she reveals, Gounod had to be put to bed "almost as if he were intoxicated." Although this scarcely constituted obscene behavior for a student, he and his friends also had been calling Ludwig van Beethoven a blackguard. Now that's a venal sin, especially if it's a Frenchman.

It is intriguing to those of us who are Unwashed that a composer who is "dramatically weak" would choose Goethe's *Faust* and Shakespeare's *Romeo and Juliet* as his source material . . . and even more intriguing that he then would produce a world-beater with one and a remarkably popular opera with the other. Hard work is one answer; Gounod was a much more meticulous composer than Fast-food Donizetti. It took him two years to write *Faust.* Significant talent is a second; although he was not a genius like Monteverdi or Mozart or Bach,

Gounod was a talented artist, more so than fellow Frenchman Ambroise Thomas. Still, his ability to produce "supreme melody" is the key.

Gounod was born in Paris into an arty family, headed by an established painter. He began studying music early, attended the Paris Conservatory, and won both the Prix de Rome and the Grand Prix de Rome. The latter scholarship gave him two years of study in Rome and a third financed year abroad. His third year was in Vienna and Berlin—and in Leipzig, where he stayed four days with Felix Mendelssohn and became familiar with the music of two classical music greats, Mendelssohn and Robert Schumann.

In 1845 he returned to Paris, became a church organist, studied for the priesthood, decided against joining it, composed a well-known mass (Messe solennelle *Sainte-Cécile*), and throughout his life remained closely aligned with the church, albeit as one who did not disavow the pleasures of the flesh. Someone called him the "philandering monk," an unfair characterization not as to his philandering but in that he never actually entered the priesthood. He was married in 1852 to Anna Zimmerman, daughter of a famous piano teacher. Later he spent five years—1870 to 1875, during the Franco-Prussian War—living in London, where he founded the Gounod Choir.

While in London he also was involved in one of music's more interesting love affairs, which involved Mrs. Georgina Weldon, the wife of Captain Harry Weldon. When the affair began, the Gounods were staying at the home of the Weldons (onetime home of Charles Dickens). After Anna Zimmerman Gounod indignantly left London for Paris, the remaining three lived cosily together. Anna sent their grown son to London to report back on matters, but his contribution to family harmony was his own attempted seduction of Georgina. Outraged, Georgina threw the callow youth out of the house. Gounod eventually tired of the threesome and went home to Paris. The menage à trois spirit was broken, however, and the Weldons not only seized all his music but also sent him a large bill for room and board for three years. There is a moral there somewhere, possibly that if one is participating in a romantic threesome he should send home his packed trunk first before saying his good-byes.

It was not until age thirty-three in 1851 that Gounod completed his first opera, *Sapho*, produced at the Paris Opéra. *Faust* came three operas later. In the wake of *Faust* were *Mireille*, in 1864, a major success, and, in 1867, *Roméo et Juliette*. One well-known critic recently described *Mireille* as "a charming opera, tender, unpretentious, delicate in its workings, conceived and executed in happiness and high spirits." That's pretty good. For years it was a staple of the Paris Opéra and a favorite of French provincial theaters.

After *Roméo et Juliette* and *Mireille*, Gounod wrote three other operas, the last in 1881. None caught on. He spent his last dozen years composing successful religious music.

The Metropolitan Opera House playbill for opening night of Faust

Number 6. *Faust*

Premiere at Théâtre-Lyrique, Paris, 1859. Text by Jules Barbier and Michel Carré based on Carré's Faust et Marguérite *and Johann Wolfgang von Goethe's Faust.* Five acts.

KEYNOTE

Satan helps lovesick philosopher meet dream girl. Gounod's masterpiece. For many years the world's most popular opera. Less frequently performed today but still overflowing with melody and spotted with magic. The moral: It rarely pays to sell your soul to the Devil.

PLOT

Sixteenth century, Germany. Faust, or Dr. Faustus (tenor), is an old philosopher, bitter because life has passed him by. He considers taking poison but stops when he hears the happy singing of women and workmen outside. Cursing human learning, hope, patience, prayer, and the life that now is gone, he rejects God and calls upon Satan (Méphistophélès) to help him. Wealth and power don't interest him, but when Satan (bass, what else?) conjures up a vision of the beautiful Marguérite (soprano) at a spinning wheel he signs a pact to sell his soul for youth, desire, and an orgy of the senses. A smug Méphistophélès, foppishly dressed in the clothes of the day, including top hat, is glad to make him young again and to promise the passion.

The Devil Made Me Do It

The Devil's henchmen are in the wings in several Collection operas, but his presence is especially felt in the following ones:

Gounod's *Faust,* who trades his soul for sensual gratification. He wins Marguérite, but kills her brother in a duel when the Devil guides his sword. Faust lives, and Marguérite goes to heaven after dying in prison of grief and a broken mind.

Boito's *Faust,* who is rejuvenated by Mefistofele and has a thing with Margherita, but dies redeemed. Margherita drowns her illegitimate son, is accused of poisoning her mother, and goes mad before her execution.

Max in *Der Freischütz,* who kills Caspar when the magic bullet he fires at a dove is guided by Samiel, the "Black Huntsman." Caspar dies, cursing heaven and hell.

The Dutchman in *The Flying Dutchman,* forced by the Devil's curse to sail the seas until Judgment Day, landing only once every seven years.

Tom Rakewell in *The Rake's Progress* (Twentieth-century European Package), whose life is destroyed by Nick Shadow, A.K.A. the Devil. Tom saves his soul in a card game, but Nick condemns him to insanity.

In an inn outside the city gates, Valentin (baritone) and Siébel (trouser-role mezzo) discuss Valentin's sister, Marguérite. Méphistophélès appears, infuriates Valentin by the way he mentions Marguérite, and the two duel. When

Valentin's sword mysteriously breaks in two, he recognizes that he has taken on the Devil but protects himself by holding up the cruciform hilt of the sword. Other soldiers make the sign of the cross with their swords, and Méphistophélès temporarily cowers. But he returns later with a young Faust, who now meets the Marguérite of his earlier vision.

One of opera's most unfair competitions follows. Siébel tries to woo Marguérite with a bouquet of flowers left at her door, but Méphistophélès causes them to wither. For young Faust, however, he provides a box of jewels to put at her front stoop. It is a tribute to the sixteenth-century German townspeople that no one steals them, but apparently that was not even a consideration. Don't try this at home on Manhattan's East or West Side.

Marguérite is a young, innocent girl. The jewels and some prodding by the Devil do the job, and Faust succeeds in seducing her. Satan howls loudly, cynically, and victoriously and Faust abandons her and their illegitimate child.

Returning with his regiment, Valentin finds he has been dishonored and disgraced by his sister's sins and demands satisfaction from Faust. They duel, and with Méphistophélès guiding the sword, Valentin is killed. Marguérite arrives in time to hear him blame her and damn her for eternity with his dying words.

Marguérite turns to the Church, looking for comfort in God. In her anguish she has killed her child. Later, in prison, where she has been sent for the murder, she prays for redemption. When Faust comes to see her and begs her to escape with him, she scarcely recognizes him. The Devil arrives to condemn her and she dies, but her soul is saved as a choir of angels takes her to heaven. Faust falls on his knees in prayer, and the Devil turns away.

HIGHLIGHTS

Act I: The first-act tenor-bass duet "A moi les plaisirs," between Faust and Mépistophélès: "Now for the good life of youth and love. Now to be young and happy again."

Act II: The waltz, with villagers and chorus.

Act III: Siébel's "Flower Song": "No flower can be as fair as she, but I trust the flowers to speak for me." Faust's "Salut! demeure": "Chaste and pure. To the home of my beloved I bring my heart's devotion." Marguérite's "Ballad of the King of Thule," "Il était un roi de Thule": "There once was a king of Thule who stayed faithful all his life to his lady and kept a golden goblet in her memory." Then, immediately, Marguérite's famous "Jewel Song," one of opera's most famous pieces for a lyric soprano: "Oh my God! Such jewels! I have never seen such riches."

Act IV: The "Soldiers' Chorus": "Hail to the glory of men who have fought before, heroes of many ancient wars." And Méphistophélès's serenade, "Vous qui faites l'endormie" ("You who pretend to be asleep"); after Faust has seduced Marguérite and left her pregnant: "Don't give him a kiss, my lady, until his ring is on your finger." A long Faust-Marguérite love duet: "Love's flame will always burn in us."

Act V: The ballet music and dances. The prison-death scene, with trio music you'll recognize.

COMMENTARY

Gounod's opera suffers in some eyes because *Faust* is woefully deficient weighed against Goethe's work. Goethe was a seminal figure in the history of literature; Gounod was a gifted composer. Beethoven was Goethe's equal; Gounod was not.

So perhaps the wise approach is to ignore Goethean standards, as the public always has. *Faust* isn't high drama, and Gounod need not be measured against one of history's great intellectuals. It's an opera, an entertainment, to be sung, for the public to see, hear, and enjoy. Gounod's Devil is a top-hatted dapper chap, something of a man-about-town Satan, almost likable but when push comes to shove still evil at heart.

Despite its long popularity, the professional consensus is that *Faust* is "flawed," that it needs editing, that Gounod lacked great theatrical instinct, and even that it contains some pedestrian music. It isn't a perfect opera, not nearly as close to perfect as *Carmen*, let alone Mozart's *Marriage of Figaro*. Few are swept away by the drama. But the melody has been the bait for many of opera's greatest singers.

It was staged at the Met as recently as 1991 and is scheduled for the 1996–97 season, evidence that it ain't dead.

The librettists didn't try to use Goethe's whole drama, concentrating instead on the love story between Faust and Marguérite. Actually, that story wasn't part of the legends from which Goethe worked. Technically, the opera was "comique" in that the original version had spoken dialogue (although it was very quickly provided with recitative), but obviously it was tragic.

Among the leading Méphistophélèses was the first great Russian basso, Feodor Chaliapin who became even better known for Boris in *Boris Godunov*. Other basses identified with Méphistophélès include Boris Christoff and Nicolai Ghiaurov, both Bulgarian.

MET PERFORMANCES

Six hundred and ninety-six performances over seventy-two seasons, from 1883 to 1991. Ten performances are scheduled for the 1996–97 season.

RECORDING

CD—Angel/EMI Dig. CDCC 54228 (3). Cheryl Studer, Martine Mahé, Richard Leech, Thomas Hampson, José van Dam. French Army Chorus and Orchestra of the Capitole de Toulouse. Michel Plasson. 1991.

VIDEO

Kraus, Scotto, Ghiaurov, Saccomani. Japanese television. French; Japanese subtitles. Ethuin, conductor. 1973. Legato-Lyric. LCS.

Number 25. *Roméo et Juliette*

Premiere at the Théâtre-Lyrique, Paris, 1867. Taken over by the Opéra-Comique, 1873. Text by Jules Barbier and Michel Carré. Taken from Shakespeare's 1596 play. Five Acts.

KEYNOTE

Tracks Shakespeare closely. Another collaboration of Gounod, Barbier, and Carré, another melody-filled work, another weak drama, declining in popularity but far from dead. Scores of twentieth-century composers would kill for the attention it still gets.

PLOT

Fourteenth century, Verona. After a Prologue, Roméo (tenor) and his friends appear at a masquerade ball at the home of the Capulets. Juliette (soprano) is introduced with her nurse and sings a waltz, "Je veux vivre." Roméo sees Juliette and they fall in love. The famous balcony scene with Roméo in the Capulet garden follows.

Later, in Friar Laurence's (bass) cell, the two lovers are married secretly and hope their nuptial will end the feud between their families. But in the street in front of the Capulet mansion, Capulet's nephew Tybalt (tenor) kills Roméo's friend Mercutio (baritone). Avenging his friend, Roméo kills Tybalt and is banished from Verona.

Roméo returns from exile and goes to Juliette's chamber to celebrate their marriage. Capulet (bass), however, tells her she must marry someone else. After Roméo has again left, Friar Laurence gives her a sleeping potion, which puts her in a deathlike trance. News of her "death" reaches Roméo in Mantua, and he rushes back, bringing a vial of poison with him to her tomb. Thinking she's dead, he takes the poison, giving her a farewell kiss. She awakens for him to die in her arms and then kills herself with a dagger.

HIGHLIGHTS

Act I: Juliette's waltz song, "Je veux vivre" ("Let me live in my dream"): "I want to live in the dream that transports me, to keep this sweet flame as a treasure." The first of four Roméo-Juliette love duets.

Act II: Roméo's song in the garden scene, "Ah! lève-toi, soleil": "Ah! Rise, fair sun! Make the stars turn pale. Love, carry my vows to her . . ." The second love duet.

Act III: Stephano (soprano trouser role) is Roméo's page. His "Que fais-tu, blanche tourterelle?" as he stands in front of the Capulet mansion and mocks them: "What is this turtle dove doing in that nest of vultures?"

Act IV: The third love duet. Roméo's "Ah! Jour de deuil" ("Oh! Day of mourning") after he has been banished by the Duke.

Act V: The scene in the tomb. The last of the four love duets.

COMMENTARY

Expert comment from a composer and two critics:

Giuseppe Verdi in a letter to a friend—

"Gounod is a great musician, a great talent, who composes excellent chamber and instrumental music in a manner all his own. But he isn't an artist of dramatic fiber. *Faust* itself, though successful, has become small in his hands. *Roméo et Juliette* . . . will be the same. In a word, he always does the intimate piece well, but his treatment of situations is weak and his characterization is bad."

George Bernard Shaw, often a harsh critic, reviewing a production in 1889—

". . . the spell of the heavenly melody, of the exquisite orchestral web of sound colors, of the unfailing dignity and delicacy of accent and rhythm."

More recently, Ernest Newman, the great English critic and biographer, about the wisdom of basing an opera on *Romeo and Juliet*:

"One of the incurable delusions of the musical world is that *Romeo and Juliet* is ideal material for an opera. Both composers and librettists have failed to perceive that apart from those two there is very little in the play that lends itself readily to the purposes of opera. Romeo and Juliet themselves have their defects in this regard . . . Each of them is good for one aria and together they are good for a love duet and a death duet. That, however, is about as far as the opera composer can possibly go with them. For the rest, there is hardly anyone in the play of sufficient importance to be worth wasting much time over in an opera, or with a dramatic physiognomy definite enough to lend itself to musical characterization."

Nonetheless, for many years the opera was in the standard repertory of major opera houses all over the world. And it was revived at the Met in 1996.

Among leading stars who performed in it at the turn of the century were Geraldine Farrar, Jean and Edouard de Reszke, Nellie Melba, Adelina Patti, and Emma Eames. A more recent (1947) pair of lovers were Brazilian soprano Bidú Sayão and the magnificent Swedish tenor Jussi Bjoerling.

MET PERFORMANCES

Two hundred and eighty-four performances over thirty-nine seasons, from 1891 to 1996.

RECORDING

CD—Angel/EMI CDCC 47365 (3). Catherine Malfitano, Ann Murray, Alfredo Kraus, Gino Quilico, José van Dam, Gabriel Bacquier. Midi-Pyrénées Regional Chorus. Chorus and Orchestra of the Capitole de Toulouse. Michael Plasson. 1983.

VIDEO

Alagna, Vaduva. Panzarella, Royal Opera House, Covent Garden. French; English subtitles. Mackerras, conductor. 1994. Royal. Pioneer laser disc.

❧

One Warhorse by Ruggerio Leoncavallo
March 8, 1857–August 9, 1919
PAGLIACCI *(Number 8)*

In Egypt or Greece or Turkey, in the same kind of little gin mill in which Sam played for Rick, you might have found Ruggerio Leoncavallo at the keyboard.

"Play it, Ruggerio. Play 'As Time Goes By.' "

It doesn't go very trippingly on the tongue. Maybe it works better in Italian.

But without Bogart, Bergman, Greenstreet, Rains, and Lorre, Signor Leoncavallo created a classic for himself after several years of playing cafe piano in foreign countries by composing the *Pag* half of two operas often presented together, *Cavalleria rusticana* and *Pagliacci*.

Someone has called *Cav* and *Pag* fraternal twins. Both premiered in the early 1890s. They are the two most famous verismo operas. Both offer adultery, jealousy, crimes of passion, and deadly revenge. One is set in very poor Sicily, the other in very poor Calabria. Both feature contemporary blue-collar people in contemporary dress. No kings, lords, wealthy Parisian courtesans, or upper crusties.

Adulterous sex, stabbing, and misery.

The similarities continue. *Pag* followed *Cav* by two years. It also achieved instant international success. Leoncavallo, like Pietro Mascagni, never came close to another smash hit. And for more than one hundred years, both have been denigrated by some critics.

Certain types of elitist critics seem to have a grudge against highly successful operas. Perhaps if no one ever came to see *Cav* 'n' *Pag*, we might hear more about Leoncavallo as quite a significant librettist, both composers as knowledgeable dramatists, and their works as standing out from almost all of the competition of their day. Not Mozart, Wagner, and Verdi, or Monteverdi, or burgeoning Richard Strauss, but quality operas.

What appears to irk some of the hoity-toity about these two compositions (the same thing that piques them about the melody-filled works of Puccini) is their fabulous success with the public. The complaint sounds like this: "If the public knew more about music and opera, it would be less enthusiastic over these things. I mean, they're okay, but they don't deserve *that* kind of attention. It isn't warranted, and this degree of public support simply isn't dignified."

The operagoers need no defense for their likes and dislikes, but a small search of professional writings yields many favorable comments about *Pag*, to wit:

- "As a librettist, Leoncavallo showed uncommon dramatic ability."
- *Pagliacci*: "A fascinating hybrid, one of those rare operas in which the story takes complete possession of the music and fuses with it perfectly."

- *Pagliacci*: "The libretto is a little masterpiece of concise, clear storytelling."
- *Pagliacci*: "In fact, the final moments are among the most emotionally compelling of all operatic finales."

Leoncavallo was born in Naples in 1858, the son of a circuit judge. He studied music at the Naples Conservatory, leaving at eighteen, something of a prodigy, with a degree of master. He began studying literature at the University of Bologna and also started work on *Chatterton*, his first opera, the story of the English poet Thomas Chatterton, from the 1835 drama by French Romantic man of letters Alfred de Vigny. Shortly before the premiere, the impresario with whom he had been working took off with all the money, leaving Leoncavallo broke, a condition that lasted for a considerable time. He supported himself in an adventurous life as a traveling pianist playing in cafes in several countries, but nothing good happened to him musically. Returning to Italy after several years, he began an ambitious project to write an operatic trilogy on the Renaissance period of Italy. But that didn't work out either, and three years later—after the premiere of *Cavalleria rusticana*—he shifted to the publishing house of Sonzogno, one that had sponsored a competition Mascagni had won with *Cav.*

He promptly wrote *Pag*, which was introduced in Milan in 1892, thanks in large part to the muscle of the Sonzogno house. The conductor was Arturo Toscanini. Claude Trevor was there:

"Well do I remember that eventful evening when it first saw the light," he wrote. "No one knew anything much about it except that it was a novelty, and of sufficient importance to have attracted the attention of Maurel, who created the baritone part. The crowded Dal Verme theater was literally in a frenzy on the above occasion, and at the fall of the curtain a scene of such wild enthusiasm took place as is to be seen only rarely."

First TV Opera

Pagliacci was the first opera to be televised in the United States. The network was NBC, the date March 10, 1940. It also was part of the first radio broadcast from the stage of the Metropolitan Opera House. That was thirty years earlier, on January 20, 1910, when portions of both *Cav* and *Pag* were broadcast and picked up by some fifty radio amateurs, several ships in the Brooklyn Naval Yard, and a group of invited guests in a Times Square Hotel. The singer was Enrico Caruso.

Leoncavallo's other operas included *I Medici*, 1893, a failure; a version of *La Bohème*, 1897, which suffered alongside Puccini's work; and *Zaza*, 1900, a moderate success and an effort respected by the French classical music master Gabriel Fauré. Kaiser Wilhelm II commissioned *Der Roland von Berlin*, 1904, which didn't do well, and thereafter Leoncavallo settled for a series of what the music people call "trivial" operettas. He made one more effort at a major work, *Edipo Re*, 1920, but it didn't succeed either.

Basically, Leoncavallo's reputation rests on this one melodrama even more than Mascagni's on *Cavalleria rusticana*.

The professionals advise us that the word "pagliaccio," although often translated as "clown," means "player" or the buffoon who receives the hard knocks in an Italian comedy rather than a circus-type clown. The plural "pagliacci" refers to the whole troup of actors playing in such a comedy. The word "pagliacci" literally means chopped straws, which strolling players wore in their hair for identification as they entered a new town.

A playwright accused Leoncavallo of plagiarizing his work and sued him, but he withdrew his suit when the composer established that he had based his work on an actual event from the past. His father had presided over a trial in which an actor had killed his wife after they had performed together in a play.

Although *Pag* usually is twinned with *Cav*, where it almost always is performed second, it also has appeared with Gluck's *Orfeo ed Eridice*, *Giani Schicci*, other short works, and on its own.

Voice of the Critic

After the successful reception of *Pagliacci*, Leoncavallo turned to the story of *La Bohème* and began work on it. Puccini, however, stole the idea from him and beat him to the stage by more than a year. The Leoncavallo version premiered in Venice, in 1897. It was later conducted by the famous composer and conductor Gustav Mahler, although Mahler made it clear that he disliked both the opera and its composer.

Another well-known figure who felt the same way was Eduard Hanslick, Vienna's most powerful late-nineteenth-century critic. He wrote: "No creative force, no personality, no sense of beauty—a caricature of Italian music."

This *Bohème* was pulled off the stage after six performances but is occasionally produced now, especially in Italy.

Number 8. *Pagliacci (The Strolling Players)*

Premiere at Teatro dal Verme, in Milan, 1892. Text by the composer, based on a real incident. Prologue and two acts (or two scenes).

Enrico Caruso in Pagliacci

KEYNOTE

Verismo. Truth. Naturalism. Rage. Vengeance. Blood. Jealousy. Violence. Tell-it-like-it-is. Make my day. If Clint Eastwood could sing, the verismo operas would be his thing.

PLOT

The Feast of the Assumption, August, about 1865–1870. Montalto, in Calabria, Italy. The opera opens with a Prologue. After an instrumental introduction, Tonio (baritone), dressed as a clown, pokes his head through the curtains and, in song, tells the theater audience that it's about to see a play based upon life, with players who are not mere actors but real human beings. The audience should not be deceived by the foolish costumes. Love and hate will appear as they actually are. This will be life as all of us know it.

The opera then begins in a small village, with a troop of strolling players. Their tent is in the background. Four are dressed in the costumes they will be wearing for the play they will perform that night. Canio (tenor) is the leader, beating a drum. He will be playing Pagliaccio, First Clown. Tonio, dressed as Taddeo, Second Clown in the play to come, brings up in the rear. His back is deformed. Canio tells the crowd that in the play they'll see the troubles of poor Pagliaccio and the vengeance he takes. When Tonio tries to help Canio's wife Nedda (soprano) down from a cart, Canio slaps him, the crowd mocks him, and he goes off muttering that he'll have his revenge for being humiliated.

Later, in their offstage clothes, Tonio tells Nedda he loves her and tries to kiss her. When first she mocks him and then bloodies his face with a whip for daring to approach her, he again vows revenge. Shortly thereafter he overhears a love scene between Nedda and a young villager named Silvio (baritone) and learns that they're having an affair. She plans to leave Canio and meet Silvio at midnight to elope. Smelling sweet revenge, Tonio runs to the tavern to tell Canio, who arrives in time to hear his wife calling out her love to a man as he is leaving the scene (or, in some productions, finding them on the ground together). Although Canio rushes after him, the unknown lover escapes, unseen.

Canio demands to know his name, but Nedda says she'll never tell. Infuriated, he tries to stab her, but others hold him back. Savoring their problems and anxious for even greater revenge, Tonio advises Canio that he'll be able to identify the lover at the play that night when Nedda unwittingly makes some gesture to betray him. Here Canio sings one of the most famous arias in opera, "Vesti la giubba" ("Put on the costume") or "Ridi, Pagliaccio" ("Laugh, then, Clown"). He must go on with tonight's show, smiling though his heart is breaking.

In Act II (or Scene 2), the play within a play begins, the plot resembling what has taken place "in real life." Canio, in his role, demands to know the name of Nedda's in-play lover. She tries to keep up appearances, he grows furious and picks up a knife, she screams "No" . . . and the audience begins to suspect this is no longer acting. To escape him, she darts into the onstage "audience" of the play. Silvio, who has been watching the troupe, knocks over benches as he tries to push his way through the stage audience to reach her. Canio catches her first and stabs her as she cries out for Silvio's help. When he does fight his way to them, Canio savagely stabs him too. The orchestra plays "Ridi, Pagliaccio." Canio stands in a daze, drops the knife, faces the real audience, and, as the curtain falls, declares, "La commedia è finita" ("The comedy is over").

HIGHLIGHTS

Prologue: Tonio's precurtain number, "Sio può." This is a revival of opera prologues from the seventeenth century.

Act I: Nedda's envy of the freedom of the birds, "Stridono lassù: "Hear them call and cry, never faltering through storms. May life never confine them." The Nedda-Silvio illicit love duet. Later, Canio's "Vesti la giubba," with its "Ridi, Pagliaccio," which closes the act and is familiar to people who know no more about opera than they do about cricket. In essence: Laugh while your heart is breaking: "Put on the costume, and powder your face for the people who come here to laugh . . . Ah! Laugh, Clown, at the pain that is destroying your heart."

COMMENTARY

In both *Pagliacci* and *Cavalleria rusticana*, many analysts tend to pay more attention to the "naturalism" and "verismo" of the plot than to the music. "Naturalism" came on the art scene in the late 1800s and early 1900s. "Truth" was the order of the day—or what was seen as "truth" by those looking for the bad and the ugly rather than the good. Veristic dramas tried to capture life in the raw, with instincts and passions running wild, mindlessly, without discipline. No one smelled the roses along the way.

In England, critic George Bernard Shaw addressed the issue of verismo and both operas in 1894, after seeing *Pagliacci*: "It is true that Leoncavallo has shown as yet nothing comparable to the melodic inspiration of Donizetti, but the advance in serious workmanship, in elaboration of detail, in variety of interest, and in capital expenditure on the orchestra and the stage is enormous. There is more work in the composition of *Cavalleria* than in [Donizetti's] *La Favorita*, *Lucrezia* and *Lucia* put together."

Shaw concluded: "Though I cannot think—perhaps this is only my own old-fashionedness—that any part of it [*Cav*] will live as long or move the world as much as the best half-dozen numbers in those three obsolete masterpieces."

Many musicologists today are skeptical of Shaw's critical musical opinions, but he could write circles around nearly everyone, is a delight to read, and has turned out to be both right and wrong.

Unlike *Cav*, *Pag* was not instantly successful in this country at the Met but became a huge hit beginning in 1903, when Enrico Caruso assumed the role of Canio, a part he sang seventy-six times. Other famous tenor Canios include Giovanni Martinelli, who died in 1969, Giovanni Zenatello who died twenty years earlier, the great Beniamino Gigli, and Carlo Bergonzi, a leading Italian tenor. Luciano Pavarotti sang it for the first time in a performance at the Met in 1994.

MET PERFORMANCES
Six hundred and sixteen performances over seventy-two seasons, from 1891 to 1995. Performances of *Cav* and *Pag* are scheduled for the 1996–97 season.

RECORDINGS
CD—Angel/EMI CDCC 47981 (2) (mono). Maria Callas, Nicola Monti, Giuseppe Di Stefano, Tito Gobbi, Rolando Panerai. La Scala Chorus and Orchestra. Tullio Serafin. 1954.

or

—Deutsche Grammophon 419 257-2 (3). Joan Carlyle, Ugo Benelli, Carlo Bergonzi, Giuseppe Taddei, Rolando Panerai. La Scala Chorus and Orchestra. Herbert von Karajan. 1965. (With *Cavalleria rusticanna*.)

VIDEO
Domingo, Stratas, Pons. A film by Franco Zeffirelli. Italian; English subtitles. Prêtre, conductor. 1982. PGD.

Seven Warhorses by Richard Wagner
May 22, 1813–February 13, 1883

LOHENGRIN *(Number 10)*
TRISTAN UND ISOLDE *(Number 12)*
DIE MEISTERSINGER VON NÜRNBERG *(Number 16)*
TANNHÄUSER *(Number 17)*
PARSIFAL *(Number 22)*
(Including Two of the Four Operas
from *The Ring of the Nibelung*)

DIE WALKÜRE *(Number 13)*
SIEGFRIED *(Number 24)*

(Plus the other two *Ring* operas
in The Collection.)

The Five Non-Ring Operas
A lot of people say that Richard Wagner changed the face of opera forever. A lot of others say that he had no true disciple and that no "Wagner school of opera" ever has developed.

Richard Wagner

Both are true.

Some—led by Wagner himself—say he created the music of the future. Others—led by such composers as Claude Debussy—say he was the beautiful sunset of the music of the past.

Certainly he transformed the system.

The system suggests that the emotions of operatic characters are to be expressed chiefly through their vocal music. The orchestra sets the atmosphere and creates the dramatic emphasis. In the movies, you don't hear *Pink Panther* music in *The Silence of the Lambs*.

More than others, Wagner relied on the orchestra to perform both functions. His own writings frankly acknowledge extra reliance on the orchestra but deny intent to shortchange the voice. Reading his books, we might conclude it will be sixty-forty, but it turns out to be a little more lopsided—maybe, say some, as much as eighty-twenty.

Foul, cry the Wagnerians. *Wrong*. *Despicable*, unfounded allegations by Italian canaries.

In fact, the charge by extremist Italian opera fans that Wagner virtually ignored the vocal line collapses in face of the large number of great singers who have made magnificent careers from their abilities to interpret Wagner. Just a few, from relatively recent times: Kirsten Flagstad, Birgit Nilsson, Martha Mödl, Leonie Rysanek, Astrid Varnay, Lauritz Melchior, Wolfgang Windgassen, Jon Vickers, Gerhard Stolze, Hans Hotter, Dietrich Fischer-Dieskau, Hermann Unde, Kurt Böhme, and Josef Greindl.

Even nonprofessionals familiar with Wagner can find a good number of moments that are truly vocal challenges and in which the orchestral expression, while undeniably there, is secondary to the voice: Wolfram's "Evening Star" song in *Tannhäuser*, Lohengrin's farewell aria and Elsa's arias and duet with Ortrud in *Lohengrin*, and Wotan's "Farewell" in *The Ring* are a few examples.

Well, it's a debate. It isn't always orchestra eighty and voice twenty, but it's usually a good bit heavier on orchestra than sixty-forty. You be the judge as you get into Wagner.

RED ALERT:

Be on your guard if you are one of the many who approach Richard Wagner with a predisposition to be bored. You must be careful with this composer. The virus he transmits is treacherous, perfidious, insidious, and pernicious. It's impossible to like the man, but the musician can invade you in a hard-to-combat manner. This is not Charpentier or Flotow. This is a clear and present danger to your prejudices. This is like that friendly oaf your daughter is about to marry. I mean, there he is. Beyond all belief, there he is . . . in the church . . . and your daughter is radiant . . . and the minister is smiling. It's time to take that young man seriously.

So beware. If you get hooked in spite of yourself, even on the Big One, the unique and indescribable *Ring*, don't say you weren't warned here.

Eight things to know about Wagner:

1. There are at least three Wagners, probably more. One wrote reasonably conventional operas, three of which are in The Collection. *Lohengrin* is an example. An older Wagner turned to what he called "music drama." Six of these, including the *Ring* four, are also in The Collection. *Parsifal* is an example. Another Wagner composed a late-in-career comedy, *Die Meistersinger von Nürnberg*.

2. He described "music drama" as a total work of stage art designed to unify dramatic, musical, poetic, and scenic aspects. Although he insisted that this fusion of art constituted a giant conceptual advance, the *goal* itself was not all that different from that of many composers, beginning with Monteverdi. Wagner, a certifiable gabby mouth with a world-class ego, did talk and write much more about unity, but he also had an uncanny knack of making his biggest musical moments also his biggest scenic moments. Nobody else, his followers say, came close to him in this regard. Wagner had a name for his new approach to opera: "Gesamtkunstwerk," or Universal Art Work. In his own mind this was what made him special and what put his own work beyond the spoken theater, beyond opera and beyond instrumental music, into a new art form.

3. In the music dramas, he features "endless melody," a full-time song line

for his vocalists that was more than sing-talk recitative and less than a big set vocal number. This is a different kind of opera, theoretically without the virtuoso arias or duets that bring applause and interrupt the drama.

4. The Wagner orchestra frequently dominates not only the singing voice but also everything else on the stage. At times the singers scarcely move a muscle while the orchestral music carries the day, presumably telling the story, presumably expressing the emotions, and certainly capturing the ear.

5. The "leitmotif," the leading motif, is an integral part of Wagner. He identifies these short special musical themes with individual characters, emotions, or ideas. During an opera one leitmotiv often runs right into another to become forged parts of the orchestral "endless melody." Leitmotif detectives have searched for them in every line of late Wagner—and found them in many. Curiously, perhaps, they were not as important to the composer himself as they have become to his analysts.

6. To a lesser extent in the earlier operas and to the maximum degree in the later music dramas, symbolism is rampant. He went through one Buddhist period, but even without that no composer is so besotted with philosophy, psychology, mysticism, and what makes the human condition Good and Evil.

7. His unique epic composition, the Big One, is the set of four full-scale operas called *The Ring of the Nibelung*, initially meant to be performed one night and then over four days in a near row for a total time of sixteen to eighteen hours—say Monday, Tuesday, Thursday, and Saturday. Although these four works are the primary examples of what he called "music dramas," they are not the only ones.

Wagner Orchestral Gems

Venusberg Music	*Tannhäuser*
Dance of the Apprentices	*Die Meistersinger von Nürnberg*
Entrance of the Gods into Valhalla	*Das Rheingold*
Forest Murmurs	*Siegfried*
Good Friday Spell	*Parsifal*
Grand March	*Tannhäuser*
Magic Fire Music	*Die Walküre*
Ride of the Valkyries	*Die Walküre*
Siegfried's Funeral Music	*Götterdämmerung*
Siegfried's Rhine Journey	*Götterdämmerung*
Transformation Scene	*Parsifal*

All are performed in the concert halls of the world and are available as orchestral excerpts on cassettes and compact discs. Vocalists need not apply.

---

8. As an opera composer, he was almost certainly a genius, a person of considerable intellectual capacity and great inventive ability. But don't be misled by his critics, who ignore another side of him. The secret of his hold on audiences is not intellectual at all, but his ability to grab them by the emotional throat. Evidence: He's the only multiopera composer whose entire mature production is in this anthology of most frequently performed works. Intellect and intellectual music didn't accomplish that.

The professionals—those who worship him, those most critical of him, and those content to weigh his pluses and minuses—have gone over his operas note by note and line by line. The public, meanwhile, for more than one hundred years seems to have found good news and bad news about Richard Wagner.

The good news for lovers of orchestral music is that he took the German symphony off the concert stage, put it in the opera pit, and blended it with dramatic action.

The bad news about that good news is that the dramatic action sometimes fails to come off—in part because the orchestra has been asked to do so much, in part because the whole work is so symbolic, in part because he was a lousy editor and, Wagner defenders insist, in part because too often the opera productions are fouled up by companies that can't afford to handle his work properly or a director who adds "clever" symbolic ideas of his own.

The good news about that bad news is that we amateurs don't have to worry about any of it. We can just listen to the music, enjoy the great stage effects, and absorb the whole. We don't need to concern ourselves with what the Rhine gold "really" means.

All but three of Wagner's ten Collection operas are Warhorses, and one of them, *Götterdämmerung*, is Number 26 and just misses by a step. The remaining two are the other opera of the *Ring* cycle, *Das Rheingold*, Number 43, and *The Flying Dutchman* Number 45. Because it makes no sense to separate them, all four *Ring* operas are kept together and explored here.

The ten Collection works fall into these periods:

The early three, before Wagner got into later music drama:

The Flying Dutchman, 1843 (Number 45). A deal with the Devil.
Lohengrin, 1850 (Number 10). Magic swan, magic dove, and the Holy Grail.
Tannhäuser, 1845 (Number 17). Carnal love with Venus. As in *The Flying Dutchman*, redemption comes from a woman's love and sacrifice. As in *Die Meistersinger*, a song contest is pivotal.

Two later-in-life serious operas that qualify as music dramas:

Tristan und Isolde, 1865 (Number 12). A love potion at work.
Parsifal, 1882 (Number 22). A sacred spear and the Holy Grail.

A gentle romance from his later years:

Die Meistersinger von Nürnberg, 1868 (Number 16). Nobody dies, nobody is redeemed, no supernatural is at work, and the lovers live happily ever after.

The four works that make up *The Ring of the Nibelung* took twenty-seven
years to complete. Either a supreme masterpiece, a supreme bore, or something
of each.

Das Rheingold, 1869 (Number 43)
Die Walküre, 1870 (Number 13)
Siegfried, 1876 (Number 24)
Götterdämmerung, 1876 (Number 26)

He drove to the maximum his own artistry and created something unlike
what had gone before or has come after. That he *was* a musical giant—a cad, a
bigot, a womanizer, a wife stealer, amoral, anti-Semitic, contemptuous of others, but a musical giant—is accepted generally by the music world, although
not unanimously. It isn't logical to challenge his musical stature either on the
grounds of his character or because, years after his death, Adolf Hitler wor-
shiped his works and writings and reveled in his anti-Semitism. Whether one
chooses to listen to his music is an issue of individual judgment.

Many musicologists make the case that his *orchestral works* had a significantly greater impact on twentieth-century classical music than did his opera.
Some even cite one chord, which follows the first four notes of the Prelude to
Tristan und Isolde, as the "beginning of modern music," a citation too technical
for us to consider (though it does seem rather an extravagant statement).

Such exceptional classical music composers as Debussy and such astute observers as George Bernard Shaw, turn-of-the-century music critic in London,
saw him as the culmination of the past rather than the first step into the future.

One wonders whether it is not feasible to be both.

Some of the words for him from the critics: "Inept poet-playwright," "insuffer-
able philosopher," "bombastic," "pompous." And: "Repetitious." "Repetitious."

Other words for him: "Towering genius," "superb musician," "the greatest
of all composers for the theater," "operatic heights never before reached," "the
most commanding figure of the Romantic period."

Gesamtkunstwerk notwithstanding. One theory I like is that if you can't
pronounce *Gesamtkunstwerk* you're unlikely to understand Wagner. But there's
a catch. Even without understanding him, you still may be bitten by that pernicious bug.

It is far from Verdi music. Verdi was music from the tradition of great Ital-
ian voices; Wagner is music from the tradition of great German symphonists:
Vienna's Magnificent Seven: Franz Joseph Haydn, Mozart, Beethoven, Franz
Schubert, Johannes Brahms, Gustav Mahler, and Anton Bruckner, plus Robert

Schumann and Felix Mendelssohn from the north. They portray the German heritage; Wagner simply moved it off the concert stage.

If you go to the concert hall or look in music stores for opera excerpts without vocalists, you aren't apt to find the opera music of Rossini, Donizetti, Bellini—or yet Verdi or even mighty Mozart. Overtures are commonly available, of course, like Rossini's *William Tell* (else the Lone Ranger would be unhorsed). But there are not many highlights of nonvocal music from the opera proper.

This is not the case for Wagner's operatic music, especially for his later works. The early ones were in the mainstream of the opera of the time—the French grand opera of Meyerbeer, the Italian opera of Bellini, the early German Romantic opera of Weber, or combinations and modifications thereof—and these *do* have conventional arias and duets.

Wagner used orchestral leitmotifs to convey symphonic and dramatic development. The music encyclopedia defines leitmotif this way: "A clearly defined theme or musical idea, representing or symbolizing a person, object, idea, etc., which returns in its original or altered form at appropriate points in a dramatic [mainly opera] work." The term was coined in the 1870s, but composers had been using leitmotifs for years. They weren't new when Weber used them in his early German Romantic opera when Wagner was a teenager. But Wagner took the concept far beyond anyone else.

Gross oversimplification of leitmotifs: If the opera is about Washington, everytime the President is involved, on stage or off, you hear the leitmotif of "Hail to the Chief." If war is involved, you hear the leitmotif of "Taps." And more leitmotivs to represent the State Department, Lying-to-Congress, the Bully Senator, and Congressional Leaks-to-Media.

The difficulty with that gross oversimplification is that it isn't quite right. The interesting point—Wagnerians would say the wonderful point—about his leitmotifs is that, unlike "Hail to the Chief," which halts all action, they don't interrupt the onward flow of things. Also, leitmotifs take on various musical shapes from an original base. A basic motif signaling "nature" might have a variant signaling "brook."

Let's move to Wagner's life. He once introduced himself this way: "My name is Wilhelm Richard Wagner and I was born in Leipzig in 22 May, 1813. My father was a registrar in the police department, he died six months after I was born."

Leipzig was the second largest town in the Kingdom of Saxony, a Protestant German state with a population of some 33,000, an important trading center since the Middle Ages.

Wagner biographers raise a question about the identity of his father, citing some evidence that it was actually an actor, playwright, and painter named Ludwig Geyer, whom Wagner's mother later married. There is some indirect evidence—presented by Nietzsche among others—that Geyer was Jewish, interesting in that Wagner later made no secret of his own ardent anti-Semitism.

In any case, his "legal" father died when he was six months old, shortly thereafter his mother married Geyer, and six months after that marriage she bore Geyer a daughter. The family moved to Dresden, where Richard, although surrounded by Geyer's artistic friends, showed little interest in the arts.

Early Start

Richard Wagner was no child-prodigy Mozart, but he did teach himself to play the piano by pecking out the notes from the overture to Carl Maria von Weber's opera *Der Freischütz*. Weber was a down-the-street neighbor. Wagner's own father was not in favor of the boy fussing around with music.

Later in life Wagner became a big admirer of Weber, although the only hero he was passionate about was a fellow German who wrote only one opera but also was into symphonic music, Ludwig van Beethoven.

Then, at age fifteen, he decided to become a composer and taught himself by listening to Beethoven symphonies. In 1831 he attended the University of Leipzig for a short time and made a small reputation for himself as a nonstop talker who enjoyed drinking and gambling. Few successful composers had as little formal training.

In 1833, at age twenty, he wrote *Die Feen, (The Fairies)* his first complete opera. It didn't go and never has. That year he also wrote the first of many polemical treatises. Four years later, after having lived in Magdeburg and Königsberg, he joined an opera company in Riga. Meanwhile, he had met and married an actress, Minna Planer, who at one time went back home to mother, in part because they lived on borrowed money while he worked on a second unsuccessful opera, *Das Liebesverbot*. Then, while conducting at the theater in Riga, he began a grand opera based on Edward Bulwer-Lytton's historical novel *Rienzi, the Last of the Tribunes*. After finishing only two acts, he was fired from the theater because he was too demanding.

Ducking creditors, and with the *Rienzi* manuscript in a suitcase, he left Riga in 1839 for Paris. That stormy sea voyage that took him via London was his inspiration for *The Flying Dutchman*, his next opera and the one he later regarded as his first mature effort.

Despite support from Meyerbeer, then at the peak of his grand opera popularity, Wagner was poor, miserable, and unnoticed in Paris, although he did finish *Rienzi* while there and began work on *The Flying Dutchman*.

In 1842, when the Dresden Opera accepted *Rienzi*, allegedly he gazed at the Rhine and "with great tears in his eyes swore eternal fidelity to the German fatherland." Well, it's not on tape anywhere, but maybe he did. *Rienzi* was successful and is infrequently performed today. It was a grand opera in the style of the popular French grand opera of the day. At this time the young Wagner was a disciple of Meyerbeer, who owned opera in Paris, and *Rienzi* was designed for a Paris audience—five acts, historical setting (fourteenth-century Rome), massive choruses, big ensembles, everything on a huge scale. Everything, in fact, that Wagner later came to detest. But it isn't a sin to write one kind of opera at twenty-nine when you are hungry in Paris and another kind later in life.

Rejection

Young—and broke—Richard Wagner submitted the score of his *Rienzi* (with the help of Giacomo Meyerbeer) to the directors of the Opéra in Paris. They had zero interest. Although this was the type of opera he later rejected, Wagner was intensely disappointed. His later reaction: "I had a splendid grand opera before me and my ambition was not only to imitate, but with reckless extravagance to surpass, all that had gone before, in brilliant finales, hymns, processions, and musical clang of arms."

The Flying Dutchman was performed in Dresden the next year. More a German Romantic work like Weber's *Der Freischütz* than a Meyerbeer-type grand opera like *Rienzi*—and from a German legend rather than ancient history—*Dutchman* is filled with nature and supernatural forces. Although the opera ran for only four performances, Wagner now was well enough known to be named director of the Dresden Opera and conductor to the King of Saxony. (See more on *Dutchman* under its own title at Number 45.)

During the next several years in Dresden he wrote two more German Romantic operas—*Tannhäuser* and *Lohengrin*, two Warhorses, again both influenced by Weber. Both use subjects derived from medieval German epics, rely on the supernatural, and glorify Germany and its people (although less so than his later works).

Wagner was a dedicated artist who made few concessions to popular taste and who dreamed the grandest dreams. A fanatical reformer, he was convinced that the theater around him was corrupt and badly in need of revision and improvement.

Indeed, he felt the current world around him also was badly in need of reform. In 1848, many countries in Europe experienced liberal revolts against established monarchies. These began in Paris in February and spread to Vienna the following month. In Dresden, barricades were erected and the King was presented with demands for democratic reform. Wagner sided with the insurrectionists, writing: "The present order is crumbling to ruin. A new world will be born from it" (shades of *The Ring*).

In May 1849, revolution broke out in Dresden, the King of Saxony fled, the King of Prussia crushed the uprising, and a warrant was issued for Wagner's arrest. With the help of his friend Franz Liszt in nearby Weimar, he fled to Zurich, where he was to remain in exile until a political amnesty was proclaimed in 1860.

The Zurich years were busy ones. For the first several, he wrote no music, concentrating instead on a series of essays in which he argued for something new, which he called "music drama." After beginning work on *The Ring*, he veered off to write *Tristan und Isolde* (1857–1859) and to start *Die Meistersinger* (1862–1867).

The period after *Tristan* was not a happy time: Not one of his operas was being performed, he and Minna became estranged, and he had a series of relationships with married women. When he turned fifty in 1863, he had experienced no significant success since *Rienzi* years earlier.

Then he hit the multimillion-dollar lottery. Ludwig found him and his entire life changed.

Wagner later wrote: "I was never again to feel the weight of everyday hardships of existence, under the protection of my exalted friend."

Ludwig was King Ludwig II of Bavaria, eighteen, tall, blond, and handsome, a homosexual devoted to music. *Lohengrin* was his favorite German legend, and in 1864, after becoming familiar with the opera, he summoned Wagner to Munich. He fell in love with Wagner's music and, some biographers say, quite possibly with Wagner himself. Ludwig's financial support lasted the rest of Wagner's life.

Soon both *Tristan* and *Die Meistersinger* were produced and the King commissioned the completion of *The Ring*. Wagner fell in love with Cosima, illegitimate daughter of his old friend, Franz Liszt. She was married, to conductor Hans von Bülow and had children, but that never bothered the amoral (to employ a kindly adjective) Wagner. She joined him in Bavaria, and nine years later, after Minna's death, they were married.

Europe loved the new Wagner. His Germany won the Franco-Prussian War (it hasn't won one since) and Wagner was the hero artist of Bismarck's German Empire. The *Ring* cycle was completed in 1874. A Wagner music temple at the city of Bayreuth in Germany, designed by Wagner and the architect Otto Brückwald, was built especially for his works. The first complete performance of *The Ring* was held there in 1876 as a four-day festival event. (That Bayreuth summer festival, interrupted in some war and postwar years, has been held continuously since 1951.) Approaching seventy, he had only to write his last opera, *Parsifal*. He died shortly after its first performance and is buried in his garden at Bayreuth.

If you stay on the edges of Wagner, probably you can walk away without infection. If you get into him, it's ten-to-one that the resolute bug will bite. Remember what William Shakespeare put in the mouth of Macbeth more than two hundred years before Wagner was born:

"Such welcome and unwelcome things at once 'tis hard to reconcile."

Except for the *Ring* operas, saved here until last so that they are kept together, these are in Collection order:

Number 10. *Lohengrin*

Premiere at the Weimar Opera, 1850, (Franz Liszt conducting). Written, 1846–1848. Text by Wagner from various sources, including several from the thirteenth century. Three acts.

KEYNOTE

The Holy Grail is greater than human love. Hear opera's most famous march and Wagner's most melodious music. The last great German Romantic opera and the first large step toward Wagner's music drama of the future.

PLOT

Antwerp, first half of the tenth century. Lohengrin (tenor) arrives by swan boat at the court of King Henry the Fowler (bass), wearing shining armor, to be the defender of Elsa of Brabant (soprano). She has been falsely accused by her guardian, Frederick of Telramund (baritone), of murdering her young brother, Gottfried (who disappeared after she took him into the woods), in order to seize the throne. Lohengrin agrees not only to champion but also to marry her. The condition is that she never ask his name, rank, or birthplace, or else he must leave. He does defeat Telramund in a duel, thus establishing her innocence. Telramund and his wife, Ortrud (mezzo-soprano), however, plant doubts in Elsa's mind about Lohengrin's character. After the famous "Here Comes the Bride" wedding march, and after being further misled, she becomes hysterical, breaks the rules, and demands to know who he is and where he comes from. Now he must reveal that he is a Knight of the Holy Grail, but then he no longer can stay among mortals as a champion of right against wrong, drawing on the force of the Grail. As he leaves, in a boat drawn by a swan, the bird vanishes and its place is taken on the riverbank by Elsa's missing brother, Gottfried. Elsa then dies in her brother's arms, crying out for her husband, as the dove of the Holy Grail descends to draw Lohengrin's boat away.

HIGHLIGHTS

The Prelude.

Act I: "Elsa's Dream," "Einsam in trüben Tagen," in which a handsome knight promises to champion her if he is needed: "Alone in somber days I sought help from the Lord. I poured out my painful heart in prayer."

Act II: The procession to the minister.

Act III: The "Bridal Chorus"—(We say "Here Comes the Bride," although Wagner didn't)—opera's most frequently played music. One of several outstanding Wagner choral works. Also the scene in which Lohengrin reveals his identity as a Knight of the Holy Grail, son of Parsifal, in "In fernem Land": "In a distant land that you cannot reach, there is a citadel named Monsalvat where a shining temple stands."

Wagner on Lohengrin

Wagner pictured *Lohengrin* this way:

"Out of the clear blue ether of the sky there seems to condense a wonderful yet at first hardly perceptible vision; and out of this there gradually emerges, ever more and more clearly, an angel host bearing in its midst the Holy Grail. As it approaches earth, it pours out exquisite odors, like grams of gold, ravishing the senses of the beholder. The glory of the vision grows and grows until it seems as if the rapture must be shattered and dispersed by the very vehemence of its expansion . . . The flames die away and the angel host soars up again to the ethereal heights in tender joy."

COMMENTARY

This isn't music drama, but Wagner does move away from set arias standing by themselves and toward long and expressive recitative. The professionals say it shows monumental musical development from his prior operas. Franz Liszt wrote: "With *Lohengrin*, the old world of opera comes to an end."

Listen to the Prelude a half-dozen times. One Wagnerian told me it portrays "the magical, ethereal coloring of the whole score, the wonderful choral and processional writing, and the opera's special place as the last refuge of pure vocal melody in Wagner's work." He likes it.

Without cuts and not counting intermissions, *Lohengrin* takes three and a half hours. Interestingly, it wasn't well received at first, although for decades it has been the public's favorite Wagner opera, despite the unhappy ending in which one lover dies while the other lives on. The governing theme is not their love for one another but rather the obligation owed the Holy Grail.

Though *Lohengrin* is early Wagner, the symbolist detectives have a field day with it. Some see a sort of Christian mysticism tie-up with the Holy Grail versus the villains Frederick and Ortrud, who worship pagan gods. Some see the artist versus common humanity and some the outsider versus the insiders. And most see a theme similar to *The Flying Dutchman*: the search of man for a woman who trusts him totally and always will be faithful.

The Prelude to Act III is one of the best-known Wagner orchestral numbers, heard on classical radio and used as a concert piece.

MET PERFORMANCES
Five hundred and ninety-eight performances over sixty-nine seasons, from 1883 to 1986.

RECORDING
CD—Decca/London Dig. 421 053-2 (4). Jessye Norman, Eva Randová, Plácido Domingo, Siegmund Nimsgern, Hans Sotin. Chorus of the Vienna Sate Opera, Vienna Philharmonic Orchestra. Georg Solti. 1986.

VIDEO
Domingo, Studer, Vejzovic, Lloyd. Vienna Staatsoper. German; English subtitles. Abbado, conductor. 1990. HOME VISION.

Number 12. *Tristan und Isolde*

Premiere at the Munich Opera, 1865. Written, 1857–1859. Text by Wagner, drawn loosely from a thirteenth-century German poem by Gottfried von Strassbourg, which came from old Celtic legends. Three acts.

KEYNOTE
An epic love story, probably Wagner's finest work, and arguably the most passionate of all operas. Drama, friendship, fidelity, faithlessness, forgiveness, treachery . . . and love.

PLOT
Legendary time, a ship at sea, a Cornwall castle, a Kareol castle. The background: Tristan (tenor), who lost his parents in infancy, has been brought up at the court of his Uncle Marke (bass), King of Cornwall. Tristan had fought and killed an Irish knight named Morold in a dispute over whether Cornwall would continue to pay tribute to the King of Ireland. Back in Ireland, Morold had been engaged to Isolde (soprano), the daughter of that Irish King. Having been badly wounded in the fight with Morold, Tristan had put himself under the care of Isolde, whose mother had been a sorceress and who thus was skilled in magic healing. At first he hadn't identified himself, but even after Isolde realized that he had killed her fiancé, she looked into his eyes and wasn't able to harm him.

When Tristan returns to Cornwall, King Marke orders him to go back to Ireland with the assignment of escorting Isolde to Cornwall to become *his* wife and Queen. Loving Isolde as he does, this is an unhappy mission for Tristan, but he has no choice. When the curtain rises, the pair are on a ship bringing them to Cornwall and King Marke. Isolde, who still loves Tristan, is bewildered—and furious—that he's taking her to another man. Neither is aware of

Kirsten Flagstad as Isolde

the other's love. She decides that both of them must die from a death potion, but without her knowledge her maid/confidante Brangäne (mezzo-soprano) substitutes a love potion for it. Tristan and Isolde drink it together, expecting to die, but instead recognize their love for one another and intensify their lust. One description says they "face each other with ardent passion" and another that the potion "rouses their love to irresistible passion." In any case, there's a lot of fervor.

High Praise for Tristan

No Wagner opera is more intense and more passionate in feeling than *Tristan*. Musicologist Harold Schonberg, normally not extravagant, writes in *The Lives of the Great Composers*: "Never in the history of music had there been an operatic score of comparable breadth, intensity, harmonic richness, massive orchestration, sensuousness, power, imagination and color."

The second act is dominated by a garden love scene in King Marke's castle. The night is their friend, the sunlit day their enemy. The King has gone hunting, and the lovers are together for one of opera's longest and most passionate love scenes. Led home by Melot (tenor), presumably a friend of Tristan's but actually a sneak who wants Isolde for himself, the King finds Tristan and Isolde making love and denounces Tristan for his treachery. Melot stabs Tristan, who, though unconscious and sorely wounded, is taken by his dedicated henchman Kurwenal (baritone) to Kareol (Brittany). When he regains consciousness, he learns that Kurwenal has sent word to Isolde to join them. No ship appears, no ship . . . and then one is sighted. It will founder on the rocks; no, it will reach shore safely. Tristan is ecstatic and in his excitement tears off his bandages and rises from his couch. But then a second ship, bearing King Marke and some of his men, is seen. Trying to protect the two lovers, Kurwenal attempts to stop them and kills Melot. The King, whom Brangäne has told of the love potion, actually has come to tell his dear friend Tristan, faithless yet most faithful, that he has forgiven him, but the lovers don't know this. By the time the King gets to them, Tristan has died of his wounds, which were aggravated by his frenzied reaction to Isolde's arrival, and she has died of grief in his arms.

HIGHLIGHTS

Without conventional set arias, this is a difficult opera to highlight. I make an effort here, but a better idea is to listen to thirty minutes of a compact disc, including the central section of Act II. If it doesn't turn you on, buy some Geritol.

The Prelude to Act I: A love-poem symphony, unique in opera.

Act II: The great forty-minute love duet between Tristan and Isolde, in six sections, known as the "Liebesnacht." (Verdi's famous Otello–Desdemona duet lasts nine minutes.) "Oh night of love, sink upon us." Hear the "Liebestod" at the end.

Act III: The entire act. The "Liebestod," the Love-Death hymn at the end of the opera, sung by Isolde over Tristan's dead body.

COMMENTARY

Often called Wagner's most musical opera, *Tristan and Isolde* is a mystical work of sex and of a love so overwhelming and powerful that it can be realized only in death. Tristan's honor forbids any other true long-term union. Many analysts call it the father of twentieth-century music; others say no finer love music has ever been written. Some operagoers who are turned off by *The Ring* find this to be a wonderful fulfillment of Wagner's music drama, the most perfect of his lyric tragedies. Although negative critics say the dramatic unity Wagner sought is overwhelmed by the force of the orchestral music, Wagnerians insist that the dramatic unity is *in* that orchestral music. That would be my view, but I've been infected by the Wagner bug. You decide.

Tristan was composed during Wagner's passionate love affair with Mathilde Wesendonck; opinions differ as to whether the ardent affair led to the passionate opera or the ardent opera to the passionate affair. Most likely they enhanced each other.

Few operas have been more analyzed (The *Ring* is an exception). Long books dissect it. No Wagner "concept" heroine like Kundry in *Parsifal*, Isolde is a flesh and blood woman. It is not permitted for opera beginners to pass judgment on Wagner before reading the story in detail and then watching a laser disc or good videotape of *Tristan und Isolde*—and then, let's hope, a live opera.

MET PERFORMANCES

Four hundred and thirty performances over sixty-six seasons, from 1886 to 1983.

RECORDING

CD—Angel/EMI CDMD 69319 (4). Helga Dernesch, Christa Ludwig, Jon Vickers, Walter Berry, Karl Ridderbusch. Chorus of the Deutsche Oper. Berlin Philharmonic Orchestra. Herbert von Karajan. 1972.

or

—Deutsche Grammophon. Birgit Nilsson, Christa Ludwig, Wolfgang Windgassen, Eberhard Wächter, Martti Talvela. Bayreuth Festival Chorus and Orchestra. Karl Böhm. 1966.

VIDEO

Kollo, Meier, Schwarz. Bayreuther Festspielhaus. German; English subtitles. Barenboim, conductor, 1983. PGD.

Number 16. *Die Meistersinger von Nürnberg*

Premiere at the Royal Court Theatre, Munich, 1868. Written, 1862–1867. Text by Wagner. From German history and literature. Three acts.

KEYNOTE

Wagner's only comedy, his warmest opera, and the one that's easiest to enjoy. Hear the Prelude five times and then look into the mirror and say you can't stand Richard Wagner. Meet opera's favorite shoemaker and then argue that Wagner is too intellectual and not human enough.

The Old and the New

Q: What do Richard Wagner, Hermann Goering, the imperial jewels, and gingerbread have in common?

A: Nuremberg. Wagner thought of his opera while looking for musicians there. The Nazi thug Goering was tried there for war crimes after World War II. The imperial jewels were stored behind the walls for safekeeping during the Holy Roman Empire six-hundred years ago. And gingerbread is the city's most famous commercial product, sold all over Germany today.

PLOT

Mid-sixteenth century, Nuremberg. In the Church of St. Katharine, Walther (tenor), a young knight who is passing through town, tries to attract the attention of Eva (soprano), daughter of the goldsmith Pogner (bass). She is with her nurse, Magdalena (mezzo-soprano). Walther learns that the next day Eva will be betrothed to the winner of a singing contest held by the Guild of Mastersingers. An apprentice shoemaker named David (tenor), who is one of Magdalena's admirers, explains the technical rules of the contest to Walther. David also discloses that he's studying singing and poetry as well as shoemaking.

When the mastersingers enter the church for a meeting, they're led by Pogner and Beckmesser (bass-baritone), a small-minded town clerk who also has his eyes on Eva. Hans Sachs (bass-baritone), a wise and fair-minded cobbler who doubles as a poet, also enters. Walther is introduced as a candidate for the guild and invited to sing a song, but he is given poor marks by Beck-messer, the designated marker (scorekeeper), who knows a rival when he judges one. Sachs, one of opera's nicest guys, is the only one to see potential in Walther, who inadvertently broke the rules by rising from his chair as he sang. The meeting breaks up in disorder.

Hold the Metaphysics: Boy Marries Girl

American composer/critic Virgil Thomson, admittedly no fan of Wag-nerian opera, wrote about *Die Meistersinger* in 1945:

"It is all direct and human and warm and sentimental and down to earth. It is unique among Wagner's theatrical works in that none of the characters gets mixed up with magic or takes drugs. And nobody gets redeemed according to the usual Wagnerian pattern, which a German critic once described as 'around the mountain and through the woman'. . . . The hero merely gives a successful debut recital and marries the girl of his heart. And Wagner, without his erotic meta-physical paraphernalia is a better composer than with it. He pays more attention to holding interest by musical means, wastes less time pre-dicting doom, describing weather, soul states and ecstatic experiences . . . The whole score is reasonable. It is also rich and witty and roman-tic, full of interest and of human expression."

In the next act, the apprentices are closing Sachs's shop as he and Eva dis-cuss the singing trial. Sachs also loves Eva, but he's wise enough to know that he's too old for her. When he teases her, she rushes home in tears. As for Walther, he has been discouraged by the reaction to his singing, has given up hope of winning Elsa in the singing contest, and has convinced her that they should elope. Sachs, realizing that a successful elopement would be a disastrous move for the lovers and wanting to help them by preventing it, opens a win-dow and lets light stream across the roadway so that they will be discovered by the townspeople. At the same time, Beckmesser arrives to serenade Eva. While working on shoes for Beckmesser, Sachs plays the role of marker and hammers each time Beckmesser makes a mistake. Beckmesser sees a figure in the window above. This is Magdalena, dressed in Eva's clothes, but Beckmesser mistakes her for Eva. The serenade and the hammering awaken the neighborhood, Beckmesser receives a drubbing, and during the tumult Sachs prevents the couple from running off.

In Act III, Sachs soliloquizes on the madness of the world and the love of the young couple. When Walther tells Sachs of a song that came to him in a dream, the cobbler writes it down, considering it a real winner even though the last stanza is missing. Sachs then sees Beckmesser stealing the script but says nothing and allows him to keep it, realizing that without an ending it will get Beckmesser in trouble and thus help the lovers. Walther enters; after seeing Eva, he's been inspired to write the missing last stanza. David and Magdalena are summoned, David is promoted from apprentice to journeyman, and the five rejoice at the dawning of new hope and love as they depart for the festival.

On the banks of the river, the apprentices and guildsmen assemble. Amid dancing, the masters arrive to take their places on the stand. Beckmesser makes a fiasco of the stolen song, and Walther then sings it properly, winning both the contest and Eva. But he's still smarting from his earlier treatment, and when Pogner moves to invest him into the guild he brushes aside the invest-ment chain. Sachs soothes him, explaining that the purpose of the master-singers is to preserve German song. Walther now accepts the investment chain, Sachs is thanked for being the sort of person he is, and the opera ends with everyone shouting approval.

HIGHLIGHTS

Prelude to Act I: With its leading motifs, which will come back through-out the opera.

Act I: The beginning of Walther's trial song, "Am stillen Herd."

Act II: A Hans Sachs monologue, "Wie duftet doch der Flieder," in which the cobbler thinks about the beauty of Walther's song.

Prelude to Act III, made up partly of the soliloquy Hans Sachs sings in Scene 1 and partly of a chorale sung in his honor in Scene 2.

Act III: Hans Sachs's monologue, "Wahn, wahn," in which he reflects on the madness of the world. Walther's "Prize Song," "Morgenlich": "In the rosy morning, the air heavy with blossoms, I went to a garden. There under a lovely fruit tree, in a dream of love, I saw the most beautiful woman: Eve in Paradise." A famous quintet that ends Scene 1, with Hans Sachs, Eva, Walther, David, and Magdalena. In Scene 2, the chorale honoring Hans Sachs, heard earlier in the Prelude to Act III, and, again, the "Prize Song."

COMMENTARY

Wagner was in the midst of writing *The Ring* when he composed *Die Meis-tersinger*, which is modeled after a movement of poet-singers who actually existed.

Although the last act alone is longer than Verdi's great comedy, *Fal-staff*, Wagnerians and normal people agree that the opera is a warm, mellow winner, a simple human love story, laced with nice humor and full of song and whimsy. No gods or legendary heroes are involved, only real people in real sixteenth-century circumstances. Sachs is an especially good fellow, perhaps Wagner's best hero, and one who makes you feel good about the world as Siegfried never does.

Despite Wagner's asserted dislike of Italian ensemble numbers—"Italian tinsel"—he has several big ensemble scenes plus another self-designated no-no, an action-stopping quintet in the last act. Wagner always had a purpose; his use of the ensemble finale was done consciously as he deliberately mingled the past and the future.

To make the opera work, the experts say, there must be a great tenor, a first-rate soprano, and a wise and warm bass-baritone for Sachs.

Author's note: This is a warm comedy. Don't leave Wagner without it.

Die Meistersinger is one of several operas in The Collection that merits special attention. For improved understanding, here are a few sound-bite-sized keynotes:

- *Die Meistersinger* follows convention for a German Romantic opera—it's from actual German history, it deals with real people, not gods or legends, and nature plays a significant part. Present, too, is strong nineteenth-century nationalism, with great pride in German artistry and tradition.
- Though called a "comedy of romance," it's closer to romance than comedy, dealing more with a gentle philosophical view of humanity than with actual laughter. Consider the other most famous comedies: Mozart's *Marriage of Figaro* does offer outright laughter, albeit with a social purpose as the servants outwit the arrogant nobility, and it also has touching sadness. Rossini's less profound *Barber of Seville* is more pure fun. Donizetti's *Elixir of Love* is delightful fluff in theme (but not in music). Verdi's *Falstaff* is a wise veteran's musical and dramatic masterpiece.
- The foppish, foolish character of Beckmesser was modeled after an avidly anti-Wagner Vienna critic, Eduard Hanslick, and all other narrow-minded critics (and audiences) who refused to recognize Wagner's genius. Hans Sachs—who admired good, fresh music even if it was beyond the boundaries of accepted conventions—was in that sense Wagner's sort of guy, representing enlightened public opinion. (Hans Sachs was a real shoemaker and a real poet of note who lived from 1494 to 1576. Biographies of him were one source for the opera.)
- Particularly appealing to Wagner were the scenic possibilities of old Nuremberg, one of the great German cities of its day. He studied the architecture, and the sets re-create actual parts of the heavily walled city (too well walled and defended ever to be damaged by war, until World War II).
- Wagner's original idea was that this would be a one-act production, fun to see and easy to perform. Hah! Like so much of his work, it got away from him. Uncut, *Die Meistersinger* takes four and a half hours to stage. His simple little comedy was the longest opera ever written up to that time. Like good old Hubert H. Humphrey—who would have despised Wagner's prejudices and character—Wagner never knew how to stop.
- Though a romance rather than an epic music drama, the music is more in

the style of Wagner's endless melody than the music of *Tannhäuser* and his other early works. Walther's two competitive songs aside, you don't hear the "tunes" associated with the operas of most other composers. In late Wagner, there was no recitative followed by a set piece. But the "Prize Song" is the best example in Wagner of his ability to write a beautiful lyric melody when he chose to do so.

- As expected from Wagner, the orchestra is in control of the music, even while the singers are singing. (The story goes that Richard Strauss, years later conducting his *Elektra*, told the orchestra: "Play louder; I can still hear the singer." Although Strauss said it, Wagner might have.)

- Although fairly straightforward, there are morals in *Die Meistersinger*. With Wagner, always morals. The unconventional "Prize Song" is seen by Sachs as music with the potential of leading art from established tradition to a new and better ideal. This is what Wagner was all about; his music of the future was to pave the way toward greater artistic glory.

- Trick of the trade: When the opera is involved in tradition, featuring the stately mastersingers, the melodies are traditional, with little dissonance. When his characters muse about an uncertain future, Wagner abandons conventional music and becomes more dissonant, anticipating twentieth-century sounds.

- Leading motifs. Seven different themes are heard in the short Prelude. All come back many times during the opera. Listen for them; they're not hidden, and identifying them is fun. Frequently one moves right into another, most lasting only thirty or forty seconds. In order they are:

    1. The mastersingers as a group, in their corporate capacity. Stately and dignified.

    2. Walther's wooing of Eva. Lyrical.

    3. The banner of the mastersingers under which they march. Although slightly different, it is spawned from the basic mastersingers' motif.

    4. The role of the mastersingers as guardians of poetry and music.

    5. Walther's romantic yearning. Longing.

    6. The beauty and love of earth in the spring.

    7. The apprentices. Ridicule.

MET PERFORMANCES

Three hundred and ninety performances over sixty-five seasons, from 1886 to 1995.

RECORDING

CD—Deutsche Grammophon 415 278-2 (4). Catarina Ligendza, Christa Ludwig, Plácido Domingo, Horst R. Laubenthal, Dietrich Fischer-Dieskau, Roland Hermann, Gerd Feldhoff, Peter Lagger. Chorus and Orchestra of the Deutsche Oper, Berlin. Eugen Jochum. 1976.

VIDEO

McIntyre, Pringle, Frey, Dose. Australian Opera. German; English subtitles. Mackerras. 1990. HOME VISION.

Number 17. *Tannhäuser*

Premiere at the Dresden Opera, 1845. From two separate medieval legends. Written, 1842–45. Text by Wagner. Three acts.

KEYNOTE

Wagner's second major opera, written three years after *The Flying Dutchman*. Virtue versus Venus. Closer to his music drama than the *Dutchman*, but still far away. Look for the Evening Star. A typical Wagner plot: man's redemption through woman's sacrifice.

Wagner Fatality

Copenhagen, Denmark, Aug. 10. 1994 (AP)—Opera may be sweet to some people's ears. But to one animal, the strains of Wagner were fatal. The Copenhagen Zoo said Tuesday that one of its okapis—a rare African mammal related to the giraffe—died from stress apparently triggered by opera singers rehearsing three hundred yards away in a park. The six-year-old okapi, Katanda, collapsed after Royal Theatre performers were singing selections from *Tannhäuser* on Friday, zoo spokesman Peter Haase said. "She started hyperventilating, went into shock and collapsed," he said. "We did all we could, but she died Saturday."

PLOT

Early thirteenth century, near Eisenach. The minnesinger (type of German troubador) Tannhäuser (tenor) has abandoned the world to spend his days and nights making love to Venus (soprano or mezzo-soprano) in her court, but eventually he tires of twenty-four-hour-a-day sex and yearns to return to earth. When he prays to the Virgin, his prayers are answered and he finds himself in a valley on earth. A band of pilgrims en route to Rome urge him to join them and expiate his sins. But he also encounters a group of fellow minstrel knights, including an old friend named Wolfram (baritone) and the Landgrave Hermann (bass), both of whom urge him to return with them to the Wartburg (a castle). When he's reminded that the lovely Elisabeth (soprano), whose heart he had once won, lives there, Tannhäuser recalls the beauty of earthly love and devotion as opposed to that nasty orgiastic sex with Venus. He joins them.

Geraldine Farrar as Elisabeth in Tannhäuser

In the Wartburg, where Elisabeth gives him a warm greeting, a singing contest for her hand has been scheduled. The other knights sing appropriately of pure and chaste love, but Tannhäuser shocks everyone by singing of the carnal delights of the Venusberg. Distressed by his lack of couth, the knights threaten to run him through with their swords, and he's saved only by Elisabeth's pleas. The Landgrave then advises him that only the Holy Father in Rome can forgive his terrible sins. Tannhäuser leaves for Rome and is gone for many months, while a grieving Elisabeth looks futilely for him in each band of returning pilgrims. Although Wolfram prays to the evening star to protect her, she dies of a broken heart.

Meanwhile, the weary Tannhäuser finally does return, having failed in his pilgrimage. The Pope has told him there will be no pardon for him until the papal staff has sprouted leaves. Despairing, Tannhäuser is called by Venus to return to her sinful charms, but he resists when Wolfram tells him one angel—Elisabeth—is praying for his soul. When a procession carrying her body comes past him, he dies at her side. A moment later, pilgrims from Rome arrive with the soul-saving news that the Pope's staff miraculously has sprouted leaves. God has forgiven Tannhäuser; redemption for him has come through Elisabeth's love and sacrifice.

HIGHLIGHTS

Lohengrin has the greater total vocal melody, but *Tannhäuser* has more vocal highlights than any Wagner opera.

The Overture: Including themes of the "Pilgrims' Chorus" and the "Venusberg Music," the overture sets the tone for the entire opera. It is a popular piece for symphonic orchestra in concert halls everywhere.

Act I: Tannhäuser's "Hymn to Venus" and the sensual orchestral "Venusberg Music." It you're into carnal love, don't miss this scene. If you aren't, and want to be, don't miss this scene.

Act II: Elisabeth's aria greeting the Hall of Song, "Dich, teure Halle": "You, dear hall, I joyfully greet you again. You are proud and noble." The "Tannhäuser March," familiar to nonopera folks, starting with trumpets, as people gather for the song tournament. Wolfram's song that opens the contest, "Blick' ich umher": "The sight of this noble circle makes my heart glow. So many valiant and wise German knights in this magnificent oak forest." A love duet between Elisabeth and Tannhäuser, before he gets into trouble defending carnal love.

Act III: The "Pilgrims' Chorus," sung by pilgrims as they pass a roadside shrine. Elisabeth's prayer to the Virgin that she may find peace in death and Wolfram's famous "Ode to the Evening Star" as he asks it to guide her soul, "O du mein holder Abendstern": "O you my lovely Evening Star, I have always welcomed you with pleasure. From the heart that has never betrayed her, greet her when she passes by you." More "Venusberg Music" and more of the "Tannhäuser March."

COMMENTARY

Although *The Flying Dutchman* is popular enough to be in The Collection, *Tannhäuser* is the first of Wagner's works to be a permanent part of international repertories.

This is a story of sacred versus profane love—or, most bluntly, pure love versus rank sex. Wagner said the sensual versus the spiritual. Initially, it wasn't much of a success, in part because it put more stress on the drama than Dresden audiences were accustomed to and had something less of the conventional distinction between the recitative and the arias—more distinction between them than any Wagner opera that came later but less than Dresden wanted. Audiences couldn't take those early suggestions of his continuous song-speech.

When it was introduced in Paris in 1861, Wagner added an opening ballet that now is known as the "Venusberg Music." For political reasons, upset that the unpopular Princess Pauline Metternich had negotiated the production, members of the fashionable Paris Jockey Club hooted, howled, and whistled during the opening performances, and it closed after three shows.

MET PERFORMANCES

Four hundred and fifty-four performances over sixty seasons, from 1884 to 1992.

RECORDING

CD—Decca/London 414 581-2 (3). Helga Dernesch, Christa Ludwig, René Kollo, Victor Braun, Hans Sotin. Vienna State Opera Chorus. Vienna Boys Choir. Vienna Philharmonic Orchestra. Georg Solti. 1971.

VIDEO

Cassilly, Marton, Troyanos, Weikl. Metropolitan Opera. German; English subtitles. Levine, conductor. 1982. PAR.

Number 22. *Parsifal*

Premiere, Bayreuth, 1882. Written 1857 to 1882. Text by Wagner, based on a medieval legend and a poem by Wolfram von Escherbach. Three acts.

KEYNOTE

Wagner's last music drama, presumably religious. We've had carnal love, deep romantic love, and passionate love. Now spiritual love and the holy relics of Christ. Meet the two Kundrys and the innocent fool.

PLOT

Spain, in the Middle Ages, in and near the Kingdom of the Grail. The Knights of the Holy Grail, including an old one named Gurnemanz (bass), live in a forest castle at Monsalvat. There they had guarded two holy relics: the spear that pierced Christ and the Cup—or Grail—from which He drank at the Last Supper, containing His blood shed at the cross. Their king, Amfortas (bass-baritone), son of former King Titurel (bass), is wounded and ill. He can be cured only if his wound is touched by the holy spear held by a man pure at heart—"an innocent fool, made wise by pity."

The audience learns that Amfortas earlier had tangled with an evil sorcerer name Klingsor (bass) and his band of beautiful maidens, whose mission was to seduce pure men. Amfortas succumbed to the charms of a particularly sexy enchantress named Kundry (soprano or mezzo-soprano). Their lovemaking gave Klingsor the opportunity to steal the sacred spear that Amfortas had set aside.

In Act I, an innocent youth named Parsifal (tenor) wanders from the forest to the Kingdom of the Grail, where he meets Gurnemanz, who takes him to the castle housing Amfortas and the other knights. Without participating or understanding, young Parsifal watches the unveiling of the Grail and the rite of communion. Hanging out around Monsalvat is Kundry, but here she appears as a wild maiden, unkempt and sullen, with a wholly different personality, who serves as friend and messenger of the knights.

The knights send Parsifal away—with just a late fleeting thought that he might be the innocent fool, made wise by pity, who can cure and redeem Amfortas.

Victor Von Halem, left, as Gurnemanz, Ruthild Engert-Ely as Kundry, and William Pell as Parsifal in Gian Carlo Menotti's staging of Parsifal at the Spoleto Festival in Charleston, SC

When Parsifal wanders into Klingsor's woods, he's tempted first by the seduction-minded lovelies and then by Kundry, now back in her role as a beautiful enchantress. In this realm she's the slave of Klingsor, under his evil power because of her own past sins. Her assignment is to seduce Parsifal, thus rendering him helpless. Like Jimmy Carter, he lusts in his heart, and she almost brings it off. They share a mighty kiss—the same kind of sensuous kiss that in the past did in Amfortas (and a raft of other Knights of the Grail). But Parsifal is of sterner stuff. He recoils from the kiss, recalls his mother, understands now what caused Amfortas to sin, feels compassion for him, becomes "wise through pity," and recognizes that he has a redemption mission to perform: Get possession of the spear, find his way back to the knights, and touch-and-heal Amfortas.

Kundry, unaccustomed to losing in these sex scenes, calls on her master, Klingsor, for help. Klingsor responds and throws the magic spear at Parsifal, but it is mysteriously suspended in midair over Parsifal's head. Seizing it, he makes the sign of the cross, Klingsor's realm disintegrates, and Kundry is freed.

After years of wandering (Kundry has cursed all paths back to Monsalvat), Parsifal returns to Grail country as a knight in black armor, carrying the sacred spear. It is Good Friday. At first the aging Gurnemanz chides the strange knight for being armed on this sacred ground, but he then recognizes both Parsifal and the spear. Redemption is near! The now good Kundry bathes Parsifal's feet and dries them with her hair. After Gurnemanz names him new king of the Holy Grail, Parsifal's first act is to forgive and baptize Kundry. They join wounded-and-weary Amfortas, who has been trying to die since before the opera began, urging the other knights to kill him. But when Parsifal touches Amfortas's wound with the sacred spear, the wound is healed instantly. As the knights pay homage to Parsifal, he holds up the Grail, and Kundry, now forgiven for her sins and at rest, dies peacefully.

HIGHLIGHTS

Listen for the leitmotifs: Parsifal, Kundry, Grail, Bell, Spear, Communion, and many more.

Prelude: A popular concert piece, which includes themes Wagner named "Love," "Faith," and "Hope?" (The question mark is Wagner's.) The music is meant to sound religious, and does.

Act I: The "Transformation Music," as the scene changes from the forest to the Grail castle.

Act II: The Flower Maiden chorus, as Parsifal is tempted.

Act III: The "Good Friday Music" (Good Friday Spell) after Parsifal, as the new King of the Grail, baptizes Kundry. This tone painting is another of Wagner's best-known themes. Hear all of the music from the baptism of Kundry through the end of the opera.

COMMENTARY

Wagner, who had a different word for everything, called this one a "festival stage play." Once again the central theme is suffering and redemption—not, this time, redemption through sacrifice and love, but redemption via the savior Parsifal. His knowledge and wisdom results from the pain he has felt for the suffering of others.

Symbolically, Parsifal presumably personifies Christianity, Klingsor paganism, and the opera the triumph of Christianity over paganism. (Wagner, not a Christian you'd want as a godfather to your children, either in lifestyle or tolerance, didn't permit his personal life to interfere with his art.) *Parsifal* is often performed at Easter; Wagner himself promoted it as a religious drama dealing with suffering, compassion, service, renunciation, and redemption. But musicologists remind us that Wagner essentially was a nonbeliever who felt true redemption comes only through art, not God.

Don't choose *Parsifal* for a light evening out. Unstudied and unseen, on audiotape it goes on everlastingly. Much of the music, however, is glorious, whatever the debates over the symbolism, the compassion, and the carnality. If one does a little advance homework, perhaps with a book that details the leading motifs, watching a videotape with subtitles can be a grand experience. And you can consider fast-forwarding your way through, savoring the orchestral music and risking the eternal consequences of this heresy.

And Kundry is one of opera's most fascinating characters. Hans Sachs from *Die Meistersinger* is another. It is fun to imagine the two of them on a blind date.

MET PERFORMANCES

Two hundred and seventy-five performances over sixty-seven seasons, from 1903 to 1995.

RECORDING

CD—Deutsche Grammophon 413 347-2 (4). Dunja Vejzovic, Peter Hofmann, José van Dam, Siegmund Nimsgern, Kurt Moll, Victor von Halem. Chorus of the Deutsche Oper, Berlin. Berlin Philharmonic Orchestra. Herbert von Karajan. 1979.

VIDEO

Jerusalem, Meier, Moll, Weikl, Mazura. Metropolitan Opera. German; English subtitles. Levine, conductor. 1992. DG.

The Ring operas

The Ring of the Nibelung
DAS RHEINGOLD
DIE WALKÜRE
SIEGFRIED
GÖTTERDÄMMERUNG

The *Ring* cycle is alone in opera . . . and, indeed, alone in art.

It has been called the "noblest and the hugest work ever attempted by the creative mind." One who agrees is musicologist Alfred Einstein, who said:

"His feat in welding into a unified whole this cosmic drama of the curse of might redeemed by love, as mirrored in the profound Germanic myth, remains one of the greatest achievements of the human intellect."

Some opera lovers find it a colossal bore, but that's the extreme view. Many other opera lovers, and many professional analysts, find it a blend of tedious and magnificent moments. The question is whether any given listener is prepared to excuse the one for the sake of the other.

George Bernard Shaw couldn't decide whether *Das Rheingold* was a profound allegory or a puerile fairy tale. He also said *The Ring* was not opera at all but dramatic prose heavily salted with orchestral music.

Wagner spent hundreds of thousands of words telling the world what he thought his *Ring* was about. According to him, it presents—in the simplest, most inclusive, and most concentrated form imaginable—the interplay of eternal forces affecting the relation of human beings to God, to nature, and to each other in society. It's the duty of art, Wagner argues, to concern itself consciously with the eternal issues of religious, social, and economic importance. Inasmuch as he considered himself the supreme artist, obviously he had no choice but to deal with them in a gargantuan way.

To explore this interplay, Wagner employs symbols. Sometimes they are objects: a hoard of gold at the bottom of the River Rhine, Valhalla (home of the gods), the gold ring, a sword called Nothung. Sometimes they are people or peoplelike: Wotan, King of the Gods; Brünnhilde, his favorite daughter; Siegfried, his hero/grandson.

Symbols, by definition, demand various interpretations. In *The Ring*, Wagner rarely conveys his thoughts clearly. It's uncertain whether this is because he was inconsistent in his thinking, ambiguous in his symbolism, overcome by his egomania, or just a rotten communicator.

But if you could instantly see the relationship between symbols and meaning, there would be no point in employing symbols. And although Wagner was a terrible communicator as a prose writer, he was a something else as a musician. The analysts who most admire him point out that the very ambiguity of his symbolism, coupled with the sense (created largely through his music) that they deal with something absolutely basic, is essential to his work's power.

Dozens of books deal with the *Ring* meanings. A common thread is this one: Siegfried—hero of the cycle—was a shining champion inspired by the European revolutions of 1848. He was too big and too good for the existing world. His fate was to be murdered by the forces of evil. The Nibelungs, who lived deep in the earth, were the proletariat. Two earth-living giants who worked in the clouds were the exploiting class. The ring symbolized the rule of money, the false philosophy of getting and spending . . . and the ultimate destruction of life.

You may think that these are just operas, that they're not the Ten Commandments or the Bill of Rights, and that Wagner was just a fellow who made music and neither Moses nor Thomas Jefferson. Not at all.

If you see a *Ring* opera at a major opera house, freeze in place once you've sat down. To rustle a program, or to cough, can lead to serious bodily harm. This is a no-nonsense cult. There's nothing else like it in opera.

With *The Ring*, as with all of his operas, Wagner wrote both the librettos and the music. The four operas first were shown on an individual basis in 1869, 1870, and August 16 and 17, 1876. The full cycle, sometimes called a tetralogy (Wagner viewed them as three plus a prelude), was performed for the first time at Wagner's special theater in Bayreuth, Germany, on August 13, 14, 16, and 17 in 1876. As he planned it, they constituted a festival that takes three performance days and the prelude on the preceding evening—and his initial concept was that they only be performed as a foursome. From the outset, they have been attacked, defended, ridiculed, praised, condemned, and glorified.

One reason for the repetition in them is that they were created in a convoluted way. The basic stories are from two separate German myth cycles—one about Siegfried and one about the downfall of the gods. Both were based on Scandinavian myths. There is confusion from the outset because Wagner was an inept storyteller. Further, he wrote the four texts in reverse order, before composing music for any of them, discovering after completing each libretto that it needed an earlier one to explain more fully what had taken place previously.

Although the music was composed in the right sequence, the whole project took twenty-seven years, during which time he veered away long enough to turn out both *Tristan und Isolde* and *Die Meistersinger*.

By general agreement, the cycle is unique, intriguing, baffling, and staggering. One of Wagner's stated objectives was to marry the music of Beethoven and the drama of Shakespeare. Nothing wrong with that objective, but perhaps impossible to achieve with balance even by a German master with a forbidding ego.

The operas take place on three physical levels—deep within the earth, on the earth's surface, and up in the clouds, where the gods live. These represent three levels of society. The title comes from an actual finger ring, fashioned from a lump of stolen gold. Whoever wears the ring gains unlimited power to rule the universe. But to wield this power, the possessor must renounce love, once and for all. During the four operas we learn about how the ring affects the lives of all who come in contact with it and its magic force.

So what does the nonexpert do about *The Ring of the Nibelung?* Here are several options:

1. The Spineless Option. Simply ignore it, making believe it doesn't exist. An ignominious choice, not worthy of us.

2. The Easy Option. Listen to recorded orchestral excerpts from all four works. Don't worry about singing, plot, or meaning. This is a sure winner, as far as it goes.

3. The Flawed Option. With no advance preparation, attend a *Ring* opera or watch a videotape. Even with subtitles, far too much is here to absorb. Forget it.

4. The Leitmotif Detective Option. Buy or borrow any one of several books on Wagner that discuss leitmotifs in detail. Leitmotif investigators have found up to 140 in *The Ring,* running into one another, linked to current stage action, looking back to past action, or anticipating the future. In the one-act *Rheingold* alone, *Kobbé* identifies just a few of the leading motifs: The Rhine, the Rhinedaughters, the Nibelungs' Servitude, the Rhine Gold, the Renunciation of Love, the Valhalla, the Spear, Freia (Goddess of Youth and Beauty), her sister Fricka, Loge (Spirit of Fire), the Compact, the Giant, Eternal Youth, the Nibelungs' Hate, the Sword, the Rainbow—and various combinations thereof. This is a splendid option if you are retired and do little except go to the barbershop, to the bathroom, and to the yard to watch the grass grow.

5. The Sermon Option. Read the libretto in full. Wagner is a preacher—an amoral preacher, in real life, but nonetheless a Man with Social and Philosophical messages. The shortest summary of *The Ring* is this: "Go for Love, not for Money." But there's much more in the libretto, straight from Wagner—if you like sermons or if puzzles amuse you. Wagner's moralizing disturbs many within the arts who believe "intentional" preaching is unimportant to art, or downright inartistic, or an intolerable artistic objective. That debate is beyond the scope of this road map.

6. The Couch Option. Join the analysts who concern themselves with what Wagner "really is saying" with his symbolism. One set of examples from the couch people: The forest is associated with Unconsciousness, the horn with Impulse toward Consciousness, the Dwarf with Obstacle to Psychological Growth, the Sword with the Assimilation of Mother and Father, the Ring with the Forces of the Psyche, the bird both with Mother and with the Eternal Feminine, the two ravens with Reason and Memory, Fire with Man's Consciousness of Knowledge and What Love Can Bring Him, and the three norms with Mother-Wife-Daughter. Nothing wrong with this option if you are a little nutty anyhow.

7. The Little Engine That Could Option. Do solid homework in advance. Read and study plot summaries. Draw some family trees. Identify the characters. Treat it all as a good adventure story: *Indiana Jones Meets the Rhine Maidens and Sees Valhalla.* You get love, hate, murder, magic, mystery, treachery, and

sex. Then borrow videotapes, with subtitles. Buy some orchestral cassettes for the car radio. Keep saying to yourself: "I think I can . . . I think I can . . . I think I can."

In conclusion:

In one way or another, sample *The Ring* if only for the experience. I find it like watching an exquisite Hawaiian sunset while having a root canal.

Good luck. Don't forget your compass and your canteen.

Number 43. *Das Rheingold*

Premiere at the Munich Opera, 1869. A one-act prologue to the three other operas that make up the Ring *cycle. Libretto completed, 1853; music completed, 1854. Though production times vary, the one act takes 141 minutes.*

KEYNOTE

How it all begins. Swimming Rhinemaiden lovelies mock the vile Alberich and live to regret it when he steals their gold. Meet the greedy giants, Fafner and Fasolt, conned by a deal-breaking chief of gods.

PLOT

Legendary time. The bed of the Rhine, a mountainous area near the Rhine, the subterranean caverns of Nibelheim. A hoard of gold, called the Rhine gold, is hidden beneath the waters of the river, guarded by three swimming Rhinemaidens (two sopranos and a mezzo-soprano). A cunning treacherous gnome called Alberich (bass-baritone), a Nibelung, learns while trying to paw them that whoever forges the gold into a ring will have unlimited power to rule the world—but only if he gives up love for the rest of his life. Frustrated by his unsuccessful flirtation with the maidens, unable to find love elsewhere, mocked by all women, Alberich makes off with the gold and the Rhinemaidens bewail their loss.

Above the earth in the skies (the text says mountaintop) where the undying gods live, Wotan (bass-baritone), the chief of the gods, and his wife, Fricka (mezzo-soprano), are having a palace built for them by two brother giants named Fasolt (bass-baritone) and Fafner (bass). Wotan is reminded by Fricka that he has promised the giants that their payment will be her sister Freia (soprano), goddess of youth and beauty, who also supplies the golden apples that give the gods their immortality. Wotan tells Fricka he was only jesting (although in fact it was a solemn contract), and when the giants come for their payment he persuades them to accept instead all of the Rhine gold possessed by the now all-powerful Alberich. Now it's up to Wotan to make good. He and the cunning Loge (tenor), Spirit of Fire who assists the gods, descend into Nibelheim where, through trickery, they take from Alberich both the gold and the ring. (Alberich's brother, Mime [tenor], has created the Tarnhelm, a magic helmet that permits its wearer to assume any form he chooses. Remember it; it will return.) In response Alberich curses the ring, vowing that death and destruction will come to all who wear it—indeed, to all who even touch it, as Wotan has. Back in the heavens, Erda (contralto), the earth goddess, rises to warn Wotan to surrender the ring, and, also, he's been so bugged by Fricka to save Freia that he gives both the ring and the gold to the giants as their payment. The curse begins to work as the giants fight among themselves. Fafner kills Fasolt. The gods then enter Valhalla, their new palace, while far below the Rhinemaidens cry out to Wotan to return the gold to them.

HIGHLIGHTS

The Prelude: Regarded as one of opera's most original and descriptive overtures. Analysts point out that it's all based on a single chord.

Act I: The orchestral piece, the "Entry of the Gods into Valhalla." But that isn't enough. On a compact disc, listen to the entire first scene and then the last twenty minutes or so of the final scene.

COMMENTARY

Recall that there are several orders of Wagner's universe. In this opera, three of those orders are involved: dwarf, immortal gods, and giants. All three do evil—Alberich steals the gold, Wotan steals the ring and the gold, and one giant kills his brother. So all three orders now have sought the ring and its power, thus renouncing love. A fourth order of Wagner's universe, a free hero, potentially superior to all, is coming later. And there will be a fifth order consisting of a few common folk, who really don't count.

Like the other *Ring* operas, the orchestra is the leading character, the protagonist. And the fine music starts at the beginning. As Professor Paul Henry Lang notes, the audience feels from the first moments that the Rhine is flowing right into the auditorium.

MET PERFORMANCES

One hundred and thirty-seven performances over forty-three seasons, from 1889 to 1993. Four performances are scheduled for the 1996–97 season.

RECORDINGS

CD—Decca/London 414 101-2 (3). Kirsten Flagstad, Jean Madeira, Set Svanholm, Paul Kuen, George London, Gustav Neidlinger, Walter Kreppel, Kurt Böhme. Vienna Philharmonic Orchestra. Georg Solti. 1958.

or

—Deutsche Grammophon 415 141-2 (3). Josephine Veasey, Oralia Dominguez, Gerhard Stolze, Erwin Wohlfahrt, Dietrich Fishcher-Dieskau, Zoltán Kelemen, Martti Talvela, Karl Ridderbusch. Berlin Philharmonic Orchestra. Herbert von Karajan. 1967.

Lilli Lehmann as Brünnhilde in Die Walküre

Number 13. *Die Walküre*

Premiere at the Munich Opera, 1870. Libretto completed, 1852, music completed, 1856. Act I is 61 minutes, Act II, 87, and Act III, 72.

KEYNOTE

The incestuous love of the Wälsung twins, a.k.a. Siegmund and Sieglinde. He's the mortal not bound by the god's pacts, free of his soul, his own man, and the potential savior of all—but that's before his father breaks his magic sword called Nothung. She's the pregnant lady carrying the real hero.

PLOT

Legendary time. In a long monologue in Act II we learn that Wotan has come to earth with the objective of fathering a hero who will be able to recover the ring from the giant Fafner. Fafner has transformed himself into a fire-breathing dragon to protect the ring. On earth, operating under the name of Wälse, Wotan has lived with a human wife and fathered the Wälsung twins, Siegmund (tenor) and Sieglinde (soprano). They became separated early in life and, against her will, Sieglinde has been married to a forester named Hunding (bass).

As the opera opens, Siegmund—wounded and exhausted—arrives in a violent storm at the forest hut in which Sieglinde and Hunding live. Not knowing they're brother and sister, Sieglinde and Siegmund fall in love. Sieglinde slips Hunding a Mickey to knock him out, and after he goes to bed she tells Siegmund about a one-eyed stranger (Wotan) who thrust a sword into the tree that is growing in the living room of the hut, and advised that it would belong to the man who could remove it. After Siegmund pulls out the sword, he and Sieglinde exchange life stories, and she recognizes him as her brother. But that doesn't cool their passion for one another; indeed, they celebrate it in the orgiastic postlude to Act I. The incestuous nature of their relationship is sort of passed over. Indeed, throughout *The Ring* there's a good bit of fornication that's taken casually by just about everyone except Fricka. The two leave the hut and go off into the forest together.

Hunding later follows them into the mountains, where a fight is inevitable. Wotan (optimistically and mistakenly) sees Siegmund as the hero who will kill the giant, return the ring to the Nibelungs, and eventually save the world. Although Wotan desperately wants to use his god powers to help Siegmund, Fricka, who is not only Queen of the gods but also the goddess who protects marriage vows, talks him out of it—not because of the incest but because Sieglinde is cheating on her husband. If the twins aren't punished she, as guardian of the marriage vows, will be the laughingstock of mankind. In fact, she's teed off to begin with that Wotan had gone galivanting down to earth and fathered the twins. Not only must Wotan not protect Siegmund, he must render the sword powerless so that his son has no chance.

Wotan's favorite daughter is Brünnhilde (soprano), who has eight Valkyrie sisters. It is she who dashes about the stage with the music of the "Ride of the Valkyries" and the "Shout of the Valkyries," "Ho-jo-to-ho." Before Fricka intervened, she was set, joyously, to ride to earth to help Siegmund—a half brother—against Hunding. Yielding to his wife, Wotan commands her to stay out of it, but Brünnhilde ignores him and rides down to protect Siegmund. This disobedience infuriates Wotan, who puts his mighty spear between the two fighters so that Siegmund's sword is shattered on it. Hunding kills Siegmund and Wotan then knocks off Hunding with a wave of his hand.

By this time Sieglinde is pregnant with her twin brother's child, who will be called Seigfried. Brünnhilde shelters her until she dies in childbirth. This further interference from Brünnhilde makes Wotan even angrier, and he banishes her from Valhalla forever. But since she is his favorite and adored daughter, he also protects her by letting her sleep within a ring of fire, decreeing that she will be awakened by and become the bride of whoever can come through the fire ring to awaken her. Wotan has not had a good day. He now has helped kill his son, lost his mortal daughter in childbirth, banished and made mortal his favorite goddess daughter, and still not coped with Alberich's curse. But he does have a grandson named Siegfried, important to the future of the world.

HIGHLIGHTS

Act I: The love music of Siegmund and Sieglinde, his "Stürme" music, "Winterstürme wichen dem Wonnemond" ("Winter storms have waned"), and her reply ("Du bist der Lenz") that he is the spring. More generally, the whole first half of the act. One pro-Wagner analyst describes it as "the most astounding continuous outpouring of lyrical melody in the entire *Ring* cycle."

Act II: The battle cry of Brünnhilde: "Ho-jo-to-ho!" summoning the Valkyries (the nine daughters of Wotan and Erda) to help Siegmund. But steer clear of Wotan's story-to-date narration that takes up much of the act.

Act III: "The Ride of the Valkyries," Wotan's "Farewell," and the "Magic Fire Music." More generally, the entire act, especially the first ten minutes or so and the last twenty.

COMMENTARY

Wotan wants a hero who will represent a fourth and new order of humanity. Only when the ring is returned to the Rhinemaidens will the power of evil in the world be broken. Wotan is attempting to bring about this New World Order but is hampered by the existing rules, regulations, and conventions that were created for an earlier time, including Fricka's feelings on marital fidelity.

Few successful operas need editing more, and Wotan does go on and on. But, again, the orchestral music is glorious, and there are more melodious vocal passages than one is supposed to find in Wagner's music drama. Some of the analysts say the "Ride of the Valkyries" is corny, but that's because they're too Washed. We nonprofessionals, or at least some of us, think it's stirring.

Leitmotif detectives find scads of themes throughout. Many are identified in *Kobbé's Complete Opera Book*, which you should have on your bookshelf in any case. But you don't have to try to track them to enjoy the opera. My own opinion, about all of *The Ring*, is that it's essential to know the storyline in some detail if you want to experience the drama. Then leave the symbolism and the leitmotifs to the analysts, practice stretching in place if in an auditorium, or just walk around the room now and then if you're home with the VCR.

MET PERFORMANCES

Four hundred and eighty-one performances over seventy-six seasons, from 1885 to 1996. Five performances are scheduled for the 1996–97 season.

RECORDING

CD—Continuing the Solti cycle: Decca/London 414 105-2 (4). Birgit Nilsson, Regine Crespin, Christa Ludwig, James King, Hans Hotter, Gottlob Frick. Vienna Philharmonic Orchestra. 1966.

Number 24. *Siegfried*

Premiere at Bayreuth, 1876. Libretto completed 1851; music completed, 1857. Plan on four hours and fifteen minutes.

KEYNOTE

Meet the youth hero. See and hear Wagner walking in place. If you didn't like vile Alberich, try slimy brother Mime. Dragon's blood and bird talk. Wotan exits from *The Ring* and Siegfried finds Brünnhilde.

PLOT

Legendary time. By the beginning of the opera, Sieglinde has died while giving birth to Siegfried (tenor), now a young man who has grown up in the forest under the care of a dwarf named Mime, the crummy, cunning brother of the crummy, sneaky Alberich. Wanting the ring for himself, Mime knows the only way to get it is for Siegfried to slay the dragon, who used to be the giant Fafner. With the dragon dead and the ring in his possession, Mime would kill Siegfried, rule over the gods in Valhalla, and defeat Alberich's plans for a comeback.

Mime is a particularly unattractive fellow, and young Siegfried is unimpressed by his claim that Siegfried owes him a debt for having been both mother and father to him. Wotan, disguised as a Wanderer, is drifting around the forest keeping his one eye on things, hoping that Siegfried will free the gods from Alberich's curse. As the Wanderer, he advises Mime that the only way to get a dragon-killing sword is to forge together the two broken pieces of Siegmund's weapon—and that this can be done only by a man who is without fear—to wit, young Siegfried.

Siegfried does forge the sword, goes to the forest where the dragon guards the gold (with Alberich lurking outside the dragon's cave), and kills the dragon. Licking the dragon's blood from his finger enables him to understand bird talk. The Forest Bird tells him about the powers of the ring and advises him that the hoard now belongs to him. The dragon's blood also allows him to recognize that Mime will try to poison him. When Mime appears carrying a cup filled with poison, Siegfried handles this possible danger forthrightly by cutting off the little sneak's head.

Further advised by the Forest Bird, he then sets off to find Brünnhilde in her ring of fire. En route he encounters the Wanderer, Wotan, his grandfather, and in a confrontation Siegfried cuts the god chief's spear in two. His authority gone, the commander in chief of the gods leaves the *Ring* operas forever.

Knowing no fear, Siegfried zaps through the fire, kisses Brünnhilde, removes her breastplate, learns that men and women are different, and claims her as his bride. She awakens, and they sing a passionate love song, even though she realizes this relationship will cost her her Valkyrie independence. They are blind to the destruction of the world and the death of the gods.

HIGHLIGHTS

Act I: For vocal music, the "Forging Scene," in which Siegfried forges the sword and splits the anvil with it. Listen for the theme for Nothung, the sword. It doesn't go away.

Act II: "Forest Murmurs," the only frequently recorded orchestral piece from *Siegfried*, heard as he lies down under the trees, listens to birds, and tries to talk with them.

Act III: The love—and fate—duet between Brünnhilde and Siegfried at the end of the opera. (Wagner's chamber orchestral piece, the "Siegfreid Idyll," was developed from much of this material.)

COMMENTARY

Wagner regarded Siegfried as the new man in his natural state, untainted and uncorrupted by society. Scholars say Wagner believed that the common man was capable—if given the chance—of fashioning a better world. He didn't believe that the world would improve through better governments (liberal Democrats take note) but rather through perfection of the individual. Siegfried is an example of one such more evolved individual.

No one in a hurry should mess with Wagner, but if you are pressed for time try fast-forwarding through Act I. Don't, however, miss Act III.

It took Wagner fifteen years to compose *Siegfried*. Analysts find differences in the musical structure between the first two acts and the third, but we non-professionals have trouble identifying them. What we can recognize is the taxing tenor role of *Siegfried*, who must be onstage most of four hours—and then undertake the long last duet.

Several characters who were in *Das Rheingold* but not in *Die Walküre* appear in *Siegfried*, among them the Nibelungs, Alberich and Mime, and Fafner, although here he's in the form of a dragon instead of a giant.

MET PERFORMANCES

Two hundred and forty-three performances over fifty-nine seasons, from 1887 to 1993. Three performances are scheduled for the 1996–97 season.

RECORDINGS

CD—One option is to stay with Solti. Decca/London 414 110-2 (4). Birgit Nilsson, Marga Höffgen, Wolfgang Windgassen, Gerhard Stolze, Hans Hotter, Gustav Neidlinger. Vienna Philharmonic Orchestra. 1962.

or

—Philips Dig. 434 423-2 (3). Gwyneth Jones, Ortrun Wenkel, Manfred Jung, Heinz Zednik, Donald McIntyre, Hermann Becht. Bayreuth Festival Orchestra. Pierre Boulez. 1980.

Number 26. *Götterdämmerung (Twilight of the Gods)*

Premiere at Bayreuth, 1876. Libretto completed, 1845; music completed, 1874. The Prologue is 40 minutes: Act I, 74; Act II, 65; and Act III, 85.

KEYNOTE

An orchestral "Rhine Journey." Crossed identities and the confusing magic of a magic helmet. Assassination. A hall collapses, the Rhine overflows, death by drowning, Valhalla burns, suicide by fire . . . and the return of the ring. Take deep breaths.

Long-term Project

The *New Grove Dictionary of Opera* informs us that the first draft of the opera that was to become *Götterdämmerng* is dated October 20, 1848, and that the full score was completed on November 21, 1874— a period of more than twenty-six years.

PLOT

Legendary time. In the Prologue the three Norns—Norse Fates—are outside the cave in which Siegfried and Brünnhilde sleep, spinning the golden rope of Fate. It snaps, suggesting that Fate's final catastrophe is near, and the Norns sink into the earth. Siegfried will have to control his own destiny without them. At dawn, Siegfried gives Brünnhilde the ring, borrows her horse Grane, and rides out in search of more action.

After a seven-minute orchestral interlude, called the "Rhine Journey," Act I opens in the hall of the Gibichungs, where Gunther (baritone) and his sister, Gutrune (soprano), live. Hagen (bass), their half brother, and the son of the miserable little Alberich, laments that neither Gunther nor Gutrune is married. No less treacherous than his father, Hagen suggests Siegfried as a good spouse for Gutrune and Brünnhilde as the right woman for Gunther. He hopes in time to get the all-powerful ring that Brünnhilde now wears.

The weak-willed Gunther is willing, and when Siegfried arrives in town Hagen prepares a potion that will cause him not only to lose his memory but

Edouard de Reszke as Hagen in Götterdämmerung

also to fall in love with the first woman he sees. Siegfried drinks it, forgets his past, sees Gutrune, lusts for her, and obeys Hagen's instructions to go fetch Brünnhilde for Gunther.

Meanwhile, Waltraute (mezzo-soprano), a sister Valkyrie, is trying to persuade Brünnhilde that she must give the ring back to the Rhinemaidens where it belongs, thus getting rid of the curse and thereby saving the gods—and, indeed, the world. But Brünnhilde refuses, as (a) the ring now symbolizes her love for Siegfried and (b) she now doesn't seem to care all that much about the fate of her beloved father, Wotan. Siegfried arrives to execute his assignment of bringing Brünnhilde back. But he's wearing the magic helmet, Tarnhelm, which makes him look like Gunther. He tears the ring from Brünnhilde's finger and puts it on his own.

Back in the hall of the Gibichungs, Siegfried, now as himself but still without a memory and still with the hots for Gutrune, has no idea what he has done and doesn't recognize Brünnhilde. But she knows him, sees on his finger the ring taken by Siegfried-as-Gunther, senses that she is the victim of treachery, blames Siegfried (who has drifted off with his arm around Gutrune), and vows vengeance. She plots with Hagen to kill Siegfried while he is hunting the next day. They will tell others a wild boar did him in. "Let his death atone for the shame he has wrought me," she declares. "So be it."

At the hunt, Siegfried drinks an herb that counteracts the love potion so that he remembers Brünnhilde. He tells his own real life story, which Gunther, no party to the treachery, hears for the first time. As Siegfried sings, Hagen mortally wounds him by jabbing a spear into his back. Siegfried dies, but not until he recalls his meeting with Brünnhilde in a touching death song. Later, the two half brothers fight and Hagen commits his second murder by killing Gunther.

Back in the hall, a remorseful Brünnhilde finally straightens out what has happened and orders a funeral pyre for Siegfried. She lights the fire, seizes the ring, mounts her horse, and plunges into the flames to join Siegfried in death. The hall collapses, the Rhine overflows, and Valhalla burns. Rhinemaidens appear, in their element. Two draw Hagen down into the flooding river while the third holds up the ring they have taken from Siegfried's finger.

HIGHLIGHTS

Prologue: Wonderful orchestral music in the second part, including Siegfried's "Rhine Journey," which leads into Act I.

Act II: Hear the motifs, including the Ring, the Curse, Vengeance, Valhalla, Brünnhilde's Pleading, Murder, Hagen, and perhaps Babe Ruth. My favorite Wagnerian scholar gets upset by this irreverent approach, calling Act II difficult and dense but probably the most concentrated and intense act of music drama that Wagner ever wrote.

Act III: Siegfried's "Funeral March" as his body is carried off on his shield. Also Brünnhilde's long final solo ("Immolation Scene") as she seizes the ring, throws a flame into the funeral pyre, and rides her horse directly into it.

And, as *The Ring* finally ends, the soft orchestral sounds of the theme of Redemption by Love. We can rest easily; the whole world will now have a rebirth.

COMMENTARY

Notwithstanding the countless interpretations of *The Ring*, some things are reasonably clear. One is that the sordid time of the gods has gone. Another is that love is a good thing and that a new era of love has dawned that will make possible a new beginning for the world. As in both *The Flying Dutchman* and *Tannhäuser*, redemption comes through the love of a woman.

If you will, the whole thing is a morality play—heroism and fortitude are good; treachery and falsehood are bad. There must be a new mankind, one not controlled by malice, greed, envy, spite, spleen, rivalry, jealousy, covetousness, gluttony, and avarice. Man must search harder for the understanding of himself. Ecologists take heart: Natural resources are valuable.

Musically, like the other music dramas, the formal aria is gone, replaced by the continuing line of song that is half recitative and half miniaria. Like all Wagner operas, the music controls the drama.

Although the time of the action is immediately after *Siegfried*, the cast of characters and scenery are very different. *Siegfried* took place in a cave in the forest, in the forest itself, and at Brünnhilde's rock. *Götterdämmerung* has two scenes at Brünnhilde's rock and one in a forest on the Rhine, but much of the action is in the giant Hall of the Gibichungs. And there are three new and important characters in the Gibichungs' castle who have not been in any of the first three operas—Gunther, Gutrune, and Hagen.

Brünnhilde is the key role for great Wagnerian heroic sopranos. Among the most famous have been Lilli Lehmann, Olive Fremstad, Frida Leider, Kirsten Flagstad, Birgit Nilsson, Martha Mödl, Astrid Varnay, and Gwyneth Jones. Leading Wagnerian heroic tenors include Erik Schmedes, Lauritz Melchior, Jon Vickers, Wolfgang Windgassen, Ramon Vinay, Max Lorenz, Set Svanholm, and Jess Thomas.

MET PERFORMANCES

Two hundred and twelve performances over fifty-seven seasons, from 1888 to 1993. Three performances are scheduled for the 1996–97 season.

RECORDING

CD—The recommended Solti cycle continues with Decca/London 414 115-2 (4). Birgit Nilsson, Claire Watson, Christa Ludwig, Wolfgang Windgassen, Dietrich Fischer-Dieskau, Gustave Neidlinger, Gottlob Frick. Vienna State Opera Chorus. Vienna Philharmonic Orchestra. Georg Solti. 1964.

or

—The Ring. Shortcut. "Great scenes" from the Solti cycle. Decca/London 421 313-2. Birgit Nilsson, Wolfgang Windgassen, Hans Hotter, Gerhard Stolze. Vienna Philharmonic Orchestra. *Das Rheingold:* "Entry of the Gods into Valhalla." *Die Walküre:* "Ride of the Valkyries" and "Magic Fire Music." *Siegfried:* "Forging Scene" and "Forest Murmurs." *Götterdämmerung:* Siegfried's "Funeral March" and Brünnhilde's "Immolation Scene."

VIDEOS

Metropolitan Opera. German; English subtitles. Levine conductor. 1990. PGD. All available separately. A "neutral" rendition. *Die Walküre* cast includes Behrens, Norman, Ludwig, Lakes, Morris.

or

Bayreuth Festspielhaus. German; English subtitles. Boulez, conductor. 1980. PGD. All available separately. A more adventurous rendition. *Die Walküre* cast includes Jones, Altmeyer, Hofmann.

∾

One Warhorse by Pietro Mascagni

December 7, 1863 — August 2, 1945

CAVALLERIA RUSTICANA *(Number 11)*

Pietro Mascagni was regarded as an "inconsiderable" traveling opera conductor, giving him few career Brownie points there.

Later, in the 1930s and 1940s, he was a mouthpiece for Benito Mussolini and the Fascist thugs, earning him no Brownie points of any kind there.

Only one of his seventeen operas and operettas was a big success, which doesn't say a whole lot for him compared with many of the composers with whom we're dealing. He had to win a publisher's all-comers-welcome competition even to get that work performed.

An opera specialist, he left behind no instrumental music of enduring substance.

Faulty Forecast

Hugo Wolf (1860–1903), Austrian composer, referred to the popularity of Mascagni and others in 1895 as he predicted success for his own new opera, *Der Corregidor:* "People will no longer talk about anything but this opera. All of them, Mascagni, Humperdinck, 'e tutti quanti,' will be unable to compete and will fade away." But a year later it was *Der Corregidor* that had disappeared. Tragically, composer Wolf went mad, with delusions that he had been named director of the Vienna Staatsopor.

Most descriptions of his one famous opera include the words "natural," "theatrical," and "brutal," words that might be used to describe a good three-ring circus with a sadistic lion tamer.

One leading critic has written that the music of that big success is sometimes not original, sometimes commonplace, and sometimes coarse. Another has spoken of "a wealth of powerful, vulgar melody." By general agreement, that work is "musically insignificant" compared with Bizet's *Carmen*, after which it was modeled.

But the one-act *Cavalleria rusticana*—a story of seduction, adultery, Sicilian ear biting, and revengeful murder by stiletto—has been a sensational smash hit from its first performance in 1890. And if some of the music is judged commonplace, some also is judged supremely melodious. In any event, the work is Number 11 in The Collection, a Warhorse, one of the most popular of all operas.

The verists, who dominated opera's 1890s, wanted realism but also concentrated on the seamy side of life. Firefighter heroism is just as realistic as serial murder, but the verists chose the mirror's ugly reflection rather than its beautiful one. Definitions of verismo opera vary among the musicologists, but in essence:

- The times are today, not those of antiquity or history.
- By definition, then, the characters are dressed in contemporary clothing.
- The people are ordinary working people—not gods, kings, princes, and nobles, nor even today's wealthy. Verdi's *La traviata*, for example, deals with contemporary people, but they are sophisticated Parisian courtesans and fast-track socialites. Verismo deals with Joe and June Six-Pack.
- Mostly, they are people who must save their lire to buy that six-pack—men and women on, or over, the edge of poverty. Most would qualify for food stamps.

Mascagni is one of two grade A verists in The Collection; the other we have just met in Ruggerio Leoncavallo and his *Pagliacci*. A third in the same school, a little less successful, is another Italian, Umberto Giordano, with *Andrea Chénier*, and a fourth, if the borders are widened a little, the French Gustave Charpentier with *Louise*. It's interesting that among these four each had only one opera that really stuck. Puccini, once a roommate of Mascagni's at the Milan Conservatory, is a part-time verist (especially in his one-act *Il tabarro*). *Tosca* has many of the elements. *La Bohème* qualifies on some grounds but not on others since it lacks brutality, violence, revenge, and murder.

In verismo, more than in many operas, the plot is a primary element. Musically, the professionals assess Mascagni's work as conventional, pushing no boundaries, not extreme, daring, or revolutionary. That doesn't mean individual numbers aren't tuneful and lovely.

Both of the two most important verists, Mascagni and Leoncavallo, were influenced by Bizet's *Carmen*. But experts such as Paul Henry Lang point out that they were too noisy and overemphatic to grasp the finesse of the Frenchman's realism, adding "Their lovers have no tender words for each other; they break into frenzy, slashing, biting, killing. Without wishing to argue that the world is all sweetness and light, one wonders why realism should be so peculiarly unpleasant."

As a movement, verismo did not last long. Though individual operas survived, the movement appeared, dominated, and died, all in the 1890s. A reaction against it set in. Critics then, and musicologists now, agree that it was too undisciplined, that it substituted instinct for the soul, that it denied freedom of the will.

There is an Ed Sullivan/Major Bowes/Ed McMahon star-search story to Mascagni. He was born in Livorno, Italy, in 1863, the son of a baker. Like many fathers, the senior Mascagni wanted his son to become a lawyer, although the world has learned since that a good baker makes a more significant contribution to society than a good lawyer. Young Pietro had to study music on the sly, but in time a friendly uncle stepped in to support his musical ambitions. While studying, he wrote a little symphony, a cantata for solo voices, and some other pieces, enough to cause a wealthy aristocrat to pay for further education at the conservatory in Milan, which he entered at nineteen. But the discipline there was a little strong for him and he left to be the conductor—the "inconsiderable conductor"—of an inconsiderable traveling opera company. (Judgments are harsh at this level. What wonderful fun it would be to have the training and skill to conduct an inconsiderable opera company!)

Trivial Pursuit Question

What do Alfred Dreyfus, Henri Meilhac, Ludovic Halévy, and a woman named Santuzza have in common?

Answer: Verismo.

Alfred Dreyfus was a French army officer convicted of treason. His most vigorous defender was novelist Emile Zola, founder of the French literary school of naturalism, whose works deal with the brutality associated with poverty. Zola's approach influenced French music. The first successful naturalistic-like opera was Bizet's *Carmen*. Its librettists were Henry Meilhac and Ludovic Halévy. Italians picked up the naturalism approach and called it "verismo." *Cavalleria rusticana* was Italy's first verismo opera. Santuzza is its heroine.

For several years he lived almost a carnival-like life, making barely enough to live on, constantly on the move, and definitely in musical obscurity. He married, settled in the little town of Cerignola, and eked out a living teaching the piano and managing the small municipal music school.

Not much of a beginning for a Superstar composer. Soon he was twenty-seven years old and far from the fast track. Then a music publisher named San-zogno sponsored an opera-writing competition. Almost everybody plays the lottery, so what's to lose? Mascagni wrote and submitted his little one-act entry, *Cavalleria rusticana*. It won the competition and, as a result, was produced in Rome on May 17. The unknown Pietro Mascagni took twenty curtain calls. On May 18 he was a famous artist, called by critics the successor to Verdi (then nearing eighty). Nowhere in music is there more of an overnight success story. The opera spread rapidly through Italy, made Berlin the same year, London at the Shaftesbury Theatre in 1891, and Paris at the Opéra-Comique in 1892. It opened in Philadelphia on September 9, 1891, in Chicago by another company, September 30, in New York by two different companies on October 1, and at the Metropolitan on December 30.

Scared Composer

For much of his career Verdi wanted to make an opera of Shakespeare's *King Lear*. After *Falstaff*, it was rumored that he and librettist Boito would work together on that project. But when Verdi was eighty-three he offered a synopsis he had drafted to the young Mascagni.

Why, asked Mascagni, had Verdi never undertaken it himself? Verdi replied: "The scene in which King Lear finds himself on the heath terrified me."

Mascagni was made Knight of the Crown of Italy and an honorary citizen of the town of Cerignola. He was a national idol, a composer so admired that his next opera, *L'amico Fritz*, was produced simultaneously by opera companies in seven different cities.

And it was soundly hissed in five of them: Milan, Verona, Venice, Naples, and Turin. The sixth was worse; in Genoa the audience wouldn't allow the performance to be completed. Only Rome, where it had its premiere, accepted it.

Mascagni had peaked with his first effort. Later operas fared better than the second, but nothing came close to the top. The music Bible, *Grove's Dictionary of Music and Musicians*, summarizes his life this way: "Mascagni's reputation rests almost entirely upon *Cavalleria rusticana*. It owes much to its direct if somewhat brutal libretto, but the music undeniably shows a natural instinct for theatrical effect, and it boasts plenty of catchy, commonplace tunes. The speedy exhaustion of a shallow vein of musical invention, together with the carelessness engendered by a dangerously sudden success, is in great part responsible for the complete collapse of what at one time seemed a talent of bright promise."

Two years after *Cavalleria rusticana*, Leoncavallo wrote its twin, *Pagliacci*, another one-act work. Almost since the start the two have been performed together—not *a* double bill, but *the* double bill. They are spoken of in the music community as *Cav-Pag*, or the *Cav-Pag*, as if you were to say "Abb-Cos" or "Rodg-Ham."

Mascagni composed other operas between 1891 and 1921 and then a pro-Mussolini worked called *Nerone* in 1935. In the Mussolini years, he also wrote choral and orchestra works for other Fascist ceremonial occasions. Many Italian musicians turned their backs on him, including Arturo Toscanini, Italy's world-famous conductor, who had conducted *Cav* earlier. Mascagni died alone in poverty and disgrace in a Rome hotel room in the final week of World War II.

Of his other operas, at least two hang on: *L'amico Fritz*, 1891, and *Iris*, 1898. In a sense it is unfair to dismiss them lightly on the grounds that they were not as successful as the blockbuster, but Mascagni doesn't have a Big Three or even a big Two. *Iris* is a story of old Japan that prompted Puccini to turn his attention to the East and is a model for *Madama Butterfly*. The music people say that Mascagni aimed far higher here than he had in *Cav* and produced a finer work, but without enough action in the story to sustain interest. *L'amico Fritz* is rarely performed, but the music is charming and available on CD if you like unseen opera. Segments are heard on classical radio stations.

Number 11. *Cavalleria rusticana*

Premiere at the Teatro Costanzi, Rome, 1890. From Giovanni Verga's short story of the same name. One act.

KEYNOTE
Pag's other half. Modern-day sex, infidelity, revenge, and violence in Sicilian dialect on Easter. Something new for the 1890s, both in Italy and across the Alps. Like *Carmen*, a tragedy driven by jealousy.

PLOT
Before the curtain rises, the music of a prelude has set the mood for passion, revenge, and death. It is Easter day, on the village square. Lucia (contralto), a woman who keeps a wineshop, is the mother of a soldier named Turiddu (tenor), who has been involved with a young woman, Santuzza (soprano). Santuzza appears to tell Lucia that she's been excommunicated for her adultery and must find Turiddu. She begs Lucia to have pity on her, as Christ had pity on the magdalen.

A cheerful teamster named Alfio (baritone) and his singing friends arrive

Plácido Domingo as Turiddu in Franco Zeffirelli's production of Cavalleria rusticana

on the village square and a long Easter procession passes en route to church. A distraught Santuzza tells her story to Lucia in an aria, "Voi lo sapete, o mamma." She has been seduced by Turiddu, but he has deserted her for a secret affair with his old girl, Lola (mezzo-soprano), married to Alfio. Lucia is horrified at her son's behavior.

When Turiddu appears, Santuzza begs for his attention, but he'll have none of it. He denies her accusations, she curses him, he violently orders her to close her mouth, and she cries that she'll still love him even if he beats and despises her. A smug Lola arrives in the square and also mocks her. After Lola enters the church for Easter mass, Santuzza and Turiddu again scream and fight, he demanding that she stop spying on him and she begging him not to leave her. But he throws her to the ground and follows Lola into the church. Having sinned, Santuzza stays out.

In the square she encounters Alfio and angrily tells everything. At first he thinks she's lying and threatens to cut out her heart but, swearing by her own dishonor, she convinces him Lola has been unfaithful. Santuzza quickly regrets what she's done, but it's too late. Alfio will have revenge and forces Turiddu into a confrontation by refusing to drink the wine he offers him, saying it would turn to poison in his throat. The insult means a duel. The two embrace, and Turiddu bites Alfio's right ear. As any good Sicilian knows, this formally signals that the duel is soon to come.

Turiddu finally regrets his affair with Lola, begs his mother to be a mother to Santuzza, asks God's forgiveness, and leaves to meet Alfio. Lucia and Santuzza are in each other's arms when a woman rushes in to say Turiddu has been murdered. They fall fainting to the ground together.

HIGHLIGHTS

The Prelude: Includes the duet between Santuzza and Turiddu and Turiddu's "Siciliana," a Sicilian-style song, sung offstage.

Act I: A lovely, lyrical, hard-to-beat introductory chorus, worth the price of the opera: "The scent of orange blossoms fill the meadow. The larks sing . . . This is the season for tender songs . . . At day's end we will think of you and hurry home." Santuzza's "Voi lo sapete" as she tells Mamma Lucia how poorly Turiddu has treated her: "He made love to me . . . I fell in love with him. That witch forgot her husband and stole him from me. I'm desperate; I'm damned." A Turiddu-Santuzza duet, ending in her cursing him.

The most acclaimed single number is the Intermezzo, performed by the orchestra during mass when the square is empty.

Turiddu's "Mamma, quel vino è generoso," as he asks his mother to take care of Santuzza if he doesn't return.

COMMENTARY

Rustic chivalry presumably deals with the rural Sicilians' code of honor, although if one steps back a pace personal honor doesn't seem to dominate Turiddu, Lola, or Santuzza—nor, indeed, Alfio, who has stolen a soldier's fiancée. One of the different things about the opera when it was first presented was the Sicilian dialect; this is real verismo, real gut Italy. Some critics complain that the melodies are "too pretty" for the intense emotions (while others protest that the music is too coarse). That's a danger in using select quotations: Some of the music is pretty and some coarse.

This was a new thing. *Carmen*, fifteen years earlier in France, had dealt with infidelity and revenge but in a wholly different way. Carmen was a working gypsy, exotic, but not dirt poor. One lover was a noncommissioned army officer; the other a hero of the bullring. And the time was 1820, not contemporary. *Cavalleria rusticana* touches a rawer nerve. Analysts point out that the flirtatious Carmen is the cause of her own problems while Santuzza is a victim—seduced, spurned, excommunicated, and friendless. It was not much of an Easter for her.

In big-time verismo opera, a husband doesn't learn of his wife's adultery by inadvertently seeing her enter a neighborhood motel. In verismo—in *Cavalleria rusticana*—the husband is told of his wife's behavior by a woman he knows, outside the church, during mass, and on Easter Sunday.

A calm onlooker in 1891, when the music world was afflicted by Mascagnitis and a *Cav* epidemic, was George Bernard Shaw, who wrote in an essay on *Cavalleria rusticana*: "Opera now offers to clever men with a turn for music and drama an unprecedented opportunity for picturesque, brilliant, apt, novel, and yet safely familiar and popular combinations and permutations of the immense store of musical 'effects' gathered up in the scores of the great modern composers, from Mozart to Wagner and Berlioz. This is the age of second-hand music."

"The public," Shaw continued, "is trained to endure, and even expect, continuous and passionate melody."

Enrico Caruso was an early famous Turiddu, continuing in the role even after he rounded out considerably. Another great one was the magnificent tenor Beniamino Gigli, and more recently, Plácido Domingo.

MET PERFORMANCES
Six hundred and fourteen performances in seventy-three seasons, from 1891 to 1995. Ten performances are scheduled, with *Pagliacci*, for the 1996–97 season.

RECORDINGS
CD—Deutsche Grammophon 419 257-2 (3). Fiorenza Cossatto, Giangiacomo Guelfi, Carlo Bergoniz. La Scala Chorus and Orchestra. Herbert von Karajan. 1965. (With *Pagliacci*.)

VIDEO
Domingo, Obraztsova, Bruson. La Scala. Italian; English subtitles. Prêtre, conductor. 1982. PGD.

❧

One Warhorse by Gaetano Donizetti
November 29, 1797–April 8, 1848
LUCIA DI LAMMERMOOR *(Number 15)*

Gaetano Donizetti is a fascinating fellow, a bundle of contradictions.

Comedy is his most successful field, but he wrote many more serious operas than comedies, of which this dark tragedy is the best known. Spontaneous melody is his specialty, but *Lucia di Lammermoor* is most acclaimed as a dramatic masterwork.

Fifty years ago, many Upper-Crust critics found a lot not to like about Donizetti. He was a disappointment in so many ways. For one thing, he wrote some sixty-five operas, clearly an unbecoming thing to do. Really!

Something here is unfair. Franz Joseph Haydn wrote 104 symphonies, just as one part of his total musical production. There are 300-odd cantatas from Johann Sebastian Bach. When Mozart composes his three major symphonies in six weeks, he's the genius of geniuses—which, of course, he is. Yet when Donizetti writes *Don Pasquale* in eleven days and *Lucia di Lammermoor* in six weeks, when he writes eight operas including *The Elixir of Love* in three years, he's a shallow hack. Is not the important point the quality and consistency of the work produced rather than the rapidity of writing?

Another thing that bothered the Upper Crusties was that Donizetti only mildly disguised his subservience to the audience. Well, this was the way he was making his living. Opera was the entertainment of the day. Composers, unless born with a silver quill in their hands, were looking for a market share. They weren't writing for history, any more than William Shakespeare was writing for history a couple of hundred years earlier.

Opera, like Shakespeare, is a lot more fun if approached with the recognition that most of the individuals involved are real, live people, trying to buy some pasta and pay the rent. Donizetti came from poor parents; he had to accept every commission offered him. Presumably the Crusties would approve of Signor Donizetti if he had advised his agent: "Hold all calls for the next five years. I've decided to create a masterpiece. And tell the little woman not to worry."

Yeah, sure.

Another charge against Donizetti was that he was too submissive to the singers. Deliberately, consciously, willfully, with total premeditation—still worse, without the slightest sign of remorse—he was the servant of the singer. But this also was an exigency of the day in Italy. If the singers weren't with you, you weren't published and performed.

Gaetano Donizetti

And a fourth fault was that a good bit of his work was dreadfully sloppy. Even the pro-Donizetti claque today acknowledges his lapses in craftsmanship. But he also wrote passages of great glory, even if he neither sought nor achieved that perfect balance of music and drama that the purists like.

Donizetti's prestige has gone up and down like a yo-yo. At the time of his death, he was dominant. One of every four operas performed in Italy was his. Around the turn of the century, he was in the pits. Too superficial, too much a copycat. Here in the second part of our century, he's back up again—for his best tragedy, his best comedy, his best dramatic writing, his melody—and for having been a key force in Italian opera development.

In 1954, *The Grove Dictionary of Music* gave him short shrift. It said that music written as rapidly as Donizetti's could be no more than successful improvisation. He lacked Rossini's "brilliance" and Verdi's "earnest sincerity."

But the *New Grove Dictionary of Opera*—four volumes, 5,424 pages, a wonderful tool—while asserting that no single one of Donizetti's tragic operas makes the impact one would expect of an "unqualified masterpiece," summarizes him this way:

"Yet so central was he to the vitality of the tradition he served that when he retired it began to decay . . . Only Verdi succeeded in putting the Donizettian heritage to a new and valid use. Donizetti's own works survive through the grace and spontaneity of their melodies, their formal poise, their effortless dramatic pace and above all the romantic vitality that underlies their veneer of artifice."

Passing the Torch

In a 1844 letter, Donizetti wrote:

"My heydey is over, and another must take my place. The world wants something new . . . I am more than happy to have given mine up to talented people like Verdi."

Two groups have been with him from the start: the people who buy the tickets and the performers who sing his operas. One singer in this century that people came to hear was Maria Callas, and in 1954 she and the great German conductor Herbert von Karajan teamed up at La Scala on *Lucia di Lammermoor*. Five years later Joan Sutherland was a smash hit in *Lucia* at London's Covent Garden in a famous production that brought her to stardom. Beverly Sills made Donizetti one of her specialities. These three sopranos did much to revive bel canto opera and through their individual artistry helped show the music world that poor old Donizetti did have dramatic force. A Donizetti sense of drama had been there all the time but was overlooked during the decades that singers used him chiefly as a showcase for their voices.

The record should show that this Fast-food fellow played the viola, was an experienced conductor, wrote an excellent Requiem Mass in honor of Bellini and much other religious music, was a student of the works of Haydn and Mozart, composed nineteen string quartets, and even wrote some symphonies.

In addition to *Lucia di Lammermoor*, Donizetti has three operas in The Collection:

L'elisir d'amore (The Elixir of Love), opera buffa, 1832 (Number 35). The first of his two great Italian comic operas, close to perfection as a sentimental comedy.

Don Pasquale, opera buffa, 1843 (Number 56). The second outstanding Italian comic opera buffa.

La fille du régiment (The Daughter of the Regiment), 1840 (Number 61). A comedy, for the French Opéra-Comique.

A half-dozen more Donizetti operas also are performed, several with considerable frequency:

Anna Bolena, 1830, a two-act romantic tragedy, with libretto by Felice Romani, his first great tragedy, a work that helped establish him. The first of Donizetti's three operas involving Tudor queens.

Lucrezia Borgia, 1833, typical of the violent romantic Italian operas of that time. A sentimental melodrama. Musicologists call it a breakthrough from Rossini. Of three duets, none is in the Rossini form. Another libretto by Felice Romani.

Maria Stuarda (Mary Stuart), 1834, a three-act work from a tragedy by Friedrich von Schiller. A big revival of it started in the mid-twentieth century. The second Donizetti opera involving Tudor queens.

Roberto Devereux, 1837, a three-act opera partially based on the tragedy *Elisabeth d'Angleterre* by François Ancelot. The third opera involving a Tudor queen.

La favorite, 1840, a four-act grand opera that was one of seven originally written in French.

Linda di Chamounix, 1842, a serious opera, his first written for the court of Vienna, so successful that the Emperor named him court composer.

For road-map purposes, let's review for a moment where he fits in history. The bel canto school of Italian opera developed after Mozart died in 1791 and before Verdi began to take over in Italy in the 1840s. Rossini, Donizetti, and Bellini vied with one another for space and attention.

The term "bel canto" goes back to earlier Italian works that emphasized the beauty of sound and the brilliance of the performing singers rather than expressions of romantic emotion. The range of the tenor is expanded to new heights. There is a special tone, technique, and approach and a special phrasing, all featuring a lyric voice as opposed to the declamatory one favored by the Germans.

Italy loved not only voices during the bel canto period but high voices. Although women did not appear onstage near the Vatican, they did perform in more distant regions, presumably without the Pope knowing about it (or perhaps with the Pope closing an eye, since one conjectures that the Pope's agents kept him well informed).

The bel canto style of singing called for a great deal of ornamentation, characterized by one professional opera singer friend of mine as "roodle doodle." The singer who can't add roodle doodle to the aria can't have a career with Donizetti and his colleagues. Italian audiences loved roodle doodle. Operas were supposed to be fun; families went to show off the husband's prosperity, the wife's gowns, and the marriageable children. Some people in the audience ate; others played cards. Some ate while they played cards. It's a little tough to eat, play cards, and follow the plot of a fine drama—but not hard under these conditions to enjoy a beautiful aria topped with roodle doodle.

Some positive thoughts from the critics:

No other opera composer knew more than Donizetti about the beauty of the human voice. Few had a better innate feeling for singable melody. Again, none had a better sense of what the audience wanted to see and hear—and in some works he gave those audiences wonderful theatrical numbers.

Some negative thoughts from the critics:

Theater generally was not his thing. Although he chose noble themes, his style was not grand enough to handle them well. The audiences who like him best are those whose tastes are most questionable (now there's a comment that says something about its author). Much of his music is naive. His powers do show through loudly and clearly in such scenes as the sextet in *Lucia*—but rarely does he reach this height.

One senses that one of the things most troublesome to the purist professionals is that too much of the time he failed to live up to his potential. Now if he had written only ten operas . . . and not eaten well . . .

Before Donizetti, Rossini had overwhelmed the competition and totally dominated the Italian operatic stage. Donizetti and Bellini then both took what Rossini had developed and added to it the spirit of nineteenth-century Romanticism.

One opera professional gave me this comparison: Donizetti had nimble craftsmanship and great melody. The music in his early works was not as lofty as Bellini's. It was more in the vernacular—not folksy but with a folksy feeling, comfortable music that stays with you. He used the chorus a lot but as background rather than as an action-player the way Bellini used it. In late works, his melodies began to be more lyrical, vivid, and concise, foreshadowing what was coming from Verdi. With *Anna Bolena* he came into his own as a classical composer, and the librettos began to improve.

Donizetti was born in Bergamo, studied at Naples under one respected opera composer, continued to learn at Bologna under another, and returned to Bergamo as a young man. He enlisted in the army, reportedly in preference to giving music lessons as demanded by his father, and was stationed in Venice. Two early operas written during not-too-taxing regimental life earned him a modest reputation, he obtained a discharge from the army, and—competing with Rossini and Bellini—began cranking out more operas.

Anna Bolena, which premiered in Milan in 1830 when Donizetti was thirty-three, received some international recognition. He went to Paris, an opera mecca at the time, but didn't score there then. After turning to Naples for his first real blockbuster, *Lucia di Lammermoor*, he again tried Paris, this time with the premiere of *The Daughter of the Regiment*. Although not an immediate hit with the French, it traveled rapidly and well through the rest of Europe.

Still relatively young, Donizetti now was famous. Other operas tumbled out in quick order, many soon forgotten, some more popular now than ever. In 1837, his adored wife died, a loss from which his biographers say he never recovered. After a paralytic stroke in 1845, still on the good side of fifty, he spent three miserable years with mind and body failing, until he died at home in 1848. Musicologists earlier this century wrote that the stroke probably was from overwork; today they say the root problem was syphilis, probably caught when he was young and ignored or mistreated throughout the rest of his life.

Biographers portray him as a kind, gentle, gracious human being.

Number 15. *Lucia di Lammermoor*

Premiere at the Teatro San Carlo, Naples, 1835. Text by Salvatore Cammarano from an 1814 novel by Sir Walter Scott, The Bride of Lammermoor. *Three acts.*

KEYNOTE

Donizetti's greatest tragedy, arguably his finest work, and a superb example of opera seria. Meet the treacherous brother and be glad he's not yours. Hear the Sextet; see and hear the Mad Scene, a coloratura jewel. Edgardo's role was a favorite of Enrico Caruso.

PLOT

Scotland, 1700, a castle on a misty moor. (Scottish and Italian names are given here) Lucy (Lucia) Ashton (soprano) is in love with Edgar (Edgardo) of Ravenswood (tenor), although their families have been feuding for years. He's the last of his clan, since his father was killed by Lucia's brother, Lord Henry (Enrico) Ashton of Lammermoor (baritone). Lucia and Edgardo meet in the park of Lammermoor Castle before he leaves for France on a political mission, swear eternal vows, and exchange wedding rings. Before God, they will marry. He promises to write frequently.

Enrico will have none of this; he has lost his fortune, has committed treason against the King, and reasons he can be saved only if Lucia marries the powerful Lord Arthur (Arturo) Bucklaw (tenor). While Edgardo is away in France, Enrico and his henchmen block Lucia's letters, intercept his, and create a forgery to convince her he has been unfaithful and plans to marry someone else. Lucia at first says she would rather die than spend her life with anyone else, but, faced with "evidence" of Edgardo's "treachery" and influenced by the selfish pleading of her no-good brother, she reluctantly agrees to wed Arturo.

As the marriage contract is being signed, Edgardo returns and forces his way into the great hall of the castle. He is convinced she's the one who is betraying him. Furious, he throws the ring she's given him at her feet and curses her and all other members of the House of Lammermoor, past, present, and future, born and unborn.

Lucia and Arturo go offstage to the bridal chamber. It's all too much for Lucia, who loses her mind and kills Arturo with a dagger. Pale, hair disheveled, and wearing a bloody white wedding dress, she bursts back upon the partying weddings guests. She is in a trance, imagining that her Edgardo is there and that they are being married. In partnership with a flute, she sings softly of the beautiful life they will have together. This is the Mad Scene, as famous as any in opera. Begging her imaginary Edgardo to have mercy on her, she falls to the floor. In the next scene, Edgardo is wandering in the churchyard where his ancestors are buried. A church bell signals death. He learns that it is Lucia who has died, promises to join her, and stabs himself in the heart with a dagger.

Unsay

One reason translations into English have not worked better is that some of the translations were so bad.

In one production, when Edgar in *Lucia di Lammermoor* hears of the death of his beloved Lucia, he sings: "Dead! That word unsay."

HIGHLIGHTS

Act I: Lucia's ghost story about a fountain in the park, "Regnava nel silenzio": "A pale moonbeam shone on the fountain. A ghost appeared, beckoned, and vanished. The clear water was red with blood." This is followed by her song about the happiness love is giving her, "Quando rapito in estasi": "He is my only comfort. I'm caught by his burning love." The duet between Lucy and Edgar after he tells her he is leaving for France, "Verranno a te sull'aure." They will write. "The breeze will carry my love to you. The seas will sound the echo of my love."

Act II: The celebrated Sextet, "Chi mi frena in tal momento?" ("What restrains me at this moment?"), as Edgardo returns to find the signing of the marriage contract. It is sung by two tenors, Edgardo and Arturo; a baritone, Enrico; a soprano, Lucia; a mezzo-soprano, her companion Alisa, and a bass, her tutor and chaplain, Raimondo. One of opera's best-known ensemble numbers.

Act III: The Mad Scene, magnificent in mood, one of opera's most exquisite show pieces for soprano. When performed by a superstar, worth the price of any ticket. Edgar's final aria from the graveyard, "Tu che a Dio spiegasti l'ali" ("You have spread your wings to heaven").

COMMENTARY

The musicologists don't seem to know how or why Donizetti selected Sir Walter Scott's novel, must reading for anyone traveling the moors of Great Britain. *Lucia* was the composer's fiftieth opera (or thereabout, depending on how we count unfinished works), written some twenty years into his career. From the outset it has been a big success, playing in London in 1838, Havana in 1840, New Orleans in 1841. Mexico City in 1841, and New York in 1843, a great start on a popular run that has lasted to this day.

Although the Mad Scene and the Sextet are the best known, the opera contains much more fine melody. The complaints of some analysts are that for all of his strengths Donizetti could not build as strong a dramatic structure as a mature Verdi did, that his characters aren't as true to life as Mozart's characters, and that they aren't depicted musically as Mozart portrayed them. Therefore, they conclude, *Lucia* works magnificently when sung by magnificent voices but falls short when handled by ordinary opera voices.

One fault with this analysis is that not that many Verdis and Mozarts are found walking along the towpath.

Lucia di Lammermoor, a curious blend of the old and the new, is regarded as less innovative than some of Donizetti's earlier works. The first duet is "through-composed," that is, all of the words and music from the start to the end are new, with no repetition. The second is more similar to the older form used by Rossini and scads of others. The Sextet is superb music, as each character expresses a different emotion, although all use exactly the same melody.

Lucia is a role that many of the great coloratura sopranos have sung. Among those who made their New York debut with it are Adelina Patti in 1859, Nellie Melba in 1893, Maria Barrientos in 1916, and Lily Pons in 1931. Pons, musicologists say, didn't turn the role into a dramatic masterpiece the way Maria Callas did, but nonetheless was a pioneer in reviving bel canto opera in the twentieth century. Other favorites in the role include Renata Scotto, Marcella Sembrich, Luisa Tetrazzini, Jenny Lind, Amelita Galli-Curci, Joan Sutherland—it sent her off to stardom—and Beverly Sills. But always Callas.

MET PERFORMANCES

Four hundred and ninety-five performances over seventy-two seasons, from 1883 to 1994.

RECORDINGS

CD—Angel/EMI CDMB 63631 (2) (mono). Maria Callas, Giuseppe Di Stefano, Rolando Panerai, Nicola Zaccaria. La Scala Chorus. RIAS Symphony Orchestra, Berlin. Herbert von Karajan. 1955.

or

—Decca/London 411 622-2 (2). Joan Sutherland, Renato Cioni, Robert Merrill, Cesare Siepi. Chorus and Orchestra of the Academia di Santa Cecilia, Rome. John Pritchard. 1961.

VIDEO

Sutherland, Kraus, Elvira. Metropolitan Opera. Italian; English subtitles. Bonynge, conductor. 1982. PAR.

∾

Three Warhorses by Wolfgang Amadeus Mozart
January 27, 1756–December 5, 1791

DON GIOVANNI *(Number 18)*
THE MARRIAGE OF FIGARO *(Number 21)*
THE MAGIC FLUTE *(Number 23)*

"Opera, to me, comes before everything else."

We might anticipate such a comment from the specialists, from Verdi, Wagner, and Puccini, who contributed twenty-nine of the Collection operas. But the speaker was Wolfgang Amadeus Mozart.

He's one of the three Immortals of classical music, along with Johann Sebastian Bach and Ludwig van Beethoven. Strong proof that they're history's greatest is that no one questions their being placed there, whereas objections come from all four corners if that status is given other giants like Joseph Haydn or Franz Schubert.

Superlatives about Mozart are inexhaustable. Tchaikovsky called him "the music Christ." Haydn said he was the best composer he knew about. Schubert wept over "the impressions of a brighter and better life he had imprinted on our souls." Robert Schumann wrote that there were some things in the world about which nothing could be said: much of Shakespeare, pages of Beethoven, and the forty-first symphony of Mozart.

He composed forty-one symphonies, twenty-seven piano concertos, more than thirty string quartets, some of music's most acclaimed quintets, world-famous violin and flute concertos, historic piano and violin sonatas, and so forth and so forth and so forth.

But despite all that, in 1782 he said that opera came before everything else.

Mozart was born in Salzburg, the son of Leopold, a gifted court musician who was teacher, composer, and vice chapel conductor for the Archbishop of Salzburg. Three major points about Wolfgang's musical life:

1. He was an incredible child genius, unmatched in music. At age three he picked out tunes on the harpsichord; at age four he composed. His first public concert was at six. He and his sister then took a European tour, performing at courts in Austria, England, France, and Holland. By age twelve he had written ten symphonies, a cantata, and an Italian opera. At thirteen he toured Italy, playing the organ, and in Rome astonished the music world by writing out the

Wolfgang Amadeus Mozart

full score of a complex religious composition at the Sistine Chapel after one hearing.

2. He lived not in poverty but in and out of hardship (although there were many frock coats in his closet when he died and at times he moved in some pretty decent circles). These were still patronage days for musicians, when a livelihood depended on the whims of the rich—a time before money could be made from public concerts and performances. Mozart was miserable under the Archbishop of Salzburg and moved to Vienna with high hopes of more satisfactory conditions. For the most part, they were an improvement over Salzburg, but at no time in his life did he enjoy either a first-rate appointment or financial security, despite the fact that both the Empress Maria Theresa and her son, Joseph II, knew of him and were interested in music. He was pushed around by both Church and State. But, like old Johann Sebastian Bach, who died and was planted quietly in his church courtyard, no one knew they had an immortal genius on their hands.

3. He died at thirty-five. We can only dream of what might have come.

In 1783 he made a prediction to his father that turned out to be wrong.

"I don't believe that the Italian opera will keep going for long," he wrote from Vienna, "and besides, I hold with the Germans."

Well, at least he was half wrong. Italy was producing both opera seria and opera buffa. Both were on their last legs in Mozart's time. Opera seria in its old form was to disappear quickly, but opera buffa won new life in the hands of Rossini and Donizetti, both of whom also went on to a different type of serious work.

Back to the letter:

"I prefer German opera . . . Every nation has its own opera—why not Germany? Is not German as singable as French and English? Is it not more so than Russian? Very well then! I am now writing a German opera for myself."

Eight or nine Mozart operas are still bobbing about in international repertories, some more popular today than others but none off the stage for long. Two are in German, the rest in Italian. Six are particularly successful, four of which make The Collection. Additionally, a few earlier dramatic works—including an opera written at age fourteen—are revived in Mozart anniversary years and on a few other occasions.

Question: Why was Mozart writing operas in Italian when he lived in Vienna, which not only was part of Germany but also was the headquarters of Emperor Joseph II, a man who loved, encouraged, and sponsored music?

Answer: Because Italy still set the international opera standards; Italian-style opera was the kind that audiences in Vienna—and most of the rest of Europe—wanted to see.

Of his five main Italian works, the three in The Collection are:

The Marriage of Figaro, 1786 (Number 21). An Italian opera buffa. Considered by many musicologists to be one of the three perfect "popular" operas, along with Verdi's *Aida* and Bizet's *Carmen*. It is the first collaboration of Mozart with his most famous librettist, Lorenzo Da Ponte.

Don Giovanni, 1787 (Number 18). Technically an opera buffa in the Italian style, called by Mozart a "dramma giocoso" but actually an original blend of opera buffa and opera seria. By near unanimous consent today it is a towering masterwork.

Così fan tutte (Thus do all women), 1790 (Number 50). The incarnation of opera buffa in the Italian style and his last comic opera. A comedy about the human condition. Some see it as a comedy, pure and simple, and others as something darker.

His other two most successful Italian operas:

Idomeneo. Premiere in Munich, 1781, commissioned by Karl Theodor, Elector of Bavaria. Three acts. This was Mozart's third attempt in the style of Italian opera seria. (*Mitridate* and *Lucio Silla* were a decade earlier.) It was re-

vived only once in Mozart's lifetime, was heard fairly frequently in Austria
and Germany after his death, did not reach England until 1934, and was
not performed professionally there until 1951, at Glyndebourne. It was
first produced in America in 1947 at the Berkshire Music Festival at Tan-
glewood, in Lenox, Massachusetts. His first masterpiece, a superior opera
equal to some Collection choices, in its early form it had a major role for a
castrato, a voice for which Mozart later stopped writing. It was one of the
last great examples of the fading form of Italian opera seria.

Opera seria, as we have seen, was a seventeenth-century attempt to
re-create Greek tragedy, with the recitative poetry accompanied by a
harpsichord. By this time, due partly to free-wheeling freelance singers
and partly to hard artificial rules, it was a weak format, but Mozart's talent
overcame its flaws. Musicologist Alfred Einstein has described *Idomeneo* as
"one of those works that even genius of the highest rank, like Mozart,
could write only once in his life." One of my experts suggests concentrating on the last twenty minutes of Act II, including Electra's aria; the
lovely chorus, "Placido è il mar;" a trio; and the choruses heralding the
arrival of the sea monster.

La Clemenza di Tito. Premiere at the National Theatre, Prague, 1791. (Visit
Prague quickly and enjoy all three opera houses there before prices rise
and the beautiful old city is overtaken by "progress.") Two acts. Mozart's
fourth opera seria, commissioned to celebrate the coronation in Prague of
the Emperor Leopold II as King of Bohemia. Mozart was in the midst of
writing both *The Magic Flute* and his deathbed Requiem when he received
the commission. Three weeks after the coronation premiere, *The Magic
Flute* was performed, and nine weeks later Mozart was dead. Interest
in *Clemenza* had fallen until fairly recently when Italian opera seria
began a comeback, and now both this work and *Idomeneo* are performed
quite often.

One of his two main German operas is in The Collection:

Die Zauberflöte, or *The Magic Flute*, 1791 (Number 23). His last dramatic work,
technically also a Singspiel, with spoken dialogue, but actually a much
more advanced work.

His other main German opera:

The Abduction from the Seraglio (Die Entführung aus dem Serail). Premiere at the
Burgtheatre, Vienna, 1782. Three acts. A German Singspiel. The emperor, Joseph II, had founded the National Singspiel Company in 1778,
designed to promote German couth in the city of Vienna, where the
predominant culture was French. This was Mozart's first imperial
operatic commission. True to Singspiel, the action takes place almost

entirely in spoken dialogue, not recitative. Almost everyone writing about opera tells the story of the postperformance meeting between Emperor Joseph II and the composer. "Too beautiful for our ears and monstrous many notes, my dear Mozart," said the Emperor. "Exactly as many as necessary, Your Majesty," replied Mozart. The work combines elements of Italian opera seria, opera buffa, and some good warm German song. Look and listen for the Act II finale, an example in miniature of what made Mozart so great, the three big arias for Konstanze, especially "Martern aller Arten" in Act II, and Osmin's "Ha! wie will ich triumphieren" in Act III. Also the duet for Konstanze and Belmonte that follows it.

Mozart's operas receive the same extravagant praise as his instrumental music. Many professionals call *Don Giovanni* the finest opera ever written, some prefer *The Magic Flute*, and still others choose *Figaro*, arguing that no other opera equals it in portraying both the smiles and tears of life. And William Mann, noted musicologist, wrote that *Così fan tutte* contains "the most captivating music ever composed."

Mozart, like all other opera composers from the time of the Camerata, was faced with major choices between music and drama. One of his contemporaries was Christoph Willibald von Gluck, the great reformer, who insisted that drama must come first, to be attended by the music. Fifty years later, Wagner tried to make music and drama coequal, although he didn't succeed.

Mozart was unequivocal about what he wanted.

"In an opera," he said, "poetry must be altogether the obedient daughter of the music." (But, professionals note, he took great care in selecting that poetry, hammering at his librettists to be sure they produced words that could be illuminated and then transcended by his music.)

The overtures reflected his own genius in instrumental music and the operas themselves his glorious vocal music—recitative, arias, duets, quartets, choruses, and all, including "ensemble finales." As the term suggests, an ensemble is a group of more than one soloist, with or without a chorus; a finale comes at the end of an act. Look for them when watching and hearing Mozart operas; no composer did a better job of writing them.

Mozart did not create high-tension plots that keep us on the edge of our seats—but neither did William Shakespeare most of the time. The "dramatic truth" of Mozartian opera, the element that is combined with his music to move him away from the pack, is in his characters. Musicologists generally agree that no one in the opera business, before or after Mozart, ever surpassed him in understanding his fellow human beings—the best, the brightest, and the ones occupying the lower stations—and in creating characters who possessed all the complex real-person emotions.

What he provided, in words the professionals favor, was an extraordinarily truthful mirror of human conduct.

And the result is a *Don Giovanni*, still as popular as ever because nearly everyone in the opera has passion and character and all behave according to that passion and character—portrayed by Mozart with dignity, sentiment, and insight. Critic/composer Virgil Thomson wrote in the New York *Herald Tribune* fifty years ago that Mozart's characters were so real the audience blamed no one on the stage for being what he was or acting the way he acted.

Wagner on Mozart

Richard Wagner always thought in terms of the orchestra. His assessment of Mozart symphonies:

"He seemed to breathe into his instruments the passionate tones of the human voice . . . and thus raised the capacity of orchestral music for expressing the emotions to a height where it could represent the whole unsatisfied yearning of the heart."

This is one reason his operas were as contemporary in 1895 as they were in 1795—and are no less contemporary in 1995. The costumes and the customs may have changed, the wealthy chief executive officer in his Connecticut mansion may no longer legally bed his illegal alien housekeeper against her wishes, but the individual people on Mozart's stage are the same flawed individual people as our in-laws. Well, as your in-laws.

Musicologists tell us that this accent on the individual makes Mozart a bridge between eighteenth- and nineteenth-century operas. Before him, abstract emotion had been the central thing. But Mozart—anticipating the Romantic movement that was to begin soon after his death—put the spotlight on the individual.

Consider this difference between a Gluck and a Mozart. Gluck, the great reformer, typically recapitulates a situation with a chorus. The individual is lost as the chorus offers its summation. Mozart, however, typically ends a situation with an ensemble, in which several main characters sing at the same time, each expressing his or her own reactions and feelings.

Twentieth-century illustration: After the opera about a presidential election, Gluck's chorus would say: "See, the people have spoken and once again there will be a change of command without violence." But in Mozart's ensemble, four main characters speak for themselves. The winner sings of her hopes, the loser of his sadness, the third-party spoiler of his intention to run again, and the winner's spouse of his dedication to weed control.

Question: How does a composer like Mozart use *music* to mirror the human condition, to portray the whole human life, to depict human character, to communicate envy, passion, revenge, and pledge of eternal love?

For openers, respond the experts, the composer can control the tempo, pitch, and accent of the music to suggest the inflections of speech necessary to a particular character at the given moment. More important, he also can define the character by the kinds of melodies and harmonies he uses, the kinds of rhythms, the kinds of color from the supporting instruments (a flute and a tuba do not paint the same picture). (For examples, see commentary below on *Figaro* and *Don Giovanni*.)

A particularly useful tool for the composer is his choice of key, to which Mozart paid great attention. We nonmusicians don't need to be able to recognize A major from E major (or even from C minor) in order to hear that the two keys don't sound the same. Here are a few Mozart examples:

- Mozart's music for peasant scenes—for rustic life and "common people"—often is in the key of G major. Also, his melodies for commoners often sound like folk tunes. A prince never would be given folk music—unless he were masquerading as a pauper.
- For "Sturm and Drang," storm and stress, his key choice was D minor. The professionals say that this D minor music is responsible for much of the effect of *Don Giovanni*. For sensual love scenes, he liked A major, a seductive-sounding key.
- Every Mozart opera has a home key in which it is written. When the characters are in trouble, he has them sing in keys removed from that home key—the more trouble, the farther removed. As they get out of trouble, he gradually brings them back closer to the home key so that at the end no tension is left hanging. Violent rage is not expressed in the same key—nor in the same rhythm or tempo—as gentle love.
- As an example of the use of key, listen to the end of Act II of *Figaro*. One of the great comic finales in opera, it offers a fine example of character depiction through music. We who are unWashed don't identify them, but the analysts tell us that within this twenty-five minute finale, with all main players onstage, Mozart goes from character to character with E flat major to B flat major to G major to C major to F major back to B flat major and again E flat major. This helps give each principal his or her own personality. Opera can do this sort of thing; a stage play can't.
- Mozart also uses key to tell us which character is in control of a particular situation. If the heroine sings in one key and the hero responds in the same one, she comes across as the one in command of what's happening in the plot. If the hero tops her by shifting keys to one of his own, the audience can sense that he's the dominate one. By this yardstick, in *Figaro* "commoner" Susanna is in control of most of her scenes, regardless of who else is onstage. That's what Mozart wanted; his choices of key (and tempo and rhythm) help portray the kind of person she is.
- No music in *Figaro* is in a minor key until the beginning of the third act. In those days, if a scene began in a minor key it usually had to end in a major

key. Otherwise, an opera friend tells me, it was called "abuse of a minor." The same friend notes that the phrase also could apply to the castrato practice.

There is no "typical" Mozart opera. One analyst, tying the operas to Mozart's nonoperatic music, has described *Don Giovanni* as a symphonic opera, *Die Zauberflöte* as a church-type opera with the sound of his masses and Requiem, *Così fan tutte* as the opera that features woodwinds and resembles his serenades and divertimentos, and *Figaro* as the work that brings to mind his piano concertos.

Well, maybe so. That gives us something to listen for.

Mozart followed many rules of composition but broke just as many and made many of his own. He used everything in sight, all the styles of the past, borrowing and casting aside as he chose. And he was an independent chap:

- Opera seria traditionally had three acts and opera buffa two. But Mozart wrote *Figaro* in four.
- Action at this time commonly was carried out in the recitative. Arias were designed for characters to reflect on that action. But in *Figaro*, Mozart has *action* arias, something seldom done.
- Opera buffa traditionally had relied on "secco"—"dry"—recitative, accompanied only by an occasional chord on a harpsichord. But in his opera buffa Mozart also used "accompanied" recitative, in which the whole orchestra sometimes joined.

Some general operatic points of interest of Mozart times:

- Big roles in the serious operas of this time were played by castrati. For example, in *Idomeneo* the role of Idamante, son of the King of Crete, was written for a castrato. After the castration practice ended, casting for some parts became difficult. Nearly all of the operas sung by castrati are now out of the repertory, except for a few works by Handel, Gluck, and Mozart.
- Opera seria made no bones about being unrealistic. Although the personages were often real historic figures, they were presented ideologically, in terms of their noblest aspirations or strongest drives. Opera buffa was more faithful to true life, showing us the way we really are.
- In opera seria, the bass was unimportant and only minor characters were assigned bass roles. The tenor also was unimportant, inasmuch as a castrato had the hero's role.
- The writing style in opera seria was florid. Each aria was centered around an emotion—a rage aria, a love aria, a grief aria, for instance. Also, arias in these days often were written for specific singers. If a star singer didn't like the aria, the composer had to change it. Mozart had to face this problem just as the non-geniuses did, a complication when operas were performed in different cities with different singers.

Here are the three Mozart Warhorse operas. Comment is especially detailed on *Don Giovanni* and *Figaro* as works representative of Mozart's genius in the field of opera:

Number 18. *Don Giovanni*

Premiere at the National Theatre, Prague, 1787. Text by Lorenzo Da Ponte from Giovanni Bertati's 1786 libretto for an opera by Giuseppe Gazzaniga's Dramma giocoso (Mozart's words) in two acts.

KEYNOTE

His second collaboration with librettist Lorenzo Da Ponte. Meet Don Giovanni and his 2,065 conquests. Hear the stone statue speak. See the consignment to Hell. Watch the chameleon character of Giovanni and how it is portrayed by music.

Press Notice, 1764

This was published in a Paris newspaper after Mozart appeared at court in Versailles:

"The boy, who is only seven this month, is a true prodigy. He has all the talent and science of a mature musician. Not only does he give surprising performances of the works of the most celebrated masters in Europe, but he is also a composer. Guided by the inspiration of his genius, he will improvise, for hours together, music which combines the most exquisite ideas with an exhaustive knowledge of harmony. Every musical connoisseur is lost in amazement at the child, who performs feats such as would do credit to an artist possessed of the experience of a long career."

PLOT

Seventeenth century, Seville. Don Giovanni (baritone), enters the house of the Commendatore (or Commandant) (bass) to seduce his daughter, Donna Anna (soprano). Don Giovanni is masked. Her father finds them together and draws his sword. Although reluctant to take on so old a man, Don Giovanni can't avoid the fight; he mortally wounds the father and escapes without being recognized. Don Ottavio (tenor), Donna Anna's fiancé, vows to avenge her father's murder.

Don Giovanni's next escapade involves Donna Elvira (soprano), who is onstage singing of the wretch who loved her for three days and then abandoned her.

She swears she will tear his heart out. From a distance, Don Giovanni notes how sorrowful she is, pretties himself up, and approaches, bent on helping the poor soul who is in such distress. He quickly retreats when they recognize one another, leaving her in the hands of his servant, Leporello (bass). To show her Giovanni isn't worth her tears, Leporello recites a list of his master's other women—2,065 in all, including 640 in Italy, 230 in Germany, 100 in France, 91 in Turkey, and a minimum of 1,003 in Spain.

Peasants take the stage to celebrate the marriage of their friends Masetto (bass-baritone) and Zerlina (soprano). Don Giovanni encounters them and invites the group to his château, where Leporello will see to their entertainment. He delays Zerlina and attempts to seduce her. She is close to yielding to him, but they are interrupted by the reappearance of Elvira, who warns Zerlina that her fascinating admirer is a no-good dog who is not to be trusted. He explains that he's too compassionate for his own good and is just being friendly. When Donna Anna reappears with Don Ottavio, she recognizes Giovanni's voice as that of her masked attacker. Meanwhile, Giovanni steps up his efforts to seduce Zerlina, even involving Leporello in a ruse, but he doesn't make it.

Three masked persons who have joined the wedding festivities reveal themselves to be Donna Anna, Elvira, and Ottavio. They accuse Don Giovanni of horrible and shocking crimes. Ottavio sings that he can hardly believe a man of nobility could be so vile a felon. Giovanni first confronts and then eludes them. After additional escapades, he comes across a stone statue of the Commendatore (it must have been erected before the Commendatore's death) and mockingly bids Leporello to invite it to dinner. Astonishingly, it arrives and orders Giovanni to repent or be damned. He taunts the statue, refuses to renounce his lifestyle, and declares that he is fully prepared to accept the consequences. They are severe: The room becomes black, a fiery pit opens, and he is dragged down into the fires of Hell.

HIGHLIGHTS

Act I: "Madamina! il catalogo è questo," Leporello's famous catalogue of his master's triumphs: "Here are valid statistics of his conquests from border to border. In Italy, six hundred and forty, and so forth."

A tender duet between Don Giovanni and young Zerlina, inviting her to his castle, "Là ci darem la mano" ("Lay your hand in mine, dear"): "Promise to be my wife. There is my castle where we will share a happy life together . . . I wish I could believe him. My heart favors you; my reason says wait. I feel myself giving way." A short, beautiful trio with the three maskers, Don Ottavio, Donna Anna, and Donna Elvira, "Protegga il giusto cielo," asking for heaven's help. Finally, the act-ending ballroom scene, with three simultaneous dances for nobility, bourgeoise, and peasantry. Hear the music change as the mood shifts from near farce to near rape.

Act II: The Don's soft serenade to Elvira's maid, "Deh, vieni alla finestra": "Ah, come to the window, my beloved. Console my tears. If you do not respond, I'll end my life today." A big number of the opera, Ottavio's "Il mio tesoro," as he asks friends to stay with Anna while he pursues Giovanni, revenge, and justice: "Go comfort my treasure and try to dry her tears. Tell her I have gone to avenge the wrongs done her." This famous aria, regarded as a supreme test of classical song, is considered one of the most taxing arias in the tenor repertoire. It is followed immediately by Donna Alvira's "Mi tradì": "He betrayed my love and honor. Though I hate him for his shameful deeds, I still pity him. But my heart speaks of vengeance." Another beautiful aria, although it is sometimes criticized for adding little or nothing to the plot, is Donna Anna's "Non mi dir" ("Say no more"), in which she says she can't consider marriage while her thoughts are on her murdered father.

And many more.

COMMENTARY

Don Giovanni was commissioned for the opera in Prague, where *Figaro* had been a great success—and where the lovely theater in which it was premiered still stands as one of three major Prague opera houses. It is an opera with wit, satire, farce, moving drama, and tragedy and is cited today to contradict the notion—popular at one time—that Mozart was simply an ultragraceful musician without passion or depth. Despite many light moments, the Commendatore *is* murdered and the Don *is* consigned, onstage, to Hell. The characters are divided, serious and comic, with Don Ottavio, Donna Anna, the Commendatore, and Donna Elvira on one side and Leporello, Zerlina, and Masetto on the other—and the Don on both.

It is a puzzling work, neither fish nor fowl. Although called an opera buffa, much of it is typical of opera seria, but Mozart's innovative treatment hurried the old form of opera seria to its death.

Johannes C.W.T. Mozart

Mozart was christened Johannes Chrysostomus Wolfgangus Theophilus. In the official records, his father, a musician of considerable repute in his day, substituted Amadeus for Theophilus. The son preferred to style himself as Wolfgang Amadeus.

About one hundred years ago George Bernard Shaw called *Don Giovanni* the greatest opera ever composed, "eminent in virtue of its uncommon share of wisdom, beauty, and humor." Fifty years later, Virgil Thomson was no less flattering: "*Don Giovanni* is one of the funniest shows in the world and one of the most terrifying. It is all about love, and it kids love to a fare-ye-well. It is the world's greatest opera and the world's greatest parody of opera. It is a moral entertainment so movingly human that morality gets lost before the play is scarcely started."

Don Giovanni, the title character, has no conventional big aria. He has a drinking song and a serenade, but nothing showstopping. Mozart planned it that way as a deliberate change from tradition. Written so that either a baritone or bass can sing it, the role of Giovanni has been played by Ezio Pinza, a bass, a range of baritones including Antonio Scotti, Tito Gobbi, and Dietrich Fischer-Dieskau, and even some tenors.

One ever-open question is whether Don Giovanni did actually have his way with Donna Anna at the outset before she cried out—and, if so, whether it was rape or a liaison in which she willingly participated. In fact, despite his reputation, the Don never positively scores, on stage or off, during the course of the opera.

Zerlina's character is also a question mark—it's never clear how much an innocent country girl she really is and how much a saucy, wily, and ever-so-knowledgeable flirt.

Among interesting similarities between *Don Giovanni* and *Figaro* is the portrayal of marriage. In both, marriage is treated as almost a holy thing, even though it means nothing to Don Giovanni, the all-time rake. He is a chap who enjoys challenging authority—first that of society, then that of God. Because marriage is sacrosanct, it serves very well as a target for him. In fact, by Mozart's time, the story of the Spanish Don Juan was hackneyed—and not well fitted for the walled city of Vienna, then the center of culture at a time of "enlightened reason" in music and literature. The whole idea of a "Hell" was looked upon disdainfully and the notion of a stone statue walking, talking, and coming to dinner didn't fit at all into Viennese culture. The rational *Figaro* was much more in tune with that enlightenment, despite its "unfortunate" victory of the servant class over the nobility. But in far-off Prague, relatively provincial, with a different type of society, *Don Giovanni* was a smash hit.

Listen for music of one kind when noble characters are singing and another when the common folk have the stage. With your eyes closed, and no understanding of the words, soon you can tell what sort of character is performing.

The more familiar these tricks of the trade become, the more one is apt to enjoy opera. But Mozart is so creative that you have to be alert to his booby traps. For example, patter singing, as in the "Catalogue Aria," in which Leporello lists his master's sexual conquests, is typical of Italian opera buffa. This is the servant being the servant, talking about his master. But before the aria is over Leporello is aping the Don, and the music for him shifts from "common folk" music to a more pretentious style befitting of nobility.

Don Giovanni himself is a chameleon, assuming every available musical guise to get what he wants. Pretentious Donna Anna's music is formal and serious, so when he approaches her his music is aloof. The music for peasant Zerlina is more folklike, so when he is wooing her his music is in the common style. Whatever it takes to win.

When farm-girl Zerlina and Don Giovanno sing a duet, she sings *his* upper-class music, no longer the commoner's music she previously has sung. To the sophisticated opera audiences of the day, this raised the question: Is she really being conned by the Don, or is she willingly coming along every step, perhaps even leading the way?

The original Prague version is different from a later Vienna production, for which Mozart wrote in some new arias to please audiences there. These are retained in most performances today, although they are superfluous to the plot.

The overture music in *Don Giovanni* and in *The Magic Flute* comes back later in those operas, but in *Figaro* it is not heard again. Overture conventions kept changing. Rossini liked one of his so much that he used it for *The Barber of Seville, Elizabeth, Queen of England* and *Aureliano in Palmira*.

Most overtures tell a good deal. In *Don Giovanni*, it sets the scene. It is in a tragic minor key, with a lot of brass making both earthly and supernatural sounds. Now listen to the overture of *Figaro*, a much lighter opera. It is all hustle and bustle with no brass. The *Don Giovanni* overture wouldn't fit the *Figaro* story at all.

The usual practice for composers of the times was to open Act I with recitative leading up to an aria. Mozart, in his mature operas, ignores these rules and goes full-blast into the action, in this case, first with Don Giovanni and Donna Anna and then with the murder of the Commendatore.

MET PERFORMANCES

Four hundred thirty-nine performances over fifty-five seasons, from 1883 to 1996.

RECORDING

CD—Angel/EMI CDCC 476260 (3). Joan Sutherland, Elisabeth Schwarzkopf, Graziella Sciutti, Luigi Alva, Eberhard Wächter, Piero Cappuccilli, Giuseppe Taddei, Gottlob Frick. Philharmonia Chorus and Orchestra. Carlo Maria Guilini. 1959.

VIDEO

Luxon, Gale, Goeke. Glyndebourne Festival Opera. Italian; English subtitles. Haitink, conductor. 1977. VAI.

Number 21. *Le Nozze di Figaro (The Marriage of Figaro)*

Premiere at the Burg Theatre, Vienna, 1786. Text by Lorenzo Da Ponte based on Pierre-Augustin-Caron de Beaumarchais's 1784 comedy, La folle journée, ou Le mariage de Figaro. *An opera buffa in four acts.*

KEYNOTE

Sublime mixture of wit and melancholy. Meet opera's first big trouser role, successor of castrati singers. Hear the great overture. Savor the real-life characters. Mozart's first joint venture with famed librettist Da Ponte.

PLOT

The scene is the Count's château, near Seville. Figaro (bass or baritone), valet to Count Almaviva (baritone), is to marry Susanna (soprano), maid to the Countess (soprano). The Count has his eye on Susanna, hoping to get her into bed before the marriage, even though he has formally yielded his traditional "right" to have her. (The opera rests on this "droit de seigneur," the right of a nobleman to sleep with any servant of his choosing on her wedding night before she goes to the groom.) Another problem surfaces for Figaro with the arrival of Dr. Bartolo (bass), who reminds him that he has borrowed money from Marcellina (soprano or mezzo-soprano), the doctor's housekeeper, and signed a contract to marry her if he doesn't repay it. A page, Cherubino (trouser role, mezzo-soprano), is about to be banished by the Count for flirting with his wife. He comes to Susanna for help, hides when the Count arrives, and overhears him wooing Susanna.

The Countess loves the Count and is unhappy about his indifference to her. Figaro and Susanna plot to trap him, shame him into returning to the Countess, and force him into approving their marriage. The plan is to dress Cherubino as Susanna and catch the Count trying to seduce her. Meanwhile,

Christopher Trakas as the Count; Young Ok Su as Susanna; Hilda Harris as Cherubino in Gian Carlo Menotti's staging of The Marriage of Figaro *at the Spoleto Festival*

the Count hears the Bartolo/Marcellina case and rules that Figaro must abide by his promise and marry Marcellina. This would conveniently clear the road for him to have his way with Susanna.

But Marcellina turns out to be Figaro's mother. Free of his obligation to marry her, Figaro now is in a position to marry Susanna. In other action, Susanna and the Countess switch clothing so that the Countess can confront her ever-lusting husband unawares and head-on. Out and out entrapment. Figaro, ignorant of the switch and thinking the Countess is his Susanna, gets a little antsy himself. In the end, true identities are revealed, all is forgiven, and everyone goes into the palace to celebrate.

HIGHLIGHTS

The superb ensembles, both the one ending Act II and the last-act finale in which the Count begs for forgiveness. Other special features include:

The Overture: Four minutes of wonderful Mozart music. It is his best-known overture and one of opera's best known.

Act I: Cherubino's "Non so più," as he muses about adolescent love: "I don't know anymore what I am. I'm burning hot, now ice cold. Every woman makes me tremble with pleasure and pain." Figaro's "Non più andrai," as Cherubino goes off to the army: "Life in the army is tough, my adventurous young lover. Forget your finery. You'll have no romantic philandering there."

Act II: The Countess's "Porgi amor" ("God of love"), lovely and taxing, which opens the act: "Oh Lord, give me back my lord and husband. My heart is breaking." Cherubino's love song, "Voi che sapete," which has become one of Mozart's most popular tunes: "You ladies hold the key to love. It is all new to me. I find no peace, either night or day, yet I never want it to change." The finale, which involves all nine principals except Cherubino talking at once about their complicated situations. This was a favorite scene of Mozart's and is one of his greatest.

Act III: The Countess's "Dove sono," in which she sings tearfully of her lost love, as the Count has deserted and offended her. It is her most moving piece in the opera and still another famous one: "Where are the beautiful moments of tenderness and pleasure? Where did the promises go?" The duet between Susanna and the Countess, as they draft a letter of assignation to the Count, "Che soave zeffiretto": "When the breezes are blowing gently and the evening shadows fall."

Act IV: Susanna's exquisite "Deh vieni non tardar," in anticipation of her wedding night with Figaro but sung to make him think she is addressing the Count: "Night is falling. Oh come, my beloved. Do not delay, my beautiful joy."

COMMENTARY

The plot was based on a famous comedy by Pierre-Augustin-Caron de Beaumarchais, the second part of his trilogy that begins with *The Barber of Seville*, the source of one opera by Giovanni Paisiello that opened in 1782 and the other later one by Rossini. Censors banned the play locally because it portrayed a lecherous nobleman, despite (or because of) the fact that a good many lecherous nobles were bounding about in those days. But the Emperor liked Mozart's operatic rendition, so the opera was permitted—despite reported sabotage efforts by Antonio Salieri, the composer who was the villain of the play and then film, *Amadeus*.

The plot is complicated, but Mozart does such a phenomenal job on each individual character that this does not detract from the whole. It was reasonably received in Vienna (only nine performances initially, but that was at the end of the season) and a smashing success in Prague, where it was staged for six solid months.

Mozart superbly used pairs of characters to contrast the workings of human beings, in this case, the "lowly" valet resolved to save his fiancée's honor and the powerful, lusty Count determined to have sex with her.

It is hard to find a critic or musicologist willing to attack this opera. *Kobbé* calls it an "incomparable masterpiece." Lang writes of the "delectable equilibrium between mirth and sadness." Addressing both *Figaro* and *Don Giovanni*, Einstein comments on the "imperishable personages" found in the former and the "iridescent picture of the universe" painted in the latter.

Here are some *Figaro* sound bites to help characterize it:

- From the first scene, it is clearly an opera buffa. Domestic problems of the kind discussed on the stage, such as measuring to see if a bed will fit, never would be found in an opera seria.
- Some 3,600 nobles in Vienna, most of them living within the walls, were being cared for by 60,000 common folk, most of them living outside the walls. In this class-conscious society, it was most unusual in an opera for the servants to outwit their masters on a deep moral issue, onstage, right out there in front of everyone. But Mozart presents the two classes playing on a level battleground.
- Like virtually all eighteenth- and early-nineteenth-century drama, the entire opera takes place in twenty-four hours; the subtitle, in fact, is *The Follies of One Day*.
- Mozart loved the clarinet, especially in music about love. Listen for it. One good place to listen is in the extended introduction to Act II.
- Another rule was broken in Act III, when the Count has a big double aria with accompanied recitative, that is, supported by the full orchestra instead of a few instruments. This was opera seria style, rarely found in opera buffa. In Act III, the Countess has her double whopper, with the full orchestra serving to give her status, stature, and dignity. But even in opera seria, these double whoppers were reserved for characters who were both noble and important. No commoners rated them, regardless of their importance in the opera. Even Susanna, who does beat out the Count and

have her way, never gets a double whopper to sing. Mozart can defy convention enough to have the serving girl win, but he cannot—or does not—defy it so much as to give a commoner a double aria with full-orchestra recitative.

- When you hear brass instruments in opera, wake up. They signal that something important is about to happen. This forewarning is another small example of the advantage of opera over spoken drama.
- The closing lines of *Figaro* are typical opera buffa. All the characters come onstage to say, in essence: "This is now the end, and we hope everyone had a good time."
- Trick of the trade. Early in the opera, when the Count is calling the shots, he has his own rhythm. Once Susanna seizes control, she now sings in the rhythm that formerly had been his. In the same vein, the Count's music early on is in the form of a minuet, the music of the court dance. When the valet Figaro sings, his music is common folk dance music. Mozart helps Figaro become the Count's equal by taking the minuet-style music away from the Count and giving it to Figaro. By the time one scene is finished, the Count is singing in the country style, something unheard of in the opera of the day.

MET PERFORMANCES

Four hundred and twenty performances over forty-five seasons, between 1894 and 1995. Ten performances are scheduled for the 1996–97 season.

RECORDING

CD—Decca/London 410 150-2 (3). Kiri Te Kanawa, Lucia Popp, Frederica Von Stade, Jane Berbié, Yvonne Kenny, Robert Tear, Thomas Allen, Samuel Ramey, Kurt Moll. London Opera Chorus and Orchestra. Georg Solti. 1981.

VIDEO

Skram, Cotrubas, Te Kanawa, von Stade, Luxon. Glyndebourne Opera Festival. Italian; English subtitles. Pritchard, conductor. 1973. VAI.

Number 23. *Die Zauberflöte (The Magic Flute)*

Premiere at the Theatre Auf der Wieden, Vienna, 1791. Libretto by Emanual Schikaneder. Technically a Singspiel (German song play) in two acts.

KEYNOTE

A fairy-tale opera and another blend of the serious and the comic. The first German Romantic opera, anticipating Weber's *Der Freischütz* in the next century. Mozart's next-to-last opera, completed less than three months before his death. Much Freemasonery symbolism.

PLOT

The days of Ramses I, Egypt. Tamino (tenor), an Egyptian prince, is saved while unconscious from a huge (but not very terrifying) serpent by three ladies-in-waiting to the Queen of the Night (soprano), a supernatural character. But when he recovers, a comic character named Papageno (baritone), a bird catcher who is covered with feathers, takes credit for his rescue. The Three Ladies (two sopranos and a mezzo-soprano), upset by Papageno's false claims of heroism, punish him by putting a big padlock on his mouth. They also show Tamino a miniature picture of a beautiful young girl, Pamina (soprano), the daughter of the Queen of the Night, who had been abducted. Tamino instantly falls in love and commits himself to her rescue. The Queen arrives, midst darkness and thunder, to tell him that Pamina has been captured by Sarastro (bass), a High Priest, whom she describes as a tyrant and evil sorcerer. Tamino and Papageno, accompanied by three cloud-riding boys (Genii), set off on a rescue mission, for which Tamino is given a magic flute and Papageno some magic bells, both designed to protect them.

A Boring Role?

Beverly Sills has written that the Queen of the Night was the most boring and pointless role she ever sang, with one aria in the first scene of Act I, a second in the third scene of Act II, and ninety minutes backstage in between. But the challenge of it is five high F's, plus some fancy coloratura passages.

Well, who wants to take on Beverly Sills? The audience gets the Queen's beautiful voice and loads of entertainment in between her infrequent appearances.

Scene 2 is in Sarastro's realm, where he heads a secret Egyptian religious order. He has Pamina under the care of Monostatos (tenor), presumably an evil and brutal Moor, but one who usually comes across as a comic villain who wouldn't scare the average nine-year-old. Although he lusts for Pamina, he runs away after a confrontation with the befeathered Papageno, whom he thinks is the Devil. Papageno and Pamina comfort one another. He tells her a handsome youth will come to rescue her, and she tells him he'll find someone to love.

In Scene 3, outside the Temple of Sarastro, Tamino learns that Sarastro is not an inhuman tyrant as described by the Queen of the Night but rather a wise and noble priest. Pamina and Papageno reappear, chased by Monostatos, who wants to put them in chains but who starts to dance when Papageno tinkles the magic bells. Later Monostatos returns with Tamino as prisoner, but instead of the reward he expects he's sentenced to a punishment of no more than seventy-seven strokes, on the soles of his shoes. Tamino and Pamina, now together for the first time, instantly fall in love but are ordered by Sarastro to the forecourt of the Temple of Examination, house of virtue and justice, to see whether they're worthy of one another. There they are separated.

Act II. After Sarastro sings a famous aria, "O Isis and Osiris," Tamino and Papageno begin their religious instruction. They're warned against all women by two priests and against all priests by the Three Ladies, who interrupt their lessons about virtue, discretion, and charity. The next scene is in a garden, where Monostatos comes across Pamina while she's asleep, bewails the fact that he is black and has no one to love, and ponders taking his chance to kiss her. He's interrupted by the appearance of the Queen of the Night, who is determined to destroy Sarastro's realm. She gives Pamina a dagger, with instructions to kill Sarastro and deliver the mighty orb of the sun to her, or be disowned. Pamina declines, and when Sarastro learns what's happening she begs forgiveness for her mother. He instructs her that there's no thought of vengeance within temple walls. It is love, not revenge, that ties man to man.

Gounod on Mozart

Charles François Gounod, composer of Faust, was an admirer. In one translation of a comment:

"O Mozart, divine Mozart! How little do they know thee who do not adore thee—thee, who art eternal truth, perfect beauty, inexhaustible charm, profound yet ever limpid, all humanity with the simplicity of a child—who hast felt everything and expressed everything in a musical language that has never been and never will be surpassed."

Tamino is directed to take a vow of silence as part of his instruction. Pamina doesn't know about the vow, is bewildered that he won't speak to her, and considers suicide, but is forestalled by the three Genii. Papageno sings that love makes the world go round. He wishes for a wife, meets an old crone who offers herself, and reluctantly accepts. She disappears after telling him to his disbelief that she's only eighteen years and two minutes old. Tamino and Pamina meet again and, protected by the magic flute, pass together through trials of fire and water. The Queen, her attendants, and Monostatos make a last attempt to destroy Sarastro and seize Pamina but are overcome by the sounds of raging water and thunder. The old crone reappears as Papageno (soprano), now a beautiful feathered girl. She and Tamino find one another with the help of the magic bells and plan a family of many wonderful children. Sunlight floods the stage.

Sarastro receives Tamino and Pamina into the temple. All praise the temples of Isis and Osiris. Love triumphs over Evil. Courage, virtue, and wisdom prevail over the powers of darkness.

HIGHLIGHTS

Overture: Miraculous musical fairy-tale language.

Act I: Papageno's "Der Vogelfänger bin ich" ("I am the bird catcher"): "I am a man of widespread fame; I am a happy man but would like to find a girl." Tamino's "Dies Bildnis ist bezaubernd schön," one of Mozart's most beautiful tenor arias, sung after seeing Pamina's portrait: "This portrait is beautiful, a divine one that fills my heart with a new emotion. Might this be love?"

The Queen of the Night's aria "O zittre nicht" after she materializes out of the clouds: "Oh tremble not, my dear son! You are innocent, noble, and wise, and will be my daughter's rescuer!" The quintet that follows immediately, "Hm! Hm! Hm!," sung by Tamino, Papageno, and the Three Ladies when the lock has been removed from Papageno's mouth. The duet for Pamina and Papageno, "Bei Männern welche Liebe fühlen" ("The man who loves has a kindly heart"), as he assures her she soon will be rescued and she tells him love will come:

Act II: The "March of the Priests" in the opening scene. Sarastro's noble, solemn prayer, "O Isis and Osiris," as he asks for strength for Tamino and Pamina to find the light. The Queen of the Night's "Revenge Aria" with its supreme high notes, "Der Hölle rache" ("The rage of Hell"), as she orders Pamina to kill Sarastro or else stop being her daughter. Sarastro's song to Pamina advising her there is no vengeance in this temple, "In diesen heil'gen Hallen." Pamina's "Ach, ich fühl's," as she misunderstands Tamino's silence: "Ah, I sense his love has vanished. My happiness is gone." Papageno's little "Ein Mädchen oder Weibchen," a love-makes-the-world-go-round song in which he asks for a sweetheart or wife.

COMMENTARY

This opera has a wonderful reputation, but for maximum enjoyment it demands more advance attention than *Don Giovanni* or *Figaro*. Some plot summaries make it sound like a scary and sometimes lustful drama, but it can be presented as an outright farce, a treatise on wisdom and reason, or a delightful musical entertainment. Mozart began it as a popular fairy tale, but it became a mighty operatic triumph. Conductor James Levine of the Metropolitan has called it a "complete masterpiece" and a "consummate work of art." George Bernard Shaw said during the 1891 centenary anniversary of Mozart's death that the music Mozart created for Sarastro is the only music that could be put in the mouth of God. Musicologist Alfred Einstein wrote more than fifty years ago that with this one work Mozart gained for German *opera* a position equal to that held by the idealistic *drama* of Schiller and Goethe. Professor Paul Henry Lang and many other twentieth-century musicologists call it the principal foundation on which all German Romantic opera was built. It combines the comic and the serious in a way that rarely—if ever—has been surpassed in opera.

Mozart and librettist Emanuel Schikaneder were dedicated Freemasons (so were two contemporaries across the ocean, George Washington and Benjamin Franklin), and heavy comparisons are drawn between the rites of Sarastros's brotherhood and the secret rites of Freemasonry. The opera often has been characterized as an outright pitch for Freemasonry and for universal brotherhood to replace the class system of eighteenth-century Europe. In those days Freemasonry was not the anti-Catholic movement it became in nineteenth-century America. It was something in which critical minds and generally enlightened people were involved, calling for self-discipline, practical humanity, virtue, patience, and tolerance. Mozart biographer Volkmar Braunbehrens writes that in Vienna it constituted an alliance of all who worked in the spirit of the Enlightenment—scientists, artists, writers, and musicians. Composer Virgil Thomson, a chap who combined arrogance with pixiness, describes it as something between the Rotary Club and middle-of-the-road Marxism.

MET PERFORMANCES
Three hundred and sixteen performances in thirty-five seasons, from 1902 to 1995.

RECORDING
CD—Philips Dig. 426 276-2; 426 276-4 (2). Kiri Te Kanawa, Cheryl Studer, Eva Lind, Francisco Araiza, Aldo Baldin, Olaf Bär, Samuel Ramey. Ambrosian Opera Chorus. Academy of St. Martin in the Fields. Neville Marriner. 1989.

VIDEO
Araiza, Battle, Serra. Metropolitan Opera. German; English subtitles. Levine, conductor. 1991. PGD.

One Warhorse by Gioacchino Rossini
February 29, 1792–November 13, 1868

IL BARBIERE DI SIVIGLIA *(Number 19)*,
THE BARBER OF SEVILLE

Gioacchino Rossini was born the year after Mozart died.

He was called the music emperor of Europe—and he lived like one. He had homes in Italy and Paris, with a summer house in rural France. He reigned for years in Paris, granting audiences to lesser lights, holding court and offering

Gioacchino Rossini

commentary, a nineteenth-century prince, rich, famous, gourmand-stomached, often with a mistress on hand. The great classical composer Camille Saint-Saëns was in one corner of Rossini's house, waiting his turn at the piano; a famous singer was in another, preparing to entertain the bejeweled ladies.

Many considered Rossini the leading composer of Europe—not the leading composer of opera but the leading composer period. In those days his overtures were even compared—favorably compared—with Beethoven's.

At age twenty-four came this Warhorse work, which is a masterpiece of opera buffa, one of the three or four immortal examples of comic opera—*Il barbiere di Siviglia* (*The Barber of Seville*).

He has one other Collection opera, Number 69, *L'Italiana in Algeri* (*The Italian Girl in Algiers*), a comic treasure that was internationally successful. It was his eleventh opera, written at age twenty-one, and is pure frivolity. Grouches, gripers, and grumps need not attend. Nor need double-domed intellectuals; no lessons are taught here nor any symbolism employed.

And a later piece at age thirty-seven, just before hanging up his opera quill at the peak of his popularity, was an accepted masterwork of Parisian grand opera—*Guillaume Tell* (*William Tell*), with the overture America knows best. The opera is infrequently performed today and doesn't make The Collection.

Italian Bayreuth

If you are a Rossinian, try the annual summer Rossini Opera Festival in Pesaro, Italy, the Adriatic Sea town where Rossini was born. The Teatro Rossini is a five-tier horseshoe-shaped opera house where only his operas are performed, although there also is a concert hall where works of other musicians are given. Rossini's home is now a museum. Some twenty miles away is one of Italy's most picturesque towns, Urbino, where Raphael was born.

Gioacchino Rossini emerges as one of the greats of operatic history, the leading composer of opera buffa and in his day well regarded for serious opera, although none of his serious works is now often performed. He composed some forty operas and a great deal of choral music.

True to the norm, assessments of Rossini's music have gone up and down during the century and a half since his time. Even at the peak of his popularity, not everyone—certainly including the Germans—ranked his overtures with the works of mighty Beethoven, and no one today sees him in such an extravagant 1850s light. Indeed, that recklessly high evaluation was gone by the end of his own century.

Giulio Ricordi, Verdi's music publisher and publisher of much of Rossini, Bellini, and Donizetti, was among those who called Rossini "Imperator musicae." Less flattering but perhaps more objective was musicologist Alfred Einstein, who in the early 1900s wrote of the "superficial, sensuous melody of Rossini and his imitators" but nonetheless also acclaimed *The Barber of Seville* as an "opera buffa masterpiece."

If Einstein found Rossini's melody "superficial," he also found it "truly magical." It was music that demanded exceptional singers with agile voices. The impresarios saw that it reached the right places—Vienna, the political center of Europe, and later Paris, which since Gluck had been the opera center of Europe.

The overtures of several other Rossini operas became concert-hall favorites all over the world, even though they never achieved the public renown of the *William Tell* Overture, familiar to tens of millions as the Lone Ranger's theme. In 1892, the one hundredth anniversary of Rossini's birth was celebrated with the overtures to *The Siege of Corinth*, *La gazza ladra*, *Semiramide*, and *William Tell*. Among the attendees of that afternoon concert at London's Crystal Palace was the then famous critic, George Bernard Shaw.

Rossini was not "profound" enough for the learned and doughty Shaw, but even he was susceptible on that afternoon to the infectious Rossini melody. "We were exhilarated and amused," he wrote in his review, "and I, for one, was astonished to find it all still so fresh, so imposing, so clever, and even, in the few serious passages, so really fine. I felt, not without dread, that the nails were coming out of Rossini's coffin as the performance proceeded; and if I had been seated a little nearer the platform, there is no saying that I might not have seized Mr. [Conductor] Manns's arm and exclaimed, 'You know not what you do. Ten minutes more and you will have this evil genius of music alive again.' "

Now that the second Rossini centenary has come and gone, the "evil genius" remains uncorked and flourishing, with his overtures especially admired, even if people no longer link him with Haydn and Schubert.

Rossini is a bel canto composer, put in the same little compartment as Donizetti and Bellini. Debates continue today over which of those three was the more gifted musically. Among things in opera for which Rossini is known:

• Wonderful overtures
• More use of the orchestra during the opera than was customary in Italy—but never to the detriment of the singers
• Large ensemble numbers, and many of them
• Emphasis on contralto and mezzo-soprano voices
• Long streams of melodies, apparently effortless, apparently endless, and apparently produced by the snap of his fingers
• Being one of the last important composers to write castrato roles

A leap-year baby, Rossini was born in Pesaro, Italy, on February 29, 1792, and like most (but not all) great composers had a musical childhood, in his case singing operatic numbers and mastering several instruments. At fifteen he began studying at the conservatory in Bologna. By this time he already was a sexually active chap, establishing a pattern he was destined to follow for the rest of his life. At the conservatory he met and later married a Spanish soprano, Isabella Colbran—the former mistress of the King of Naples—who was to appear in many of his later operas.

Several leading classical music composers did not find themselves until their forties and even fifties. Not so Rossini. His first staged opera was a one-act farce in 1810, *La cambiale di matrimonio*. This brought him some recognition, and just over a year later he became known throughout Italy when *L'Inganno felice* was performed in Venice.

After two more reasonably successful although short-lived works came many that still are produced today. These include but are not limited to:

Tancredi, 1813, Venice, which quickly became known outside Italy
L'Italiana in Algeri, 1813, Venice, a Collection opera
Il Turco in Italia, 1814, Milan
Elisabetta, regina d'Inghilterra, 1815, Naples
Il barbiere di Siviglia, 1816, Rome, his greatest masterpiece
Otello, 1816, Naples
La Cenerentola, 1817, Rome
La gazza ladra, 1817, Milan
Mosè in Egitto, 1818, Naples
La donna del lago, 1819, Naples
Semiramide, 1823, Venice
Le Siège de Corinthe, 1826, Paris (adapted from the Italian *Maometto II*)
Le Comte Ory, Paris, 1828
Guillaume Tell, Paris, 1829

That list includes his best-known tragic and serious works: *Otello*, *Le Siège de Corinthe*, *Mosè in Egitto*, and *William Tell*.

William Tell is a little off the radar screen today but a masterpiece in its own right and proof positive that an Italian bel canto composer could handle a French grand opera if he put his mind to it. When Rossini arrived to live in Paris in 1824, he made an agreement with the French government to write three operas, of which it was the last. Set in thirteenth-century Switzerland, it's the familiar story of the Swiss leader who rallied his country against the Austrians. It was taken from Friedrich von Schiller's 1804 play based on an old Swiss legend that came down through the years as a ballad. As most nonoperagoers know, Tell is forced to prove his reported skill in archery by shooting an apple from his son's head.

This was the last opera Rossini wrote and one of the longest ever composed by anyone. Although rarely performed at full length, an uncut version lasts some six hours. It was a four-act grand opera, produced between Auber's *La Muette de Portici* at the Paris Opéra in 1828 and Halévy's *La Juive* there in 1835. Meyerbeer, grand opera King, peaked later.

An opera on steroids that Cecil B. DeMille would have loved, *William Tell* was grand opera from A to Z: a serious subject, recitative rather than spoken dialogue, a subject from medieval history rather than antiquity, political relevance to the issues of the day, long and elaborate ballets, the spectacles of a lake storm and excited Swiss patriots, and rich orchestral writing. After fifty-six performances in the original form, it was cut significantly.

> ### *How Much Is Enough?*
>
> The story goes that Rossini met the director of the Paris Opéra on the street one day after he had retired. The director advised him that the Opéra planned to revive his big grand opera *William Tell*.
>   Rossini's response: "What!!! All of it?"

When he completed it at age thirty-seven, Rossini was at the peak of his European popularity, but he never wrote another note of opera, though he lived for thirty-nine more years. That's a long time to devote to good eating, good women, and sharp witticisms. No one knows why; musicologists give the following reasons, offered here in no order of priority:

- He was a millionaire, needing neither work nor money.
- He was basically lazy; everything had come to him so easily.
- He had health problems.
- Although he had created his own grand opera in *William Tell*, he deplored the trend toward that spectacular type of opera and away from his own opera buffa.
- Like Cleveland's Jim Brown and (temporarily) Chicago's Michael Jordan, he enjoyed being the emperor and decided to quit on top.
- He wanted to devote full attention to gourmand eating and attractive women.
- He had said all he wanted to say in the last dramatic scene of *William Tell*, a cry for liberty.
- All of the above.

There is no evidence that he even flirted with another opera during all that retirement time, although he did compose two big religious works, readily available on compact discs, the *Petite messe solennelle* (which nearly all musicologists note is neither petite nor solemn) and a Stabat Mater. He died in 1868 in Passy, France, where he had a summer home. By a music calendar this was four years after the birth of Richard Strauss and the year of the premiere of Wagner's *Die Meistersinger*.

One enthusiastic fan of Rossini is superstar Marilyn Horne, who says the ultimate critics are the ticket buyers, who always are with Rossini performances from the start.

Rossini wrote number operas, usually beginning with an orchestral number, followed by a chorus number, and then an entrance aria, all separated by recitative. Verdi began to move away from this model in Italy, and by Puccini's time it was about gone completely.

Professionals make the case that Rossini, a consummate musician, did for the early nineteenth century what Handel had done for the eighteenth. That is, he took all developments of the past and shaped them into a viable opera format, creating a whole that was much greater than all of its parts.

He is respected today in part because he recognized that the Italian preoccupation with beautiful voices singing beautiful arias was turning opera into something considerably less than it could and should be. No Italian composer functioning during his lifetime could ignore the singer fixation, and Rossini was too bright to try, but he also knew Mozart's work intimately, knew what a "whole" opera could look and sound like, and proved it with *The Barber of Seville*.

When Rossini wrote his version, another *Barber of Seville* opera, also based on Beaumarchais, was already on the market from another Italian composer, Giovanni Paisiello. It had premiered back in 1782 and Paisiello, a distinguished composer of more than one hundred operas, was still alive when Rossini's *Barber* came out. It was not unusual for composers to use the same source; there were other *Barbers* between Paisiello's and Rossini's. In this case, however, Paisiello's version was well established and some of his disgruntled followers made a raucous fuss at the Rossini premiere. Musicologists a half century ago wrote that Rossini had asked Paisiello for permission, but the more recent conclusion of the scholars is that he neither did so nor was obligated to do so. Some Rossini sound bites:

- If you were a kid or a parent at the right time, you know more about the *Barber of Seville* than you think you know. Parts of its overture were heard by millions on the sound track of Bugs Bunny cartoons so popular in the 1940s and 1950s.
- In some, but not all operas, he has the orchestra playing a tune all the way through before the performer begins to sing it, thus familiarizing the audience with the music. Haydn did this in his chamber operas; Mozart did not.
- Before Rossini, no major parts in Italian opera seria were given to basses or baritones, and so it wasn't feasible to have a true "ensemble." But opera buffa did employ basses and baritones, and as those two forms were merged many more fully developed ensembles appeared.

Number 19. *Il Barbiere di Siviglia (The Barber of Seville)*

Premiere at the Teatro Argentina, Rome, 1816. Text by Cesare Sterbini. From Pierre-Augustine-Caron de Beaumarchais's 1775 play Le Barbier de Séville. An opera buffa usually in two acts.

KEYNOTE

One of opera's top delights. "I was born for the opera buffa," Rossini once wrote. No deep problems, no social statement. Keep your eye on the ensembles, one of opera's most enjoyable parts.

PLOT

Seventeenth century, Seville, Spain. Old Dr. Bartolo (basso buffo) has his eye on the money of his ward, Rosina (mezzo-soprano or soprano), and wants to marry her. She's in love with Lindoro (tenor), who is Count Almaviva in disguise. Advised and aided by Figaro (baritone), a barber and jack-of-all-trades who can handle any situation with skill and trickery, the Count tries in two different ways to get inside Bartolo's guarded household, first by pretending to be a drunken soldier who has been billeted there and then in disguise as a replacement for Don Basilio (bass), the music teacher.

When Almaviva/Lindoro eventually does manage to communicate with Rosina, they exchange vows of eternal love and plan an elopement. Figaro shaves Dr. Bartolo in order to keep him occupied so that the lovers can steal off together, but Bartolo later temporarily breaks them apart by telling Rosina that "Lindoro" doesn't want her for himself but intends to turn her over to the "vile" Count Almaviva, whom he characterizes as a man with an infamous reputation. Once convinced of this, Rosina consents to marry Bartolo.

After Lindoro reveals to Rosina that he and Almaviva are the same person, the two again pledge their love. A marriage contract that has been drawn for Bartolo and Rosina is altered to substitute Almaviva's name. Eventually the doctor accepts his fate, and his pain is eased when Almaviva turns over Rosina's dowry to him.

HIGHLIGHTS

The Overture, familiar to many of the Unwashed who may not know its source.

Act I: Figaro's famous patter air, "Largo al factotum," perhaps opera's most popular song for a high baritone: "Make room for the factotum of the town, the jack-of-all-trades. I have a wonderful life and the pleasures are great for a good barber with my talents. Everybody asks for me." Rosina's famous coloratura aria "Una voce poco fa," as she admits her love for Lindoro.

Don Basilio's aria, "La calunnia," in which he praises gossip and tells how the Count's reputation can be destroyed by slander: "Slander is a little breeze, a gentle little wind, heartless when it slips into people's ears." Dr. Bartolo's buffo aria, "A un dottor della mia sorte," as he warns Rosina that it isn't easy to make a fool of a learned man like him, a doctor in good standing. And the great Act I finale, with all major characters expressing total confusion.

Act II: The quintet "Buona sera, mio Signore" ("Fare you well, good Signore"), as Don Basilio accepts money, agrees to the story that he is suffering from scarlet fever, and withdraws. The soft elopement trio for Almaviva, Rosina, and Figaro, "Zitti, zitti, piano."

COMMENTARY

One of the most popular operas of all time, *The Barber* is based on the first play in a trilogy of comedies featuring Figaro that were written in the

1770s, 1780s, and 1790s by Pierre-Augustine-Caron de Beaumarchais—*Le barbier de Séville*, *Le mariage de Figaro*, and *La mère coupable*. Thirty years before Rossini's *Barber*, Mozart had selected the second of the trilogy for his *Figaro*.

Immortality

"My immortality?" said Rossini. "Do you know what will survive me? The third act of *Tell*, the second act of *Otello* . . . and *The Barber of Seville* from one end to the other."

He was somewhat off. Today *Tell* is not seen often in major opera houses, although Donizetti once said of it: "The first and last acts were written by Rossini, the second by God." Rossini's *Otello* has not stood up against Verdi's later one. But *Barber* alone is immortality enough.

Points of difference between Mozart's *Figaro* and Rossini's *Barber* are made by the professionals. Among them:

- Rossini was the master of catchy phrases but seldom ventured into the kind of expressive writing that makes Mozart so wonderful.
- Mozart was better at using music to depict his characters—better than Rossini, better than anyone. His work is a deeper one; his characters more true to life.
- *Barber* is pure opera buffa, and no one surpassed Rossini at writing this kind of opera. *Figaro*, although technically called opera buffa, actually is a miraculous blend of operas buffa and seria. In the wrong productions, Rossini's *Barber*, written to be a farce, sometimes degenerates into a mere showcase for singers. It's more difficult to ruin Mozart's *Figaro*.
- In composing ensembles, Mozart and Rossini were matched by few and topped by none.
- The two composers operated in wholly different ways. Mozart worked within the political and administrative structure of his time in Austria. Rossini, in his younger days, roamed through Italy like a traveling salesman. After arriving in a new town, he first got to know the townspeople and their likes and dislikes. Then he assessed the kinds and types of local singers and musicians. Perhaps, for example, he found a surplus of mezzo-sopranos, an amply supply of woodwinds, and a scarcity of strings. Now it was time to start composing. Working in this fashion, he turned out seven operas in sixteen months before he began to become famous.

Buy or borrow a videotape and watch the finale at the end of Act I. Part of the formula for opera buffa in the late 1700s and early 1800s was for the mid-opera finale to present musical chaos that summarized the confusion that would be resolved in the second half of the work. This is seen in Mozart's three Italian operas in The Collection: *Figaro, Don Giovanni,* and *Così fan tutte,* and not long thereafter in early Rossini. The rapid singing here is a Rossini trademark.

One of my favorite opera experts is Peter Fox Smith, lecturer, college professor, radio authority, and head of the Opera Society of Vermont who says of the Act I finale: "If you don't like this, there's no hope for you and Rossini." In fact, if you don't like this, there's no hope for you and comic opera. It's a wonderful example of why *opera* is more enjoyable seen than simply heard, however much one can enjoy opera *music* on radio or recordings.

This is a comedy with which the top performers have fun, especially when produced as a merry affair. Though written for a mezzo-soprano, Rosina is sung also by sopranos. Among the former is Marilyn Horne, among the latter Beverly Sills. A renowned contemporary Figaro is Thomas Hampson. The classic Bartolo is Italian Enzo Dara, who has sung the basso buffo role more than three hundred times.

MET PERFORMANCES

Four hundred and eighty-one performances over sixty-four seasons between 1883 and 1996.

RECORDING

CD—Angel/EMI CDCB 47634 (2). Maria Callas, Luigi Alva, Tito Gobbi, Nicola Zaccaria, Fritz Ollendorff. Philharmonia Chorus and Orchestra. Alceo Galliera. 1957.

VIDEO

Quilico, Bartoli, Kuebler, Feller. Schwetzingen Festival. Italian, English subtitles. Ferro, conductor. 1988. BMG (Bertelsmann Music Group).

One Warhorse by Richard Strauss

June 11, 1864–September 8, 1949

DER ROSENKAVALIER *(Number 20)*

With no true competition, this delightful fun-and-games work is the most popular German opera written in this century. And, with no true competition, Richard Strauss is the most popular twentieth-century German composer.

Richard Strauss

That's not to say there isn't a great deal of other twentieth-century German opera. Alban Berg is in The Collection, and several other fine German composers, including Arnold Schoenberg, are in the Twentieth-century European Package. But none of them challenge Strauss in popularity.

Even more than most composers, Strauss produced different types of operas during his career. Consider his four Collection works:

Der Rosenkavalier (The Rose Cavalier), 1911 (Number 20), his most charming opera, which followed quickly after two sordid shockers.

Salome, 1905 (Number 42), which appalled the opera world with disturbing plot and radical music.

Elektra, 1909 (Number 59), another people stunner, called a "ponderous orchestral orgy" by a *New York Times* critic.

Ariadne auf Naxos, 1912 (Number 70), poetic and sensitive, a mixture of comedy and tragedy with a chamber orchestra.

Strauss, unlike many Collection composers who are opera specialists, is one of history's top classical composers of instrumental music. Though he wrote fifteen operas and during a long life was considered Germany's top living opera composer, he made his music reputation with tone poems—long orchestral pieces that painted a picture or told a story—most of which were written between 1888 and 1899. These swept across the music world, establishing him as the successor to the famous Franz Liszt, who invented the tone-poem form. Strauss's included *Don Juan*, *Till Eulenspiegel*, *Death and Transfiguration*, *Ein Heldenleben*, *Thus Spake Zarathustra*, and *Don Quixote*. (You'd recognize the first movement of *Thus Spake Zarathustra* as the theme music for the movie classic *2001*).

Operatic Quacks

For years there was an open-air opera season at the zoo in Cincinnati. The great German soprano Elisabeth Schwarzkopf commented on singing *Der Rosenkavalier* there: "Everyone was terrified at the idea that some animal might make rude noise during one of his roles . . . In other performances, someone would sing 'Rispondi mi'—answer me— and immediately there would be a 'quack quack' from a nearby pond."

Richard Strauss is Big Time. Ask a dozen music people to choose the leading opera composers and most will include him shortly after they've named Mozart, Wagner, and Verdi—and possibly shortly before they've named Puccini.

After the first performance of *Elektra*—an opera about a woman's obsessive desire to kill her mother—he said to friends: "Next time I shall write a Mozart opera," a musical shift of enormous distance from the ferocious, no-holds-barred music of *Salome* and *Elektra*. Those sounds wounded the ears of opera-goers all over the world. Mozart believed no music should offend the ears, ever, under any circumstances.

Well, no one other than Mozart writes a Mozart opera. But in Strauss's case the immediate result was the immensely popular *Der Rosenkavalier*, a sparkling delight bearing no more resemblance to *Salome* and *Elektra* than *Snow White* does to *Psycho*. After *Ariadne auf Naxos*, he continued to compose through both world wars.

In his first works, Strauss was a disciple of Richard Wagner. But in addition to moving toward Mozart he also tried to veer away from Wagner for the rest of a long life. He wrote of his decision to make this shift in a 1912 letter to his longtime collaborator Hugo von Hofmannsthal while they were completing the *Ariadne auf Naxos*:

"Your cry of pain against Wagnerian music manufacture has gone deep into my heart and has pushed open the door to a quite new landscape in which, led by *Ariadne*, especially the new Prologue, I hope to make my way along the path of an entirely un-Wagnerian opera of action, mood and humanity. I now see the way clearly before me, and thank you for opening my eyes . . . I promise you that I have now cast off the whole musical armour of Wagner forever."

Analysts today suggest that this letter must be taken with a grain of salt, arguing that in most of his later operas, he was no less complex, no less willing to tackle mythological subjects, and no less orchestra-oriented than he had been back in his Wagner days. Certainly, however, he pulled way back from the intensity of *Salome* and *Elektra*.

Strauss lived from 1864 to 1949, composing actively in two centuries, a contemporary of the Italian Puccini (1858–1924), the Russian Stravinsky (1882–1971), and the French Debussy (1862–1918). He was a product first of the late Romantic period, then of the post-Romantic "New Music" era, in which most serious composers turned away from Romanticism, and finally of the twentieth-century experimentation that came next.

His operatic production includes *Guntram*, 1894; *Feuersnot*, 1901; (the four Collection works, 1905–1912); *Die Frau ohne Schatten*, 1919 (see Twentieth-century European Package); *Intermezzo*, 1924; *Die Aegyptische Helena*, 1928; *Arabella*, 1933; *Die schweigsame Frau*, 1935; *Friedenstag*, 1938; *Daphne*, 1938; *Die Liebe der Danae*, written in 1940 but not performed until 1952; and *Capriccio*, 1942.

Guntram, a Wagnerian opera, was a one-performance disaster. Little is heard of *Feuersnot* and not a great deal of *Die Aegyptische Helena*. But *Die Frau ohne Schatten* and *Arabella* today are performed frequently, both in the United States and in Europe. *Intermezzo* was an attempt at a two-act comedy. *Friedenstag*, in one act, never made it off the ground, and the one-act *Daphne* is looked upon kindly as something written in a great composer's declining years. *Capriccio*, a chamber work, his last opera, is a long speculation on the subject of words versus music in opera. It's given occasionally at opera festivals.

Conservative Forecast

Librettist Hugo von Hofmannsthal had confidence in what they were to create in *Der Rosenkavalier*. This was his reply to Strauss after the composer explained what he wanted: "If I succeed, as I confidently hope to do, the result will be something which, in its blending of the grotesque with the lyrical, will to a certain extent correspond with your artistic individuality—something which will be strong enough to keep its place in the repertory for years, perhaps for decades."

Before very long, the decades will stretch into the twenty-first century.

Despite his long successful career, the conventional assessment is that Strauss peaked with his four Collection operas, all written when he was in his forties. By this time he had become one of the biggest men on the world musical scene—the successor to Liszt with his tone poems, the successor to Wagner with his knowledge of the orchestra, one of the most respected conductors in Europe, and a leading composer of magical operas. Still, he later became musical director of the Berlin Opera and co-music director of the Vienna State Opera and continued composing for decades. He was nearly seventy when he wrote *Arabella*, now a highly respected work even if it took nearly thirty years for it to enter the repertory. And he also wrote many lovely songs over the years, including one of his most beautiful pieces of music, *Four Last Songs*, composed at age eighty-four.

It's fair to say he didn't again reach the same high level that he had achieved during the first dozen years of the century.

Born in Munich, he played the piano at five and composed at six, but due to his conservative father never experienced the trauma of being a child prodigy. He was educated at the University of Munich. In 1885 the famous conductor, Hans von Bülow, who had premiered some of his early instrumental compositions, appointed him assistant conductor of the Meiningen Orchestra. Von Bülow was one of the most powerful men in European music and an intimate friend of Richard Wagner's—at least up to the time that Wagner stole his wife. It has been my experience that this act between friends is apt to impact adversely on their relationship. Strauss went to the Munich Opera in 1886 as third conductor and later succeeded Von Bülow at the Meiningen.

He was married to Pauline de Ahna, a soprano who had sung under his direction in Munich and who was the daughter of a general. As Strauss's father was a musician and his mother came from a family of brewers, neither Pauline nor her parents considered him much of a catch from a social standpoint.

Two men greatly influenced Strauss's musical career. The first was Alexander Ritter, a violinist in the Meiningen Orchestra, who had known Wagner, had married Wagner's niece, and convinced a young Strauss that Wagner's Music of the Future was the way to go. This was at a time when Wagner, Franz Liszt, and Hector Berlioz were the radicals in Romantic classical music and Felix Mendelssohn and Johannes Brahms the conservatives.

The other big influence came twenty years later in the person of Hugo von Hofmannsthal, the librettist with whom Strauss was to work for twenty-five years. Although their first joint venture was *Elektra*, thereafter Hofmannsthal steered Strauss away from that radical style and into *Der Rosenkavalier* and the subsequent less controversial works. Hofmannsthal was a distinguished poet, dramatist, and all-around man of letters.

Not all of the music establishment today is so certain that Hofmannsthal's influence was a good thing. What might a brilliant musical artist such as Strauss have accomplished had he continued breaking new ground with works as innovative as *Elektra* instead of shifting to a safer *Rosenkavalier*? One answer might be rapid burnout. Given the continued box-office popularity of both *Salome* and *Elektra*, it can't logically be argued that he would have lost his audience. In any case, musicologists today debate whether the partnership helped turn genius into gifted talent.

You don't have to like *Elektra* to like *Der Rosenkavalier*, although I strongly recommend both. And you don't have to admire everything about Strauss, the man, to like either. Unlike Wagner, he was a decent enough fellow in his personal life, although enormously difficult to work with. He did find it convenient to stay in Nazi Germany through the Hitler years and World War II. As Germany's leading composer, he was made president of the official Reichsmusikkammer under Der Führer. He lived in Garmisch, composing, doing his own thing, and making money. He was not political, and he used a Jewish librettist—scarcely the politically correct thing to do at the time—but he didn't disassociate himself from the Hitler regime. He accepted an engagement at the Bayreuth Festival that Toscanini and other famous musicians turned down, but biographer William Mann concludes that in general he acted toward Nazi authorities with more courage and defiance than sometimes has been credited to him. Mann also finds that Strauss was prepared to tolerate any regime that facilitated the production of his music.

In addition to the four Collection operas, *Die Frau ohne Schatten*, *Die Aegyphsche Helena*, and *Arabella* have also been performed at the Met—a total of more than 600 performances for all Strauss works since it opened in 1883.

The Composer and the Librettist

Richard Strauss and Hugo von Hofmannsthal corresponded frequently during their years of collaboration. Typical of Strauss's interest in the libretto are these comments on *Der Rosenkavalier*:

May 4, 1909: "Received the first act yesterday. I'm delighted. It really is charming beyond all measure: so delicate, maybe a little too delicate for the general mob, but that doesn't matter."

July 9, 1909: "Three days of snow, rain and fog have made me come to a decision today which I don't want to keep from you any longer. Please don't get angry, but think over calmly all I'm going to say to you. Even on my first reading of Act II I felt that there was something wrong with it, that it lacked the right dramatic climaxes . . . [It] lacks the necessary clash and climax; these can't possibly all be left to Act III. Act III must overtrump the climax of Act II, but the audience can't wait as long as that: if Act II falls flat the opera is lost. Even a good third act can't save it then."

Number 20. *Der Rosenkavalier*

Premiere at the Dresden Opera, 1911. Text by Hugo von Hofmannsthal. Three acts.

KEYNOTE

A masterful romantic fairy-type story of old Vienna by a master of music, orchestra, and theater. No horror, no shock, no blood, no murder, no kissing of the lips of severed heads. Enjoy the Marschallin, one of the opera's more taxing and rewarding roles.

PLOT

The reign of Empress Maria Theresa, Vienna, mid-eighteenth century. The Princess of Werdenberg, known as the Marschallin (soprano), is having a postlovemaking breakfast in her palace boudoir with her seventeen-year-old lover Octavian (trouser-role, mezzo-soprano), the younger brother of Count Rofrano. Her husband, a field marshal, is away hunting. Her cousin, the Baron Ochs (bass), an ill-mannered, pompous ass, arrives at the palace. Hearing him coming, fearing that he's her returning husband, and lacking the time to flee, Octavian dresses as a housemaid. The Baron enters the boudoir and explains that he is betrothed to a young lady named Sophie (soprano), whose father owns twelve houses but lacks noble blood. He asks the Marschallin to choose a young cavalier to carry the traditional silver rose to Sophie as a symbol of his love. While talking to the Marschallin, the sex-minded Baron is attracted to the young "housemaid" and shows it outrageously, pinching "her," chasing "her" about the bedchamber, and suggesting an immediate romp in any convenient haystack. When the Marschallin reminds him of his finacée, he tells her being engaged doesn't make him a lame donkey. Man, after all, is the lord of creation.

The Marschallin later chooses her young Octavian to serve as the Cavalier of the Rose. When he duly delivers it to Sophie, he immediately falls madly in love. The Baron arrives, behaves boorishly, and turns off Sophie. When he leaves she and Octavian declare their love. The Baron's servants find them together and summon him. Though he's not a fighting man, he's forced by Octavian to draw his sword and during a short duel is nicked harmlessly on the arm. This causes a terrible commotion, with everyone running around the stage in distress. When Sophie advises her father that she won't go through with the wedding, he threatens to send her to a convent and have Octavian arrested. The anti-Baron element conspires against Ochs, and he receives a "love note" suggesting a rendezvous with the Marschallin's pretty "maid."

Act III takes place in a room in a nearby inn. Octavian, disguised again as the maid, is keeping his assignation with the Baron but has had the room set up so that it appears haunted, with people and ghostlike things popping in windows and up from trapdoors. The police are called, the Marschallin and Sophie's father both appear, and, faced with the resultant ridicule, the Baron agrees to call off the engagement, leaving the two young lovers free to marry. Sadly but graciously, the Marschallin consents, releasing Octavian from any obligation to her.

HIGHLIGHTS

Act I: The tenor aria from the Italian singer who appears at court to further his cause, "Di rigori armato il seno": At the end of the act comes the Marschallin's famous meditation on the passage of time, "Die Zeit, die is ein sonderbar Ding": "I can recall another young girl who went straight from the convent into marriage. Where is she now, looking at the snows of the past? Time is a mystery of life. How we bear its passing makes the difference in how we enjoy living."

Act II: The "Presentation of the Rose," the first twelve minutes of the act, as Octavian and Sophie fall in love. Ochs's waltz scene, which closes the act, the same tune heard after he first meets Sophie: "Without me, how sad every day is for you. With me, no night is too long for you."

Act III: A famous trio, "Hab' mir's gelobt," in which the Marschallin sings that she wanted to love Octavian in the right way so she could even love him when he loved another but didn't know this would happen so soon. Finally, a love duet between Octavian and Sophie, "Ist ein Traum": "It's a dream; it can't be true that we are alone together, through eternity."

Greener Pastures

The German Richard Strauss compared his *Der Rosenkavalier* with *Falstaff*, one of only two comic operas (and the only successful one) written by the Italian Giuseppe Verdi: "*Falstaff* is the greatest masterpiece of modern Italian music. It is a work in which Verdi attained real artistic perfection. If I could only bring my own comic opera up to such exalted beauty."

COMMENTARY

Although considerably less adventuresome musically than the two shockers, *Der Rosenkavalier* is regarded as Strauss's best opera.

It requires a huge orchestra, 112 instruments in all, including 32 violins. Strauss was one of the best orchestrators of all leading classical composers, and this work is characterized as a wonderful vehicle for showing off his skills and imagination in handling the instruments.

It's also a superb vehicle for vocalists, described by one opera friend of mine as a work that presents "real, honest-to-God, glorious, almost bel canto singing, reminiscent of Donizetti, Bellini, and Rossini." The find-fault critics hold that several of the musical themes are a little trite, but not to worry about that.

A case can be made that Strauss came reasonably close to his objective of recapturing the spirit of Mozart, with his individual characters showing the strengths and flaws of real people, as Mozart's did. (Strauss wrote that Mozart "solved all problems even before they are posed.")

Don't look for historical accuracy. This is a fairy story. The tradition of the silver rose never existed, so there was no need for a cavalier to carry one. Also, the opera includes several fine Viennese waltzes, even though it is set at a time in history before the waltz was part of life in Vienna.

Octavian, like the Composer in *Ariadne auf Naxos*, is a trouser role, a direct descendant of Mozart's Cherubino in *Figaro* (although Cherubino is more flirtatious and Octavian more sexually experienced).

The Marschallin is the best-known character in *Der Rosenkavalier*, although Octavian and the Baron between them can steal the show. One of the singers most closely identified with her is the German soprano Elisabeth Schwarzkopf, born in 1915. Early in her career she sang coloratura roles but then became a magnificent lyric soprano, starring from the mid-1940s for nearly three decades. After a career in Europe, she made her Met debut as the Marschallin in 1964 and went on to become the leading Mozart and Richard Strauss opera singer of her day. Other famous Marschallins have included Régine Crespin and Kiri Te Kanawa.

MET PERFORMANCES
Three hundred and forty-four performances over forty-four seasons, from 1913 to 1995.

RECORDING
CD—Angel/EMI CDCC 54259 (3). Barbara Hendricks, Kiri Te Kanawa, Anne Sofie von Otter, Franz Grundheber, Kurt Rydl. Dresden Kreuzchor. Dresden State Opera Chorus. Dresden State Orchestra. Bernard Haitink. 1990.

VIDEO
Jurinac, Schwarzkopf, Edelmann. Salzburg Festival. German; English subtitles. Karajan, conductor. 1961. KULTUR.

∾

THE OTHER SIXTY OPERAS

Number 27. *Boris Godunov*
by Modest Mussorgsky
March 21, 1839–March 28, 1881

Premiere at the Maryinsky Theatre, St. Petersburg, 1874. Text by the composer from Alexander Pushkin's 1833 play and Nikolai Karamzin's 1819–26 History of the Russian State. *Prologue and four acts.*

"Weep, weep," cried the Idiot. "Darkness is coming."

"Woe, awful woe, to Russia."

The Mad Boris is dead. The new Czar and his entourage have ridden by the village, urging all to follow them to Moscow. But the curtain doesn't fall until the Idiot has sung his song of woe. No one is left to hear him.

Modest Mussorgsky, one of the most original composers in The Collection, converted a masterwork by Alexander Pushkin into *Boris Godunov*, a masterwork of his own, as powerful an opera as you are likely to find. Opera—and classical music generally—have no finer example of raw genius and individuality.

Mussorgsky died the same year as Dostoyevsky, and many have called him the Dostoyevsky of music. His goal was a simple one: to express the soul of the Russian people—without initial regard for what pampered singers wanted to sing, what money-seeking impresarios wanted to produce, or what a paying public wanted to hear.

Just Do It

Mussorgsky on composers:

"When I think of certain artists who dare not cross the barrier, I feel not merely distressed but sickened. All their ambition is to detail, one by one, carefully measured drops of prettiness. A real man would be ashamed of doing so. Devoid of wisdom and willpower, they entangle themselves in the bonds of tradition."

The best way to handle the essence of Russia, he determined, was with a new kind of music—one that simulated speech. He listened to the unusual rhythms and melodies of Russian folksong and to early mysterious Russian church music, hearing the simple and natural style of the Russian language. He heard forgotten inflections of rich dialects. In his own words: "I foresee a new kind of melody, which will be the melody of life. With great pains I have achieved a new type of melody evolved from that of speech. Some day, all of a sudden, the ineffable song will arise, intelligent to one and all. If I succeed, I shall stand as a conqueror in art—and succeed I must."

Mussorgsky was dedicated to the Russian people: "When I sleep I see them, when I eat I think of them, when I drink—I can visualize them, integral, big, unpainted and without any tinsel."

One style of opera is something like the Italian *La Gioconda*, structured around exhibitionist arias carefully designed for six types of supervoices. Another type of a wholly different nature is *Boris Godunov*, composed in Mussorgsky's speechlike melody and, in its original version, containing no major love scenes, no ballets, and no ornamental tunes.

One of five Russian operas in The Collection, it is by far the most popular:

Boris Godunov (Number 27).
Le coq d'or. Rimsky-Korsakov (Number 57).
Eugene Onegin. Tchaikovsky (Number 65).
The Queen of Spades. Tchaikovsky (Number 66).
Prince Igor. Borodin (Number 74).

If you are Russian, if you are six feet, six inches tall, if your voice is a powerful one, you would sell your soul for the role of Boris Godunov.

Descriptions of the opera from the critics: "a sprawling canvas of life in sixteenth-century Russia," "an opera that almost completely bypasses conventional melody," "an exquisite theatrical spectacle," "comparable without blasphemy to such eternal masterpieces as Shakespeare's *Julius Caesar*."

Whew!

Mussorgsky was his own man. He ignored both musical and dramatic protocols. He paid no attention to what the world thought, and he despised composers who did. He had little money and cared for none.

Professor Paul Henry Lang, one of my preferred sources, an academic who could and did write for the uninitiated, said a quarter of a century ago: "What he sees he renders with extraordinary force and fidelity . . . The musical language in *Boris Godunov* is new and original; everything here is invention rather than elaboration, the vision of genius, some tender, some overwhelming . . . What he created is magnificent and somewhat chaotic, as was his own much-tired Russian soul, rent by pity, childlike wonderment, and unspeakable agony."

Important to the survival of *Boris Godunov* on the operatic stage is that Mussorgsky was a member of Russia's "Five," or "Mighty Five," five classical music composers of the 1870s who dedicated themselves to creating a national style in Russian music, in rebellion against the Moscow "Western" international school headed by Tchaikovsky. Based in St. Petersburg, the group was led by a trained composer, Mily Balakirev, and, besides Mussorgsky, included

César Cui, a military engineer, and two other Collection composers, Nikolai Rimsky-Korsakov, trained to be a naval officer, and Alexander Borodin, a research chemist. The Five not only constructively criticized one another's compositions but also exchanged them for intimate editing and rewriting.

As a result of this kind of collaboration, few operas have a more complex history than *Boris*. There are several major versions, the first two by Mussorgsky and two more reflecting massive revisions by Rimsky-Korsakov after Mussorgsky's death. In addition there are later editings reflecting newly found Mussorgsky notes.

Mussorgsky's 1874 Version

This form, in a Prologue and four acts, with nine tableaux, is the one now viewed as the original:

Prologue: (1) The courtyard of the Novodievichy Monastery, near Moscow, with the people confused as to why they are there. (2) The coronation of Boris as czar outside the Kremlin.

Act I: (3) Five years later, the cell of Pimen, an old monk, in another monastery. (4) An inn on the Lithuanian border.

Act II: (5) The Czar's apartment in the Kremlin.

Act III: The Polish Act. (Added by Mussorgsky after the first rejection, to include romance and a part for a soprano.) (6) Polish Princess Marina's boudoir in her castle. (7) The moonlit gardens of the palace.

Act IV. (8) The palace in the Kremlin, where the council is meeting. There is a frightening appearance of an incoherent Boris, followed by the entry of Pimen, a holy man of great age, who has a tale to tell. The death of Boris. (9) The final tableau of Act IV in the 1874 version is a revolutionary scene in the forest. As the curtain closes, it reaffirms that the people are the "heroes." They are what the opera is about, not one man, however definitive a figure. (In Rimsky-Korsakov's 1904 rendition, the forest revolutionary scene is the penultimate one and the opera closes with Boris's death.)

Mussorgsky's first score, which consisted of a series of tableaux, or pageants, was turned down by the St. Petersburg opera in 1869. Among the flaws found by the directors:

- No central female role.
- No amorous tenor.
- No ballet scene.

- No sentimental intrigue.
- Strange and unconventional music.
- An "unsingable" bass role for Boris.
- Too true. Too bleak. Too shocking.

Mussorgsky went back to the drawing board, adding three tableaux and deleting one, writing in some love passages and a few singable melodies. When this new version also was found unacceptable, he was crushed. Not until further amendments, and until individual excerpts performed in public had caught the attention of music lovers, was the opera finally heard in its entirety. The date was February 8, 1874.

Because it *was* the first performed version, that 1874 production, with nine tableaux, is now generally regarded as the "original" Mussorgsky rendition.

Neither reviewers nor public was overwhelmed. Among assessments by the critics: "patchwork revision" and "coarseness and cacophony." Even Rimsky-Korsakov, friend and Mighty Five colleague, considered it clumsy and illiterate. After twenty performances in 1875, 1876, 1880, and 1882 in St. Petersburg, and 1888 in Moscow, the opera was put on the shelf, out of the repertory. Mussorgsky had died in 1881.

After his death, his good friend Rimsky-Korsakov spent time over several years reorchestrating the entire score, rewriting parts of the music, deleting and adding. Some years later, still not satisfied, he undertook yet another revision in which he held on to most of his changes but restored some of the Mussorgsky parts that he previously had cut.

Chicken Fricasee

One unhappy Russian expressed himself this way in a letter to the editor in 1876, at the time *Boris Godunov* was being rewritten:

"Our operas resemble chickens that can't defend themselves against a powerful cook. At any day or hour of his choice some(one) . . . has the right to catch the most talented Russian opera by the wings, chop off its legs or tail, cut its throat, and cook a fricasse of his own invention. When Mussorgsky's *Boris Godunov* was being considered, I remember hearing some profound connoisseurs saying with an important mien and with their customary aplomb that the entire fifth act was quite superfluous, that it simply had to be cut off, or, at least, that it should be transposed and played before the fourth act. O God, it was just like being in the kitchen . . . Not everyone has the fortitude of a Beethoven or a Schubert, not everyone is big enough to withdraw his work rather than have it mutilated."

This second Rimsky version was produced successfully in 1908, thirty years after the Mussorgsky premiere, and is the one that became internationally famous in the twentieth century. And it is the one in which the great Russian bass Feodor Chaliapin starred for years.

Most recently, typical of today's back-to-the-original inclinations, audiences more often see and hear the nine tableaux of the 1874 rendition.

Musicologists still argue today about the many versions. On the one hand, Mussorgsky was not an accomplished craftsman; his work needed help if it was going to live in its own time. On the other, the analysts say, elements of his composition, especially his harmonies, were far in advance of his time—and in advance of the much more technically skilled Rimsky-Korsakov. With each "improvement" something of the original power is lost. Various other musical artists have attempted revisions, including one by the great Russian composer Dmitri Shostakovich in 1940, produced in Leningrad in 1959. Two back-to-the-original versions were by the Russian musicologist Pavel Lamm in 1928 and by the English conductor David Lloyd-Jones in 1975, who incorporated original sources not available to Lamm. Lloyd-Jones's is the current standard version.

Some Mussorgsky experts, including a biographer, M. D. Calvocoressi, consider the first version, pre-1874, the strongest of all.

Mussorgsky's life was a short, tragic, and tormented one, largely because he was an alcoholic. He was born in 1839 in Karevo, Russia, three hundred miles south of Moscow. His father was a landowner, comfortable economically; his paternal grandmother had been a peasant, and from her he heard his first old peasant songs. Aside from playing the piano a little as a child—he gave a small concert at age eleven—he had no early musical background. From boyhood he was earmarked for the army. He attended the Military School for Ensigns and at eighteen was a young officer in the aristocratic Preobrajensky regiment. As described by author/critic Harold C. Schonberg, by that time he "had been taught what every good regimental officer of the Preobrajensky had to know—how to drink, how to wench, how to wear clothes, how to gamble, how to flog a serf, how to sit a horse." Serf-flogging aside, it sounds like the education of most Princeton undergraduates a few generations ago. Tragically for his life and the world's opera, the drinking that began so early was to dominate his life and work.

But he continued to play the piano and also developed a fierce appetite for music, without having studied harmony or composition. Balakirev took him on as a student, and in two years he resigned his commission to concentrate on music. Few have undertaken classical composition with as little training and musical education.

For years his objective was an opera that communicated the essence of the Russian people. As an experiment in relating music to human speech—and especially Russian music to the rhythm of Russian speech—in 1864 he composed one act of *The Marriage*, based on the comic drama by Nikolay Gogol

(1809–1852), often called the father of realism in Russian literature. But this was left unfinished. Then came *Boris Godunov*.

Later he worked on another opera, *Khovanschina*, completing a piano score in 1874, but never scoring the opera for orchestra. This was done later by his friend Rimsky. Yet another operatic project, *The Fair at Sorochinsk*, also was finished by another composer, Cui. His nonoperatic work included a powerful song cycle, *Songs and Dances of Death*; *Pictures at an Exhibition* for piano (later orchestrated by Maurice Ravel into one of classical music's most popular pieces); and a lively and lovely orchestrated work, *A Night on Bald Mountain*.

The drinking that began casually in his youth became more and more serious and caused hallucinations, fits of delirium tremens, and finally a stroke. He died at the age of forty-two in 1881, having lived several years as a pitiful alcoholic, sometimes found by his friends unconscious in saloons, wearing rags . . . yet always obsessed by his music.

Pushkin, from whose play *Boris* was drawn, is the Russian Shakespeare, the man who almost single-handedly created a classical literary heritage for Russian writers: poetry, plays, novels, and short stories. Two of his famous works are *Eugene Onegin*, a novel in verse, and *Pikovaya dama* (*The Queen of Spades*), a novel in prose. Tchaikovsky, Russia's finest classical composer, turned both into Collection operas.

In 1824 Pushkin was expelled from the government as a troublemaker and banished to his estate. There he wrote *Boris*, another masterpiece, a historical tragedy, a play in blank verse. No one understood the Russian soul more than Pushkin, and both he and his work were natural sources for Mussorgsky.

KEYNOTE

A soul-stirring drama. See the intense realism of the folk scenes. Meet the Russian people. Powerful emotion and originality. No froth, fun, or games here.

PLOT

Russia, 1598–1605. Although the versions differ, the basic story is this: Boris Godunov (bass) is the chief minister and brother-in-law of Czar Fyodor, who was the son of Ivan the Terrible. To clear the way for seizing power on his own, Boris has ordered the assassination of young Dmitri, half brother of the Czar and the legitimate heir. Once this has been done, he pretends to decline the throne but has his agents incite the crowd to demand that he accept it— which he does.

In another scene, a young monk named Grigory (tenor) is in a monastery learning the history of Russia from an old monk, Pimen (bass). Grigory hears of the murder, decides to become the instrument of divine retribution for it, and leaves the monastery for Poland, where he passes as the dead Dmitri. He falls in love with Marina (soprano), an ambitious Polish princess with her own agenda, whom he later marries. In time, he assumes command of the Polish army with the purpose of leading it against Russia.

Feodor Chaliapin as Boris Godunov

In the Kromy Forest, the starving people bait a captured landlord who has been a supporter of Boris, and the unhappy children mock a helpless simpleton (whose song is to close the opera). The mob cheers Grigory-as-Dmitri as he passes by en route to Moscow and the throne. Meanwhile, Boris has heard a report that Dmitri is still alive and seeking revenge. He begins to be haunted by Dmitri's apparition. Tortured by his guilty conscience, and half insane, he turns over the empire to his son, and dies in agony. When Grigory hears of his death, he seizes power as Dmitri.

HIGHLIGHTS

The chorus throughout.

The Prologue: Boris's "Coronation Scene," biggest scene of the opera: "I have attained the highest power. Six years have passed since I first ruled Russia, but my soul has no peace . . . In darkest night I see the child Dmitri in a blood-stained shroud . . . His cry forever haunts me . . . Great God above, save me."

Act I: A long monologue by Pimen chronicling Russian history. A bass aria by the monk Varlaam about Ivan the Terrible's victory at the town of Kazan: "Forty thousand Tartars lay slain."

Act II: Boris's monologue to his son about his rule of Russia. "All this is beautiful . . . The great and mighty realm before you." One of the themes here is heard again at Boris's death scene.

Act III: The polonaise that is danced as court is paid to Marina. Also "O Czarevitch," the love duet for Marina and Grigory-Dmitri: "O my beloved, my heart is enchanted. I am yours forever."

Act IV: Boris's monologue near the end constituting his prayer and death, the opera's second major scene: "Heaven, I am lost. Forgive me for my sins. Heaven. Death. Forgive me."

COMMENTARY

The hero of the opera is the Russian people, the great masses—suffering at the time of Czar Boris, suffering when Mussorgsky was writing, suffering for a century thereafter, and not doing all that well today. The opera's chorus speaks for the oppressed peasants and children. At the beginning, the masses are easily influenced by their masters; at the end they're in open revolt.

But if the masses are the hero, the character critical to the opera's success as theater is the brutal Czar Boris, plucked by Pushkin out of Russian history, whose tormented guilt after killing a small boy leads eventually to his own death. Psychologists are fascinated by him. Some musicologists regard him as one of the great creations of the operatic stage, along with two totally different types, Mozart's Don Giovanni and Wagner's Hans Sachs from *Die Meistersinger*.

It almost goes without saying that a brutal sixteenth-century czar is a bass rather than a lyric tenor. *The* Boris of all Borises was Feodor Chaliapin (1873–1938), who in his international career was to basses what Caruso was to tenors. The scholars say he gave greater emphasis to words than to music, which fitted him ideally to the composer's speech-rhythm melody. Other leading Borises include Nicolai Ghiaurov, the Italian Ruggero Raimondi, the American Norman Treigle—and Boris Christoff, who is almost as famous in the role as Chaliapin.

MET PERFORMANCES

Two hundred and fifty performances in thirty-four seasons, from 1913 to 1991.

RECORDING

CD—Erato/Warner 2292 45418-2 (3). Galina Vishnevskaya, Vyacheslav Polozov, Kenneth Riegel, Nikita Storojev, Ruggero Raimondi, Paul Plishka, Romuald Tesarowicz. Chevy Chase Elementary School Chorus. Oratorio Society of Washington. Choral Arts Society of Washington. National Symphony Orchestra. Mstislav Rostropovich. 1987.

VIDEO

Nesterenko, Arkhipova, Piavko. Bolshoi Opera. Russian; English subtitles. Khaikin, conductor. 1978. KULTUR.

∾

Number 28. *Otello*
by Giuseppe Verdi
October 10, 1813–January 27, 1901

Premiere at La Scala, Milan, 1887. Text by Arrigo Boito from William Shakespeare's 1604 play Othello. A lyrical drama in four acts.

Otello is often called the greatest Italian opera of the nineteenth century . . . and sometimes the greatest opera of any type of any century.

The former description excludes all of Wolfgang Amadeus Mozart, always a wise thing to do when you get into the "greatest" game.

Greatest or near greatest, *Otello* is accepted generally as the prime example of Verdi's own absolute genius.

FTU (For the Unwashed): Despite the superlatives, I'd still start with *La traviata* or *Rigoletto*. But before waiting too long, at least watch a videotape of *Otello*. My own favorite version is a film by Franco Zeffirelli. It's an opera that should be seen, not just heard.

This was Verdi's next-to-last opera, ending a sixteen-year-gap after *Aida*, during which he composed his best-known nonoperatic piece, the Requiem, and began his association with the great librettist Arrigo Boito. Boito, a fine poet and an all-around literary figure, is in The Collection with his own opera, *Mefistofele*. It was his excellent libretto, combined with Verdi's lifelong love affair with the works of Shakespeare, that led the master to undertake *Otello*— and then still another opera, his last, *Falstaff*.

Most of the things Verdi liked best in his operas are found in *Otello*:

- Love.
- Power.
- Confrontation and despair.
- Hate, rage, and revenge.

- Heroic nation-building.
- Nation governing.

Verdi's was not the first *Otello*. Seventy years earlier Rossini had written one that premiered in Naples and enjoyed reasonable success, although it was quite different from Shakespeare's play.

For more general background, see the Verdi Warhorses.

KEYNOTE

Verdi's supreme masterpiece, action-loaded like Shakespeare's play, moving relentlessly toward the tragic conclusion engineered by the sinister Iago, the embodiment of evil.

PLOT

Cyprus, late fifteenth century. The familiar Shakespeare tragedy of the passionate love of the Moor Otello (tenor) for his beautiful white wife, Desdemona (soprano). Otello, a general, has led the Venetians in victory over the Turks. He is hated by Iago (baritone), his ensign, who aspires to replace Cassio (tenor) as his lieutenant.

By lies and treachery, Iago discredits Cassio in order to have him replaced as lieutenant, and worms his way further into Otello's confidence. He then plants false accusations against Desdemona, steals a handkerchief she has innocently dropped, suggests it has been in Cassio's hands and through other trickery first raises Otello's suspicions and then gradually convinces him that Desdemona and Cassio are betraying him. Innocent of wrongdoing and madly in love with her husband, Desdemona is bewildered by his changing attitude.

The Power of the People

The premiere of *Otello* was sold out weeks in advance. During the performance there were repeated calls from the audience for Verdi to take the stage. After the opera, huge crowds in the streets waited for him to appear. To show their respect, some fans unhitched the horses from his carriage and pulled it themselves through the streets to his destination.

Duped and delirious, Otello accuses Desdemona in public, curses her, and leaves her lying on the floor, distraught and humiliated. In the last act he enters her bedroom after she has said her prayers, extinguishes her lamp, kisses her, and, as she realizes that he has come to kill her, smothers her. Not until after the murder does he recognize her innocence and his horrible error. Iago escapes for the moment, but Otello, heartbroken at his actions and his loss, kills himself with a dagger.

Except for omitting most of the first act, the libretto follows Shakespeare closely.

HIGHLIGHTS

Given Verdi's different musical approach in which the songs are more part of the general texture than they were in his earlier operas, there are fewer Big-Number showstoppers than usual. Still, especially live or on videotape, look for:

Act I: The magnificent opening choral storm scene, with Otello's entrance and the bonfire chorus. The "Brindisi" ("Drinking Song"). At the end of the act, the poetic Otello-Desdemona love duet, "Già nella notte densa": "My soul is full of joy; I fear my destiny will not allow me another such divine moment." Some rate it among opera's most beautiful love music, with two of Verdi's most human characters onstage at the same time.

Act II: Iago's "Credo": "God is cruel who has made cruel humans in His image. I am wicked because I'm a man and I feel the primeval slime in me." This was Boito, not Shakespeare, but it is from Shakespearean examples of how Iago thought. The tenor-baritone duet that ends the act, as Iago convinces Otello of Desdemona's guilt.

Act III: Otello's "Dio! mi potevi scagliar": "God, try me with affliction, with misery and shame, if I have displeased you."

Act IV: Desdemona's ballad, the "Willow Song": "He asked me to go to bed and to expect him. Emilia, I beg you, spread out on my bed my white wedding gown." Also her prayer, the "Ave Maria." And Otello's death scene, "Niun mu tema," in which the music associated with the Act I love duet is again heard.

The entire final scene, much more than the sum of the numbers.

A Very Dumb Lion

Iago is the supreme mind poisoner of opera.

Otello is the dumbest general.

With due respect to Messrs. Boito, Verdi, and Shakespeare, in different careers I've known scores, perhaps hundreds, of generals. Dozens on a first-name basis. Some I've admired more than others. Two remain among my closest friends. I've known one-star generals, two-star generals, three-star generals, and four-star generals—and one five-star general. But never, in war or in Washington, have I met a general as gullible and just plain dumb as Otello, the Lion of St. Marks's.

COMMENTARY

Boito's libretto often is called one of the only ones in opera that can stand by itself as a drama. No Verdi characters are more real than Otello and Desdemona, which is what one would expect from a merger of Master Librettist Boito, Master Composer Verdi, and Grand Master William Shakespeare. As a villain, Iago is in a class by himself, the epitome of wickedness. The more misery he causes, the happier he seems to be. Puccini's Scarpia at least has objectives: Catch the escaped alleged bad guy and seduce Tosca. What's a little torture as a means to such noble ends? But Iago is relentlessly and diabolically evil, and his evil comes across as much in the opera as in Shakespeare's play.

This has been called the dramatic masterpiece that Verdi had been working on throughout his long career. The "theater" is sensational—a fifteenth-century castle, a raging storm at sea, a huge bonfire on the shore, and mobs and mobs of people. Not an easy-to-stage chamber opera. Musically, the melody is glorious and the musical characterization of his characters unsurpassed. Through music as well as voice, Iago comes across as wholly true to his creed, loosely translated as:

- I am a servant of Evil.
- I was made in the image of God, who is himself a monster.
- I come from foul seed, slimy, filthy and rotten.
- I am the obedient tool of my Devil's will.
- My vile intent must not weaken until it has reached its goal.
- All the noble words—fairness, friendship, honor—are lies, all nonsense and rot.
- Here is my faith: We all are fools of fortune, blind and senseless fortune. Life is a stupid farce. After life, nothing. Heaven is a monstrous lie.

Verdi departs significantly from the traditional approach of big set numbers that are linked by recitative. His style here is closer to the more fluid endless melody found in Wagner's music dramas. "More unified," the critics say. But he doesn't abandon individual numbers; there are solos and duets, a trio, a quartet, and some full-scale ensembles for soloists and chorus.

Especially when seeing it, live or on videotape, the Unwashed soon sense that *Otello* is of a different mold than the Big Three of *Il trovatore*, *La traviata*, and *Rigoletto*. That doesn't mean they'll like it more.

After singing the role for twenty years, by the mid-1990s Plácido Domingo has become the reigning Otello. Canadian Jon Vickers was an earlier magnificent one, perhaps more "heroic" and more powerful. It also became the most celebrated role of American James McCracken.

MET PERFORMANCES

Two hundred and sixty-nine performances over thirty-three seasons, from 1891 to 1996.

RECORDING

CD—RCA/BMG RCD2-2951 (2). Renata Scotto, Jean Kraft, Plácido Domingo, Frank Little, Sherrill Milnes. Ambrosian Opera Chorus and Boys Chorus. National Philharmonic Orchestra. James Levine. 1978.

VIDEO

Domingo, Te Kanawa, Leiferkus. Royal Opera House, Convent Garden. Italian; English subtitles. Solti, conductor. 1992. HOME VISION.

∾

Number 29. *Manon*
by Jules Massenet
May 12, 1842–August 13, 1912

Premiere at the Opéra-Comique, Paris, 1884. Text by Henri Meilhac and Philippe Gille from the Abbé Prévost's 1731 novel L'histoire du chevalier des Grieux et de Manon Lescaut. *Five acts.*

A common expression sixty-odd years ago was "The French have a word for it." When we were thirteen, we figured that word had to do with girls and hoped a friend would share it with us.

The French do have a word in music called "Massenetique," now part of their musical heritage. It means graceful, suave, warm, elegant, and flowing . . . but rarely deep.

Jules Massenet is not known for the dramatic quality of his work. But he is known for long-lined melody, technical mastery, extraordinary attention to detail, including costumes and lighting, and economy of means compared with the excesses of French grand opera. He was the central figure in French opera for the last three decades of the nineteenth century, between the death of Bizet in 1875 and the 1902 premiere of Debussy's *Pelléas et Mélisande*—in which Debussy demonstrated that opera could do things Massenet hadn't dreamed of.

Romain Rolland (1866–1944), French Nobel Prize winner for literature who wrote many musical essays, declared that the portrait of Massenet sleeps in the innermost recesses of every French heart.

Professionals outside France generally consider Massenet a "minor" composer who combined canny theatrical talent with charm, although some hold him considerably higher than that. He is not included among opera's "classic" composers—not with Mozart, Verdi, Wagner, and Richard Strauss, nor with Rossini . . . or Donizetti (especially if the right supersingers are available for his operas). And almost everyone concedes that Massenet ran out of steam many years before he died. But no critic can deny the hold he had on the public. Although he wrote considerable instrumental music of all kinds, he's best remembered today—as he was during his life—for his operas.

Tchaikovsky on Massenet

The French Massenet and the Russian Tchaikovsky were contemporaries, both born in the early 1840s. Each wrote a good many operas: One of Massenet's was *Le roi de Lahore*, 1877; one of Tchaikovsky's was *The Maid of Orleans*, 1878–79. While working on it, Tchaikovsky commented on both works in a 1879 letter to his brother: "I have a new pleasure in life, I bought some piano scores of Mozart and Beethoven quartets in Geneva and I play one each evening. You will not believe what a joy it is, and how refreshing they are. . . . I am quite in love with Massenet's *Le roi de Lahore*. I advise you to get hold of it and play it. I would give a lot for my *Maid of Orleans* to be as good."

Five years later, however, Tchaikovsky was less pleased by a Paris performance of *Manon*: "Very charming, well finished, but without one touching or impressive moment . . . Massenet was not up to the mark. He is beginning to get colourless, and boring, in spite of much effort and very fine work from beginning to end."

He also was hung up on women, which is not a mortal sin. He loved them, flirted with them, flattered them, and pleased them. Some scholars say the evidence suggests he was more talk than action. Many of his incredibly successful operas presented portraits of them, his writings included pieces on the lives of female characters in the Bible. Even his music itself is considered to have a great deal of feminine charm to it. This is not brutal Mussorgsky.

Although some elitists argue that a composer can be gloriously successful even if no one ever comes to any of his operas, a more general view is that a "successful opera" would, at one time or another, draw some kind of an audience. It may be a matter of semantics. In any case, like most opera composers, Massenet kept one eye on the public for which he was writing. This didn't endear him to all of his fellow composers, especially the less "successful" ones. The ones with purer thoughts disliked him for toadying to the public; the ones who also were toadying to the public envied him for being a superior toadier.

For what it's worth, we recall again the advice given Mozart by his father that he should not overlook all the musical ignoramuses out there. The rebuttal to that counsel is that meeting the public partway is one thing, but it's quite another to dedicate yourself to dishing out whatever the public wants.

In any event, the time in France was ripe for a Massenet. Consider the picture of Collection operas as he was maturing and writing:

Meyerbeer and grand opera had enjoyed a thirty-year stretch on both sides of midcentury. Offenbach and operetta were big in the 1860s and 1870s. Gounod produced the tuneful *Faust* in 1857 and *Roméo et Juliette* in 1869 but flopped with his next big effort in 1877. Thomas's one hit, the pleasant but lightweight *Mignon*, was in 1866; Bizet's spectacular *Carmen*, a far more substantive piece, was in 1875. Saint-Saëns was respected for his opera-oratorio *Samson et Dalila* in 1877, but none of his several other operas caught on. Delibes's operatic fame is based on *Lakmé* in 1883. Charpentier also experienced only one real success, *Louise* in 1900.

Verði, Puccini, and Massenet

In part because they both tackled the story of Manon Lescaut and in part because they were contemporaries, one French and one Italian, Massenet and Puccini often are compared. The expert consensus: Puccini had greater talent than Massenet and could produce endless melody. But they both lacked the true depth, strength, and deep passion of Verdi. Only he among those three could do justice to Shakespeare.

One or even two triumphs, however great, do not a central figure make. Thus the French field was wide open the last couple of decades of the 1800s for a talented, crowd-pleasing businessman composer to seize command. Massenet was delighted to oblige.

They saw him coming. "That little fellow is about to walk all over us," said Bizet.

The analysts say that Massenet's orchestral work was strongly influenced by Wagner, to the extent that some called him "Mademoiselle Wagner," a designation that today might be barred as being sexist or otherwise politically incorrect. The reasoning was that he had accepted some of the more superficial and stylistic aspects of Wagner—the leitmotif, for example—but that he lacked Wagner's powers of musical construction. This seems to suggest that a mademoiselle would not or could not possess Wagner's powers of musical construction. In the 1990s, with my wife, daughters, and granddaughters, I wouldn't touch that with a forty-foot pole.

The fact is that Massenet did not *try* to weave his musical themes into a Wagner-like symphonic whole, so the comparison seems meaningless. Massenet was not a lesser Wagner, but a different kind of creature altogether.

His two Collection operas came when he was at his peak in the 1880s and 1890s:

Manon, 1884 (Number 29). She dies.
Werther, 1892 (Number 77). He kills himself.

And I'd like to sneak in a third, *Thaïs*, 1894, even though it's not in The Collection. She also dies.

Other very successful works included *Hérodiade*, 1881; *Le Cid*, 1885; *Sapho*, 1897; *Le jongleur de Notre Dame*, 1902; *Thérèse*, 1907; and *Don Quichotte*, 1910, a good opera for the Russian bass Feodor Chaliapin.

Massenet was born in Montaud, France, in 1842, entered the Conservatory in Paris as a young boy, and won the coveted Prix de Rome at twenty-one. Four years later his first opera was performed at the Opéra-Comique. He was to write two dozen more before his death in 1924, although little has survived after *Thérèse*. In 1878 he was elected to the Académie des Beaux-Arts and appointed a professor of composition at the Conservatory.

He was a true nineteenth-century fellow, a Romantic in his music (even if financially a practical Romantic), and his operas are filled with sentiment and feeling. The words for him are words like "poignant," "dramatic," "tender," "passionate." This is not the Italian turn-of-the-century "realism" opera, nor is it early-twentieth-century symbolic atonal opera. The scholars describe most of it as softer "sunset" Romanticism rather than the fiercely emotional "sunrise" Romanticism of a Chopin or Schumann. It isn't strange that his popularity dimmed in the pressure-filled twentieth century.

Among Massenet's other compositions were a good many song cycles in the manner of classical masters Robert Schumann and Franz Schubert.

In his memoirs, Massenet explains how he got into *Manon*. The director of the Opéra-Comique had sent him a text of *Phoebe* by librettist Meilhac, one of the authors of *Carmen*. Unattracted to it, Massenet suggested to Meilhac that they consider the Manon Lescaut story. Meilhac invited him to lunch the following day.

Massenet recalled: "In responding to that invitation, one can guess whether I had more aroused curiosity in my heart than appetite in my stomach. I accordingly went to Vachette's [restaurant], and there, ineffable and quite adorable surprise, I found what? Under my napkin the first two acts of *Manon*. The other three acts were to follow in a few days. The idea of doing this work had haunted me for a long time. This was the dream come true."

Massenet's *Manon* was staged nine years before Puccini's *Manon Lescaut*, which was based on the same story. But circumstances for the two composers were entirely different.

Puccini's work came when he was young, down and out, struggling, trying to get off the floor. Massenet, on the other hand, was securely established when he wrote *Manon*. For Puccini, *Manon Lescaut* was the work that kept him alive in the opera business; for Massenet, *Manon* was just another success that solidified his position. Actually, Auber had used the same subject for an earlier 1856 opera, and Halévy had based a ballet on it in 1830.

KEYNOTE

Warmly approachable. More than 1,700 performances at the Opéra-Comique in Paris, still frequently performed, and arguably a better work than Puccini's.

PLOT

Amiens, Paris, and Le Havre, 1721. In the courtyard of an inn, Guillot (tenor), a nobleman roué, and Brétigny (baritone), a wealthy farmer, are dining with three "ladies." Lescaut (baritone) arrives to meet his fifteen-year-old cousin, Manon Lescaut (soprano) (they are brother and sister in Puccini's opera), who is being sent to a convent by her parents because she is too flirtatious. Guillot offers her money for a "word of love," is turned down, but nonetheless tells her his coach is at her disposal. The Chevalier Des Grieux (tenor) enters, sees Manon, and instantly falls in love. They run off together in Guillot's coach, which infuriates and humilitates him.

In Act II, Manon and Des Grieux are in a Paris love nest. Des Grieux writes his father, the Count des Grieux (bass), for permission to marry her. The father refuses in a return letter, and it's learned that he intends to abduct his son to get him away from Manon. Lescaut and Brétigny, in disguise, come and go. Although Manon loves Des Grieux, she feels she isn't worthy of him (and also wants to improve her position in life). She flees. Strangers come to the door and abduct Des Grieux.

In Act III, two years have passed. Manon now is living with Brétigny and enters a party with him. When she overhears the Count des Grieux say that his son is about to take holy orders at St. Sulpice seminary, she goes to see him. After a fight in which she admits she has behaved badly and asks his forgiveness, they are reunited in love and he gives up the priesthood. In Act IV, at a hotel casino, Des Grieux gambles with Guillot to get money for Manon and himself. Guillot, still bitter, loses, accuses Des Grieux and Manon of cheating, and leaves to get the police, who arrive and arrest them both. Manon collapses as they are taken away.

Act V is on the road to Le Havre. Des Grieux has been freed because of his father's influence, but Manon has been sentenced to deportation. After Lescaut and Des Grieux fail in an attempt to rescue her, Des Grieux bribes his way into seeing her. Now an ill and broken young woman, Manon begs him to forgive her and dies in his arms. (In Puccini, they both get to America and a "desert plain" outside New Orleans before she dies.)

HIGHLIGHTS

Act II: Manon's aria, a sad farewell to her table in the love nest she shares with Des Grieux, "Adieu, notre petite table:" "Farewell, our little table, that united us so often!"

Des Grieux's dream of Manon, "En termant les yeux,": "Closing my eyes, I see a humble, small white house, deep in the woods. Near it little brooklets sing with the birds! It is paradise! Oh no! . . . It still needs Manon."

Beverly Sills and Michell Molese in Act II of a New York City Opera production of Massenet's Manon

Act III: Manon's "Obéissons quand leur voix appelle," "Listen to the voice of youth when it calls." The aria "Ah! fuyez, douce image" by Des Grieux, who sings of how difficult it is to forget Manon: "There is nothing I now love except my faith. Ah flee, flee sweet image, too dear to my soul . . ."

COMMENTARY

Next to Bizet's *Carmen*, Gounod's *Faust*, and perhaps Gounod's *Roméo et Juliette*, this is the most popular of all French operas. Maybe Offenbach's *Tales of Hoffmann* comes close. Although it has a little spoken dialogue, for the most part the words are spoken against the orchestra and don't interrupt the music.

The melodies are lovely, even if some analysts describe them as bordering on being trite. The orchestration is pleasing, even if the naysayers declare that it lacks originality. The charm cannot be questioned, even if the drama is not overpowering.

Beverly Sills was fond of the French repertory, including *Manon* and *Thaïs*. She say in her autobiography, "Beverly": "I love Massenet—*Manon* had been a wonderful role for me—and the music he wrote for *Thaïs* is quite enjoyable and not terribly demanding in a vocal sense." Critic Irving Kolodin wrote that a skilled interpreter of Massenet's *Manon* might readily adjust herself to Puccini's *Manon Lescaut*. One who did was the Spanish soprano Lucrezia Bori, who made her debut at the Met in 1912 in Puccini's opera and is viewed by some critics as the all-time best Manon. Others include Mary Garden, Geraldine Farrar, Grace Moore, Bidú Sayão, Victoria de los Angeles, and Anna Moffo.

MET PERFORMANCES

Two hundred and thirty-five performances over thirty-seven seasons, from 1895 to 1988.

RECORDING

CD—Angel/EMI. CDMC 69831 (3). Beverly Sills, Michèle Raynaud, Hélia T'Hézan, Patricia Kern, Nicolai Gedda, Nico Castel, Gérard Souzay, Michel Trempont, Gabriel Bacquier. Ambrosian Opera Chorus. New Philharmonic Orchestra. Julius Rudel. 1970.

VIDEO

Sills, Price, Ramey. New York City Opera. French; English subtitles. Rudel. 1977. PAR.

⌒

Number 30. *La forza del destino (The Force of Destiny)*
by Giuseppe Verdi
October 10, 1813–January 27, 1901

Premiere at the Bolshoi Theatre, St. Petersburg, Russia, 1862. Premiere of the revised version at La Scala, Milan, 1869. Text by Francesco Maria Piave, from an 1835 Spanish drama by Angel de Saavedra, Duke of Rivass. Four acts.

Be careful of this one. If you watch Leontyne Price at the Metropolitan on videotape, unless you've sold your soul to the Devil, this work alone may hook you on opera.

That's in spite of the fact that it is known as a diffuse, flawed, and sprawling work for which a good road map is needed, even though Verdi involved himself deeply in a considerable amount of rewriting.

Over the years it's turned out to be one of his half-dozen most popular creations, a fact that could start a good debate about just how clean a story line must be in order to satisfy the operagoers. It proves again that characters who are true to themselves and drama that is powerful and intense can overcome a plot that barely hangs together.

The Force of Destiny (La forza del destino) is one of the four Collection operas written in Verdi's middle period, after the earlier Big Three and in the same ten-year span as *Simon Boccanegra*, 1857, Number 55; *A Masked Ball*, 1859, Number 32; and *Don Carlos*, 1867, Number 47.

By the end of the 1850s, Verdi was living a nice kind of life—rich, famous, a country gentleman content to write if a project interested him and rest if it didn't. Musically, St. Petersburg was something of the Paris of the north—if one can comprehend a Paris of the north—and he was glad to accept a lucrative commission to compose the work and oversee the opening. His wife, Giuseppina Strepponi, saw to it that he took with him 120 bottles of red wine and twenty of champagne.

Russian Review

Comments from a newspaper in St. Petersburg after the 1862 premiere:

"It is midnight. We have just left the first performance of the new opera which Maestro Verdi has written expressly for the Italian Theatre of St. Petersburg. We should not want this issue of the paper to go to press without mentioning the brilliant success of this beautiful work . . . It is our opinion that *La forza del destino*, of all Verdi works, is the most complete, both in terms of its inspiration and the rich abundance of its melodic invention, and in those of its musical development and orchestration."

Two versions survive. In the first, Don Alvaro, always a victim of the first order, throws himself off a cliff at the end, dying along with the other main characters, and in the second, commonly staged today, Alvaro lives on, desolate, despondent, and distraught, after his loved one has been murdered by her brother.

The initial librettist was Francesco Maria Piave (1810–76), who worked with Verdi on eight other operas, including *Macbeth*, *La traviata*, and an early version of *Simon Boccanegra*. At one point in *Forza*'s development, Verdi wrote Piave: "I have received your verses and, if I may say so, I don't like them . . . Now then, can't you do better, retaining as far as possible the words I sent you, but turning them into better rhymes?"

After Piave suffered a stroke, a poet named Antonio Ghislanzoni was brought into the project. An interesting chap, he also worked as a doctor, singer, and journalist.

Forza is regarded as a difficult opera to produce, in part because six principal roles must marry one another. It drifted casually in and out of the repertoire until after World War I, when it gradually became a solid international favorite.

KEYNOTE

Cruel destiny separates father from daughter, blood brother from blood brother, and brother from sister. Typical Verdi melodrama: the curse of a dying father, a blood feud, hate, sword fights, murder, and obsessive unfounded revenge.

PLOT

Spain and Italy in the middle of the eighteenth century. Leonora (soprano) and Don Alvaro (tenor) are in love. His father was a Spanish nobleman but his mother was an Indian, and although she was a princess this parentage makes him off limits for a European nobleman's daughter. Leonora's father (bass), the Marquis of Calatrova, finds them together as they prepare to elope and erroneously concludes she's been sexually dishonored. Don Alvaro takes full blame for being in her chambers and for the planned elopement but insists she is as pure as an angel. Although he's ready to die rather than fight his love's father, his pistol discharges during their confrontation and a bullet accidentally strikes the Marquis, mortally wounding him. The dying father curses his daughter. His son Don Carlo (baritone) swears revenge: He will kill not only Don Alvaro but also his sister. Opera has few more obsessive revenge seekers, nor few with so little cause.

The two lovers flee but are separated. Disguised as a boy for safety, Leonora seeks sanctuary in a Spanish monastery. At its gates she pleads her case with a wise and compassionate abbot (bass) who, after significant deliberation, grants her refuge for life in a cave on the monastery grounds.

Meantime, Don Carlo has been looking for her and Don Alvaro to avenge the death of his father. Coincidence—or destiny, if you will—now takes over. The two men, baritone and tenor, find one another in Italy, where the Spanish have joined the Italians in war against Germany. Neither knows the identify of the other. Off the battlefield, Alvaro saves Carlo's life by rescuing him from a gang of thugs. They swear eternal friendship. Later, after Alvaro is seriously wounded in battle, Carlo brings him in. Thinking he's dying, Alvaro entrusts Carlo with the mission of burning, unopened, letters in his small chest. Carlo agrees, but he finds a portrait of Leonora alongside the letters and recognizes blood brother Alvaro as his sworn enemy. He rejoices that Alvaro's wounds aren't fatal; now he'll be able to fight and kill this (now) coward who has slain his father and helped dishonor the family.

Over five intervening years, Alvaro has become a monk in the same Spanish monastery that houses Leonora, although he is unaware that she is the person living in solitude in the cave. Carlo stumbles upon him there and demands a duel. Although Alvaro tries desperately to avoid it, he cannot and he fatally wounds Carlo. When Leonora realizes what has happened, she rushes to find her brother. Unfortunately, she arrives before he dies and he has strength enough to wound her. As she dies, she prays that one day she and Alvaro will be united in death. But there are no guarantees since all have been victims of the "force of destiny." "Non imprecare, umiliati" exhorts the Abbot: "Don't curse, humble yourself."

It takes a bit of real genius to bring it all off, especially since there's no apparent valid reason in the first place for the father's curse or the son's revenge. True, it isn't known that Alvaro is the son of a Spanish nobleman and, true, his mother is Indian rather than European, and the Marquis's death is regrettable, but those facts seem scarcely reason enough for all the problem.

Still, it works gloriously.

HIGHLIGHTS

(Using a four-act version; sometimes there are five.)

Overture: One of Verdi's finest.

Act II, Scene 2: One of opera's most brilliant scenes, all outside the monastery gate. In the opera's biggest aria, Leonora sings "Madre, pietosa Vergine" ("Holy Mother, hear my prayer"), as she prays for forgiveness for her sins and contemplates her dim future. This leads to a major duet between Leonora and the abbot and that duet to one of the grand finales of all opera as the entire convent is called together and "La Vergine degli angeli" ("The Virgin of the Angels") is sung. Leonora is given sanctuary; no one shall disturb her. She will give her life to God.

Act III: Alvaro's forlorn aria, "O tu che in seno" ("Oh thou among the angels"), as he thinks Leonora is dead, protests his fate, and prays for her. A great tenor-baritone duet, between Don Carlo and Don Alvaro, "Solenne in quest'ora" ("Swear in this Hour"), in which the wounded Alvaro asks Carlo to burn the letters in his trunk without reading them.

Too Many Corpses

Librettist Francesco Maria Piave provided texts for *Ernani*, *The Force of Destiny*, *Macbeth*, *Simon Boccanegra*, *Rigoletto*, *La traviata*, and three other Verdi operas. In a note to him on *The Force of Destiny*, Verdi wrote: "We've got to think about the ending and find some way to avoid all those dead bodies."

They did. In the original version Alvaro throws himself into a ravine to his death, but in a revision he is redeemed, though miserable.

Act IV: Another famous duet between Don Carlo and Alvaro, and another one of Verdi's finest, often compared with the Otello-Iago duet in *Otello*. Alvaro, now a monk, again denies either seduction or any other dishonor and urges that both men bow to destiny, but Carlo will have his revenge: "Only your blood can wash away the stain on my honor . . . Only your death can atone for your crimes." The entire final scene in which Leonora sings "Pace, pace, mio Dio," begging peace in death: "Cruel misfortunes force me to waste away. My suffering has continued for many years . . . Who dares profane this sacred place? Maledizione! Damnation."

COMMENTARY

Despite its faults, *The Force of Destiny* is a strong, turbulent music drama on a grand scale, the only opera Verdi wrote that has an abstract idea for a title—and for a theme. No individual is dominant; domination comes from the force of destiny.

The "destiny" found in the original stage drama comes across in the opera as coincidence. But the work has glorious melody, with wonderful solos, duets, trios, and ensembles—and intense dramatic power. It isn't necessary to track each machination on the stage to drink in the music, sense what is happening, and get caught up in the emotion and drama.

It also has a big overture, possibly Verdi's finest, with haunting music in which an imaginative listener can hear the thumping of fate. The music tells us that dire things are going to happen to someone, and probably a lot of someones. Even in the milder version, father, daughter, and brother all end up as corpses.

Since the Russians had admired Italian-style opera from Mozart's day, a premiere of *Forza* at the Bolshoi Theatre in St. Petersburg was not too surprising. As an aside, don't confuse Leonoras; we have met another Verdi Leonora; the heroine in *Il trovatore*. The *Forza* Leonora goes to a monastery instead of a nunnery, the sanctuary of other Verdi women. She spends much of the opera searching for peace, finally finding it in death.

Sound bites:

- The music people point out that most of the first act is sung in something that sounds very much like the old recitative of Monteverdi.
- Because of the rambling libretto, a successful production demands a strong conductor and/or stage director to pull it all together.
- At *Forza*'s 1918 debut at the Metropolitan, the name of the man who sang Don Carlo was Giuseppe De Luca, one of the great Italian baritones of opera, and the name of the tenor who sang Don Alvaro was Enrico Caruso. The recording of the Act III duet by Caruso and Antonio Scotti, is a classic, and a good case can be made that these two singers were primarily responsible for the opera's post–World War I success. The singer who got the rave reviews at the Met debut, however, was the Baltimore soprano, Rosa Ponselle.

MET PERFORMANCES

Two hundred and nineteen performances in twenty-six seasons, from 1918 to 1996. Ten performances are scheduled for the 1996–97 season.

RECORDING

CD—RCA/BMG RCD3-1864 (3). Leontyne Price, Fiorenza Cossotto, Plácido Domingo, Sherrill Milnes, Gabriel Bacquier, Bonaldo Giaiotti. John Alldis Choir. London Symphony Orchestra. James Levine. 1976.

VIDEO

L. Price, Giacomini, Nucci. Metropolitan Opera. Italian; English subtitles. Levine, conductor. 1984. PAR.

∿

Number 31. *Hänsel und Gretel*
by Engelbert Humperdinck
September 1, 1854–September 27, 1921

Premiere at the Hoftheatre, Weimar, 1893. Text by the composer's sister, Adelheid Wette, based on the famous Grimm fairy tale. Three acts.

Charles Dodgson and Engelbert Humperdinck each set out to write a little something for the kids—one for young Alice Liddell, the daughter of a friend, the other for his nephews and nieces.

Dodgson, who wrote under the name Lewis Carroll, was a mathematician. He wrote "Alice in Wonderland."

Humperdinck, who wrote under his own improbable name, Engelbert Humperdinck, was a student of architecture until age twenty-five. He wrote the fairy-tale opera *Hänsel und Gretel.*

Dodgson did better . . . but Humperdinck did well.

Well enough, in fact, so that some forty years later *Hänsel und Gretel* was the first opera to be broadcast in its entirety to a nationwide audience in the United States. The time was December 25, 1931, the place the stage of the Metropolitan Opera in New York.

When the work was produced in 1893, Europe was agog over the versismo (realism) work of Mascagni. His lurid *Cavalleria rusticana*, produced in 1890, had spread rapidly across the Continent and the English Channel to London. Operagoers latched onto this brutal work as something different from both Richard Wagner and the aged Verdi, but they also latched onto the equally different childlike fairy aspects of *Hänsel und Gretel.*

To reset the clock: It had been forty years since Verdi's *La traviata*, nearly twenty since Wagner's *Ring*, and eight since Massenet's *Manon*. Puccini's Big Three (*La Bohème*, *Madama Butterfly*, and *Tosca*) were yet to come.

Humperdinck was born in Siegburg, Germany, and studied at the gymnasium at Paderborn with the intent of becoming an architect. But he turned to music and showed astonishing aptitude, winning top prizes in Cologne, Frankfurt, Munich, and Berlin. These enabled him to travel to Italy, where he met Richard Wagner, under whom he then worked for a year at Bayreuth preparing for the premiere of *Parsifal*. He remained a close friend of Wagner's, acting as one of a small group of Bayreuth faithful who attended their master until his death in 1883.

After winning still another award, the Meyerbeer Prize of Berlin, he traveled again in Italy, France, and Spain before settling for two years in Barcelona, where he taught music theory at the conservatory. From 1890 to 1896 he was a professor at the Hoch Conservatory in Frankfurt and taught harmony in a vocal school there. In 1900 he was appointed director of the Akademische Meislerschule in Berlin. He died near Berlin in 1921.

Kind Words from Strauss

Among the admirers of *Hänsel und Gretel* was Humperdinck's fellow German, Richard Strauss, who wrote him:

"Dear Friend: I have just looked through the score of your Hansel and Gretel and sit down at once to try to tell you how greatly your work has delighted me. Truly, it is a masterwork of the highest quality, on the completion of which I offer you my heartiest congratulations. Here, for the first time in a long while, is a composition that makes a deep impression on me. What refreshing humor, what preciously naive melodic art, what skill and subtlety in the treatment of the orchestra, what perfect art in the shaping of the whole work, what rich invention, what splendid polyphone—and everything original, new, and thoroughly German. My dear friend, you are a great master who has bestowed on the dear Germans a work which they hardly deserve, but which I hope they will continue to appraise at its full value."

It was during his teaching time in Frankfort that he wrote the opera that made him famous, the one that has endured most successfully, and the one strongly recommended for children of all ages.

After he had dashed off a play for his sister's children, she asked him to compose an appropriate musical setting for it. He did so, was drawn to the story, and extended his small work to opera size. He then sent it to Richard Strauss, conductor at Weimar, who was thrilled by it.

In 1895, the opera was transported to the United States by Sir Augustus Harris, a well-known London manager, who decided to use an English-language version. The *New York Herald* said the next day: "When Sir Augustus stepped in front of the curtain at Daly's Theatre last evening and in an amusing speech impressed upon his listeners that in *Hänsel und Gretel* he had brought to this country not only a novelty but what was broadly considered the most important lyric work of the last decade, he told the truth if ever a man did."

Actually, that production was weak and ran only for six weeks. But it returned in 1905, this time to the Metropolitan, in the original German, and it has never gone away.

Teresa Stratas in Act I of Hänsel und Gretel *in a Metropolitan Opera production*

Humperdinck was the main man in initiating a long string of German fairy-tale operas, with texts drawn from German folklore and fairy tales and music based on German folk tunes. Composers in this school, none in The Collection, include Ludwig Thuille, Friedrich Klose, Hans Sommer, Leo Blech, and Wagner's own son, Siegfried.

In a sense, this was a throwback to the days of their grandparents, who had attended the early German Romantic operas founded by Carl Maria von Weber, operas involved with something of the supernatural, something of forest scenes, and something of the songs and dances of the folk people.

Humperdinck's other operas are *Dornröschen* (1902), *Die Heirat wider Willen* (1905), *Die Königskinder* (1910), *Die Marketenderin* (1914), and *Gaudeamus* (1919).

KEYNOTE

Talented composer hides his sophistication. The kids take on the bad witch, and there's no contest. A longtime international favorite.

PLOT

Fairy-tale land. Hänsel (mezzo-soprano) and Gretel (soprano) are from a poor family and are bored and restless. After their mother (mezzo-soprano) chastises them for not having done their chores, she sends them to the woods to pick strawberries. When their father (baritone), a broom maker, comes home, he is appalled that they have been allowed to go into the forest where a wicked Witch turns children to gingerbread. Both parents set out to find them. In Act II, Hänsel and Gretel are in the woods gathering berries when twilight comes. After they get lost in the shadows, a friendly bearded Sandman (soprano) comes to put them to sleep and fourteen guardian angels watch over them during the night. In Act III, in the morning, they see a Witch's gingerbread hut and begin to nibble on it. With the help of a hocus-pocus spell, the Witch (mezzo-soprano) catches them and plans a nasty witchlike future for both. Hänsel is to be fattened up with apples and raisins, and put in the big oven, to become a feast. Gretel is to help the Witch, whose custom is to capture, bake, and eat little children. By trickery, they maneuver the Witch into her own oven, an act sure to bring applause from the audience. Upon her death, all the other children she has captured are released. This results in a happy ending for everyone except the bad Witch, who gets what she deserves and is pulled out of the oven as a giant honey cake. No one was concerned over whether it was politically correct to eat a witch-turned-honey cake.

HIGHLIGHTS

The Overture: Based on motifs from the opera, including the "Evening Prayer," a piece frequently played by itself on classical radio.

Act I: The dance song-duet for the two children, "Brother, come and dance with me," with its tap-tap-tap and clap-clap-clap.

The Prelude to Act II and the ominous music of the "Witch's Ride" that sets the tone for the appearance of the Witch.

Act II: The "Sandman's Song," the "Evening Prayer," and the Angel pantomime.

Act III: The Witch's big solo, "Hurr, hopp," as she gets more and more excited about her evil plans for the children, the children's happy "Gingerbread Waltz," and a reappearance of the "Evening Prayer."

COMMENTARY

Hänsel und Gretel is a good reminder that a lot of composers of lesser stature than Guiseppe Verdi have turned out a lot of splendid operas that have been and are enjoyed by a lot of people, including great musicians. Do not cast into darkness all composers except those who are most possessed by genius.

The story is clear, and the action is easy to follow. The atmosphere is picturesque. Unless you are a child-eating witch, the conclusion is happy. The vocal line is simple, folklike, tuneful, and, above all, singable. And the orchestra, though not Wagner, is characterized as Wagnerian in its richness.

Take that, Iago and Scarpia.

Among pairs of mezzo Hänsel and soprano Gretel have been Brigitte Fassbaender and Lucia Popp, Frederica von Stade and Ileana Cotrubas, von Stade and Judith Blegen, and Anne Sofie von Otter and Barbara Bonney.

MET PERFORMANCES

Two hundred and twenty-six performances over thirty-seven seasons, from 1905 to 1989. Seven performances are scheduled for the 1996–97 season.

RECORDING

CD—Angel/EMI CDCB 54022-2 (2). Barbara Bonney, Anne Sofie von Otter, Hanna Schwarz, Marjana Lipovšek, Andreas Schmidt, Eva Lind, Barbara Hendricks. Tölz Boys' Choir. Bavarian Radio Orchestra. Jeffrey Tate. 1989.

VIDEO

Fassbaender, Gruberová. A film. German; English subtitles. Solti, conductor. 1981. Unitel, Munich.

&

Number 32. *Un ballo in maschera (A Masked Ball)*
by Giuseppe Verdi
October 10, 1813–January 27, 1901

Premiere at the Teatro Apollo, Rome, 1859. Text by Antonio Somma, based on Eugenè Scribe's libretto for French composer Daniel-François Auber's 1833 opera Gustavus III. *Three acts.*

Some of us remember where we were on V-E Day (Victory in Europe) on May 8, 1945, and many more remember where we were on November 22, 1963. But where were you on January 7, 1955?

If you were very lucky, you were at the Metropolitan Opera in New York, when Marian Anderson became the first black operatic singer to appear at the Met. The opera was *A Masked Ball*. True, it was late in her singing life, and, true, they chose to cast her as a black sorceress/fortuneteller, but it's a strong part and the audience loved her.

Verdi, a republican who spent years seeking a unified and independent Italy, was always battling government censors. When he first submitted this libretto, the censor for the San Carlo theater in Naples rejected it because it dealt with the onstage assassination of a monarch, in this case the King of Sweden. The Pope also said no, perhaps because the King had been a good Catholic. The story was true to history; a Swedish king actually had been shot in the back during a masked ball in Stockholm in 1792.

When the work was withdrawn, a revolution nearly broke out in Naples, with people parading in the streets shouting "Viva V-E-R-D-I."

Verdi took his libretto to Rome, where the censor suggested a solution: Change the locale to early Boston, over there in the New World! It worked; no one cared about the murder of the colonial governor of Boston. (Yes, a Boston governor. Richard Wagner, a better researcher than Verdi, would have established that Boston was lacking a governor.) A later version used in the Paris premiere in 1861 set the story in Naples. Today both versions are seen, one taking place in eighteenth-century Sweden and another in Boston in the late seventeenth.

Censorship

The censors were extremely uncomfortable with much of A Masked Ball. Among their original demands were these:

Change the hero into an ordinary gentleman with no suggestion that he is a king or of royal blood.
Change the wife into a sister.
Alter the scene with the fortuneteller, and set the opera back in a time when people truly believed in fortunetellers.
Kill the ball, masked or unmasked.
Move the murder offstage.

Arturo Toscanini, longtime head of the NBC Symphony, a radio orchestra, was so fond of the work that he chose it in 1954 for his last complete broadcast opera.

This was one of the Verdi operas written during his "slow" period. In the fourteen years up to La traviata he had turned out sixteen; in the eighteen subsequent years only six.

See Verdi Warhorses for additional background.

KEYNOTE

Verdi's friendship opera. A triangle conflict involving the deep friendship of two men and the guilty (if chaste) love between the wife of one and the other. For many years, the only Verdi opera composed between La traviata and Aida that was regularly performed. Tight and fast-moving, though neither man would be my recommended choice for best friend.

PLOT

Boston, at the end of the seventeenth century. Using "Boston" names: Riccardo, Count of Warwick, the governor of Boston (tenor), is going over the guest list for a masked ball with his page, Oscar (trouser role, soprano). When he sees the name of Amelia (soprano), wife of his aide and dearest friend, Renato (baritone), Riccardo sings of his secret passion for her. Renato brings word that traitors are plotting against Riccardo's life, but Riccardo shrugs off the news, saying he'll be protected by the love of the citizens. When charges of witchcraft are leveled against Ulrica (contralto), a fortuneteller, Riccardo and his associates visit her in disguise to check her out for themselves. She warns him that he will be murdered—by a friend, the next man who shakes his hand. No one will take his hand until Renato arrives, who has not heard the prophesy. Confident of Renato's loyalty, Riccardo laughs at Ulrica's poor fortune-telling skills. Amelia also comes to see Ulrica to ask her counsel on how to cure a guilty love. They are overheard by Riccardo, who learns now that Amelia has the same passionate feelings for him that he has for her. He also hears Ulrica's suggested remedy, which involves Amelia picking herbs at midnight from the field where the hangman's gallows is located.

A Favorite Role

Verdi was especially fond of the role of Oscar, the bumblebee page. "I would rather the opera be not given," he said, "than that such a very important part be spoiled."

When Amelia goes to the gallows field for her herbs, Riccardo appears, declares his love, and urges her to acknowledge her love for him. At first she refuses. I belong to your dearest friend, she says, the man who would give his life for you. But as he presses her she admits her love, and it takes best-friend Riccardo about thirty seconds to say, "Let friendship and remorse both disappear." When Renato arrives to warn Riccardo that the conspirators are about to ambush him, Amelia covers her face with a veil so she won't be recognized. Riccardo leaves by a back route after instructing Renato to escort home the veiled lady. Renato and Amelia encounter the conspirators, Amelia's veil falls and Renato is humiliated for having a midnight assignation with his own veiled wife.

Angry and betrayed, Renato abandons his allegiance to Riccardo and the government and joins the plotters. Convinced that Amelia and Riccardo have betrayed him, he tells her she must die. She concedes her love, denies that she has been unfaithful, and goes to say farewell to their child. Renato then changes his mind about killing her but vows that he won't spare Riccardo. He and the plotters draw lots for the privilege of murdering the governor, and his name is drawn. Amelia has overheard them and sends Riccardo an anonymous letter warning him that an assassination attempt will be made at the ball, but he ignores it. At the ball, Amelia urges him to flee, but he refuses, saying that this would dishonor his friendship. He tells her he is resolving the issue by promoting Renato and sending them both back to England. He is saying good-bye when a masked man moves in and stabs (or shoots) him. Oscar rips off the mask to reveal Renato. As Riccardo dies (nearly everyone in the opera gives speeches and sings songs once mortally wounded), he declares Amelia's innocence and tells the people to forgive Renato and all the conspirators.

HIGHLIGHTS

Act I: Riccardo's "La rivedrà nell'estasi" ("I shall see her again"), singing to himself about his love for Amelia. Ulrica's invocation, "Re dell'abisso."

Act II: Amelia's recitative and aria, "Ma dall'arido stelo divulsa" (sopranos say an exceedingly difficult number), as she looks in the gallows field for a magic herb that will destroy her love: "What is left when love is lost." The love duet between Amelia and Riccardo, "O qual soave brivido," one of Verdi's best-known pre-*Otello* love duets. Riccardo begs for her love; she reminds him her husband is his best friend.

Act III: The opera's best-known tune, Renato's "Eri tu," sung in front of Riccardo's portrait. He decides to punish Riccardo but not his wife: "It was you whom I trusted and who poisoned the universe for me . . . It is all over, only hatred and death remain in my heart."

COMMENTARY

Unlike most Verdi operas, the best male part in this one goes to a tenor. It's a splendid opera that many experts, including two of my personal advisors, suggest should be grouped with Verdi's Big Three, *La traviata, Il trovatore,* and *Rigoletto,* although the public hasn't been quite that supportive. Music detectives say the harmonies here are more adventurous than those heard in *La traviata,* composed six years earlier, or in any previous Verdi work.

Although it's much better written and put together than *The Force of Destiny,* his next opera, which premiered three years later, both works offer Verdi melody and Verdi melodrama. There is a comic side in this one, found in the character of Oscar, which gives it a touch of the lighter side of French opera to blend with the Italian serious opera. Some have called it Verdi's *Tristan and Isolde,* in part because of the big Act II love duet, but this seems a considerable reach.

MET PERFORMANCES

Two hundred and forty-one performances over twenty-nine seasons, from 1889 to 1995.

RECORDINGS

CD—Angel/EMI CDCB 47498-8 (2) (mono). Maria Callas, Eugenia Ratti, Fedora Barbieri, Giuseppe di Stefano, Tito Gobbi. La Scala Chorus and Orchestra. Antonio Votto. 1956.

or

—RCA/BMG 6645-2-RG (2). Leontyne Price, Reri Grist, Shirley Verrett, Carlo Bergonzi, Robert Merrill. Chorus and Orchestra of RCA Italiana. Erich Leinsdorf. 1966.

VIDEO

Pavarotti, Ricciarelli, Berini, Blegen, Quilico. Metropolitan Opera. Italian; English subtitles. Patane, conductor. 1980. PIO.

❧

Number 33. *Manon Lescaut*
by Giacomo Puccini
December 22, 1858–November 29, 1924

Premiere at the Teatro Regio, Turin, 1893. The first collaboration of Puccini and his major librettists, Giuseppe Giacosa and Luigi Illica. From the Abbé Prévost's 1731 novel L'histoire du chevalier des Grieux et de Manon Lescaut. *A lyric drama in four acts.*

It's not the most important aspect of the work, but Manon sets an opera record here for rapid bed jumping. Although her romantic relationships involve only two men, she leaves the stage to live with one at the end of Act I and shows up at the beginning of Act II in her luxurious boudoir in the home of another.

Many Lovers

Commenting on the issue of both Massenet and himself writing operas based on the same story, Puccini said: "Why shouldn't there be two operas about her? A woman like Manon can have more than one lover."

And, indeed, within the opera, did.

With this heroine, you've got a choice: this Puccini version or an earlier one by Jules Massenet, *Manon*, Number 29 in The Collection. Lustful Italian ardor or more delicate French romance?

Puccini, hot-blooded Italian and scarely an objective commentator, compared the two versions this way: "Massenet has felt the subject as a Frenchman, with powder and minuets . . . I feel it as an Italian, with despairing passion."

Manon Lescaut, a fatalistic tragedy, was Puccini's third opera but his initial success, coming three years before *La Bohème*, the first of his Big Three. He desperately needed a hit. His first opera, *Le Villi*, had failed. Verdi had succeeded once again with *Otello*. Puccini worked five years on *Edgar*, another failure. Then Pietro Mascagni made it big with *Cavalleria rusticana*, followed two years later by Leoncavallo, who triumphed with *Pagliacci*. In contrast to the master and the two new bright stars, Puccini, in his early thirties, was broke, unsuccessful, and depressed.

After a fabulous premiere in Turin, *Manon Lescaut* had considerable good fortune elsewhere in Italy before moving to London in 1894. Despite a good notice from George Bernard Shaw, it had only one more performance in London before being put on the shelf for ten years. Shaw, who had been disappointed by the Italian verists Mascagni and Leoncavallo, wrote in his review:

"Italian opera has been born again," and "Puccini looks to me more like the heir of Verdi than any of his rivals." But the management of Covent Garden didn't agree; in fact, their distaste for Puccini was sufficiently great that they turned down *La Bohème* three years later, a decision that did not impact on the general applause elsewhere in Europe for *Manon Lescaut*.

This was not the only time Puccini chose to challenge another man's operatic story. Later, he and Leoncavallo were writing Mimi's *La Bohème* story at the same time.

See Puccini Warhorses for additional background on him.

Puccini on Pigs

When the public bought tickets in record numbers after the reviewers had panned *Manon Lescaut*, Puccini poured out his feelings in a letter, characterizing the gentlemen of the press as pigs, noting that they were full of bile, and declaring that he didn't give a fig about them so long as the public took his side.

KEYNOTE

Puccini's first hit, establishing him as a first-level composer. Floods of melody and two dramatic acts. Compare with Massenet and choose your Manon.

PLOT

Amiens, Paris, Le Havre and the Louisiana desert, eighteenth century. Young Manon Lescaut (fifteen in the novel, although described as eighteen in the opera) is being taken to a convent by her brother, Lescaut (baritone). At an inn en route she catches the eye of Géronte (bass), an arrogant and rich senior citizen who is the treasurer-general. He plans to spirit her away to Paris in a carriage, but she and the handsome young Chevalier Des Grieux (tenor) have fallen in love at first sight. Géronte's plot is overheard by a student, Edmondo (tenor), who advises his friend Des Grieux, and the two young lovers run off together to Paris in the carriage Géronte has ordered. Big brother Lescaut, more of an operator/manipulator than one would like in a big brother, tells Géronte to be calm and philosophical, and not to worry. He knows Manon; he's confident she will be available once Des Grieux's money has run out, as certainly it soon will.

Lescaut was right on. Act II finds her living in luxury with Géronte, having left Des Grieux for the old goat's money without so much as a word or a good-bye kiss. Her life is one of jewelry, beautiful gowns, fatuous madrigals written for her by Géronte, dancing lessons, and chamber music in her honor. In her boudoir, she confides to her brother that she's bored. He tells her Des Grieux is gambling, trying to make enough money to get her back. Later he brings Des Grieux to the mansion. Initially he's teed off at Manon for her fickleness, but after he cools down the old fires burn again and they have a long love duet. When Géronte finds them together, she unkindly thrusts a mirror before his face. Why would I want you when I can have him? Géronte leaves, telling them both to get out of his house. But she and her rather worthless brother delay long enough to sweep together a good bit of the jewelry Géronte has given her, despite Des Grieux's pleading that her lips are treasure enough for him. The delay is a disaster as the police, led by a gleeful Géronte, arrive to arrest her. He's even more satisfied when he sees she's also a petty little thief, and she is sentenced to be exiled.

The next act takes place at the harbor of Le Havre, where Manon is to be deported to Louisiana. Fifty-odd years ago, after D-day in Normandy, the small ship on which I served and hundreds of other vessels moving in and out of the harbor would have been overjoyed to take a good-looking French girl and her friend to America. But back to the opera: A plan to rescue Manon from prison fails and she is loaded onto the exile ship along with a group of prostitutes who also are being sent to the New World. In a pleaful and dramatic song, Des Grieux persuades the ship's captain to let him sail as a cabin boy.

In Act IV they have landed in America. Des Grieux has helped Manon escape, and they are on the run on a "plain (or desert) near New Orleans." In some productions it looks more like a lunar moonscape than any land that might be found within several hundred miles of that city, but there they are, alone, exhausted, despairing, and far from help. Watching the opera, it's a little uncertain how they got into this predicament. They are together, however, although she is exhausted from the sea journey and whatever land tribulations they have experienced. She begs Des Grieux to leave her and save himself while she dies alone, but he returns after failing to find shelter and water and she dies in his arms. He collapses by her side at the end of their long death duet in which they vow that their love will last forever.

HIGHLIGHTS

Act I: Des Grieux's aria on first seeing Manon, "Donna non vidi mai simile a questa!": "I have never seen a woman such as this one! When I tell her I love her, a new life is awakened in my heart." And their following love duet.

Still a Third

The first opera from Prévost's novel came long before either Massenet or Puccini. Also called *Manon Lescaut*, it was by a famous French composer, Daniel-François-Esprit Auber, and it premiered at the Opéra-Comique in Paris in 1856. The librettist was the most famous of his time, Eugène Scribe.

Auber, a high-class talent, was in the original Collection with *La muette de Portici* before I cut it from one hundred to eighty-five operas. In the Twentieth-Century European package, we'll meet Hans Werner Henze, German composer who based his *Boulevard Solitude* (1952) on the Manon story.

Act II: The opera's most famous aria—one of Puccini's most beautiful—is "In quelle trine morbide," in which Manon sings of her luxurious life in Géronte's home and the death of her old love: "In this gilded home reigns an icy, deadly silence that chills me! Then I had passionate embraces and kisses in our humble dwelling." Also the Manon–Des Grieux duet "Tu, amore! Tu?" as past differences are forgotten and they tell one another of the magic of love. It's a little hard for onlookers to think he's getting much of a bargain, but love is love.

Act III: Des Grieux's strong aria "No! pazzo son! guardate!" ("Have a care; I'm going mad"), as he sings the captain into taking him aboard.

An orchestral intermezzo.

Act IV: The final eighteen-minute death duet, which includes Manon's "Sola, perduta, abbandonata," when she fears she has been abandoned. Irreverent snipers in the music world describe it as her "Call me wretched" number: "Lonely and abandoned in this desolate country. The skies are darkening. I'm lost . . . I'm dying . . . How cruel is fate . . . Oh, wretched and hapless woman. Let me not die . . . All hope is over . . . No, no, let me not die." Well, die she does, in spite of this strength and courage, but the entire act is dramatic and beautiful.

COMMENTARY

The expert consensus seems to be that Puccini's version is better music, that Massenet's is better drama, and that Massenet's may be the all-around better opera. But then some musicologists consider Massenet to be an all-around better opera composer, although most who think that way tend to have French blood.

Puccini was young, not yet an experienced composer, and this had some beneficial results. He had fewer inhibitions about unloosening his torrents of melody, like a young fireball baseball pitcher who doesn't know any better.

Some sound bites from the musicologists:

More than in Puccini's two earlier operas, *Manon Lescaut*'s characters communicate their personal feelings. This isn't a work filled with abstract emotion.

Puccini uses some of Wagner's leitmotif techniques but much more of the recitative and the kinds of arias and duets that had been typical of Italian opera for years.

The orchestration is a little heavy-handed, a charge leveled at many operas of this time—and one reason these works helped ruin a lot of voices over the years as the singers strained to be heard.

MET PERFORMANCES

Two hundred and six performances over thirty-two seasons, from 1907 to 1990.

RECORDINGS

CD—RCA/BMG 60573-2-RG (2) (mono). Licia Albanese, Jussi Bjoerling, Mario Carlin, Robert Merrill, Franco Calabrese. Rome Opera Chorus and Orchestra. Jonel Perlea. 1954.

or

Deutsche Grammophon Dig. 413 893-2 (2). Mirella Freni, Plácido Domingo, Robert Gambill, Renato Bruson, Kurt Rydl. Chorus of the Royal Opera House, Covent Garden. Philharmonia Orchestra. Giuseppe Sinopoli. 1983.

VIDEO

Scotto, Domingo, Capecchi. Metropolitan Opera. Italian; English subtitles. Levine, conductor. 1980. PAR.

&

Number 34. *Fidelio*

by Ludwig van Beethoven

December 16, 1770–March 26, 1827

Premiere at the Theatre an der Wien, Vienna, 1805, in three acts. First performed in its present two-act form at the Kärnthnerthor Theatre, Vienna, 1814. Text by Joseph Sonnleithner and Georg Friedrich Treitschke from Jean-Nicolas Bouilly's drama Léonore, ou l'amour conjugal.

In 1788, George Washington was elected president of the United States, a revolution was fomenting in France, and an opera company was formed at the Electoral Court in Bonn.

One of the youths hired to play viola in its orchestra was the son of a tenor in the Elector's chapel choir. This was the young man's first intimate experience with opera, and it gave him a chance to hear and learn the successful works of the time, including those by Christoph Willibald Gluck, the great reformer, and newer ones by an artist named Wolfgang Amadeus Mozart.

Some of these were sentimental German Singspiel, a popular form dealing with everyday people and their everyday lives. Some were Italian-style works (including Mozart's *Don Giovanni* and *Marriage of Figaro*), which the serious young violist considered either "immoral" or "frivolous." Mozart's fairy-tale *Magic Flute* was soon to become popular, but this was thirty years before Carl Maria von Weber's *Der Freischütz* and there was no such thing as national German opera.

A few years later, after the turn of the century, the now mature violist, Ludwig van Beethoven, began a heavy fifteen-year period of composition during which his work included eight symphonies, three concertos for piano, a concerto for violin, three sonatas for piano, eleven string quartets, and much other chamber music.

Intellectual Opera

The German critic Paul Bekker, in a 1911 biography of Beethoven, writes: "He [Beethoven] believed in the possibility of opera as a field for the intellect, as a bearer of ideas . . . Although thanks to the impetuous force that resides in it, it established itself upon the stage, it has never really captured the theater."

By the early 1800s the name of Beethoven was already big in Vienna music circles, opera was the form of music most open to the paying public, and impresarios could add two and two to make money. In 1803 the director of the Theatre an der Wien, a hot competitor of Vienna's Court Opera, was looking for new properties. Mozart was dead, and the director commissioned Beethoven to write one.

This was to be his only opera. It didn't come easily. Donizetti is at his best in opera, Beethoven in instrumental composition. Among charges leveled against his operatic prowess:

• That he was unskilled and uninterested in the theater. Well, in 1801 he wrote a ballet, *The Creatures of Prometheus*. He followed this with incidental music and overtures for several plays, including *King Stephen*, *Egmont*, and *Coriolanus*. And he wrote an oratorio, *Christus am Oelberg* (*Christ on the Mount of Olives*). Still, all of these are a far cry from opera.

- That he knew little about the human voice. Well, one of his most magnificent works is his Missa Solemnis. He also wrote an earlier Mass in C, a Choral Fantasy for Piano, Chorus and Orchestra, and more than sixty songs. Still, for his opera, there are 346 pages of sketches, including sixteen for the opening of Florestan's first air, which does suggest that he was more interested in the theme structure of his music than in the vocal aspects.
- That opera was new and strange for him. Well, in addition to his work in the Bonn opera orchestra, he had attended many operas, had studied and enjoyed the works of opera composers, and had associated with them. Biographers say there was hardly a year between 1800 and 1813 that he was not dallying with some operatic proposal.

Conclusion: True, the Beethoven genius *was* centered more around instrumental than vocal music. True, "theater" and "spectacle" were not his primary interests. And true, he was more at home with choral music than with music for the individual voice. But none of this makes his only opera an "amateur" effort undeserving of our attention. By common agreement, it's a masterpiece, even if an imperfect masterpiece.

Fidelio is Number 34 in The Collection. Paying customers haven't thrown this much money down the drain for nearly two hundred years for the honor of attending an immortal composer's weak opera—a curiosity, a sport.

This isn't Winston Churchill, whom readers over fifty know relaxed in times of stress by laying bricks. People came to see *that* work because he *was* Winston Churchill, not because of a unique skill with trowel and mortar that shook up the union and revolutionized the craft.

Fidelio survives because it contains some magnificent music—some intense drama in the second half that includes a duet of joy that's one of the great moments in all German opera.

Is it the Third or the Fifth or the Ninth Symphony? Certainly not. Neither are the Second, Fourth, and Eighth.

No one characterizes *Fidelio* as "superb" theater. Some professionals even say that Umberto Giordano may have written a "better" all-around opera with *Andrea Chénier*, an equally popular work, Number 36 in The Collection.

Decide for yourself. As a nonmusician, I have no quarrel with Signor Giordano—and in any event would hesitate to declare it publicly. But if the hangman is coming at dawn, and my final hours must be spent with either Umberto Giordano or Ludwig van Beethoven, I think I'll go along with the Immortal One and leave a finer "sense of theater" and a superior "lyric gift" to the fellow in the next cell.

After accepting the commission for an opera, the question was obvious: What text was appropriate for Beethoven, the Immortal Thunderer, the Prometheus of music? Tchaikovsky was to call him "the God Jehovah." Bizet was to couple him with Shakespeare, Dante, Homer, and Moses. He was the ultimate master of the symphonic orchestra, soon to compose the mighty Ninth, which would stand alone—or close enough to alone to intimidate Johannes Brahms, Anton Bruckner, Gustav Mahler, and many symphonists to follow. Where was there a text suitable to his proud and independent makeup?

The Opera Gift

American composer/critic Virgil Thomson wrote: "Not all masters have had the opera gift. Handel and Mozart did, certainly. Bach and Brahms did not. And Beethoven, like Stravinsky, wrote more effectively for chorus than for solo singers. He lacked, too, the instinct for stage timings and stage pacings. I am inclined to think that Beethoven's *Fidelio* and Stravinsky's *Rake* share this ineptitude."

Some seventy-five years ago, one musicologist wrote: "A century after his death, why does Beethoven remain the central—if not the chief—figure in music? For one thing, because he was perhaps an even greater master of construction than the men who made the frieze of the Parthenon, Macbeth, the Sistine Frescoes, the B Minor Mass and the Chartres Cathedral."

He thought he had found the proper vehicle when he came across an opera called *Léonore ou l'amour conjugal* (*Leonora, or Married Love*), by Fredinando Paër. The French librettist was Jean-Nicolas Bouilly. Beethoven liked the glory of the plot and accepted a translation into German by a friend, Joseph Sonnleithner. The heroine's name was Leonora (Léonore in French), but at times she was disguised as a young man named Fidelio.

It's the story of the heroic deeds of a devoted wife who saves her husband from a killer governor and frees him from dungeon chains: Freedom . . . Liberation . . . Devotion . . . Heroism . . . Sacrifice. Now that's Beethoven, who on his deathbed shook his fist at thunder. Well, that's the story, and it's one worth preserving.

"Freedom above all," he once said. Artistic freedom, political freedom, personal freedom, freedom of all kinds.

Critics say that the libretto has obvious technical flaws that Beethoven could and should have had corrected, and scarcely anyone really likes the whole text.

But he worked hard—Beethoven always worked hard—and his opera was produced in November 1805 before an audience consisting largely of French officers from Napoleon's occupation army, the court having fled Vienna to Schönbrunn. It was in three acts, with an overture now known as Léonore No. 2.

Vienna was able to contain its enthusiasm. The opera was too long, it was poorly arranged, and the mood of the city was gloomy. Andrew Lloyd Webber had a thousand times the success in the same Theatre an der Wien nearly two hundred years later with an entertainment called *Cats*.

Wagner on Beethoven

Richard Wagner said: "Through Beethoven, melody has become emancipated from the influence of fashion and fluctuating taste, and elevated to an eternally valid type of pure humanity."

The opera was reworked, cut to two acts, and produced again four months later, this time with a piece now called Léonore No. 3 as the overture. The city was at peace and the reception was reasonably good, but the ever-crusty composer had a brawl with management over royalties and, in a typical huff, pulled his opera out of circulation.

It was not heard again until May 23, 1814, this time at Vienna's Kärnthnerthor Theatre. Beethoven now had made significant changes and had brought in a new librettist, Georg Friedrich Treitschke. This became the definitive version of *Fidelio* that has been in the repertory ever since. The music people say that many of the things that have kept it healthy were not in the earlier drafts.

Fidelio is a serious "Curses, Foiled Again" opera, the kind of melodramatic story that in 1930s movies has the frustrated villain curling his mustache at the end just before the good guys take him away. It is less ostentatious than the spectacular grand opera that was coming to Paris, heavier than the light German Singspiel that had become popular, and much more high-minded than the sometimes frivolous Italian opera buffa, although its spoken dialogue (true to Singspiel form) is "lighter" musically than opera buffa's recitative. A rescue opera, it reflected the spirit of the French Revolution.

Aside from Weber's *Der Freischütz*, which is revived today partly on historical grounds, *Fidelio* is the only major German opera between Mozart and Wagner that survives in the international permanent repertories. Recall that some consider Mozart's *Magic Flute* to be Germany's first "great opera," *Fidelio* the second, and *Der Freischütz* the third.

Beethoven was born in 1770, began studying music at four, and published his first works at eleven. His most creative period was between 1800 and 1815, even though he was growing deaf during this time. Many of us think of him as having lived a long life, challenging the Heavens at age ninety-four, but in fact he died in Vienna in 1827 at fifty-six.

KEYNOTE

Titans don't mess with commonplace Singspiel, frivolous Italian subjects, or fairy tales. Titans tackle tyranny and injustice. For Beethoven, freedom and independence were everything. Love and heroism were what life was about. Souls must be tried . . . and found worthy.

PLOT

Eighteenth century, a fortress near Seville. Rocco (bass) is the jailer of the prison at Seville. His daughter, Marzelline (soprano), is loved by his assistant, Jacquino (tenor), although she pays little attention to him. She has a thing for another assistant, Fidelio (soprano), unaware that Fidelio is a woman in disguise—Léonore, wife of Florestan (tenor), a political prisoner of Don Pizarro (bass-baritone), the brutal governor of the prison fortress. Florestan has been seized secretly (and unjustly) and hidden deep within the jail. Fidelio is working there only to find and rescue her husband.

Eventually she learns that a secret prisoner is hidden deep inside. Learning that Minister of State Don Fernando (bass) is coming on an inspection tour, and fearing he'll come across Florestan, Pizarro decides to kill the prisoner and hide the body. He orders Rocco to dig a grave in Florestan's cell.

After being instructed to help Rocco, Fidelio persuades him to let the prisoners out for some sunlight, but when they stream out of their cells Florestan isn't among them. Going down into the dungeon, she finds him chained and half out of his mind, without food, air, or light. Showing no emotion, she helps Rocco dig the grave, but when Pizzaro is about to stab Florestan she throws herself between them and stops him with a pointed pistol. Before she shoots, a dramatic flourish of trumpets announces the arrival of Fernando. It is the cavalry; Léonore has saved her husband. Pizarro is arrested and sent off in disgrace and Léonore herself is given the joy of unshackling her husband. Wife and husband are united; joy abounds; freedom has triumphed.

HIGHLIGHTS

The four overtures.

Act I: A quartet, "Mir ist so wunderbar" ("It is wonderful to me"), for Léonore, Rocco, Marzelline, and Jacquino. Called the "canon quartet," it is considered one of the great ensemble pieces of opera. Also Léonore's reaffirmation in the power of love and her confidence that she will find her husband, "Abscheulicher!" the big soprano aria of the opera: "Abominable man, where are you rushing to in your savage anger? . . . But I will not falter in my duty; true married love will give me strength. I will force my way to Florestan." Then the highly dramatic finale to Act I, the "Prisoners' Chorus," as they emerge from the dungeons into the light, the sun, the fresh air, and temporary freedom: "O welche Luft" ("O what joy"). Soaring music celebrating freedom. The analysts call it sublime, Beethoven at his best.

Act II: Florestan's cry of despair, "Gott! Welch Dunkel hier" ("God! how dark it is here"), a favorite of many tenors, and his "In des Lebens Frühlingstagen" ("In the spring of life") as he accepts his fate and sees an angel, Léonore, leading him through golden mists to heaven. The "joy-beyond-expression" love duet after she has saved his life.

The Composer's View

Beethoven himself was to say: "This work has won me the martyr's crown." But then, he always did a lot of griping. "Mr. Congeniality" he was not.

COMMENTARY

Some sound bites:

- Despite improvements between 1805 and 1814, even the latest libretto is not Shakespearean.
- Much of Act I is akin to German Singspiel, involving Marzelline, Jacquino, and Fidelio, a romantic triangle that didn't capture Beethoven's enthusiasm. Most operas in the early 1800s were spotted with miniplots featuring minor characters; like grits in the south, the customers expected them and they "came with," whether ordered or not. But in Act II we get rolling into gravedigging, dungeons, and near death. The drama is intense. This is Beethoven's kind of stuff. The analysts say that in this act he was interested in his characters and did a much sharper job of portraying them as living figures—with Mozart dead, better by far than his contemporaries.
- As a whole, the opera has "many ungrateful pages for singers." Critics like the word "ungrateful," as they do "ambitious" and "ingratiating." Let's say some of the arias are difficult to handle for many performers.
- Not surprisingly, *Fidelio* is more symphonic than vocal in nature. And, not surprisingly, the overtures are regarded by some professionals as the most inspiring music of the opera.
- Beethoven was dedicated to the idealism in it. He had a Message of the Human Spirit to convey. If your music is supreme, spirit conveyance is feasible—but opera generally is regarded more as a vehicle for the human voice than as one for message delivery.
- My experts don't quite agree with one another. In the earlier part of the century, Alfred Einstein said: "But his only opera plainly shows how uncongenial the great man found the historic opera forms." Some years later, Professor Paul Henry Lang wrote: "After the scene with the prisoners,

Beethoven composes a traditional ending finale with all hands participating. It is a very good piece that once more shows Beethoven to be thoroughly familiar with operatic conventions and techniques."

- The overture usually played today is called the "Fidelio." There are three others. Léonore No. 1 (misnamed; chronologically it is the second one written), composed for a projected performance in Prague; Léonore No. 2, the one written for and played at the 1805 premiere, and Léonore No. 3, often now done as an orchestral interlude between the scenes of Act II (although it also had been performed between Acts I and II). All four are played in concert halls and heard on classical radio.

- *Fidelio* is one of several masterpieces set in Spain (one of my professional sources calls it "as Spanish as a pretzel"). Others include *The Marriage of Figaro, Don Giovanni, The Barber of Seville, Carmen, Il trovatore, Don Carlos,* and *The Force of Destiny*. One analyst has figured out that if you take the top twenty-five or thirty operas most frequently performed and subtract the ones set in the composer's home country, more are in Spain than anywhere else.

- Plácido Domingo sang Florestan's aria in a film made in the ruins of Rome. Florestan was a favorite of Canadian tenor Jon Vickers, who sang it at the Met for nearly a quarter of a century. Famous Léonores have included Lilli Lehman, Kirsten Flagstad, Leonie Rysanek, Jessye Norman, Hildegarde Behrens, and Eva Marton.

MET PERFORMANCES
Two hundred and two performances over forty seasons, from 1884 to 1993.

RECORDING
CD—Angel/EMI CDMB 69324-2 (2). Christa Ludwig, Ingeborg Hallstein, Jon Vickers, Gerhard Unger, Walter Berry, Gottlob Frick, Franz Crass. Philharmonia Chorus and Orchestra. Otto Klemperer. 1962.

VIDEO
Söderström, de Ridder, Allman. Glyndebourne Festival Opera. German; English subtitles. Haitink, conductor. 1985. VAI.

Number 35. *L'elisir d'amore (The Elixir of Love)*
by Gaetano Donizetti
November 29, 1797–April 8, 1848

Premiere at the Teatro della Canobbiana, Milan, 1832. Text by Felice Romani from Eugène Scribe's libretto for Daniel-François Auber's 1831 opera Le philtre. A comic opera in two acts.

Although many comic operas were to come, a good case can be made that Gaetano Donizetti's *The Elixir of Love* and his *Don Pasquale*, 1843 (Number 56), are the last bona fide works of true opera buffa, the form that began in Italy way back in the seventeenth century. Rossini, who outlived Donizetti, might have written another, but he stopped composing.

These were Donizetti's two finest comedies. *Elixir* is an out-and-out opera buffa about a very good-hearted fellow who wins the girl against some pretty stalwart opposition, the most frequently performed of his works during his lifetime and one that's been in the international repertory ever since.

His greatest dramatic tragedy, and arguably his greatest opera, was *Lucia di Lammermoor* (see Donizetti Warhorses).

Analysts who like to compare the three big bel canto composers offer these sound bites:

- Like Bellini, Donizetti took the Rossini operatic form and added to it the spirit of nineteenth-century Romanticism. Before them, Rossini had dominated the Italian operatic stage.
- Donizetti had nimble craftsmanship and great melody. The music in his early works was less lofty than Bellini's and more in the vernacular—not folksy but with a folksy feeling, comfortable music that stays with you.
- The longer he wrote, the more lyrical, vivid, and concise Donizetti's melodies became, foreshadowing Verdi's music.

KEYNOTE

Donizetti's earliest opera buffa and generally considered his best. (Though don't miss *Don Pasquale*, my choice.) Hear one of opera's hit tunes, the one that launched Enrico Caruso in Milan sixty-nine years after the Milan premiere. Buy the elixir.

Deadline

Librettist Felice Romani (1788–1865) worked with all three major bel canto composers—and scores of others. Among his other important collaborations with Donizetti were *Anna Bolena* and *Lucrezia Borgia*.

Regarding *Elixir*, Donizetti wrote him: "I am obliged to write an opera in fourteen days. I give you a week to do your share."

PLOT

Nineteenth century, a small Italian village. Two men love Adina (soprano), a wealthy flirt who believes in changing sweethearts every day. One is

Nemorino (tenor), a gentle farmer; the other Belcore (baritone), a preening army sergeant. Adina keeps both in a state of flux with her fickle approach to love. She reads aloud about the love potion in *Tristan und Isolde*, which plants an idea in Nemorino's mind. Dr. Dulcamara (buffo bass), a snake oil peddler (and wonderful charlatan character), arrives at the village. He is selling an elixir that promises to cure all ills, including rats, bedbugs, diabetes, and toothaches. Nemorino, thinking of Tristan, asks if Dulcamara has anything like that—and, of course, he does. Actually, like all of the peddler's elixirs, it is cheap Bordeaux. Nemorino buys it for a coin, gets drunk, and acts so silly that he turns off Adina, who promises to marry Belcore a week later.

In Act II, the villagers gather to witness the signing of the marriage contact and Adina, Belcore, and the notary go off for the ceremony. Nemorino enters. He's broke and tries to get Dr. Dulcamara to give him a potion so that he might win Adino, but the delightful quack doesn't take American Express or other plastic.

Belcore appears, unhappy because Adina keeps putting off the marriage ceremony. Learning that Nemorino needs money, and seeing a way to get rid of a rival, he talks him into enlisting in the army for a cash recruitment bonus of twenty crowns. Nemorino agrees, marks the recruitment paper with his X, buys a second bottle of the elixir, again drinks too much, and again shows it. Word spreads that Nemorino's rich uncle has died, leaving his money to Nemorino. The village girls show a lot of interest in him: He's not only an army man, with the status that goes with that, but now he also has money. This makes him a great catch.

Nemorino hasn't received the news that his uncle is dead and credits the love potion for his sudden popularity. The attention he gets makes Adina jealous, and she recognizes he's the one she wants, frees him from the army by buying back his enlistment, and tells him she loves him. His response is the famous aria "Una furtive lagrima," as he sees one tear in her eye. Belcore behaves like the good soldier he is, declares there's always another woman in the next town, and accepts the outcome. The villagers credit Dr. Dulcamara, who sells all of his elixir at a fine profit. It's a no-lose opera.

HIGHLIGHTS

Act I: A tender love song by Nemorino about Adina, "Quanto è bella": "How beautiful she is, and how I adore her." Dr. Dulcamara's comic introduction of himself to the villagers, "Udite, udite." The great finale with a show-stopping ensemble, "Adina, credimi," begun by Nemorino.

Act II: A string of fun duets, one after another, leading to the most famous aria in the opera—and perhaps in all of Donizetti—Nemorino's "Una furtiva lagrima" ("A tear on her cheek"), as he says he would die to comfort her: "A furtive tear showed in her eyes. What more could I ever want. She loves me. One could die of love. I ask nothing more." The whole tune is played in the instrumental introduction to the aria, with a mood-setting bassoon.

COMMENTARY

Donizetti wrote to entertain, and there's no better example than this work. By bel canto standards none of the music is especially difficult. We know from movies or stage plays that for comedy to work the actors—and the singers—must have sound acting ability and a sense of timing. When *Elixir* is performed well, with singer-actors outdoing one another, it's an engaging, sometimes sentimental, farce. If it's performed poorly, you still hear a lot of good tunes.

The score is harmless and charming, the melodies are graceful, there's nothing not to enjoy. And the two main characters grow before our eyes. Nemorino becomes more outgoing (helped by the Bordeaux) and Adina less fickle as she recognizes a good thing when she sees one. For the most part, though, Nemorino still comes across pretty much as a wimp, leading one Peabody Institute friend to tell me: "The Nemorino role makes the tenor seem like a cocker spaniel. We baritones like to see that."

Among successful Nemorinos are Luciano Pavarotti, Giuseppe Di Stefano, José Carreras, Nicolai Gedda, Tito Schipa, Beniamino Gigli—and a particularly outstanding one, the Peruvian tenor Luigi Alva.

Refresher Definitions

Grand opera: An elaborate serious opera in four or five acts, sung throughout. *Aida.*

French grand opera: Meyerbeer extravaganza in five spectacular acts, sung throughout. *Les Huguenots.*

French lyric opera: An opera in five acts, sung throughout, but less spectacular than grand opera. *Faust.*

French opéra comique: A comic or tragic opera in three acts with spoken dialogue. *Carmen.*

French opéra bouffe: A light comic opera in three acts with spoken dialogue. *La Pèrichole,* by Collection composer Offenbach.

Italian opera buffa: A comic opera with graceful melodies often in two acts, sung throughout. *The Elixir of Love.*

MET PERFORMANCES

Two hundred and ten performances over thirty-one seasons, from 1904 to 1995. Nine performances are scheduled for the 1996–97 season.

RECORDING

CD—Decca/London 4214 461-2 (2). Joan Sutherland, Luciano Pavarotti, Dominic Cossa, Spiro Malas. Ambrosian Opera Chorus. English Chamber Orchestra. Richard Bonynge. 1972.

VIDEO

Pavarotti, Blegen, Bruscantini. Metropolitan Opera. Italian; English subtitles. Rescigno, conductor. 1981. PAR.

∾

Number 36. *Andrea Chénier*
by Umberto Giordano
August 27, 1867–November 12, 1948

Premiere at La Scala, Milan, in 1896. Text by Luigi Illica, based on a historical character. Four acts.

No one says Umberto Giordano was a great composer, and everyone says he wasn't an original one. He is regarded as superficial and easily satisfied with musical clichés. Even his parents opposed his musical dreams and wanted him to be a fencing master.

Yet here is *Andrea Chénier*, one of twelve operas he wrote (or helped write), and one that has lasted nearly one hundred years.

The third most successful Italian verismo opera, it was performed first in 1896—six years after Mascagni's *Cavalleria rusticana* and four years after Leoncavallo's *Pagliacci*. Giordano was an obscure composer at the time who quickly became famous and continued to write operas until 1929.

Set at the time of the French Revolution, it is a rescue opera without the rescue. As in Beethoven's *Fidelio*, the heroine joins the hero in a death cell. Unlike *Fidelio*, both die.

Negative critics say it's too emotional and too loosely organized, but let's look for the good news.

The real André Chénier was a fine Greek scholar, a young poet, a gentleman cadet in the French army, and an honorable midlevel French career diplomat. During the French Revolution he supported the revolt of the middle classes, deplored the violence and the Reign of Terror, and denounced the notion of Frenchmen killing Frenchmen. He did all this publicly in published articles and essays. Then he was arrested by mistake in 1794, accused of crimes he hadn't committed, condemned to death, and guillotined. One bit of good news, then, is that Giordano chose a noble fellow for his opera, even if his librettist strayed considerably from Chénier's actual life.

More good news, for Giordano, is that at the end of the nineteenth century the Italian heart still was throbbing with its own nationalism. Unification had been completed a couple of decades earlier, and although the Chénier story was one hundred years old and from a different revolution, emotional Italian operagoers found it appropriate for the times.

The best news is that great tenors consider Chénier a role to kill for.

Umberto Giordano was born in Foggia, Italy, in 1867. He studied for nine years at the Naples Conservatory and entered an opera named *Marina* in publisher Sanzogno's contest that was won by Mascagni's *Cavalleria rusticana*. It placed sixth, good enough for Sanzogno to pay him three hundred lire a month to write more operas.

Five years later, after one failure and one limited success, Giordano teamed with veteran librettist Luigi Illica (who had worked with Puccini) to create *Andrea Chénier*. People loved it, in Italy, elsewhere in Europe, and across the waters in America, where the New York premiere was also in 1896.

An Okay from Verði

Writing a half century ago, David Ewen tells a great story about how Giordano won his wife. She was the daughter of a Milan hotel proprietor who was unwilling to approve her marriage to the composer until he was satisfied that Giordano would amount to something. To decide the issue, Ewen writes, the father took an unfinished score of *Andrea Chénier* to the great Verdi for his opinion. Two days later Verdi returned the score with this note: "You may safely consign your daughter to the man who composed a work such as this."

A good reporter would suspect that either (a) someone made up the whole story or (b) the musicians' good-ole-boy union was at work and Giordano reached Verdi before the note did. In any case, the two were married.

Having never done as well again, Giordano often is put in the One Big Opera category with Mascagni, Leoncavallo, Ponchielli (*La Gioconda*), Boito (*Mefistofele*), Charpentier (*Louise*), and even Bizet (although as we have seen that tag actually is a little unfair to most of them). In this case, Giordano's *Fedora*, which premiered in 1898, still is performed in Italy and occasionally elsewhere, and to a lesser degree so is *Madame Sans-Gêne*, first produced in 1915.

KEYNOTE

Built from scratch for a superstar tenor. An opera about the French Revolution served up to Italians keen on nationalism and independence. Ardent drama and lyrical melody from a potential heir apparent to Verdi.

PLOT

Before and during the French Revolution, in Paris, 1789–94. At a party in the château of the Countess of Coigny (mezzo-soprano), the poet Chénier (tenor) speaks out against the misery of the peasants and the selfishness of the clergy, who grow fat while the poor people suffer. Carlo Gérard (baritone), a servant who opposes the cruelty of the aristocracy, is secretly in love with the Countess's daughter, Maddalena (soprano). Before the party ends, Gérard leads a group of beggars into the château and rips off his serving coat, denouncing it as a sign of slavery that he'll no longer accept.

Three years have passed when Act II opens. Chénier sits at a table in a Parisian cafe. He has received several anonymous letters from a secret admirer, a lady who signs herself "Hope," and has fallen in love with her. Although advised by friends to leave Paris for his own safety, he chooses to stay and meet the lady. When she arrives he finds she is Maddalena, the daughter of the Countess. As they are about to rush off together they are intercepted by Gérard, now a leader in the people's revolutionary army but still in love with Maddalena. He and Chénier do not recognize each other. They duel and Gérard is wounded, not realizing until he falls that he has been fighting with the patriot poet. He warns Chénier to be on his guard, since somehow Chénier himself has been listed as a counterrevolutionary, and also asks him to protect Maddalena.

In Act III, at the Hall of the Revolutionary Tribunal, Mathieu (baritone) speaks of the country's danger. Gérard, recovered from his wounds, enters. He is jealous over Maddalena and, despite a guilty conscience, is persuaded to sign a baseless indictment against Chénier. When Maddalena is brought in, Gérard admits that Chénier has been arrested on his personal orders and also acknowledges that his love for her played a role in that arrest decision. In a dramatic scene, she offers herself to Gérard in exchange for Chénier's freedom. She then speaks of her misery: The château has been burned by the mob, and her mother has died in the flames.

Chénier is brought in with other prisoners. He defends himself as a patriot, and Gérard, to the astonishment of his colleagues, steps forward to support him, declaring that he has been accused falsely. But the poet is sentenced to death in spite of Gérard's intervention.

Act IV takes place in the prison courtyard. Chénier waits for dawn, when he will be guillotined. He reads his last poem to Roucher (bass), a friend. Maddalena is put into his cell, having bribed a jailer to substitute her name on the condemned-to-die list in order to be with him. They sing a heroic duet and prepare to die together, loving one another, victims of the revolution.

HIGHLIGHTS

Act I: Chénier's aria, "Un dì all'azzurro spazio" ("One day in the blue heaven"), as he sings a poem about his love for his country and contrasts man's misery and nature's beauty.

Act II: Chénier's "Credo a una possanza areana" ("I believe in a sovereign power").

Act III: Gérard's great scene as he questions whether he can denounce Chénier, "Nemico della patria?" ("An enemy of his country?"), and reflects on his own principles.

Maddalena's "La mamma morta," telling of love and how her mother died to save her. Movie fans heard Maria Callas sing it in the background in a touching Tom Hanks scene in the 1993 film *Philadelphia*. The scene helped Hanks win an Oscar. Chénier's "Si, fui soldato," defending himself as an honorable man.

Act IV: Chénier's "Come un bel dì di maggio," comparing life to the end of a beautiful morning in May.

COMMENTARY

Andrea Chénier offers some great spectacle and local color but some analysts are critical of its old-fashioned harmonies.

Despite old harmonies, not many composers have written operas that the paying public has enjoyed for nearly one hundred years. It isn't a Warhorse, but people like it because it's melodious and singable, because Giordano had a strong feeling for the theater, because it's a melodrama with French Revolution crowd scenes, and because leading tenors go for a role that combines big passion, big heroism . . . and good schmaltz. It also has a stirring rendition of "La Marseillaise," and as all admirers of *Casablanca* know, there's nothing like "La Marseillaise" to drown out the bad guys and get the juices flowing.

For all who believe that life is improved by sound doses of blatant emotionalism and/or musical excesses, *Andrea Chénier* offers something quite satisfactory. Do not be intimidated by the opinions of the blasé and dispassionate, most of whom live in Manhattan and deserve our understanding.

The title role is a favorite of tenors. Among the most famous ones who have tackled it are Beniamino Gigli, one of the most beautiful voices of the century; Italians Mario Del Monaco and Franco Corelli, and the "three tenors," Plácido Domingo, Luciano Pavarotti, and José Carreras.

MET PERFORMANCES

One hundred and fifty-six performances over twenty-four seasons, from 1921 to 1996. Six performances are scheduled for the 1996–97 season.

RECORDING

CD—RCA/BMG RCD-2-2046 (2). Renata Scotto, Plácido Domingo, Sherrill Milnes. John Alldis Choir. National Philharmonic Orchestra. James Levine. 1976.

VIDEO

Carreras, Marton, Cappuccilli. La Scala. Italian; English subtitles. Chailly, conductor. 1986. PIO (Pioneer Laserdisc).

∿

Number 37. *Samson et Dalila*
by Camille Saint-Saëns
October 9, 1835–December 16, 1921

Premiere at the Hoftheatre, Weimar, 1877. Text by Ferdinand Lemaire based on Judges 14–16 from the Bible. Three acts and four tableaux.

Camille Saint-Saëns, virtuoso pianist and organist, held elegant Monday musical receptions at his Paris home. On one occasion, a mother persuaded him to accompany her two daughters singing a duet. They sang so poorly together that he turned to the mother and asked: "Madame, *which* of your daughters do you wish me to accompany?"

Samson et Dalila is a spectacle opera, close enough to the Meyerbeer grand opera vein to cause music scholar Alfred Einstein to describe it as a "draught of 'Meyer-beer,' strained through a Charles Gounod filter."

After the performance of only one act, one Cologne critic wrote that there never had been such a complete absence of melody.

Paris opera houses in the composer's own city didn't even show the one act. Nobody was interested, until Franz Liszt, Hungarian King of the Keyboard, who swept away conventional wisdom with one imperial hand and arranged for a production of the whole opera for his friend Camille in distant Weimar in 1877. Liszt, history's most famous piano virtuoso, made his own rules. Few great composers were as generous to their colleagues as he, and the story goes that he promised the production to Saint-Saëns without even having seen the score.

Then the work made its way to Brussels, Rouen, and a second-echelon house in Paris, the Théâtre Lyrique.

By now it's lack of success was getting embarrassing. Camille Saint-Saëns was no twenty-five-year-old unknown Italian, looking for his first break. He was a leading French classical composer, on his way to lasting fame as one of the half-dozen all-time top musical artists of France. Hector Berlioz, Claude Debussy, Maurice Ravel, George Bizet for *Carmen*, François Couperin, Gabriel Fauré, Rameau. Few other Frenchmen challenge Saint-Saëns.

In 1868 he had been made a Chevalier of the Legion of Honor, and in 1881 he had been elected to the Institute de France. He also was a founder of the Société Nationale de Musique in Paris in 1871. Furthermore, he had spent nine years writing this opera. This elegant, highly respected Frenchman was not a Donizetti, prepared to score big with one effort and miss with the next.

Finally on November 23, 1892, after the opera succeeded at the Théâtre

Lyrique, the arrogant Paris Opéra gave in. *Samson* was a triumph. Fortunately, the composer had been eating well in the interim seventeen years. Over the next thirty years *Samson* had five hundred performances at the Paris Opéra alone.

There were several reasons for the long germination period. First, the religious subject matter. The Bible was fine for oratorios, but not for operas. Operas were entertainment. Second, politics. Saint-Saëns was a defender of young artists, and the conservative elements of the Establishment were hostile to him. Third, the musical caste system. He was a performing pianist, a famous virtuoso, even if not quite in the class of Franz Liszt. Star pianists—Mozart, Beethoven, and Liszt are exceptions—were regarded primarily as performers, not composers.

Although a respected and productive classical composer, Saint-Saëns never was considered an "exciting" one. The music people speak of his excellent technique, his sense of proportion, his lucidity, his versatility, his unfailing craftsmanship. He was a man who knew his bounds and worked to perfection within them. Frank Sinatra didn't try to be Enrico Caruso; Camille Saint-Saëns didn't try to be an inventive, powerful Hector Berlioz, although in 1867 Berlioz had called him "one of the greatest musicians of our epoch."

In the French line of opera, Saint-Saëns was one of the group who followed in the wake of Thomas, Gounod, and Bizet—creators of the French lyric opera of the late nineteenth century. A main same-age contemporary was Edouard Lalo, who wrote a well-known opera, *Le Roi d'Ys*, in 1888. Just ahead was the most popular French opera composer of the last part of the century, Jules Massenet, who wrote *Manon* in 1884 and *Werther* in 1892, both in The Collection.

Massenet was an opportunist, Saint-Saëns a perfectionist. Not many perfectionists make the heart pound. Some hearts don't even respond to Perfectionist Bach, confusing and distressing, but true.

Although opera was part of the portfolio of nearly every Parisian composer and although *Samson et Dalila* is his best-known opera, Saint-Saëns is most respected for his instrumental music. Of a dozen other operas, *Ascanio*, 1890, is rated by some experts to be at least the equal of *Samson* if not its superior, but *Samson* is the only one in the international repertory today.

The best-known Saint-Saëns classical works include his Symphony No. 3 in C Minor, often called the *Organ* Symphony; a symphonic poem, *Danse macabre*; *The Carnival of the Animals* (which includes *The Swan* for solo cello); a Cello Concerto in A Minor; the Piano Concerto No. 2 in G Minor, and the Introduction and Rondo Capriccioso for Violin and Orchestra. He also composed a fine violin sonata.

Saint-Saëns was an interesting fellow. He was one of the great child prodigies, like Mozart and Mendelssohn, identifying music at two, composing sketches at five, giving public performances of Beethoven's music at ten. In addition to being a concert-hall pianist who performed all over Europe, he was one of the finest organists of his time—perhaps the best. He was an amateur comedian and a caricaturist and had an interest in science, astronomy, and mathematics. No classical composer was a keener student of Bach. His tongue could be sharp, but he also befriended young musicians. Early in his career he was an admirer of the radicals—Liszt, Berlioz, and Wagner—but late in life he became quite conservative and very critical of the new music of Claude Debussy.

No one questions Saint-Saëns's technical mastery. He is not "inventive" enough, "inspired" enough, "imaginative" enough for some critics—the same faults they found in Felix Mendelssohn. We should be so lucky as to have the faults of Felix Mendelssohn.

Saint-Saëns was born in Paris in 1835 and entered the Paris Conservatory in 1848. His first job was organist in a small Paris church, St. Severin, and while working there he composed his first symphony. In 1858 he became organist at the famous Madeleine church, where he played for twenty years. Although he loved to travel, his home always was Paris. He died at age eighty-six in 1921.

An Election

A favorite Saint-Saëns story: When the younger Jules Massenet was elected to the prestigious Institut de France before the long-established and respected Saint-Saëns, he sent Saint-Saëns a wire: "My dear colleague, the Institut has made a terrible mistake," Saint-Saëns replied: "I entirely agree with you."

Samson has been given as an oratorio as well as an opera, sung in this country in English with the English title *Samson and Delilah*. The first performance in the United States was in that form at Carnegie Hall in 1892 by the Oratorio Society of New York under the direction of Walter Damrosch. In fact, Saint-Saëns's original intent was to write an oratorio, but a young relative talked him into making it an opera. (As we have seen, an oratorio is a composition, usually with a religious text, traditionally performed in a concert hall or a church without scenery, costumes, or action. But some directors now stage them.)

KEYNOTE

If you read the book, you'd scarcely recognize the opera. How a wily woman uses deception and sex to win a battle but lose a war. Passionate love scenes, but one lover doesn't mean a word of it. Still, see the crushed Philistines as the temple collapses. An unemotional composer's most emotional work.

PLOT

A biblical drama, B.C., in Gaza. It is the Gaza public square, with the Temple of Dagon in the background. Israelites complain that the Philistines have enslaved them and are forcing them to work. They have given up hope. Samson (tenor), a Hebrew warrior and strongman, tries to rally them, telling them to have faith in God's promise of liberation. He kills Abimelech, satrap of Gaza (bass), a whip-bearer, and leads a revolt against the Philistines. Dalila (French spelling of Delilah) (mezzo-soprano), Philistine temptress, is urged by the High Priest of Dagon (baritone) to seduce Samson and discover the source of his strength. She and Samson have had a past relationship, but he left her couch for the battlefield and she now hates him and is looking for personal revenge as well as wartime advantage. She turns down the High Priest's offer of gold, hating Samson enough to do him in without it.

Samson appears. Though he loved Dalila passionately, he intends only to say good-bye before going back to battle. Drawn on by her "tender" recollections of their past intimacy and her false claims of love, however, he confesses that he still loves her. Knowing his duty is to lead the Hebrews in battle, he pauses before becoming involved with her again, but his strong attraction causes him to follow her into her house. As we all know, this constituted a major blunder. She cuts off his hair to deprive him of his superhuman strength, cries out in triumph, and he is easily overcome by the Philistines, who have been hiding and waiting for her signal.

"Perfection of Form"

Camille Saint-Saëns is one of those composers who is respected by the critics for one body of work and popular with the public for another.

A child prodigy who composed his first piece at age three, Saint-Saëns always has been held in high esteem as a music mechanic but for decades was criticized for being too elegant and superficial. He even said of his music: "I ran after the chimera of purity of style and perfection of form."

His most popular works are an orchestral piece called The Carnival of the Animals, a symphonic poem called the Danse macabre, and Samson et Dalila, the third of his twelve operas. The experts, however, say that these are among his weakest works and that his best are much less known: a septet for trumpet, strings, and piano; a violin sonata; and a piano quartet.

In Act III Samson is chained in a dungeon, shorn of his hair, blinded by the Philistines, pulling a mill wheel and depressed by his weakness. Filled with remorse, he offers his life as repentance. The Philistines bring him to the Temple of Dagon, where they are preparing a sacrifice and celebrating in a wine-flowing orgy. As they ridicule him he prays for the return of his strength. When the High Priest tells a boy to lead him to the middle of the temple, Samson whispers to the boy to take him instead to the two main marble pillars that support the building. Calling on God for vengeance, he seizes both pillars and brings them down, causing the temple to crash to the ground and killing himself and all the assembled Philistines.

Singer Tags from the Collection

If Oscars were awarded to characters:

Sexiest—Carmen
Most villainous—Scarpia
Greatest jerk—Pinkerton
Most overly protective parent—Rigoletto
Best Teflon seducer—The Duke of Mantua
Least trustworthy sibling—Enrico Ashton
Most famed stud—Don Giovanni
Biggest oaf—Baron Ochs
Most bipolar character—Kundry
Most gullible males—Otello and Nemorino
Most gullible females—Fiordiligi and Dorabella
Most immoral heroine—Manon
Most uninhibited kids—Hansel and Gretel
Most heroic female—Léonore
Least real heroine—Olympia
Most unyielding heroine—Turandot
Most supercilious hero—Eugene Onegin
Most decadent heroine—Salome
Best impersonator—Gianni Schicchi
Most unlikely seducer—Falstaff
Most nagging wife—Fricka
Most inquisitive wife—Judith and Elsa
Worst disobediance to instructions—Orfeo
Best candidate for psychiatrist's couch—Wozzeck

HIGHLIGHTS

Act I: Dalila's charming song, "Printemps qui commence" ("Spring has come"). And the Dance of the Priestesses.

Act II: Dalila's "Amour! viens aider ma faiblesse," as she prays for the removal of Samson's power: "Love, come help my weakness! See that Samson, defeated by my skill, will be in chains tomorrow." The very famous number, one of opera's most beautiful arias, and one of my personal favorites Dalila's lovely "Mon coeur s'ouvre à ta voix," as she sees Samson weakening. "My heart opens up at the sound of your voice as the flowers open up at dawn."

Act III: The ballet music. The wine-flowing orgy.

COMMENTARY

Saint-Saëns was never one for melodrama, in opera or other classical music, which some regard as a point in his favor. But his music also lacks passion or fire. Rarely, if ever, do you need to hold on to your heart (although one opera-expert friend who has read this manuscript insists that he does hold his heart at the end). No critic ever accused Saint-Saëns of lush emotionalism, as they do Tchaikovsky. If you are looking for a ten-Kleenex sentimental journey, your man is not this logical, orthodox composer, and *Samson* is not your opera.

Yet it has the same all-around class of other Saint-Saëns compositions. The analysts praise the simple Act I prelude, which sets the atmosphere, the treatment of the ballets, the excellence of the chorus work, and the quality of the workmanship.

Some say that perhaps the most "passionate" and intense music Saint-Saëns ever wrote is found in the second act, when Dalila plays Ms. Scissorhands with the familiar result.

A 1915 cast at the Met included Margarete Matzenauer and Enrico Caruso. Among recorded Samsons are Plácido Domingo, José Carreras, and Jon Vickers. Recorded Dalilas include Belgium's Rita Gorr, Greece's Agnes Baltsa, and Russia's Elena Obraztsova.

MET PERFORMANCES

One hundred and eighty-four performances over twenty-nine seasons, from 1895 to 1990.

RECORDING

CD—Angel/EMI CDCB 54470-2 (2). Plácido Domingo, Waltraud Meier, Alain Fondary, Jean-Philippe Courtis. L'Opéra-Bastille Chorus and Orchestra. Myung-Whun Chung. 1991.

VIDEO

Domingo, Verrett, Brendel. San Francisco Opera. French; English subtitles. Rudel, conductor. 1989. HOME VISION.

❦

Number 38. *Pelléas et Mélisande*
by Claude Debussy
August 22, 1862–March 25, 1918

Premiere at the Opéra-Comique in Paris, 1902. Text by Debussy from the 1892 play by Maurice Maeterlinck. Five acts.

Ludwig van Beethoven, one of Germany's best, is among music's top two or three composers.

Claude Debussy, one of France's best, is among music's top two or three dozen.

Most musicologists say that Beethoven's music set the tone for the nineteenth century, and many say that Debussy's was the model for the twentieth.

Beethoven wrote only one opera—a fine one, but regarded by no one as the masterwork of his musical life. Debussy, too, wrote only one opera—a unique one that *is* considered the masterwork of *his* musical life.

Critic and Pulitzer Prize–winning composer Virgil Thomson wrote of Debussy in 1948: "It is doubtful, indeed, whether Western music has made any notable progress at all since his death."

Debussy is to classical music what Stéphane Mallarmé is to symbolist poetry and Monet and Renoir to impressionist art. By using various techniques of composition, he created a new, different, and imaginative type of music—music that made *Pelléas et Mélisande* one of the century's most unusual operas.

"Things must be hinted," Mallarmé wrote, "not said."

Debussy's music is hinted, not said. Listen to any of his instrumental music. It is mysterious, shimmering, shadowy. When other musicians wrote about the sea you might hear waves crashing and feel wind blowing. When Debussy composed a famous piece called *La Mer*, he expressed the emotions and dreams the sea might inspire.

Pelléas et Mélisande is that kind of opera, in both text and music.

"How old are you?" asked Prince Golaud.

"I'm beginning to feel cold," replied Mélisande.

That's poet Mallarmé and/or symbolist playwright Maurice Maeterlinck and/or composer Debussy. Does it answer the question? Well, we have to think about that. What, after all, is age?

Or: "Who are you, Mélisande?"

"I have a crown which he gave me," she explains.

But we never learn more than that, including who "he" is.

"Music is all colors and rhythms," Debussy said.

Debussy's music uses free forms, exotic scales from the Far East, and what the music people call "unresolved discords." We might call that stopping the sentence in midair, without finishing the thought. The experts say he "freed" harmony.

The best preparation for *Pelléas et Mélisande* is to Debussify oneself—not by reading, but by hearing. Listen to the *Prélude à l'après-midi d'un faune (Prelude to the Afternoon of a Faun)*, to the three *Nocturnes—Nuages (Clouds)*, *Sirènes (Sirens)*, *Fêtes (Festivals)*—to *La Mer (The Sea)*, and to *Clair de lune* from *Suite bergamasque*. All are short. We need no knowledge of composition to hear that Debussy is writing a different kind of music, with different melodies, harmonies, and rhythms. One critic said these three, the holy trinity of music, were unknown to him.

(Later, when we get to Alban Berg's *Wozzeck*, the same technique, then called Bergification, is advised.)

Arbitrary and Absurd Cuts

During the production and rehearsal period, Maurice Maeterlinck, the man who began it all, was not pleased with the opera. He fell asleep during the audition, pipe burning. He attacked both the management of the Opéra-Comique and the opera itself. In a letter to *Le Figaro* dated April 14, 1902 (which was before the premiere), he described the work as strange and hostile to him. He wished for its immediate failure and protested against the arbitrary and absurd cuts that had been made in his original play.

He also rushed to Debussy's house one day with a cane, threatening to bash the composer with it. When Debussy sank into a chair and required smelling salts, Maeterlinck had no alternative but to retreat.

Later, however, after soprano Mary Garden had taken the part of Mélisande at the Metropolitan, he wrote her: "I had sworn to myself never to see the lyric drama *Pelléas et Mélisande*. Yesterday I violated my vow, and I am a happy man. For the first time I have entirely understood my own play, and because of you."

And still later, discussing his quarrel with Debussy, he said in an interview: "Today I find that I was completely wrong in this matter and that he was a thousand times right."

Nobel Prize winner Romain Rolland was a strong supporter of Debussy and his opera, calling its premiere a notable event in the history of French music. He said it was one of the three or four red-letter days in the history of the French lyric stage.

And he described Debussy's orchestration this way: "It possesses the aristocratic disdain for those orgies of sound to which the art of Wagner has accustomed us; it is sober and refined, like a fine classic eighteenth-century phrase.

Not a note too many—such is the artist's taste. Instead of amalgamating timbres for mass effects, he either releases their personalities from one another or he delicately ties them without perverting their own distinctive nature. Like the Impressionist painters of his time, he paints in pure colors, though with a delicate sobriety."

At another time, defending Debussy's music from critics, Rolland said:

"I don't like your modern French music very much. But what I can't understand is that, being so poor in artists, you have to quarrel with the greatest one you have."

Instead of arias or conventional recitative, *Pelléas* has declamation—a semirecitative, speechlike song, with the orchestra in the background.

The music was called "decadent," "morbid," "pernicious." The score was described as "spineless" and the singers as "unnecessary." Today it's almost impossible to find anyone anywhere in music who would agree with a single word of that.

But the music at the time also was hailed as "tender," "intensely artistic," "full of originality," "never monotonous." One professional critic said that Debussy had taken his place among the great sensualists of music, "of whom Mozart was the greatest." That's one Debussy should have framed and hung on the wall.

The opera is about a love triangle. The husband kills his brother who has betrayed him; the wife dies. But it is a mood piece, not an action drama. Debussy said that the plot is unimportant background. By his own definitions, his objective was to compose musical statements for the sentiments expressed by the characters and what lay behind them—"the borderline world between consciousness and dream, reality and imagination." When not everyone liked what they heard, Debussy offered this explanation:

"I tried to obey a law of beauty which appears to be singularly ignored in dealing with dramatic music. The characters of the drama endeavor to sing like real persons, and not in an arbitrary language or antiquated traditions. Hence, the reproach leveled at my alleged partiality for monotone declamation, in which there is no melody . . . To begin with, this is not true. Besides, the feeling of character cannot be continually expressed in melody. Also, dramatic melody should be totally different from melody in general.

"I do not pretend to have discovered anything in *Pelléas*; but I have tried to trace a path that others may follow, broadening it with individual discoveries which will, perhaps, free dramatic music from the heavy yoke under which it has existed for so long."

Debussy is often called the most original composer of this century and, with Igor Stravinsky, one of the greatest. He was born in 1862 near Paris in the town of St. Germain-en-Laye, where his parents kept a china shop. He entered the Paris Conservatory at eleven, astounding (and alarming) the professors with his creative composition. At twenty-one he wrote a friend about the kind of music he wanted to create: "supple enough to adapt itself to the lyrical effusions of the soul and the fantasy of dreams."

No Success Intended

Virgil Thomson in *The New York Review of Books* on December 9, 1965: "The last time it was in repertory at the Metropolitan, quite several years ago, a well-meaning person is said to have asked the conductor, Pierre Monteux, 'Do you suppose *Pelléas* will ever be really a success?' He answered: 'It was never intended to be.' "

Lyrical effusions of the soul normally cannot be relied upon to fill the opera house. (Well, maybe that's what Massenet did, with significantly less genius.)

Pelléas et Mélisande, which is virtually a setting of the symbolist drama by the Belgian Maeterlinck, took Debussy more than ten years to complete. Despite the negative critics, the premiere in 1902 brought him fame.

Most of his best-known instrumental pieces came in the 1890s and early 1900s, when he was writing in the impressionist mode. He composed slowly, lived only fifty-five years, and was not very prolific. Greatly disheartened by all the deaths of World War I, he worked still less during those years and died in March 1918 while Paris was being bombarded by the Germans.

KEYNOTE

A watershed event, to symbolism what *Carmen* was to realism. Hear gorgeous music composed around new theories of light and color. Expect a text that is cryptic, baffling, enigmatic, obscure.

PLOT

An indefinite medieval time in an indefinite place. Golaud (baritone), grandson of King Arkel (bass), is out hunting when he finds Mélisande (soprano) weeping at a fountain and falls in love. She agrees to accompany him home after he admits that he also is "lost." In another scene, Geneviève (contralto or mezzo-soprano), mother of Golaud and his half brother Pelléas (baritone), reads to blind King Arkel from a letter Golaud has written Pelléas, telling him about the mysterious woman he has found.

After receiving permission from Arkel, Golaud takes Mélisande to the castle as his wife. Pelléas is intrigued by her, finds he can't resist her beauty, and gradually they fall in love.

While Pelléas and Mélisande are together, she loses her wedding ring in a fountain. She lies about it to Golaud, who becomes suspicious of the time she and Pelléas spend with one another and asks Yniold, his young son from his first marriage, to spy on them. Although Arkel sees innocence in the eyes of Mélisande and predicts that youth and beauty will make everything turn out all

Mary Garden as Mélisande in Pelléas et Mélisande

right, Golaud is so tormented by Pelléas's deceptions that he drags Mélisande across the floor by her long blond hair. She loves Pelléas, but won't agree to leave Golaud and the castle with him. When Golaud finds them together in a passionate kiss, he kills Pelléas with his sword without speaking a word.

Mélisande runs off into the woods, crying out that she has no courage, and later is found dying, having given birth to a child. Mélisande admits to Golaud that she loved Pelléas but denies she was unfaithful. She dies, with Golaud doubting her and still demanding the truth.

HIGHLIGHTS

Influenced by the "endless melody" style of Wagner, Debussy has no big solo arias of traditional opera form.

Act III: The tower love scene, with no love spoken, between Pelléas and Mélisande as her long hair falls over his head.

Act IV: Two of the opera's most dramatic scenes: the last meeting of Pelléas and Mélisande, aware that fate will end their love, and Golaud's interruption of their passionate kiss followed by his instant murder of Pelléas. At the climax of the love scene the music stops for the only time in the opera and the characters whisper, "Je t'aime" and "Je t'aime aussi." It's a goose-bumps moment.

COMMENTARY

This, as noted, is unlike any other opera. The characters often speak in noncommittal phrases. The emotions all are intermingled: intimacy, innocence, jealous rage, love, and death. It is uncertain which is which . . . or why. Like Berlioz's *Les Troyens*, it's a work that some devotees insist should be shown over and over again until opera audiences come to appreciate it fully. If you see it, or watch a videotape, you may decide they are right.

Some analysts say it takes opera back to Monteverdi as a blend of poetry and music, however great the differences in three hundred years. It *is* a blend of poetry and music, precisely what one might expect from a marriage of Maeterlinck and Debussy—except that nothing is precise about it, which, logically, also is what one might expect from such a marriage.

Insult Wanted

Virgil Thomson also tells the story of Isidor Philipp, the great piano instructor, who was visited by Béla Bartók in Paris. Philipp offered to introduce the Hungarian to several different celebrities, but Bartók wasn't interested.

"Who would you like to know?"

"Debussy," said Bartók.

"But he's a horrid man," said Philipp. "He hates everybody and will certainly be rude to you. Do you want to be insulted by Debussy?"

"Yes," said Bartók.

One professional suggests that we consider *Pelléas* as a counterpart to Wagner's *Tristan und Isolde*—the same period, the same general theme, many of the same plot elements, everything treated in wholly different ways.

The role of Pelléas was written for a high lyric baritone, almost a tenor. But, my singing friends tell me, there aren't many baritones who can sing it well, so often it's given to a tenor, even though tenors don't like it because there aren't enough high notes. The first Mélisande, in Paris, was Mary Garden. She also recorded the role accompanied on the piano by Debussy himself. Other Mélisandes included the Spanish soprano Lucrezie Bori, Sweden's soprano Elisabeth Söderström and the American mezzo-soprano Frederica Von Stade.

MET PERFORMANCES

Ninety-six performances over twenty-four seasons, from 1925 to 1995.

RECORDING

CD—DG Dig. 435 344-2 (2). Francois Le Roux, Maria Ewing, Jose Van Dam. Vienna Konzertvereingung, Vienna Philharmonic Orchestra. Claudio Abbado.

VIDEO

Gagley, Walker, Archer, Maxwell, Cox. Welsh National Opera. French; English subtitles. Boulez, conductor. DG.

Number 39. *Les contes d'Hoffmann* *(The Tales of Hoffmann)*
by Jacques Offenbach
January 20, 1819–October 4, 1880

Premiere at the Opéra-Comique, Paris, 1881. Text by Jules Barbier and Michel Carré after E.T.A. Hoffmann's stories. Three acts, plus Prologue and Epilogue (or in five acts, depending on the production).

Continental Europe's two most successful "popular" composers in the nineteenth century were Johann Strauss the Younger and Jakob Eberst.

Who?

Johann Strauss and Jakob Eberst.

Jakob who?

Eberst. Some spell it Eberscht.

Never heard of him.

How about Jacques Offenbach? He was the toast of the Second Empire.

Is that the Empire that Struck Back after Star Wars? Just kidding. I'm not sure I've ever heard of him either.

We now embark on a detour that will, in time, take us back to *The Tales of Hoffmann.*

Jakob Levy Eberst was the son of a Jewish cantor, born in German Cologne. He changed his name to Jacques Offenbach and became a Parisian conductor, composer, entrepreneur, and boulevardier. And he wrote more than one hundred pieces for the stage. Rossini called him the Mozart of the Champs-Elysées.

For a good many years he made his living as a cellist. Later he opened his own theater when existing ones would not produce his compositions.

Although you wouldn't know it from his Collection work, he specialized in what the music people call "lighter fare." The manner in which they say "lighter fare" is related to the elevation of their brows. He wrote "operettas," also called "light operas," which leads us to definitions.

I have before me a *Harper Dictionary of Music*, a *Harvard Dictionary of Music*, a *Norton/Grove Concise Encyclopedia of Music*, a David Ewen *New Encyclopedia of the Opera*, and the four-volume *New Grove Dictionary of Opera*. From these come the following data:

An operetta is less serious in both subject and its treatment than a serious opera. In the seventeenth and eighteenth centuries the term was used for a variety of stage works shorter or *less enterprising* than an opera. In the nineteenth and twentieth centuries it has been used for a light opera with spoken dialogue (rather than recitative) and dances. The subject is usually sentimental, or humorous, or occasionally satirical, or a combination of the three. The music usually is popular in nature. The modern operetta originated in Vienna with Franz von Suppé (1819–95) and in Paris with Jacques Offenbach. An operetta can be described as a romantic play with songs and musical numbers. It is usually shorter than an opera. The score is "more ambitious" than that of a typical Broadway musical but "less ambitions" than that of an opera. (But the scores of Stephen Sondheim, composer of *Sweeney Todd*, *A Little Night Music* and other outstanding works for Broadway are very close to opera.)

In Vienna, the operetta gained international fame from Johann Strauss the Younger, who wrote sixteen operettas, including The Collection *Die Fledermaus* (*The Bat*), 1874. That Viennese tradition was continued by Franz Lehár with *The Merry Widow*, 1905. England enjoyed the work of Gilbert and Sullivan, and United States audiences the compositions of Victor Herbert, Rudolf Friml, Sigmund Romberg, and Jerome Kern, among others.

Does "less ambitious" mean that the composer was less gifted? Might it mean that he simply preferred the operetta form to the opera form?

Jacques Offenbach puts to rest some of those questions, inasmuch as he wrote many highly successful operettas and then, in the last year of his life, one much-acclaimed opera. On the other hand, Johann Strauss the Younger, the "Waltz King," wrote one fabulously successful operetta, *Die Fledermaus*, another almost as successful, *Die Zigeunerbaron*, and fourteen more, but never a "serious" opera despite his longing to do so.

So where does that leave us? Can we now tell an operetta from an opera?

President Lyndon Johnson once said to me at a "rehearsal" meeting in the

Oval Office before a news conference that would center on civilian casualties in North Vietnam: "Goulding, you are a hell of a lot better at asking these questions than you are at answering them."

It seems more profitable to look at each individual work rather than a composer or a composer's total production.

Major opera houses do sometimes produce operettas, and music critics then invariably speak of them as "popular favorites." That's a fact; good operettas are popular with the public . . . and with the musicians . . . and with the money counters operating the opera house.

It doesn't take a Stanford degree in musicology to recognize that a wonderful operetta by a talented Offenbach is better music than a ponderous opera by a respected classical composer who lacks understanding of the theater and knowledge of the human voice.

Who's the Genius?

Friedrich Nietzsche wrote of Offenbach: "If by artistic genius we understand the most consummate freedom within the law, divine ease and facility in overcoming the greatest difficulties, then Offenbach has more right to the title of genius than Wagner."

Nietzsche proves two points: (1) Great philosophers may construct their own definitions. (2) No highbrow he.

Back to square one. An opera is a play *in* music. An operetta is more apt to be a play *with* music.

One view of the musicologists is that there's a great gap between the music of the "creative artist" (presumably the opera composer) and the large mass of people looking for their musical pleasure from "different sources of doubtful quality such as operetta and hit song." This is the sort of elitist view that scares people away from opera. Is all operetta of "doubtful quality?" With respect to my betters, that's clearly nonsense.

One appealing and enlightening approach by the scholars examines the differences between operetta and opera in terms of how each portrays human life. It argues that operetta, limited by its sentimental aspects, is most apt to present only limited elements of the human condition, whereas opera—good opera—presents the whole of the human condition. Under this theory, characters in operetta generally come in one dimension and don't develop during the performance, whereas characters in opera are less static and do change. Of course, second-tier opera composers—not Mozarts or Verdis—also are criticized for producing characters that are essentially static.

As for opera houses performing operettas, all of us can recognize that is management's individual decision. The U.S. Congress has not intervened. If you're dictator of the Metropolitan, and want an operetta, you can have an operetta. But the Met would want that operetta to demand an operatic voice. One wouldn't expect to find in an opera house a Broadway musical comedy starring the late, wonderful Ethel Merman.

In an operetta, or in musical comedy, hero, heroine, and chorus often sing identical music. In an opera, the music of a hero is more apt to reflect his dramatic state of mind and the different music of the heroine to reflect hers.

Summary: Operettas always have spoken dialogue. Unlike many Broadway musicals, they demand an operatic voice. But the characters don't develop from curtain rise to curtain fall. And even in their one dimension, they are depicted by plot, not by music. When duets or quartets are sung, everyone is apt to be singing the same music; there are not attempts to approach a Mozartian finale. Is the music in an operetta "not as important" as the music in an opera? Define important. How important is Louis Armstrong's music? As the President said, it's easier to ask the questions than to answer them. We'll return to the subject in the Johann Strauss section.

Back to Jacques Offenbach. He didn't "invent" operetta; that honor is given to Von Suppé in Vienna. But Offenbach seized it, made it his own, and became rich and famous through it.

After he and his brother arrived in Paris from Germany when he was fourteen, he wheedled his way into the Conservatory despite the fact that it didn't take foreign students. Later he earned eighty-three francs a month playing the cello in the orchestra of the Opéra-Comique. When he tired of the orchestra (and it tired of him), he gave music lessons and copied music manuscripts in Paris for three years and then toured Germany and England as a performing cellist.

Returning to Paris, he became a Catholic, married a Spanish girl named Herminie de Alcain, skipped back to his native Germany when the 1848 revolution in Paris broke out, and came back a year later as conductor of the orchestra at the Théâtre Française. The orchestra provided incidental music for the plays presented there and played between the acts.

In 1855 he scraped together enough money to lease a very small theater in the Champs-Elysées, for which he secured a license from the government to present meager musical plays.

He named the theater the Bouffes-Parisiens and began producing his own small, light, very popular musical dramas, which became so popular that he soon took a lease on a second theater closer to downtown Paris, the Salle Choiseul. In time, as his name became well known, other theaters wanted some of his works.

A long, long string of successes included *Orpheé aux enfers*, 1858; *Geneviève de Brabant*, 1859; *La belle Hélène* 1864; *Barbe-Bleue*, 1866; *La vie parisienne*, 1866; *La Grande Duchesse de Gérolstein*, 1867; *La périchole*, 1868; *Madame l'Archiduc*, 1873, and *La fille du tambour major*, 1879.

To Swing a Cat

The *New York Tribune* in 1863 describing Offenbach's theater: "The Bouffes-Parisiens is so little as to be almost a joke. You laugh when you get inside it, at its tiny proportions . . . There is, in fact, hardly room enough to swing a cat in. People do not, however, go to the Bouffes for the purpose of swinging cats. They go to listen to the brightest and newest music, to witness the best acting, of its order, that the French stage affords. And they are never disappointed. Absolutely never."

His last theatrical venture was with still a third theater, the Gaîeté, leased in 1872, but this time with unhappy financial results. He died in Paris in 1880.

Offenbach's operetta music is gay, infectious, exhilarating, and always tuneful. Most of his works are ironic and witty. One critic called them "salty satire." Another, a Wagner biographer, preferred "elegant frivolity."

One who gave him high marks was the famous Viennese music critic Eduard Hanslick—an anti-Wagnerian—who wrote an Offenbach obituary: "Offenbach was always original. We recognize his music as Offenbach-ish after only two or three bars, and this fact alone raises him high above his French and German imitators, whose buffo operas would shrivel up miserably were we to confiscate all that is Offenbach-ish in them. He created a new style in which he reigned absolutely alone."

Freedom and originality are among the key words for the Offenbach style. His medium was new; there were no long-time conventions to be followed for something called an operetta, no tradition, no history. It had to be amusing, but it could be political. It might have a moral, it could be maliciously satirical, it often was irreverent—and it could persuade the citizens of Paris that it was talking about *them*.

Professor Paul Henry Lang said that there was a good bit of Molière in Offenbach, high praise indeed. Jean-Baptiste Molière, French actor and playwright, 1622–1673, was the greatest of all French comedy writers . . . and one of the greatest French writers of any description.

Orphée aux enfers (*Orpheus in the Underworld*), the work that contains the famous cancan, is regarded by many as Offenbach's opéra bouffe masterpiece. It was a brilliant and subtle mockery of the Olympian gods, a parody of Christoph Willibald Gluck's famous opera. Unlike the Gluck (and Monteverdi) versions, Orpheus and Eurydice are unhappily married, Orpheus lusts for Chloë, the shepherdess, and Eurydice fancies Aristeus. Much to Orpheus's delight, those two elope to Hades. Even Jupiter gets involved. The gods make Orpheus go to Hades to retrieve Eurydice with the traditional condition that he must not look back until she is safely above ground. Jupiter, however, has fallen for Eury-dice, and he throws a bolt of lightning into Hades, forcing Orpheus to turn his head. This causes him to lose Eurydice, which allows Jupiter to get her while Orpheus can return to Chloë.

In short, Jupiter screws up a two-thousand-year-old plot because he gets the hots for the heroine, and the Parisians loved it.

True Parisian

Offenbach lived in the Montmartre section of Paris for many years and was buried in Montmartre, his funeral cortege passing by the the-aters he had made famous. When the Germans advanced to the out-skirts during the Franco-Prussian War of 1870–71, he said, "I am deeply saddened to have been born on the Rhine River . . . I am a Parisian through and through."

He was at his peak in the 1860s, when Paris was hosting a World Ex-hibition and pushing under the rug its slums, poverty, and child labor. The operettas he wrote were critical while other composers were dealing in melodrama; they were satirical while others were offering sentiment.

Now . . . where does all this leave us with Offenbach's Collection opera?

Offenbach's most serious work, the one for which he is most remembered, and his only one that is sung throughout (recitative, with no spoken dialogue), is *The Tales of Hoffmann*. Although he wrote more than one hundred produc-tions for the stage, he spent substantially more time on this than on any other. It was designed as his musical masterpiece, and he arranged for it to be pro-duced at the Opéra-Comique. But he died four months too soon, before he had put his final touches on it, leaving unsaid what he expected the end product to look like—or sound like. Obviously, he never saw it staged.

The real Ernst Theodor Wilhelm Hoffmann, on whose stories the opera is based, lived from 1776 to 1822. He was a composer of operas in his own right, as well as being a writer, critic, and illustrator. To honor Mozart, he used Amadeus for his third name when composing and thus was known as E.T.A. Hoffmann. Among his writings were tales of the supernatural, which led the way to a stage play by the men who became the librettists for Offenbach's opera.

KEYNOTE

Intriguing fantasy opera from the man who created French operetta. One of France's most popular operas and a favorite on hundreds of stages in scores of countries. Enjoy windup Olympia. Strong music and great theater.

PLOT

The nineteenth century, Nuremberg, Munich, and Venice. Because it is unfinished, producers and directors do their own thing here even more than usual. The second and third acts often are performed in different order.

Prologue: Town Councillor Lindorf (bass-baritone) is in a wine cellar in Nuremberg, next to an opera house. (The singer playing the role of Lindorf is an "evil genius" who appears as Hoffmann's adversary in a different role in each act: Coppelius, a scientist; Dapertutto, a sorcerer; and Dr. Miracle, a medical doctor.) Hoffmann (tenor), a poet, appears in the tavern, accompanied by his friend Nicklausse (mezzo-soprano). Hoffmann is waiting to meet his beloved Stella (soprano), an opera singer who is performing next door. He doesn't know that Lindorf has intercepted her love letter to him, in which she had put a key to her boudoir. While he is waiting, Hoffmann is persuaded by the other drinkers to tell the story of three episodes in his unhappy love life—the three "tales" of Hoffmann.

Each act tells a separate story. Tale One (Olympia): His first love is a life-sized mechanical windup doll, Olympia (soprano), invented by a physician, Spalanzani (tenor) and (the evil) Coppelius. Hoffmann is sold a pair of magic spectacles, through which Olympia seems human to him. Eventually Spalanzani and Coppelius quarrel, Coppelius smashes Olympia into small pieces, and a disillusioned Hoffmann learns he has been in love with a windup woman.

Tale Two (Antonia): Hoffmann is in Munich, where he has fallen in love with Antonia (soprano), an ailing young singer, daughter of Crespel (bass or baritone), a violin maker. Ill with consumption inherited from her deceased mother, Antonia has been advised that she is too weak to sing. But (the evil) Dr. Miracle appears, summons up the voice of her mother to influence her, insists that he can cure her, and pleads with her not to silence her beautiful voice. She is persuaded to sing, and he accompanies her on his violin. But he leads her voice higher and higher until it exhausts her strength and she falls dead. Crespel blames Hoffmann, who now not only has lost his second love but also is accused of her murder.

Tale Three (Giulietta): In Venice, Hoffmann has given up "ideal" love for plain ordinary old sensuous sexual love. He is chasing a beautiful courtesan named Giulietta (soprano), who is in the power of (the evil) Dapertutto, whose objective is to capture Hoffmann's reflection/shadow/soul. Another suitor of Giulietta's is Schlemil (bass). Dapertutto incites a duel between the two suitors and uses his magic to guide Hoffmann's sword to kill Schlemil. When Hoffmann rushes to find his Giulietta, he sees her floating away in a gondola with the dwarf, Pittichinaccio (tenor). Strike Three.

Epilogue: Back in the tavern, Hoffmann has finished telling his stories and is drinking heavily. Nicklausse remarks that Stella is the personification of the three types of women in Hoffmann's stories. Mozart's *Don Giovanni*, the opera Stella is singing next door, has ended. When Stella arrives for the planned rendezvous with Hoffmann, he's dead drunk. The Muse of Poetry appears to claim him for her own. Lindorf leads Stella away as she tosses a flower toward Hoffmann, who by this time is in too much of an alcoholic stupor to care. But he is in the hands of the Muse.

HIGHLIGHTS

Prologue: Hoffmann's Legend of Kleinzach.

Act I (Olympia): Hoffmann's "Ah, vivre deux," as he sings of his love for Olympia. Olympia's famous "Doll Song," "Les oiseaux dans la charmille": "The birds in the arbor, the sun in the skies, everything speaks to the young girl of love."

Act II (Antonia): Antonia's song, "Elle a fui, la tourterelle," telling of her loneliness and longing for the man she loves who is not there: "The turtle dove has fled. Ah, sweet memory." The violin scene as Dr. Miracle kills Antonia.

Act III (depending on the order of the particular production, and the designation of Prologue and Epilogue, the Giulietta act): This is sometimes also called the Barcarolle Act because it is opened and closed by the best-known number of the opera, and one familiar to nonoperagoers, the famous Barcarolle. (A barcarolle imitates the rhythm of songs sung by Venetian gondoliers.) Also Dapertutto's "Diamond Aria," "Scintille diamant," as he sings about his jewel: "Sparkle, diamond, mirror that catches the lark. Fascinate and attract her. The lark or the woman comes to this bait. The lark loses its life, the woman her soul." Then Hoffmann's "O Dieu de quelle ivresse," his love song to Giulietta: "Heavens, with what rapture do you set my soul on fire." And a duet between the two, "Si ta présence m'est ravie."

COMMENTARY

This work is "ambitious" enough in scope for the harshest critics—the picture of a loser, both in love and in life, who can't cope with evil fate no matter what he does (although he does have his poetry). The professionals find it witty, sophisticated, original, appealing, and "profound." (When the critics are on hand, it's good to be profound, just as it's good for a State Department diplomat to be "pragmatic." For decades in Washington the successful diplomat invariably was described as both "pragmatic" and "pipe-smoking." "Pragmatic" is still an in-thing, but pipe-smoking is out.)

Unlike the gay operettas, this opera is a bitter story of tragic disillusionment. Offenbach was not well when he composed it, suffering from gout, melancholia, a terrible cough, and general discontent, some of which was caused by a disastrous tour of the United States during which he pleased few of the public and virtually none of the critics.

It is a favorite of set designers since they have four different locations to play with.

Plácido Domingo has sung the role of Hoffmann often and with great success. Beverly Sills, who was fond of French operas, learned it as a seventeen-year-old girl and became famous for her portrayal of all three soprano characters. Customarily, the three "evil geniuses" in the tales (plus Lindorf) are performed by the same bass-baritone singer but it is much more difficult to find a soprano who can handle the three very different kinds of female roles of Antonia, Olympia, and Giulietta, which were not written for the same voice.

MET PERFORMANCES

Two hundred and ten performances over twenty-seven seasons, from 1913 to 1993. One of the three operas on the Met's 1988 Japan trip.

RECORDING

CD—Decca/London 417 363-2 (2). Joan Sutherland, Huguette Tourangeau, Plácido Domingo, Gabriel Bacquier. Swiss Radio, Lausanne Pro Arte, and Du Brassus Choruses. Orchestra de la Suisse Romande. Richard Boynge. 1972.

VIDEO

Domingo, Serra, Baltsa, Evans. Royal Opera House, Convent Garden. French; English subtitles. Prêtre, conductor. 1981. HBO.

∾

Number 40. *La Gioconda*
by Amilcare Ponchielli
August 31, 1824–January 17, 1886

Premiere at La Scala, Milan, 1876. Text by Arrigo Boito. Based on Victor Hugo's 1835 drama Angelo, tyran de Padoue (Angelo, Tyrant of Padua). *A big opera in four acts.*

Picture the network vice president in charge of soap operas.

"What I want," he says, "is number ten melodrama. Blood and thunder. Get out your notepads.

"Start with adultery. Nothing goes like adultery. And revenge. Revenge is big. We'll need a mother in danger. Maybe she's being accused of witchcraft. And she's blind. Then arson, poisoning, stabbing, kidnapping, and suicide.

"Time's a little short. Give me something by close of business Friday.

"Hold it. We need more. Work in a lynching. Maybe the cops strangle the blind mother. And think about stealing a body from its coffin.

"Any questions? Okay, go. C.O.B. Friday. Call it *La Gioconda*. That's Italian for *The Joyous One*. Plenty of Italians in our biggest markets."

As the writers file out, one admirer expresses the enthusiasm of them all for their boss: "By God, he's done it again!"

La Gioconda is another once exceedingly popular opera, long past its peak but still on the sidelines like the verismo *Andrea Chénier* and many more. It's another that has endured a lifetime of severe criticism from critics and other composers. Like the bel canto operas of Italy earlier in the nineteenth century, the singers love it. It is the only Italian grand opera besides *Aida* that has stayed healthy.

The librettist who concocted this violent mishmash is one of the most famous of opera authors, Arrigo Boito, who not only provided texts for Verdi's *Otello* and *Falstaff* but also wrote a Collection opera of his own, Number 73, *Mefistofele*.

When *Gioconda* first appeared in 1876, one first-night reviewer was impressed: "Ponchielli's score shows that he has fully grasped the poet's intentions," wrote the critic. "True to the school of which Boito made himself the champion, and after many years of hard struggle, Ponchielli has endeavored to write dramatic music which being descriptive of action abounds in coloring and instrumental effects . . . *La Gioconda* is an energetic and laudable effort to infuse fresh vigor into Italian opera."

Teacher's Pet

Part of a letter from Ponchielli to Puccini's mother dated January 8, 1883: "Your son is one of the best pupils in my class, and I am well satisfied with him."

A few years later, however, in 1884, critic/composer Hugo Wolf (Austrian who is most famous for his magnificent songwriting) called the melodies "banal and flat" and described the libretto as "a book of horrors"—"trivial, dirty [and] cannibalistic."

No real cannibals; Wolf meant that the composer had stolen from Gounod, Verdi, and Meyerbeer.

Still, a musicologist at the turn of the century called Ponchielli a genius, although a genius of the second rank. I'm uncertain what that means.

Of several operas, *La Gioconda* is Ponchielli's only enduring success. It is a lurid melodrama, grand opera in style, with big choral scenes and big ballet, involving a street singer who promises herself to a satanic Inquisition spy in payment for the release of her lover and eventually kills herself rather than submit to him.

Not a cheerful piece. Not Snow White, although music of a famous ballet in it, the "Dance of the Hours," was used in Walt Disney's *Fantasia*. It also is the source of humorist Allan Sherman's 1963 hit record, "Hello Muddah, Hello Faddah."

Ponchielli was born near Cremona and studied at the Milan Conservatory. He composed his first opera soon after graduation, but his first success didn't come until he was in his late thirties, in 1872, when he revised an earlier effort, *I promessi sposi*, based on the novel by the Italian novelist and poet Alessandro Manzoni. This historical study of seventeenth-century Italy is considered a model for Italian prose and was perhaps more responsible than the music for the opera's success.

In later life, Ponchielli taught at the Milan Conservatory, where he was considered the "gentle professor." Among his students were Giacomo Puccini and Pietro Mascagni. Ponchielli's focus on violence and brutality made him something of a godfather of the Italian verismo movement, exemplified by Mascagni's *Cavalleria rusticana* and Leoncavallo's *Pagliacci*.

Ponchielli, like Mascagni, Leoncavallo, and Umberto Giordano, strove to be the heir of the great master, Verdi. But the Italian who came closest, leaving the others far behind, was a fifth named Giacomo Puccini.

KEYNOTE

Meyerbeer-like spectacle: opulent settings, huge orchestra, exciting choruses, and a captain who burns his own ship. Meet Barnaba, almost as villainous as Scarpia and Iago. He loves La Gioconda who loves Enzo who loves Laura who is married to Alvise. An old-fashioned melodrama.

Tears for Plácido

From his autobiography: "At the age of twenty-nine I finally made my hometown debut, singing my very first performance of *La Gioconda* at Madrid's Teatro de la Zarzuela. It was an emotional moment for me. The ovation after my aria, 'Cielo e mar,' was so great and so warm that I could not help myself—I began to cry. Some terribly difficult phrases in a rough tessitura follow soon after the aria, in the duet with Laura, and the crying was obstructing my voice. I finally managed to get hold of myself and proceed normally."

PLOT

Seventeenth-century Venice. The tortuous plot defies a logical, brief, action-describing summary. Barnaba (baritone), ballad singer and spy for the Inquisition, lusts for Gioconda (soprano), a street singer. She supports her blind mother, La Cieca (contralto), and is engaged to Enzo (tenor), a Genoese prince disguised as a sea captain. Barnaba accuses La Cieca of witchcraft in order to get Gioconda in his power. Alvise (bass), one of the Inquisition chiefs, is married to Laura (mezzo-soprano), a Genoese lady. He orders La Cieca to be arrested and tortured, but when she is brought before the courts, Laura sees a rosary she is wearing and intervenes successfully for her. Meanwhile, Laura and Enzo recognize one another from the past. Enzo loves Gioconda like a sister, but his real passion is for Laura. When Barnaba learns of this he arranges for Enzo and Laura to meet on Enzo's ship and elope. He plans to trap them there so the way will be cleared for him to have Gioconda.

Gioconda appears unexpectedly on the ship, confronts Laura, and is about to stab her when she recognizes her as the woman who saved her mother's life. Gioconda gives Laura her mask so that she can get away and extricate herself from this situation. Enzo arrives, is distressed to find Gioconda there, sees Alvise approaching by boat, sets fire to his own ship, and leaps into the water.

In his palace, Alvise tries to poison Laura to avenge his family's honor, but Gioconda substitutes a sleeping potion for the poison. Barnaba drags in La Cieca, and again accuses her of witchcraft. Enzo, who is there in disguise, reveals himself, and Alvise orders him seized. Gioconda promises Barnaba she'll submit to him if he frees Enzo. Laura's apparently dead body is on display, and funeral bells toll for her.

Later, Enzo arrives in a courtyard by the canal, not knowing why he has been released and unaware that Laura is still alive. Laura's "body" is with Gioconda. Enzo is about to stab Gioconda when she explains what she has done and tells him she has a boat in which he and Laura can escape together. When Barnaba arrives to claim Gioconda, she kills herself with a dagger, without hearing him reveal that he has killed her mother out of spite.

HIGHLIGHTS

Act I: La Cieca's "Voce di donna," as she thanks Laura for interceding for her.

Act II: A great tenor aria by Enzo, "Cielo e mar": "Will my angel come from heaven or from the sea?" Also, a famous duet between the two rivals, La Gioconda and Laura, the work's most dramatic number, "L'amo come il fulgor del creato" ("I love him as the light of creation").

Act III: The opera's most familiar music is the ballet, the "Dance of the Hours." You'll recognize it.

COMMENTARY

La Gioconda has endured (especially in Italy but also for many years as a U.S. favorite in the big houses that can afford to stage it) for a combination of reasons:

- Big, lyrical arias for big voices—six types of big voices, from soprano and tenor down.
- No intellectual activity is required.
- The melodramatic plot is nice and bloodthirsty.
- Crashing finales.
- All the sexy emotions: love, hatred, jealousy, and revenge. Plus gratitude.
- The famous, charming ballet, the "Dance of the Hours."
- A big assist in midcentury from Maria Callas.

Daniel Snowman, a Domingo biographer, says of it: "*La Gioconda*, by the gentle, professorial Amilcare Ponchielli, written in the 1870s, is one of those works that, unlike its heroine, refuses to die . . . Dramatically and emotionally overblown, hard to cast at full strength, and difficult for producer or conductor to hold together convincingly, *La Gioconda* is not one of the staples of the operatic repertoire. But when it is mounted well its surges of gloriously ingratiating music make it a work to treasure, and American audiences in particular always seem to have had a soft spot for it."

It's the last well-known opera to be written around specific arias, in this case, showpiece arias for all voices. La Gioconda is a soprano, Laura a mezzosoprano, and La Cieca a contralto; Enzo is a tenor, Barnaba a baritone, and Alvise a bass.

The Met chose it for its opening season in 1883. In 1904 Enrico Caruso entered the picture as Enzo, and for several years it was second only to *Aida* as the Met's season opener. Much later, in 1947, a performance in Verona brought Maria Callas, in her Italian debut, to the attention of the public. Emmy Destinn, Rosa Ponselle, Zinka Milanov, and Renata Tebaldi were other famous Met Giocondas. Best-known Enzos have included the great Beniamino Gigli, Richard Trucker, Domingo, and Pavarotti.

MET PERFORMANCES
Two hundred and seventy-four performances over thirty-eight seasons, from 1883 to 1990.

RECORDING
CD—EMI/Angel CDS7 49518-2 (3). Maria Callas, Irene Companeez, Pier Miranda Ferraro, Ivo Vinco, Fiorenza Cossotto, Piero Cappuccilli. La Scala, Milan, Chorus and Orchestra. Antonio Votto. 1959.

VIDEO
Marton, Domingo, Manuguerra. Vienna Staatsoper. Italian; English subtitles. Fisher, conductor. 1986. HOME VISION.

∾

Number 41. *Turandot*
by Giacomo Puccini
December 22, 1858–November 29, 1924

Premiere at La Scala, Milan, 1926. Text by Giuseppe Adami and Renato Simoni. Based on Carlo Gozzi's 1762 play King Turandot. *Three acts. Not completed by composer.*

What phantom dies each dawn but each night is reborn in the heart?

What blazes up when you think of great deeds, is hot in love, and grows cold when you die?

What is the ice that sets you on fire?

If your answers are Hope, Blood, and Princess Turandot, you have escaped beheading and, presumably, have won Turandot herself, although it's a little uncertain why you'd want her as she is at this stage of the opera.

Turandot is always around but never has truly taken off. Initial receptions in London and New York weren't particularly strong. At the Metropolitan, after twenty-one performances over four seasons, it was put on the shelf for almost thirty years before being revived in 1961 with Leopold Stokowski conducting. Though solid in the Met repertory, it never has reached the popularity level of *Bohème*, *Butterfly*, or *Tosca*.

Puccini died on November 29, 1924, before completing the last act. Franco Alfano (1876–1954) composed the final big duet between Turandot and Calaf and the last scene, both of which were then revised by the conductor, Arturo Toscanini. Puccini had designed these as essential to the opera, but most analysts say that they don't measure up to his standard and therefore Turandot's transformation from cruel ice princess to alluring woman doesn't come off as it would have if he had lived.

Puccini on Turandot

In a letter to one of his two librettists, Renato Simoni, Puccini wrote:
"I am sad and discouraged. I think of Turandot. It is because of Turandot that I feel like a lost soul. I cannot find a way out. . . ."

He also wrote his other librettist, Giuseppe Adami, that Turnadot gave him no peace.

KEYNOTE

Bad girl gets the guy. Puccini's valedictory masterpiece, his most mature work, and his greatest spectacle opera. The last Italian opera to hold the international stage. Meet the cruel Chinese princess who does a 180° turn at the end . . . and meet the slave girl worth two of her. Know Love if you would know the Kinder, Gentler world.

PLOT

Legendary times, Peking, China. Princess Turandot (soprano), proud, chaste, and vengeful daughter of the Emperor, will marry any suitor of royal blood who can answer her three riddles. If they fail, they are beheaded. Twenty-six have failed. If they succeed, they win not only the princess but also the throne of China (which apparently the suitors feel is worth having, even if Turandot comes with it). The cruelty is her means of avenging a female ancestor who was betrayed and murdered by a warlord stranger. Prince Calaf (tenor), new man in town, is the son of Timur (bass) the blind, banished King of Tartary. In a crowd scene celebrating the head-chopping of the Prince of Persia (number twenty-six) (tenor), Calaf stumbles upon his father and the slave girl Liù (soprano), the old man's friend and guide. Overwhelmed by Turandot's beauty, Calaf disregards the advice of father, slave girl, and three Chinese ministers, Ping (baritone), Pang (tenor), and Pong (tenor), who yearn for the good old days before Turandot, and enters the contest.

Calaf answers the questions, but Turandot is one of opera's great welshers. She will be possessed by no man. A vow is a vow, the Emperor says, but Calaf lets her off the hook, declaring that he wants her only if she is also burning for him. He poses a challenge of his own: Find out my name by morning. If you succeed, I'll forfeit my life. Timur has kept secret the birth of a son, fearing that the same plotters who seized his throne would kill a young prince if they knew about him.

Toscanini at the Podium

Arturo Toscanini conducted the premiere of *Turandot* after Puccini's death. In Act III, when Liù grabs a dagger to stab herself, Toscanini stopped conducting, turned to the audience, and said: "At this point the Maestro laid down his pen."

The curtain fell, and the audience sat silent.

Turandot puts out the word: No one in Peking shall sleep tonight until the name of the stranger is discovered. Calaf is tempted by luscious lovelies, chests of jewels, and promises of glory, but he'll have none of it. Timur and Liù, however, were seen earlier speaking to Calaf, and Turandot plans to torture the old man to get the name from him. Fearing for Timur's life, Liù steps forward, proclaims that only she knows the name, pledges that it can't be tortured from her, and then seizes a dagger and fatally stabs herself. Calaf upbraids Turandot for her cruelty and kisses her passionately. It is one of opera's most powerful kisses, and, coming in the wake of Liù's sacrifice for love, it breaks the spell. Turandot now is overcome by passion and shame; her strength wastes away, and her cruelty is ended. She begs Calaf to leave, but instead he tells her his name, thus putting his life in her hands. A wiser Turandot tells the Emperor and the people that she has learned the stranger's true name . . . and that it is Love.

HIGHLIGHTS

Act I: Liù's plea for Calaf to steer clear of the riddles, "Signore, ascolta": "My Lord, listen to me. My heart is breaking! How far have I walked with your name in my heart, with your name on my lips." His response, "Non piangere, Liù" ("Do not weep, Liù"): "If my father, your master, is alone tomorrow, take care of him."

Act II: Turandot's "In questa reggia" (within this palace), as she tells the story of her betrayed ancestress.

Act III: Calaf's "Nessun dorma," when he feels sure he will win Turandot: "None shall sleep, including you, my Princess. In your cold room you will look at the stars that tremble with love and hope, but my secret is mine and nobody shall know my name. Let the night end and the stars disappear. At dawn I shall triumph. Nobody shall know my name." (This became familiar as the BBC theme song for the 1990 World Cup soccer matches). Also Liù's "Tu, che di gel sei cinta": "You, who wrap yourself in ice, will be conquered by flame, and will love him! Before dawn I shall close my weary eyes, never to see him again."

COMMENTARY

Professionals are intrigued by *Turandot*. One popular view is that this is Puccini's most ambitious work, in which he tried to reach higher than he had in any other opera, but that he lacked the genius to succeed as Verdi would have with the same libretto.

Example from analysts: Puccini tries to draw a cold, cruel, heartless, sadistic Turandot to contrast with the loving, caring, warm, and dedicated Liù. But does the music itself express the great differences between them as Verdi's would have? Test it yourself: If you ignore the text, what emotions are depicted to you by the music alone? *La Bohème* is a much less "ambitious" work, where the contrasts onstage are not great, and it works beautifully. There, the characters *are* made human by the music. But *Turandot*'s characters are much more complex and far more difficult to draw musically; they tend to come across not as real people but as actors on a stage.

However, that's what makes opera interesting. The flaws don't negate *Turandot*'s wonderful melodies, great choral scenes, and superb orchestration, nor devalue the reach attempted by Puccini in his last work. Indeed, the professionals advise us that his orchestral music is significantly more "adventurous" than it had ever been before, more "twentieth century," even if still deeply rooted in the nineteenth.

One strong supporting view for *Turandot* came from *The* (London) *Observer* critic, who wrote after a Covent Garden performance in the mid-1960s: "*Turandot* is the summit and synthesis of everything that Puccini achieved. In this great work . . . the lyrical sweetness of *Bohème* is married to the sombre expression of *Tabarro*; the delicate exoticism of *Butterfly* is combined with the harsh brutality of *Tosca* . . . In all the dimensions and range of its idiom, *Turandot* towers over all its predecessors."

Turandot is Puccini's most ferocious heroine and the role is known as a soprano-killer, perhaps as difficult to handle as Wagner's Isolde. Two of the great ones have been Eva Turner and Birgit Nilsson. A third was Maria Callas. Joan Sutherland never tried her onstage, preferring the French and bel canto repertory, but she did make a much-acclaimed recording, recommended below. A chosen Puccini soprano of Vermont's expert Peter Fox Smith is Licia Albanese, who does a spectacular job in the role of Liù.

MET PERFORMANCES

One hundred and eighty-three performances over nineteen seasons, from 1927 to 1996.

RECORDING

CD—Decca/London 414 274-2 (2). Joan Sutherland, Montserrat Caballé, Luciano Pavarotti, Peter Pears, Tom Krause, Nicolai Ghiaurov. John Alldis Choir, Wandsworth School Boys' Choir. London Philharmonic Orchestra. Zubin Mehta. 1973.

VIDEO

Marton, Carreras, Ricciarelli. Vienna State Opera. Italian; English subtitles. Maazel. 1983. MGM.

∾

Number 42. *Salome*
by Richard Strauss
June 11, 1864–September 8, 1949

Premiere at the Dresden Opera, 1905. Text after Oscar Wilde's 1893 drama Salomé. One act.

You're not allowed to have an opinion of this grisly psychological shocker with its strongly dissonant orchestral music without hearing a full recording and seeing at least a videotape.

The play from which it came and the opera itself were easy pickings for censors in the early years of this century. But *Salome* is a notable opera with outstanding music, even though it's difficult to make that discovery simply by reading about it. Almost inevitably, word descriptions present the base side without the beautiful side.

After the 1907 New York premiere, at the Met, the *New York World* published this review:

Hark! from the pit a fearsome sound
that makes your blood run cold.
Symphonic cyclones rush around—
and the worst is yet untold.

The muted tuba's dismal groan
uprising from the gloom,
and answered by the heckelphone,
suggest the crack of doom.

Mama! is this the earthquake zone?
What ho, there! stand from under!
or is that the tonitrone
Just imitating thunder?

Nay, fear not, little one, because
of this sublime rough-house;
'tis modern opera by the laws
of Master Richard Strauss.

Singers? they're scarcely heard nor seen—
in yon back seat they sit,
the day of Song is past, I ween;
the orchestra is it.

And the orchestra was it in the early days of Richard Strauss (no relation to the Viennese waltz kings). Strauss's father was the principal horn at the Munich Court Opera, the finest horn player in Germany, and one of the most violently anti-Wagner musicians in Europe. Despite (or because of?) his father's views, young Richard became a Wagner disciple early in his composing career. We have seen how Wagner favored the orchestra over the singers and the *New York World*'s reviewer indicates that Strauss—at this stage of his career—did no less.

Dr. Paul Henry Lang calls *Salome* a "sordid splendor of extraordinary intensity." Sordid splendor, indeed. That accurately sums it up, the first of two shocker operas written by Richard Strauss before he turned to more pleasant themes. When you choose the story of a young sixteen-year-old girl who demands the head of John the Baptist and kisses the bloody lips of that severed head, you must anticipate some limited disapproval.

Quotes from various musicologists and biographers are much too graphic to pass up.

In the *History of Western Music*, Christopher Headington writes: "Strauss undoubtedly found suitable music for his subject; it shifts and seethes like a pit of snakes; the large orchestra is used luxuriantly throughout; and the harmony, at times seductive, can also be very bold in its sinister dissonance . . . *Salome* exemplifies a kind of ruthless realism in art which is not at all the same as [play-wright] Wilde's hypersensitive aestheticism. Strauss seems to enjoy above all the powerful drama."

One of the most vivid descriptions of Salome once Herod has acceded to her wish comes from William Mann's *Richard Strauss: A Critical Study of the Operas*: "Salome is listening by the cistern. Her heart pants horribly . . . Her self-control has vanished, she is wrought up, and stammers impatient commands to all the servants; they must expedite the gift that is hers by promise. At last in the silence, a huge black arm, that of Naaman, lifts Jokanaan's head, on a silver dish, out of the cistern. Salome grasps it in ecstasy, and begins her terrible song of love . . . This is the head that refused her love, and now must accept it. Jokanaan never looked at her; had he done so, he would have loved her. He despised her; now his head is for her to throw to the dogs or vultures. His body was infinitely desirable . . . Now she may feast herself inexhaustibly upon his mouth. He would have loved her, and the secret of love is greater than the secret of death.

"The moon is shrouded. The drums pound gently as she falls upon her prey in the darkness. Herod shudders at what he sees. Herodias is icily approving; she would doubtless claim that Salome has grown to woman's status. Herod moves away. In the blackness Salome is heard crooning blissfully to the object that has fulfilled her first longings; has she tasted blood or love? . . . she cries: 'I have kissed your mouth, Jokanaan'. . . .

"[The music] calls out of the darkness, but the moon shines out and illuminates this loathsome scene. Herod, on the stairs, sees it and calls to his guards: Kill that woman. The soldiers batter Salome to death with their shields."

Well, that's *Salome*.

Initially scheduled for a premier in Vienna, it was turned down by the censors as unshowable and denounced by the singers as unsingable. But, it was accepted by Dresden, where the enthusiastic audience gave it thirty-eight curtain calls, much to the surprise of the media.

Not a Kinky Sex Kitten

Strauss pictured Salome this way: "Anyone who has been in the Orient and has observed the decorum of its women will appreciate that Salome should be played as a chaste virgin, an Oriental princess, with but the simplest, most dignified gestures, if . . . [she] is to arouse."

The *Allegemeine Musikzeitung* wrote: "It was considered almost certain that the intelligent and educated Dresden public . . . would protest angrily and loudly at an opera whose story exceeds in gruesomeness and perverted degeneracy anything that has ever been offered in a musical work for the stage. The fears were not realized for the opera had a thunderous, stormy and unanimous success."

The opera's text tracks the play by Oscar Wilde, written in 1893 by that Irish-born poet, dramatist, and wit who was jailed for homosexual practices and who founded an aesthetic movement that advocated "art for art's sake." Although Wilde's play had been accepted in England, authorities there initially banned the opera.

After the Met's 1907 premiere, one critic wrote that "the stench of Oscar Wilde's play has filled the nostrils of humanity" and another called it "a decadent and pestiferous work." In a noteworthy exhibition of courage, the Metropolitan directors demanded its withdrawal.

Salome was followed in 1909 by *Elektra*, Number 59 in The Collection, in which the heroine lives only to avenge the murder of her father by her mother and her mother's lover. They are two of the most powerful operas of the twentieth century, musically and dramatically representing a new opera world. It's a far cry from the world of *The Elixir of Love*, but the opera stage is large enough for both.

For much more background on Strauss, see the Richard Strauss Warhorse, *Der Rosenkavalier*, Number 20, and *Elektra*, and *Ariadne auf Naxos*, Number 70.

KEYNOTE

A psychological Strauss career-starter. Sexy, lurid, and dissonant. It's a strong voice that doesn't get drowned out by the orchestra. Don't miss the sensuous "Dance of the Seven Veils."

PLOT

About 30 A.D., the palace of Herod in Galilee. The bare bones of this are in the New Testament (Matthew, Chapter 14), but the flesh is from the treatment of those bones by Oscar Wilde. Herod (tenor) is Tetrarch of Judea, a sex-hungry man with a lusty eye on his young and sensuous stepdaughter, Salome (soprano). Salome has had a tough life; her mother, Herodias (mezzo-soprano), murdered her father in order to marry Herod, and she has been brought up in a corrupt court. Imprisoned in Herod's castle is John the Baptist (baritone) (known as Jokanaan in the German version), who can't stop speaking of the coming of Christ.

When Salome hears him cursing the vile deeds of her mother, she is physically attracted to him, and asks that he be brought before her. He is in rags, but the more he denounces the wickedness around him the more turned on she becomes. She repeatedly cries that she wants to kiss his mouth, and he repeatedly rejects her as a harlot. Narraboth (tenor), a young captain of the guards who is attracted to her, becomes so upset that he kills himself with his sword. After Jokanaan is returned to his cell, lusty Herod licks a piece of fruit that Salome has tasted in order to taste her lips. This passion for his stepdaughter infuriates

Birgit Nilsson with the head of John the Baptist in Salome

his wife. While Jokanaan's cries of doom come from the prison, Salome yields to Herod's pleas that she put on a solo dance especially for him . . . but only on the condition that he then will give her anything she wants.

She chooses the ultraseductive "Dance of the Seven Veils," performs it, and for payment demands Jokanaan's head. After failing to talk her out of it, Herod makes good on his commitment. The head is brought before her on a silver platter. She has a long monologue with it and passionately kisses its lips. A horrified Herod orders his soldiers to crush her to death with their shields as the audience hears her dying shrieks.

HIGHLIGHTS

Act I: Salome's "Dance of the Seven Veils," perhaps the most sensual eight minutes of music in opera. Also her last monologue, one of opera's most hauntingly decadent passages.

COMMENTARY

Despite the plot, the dance, and the horror, the dominant role belongs to the orchestra, not surprising for a Richard Strauss under the influence of a Richard Wagner. The scenes are sheer madness, and the orchestra captures every mad moment of them. Recall that Strauss was famous for his orchestral tone poems—the avant-garde Romantic answer to the symphony—considerably before he wrote this opera.

This is hard-core music drama demanding controlled acting and powerful singing. No opera is farther from pretty voices singing pretty songs, although *Elektra* and some very modern works are as far.

A famous salome was Ljuba Welitsch, Bulgarian soprano born in 1913, who sang it at Covent Garden in 1947 and debuted at the Met with it in 1949 in one of the greatest nights in the house's history. Other known Salomes include Hildegard Behrens, Birgit Nilsson, Montserrat Caballé, Eva Marton, Cheryl Studer, Marjorie Lawrence, Grace Bumbry . . . and Maria Ewing. Find a videotape of Ewing raving about Jokanaan's "vile" white leperlike body, his gruesome hair, a "tangle of black snakes," and the red band of mouth she is obsessed to kiss.

A question to ask yourself. Does Salome do her own dance or does a substitute dancer fill in? Does she remove the seventh veil? Nowadays, most Salomes do attempt some semblance of dance, although all formerly used dancing stand-ins. And Maria Ewing does seem to get completely naked.

MET PERFORMANCES
One hundred twenty-five performances over twenty seasons from 1907 to 1996.

RECORDING
CD—Deutsche Grammophon 431 810-2 (2). Cheryl Studer, Leonie Rysanek, Horst Hiestermann, Bryn Terfel. Berlin Opera Chorus and Orchestra. Giuseppe Sinopoli. 1990.

VIDEO
Ewing, Devlin, Riegel, Knight. Royal Opera House, Covent Garden. German; English subtitles. 1992. HOME VISION.

Number 44. *Falstaff*
by Giuseppe Verdi
October 10, 1813–January 27, 1901

Premiere at La Scala, Milan, 1893. Text by Arrigo Boito, from Shakespeare's 1598 Merry Wives of Windsor, with a touch of his 1597 Henry IV.

We've met Arrigo Boito in the *Otello* section—man of letters, poet, composer of his own operas, and, most of all, librettist for the last two operas of Verdi's long career, both from Shakespeare, the tragedy *Otello* and the comedy *Falstaff*.

At the party after the opening night of *Otello*, almost six years earlier to the day before *Falstaff*'s premiere, Boito raised his glass to Verdi and said, "A toast to the fat knight," a reference to Shakespeare's engaging character.

Boito's mind already had been at work on one final opera with Verdi, and he triggered their joint venture of *Falstaff*. Some analysts call *Otello* the climax of Italian tragic opera and *Falstaff* the ultimate in Italian opera buffa.

But it's not really conventional opera buffa. Professor Paul Henry Lang describes it as a "unique work" and quotes Boito himself characterizing it as "an absolutely new art form."

Verdi's biographers advise us that he composed *Falstaff* purely for his own pleasure, with no real intent for a public performance. That's a game one plays at this time of life; my guess is that the old codger either was kidding his friends or kidding himself. Who would not produce a Verdi opera?

In any event, Boito sent him a copy of a proposed libretto in July 1889, when the master was seventy-five. This, in turn, caused Verdi to reread four Shakespeare plays—*The Merry Wives of Windsor*, the two parts of *Henry IV*, and *Henry V*—to bring himself up to date on Sir John Falstaff, a fascinating buffo character of significant physical proportions—arguably opera's fattest hero—if, indeed, he is a hero.

See Verdi Warhorses for additional detail.

Shared Genius

A 1910 commentary on Verdi's last opera:

"Mozart is rather the master that Verdi's *Falstaff* recalls. It has his exquisite lightness of touch, his rhythmic fertility, his command of a perennial flow of delicious melody, and his charming snatches of tenderness which make so welcome a contrast to the ebullient high spirits of the work as a whole. Viewed from any and every point of view, *Falstaff* approaches the miraculous, not least in this: that it was written in his eightieth year by a man who until then had dealt almost entirely with subjects of the most tragic description."

KEYNOTE

Verdi's last opera, written at age seventy-nine. His only mature comedy. Never as popular with the public as some others of his works, chiefly because he almost does away with big arias. But you can't not love Sir John who—like the Golden Ager composer—never gives up on life or living. Professional judgment: an incomparable masterpiece.

PLOT

Windsor, in the reign of Henry IV of England. Sir John Falstaff (baritone), a very stout, good-humored rascal who considers himself a great lover, writes similar love letters to two married women, Alice Ford (soprano) and Meg Page (mezzo-soprano). A shameless but relatively harmless rogue, his stated plan is to woo both of them, in part for the joy of wooing and in part as a means of getting at their husbands' money. He seeks the assistance of his henchmen, Bardolph (tenor) and Pistol (bass), but they refuse, saying their honor is at stake. What humbug, muses Falstaff, as he sings the essence of himself: "Può l'onore riempirvi la pancia?" ("Can honor fill a belly?") Unfortunately for him, the ladies compare their letters and decide to do him in. He is advised by mail that both wives love him but only Alice will have time to entertain him.

There is a side love affair throughout the opera between Nannetta (soprano), the Fords' daughter, and Fenton (tenor).

After accepting an invitation to Alice Ford's home, where he expects a little romance, Sir John is forced to hide in the clothes basket when Mr. Ford (baritone) comes home to interrupt them. To the hilarity of the people in the street, and to his humiliation, he and the clothes are dumped from the basket out of the window into the river. With a never-say-die attitude, he later invites Alice to a rendezvous in Windsor Park. During this courtship, he is attacked by Ford and friends, dressed as elves and nymphs, and given a good beating. Realizing he has been shamed before the entire village, Sir John promises to mend his ways. The opera ends with agreement by the entire cast: "Tutto nel mondo è burla." Everything in the world is a joke.

Thoughts of a Senior Citizen

Verdi and Arrigo Boito worked nearly four years on *Falstaff*, beginning in 1889 when Verdi was seventy-six. As the project was getting under way, the composer wrote the librettist of his doubts:

"In tackling *Falstaff*, have you ever thought of my enormous weight of years? . . . What if I could not stand the strain? What if I could not finish the music? Then you would have wasted time and trouble for nothing."

On the other hand: "What a joy to be able to say to the public, 'Here we are again!! Come and see us!!' "

HIGHLIGHTS

There are streams of melody throughout, but no showstopper hits since Verdi consciously has moved away from the set pattern of big aria–recitative–big aria. This is wit-and-scalpel work. But there are delicious scenes, including:

Act I: The Nannetta-Fenton duet.

Act II: A great Ford-Falstaff duet, followed by Ford's jealousy aria, "È sogno? o realtà": "Is this a dream, or realty . . . Two enormous horns are growing on my head. Is it a dream? Master Ford! Are you asleep? Wake up! Come. Get up!"

Act III: Fenton's light lyric tenor's serenade to Nannetta. Her light lyric soprano aria as a disguised Fairy Queen, "Sul fil d'un soffio etesio" (From secret caves). The whole magic of the final scene.

COMMENTARY

Analyst assessment: The orchestral music is brilliant. The orchestration is the best of Verdi's career, in places more symphonic than in any of his other operas. The marriage of music and text is unsurpassed. Musically, it's the most "sophisticated" of all Verdi operas, one reason, perhaps, why it never has been as popular with the public as the simple, more spontaneous Big Three.

Verdi obviously loved the character of the giant-bellied Sir John, who dominates the proceedings. Because of him, *Falstaff* is not only delightfully fresh but also delightfully funny, unlike Richard Wagner's only humorous opera, *Die Meistersinger von Nürnberg*, more of a social comedy. Sir John must be taught humility, but he's so outrageously vain with such panache that you have to love him. Wagner's Hans Sachs, *Die Meistersinger*'s gray eminence and "second" hero, is admired and respected, but not loved.

It is the only libretto in which Verdi did not change a single comma, accepting it exactly as Boito had written it. Caution: If you go to see *Falstaff*, study that libretto first. So much is going on that you can miss a lot if you're not familiar with the plot. But with a little homework, this masterpiece can give you as much fun as any other single night in opera. Much depends on the conductor; this is a delicate work and professionals advise that it requires a graceful hand at the controls.

MET PERFORMANCES

One hundred and fifty-eight performances over nineteen seasons, from 1895 to 1996.

RECORDINGS

CD—RCA/BMG 60251-RG-4 (2) (mono). Herva Nelli, Teresa Stich-Randall, Nan Merriman, Cloë Elmo, Antonio Madasi, Giuseppe Valdengo, Frank Guarrera. Robert Shaw Chorale. NBC Symphony Orchestra. Arturo Toscanini. 1950.

or

—Deutsche Grammophon 410 503-2 (2). Katia Ricciarelli, Barbara Hendricks, Brenda Boozer, Lucia Valentini Terrani, Dalmacio Gonzales, Renato Bruson, Leo Nucci. Los Angeles Master Chorale. Los Angeles Philharmonic Orchestra. Carlo Maria Giulini. 1982.

VIDEO

Bruson, Ricciarelli, Nucci. Royal Opera House, Covent Garden. Italian; English subtitles. Giulini, conductor. 1982. HBO (Warner Home Box Office).

∽

Number 45. *Der fliegende Holländer (The Flying Dutchman)* by Richard Wagner

May 22, 1813–February 13, 1883

Premiere at the Hofoper, Dresden 1843. Text by Wagner from several versions of an old legend, modeled after Heinrich Heine's Memoirs of Herr von Schnabelewopski. Three acts, sometimes performed without intermission.

Richard Wagner sold the original scenario to the Paris Opéra for five hundred francs. He wrote later that he needed the money to buy a piano on which he could compose the opera itself. But Wagner scholars say you never quite know how true Wagner's stories about himself are.

The Flying Dutchman (Der fliegende Holländer) came after *Rienzi*, a five-act grand opera that's not in The Collection, and is the first of his early three successes before he turned to his later "music drama." The others (see Wagner Warhorses) are *Tannhäuser* and *Lohengrin*.

The time spent writing *Dutchman* was not a happy period in Wagner's life. He was in his late twenties, and he spent two and a half miserable years in Paris, from 1839 to 1842, not only broke but so much in debt that he was threatened with debtor's prison. One of the ways he made a little money was as a music journalist, attacking what he considered mediocre operas appearing at the Paris Opéra.

Wagner Invades England

The Flying Dutchman was the first of Wagner's operas to be in England. The year was 1870, and the language was Italian. It was requested by Queen Victoria. The first American performance was in Philadelphia in 1876, also in Italian. It opened the Met's 1889–90 season, in German.

KEYNOTE

Wagner's first mature opera. Typically for him, a work from myth and legend. A suffering sea captain redeemed by the love of a faithful woman.

PLOT

The Flying Dutchman is a phantom ship whose captain had vowed with a blasphemous oath that he would sail around the Cape of Good Hope through a raging storm even if it took him all eternity. The Devil was offended by the oath and condemned the captain to stay at sea until Judgment Day, sailing indefinitely, until he found a woman who would be faithful to him until death. Once every seven years he is allowed to dock and look for such a woman. In a Norwegian port, the Dutchman comes upon Senta, daughter of Captain Daland. She falls in love with him and wants to marry him, even though she is involved with a young hunter named Erik. When the Dutchman later sees them talking, he erroneously suspects her of being unfaithful, concludes that she can't be the one who will redeem him, and puts out to sea. Senta breaks away from Erik, rushes to a cliff overlooking the waters, sees his ship leaving, is disconsolate, proclaims her fidelity, and hurls herself into the fjord. Her sacrifice frees the Dutchman from the Devil's curse. His phantom ship sinks, he drowns, and the two lovers are united under the waters in one another's arms.

HIGHLIGHTS

The Overture: A musical recap of the opera, containing several leading motifs, among them the Dutchman, Senta, and the stormy Ocean.

Act I: The Dutchman telling his story, "Die Frist ist um": "Once again seven years have passed. The sea throws me back to land. There is only the one hope that remains for me." The Dutchman/Daland duet.

Act II: The "Spinning Chorus," sung by Norwegian girls, another of Wagner's great choral numbers. "Senta's Ballad," in which she says she will be the Dutchman's faithful woman forever: "Yo ho ho! Did you encounter the ship on the sea? The sails are blood red and the mast is black . . . Pray to heaven that soon he will find a woman who will stay faithful to him." The Senta/Dutchman duet.

Act III: The final scenes as the Dutchman's ship sinks.

COMMENTARY

This early composition of Wagner's is a nice melodious German Romantic opera, not all that different from Verdi's works or others of the same time period. It is gloomy and somber, but has good tunes, fine arias, and sound choruses and ensembles, unlike the music dramas Wagner later wrote. It is good theater; it makes an interesting evening at the opera house or in front of the television. Some conductors, the music analysts complain, become too obsessed with the storms at sea and lose track of the rest of the work.

Wagner wrote that most of the music was built out of the seeds in "Senta's Ballad": "I will remember that before passing on to a realization, properly speaking, of *The Flying Dutchman*, I composed the text and melody of 'Senta's

Ballad' in the second act. I deposited in this number the thematic germs of the entire score. It was a concentrated image of the whole drama as it outlined itself in my thoughts." It isn't fun and games, but with the exception of *Die Meistersinger*, you don't get fun and games from mature Wagner. The theme, as we have seen, is a Wagner favorite: the redemption of man's soul through the love, trust, and sacrifice of a woman.

MET PERFORMANCES
One hundred and thirty-eight performances over twenty seasons, from 1889 to 1994.

RECORDING
CD—Philips Dig. 434 599-2 (2). Lisbeth Balslev, Robert Schunk, Simon Estes, Matti Salminen. Chorus, Supplementary Chorus, and Orchestra of the Bayreuth Festival. 1985.

VIDEO
Estes, Balslev, Salminen. Bayreuth Opera House. German; English subtitles. Nelsson. 1985. PGD.

∾

Number 46. *Gianni Schicchi*
by Giacomo Puccini
December 22, 1858–November 29, 1924

Premiere at the Metropolitan Opera, New York, 1918. Text by Gioachino Foranzo. The third of three one-act operas, entitled overall Il trittico. *Based on an episode in Dante's* Inferno. *One act.*

In thirteenth-century Florence, the punishment for helping falsify a will was the loss of one hand and banishment for life.

That's severe, and fear of it helped a shrewd peasant named Gianni Schicchi foil his coconspirators and perpetrate one of the great con jobs of opera.

This is a genuine opera buffa, appealing even to Puccini's toughest critics. Some consider it the funniest opera ever written. Certainly not Puccini's most ambitious work—*Turandot* gets that award—but unquestionably his most delightful one, as Italian, the music people declare, as *Die Meistersinger* is German. Someone has said it is as close as Puccini got to Mozart.

Well . . .

There's a lot of history about Mr. Schicchi. For one thing, he really lived and, apparently, really pulled off the swindle on which the opera is based. For another, the great poet Dante put him in the thirtieth Canto of his *Inferno*, right alongside Myrrha of Cyprus. Myrrha's sins were considerably more serious. The mother of Adonis in Greek legend, she had an incestuous relationship with her father and was turned into a myrtle tree.

Gianni Schicchi is one of three one-act operas devised by Puccini as an evening-at-the-opera. They are a mixed lot: *Il tabarro* (*The Cloak*) is a shocking verismo work in which a husband chokes his wife's lover to death, and *Suor Angelica* (*Sister Angelica*) is a sentimental drama. They are still sometimes performed together as a night's entertainment; other times each is apt to be paired with some other short work, including *Pagliacci, Cavalleria rusticana,* or *Elektra.*

KEYNOTE

Puccini's only comic opera, a not-to-be-missed gem. How to impersonate a corpse and dictate a new will from the deathbed in order to inherit well.

PLOT

Florence, 1299. The scene is the bedroom of Buoso Donati, who has just died and whose body is lying in bed. Relatives gather around him. It is rumored that in his will he's left his money to a monastery. His relatives don't think much of that decision and want to change the will to their own benefit. They're advised that there might be some hope of fooling the authorities as long as the will is still in the house and not yet in official hands or the hands of the lawyers. After a frantic hunt, the will is found.

Gianni Schicchi (baritone), a resourceful and cunning fellow, is called in to help family members cheat the monastery and keep the money for themselves. He agrees to do so, chiefly because his daughter, Lauretta (soprano), is in love with Rinuccio (tenor), the nephew of Buoso's cousin Zita (contralto). No death announcement has been made, no one outside the family yet knows that Buoso has died. When the doctor arrives, Schicchi impersonates Buoso's voice from behind a curtain. After the doctor has left, the plan is made. A lawyer and two witnesses are to be called, Schicchi will put on nightclothes, climb into bed, impersonate Buoso, and dictate a new will to favor the relatives. He warns them of the serious punishment they all will suffer if the notary, in his official capacity, discovers the trickery. The greedy relatives are anxious to take the chance, and each tries to talk Schicchi into giving him or her the best deal.

The lawyer and witnesses arrive. In bed, disguised as Buoso, Schicchi dictates a new will according to plan—but unaccording to plan his changes leave the primary assets to "his friend Gianni Schicchi" and the house to Lauretta and Rinuccio. Having been party to the scheme and tricked both doctor and lawyer into believing the "dying" man is Buoso, and given the harsh punishment if they are found to be part of a will-changing plot, there's nothing the avaricious relatives can do except sit in silent fury and frustration.

Toscanini on Il trittico

Famed conductor Arturo Toscanini was the principal conductor at La Scala in Milan, of the Metropolitan in New York, and of the New York Philharmonic and the NBC Symphony Orchestras. His assessment of the three one-act operas that make up *trittico*:

"*Suor Angelica*—no good! *Il tabarro*, also no good. But *Gianni Schicchi*—a little masterpiece."

HIGHLIGHTS

The enjoyment comes chiefly from the superb plot, the characters, and the ensemble music, which is almost continuous. But one detachable, popular, and beautiful number (background music for the film *A Room with a View*) is Lauretta's "O mio babbino caro" ("Oh, my beloved daddy"), as she asks her father for help. It is one of Puccini's most delicious melodies. Some spoilsports protest that when Puccini composed it he was thinking too much about the public's taste and not enough about the character, but other analysts view it as deliberate tongue-in-cheek writing . . . and listeners seem committed not to care, one way or the other.

COMMENTARY

In *Turandot*, Puccini is charged with creating such sharply contrasting characters that he was incapable of depicting them in music. With Gianni, he succeeds beautifully.

The Earl of Harewood, in *The New Kobbé's Complete Opera Book*, writes: "Puccini owes an obvious debt to Verdi (for *Falstaff*), but it would be churlish to deny him his achievement in writing music of such dexterity and brilliance, even if it falls short of the magnitude and humanity of its greater predecessor. *Gianni Schicchi* makes use of a side of the composer's make-up only revealed in such passages as the interplay of the Bohemians in *Bohème* and the entrance of the Sacristan in *Tosca*; in *Schicchi*, however, the wit is sharper and the tempo of movement faster than anywhere else in his output."

Some musicologists say this is Italy's finest comic opera but immediately justify their position by explaining that Verdi's *Falstaff* is so good that it's more than just a comic opera and belongs in another category. Professor Paul Henry Lang flatly calls this one a "masterpiece." So does Professor Joseph Machlis. Alfred Einstein describes it as an appealing and genuine opera buffa. Highly recommended viewing—and hearing. Victoria de los Angeles is a lovely recorded Lauretta.

MET PERFORMANCES

One hundred and fourteen performances over eighteen seasons, from 1919 to 1981.

RECORDING

CD—Decca/London 411 665-2 (3). Renata Tebaldi, Agostino Lazzari, Fernando Corena. Orchestra of the Maggio Musicale Fiorentino. Lamberto Gardelli. 1961. With the other two short operas that make up *Il trittico*.

VIDEO

Il trittico: Gianni Schicchi, Suor Angelica, Il tabarro. Gianni Schicchi with Pons, Gasdia. La Scala. Italian; English subtitles. Gavazzeni, conductor. 1983. PIO.

∾

Number 47. *Don Carlos*
by Giuseppe Verdi
October 10, 1813–January 27, 1901

Premiere at the Opéra, Paris, 1867. Text by Joseph Méry and Camille du Locle from Friedrich von Schiller's 1787 drama and Eugene Cormon's 1846 play Philippe II, roi d'Espagne. *A grand opera in five acts. Frequent revisions over many years led to a four-act version that premiered at La Scala, Milan, in 1884.*

For its Exposition of 1885, on the Champ de Mars, Paris got the Eiffel Tower, all 984.25 feet of it.

For its Exposition of 1867, it got a big grand opera from Giuseppe Verdi called *Don Carlos*, all five spectacle-filled acts of it.

We will soon meet Giacomo Meyerbeer, the crown prince of Parisian grand opera (*Les Huguenots*, Number 53). If you wanted your opera to play in Paris in the 1860s, it was a good idea to construct it in the Meyerbeer fashion. Verdi biographers suggest he wasn't particularly fond of that fashion, but he accepted it for this work. It was written in his late middle years, ten to fifteen years after the Big Three and his last work before *Aida*. Too lengthy for audiences outside of France, it was not immediately popular.

Friedrich von Schiller (1759–1805) was Verdi's third favorite author, after Shakespeare and Victor Hugo. The famed German dramatist, poet, and historian knew and worked closely with the great Goethe. Schiller favored fast-moving dramatic action, and his characters, literary scholars tell us, generally were not as deep as Goethe's but were more clearly defined.

The opera is known as both *Don Carlos* (French) and *Don Carlo* (Italian). The reason: Nearly twenty years after writing it for Paris, Verdi decided to convert it into an Italian opera. The result is what we (usually) see and hear today.

Verdi was commissioned to write it in 1850, giving him plenty of time to have it ready for the big 1867 fair, but he didn't actually begin it until 1865.

See the Verdi Warhorses for additional background.

KEYNOTE

Big canvas. Tyranny, nobility, liberty, and the conflict of church and throne, all put into Verdi's longest work, made to order for the spectacle-crazed French grand opera audience.

PLOT

France and Spain, about 1560. A historical note: King Philip is a real figure in history (1527–98) who became King of Spain in 1556. His empire included the Philippines, which were named after him. Elisabeth was the third of his four wives, but there is no evidence that she and Carlos—Philip's son by his first wife—had an affair. Carlos *was* imprisoned by Philip as he was about to flee to the Netherlands, and died in prison; but whether Philip murdered him seems to be an open question.

Rodrigo did not exist, but the real Philip did have a close advisor, William the Silent, who constantly warned him against his repressive policy in Flanders. Despite the Inquisition and other measures, Philip couldn't force the Flemish to accept Roman Catholicism.

Don Carlos (tenor), prince of Spain, is in France secretly to see his fiancée for the first time. She is a titled Frenchwoman, Elisabeth de Valois (soprano). But after they meet accidentally in a forest and fall in love a cannon signals a joyous announcement. To keep peace between France and Spain, a marriage has been arranged between Elisabeth and Carlos's father, King Philip II (bass). Happy French people spill into the forest, celebrating the peace. The final choice has been left to Elisabeth, but she realizes she has no real alternative.

Kinder and Gentler Ending

In Schiller's play, King Philip turns Carlos over to the Grand Inquisitor, who will put him to death. In the opera, it is uncertain what Carlos's destiny is to be, but he's in good hands as he's led safely inside Charles V's tomb.

In Spain, Carlos cries his heart out in the palace chapel where his grandfather, Emperor Charles V, is buried, and which is allegedly inhabited by the emperor's ghost. Carlos is joined by his close friend, Rodrigo (baritone), a champion of liberty for the commoner and an opponent of the Inquisition. When he hears of Carlos's romantic dilemma, he urges the prince to get out of Spain and go to Flanders (the Netherlands), where he can reform the government and help the oppressed. In a dramatic meeting with the new Queen, Carlos asks her to help talk his father into letting him go help the Flemish, but he loses control of his feelings and tells her he still loves her. Though she also still loves him, she points out in regal fashion that they could be together only if he murdered his father and, covered with blood, took his "mother" to the altar.

Meanwhile, Princess Eboli (mezzo-soprano), Philip's former mistress, has fallen in love with Carlos. When they meet at night in the Queen's garden she is thrilled when he tells her he loves her, unaware that he has mistaken her for the Queen. Both are dismayed when they discover their error—and she is furious and swears vengeance. As part of her intrigue, she lies to the King, telling him that his new wife has been unfaithful.

In a spectacle scene in the square of Madrid, preparations are made to burn heretic Flemings at the stake. Carlos, as heir apparent, demands that his father make him deputy King of Flanders so that he can stop the suffering, terror, and executions there. When Philip calls this suggestion madness, Carlos draws his sword, an unforgivable act in the presence of the King. Philip's guards are slow to respond to his cries to disarm their prince, but Rodrigo—protecting his friend and his King—steps between them, and Carlos surrenders his sword to him. Rodrigo is made a duke on the spot, and the execution of the Flemish heretics goes forward.

Though torn between his human feelings as a father and his duties to the church and its Inquisition, Philip has Carlos thrown into prison for rebellion. The Grand Inquisitor (bass) chastises the King for making Rodrigo his confidante and principal advisor, warning Philip that Rodrigo is by far a greater threat than Carlos to the church and the realm. Why do you have the title of King if a lesser man is your equal? he asks. The power of the Roman Catholic Church is sacred. Do your duty at once and strike down this sinner.

The King finds a portrait of Don Carlos in his Queen's jewel casket and falsely accuses Elisabeth of infidelity. A repentant Eboli tells the Queen she has not only lied to the King about the Queen and Carlos but also has been the King's mistress. When Rodrigo visits Carlos in prison, the King has him murdered as a dangerous rebel. The King then has second thoughts about Carlos and tries to give him back his sword. The commoners help free Carlos, who promises to devote his life to the people who are stretching out their hands to him, even if rivers must run red with blood. Carlos and Elisabeth meet and agree that it must be for the last time, because honor is even stronger than love, and Philip prepares to turn Carlos over to the Grand Inquisitor to be executed. Carlos and Elisabeth are saying good-bye at Charles V's tomb when the King and his men burst in to seize him. As he is defending himself, the solemn voice of Charles V is heard, and the Emperor appears within the tomb. Or, more accurately, there is a mysterious appearance of a monk in royal robes who may or may not be the spirit of the real Charles V. Verdi leaves it uncertain. In any case, to the bewilderment of Philip and the people, the monk-or-spirit leads Carlos to safety inside the tomb.

No Songs, No Glory

Plácido Domingo has said that he considers *Don Carlos* and *Falstaff* to be Verdi's greatest masterpieces. As a tenor, however, he has a major problem with the role of Carlos, who has a very difficult aria at the very beginning of the opera but no other solo number, despite the fact that he appears in seven of the eight scenes.

HIGHLIGHTS

(Listed in the five-act version):

Act II: A duet between Don Carlos and Rodrigo as they pledge their friendship under God, who gives them liberty, "Dio, che nell'alma infondere amor" ("God, who has filled our hearts with love"). "We will live together and die together." One scholar calls this a noble expression of feeling; another lists it among Verdi's most banal tunes!

Act III: The trio of Carlos, Eboli, and Rodrigo in the Queen's garden, as Carlos mistakes Eboli for Elisabeth and Rodrigo intervenes. The grand spectacle of the piazza scene in front of the cathedral as Carlos challenges the King and solemn preparations are made for the execution of heretics.

Act IV: The entire scene of Philip's soliloquy, "Ella giammai m'amo": the struggles he faces; no one loves him; he will always be alone. This is one of Verdi's top climactic arias and perhaps his best for a bass. A famous aria by Princess Eboli, "O don fatale" ("Oh fatal gift"), in which she curses her beauty and grieves that she has sacrificed her Queen because of her own spurned love.

Act V: The Carlos-Elisabeth duet as they say farewell forever, and the rest of the act.

COMMENTARY

Don Carlos shrieks of Verdi's views on liberty, independence, statesmanship, and sacrifice for your country. Consider Mozart and Verdi as two of the three opera supercomposers. There is none of this in Mozart and no better example of the difference in the kinds of operas that interested them.

Chronologically and substantively it fits in between Verdi's Big Three and *Aida*. The music people call it Verdi's "most aspiring" work to date—more elaborate than prior operas, bigger ensembles and climaxes, and more secondary episodes to fit the grand opera scheme, all put into a political framework. Verdi loved to write about authority figures, and King Philip is perhaps his most profound. Another fine bass role is the Inquisitor, and Princess Eboli is one of the best of his mezzo-soprano roles if not as intriguing as Azucena in *Il trovatore*. Elisabeth and Carlos also have outstanding singing parts.

The personal lives of the main characters are all tangled up in conflicts bigger than they are: Catholic versus Protestant, father versus son, independent thinker versus established authority, and state versus church.

Some musicologists suggest that Verdi comes close in this work to Mozart and Wagner in the depth and detail of his musical characterization. Look for many confrontational duets, musically and dramatically powerful, which overshadow the individual arias.

MET PERFORMANCES

One hundred and fifty-nine performances over twenty-two seasons, from 1920 to 1992.

RECORDING

CD—Angel/EMI CDCC 47701-8 (3). Montserrat Caballé, Shirley Verrett, Plácido Domingo, Sherrill Milnes, Ruggero Raimondi, Giovanni Foiani. Ambrosian Opera Chorus, Orchestra of the Royal Opera House, Covent Garden. Carlo Maria Giulini. 1971.

VIDEO

Domingo, Freni, Bumbry, Quilico. Metropolitan Opera. Italian; English subtitles. Levine, conductor. 1983. PAR.

Number 48. Norma
by Vincenzo Bellini
November 3, 1801–September 23, 1835

Premiere at La Scala, Milan, 1831. Text by Felice Romani from Alexandre Soumet's 1831 five-act tragedy in verse, Norma. *Two acts (later changed to four).*

"Fiasco! Fiasco! Serious fiasco!"

So reported a disappointed Vincenzo Bellini to a friend the night his *Norma* opened at La Scala in Milan.

Bellini was hidden in the orchestra pit for the premiere and there heard the hissing and cries of disapproval from the audience. But the second performance did better and was followed by forty-three more. Today *Norma* is still performed fairly often. Another fine Bellini opera, *La sonnambula*, is Number 58.

Bellini is the youngest of the three bel canto composers traditionally grouped together. We have met Rossini, born in 1792, and Donizetti, born in 1797.

For years, most music people considered Rossini the first among equals of the three, the only one they tagged with the term "genius." Some opera singers with the understandable desire to show off the range of their voices had a preference for Donizetti. And some professionals gave Bellini the highest marks for integrity as an artist and for craftsmanship. But Rossini rated higher as a total master.

Wagner: "A Masterpiece"

One later supporter was Richard Wagner, who called *Norma* a "master-piece," writing: "The action, bare of all theatrical coups and dazzling effects, reminds one of the dignity of Greek tragedy . . . Those who can hear in *Norma* only the usual Italian tinkle are not worthy of serious consideration. This music is noble and great, simple and grandiose in style. The very fact that there is style to this music makes it important for our time, a time of experiments and lack of form."

In today's oh-so-correct world, one of my advisors says no one would attempt to "rank" the three.

"Rossini," he says, "holds pride of place chronologically as the founder of the bel canto school, and in his day he was the most famous. Bellini was the most even, the greater melodist, and the most influential on other composers, including Chopin, Berlioz and Wagner. Donizetti, in his serious operas, may have been the most forward-looking, but his reputation has suffered for that, since he paved the way for Verdi, who then took over and eclipsed him."

All three were opera specialists. Unlike the other two, Bellini wrote no opera buffa. He died early, at thirty-three, even younger than Mozart (although not as young as classical composer Franz Schubert, who was only thirty-one). At his death he had completed ten operas; at age thirty-three Rossini had written thirty-four and Donizetti thirty-five.

Bellini was more painstaking in his work, more skilled than the other two at recitative and the union of words and music. In terms used by the analysts, he was more sensitive to the text. In *Norma*, the experts say, music and words are perfectly welded.

Even more than Rossini and Donizetti, however, Bellini composed golden melody—extended, flowing, graceful melody. Italian melody. Melody that glides. My singing friends say it takes a special vocal technique to bring it off, a certain type of artistry.

The master Verdi was taken by it: "Long, long melodies," he wrote, "such as no one before has written."

Many musicologists speak of similarities between the elegance and grace of Bellini's music and that of Chopin's, the Polish-born Parisian who wrote almost exclusively for the piano. The two were close friends, often seen together in Paris—both slim, aristocratic-looking, elegant. Both had tuberculosis, and both died young.

In the bel canto period, opera belonged not to composers, conductors, librettists, or proprietors, but to the singing stars. The public was not looking for the ideal blend of drama and music, for unity of structure, for character development, or for Shakespeare-like understanding of the human condition. It wanted to hear the superstars belt out the arias. Bellini wrote operas for these demands.

Also, more than the other bel canto composers, Bellini involved the chorus in the action, rather than just having it stand alongside.

Sills on Shoes

Beverly Sills has a sound tip for young sopranos who take on the role of Norma: Wear comfortable shoes. (Birgit Nilsson gave the same advice for Isolde.) The role is not vocally tiring, she says, but it is a very long one.

But Sills is Sills. Other professionals say (1) young singers shouldn't even think of Norma, (2) the role *is* tiring, almost impossible to sing, and (3) trying it was the worst debacle of Renata Scotto's career.

Bellini was born in Catania, Sicily, the son of an organist. With the support of a local nobleman, he studied at the Naples Conservatory, moving from there to Milan, where his third opera, *Il pirata*, was given in 1827. A famous tenor named Giovanni Battista Rubini sang it, and his performance turned on the natives. It was soon given in Rome and Paris. Another opera, *La straniera*, followed in 1829, then a failure, and then a version of *Romeo and Juliet*, *I Capuleti ed i Montecchi*, which one of my opera friends describes as a magnificent work that will top everything but *Norma* someday. His first great success, however, was with *La sonnambula* in 1831, followed by *Norma* the same year, then another failure, and finally *I Puritani*, in 1835. He died just outside Paris that same year.

Heinrich Heine, who wrote on the Parisian scene, was a German playwright and novelist and a close friend of Meyerbeer's. His description of Bellini:

"A tall, up-shooting slender figure who always moved gracefully; he was coquettish, ever looking as though just removed from a bandbox; a regular but large, delicately rose-tinted face; light, almost golden hair worn in many curls; a high, very high, marble forehead, straight nose; light blue eyes; good-sized mouth and rounded chin . . . [His face showed a] pointless shallow sorrow that the young maestro seemed most anxious to represent in his whole appearance. His hair was dressed so fancifully, his clothes fitted so languishingly around his delicate body, he carried his cane so idyll-like, that he reminded me of the young shepherds we had in our pastorals with their crooks decorated with ribbons . . . The whole man looked like a sigh, in pumps and silk stockings. He has met with much sympathy from women but I doubt if he ever produced strong passion in any one."

Heine makes him sound very much like a middle linebacker en route to a couple of beers with the guys after a December game in Green Bay's partly frozen mud.

Bellini's last work, *I Puritani* (*The Puritans*), premiered in Paris at the Théâtre des Italiens. Rossini had urged the younger composer to come to Paris for the purpose of writing it for the Italian theater there. It is one of the many operas outside The Collection that still is performed and enjoyed.

Bellini took the formula for Rossini's operas and turned them into a more lyrical art form, more typical of the Romantic era that was beginning. In pure melody, arguably he outdid not only Rossini and Donizetti but also Verdi. His career was short, but he had found his bent early and produced some beautiful work.

KEYNOTE

Bellini's best. Arguably Maria Callas's best. A melody-filled lyric tragedy with a sinning high priestess who is dumped. Hear "Casta Diva." Then hear it again. And listen for the duets.

PLOT

Roman occupation of Gaul about 50 B.C. In violation of her sacred vows of chastity, Norma (soprano), the high priestess of the Druids, has been involved secretly with the Roman proconsul, Pollione (tenor). They have had two children together, but he now has fallen in love with Adalgisa (soprano), a young priestess in the temple of Irminsul.

Callas and Norma

Maria Callas sang Norma ninety times in eight countries, more often than any other role in her repertoire. She said in 1961: "Maybe Norma is something like my own character. The grumbling woman who is too proud to show her real feelings and proves at the end exactly what she is. She is a woman who cannot be nasty or unjust in a situation for which she herself is fundamentally to blame."

Norma is also torn over politics, since she must function as leader of her people during the Roman occupation. Although she's willing to rise up against the Romans if necessary, her preference is to avoid battle and wait for Rome to fall of its own internal weaknesses. The Druids earmark Pollione to the first target when the fighting begins. In the aria "Casta Diva," Norma calls upon the chaste goddess of the moon for peace.

Pollione is returning to Rome and urges Adalgisa to come with him. She agrees and confesses to High Priestess Norma, whom she loves and respects, that she is in love and has been untrue to her faith. She begs to be freed of her vows. Norma is sympathetic and consents, without knowing that the man with whom Adalgisa is involved is Pollione. When she learns this, she curses him for being unfaithful, and when Adalgisa learns of the love affair between Norma and Pollione she turns away from him.

To revenge herself, Norma considers murdering the two children fathered by Pollione. But she's the mother, and can't bring herself to do it. The situation is unbearable, and she decides to take her own life, ordering Adalgisa to marry Pollione and raise the two children. Adalgisa, moved by Norma's sacrifice and nobility, refuses. When the Druids capture Pollione as he comes to the temple for Adalgisa, he's brought before Norma, who now gives him the choice of renouncing Adalgisa or dying. Brave Roman that he is, he chooses death. But Norma's anger changes to pity and she promises the Druids as their sacrifice a new virgin who has sinned. They are astounded when she removes the sacred wreath from her head and declares that it is she, their high priestess, who has fallen. She confesses everything, consigns her children to the care of her father, and mounts the funeral pyre that has been erected. Pollione, his love rekindled, and overwhelmed by the greatness of her spirit, joins her in the flames.

HIGHLIGHTS

(Two-act version)

Act I: The tenor aria by Pollione, "Meco all'altar di Venere," vowing that he will take Adalgisa to Rome despite an ominous dream. Norma's coloratura "Casta Diva," the most famous aria in the opera, in which she warns against impatience, prays to the goddess of the moon, asks for peace but promises battle if necessary . . . and, privately, speaks of her love: "Chaste Goddess, who shines in silver on these trees, soothe the fire in these warring hearts." In bel canto opera, we hear a lot about the "long bel canto line." "Casta Diva" is the supreme example of a long, long, *long* bel canto line.

Act II: A duet by the two women, Norma and Adalgisa, "Mira, o Norma," as Norma contemplates suicide. The climatic scenes between Norma and Pollione involving two great duets, "In mia man alfin tu sei" and the final "Qual cor tradisti" as they go to the flames.

COMMENTARY

Norma is Bellini's masterpiece, a work in which he combined his wonderful melody with significant dramatic tension. He said of it: "If I were shipwrecked on a desert island, I would leave all the rest of my operas and try to save *Norma*."

He was wrapped up in the melodic world of Italian song and didn't try to replace or reform it, here or in his other works. But although he's still more about melody than about theater, drama, and grand opera spectacle, *Norma* has its theatrical and spectacular moments.

Olivia Stapp as Norma; Robert Grayson as Pollione in a New York City
Opera production of Norma

More than most operas, *Norma* has been identified with the artistry of the soprano who sang the title role. It was created for superstar Giuditta Pasta, whose outstanding performances saved it in Italy and England. She was succeeded by another superstar, Giulia Grisi, who had sung Adalgisa at the premiere. Years later, in 1890, the first Met Norma was German soprano Lilli Lehmann, followed by American Rosa Ponselle, Italian Gina Cigna, Polish Rosa Raisa, and Croatian Zinka Milanov. More recently, leading Normas have included Joan Sutherland, Beverly Sills, and Montserrat Caballe—and, in 1956 at the Met, Maria Callas.

MET PERFORMANCES
One hundred and thirty-two performances over nineteen seasons, from 1890 to 1981.

RECORDING
CD—Decca/London 425 488-2 (3). Joan Sutherland, Marilyn Horne, John Alexander, Richard Cross. London Symphony Orchestra and Chorus. Richard Bonynge. 1964.

VIDEO
Sutherland, Elkins, Stevens, Grant. Australian Opera. Italian; no subtitles. Bonynge, conductor. 1978. HOME VISION.

❧

Number 49. *Die Fledermaus*
by Johann Strauss the Younger
October 25, 1825–June 3, 1899

Premiere at the Theatre an der Wien, Vienna, 1874. Original book and lyrics by Henri Meilhac and Ludovic Halévy for their 1872 vaudeville Le Reveillon, *based on Roderich Benedix's 1851 comedy. Adapted for Strauss by Carl Haffner and Richard Genée. An operetta in three acts.*

J. Strauss versus Offenbach

Johann Strauss, one professional source says, is "sentimental Austrian temperament." Offenbach is "reckless Parisian drollery."

"He has brought the café to the opera house," inveighed the negative critics. "He has brought the café to the opera house," extolled the positive critics. Horrors!

Hooray!

And so he had. Everyone knows the music of Johann Strauss Junior, the Waltz King, son of Johann Senior, who was Vienna's waltz spokesperson in his own right before the younger seized the crown. Everyone knows "The Blue Danube" and "Tales from the Vienna Woods."

Die Fledermaus (The Bat) is an operetta—not grand opera, rescue opera, French lyric opera, Italian opera buffa or opera seria, opéra-comique, German Romantic opera, or verismo opera.

What's the difference? What makes it an operetta?

We go around this circle several times in the book (see Offenbach and *The Tales of Hoffmann*), but another trip may be useful, even if no destination ever is reached.

You're doomed if you choose one element of distinction and attempt to use it to illustrate the difference between operetta and "true" opera. For example:

"Operettas often have silly plots." Gadzooks! Sillier than *Il trovatore*?

"Operetta has spoken dialogue." So, of course, does *Fidelio*.

"Operetta is sentimental." *La Bohème* is dry-eyed and unemotional?

"Operetta is less demanding of the singer." *Pelléas et Mélisande* demands Caruso?

Operettas are favorites of stock companies and amateur groups, many of whose performers could not effectively handle the vocal range of true opera. Operettas must and do offer songs that become popular in themselves. Everyone with a singing bent can do something in the shower with "Here Come the Mounties" or "Sweethearts," but very few can tackle "Celeste Aida."

One word that goes with almost every successful operetta is "sparkle," not a word generally associated with Wagner, Verdi, Gluck, Monteverdi, or Beethoven.

Some (not all) elitists are especially highbrowed about operetta. Writing of Victor Herbert's works, one musicologist says: "That nearly all suffer from dated and inferior librettos is now conceded, but they pleased a vast public in his day and Herbert achieved his distinction *in spite of them*" (emphasis added).

Other experts prefer to dwell on the "gaiety" of good operetta and on its "high spirit."

In summary: Almost without exception, operetta doesn't reach the highest levels of art because neither the text nor the music is powerful enough. It's much more apt to be limited to the sentimental aspects of life rather than the whole of life. It's rarely tragic. (I'd say never, but don't dare.) It has no recitative and more spoken dialogue than most spoken-dialogue operas. The characters are more apt to be comic, frivolous, and, most important, one-dimensional. An operetta is lighter in character than an opera. It's rarely as "sophisticated" or as "complicated." Often the text is more important than the music. Demands on the singers are usually considerably less.

None of this prevents an operetta from giving us great pleasure—and the composer who writes it may be a true music genius such as Johann Strauss, with greater talent than many opera writers—but almost no operetta is designed by its composer to elevate us, to make us more noble.

One way to draw the distinction is by polarizing: Put *Aida* at one end of the spectrum and a flimsy operetta at the other. Any seven-year-old listener will know which is which. It gets trickier if you choose the lightest example of early French opéra comique, all of which has spoken dialogue, and assess it against something as good as *Die Fledermaus*.

Black Friday

Devoted though Vienna was to Johann Strauss and his waltzes, and outstanding though his operetta was, it ran only for sixteen performances when it opened. The problem was financial. On May 7, 1873, the Vienna Stock Exchange experienced a Black Friday. Most shares dropped by almost a hundred percent. In the weeks and months that followed, Vienna became an ugly city, with many suicides, too distressed for the gaiety of *Fledermaus* music.

Still: In *Fledermaus*, Eisenstein is going to jail because he has insulted the tax collector. This insult, however praiseworthy, reasonable, and responsible, is central to the plot. An insult to a tax collector is less apt to occupy that pivotal position in real opera.

One might ask about Don Giovanni's 1,003 sexual conquests, in Spain alone. Are we to take them seriously?

The answer is that the "Catalogue Aria" in Mozart's *Don Giovanni* is used to make a serious point. The opera starts with rape (or near rape, or seduction, depending on the producer) and murder. And it ends with the central figure being drawn down into Hell. Operettas have happy endings.

Long before Johann Strauss, many eighteenth-century comic operas appealed to what now would be called a "musical comedy" audience. Musicologists say that the title "operette" was used first by a French composer named Florimond Ronger, known as Hervé, with the music in his little works known as "musiquette." Then along came Jacques Offenbach with his own Parisian theater and several score operettas, the most popular in the 1860s and 1870s.

Johann Strauss was born in Vienna in 1825, took violin lessons secretly as a young boy, and came out of the music closet when his father abandoned the family. In 1844 he made his debut as a composer and the music master of a coffeehouse. Before long he and his waltzes were the idol of Vienna. Among the best-known are "On the Beautiful Blue Danube," "Artists' Life," "Vienna Blood," "Tales from the Vienna Woods," "Wine, Women and Song," the "Emperor Waltz," and "Voices of Spring."

His first of seventeen operettas, *Indigo and the Forty Thieves*, or *A Thousand and One Nights*, was produced in Vienna in 1871. *Die Fledermaus* came three years later—by chance, at a time when Offenbach had fallen from grace in Paris after years of incredible popularity. At first it didn't go over in Vienna, but shortly thereafter was a sensation in Berlin, and then throughout Europe. Another big hit, *Die Zigeunerbaron (The Gypsy Baron)* was introduced eleven years later. Although viewed by some experts as more "substantial" than *Fledermaus*, and although successful in its own right, it has not been as popular.

Johann Strauss is the unchallenged King of Waltz, not the unchallenged King of Operetta. But through those two operettas alone—or, given only *Fledermaus*—he made an exceptional mark in the field.

In 1872 he toured the United States, appearing in concerts to help celebrate the centenary of American independence. Much of Vienna joined in 1894 for a one-week celebration of his fiftieth anniversary as a conductor.

Herr Strauss often rates no more than a one-line mention in opera books and sometimes no mention at all in books on instrumental classical music. In one sense this is reasonable, inasmuch as he composed neither operas nor conventional classical music. Still, *Die Fledermaus* is such a classic in its own right that the largest and most prestigious opera houses have presented it for years. It was first shown at the Metropolitan in New York in 1905, was revived there in 1950, and was last staged in 1996.

Johann Strauss was the favorite composer of crusty, prickly, difficult Johannes Brahms, who autographed a fan for Mrs. Strauss with a few bars from "The Blue Danube" and the words "Not by me—unfortunately." Among other Collection composers who esteemed him highly were Offenbach, Verdi, Wagner, Gounod, Berlioz, and Richard (no relation) Strauss.

Hector Berlioz wrote: "Now that I have heard the terrifying great Beethoven, I know exactly where musical art stands; the question is to take it from there and push it further."

And: "It is no longer just music; it is now art."

Berlioz compared Beethoven and Johann Strauss this way: Beethoven's work was so exalted that it affected only a minority of listeners. But Strauss deliberately appealed to a popular audience, and thus was copied by many imitators, and they spread his influence to the four corners.

Strauss on Strauss

Richard Strauss said: "Of all the God-gifted dispensers of joy, Johann Strauss is to me the most endearing . . . In particular, I respect in Johann Strauss his originality, his innate gift."

KEYNOTE

Words from the *Fledermaus* waltz: "Happy is he who forgets that which cannot be changed." Devour and enjoy, without changing a note or a word. Fun, games, and exquisite music in prime-time Vienna.

PLOT

Vienna, late nineteenth century. Rosalinda (soprano) is being serenaded by Alfred (tenor), an opera singer, and longtime admirer. Eisenstein (tenor), her husband, is about to go to jail for having insulted the tax collector. Dr. Falke (light baritone) comes to escort him. Although an old friend, Dr. Falke has a score to settle with Eisenstein, who once had made him walk through the city at high noon dressed as a bat (a Fledermaus). He suggests that they delay going to jail until the next morning so that they can spend the evening at a party being given by Prince Orlofsky (trouser role, mezzo-soprano, although today some tenors are singing it). Many girls will be there.

After they have left, former suitor Alfred returns for another little tête-à-tête with Rosalinda. It is interrupted by the arrival of the prison governor, Frank (baritone), who has come to take Eisenstein away. Finding Alfred and Rosalinda together, he assumes that Alfred is the law-breaker and mistakenly collars him. Still out to even the score with Eisenstein, Dr. Falke has also arranged to have Rosalinda invited to the prince's big ball. She attends, masquerading as a Hungarian countess. Unaware that she is his wife, and falling into Dr. Falke's trap, husband Eisenstein flirts outrageously with her. Adele (soprano), maid in the Eisenstein house, also has come to the party, wearing one of Rosalinda's dresses and posing as an actress. She takes the opportunity to sing a song poking fun at her employer. All enjoy a big ballet.

The ball lasts until six in the morning, when Frank and Eisenstein rush off to jail, where Alfred is singing in his cell. Alone and in pairs, the other main characters drift in, and matters straighten themselves out. The power of champagne, not human frailty, is blamed for any mild indiscretions.

One Hundred and One Conductors

Strauss wrote of a trip to America: "On the musicians' tribune, there were twenty thousand singers, in front of them the members of the orchestra—and these were the people I was to conduct. A hundred assistant conductors had been placed at my disposal to control these gigantic masses, but I was only able to recognize those nearest to me, and although we had had rehearsals there was no possibility of giving an artistic performance, a proper production. But if I had declined to conduct, it would have been at the cost of my life.

"Now, just conceive of my position face to face with a public of a hundred thousand Americans. There I stood at the raised desk, high up above all the others. How would the business start, how would it end? Suddenly, a cannon shot rang out, a gentle hint for us twenty thousand to begin playing the 'Blue Danube.'

"I gave the signal, my hundred assistant conductors followed me so quickly as well as they could and then there broke out an unholy row such as I shall never forget. As we had begun more or less simultaneously, I concentrated my whole attention on seeing that we should finish together too! . . .

"The next day I was obliged to take to flight before an army of impresarios, who promised me the whole of California if I would undertake an American tour. I had quite enough after that one musical entertainment and returned to Europe as quickly as I possibly could."

HIGHLIGHTS

A very popular overture, which includes several melodies from the operetta.

Act I: The farewell trio when Rosalinda, Adele, and Eisenstein all anticipate the evening ahead.

Act II: Adele's light soubrette aria "Mein Herr Marquis," as she makes fun of Eisenstein, telling him she is a lady of some status: "Dear Marquis, a man like you ought to know better, therefore I advise you to look more closely at people. This hand no doubt is much more graceful than any chambermaid's." Rosalinda's mock-Hungarian full lyric soprano aria. Then, after a ballet, the *Fledermaus* waltz, the most famous piece from the work.

A reported three billion televiewers heard *Fledermaus* music repeated for hours during the gymnast floor exercises of the 1996 Olympic Games.

COMMENTARY

The spirit of Strauss's fun work is expressed in Rosalinda's words:

My husband is a monstrous man
I can't forgive and never can
His faithless and disgraceful ways.
He spent the whole of yesternight
With pretty ladies, young and bright
Who did not have to force him
But let the villain now beware—
If he comes home again to me
I'll scratch him 'til he cannot see
And then I shall divorce him.

Although some of the music analysts say he tried to reach a little higher with *The Gypsy Baron*, *Die Fledermaus* is Strauss's accepted masterpiece, the finest product of Viennese operetta.

Plácido Domingo conducted the work at Covent Garden in London in a 1983 revival. Discussing that production and the relationship of the operetta to opera, a biographer, Daniel Snowman, writes:

"A problem child can often be the most lovable in the family and so it is to many operagoers with Johann Strauss's *Die Fledermaus*. *Fledermaus* is a problem because, quite simply, it is not an opera. Operetta, certainly, and a leader in the category that includes the finest works of Offenbach, Gilbert and Sullivan, Lehár, and perhaps Richard Rodgers or Lerner and Loewe. But with its improbable story and characters and its succession of light musical numbers linked by lengthy dialogue, *Fledermaus* is scarcely the same genre as *Figaro*, *Falstaff*, or *Der Rosenkavalier*."

Snowman goes on to emphasize that the work contains some of the most delicious music ever written for the stage, a feast of solo and ensemble singing and orchestral writing that overflows with sentiment and sparkle . . . "in short, a work few opera lovers—or opera managements—have been able to resist."

Note that Snowman takes the easy way out and compares Johann Strauss's work not with a light comic opera such as Flotow's *Martha* but rather with Mozart, Verdi, and Richard Strauss, three of opera's biggest heavyweights. That's sort of cheating.

The 1905 Met premiere featured Marcella Sembrich and Edyth Walker and the German tenors Andreas Dippel and Albert Reiss. A revival in 1950 starred Patrice Munsel, Risë Stevens, and Richard Tucker. Rosalindas have included New Zealand's Kiri Te Kanawa and Lucia Popp from the former Czechoslovakia. A zillion other big names who have performed in this favorite include German soprano Lotte Lehmann, Plácido Domingo, and German lieder superstar Dietrich Fischer-Dieskau.

Bing Crosby was offered a role in a 1955 British movie of *Fledermaus* called *Oh, Rosalinde!* but turned it down. So did Maurice Chevalier, Noël Coward, and Orson Welles.

MET PERFORMANCES
Three hundred and thirty performances over twenty seasons, from 1905 to 1996.

RECORDING
CD—Philips Dig. 432 157-2 (2). Kiri Te Kanawa, Edita Gruberová, Brigitte Fassbaender, Wolfgang Brendel, Richard Leech, Olaf Bär, Tom Krause. Vienna State Opera Chorus. Vienna Philharmonic Orchestra. André Previn. 1990.

VIDEO
Sutherland, Austin, Brynnel. Australian Opera. English; no subtitles. Bonynge, conductor. 1985. SVS (Columbia/Tri-Star).

∾

Number 50. *Così fan tutte*
by Wolfgang Amadeus Mozart
January 27, 1756–December 5, 1791

Premiere at the Burgtheatre, Vienna, 1790. Text by Lorenzo da Ponte, commissioned by Emperor Joseph II. Opera buffa in two acts.

You are scarcely settled in your seat at *Così fan tutte* when the plot is given away by Don Alfonso. In Act I, Scene 1, he says:

"They're all the same. Women's fidelity is the purest fiction. Like the Arabian phoenix, everyone says it exists but nobody knows where it is."

The fourth Mozart opera in The Collection, and the only non-Warhorse, this is one of his three Italian comic operas, all in the same style, all written for a small theater, all designed for a small company, and all by the same librettist, Lorenzo da Ponte, who merits a word or two on his own.

He was a poet in London and a bankrupt printer who had to flee England for New York. He held a chair in Italian studies at Columbia University. He wrote a racy autobiography that makes him sound like Don Giovanni. He was among the first to bring opera to the United States, and he founded the Italian Opera House in New York.

Forty years earlier, he was thrown out of Vienna by Leopold II. Many years before that, he was thrown out of a seminary for making love to married women.

After that adultery and before New York he was in the business of producing opera librettos. He wasn't particular; he wrote about fifty of them; he had many collaborators.

Today he's known for neither bankruptcy nor sexual conquests, but rather for three librettos written for Wolfgang Amadeus Mozart: The first, *The Marriage of Figaro*, which premiered in 1786; the second, *Don Giovanni*, which premiered in 1787; and the third, *Così fan tutte*, which premiered in 1790.

The moral of the story is that a secure place in history rests less upon an adventurous life style than upon aligning one's self with the next Mozart who comes along.

The usual translation of *Così fan tutte* is "Thus do all women," or "They all do it," or sometimes "Girls will be Girls," or other titles that were accepted at the time but considered sexist today.

Some critics find it a shallow and wholly unfair portrayal of women in the late eighteenth century. On the other hand, a strong case can be made that the conniving men don't come across as steadfast fellows either. Not only do they deceive and entrap the women they love, which is a little on the shabby side, but they also seem to enjoy the game and even, perhaps, marry one another's fiancées.

The opera was commissioned by Emperor Joseph II. It was quite popular for several years, faded away for much of the nineteenth century, and today is back in favor with both the public and most critics, who see it as deliberately artificial.

KEYNOTE

Not on the Women's Lib Top 10. The two women are shown as vain, irresponsible, fickle, and flirtatious. But whether a harmless farce or a darker commentary, Mozart's music is even more magical than usual.

PLOT

Naples, eighteenth century. Don Alfonso (baritone), a cynical older man-about-town who is confident that he knows what makes people tick, makes a bet with two young officers, Ferrando (tenor) and Guglielmo (baritone), to test the twenty-four-hour fidelity of their fiancées, Dorabella (mezzo-soprano) and her sister, Fiordiligi (soprano). According to plan, the officers board a boat and presumably leave town and Dorabella sings of her distress.

Soon the men return, disguised as Albanians, and set out to try to seduce the ladies. The sisters have a maid, Despina (soprano), who believes in living for the day and who also has been bribed by Alfonso to keep the action going. At first she fails to interest the ladies in the rich strangers, even though she advises them that soldiers are never faithful and urges them to have a little fun of their own. Although the ladies weaken for a moment, Fiordiligi declares that she can withstand anything. When the Albanians pretend to commit suicide in despair by taking poison, Despina appears as a physician and "saves" their lives with a big magnet with which she draws the poison from their bodies.

Urged on by Despina, the ladies decide that there's nothing wrong in a little flirtation, and they divide up the "strangers," each (unknowingly) taking the other's man. As Dorabella begins getting involved with the disguised Guglielmo, she gives him a picture of her real betrothed, Ferrando. Ferrando is furious when he learns this and retaliates by turning his attention to Guglielmo's fiancée, Fiordiligi. He wins her affections.

Despina, still prodded by Alfonso, disguises herself as a notary and brings marriage contracts for the now reversed couples. Then news arrives that the military has returned. After being hidden by the sisters, the Albanians flee, reappear as themselves, and confront the faithless fiancées. Alfonso, having won the bet, explains everything. The ending used to be considered happy and weddings will result, although Mozart leaves it unclear which man will marry which woman, a condition that unsettles some audiences.

HIGHLIGHTS

Look and listen for all the ensembles. If you wait for the arias you miss the best parts.

Act I: The incomparable sequences of ensembles in the second scene, when the men say good-bye to the women. Dorabella's aria, "Smanie implacabili," a mock-heroic parody after she learns her guy has gone to war: "Implacable passions rage in this heart and will not stop." Fiordiligi's "Come scoglio," vowing that she and her sister are hard to get: "Brazen men, get out of here . . . I am steady as a rock, unmoved by storm, strong forever in faith and love." (Mozart is said to have disliked the woman playing Fiordiligi, who was Da Ponte's mistress, so he gave her a difficult-to-sing aria that jumps from the top to the bottom of the soprano range. In some productions, watch her head bob as she tries to handle it all.) The finale sextet, which fluctuates between farce and beautiful, touching music.

Act II: Fiordiligi's long and well-known aria, "Per pietà" ("Ah my love, forgive my madness"), in which she is still fighting off Ferrando's advances. The drinking canon in the Act II finale.

COMMENTARY

The musical key is the ensembles, lots of them, involving both sets of lovers in their various roles plus the third duo consisting of the troublemakers, Alfonso and Despina.

In the text and the music depicting the characters, Mozart and Da Ponte establish the point that human beings are imperfect and vulnerable. Some productions present the opera as basically frivolous and fun, and others put more emphasis on the inconstancy of human beings, of both sexes. Still others work in a turn-of-the-tables angle in which Despina changes sides and alerts her mistresses to the situation.

Così fan tutte often has been called the very incarnation of opera buffa—pure, simply comedy. But you have to be a little careful about that. Mozart, like Shakespeare (and Charlie Chaplin) was a comedian of genius. His opera is not a pie-throwing farce but an ironic satire that mirrors the human condition—a blend of comic and serious elements. The genius often lets the joke go right to the boundary but never lets it go too far.

As an example of character depiction, watch how Mozart uses his music to portray Fiordiligi, the older sister. Her personality is stronger, she is less tempted by the men than her younger sibling—and she has many more low, low notes in her arias.

The Collection's Bizarre Love Objects

Siegmund—Twin sister Sieglinde
Salome—Severed body part
Don Giovanni—Anyone in skirts
Tannhäuser—Venus, goddess of erotic love (whom he two-times for
    chaste Elisabeth)
Hoffmann—Life-sized mechanical doll
Siegfried—Aunt Brünnhilde
Fiordiligi and Dorabella—Sister's boyfriend
Count Almaviva—Wife's maid, Susanna
Bartolo—Young ward Rosina
Marcellina—Son Figaro
Werther—Friend's wife
Riccardo—Secretary's wife
Pelléas—Half-brother's wife
Don Carlos—Father's wife
Elisabeth de Valois—Husband's son
Baron Ochs—Octavian, a man in drag, even if played by a woman

---

MET PERFORMANCES

One hundred and forty-two performances over nineteen seasons, from 1923 to 1996. Nine performances are scheduled for the 1996–97 season.

RECORDING

CD—EMI/Angel CDMC 69330 (3). Elisabeth Schwarzkopf, Christa Ludwig, Hanny Steffek, Alfredo Kraus, Giuseppe Taddei, Walter Berry. Philharmonia Chorus and Orchestra. Karl Böhm. 1962.

VIDEO

Roocroft, Mannion, James, Trost, Gilfry, Nicolai. Monteverdi Choir, English Baroque soloists. Italian; English subtitles. Gardiner, conductor. Archiv VHS.

∾

Number 51. *Les Troyens*
by Hector Berlioz
December 11, 1803–March 8, 1869

Premiere of Part II at the Théâtre Lyrique, Paris, 1863. World premiere of Parts I and II in Karlsruhe, 1890. Text by the composer based on Books I, II, and IV of Virgil's Aeneid. A lyric opera in two big parts and five acts.

You like Big? Hector Berlioz is your composer.

To portray Judgment Day in his Requiem, he demanded a huge orchestra supplemented by four brass bands, one each facing east, west, north and south.

His dream orchestral composition contemplated an orchestra of 450 performers, including 242 strings and 30 harps, plus a chorus of 350 singers.

Then there's opera. It takes five hours to stage *Les Troyens (The Trojans)*, his remarkable epic opera about the Trojan War. Nothing is in the same league except Wagner's four-opera *Ring*. *Les Troyens* is so big Berlioz had to break it into two parts—and the first was not performed until twenty-seven years after the second.

Parisian musical culture didn't treat Berlioz well while he was alive. Toward the end of his life he offered an opinion of that culture: "Everything is dead," he said, "save the authority of fools."

Arguably France's all-time greatest classical composer, Berlioz also is one of the most original figures in music. The first true French nineteenth-century Romantic, he was a flamboyant radical, a rule-breaker who took to musical journalism in part to beat the drums for his own out-of-step work.

One critic wrote that Berlioz believed in neither God nor Bach. In the world of music, one doesn't find many of that species. It has become okay to burn the American flag, and atheism is not unique to Berlioz. But to deny Bach? That's going too far.

Berlioz did have gods—Christoph Gluck, the great reformer, and Ludwig van Beethoven, the great, period. What he sought from opera was dramatic truth—"cosmic" truth. He loved literature as much as he loved music— Goethe, Shakespeare, and the classics. *Les Troyens*, from Virgil's *Aeneid*, was a natural for him. What could appeal more than an epic twelve-book poem glorifying the legendary Trojan origin of the Roman people?

Wagner once wrote that there were only three living composers worthy of note: the Hungarian piano virtuoso Franz Liszt, the French Hector Berlioz, and, of course, himself. The three were born within a decade of one another—Berlioz in 1803, Liszt in 1811, and Wagner in 1813.

Smitten

Henrietta Smithson was a well-known Shakespearean actress with a touring company that played in Paris. Berlioz fell in love as he watched her play Ophelia in *Hamlet*. One of his courtship letters: "If you would not see me dead, in the name of pity—I dare not say of love—let me know when I can see you. I ask for mercy, pardon at your hands, on my knees and in tears! Miserable being that I am, I cannot believe that I deserve my present sufferings; but I bless the blows that come from your hands. I await your reply as I would the sentence of my judge."

Many musicologists call Berlioz the father of the modern symphony orchestra. Along with Franz Liszt he was a founding father of "program" music—music that tells a story or describes an emotion, as opposed to "absolute" music or music for music's sake as written by Handel or Bach or Mozart or Beethoven.

A contemporary of the Italian Rossini, Berlioz looked to the future while Rossini's operatic masterpiece, *The Barber of Seville*, was the supreme example of the Italian opera buffa of the past.

He wrote very little opera—only a two-act opéra comique called *Béatrice et Bénédict* based on Shakespeare's *Much Ado About Nothing*; *Benvenuto Cellini*, a work initially slaughtered by the critics; and *Les Troyens*. Although in time all were produced, during his life Berlioz was not viewed as a composer for the theater, and many years passed before his operas began to be revived by the world's opera houses.

The opinion that Berlioz is one of classical music's great composers has developed gradually over 150 years, and as it has grown the music theater world has reconsidered his operatic works. But in *Les Troyens* he gave that world a lot to swallow.

In other music he is best known for his *Symphonie fantastique*; two "dramatic symphonies" called *Harold in Italy* and *Roméo and Juliette*; a concert opera, *The Damnation of Faust*; and an oratorio, *L'Enfance du Christ*. Other choral music—and some professionals say his most powerful works are in the choral field—include a Requiem and a Te Deum.

No supporter is more enthusiastic about his big opera than the learned musicologist Donald Jay Grout, who writes: "*Les Troyens* is quite possibly the most important French opera of the nineteenth century, the Latin counterpart of Wagner's Teutonic *Ring*; its strange fate is paralleled by nothing in the history of music unless it is the century-long neglect of Bach's *Passion According to St. Matthew*. One can account for this in the case of Berlioz's work: it is long, it is extremely expensive to stage, and its musical idiom is so original, so different from the conventional operatic style, that managers (no doubt with reason) have been unwilling to take the redoubtable financial risks involved in mounting it.

Berlioz on Wagner and Music of the Future

"If by futurism we mean that music . . . is emancipated, free, does what it wants . . . then Wagner and I are of the same school, body and soul. . . . But if futurism means to say that one must contradict what the rules teach us, that we are weary of melody, of melodic design, of arias, duos, trios . . . that the ear is to be scorned . . . then I am far from confessing it. I never have, am not about to, and never will. I raise my hand and swear: 'Non credo.' "

"There is no overwhelming public in any country for Berlioz, as there is for Wagner, Verdi and Puccini, and not even all connoisseurs are agreed about *Les Troyens*. But, public or no public, the work ought to be produced regularly until conductors, singers and audiences are brought to realize its greatness."

Well, it hasn't happened yet that often, but there is progress. For example: Before World War II, it hadn't been produced at London's Covent Garden. But between the end of the war and 1960, it was staged eighteen times (in two different productions), about the same as *Pagliacci* and *Cavalleria rusticana*, Smetana's *Bartered Bride*, Verdi's *Otello*, and Wagner's *Lohengrin*.

Not until years after it was completed could Berlioz interest anyone in performing it. Even then, in 1863, despite lengthy negotiations with the Paris Opéra, it was performed at the less prestigious Théâtre Lyrique—and only Part II was staged. The reception generally was good, but it was dropped after twenty-one performances. The first complete production was not until 1890, with a German version in Karlsruhe. Berlioz figured the time per act: Act I, 52 minutes; Act II, 22; Act III, 40; Act IV, 47; Act V, 45—a total of 206 minutes, without counting intermissions. And some of the intermissions are long because of elaborate set changes.

According to *Kobbé—The Definitive Kobbé's Opera Book*, which every household should have on its shelf next to the dictionary—"there is no doubt that Berlioz has put many obstacles between score and public, some of them probably unavoidable. There is equally little doubt that the work ranks among the major operas."

KEYNOTE

Dramatic epic by an all-time great French composer. History, not heroes. Unique. Too big for routine presentation but sometimes staged and definitely worth knowing about.

PLOT

The twelfth or thirteenth centuries B.C., in Troy and Carthage. Part I, the first two acts, is called *La prise de Troie* (*The Capture of Troy*) and Part II, the last three acts, *Les Troyens à Carthage*. (*The Trojans at Carthage*).

Part I: The capture of Troy. The Greeks have given up the siege of Troy but have left behind a great wooden horse, presumably as a tribute to the goddess Pallas Athene. It's discussed by Trojan soldiers. Achilles, the great Greek captain, is dead. Cassandra (mezzo-soprano), daughter of King Priam, appears. With her gift of prophecy—prophecy that always comes true but is never believed—she predicts Troy's destruction. True to form, she's ignored, even by her lover, Chorèbe (Chorebus) (baritone).

Aeneas (tenor), a Trojan hero, son of Aphrodite, brings disturbing news: the priest Laocoön, suspecting treachery ("I fear Greeks when they bear gifts"), has thrown a spear into the wooden horse, whereupon two serpents have come from the sea and devoured him and his sons. The Trojans sacrifice to the gods beneath the walls of the town. Cassandra again prophesies the fall of Troy, but the people pay no attention to her and drag the wooden horse into the city. The ghost of Hector (bass), brother of Cassandra, appears to Aeneas, telling him Troy is doomed and urging him to build a new empire in Italy. Pantheus (bass), friend of Aeneas, reports that Greek warriors have rushed out of the giant horse and set the town on fire. Aeneas has fought and escaped. As the victorious Greeks storm in, Cassandra and her priestesses kill themselves with daggers.

Part II (Act III): The Trojans at Carthage in North Africa, in Queen Dido's throne room. Dido (mezzo-soprano) tells how she and her Carthaginian subjects had fled there seven years earlier after the fall of Troy and established a community. A storm forces a foreign fleet into the harbor, and its leaders ask to see the Queen. She grants an audience. One boy among the men who come is Ascanius (trouser role, soprano), fifteen-year-old son of Aeneas, who is in disguise among the other sailors and has designated Ascanius as his spokesman. Hearing that Carthage is about to be invaded by a superior force of Numidians, Aeneas throws off his disguise and offers Dido the use of his forces with himself as leader. She willingly accepts.

Act IV. A forest near Carthage. There is a famous symphonic "Royal Hunt

Nell Rankin as Cassandra in The Trojans *at La Scala*

and Storm" scene in which water nymphs dash and glide about and hunters enter. Dido, dressed as the goddess Diana, appears with Aeneas. They disappear into a cave, and cries of "Italie" are heard in anticipation of the future. The next scene is in Dido's garden, after the battle against the Numidians has been fought and won. Dido and Aeneas fall in love and sing a famous love duet, but even as they go off to make love a statue of the god Mercury (bass) comes to life and calls out "Italie," "Italie."

Act V is set in the Trojan camp in the harbor. Aeneas feels he must do his duty, which is to go to Italy and found the great new city (which will be Rome) that Hector's ghost had told him about. This is his destiny. Dido begs him to stay; she would defy the gods for love. But he cannot. He is urged to go not only by the gods but also by the ghosts of Priam, Hector, and Cassandra. As he sails for Italy, a disconsolate Dido mounts a funeral pyre and kills herself with a sword he has left behind.

HIGHLIGHTS

Act I: Cassandra's lament, "Malheureux roi!" ("Unhappy King!"), predicting the doom of Troy. The "Trojan March" as the horse is drawn into the city, the chorus singing the sacred hymn of Troy, "Du roi des dieux."

> ### *Berlioz on his Masterwork*
>
> *Les Troyens* is Berlioz's supreme masterpiece and one of France's great-
> est operas. Yet, to his anguished regret, it was not performed in its en-
> tirety during his lifetime. It is so gigantic that even today it demands
> the resources of the world's major opera houses and companies to
> handle the ballets, soloists, choruses, scenery, and total pageantry.
>
> Recognizing the problems ahead for his epic, the composer wrote
> in its foreword: "Oh, my noble Cassandra, my heroic virgin, I must
> then be resigned. I shall never hear thee."

Act II: The chorus when Cassandra and the Trojan women kill themselves, "Complices de sa gloire." The cries of "Italie."

Act III: The chorus of celebration in Carthage, hailing Dido, "Gloire à
Didon." Also, again, the "Trojan March."

Act IV: The big orchestral interlude at the scene of the hunt, "Royal Hunt
and Storm" (sometimes placed earlier). The recurring cries of "Italie."

Act V: The sailor's (tenor) homesick song in Scene 1, "Vallon sonore."
The long soliloquy of Aeneas, beginning "Inutiles regrets," as he is torn between love and destiny, one of the great tenor scenes in opera. Dido's "Je vais
mourir . . . Adieux, fière cité," as she contemplates death. The final tableau,
Dido's death scene.

COMMENTARY

In some superficial ways *Les Troyens* resembles a Meyerbeer grand opera—
big ballet scenes, big choral numbers, big arias, all-around big spectacle. A
famous hunt scene is a complete symphonic poem in itself.

Few operas are more faithful to the source text, however, and it's regarded
as a work of art rather than a Meyerbeerian entertainment—a major reason, of
course, why a public looking for entertainment in its opera rather than art has
not turned to it. Berlioz himself took it very seriously; listen to how he describes his own feelings during its composition: "At one time it is passion, joy,
tenderness worthy of an artist of twenty. Then come disgust, coldness, and an
aversion to work."

Various versions with different numbers of acts are performed.

Frequent comparisons with Wagner's *Ring* result more from the magnitude
of the two projects than similarities in their approach to opera. One of Berlioz's
objectives was to bring back to opera the set arias, duets, and other vocal numbers that Wagner was decisively rejecting. But in doing this Berlioz didn't
indulge the singers as Italian composers were inclined to do.

Les Troyens is not often performed in the United States, but a Boston production of the complete opera conducted by Boris Goldovsky in 1955 was one of the first to launch the revival of interest in it. Sarah Caldwell, famed head of The Opera Company of Boston, has done it more recently, and so has the Los Angeles Company. It also was chosen to open the Met's 1983–84 centennial season and was performed eight times at the Met in 1993–94.

Dido was written for a mezzo-soprano and Cassandra for a soprano, although sometimes a mezzo and a soprano have swapped roles. In a complete production in San Francisco in 1966, French soprano Régine Crespin was both Dido and Cassandra and Canadian tenor Jon Vickers was Aeneas. Crespin sang both roles many times.

To enjoy superb singing and acting, find a videotape of the 1983 Met production with Jessye Norman, Tatiana Troyanos, and Plácido Domingo.

MET PERFORMANCES
Twenty-eight performances over three seasons, 1973, 1983, and 1994.

RECORDING
CD—Philips 416 632-2 (4). Berit Lindholm, Josephine Veasey, Heather Begg, Jon Vickers, Ian Partridge, Ryland Davies, Peter Glossop, Roger Soyer. Wandsworth School Boys' Choir. Chorus and Orchestra of the Royal Opera House, Covent Garden. Colin Davis. 1969.

VIDEO
Domingo, Norman, Troyanos. A film. Metropolitan Opera. French; English subtitles. Levine, conductor. 1983. PAR.

Number 52. *Orfeo ed Euridice*
by Christoph Willibald Gluck
July 2, 1714–November 15, 1787

Premiere in Vienna, 1762, in Italian. Revival in Paris, 1774, in French. Text by the poet Ranieri de Calzabigi from Greek mythology. An opera seria in three acts.

My late great psychiatrist brother knew a fellow we'll call Jerry. For perhaps fifty years Bob didn't once refer to him simply as Jerry. It always was: "Jerry, the cheap son of a bitch." As in: "I went fishing with Jerry, the cheap son of a bitch. We camped in Yellowstone and caught a lot of fish. I caught seventeen; Jerry, the cheap son of a bitch, caught twelve. We had a good time."

Similarly, the Homer we read in school spoke repeatedly of the "early rosy-fingered dawn." Rarely did the Greeks and the Trojans see just plain dawn.

So it is with Christoph Willibald Gluck. Musicologists don't allude to Herr

Gluck from Vienna or Monsieur Gluck from Paris or Composer Gluck but invariably to "Gluck, the great reformer."

Gluck, the great reformer, lived from 1714 to 1787, overlapping with Mozart. He was the son of a forester, born in Erasbach in the Upper Palatinate near what would be the German-Bohemian border. After performing as a musician in Prague, Vienna, and Milan he wrote ten operas in Milan with no hint of what was to come later. He went to London to compete with Handel, composed two operas there, recognized opera seria was becoming passé, and moved back to the Continent. After marrying well and becoming financially independent, he spent several years as Kappelmeister (conductor-plus) to the Empress Maria Theresa in Vienna, where he upset the music world with his new approaches to opera. He also became familiar with French opéra comique, managed to antagonize the Establishment, and finally in 1773 abandoned Vienna to try his luck and his new-style opera in Paris.

Corot on Gluck

Jean Baptiste-Camille Corot lived from 1796 to 1875 and was one of the eighteenth century's finest artists. He loved music, especially Beethoven, Haydn, Mozart, and Gluck, the great reformer. One of Corot's masterpieces is *Orpheus Leading Eurydice from the Underworld*, painted in 1861, depicting a scene at the beginning of Act III of Gluck's *Orfeo ed Euridice* when the two start their return journey out of Hades. The painting's home is Houston's Museum of Fine Arts.

Marie Antoinette had been his singing pupil at the imperial court in Vienna, and in Paris she gave him royal financial subsidies and supported him in political music skirmishes. He continued battles against the opposition, won most of them, and produced more "reform" operas. France, with its background in drama, ate them up. He returned to Vienna for his final years.

Among his best-known works are *Orfeo ed Euridice* in 1762 (that is the Italian spelling; in English the title is *Orpheus and Eurydice*, and in French *Orphée et Eurydice*), *Alceste* in 1767, *Iphigénie en Aulide* in 1774, *Armide* in 1777, and *Iphigénie en Tauride* in 1779.

Some musicologists hold that "modern" opera began with Wolfgang Amadeus Mozart, and others that Gluck's rendition of the Orpheus legend is the earliest of the standard repertory operas. Both positions are supportable. Mozart's operas are the firstborn among the Warhorses; *The Marriage of Figaro* (1786) and *Don Giovanni* (1787) are performed so often that—like well-produced Shakespeare—they seem almost contemporary.

Yet Gluck's *Orfeo*, though staged much less frequently, is considerably more than a museum piece. It has had eighty-two performances by the Metropolitan Opera alone and continues to pop up elsewhere. Also, Gluck's *Alceste*, *Armide*, and *Iphigénie en Tauride* all have been produced at the Met, although not for a while.

How much of a reformer was the great reformer? Well, it seems to depend on the individual musicologist and on definitions. For some, there is no more important figure than Gluck in the evolution of opera. His operas were remarkably different from the norm.

According to musicologist Alfred Einstein, Gluck's actual achievement was "the building and shaping of a new form of opera." He attacked prevailing tradition, cutting the singers down to real-life size and changing the nature of the libretto.

He simplified the plot, returning the story to its clearest form.

He substituted genuine passion for mechanical heroism.

He brought music and drama more into balance.

He started using the orchestra to show a "subtext," that is, a suggestion that all might not be as the singer thinks it is.

He had the insight and intellect to create fully dimensional characters, not plaster antiques, and the musical ability to communicate the depth of these characters.

This whole key notion of "depicting character in music" is difficult for us nonmusicians to understand. We know how words can do this, either spoken or sung. And we can tell the poetic difference between "I swear it, darlin' girl, by gosh, I sure do swear it," on the one hand and, on the other, Mr. Shakespeare's "Lady, by yonder blessed moon I swear, that tips with silver all these fruit-tree tops." And all of us can tell "Here Comes the Cavalry" music from *Psycho* music. But the genius in opera is having the character come to life through his or her own music. That is what opera is, or should be, about. Professor Einstein says Gluck accomplishes this with wholly diverse characters:

"Orpheus, the hard and fond young husband; Alceste, the self-sacrificing wife; the effeminate Phyrgian Paris, contrasted with Helen, the vigorous Spartan; the warlike Achilles; Agamemnon, distraught by his terrible dilemma as father and king . . . Gluck saw into the nature of them all and portrayed them with elemental rhythm, virile austerity and a minimum of purely 'musical' music, straining his untiring energies in the attainment of subtle dramatic interpretation."

Like Monteverdi, Lully and Rameau, and Richard Wagner, Gluck favored music drama. (So did Mozart, of course, but his genius was such that he just plain did it without the polemics that accompanied Lully, Rameau, Gluck, and Wagner.)

The Italians were turning their operas into pomp and pageantry; Gluck was against that. They were cluttering their operas with superficial arias and putting halos around their singers; he was opposed to that. Their orchestral accompaniment was weak; he wanted to strengthen that.

One example of his changes: *Orfeo* is the first opera in which all of the recitative is accompanied by instrumental music.

The pro-Gluckians say that he "thrust open the doors of opera and allowed the daylight of human naturalness to fall upon the opera world of the time." That is impressive.

But if a "great reformer" means one who establishes a school of disciples, then Gluck, in the view of such experts as American composer-critic Virgil Thomson, left something to be desired. Underwhelmed by Gluck, Thomson characterizes him as an intellectually fashionable composer with a gift for making himself the center of controversy and excitement.

"As a career boy," writes Thomson, "he made his fortune and got knighted by the Austrian emperor. He was a second-class composer nevertheless. As a reformer, he was a washout."

A "second-class composer" and a "washout" as a reformer!

Professor Paul Henry Lang, longtime of Columbia University, also challenges the "great reformer" label, on the grounds that Gluck had no influence on any subsequent operatic composition.

But if we return to Professor Einstein: "*Orfeo ed Euridice* marked an epoch not only in Gluck's work but in the whole of operatic history."

We don't have to take sides. Christoph Willibald Gluck, mover-and-shaker or washout, is an integral part of the story of opera, initially in Vienna, where his reforms began with the first version of *Orfeo ed Euridice*, and later in Paris with the revision of it and with other works. (He also was a key player in a Paris musical war filled with literary and musical intrigue.)

KEYNOTE

The great reformer's first great reform work. Simple, straightforward plot. Excesses eliminated. While the critics argue revolutionary reform, you listen to the "Che farò" lament in Act III.

PLOT

The legendary story told by the Roman poet Virgil in his *Georgics*, in which Orpheus (Orfeo) resolves to recover his wife, Eurydice (Euridice) from the dead. He travels to Hades, finds her, and is leading her out to safety when he does what he swore he would not do; he violates the conditions of the rescue and turns to look at her. She vanishes back to Hades (see Monteverdi's Number 81).

But Gluck chooses a happy ending. On her death, Orfeo sings one of the best-known arias in opera, "Che farò senza Euridice?" He does such a good job of communicating his love and grief that Amor, the God of Love, appears, touches Euridice, restores her to life, and leaves her in her husband's arms.

HIGHLIGHTS

Act II: The "Dance of the Furies" and the subsequent "Dance of the Blessed Spirits," with its flute solo.

The Poet's the Thing

Ranieri de' Calzabigi (1714–95) was a poet, librettist, and operatic theorist who wrote the words of Gluck's first reform operas, including *Orfeo ed Euridice*. The composer gives him full credit in a 1773 letter to the editor: "I feel bound to admit that it is to him I am indebted, since it is he who made it possible for me to develop the resources of my art . . . These works are full of happy situations, of those elements of terror and pathos which give a composer the opportunity to express great passion and to create forceful and moving music.

"Whatever talent the composer may have, he will never create more than mediocre music, if the poet does not arouse in him that enthusiasm without which all artistic productions are weak and spiritless; to imitate nature is the acknowledged aim they must all set themselves . . . This is the reason why I do not employ the trills, passages and cadenzas in which the Italians revel."

Act III: A famous scene with Euridice's "Che fiero momento," in which she prefers to die as she thinks she has lost his love. Orfeo's lyric mezzo-soprano aria "Che farò senza Euridice," as he questions how he possibly can live without her. This is Gluck's most famous aria: "What will I do without Euridice? Where will I go without my beloved? What will I do?"

COMMENTARY

Several changes were made between the Vienna and Paris versions, including alterations of "Che farò." The Vienna production, only ninety minutes long, didn't incorporate some Gluck "reform" elements that came in other works.

The analysts give much credit to Gluck's librettist, Calzabigi, for helping him move away from the exaggerations of Italian opera seria and toward simpler opera that was closer to dramatic truth.

Musicologists don't suggest that the aria and duets in *Orfeo* are superior to others of the day. What they do praise is the strong orchestral writing, the increased emphasis on the drama, and the greater unity of text and music.

Among Gluck's champions is Collection composer Hector Berlioz, who in 1859 at the Théâtre Lyrique in Paris directed an *Orfeo* revival that ran for 159 nights. Another supporter was Nobel Prize winner Romain Rolland, who wrote: "The greatness was more in the soul than in his art. And that is as it should be, for one of the secrets of the irresistable fascination of that art was that it came from a breath of moral nobility, of loyalty, of honesty, and of virtue . . . By 'virtue,' this composer endears himself to other men; in that he was like Beethoven, something finer than a great musician—he was a great man with a clean heart."

That's the kind of review that draws in new customers.

The original Orfeo was Gaetano Guadagni, the most distinguished castrato of the day, but the role has since been played both by tenors and contraltos. Among women who have sung it are Marilyn Horne, Shirley Verrett, and Britain's Dame Janet Baker.

MET PERFORMANCES

Eighty-two performances over eighteen seasons, from 1885 to 1972.

RECORDING

CD—Erato/Warner Dig. 2292 45864-2 (2). Elizabeth Gale, Elisabeth Speiser, Janet Baker. Glyndebourne Chorus. London Philharmonic Orchestra. Raymond Leppard. 1982.

VIDEO

Baker, Speiser, Gale. Glyndebourne Opera Festival. Italian; English subtitles. Leppard, conductor. 1982. PIO.

∾

Number 53. *Les Huguenots*
by Giacomo Meyerbeer
September 5, 1791–May 2, 1864

Premiere at the Opéra, Paris, 1836. Text by Eugène Scribe and Emile Deschamps. A grand opera in five acts.

His operas were bombastic, grandiose, spectacular, flamboyant—and often uninspired.

Classical music great Robert Schumann not only loathed them but made a near-career of expressing his loathing, and the esteemed musicologist Alfred Einstein, rarely downright hostile in his criticism, called them "repulsive operatic humbug."

But Giacomo Meyerbeer was painstaking in his work, theatrically dramatic, innovative, and an undisputed reigning King of Opera in Europe for some two decades.

In the polite terminology of the academics, he didn't hesitate to sacrifice dramatic verities for pageantry and display. In our language, he played to the paying public. But it doesn't follow that he lacked exceptional musical talent.

Perhaps that's what bugs the elitists. They don't like what he did with his talent. Operagoers did—and, to a vastly lesser extent, some still do.

More than any composer, Meyerbeer is the father of French grand opera, even if the term has become imprecise. Immediately before him, in the early years of the nineteenth century, the most popular operas of Europe were the Italian bel canto works of Donizetti, Rossini and Bellini. During the Meyerbeer period, these were nudged aside by his grand operas and those of a handful of Collection contemporaries.

Daniel-François Auber wrote the first grand opera, *La muette de Portici*, which premiered in 1828. It is rarely seen today and is not in The Collection. Early this century Alfred Einstein offered these opinions on the growth of grand opera after it:

"Within the next few years appeared the works in which grand opera was wholly realized—Rossini's *Guillaume Tell*, Meyerbeer's *Robert le diable*, Halévy's *La Juive*, and Meyerbeer's *Les Huguenots*. What it demanded were striking subjects, handsome historical costumes, and sensational situations; it showed no conception of an organic scheme, but only a variety of such situations in a monstrous five-act frame. It required the most arresting melodic inventions, but relegated the inspirations of genius to an arbitrary and therefore inartistic whole. It is these 'effects without causes' that render Meyerbeer's operas, in particular, such detestable examples of irresponsibility and lack of taste."

One suspects here that Einstein was not pleased with Meyerbeer's efforts.

Still, while Richard Wagner (born in 1813), was theorizing, constructing new harmonies, writing early operas, and planning what he called the music of the future, the people were coming to hear and see Meyerbeer.

Wagner on Meyerbeer

Meyerbeer and German master Karl Maria von Weber had a lasting friendship. Meyerbeer and German master Richard Wagner did not, despite the fact that an established Meyerbeer had attempted to befriend a young Wagner in Paris.

Much later, when successful, this was Wagner's gracious characterization of the man who had helped him:

"A miserable music-maker." And: "A Jew banker to whom it occurred to compose operas."

Opera in Paris in the mid-1820s meant the Paris Opéra, and that house, which catered to the aristocracy, was in sore need of a shot of get-up-and-go. Auber and Fromental Halévy, and then Meyerbeer especially, supplied the melody and singing that could be geared to the spectacle which the Opéra's resources could contribute.

New blood came to the Opéra itself from an audience-oriented director named Louis Verón and a crackerjack official librettist named Eugène Scribe. Although Scribe is associated chiefly with Meyerbeer, he also worked with several other Collection composers, including Bellini, Donizetti, Gounod, Offenbach, and Verdi.

In 1901, William Foster Apthorp, in *The Opera, Past and Present*, pointed out that for all of his "deplorable elasticity of artistic conscience" Meyerbeer had served the Opéra well by "loosening the bonds of musical form" and "rendering traditional forms more scenic."

Long in the Oven

Although a crowd-pleaser, Meyerbeer was far from a frivolous composer. It took him thirteen years to produce *Le prophète* and twenty-seven to compose *L'Africaine*.

Although he was to capture Parisian opera, Meyerbeer was born in Berlin in 1791 of a rich German Jewish banking family. His real name was Jakob Liebmann Beer, and he was a child prodigy at the piano, playing a Mozart concerto in public at age seven en route to becoming one of the fine pianists of Europe. He studied music at Darmstadt along with fellow student Carl Maria von Weber, the first true German Romantic composer and creator of *Der Freischütz*, Number 68 in The Collection.

Urged by his teachers to go to Italy to learn about the human voice, he moved to Venice, where he sopped up the works of the popular Rossini and wrote several copycat Italian-style operas of his own. Weber and others attacked him for being too much of an imitator, and their criticism led him to give up composing for seven years. During this time he studied Lully and other French artists, moved to Paris, settled there, and then began writing again.

In 1831 Meyerbeer threw a real ten strike with a *big* grand opera, *Robert le diable*, which was an immediate success in Paris and soon in hundreds of European theaters.

Three major Meyerbeer operas followed:

Les Huguenots, 1836 (Number 53)
Le prophète, 1849
L'Africaine, 1865

All had remarkable success. No earlier composer in Europe—not even Rossini—had achieved his kind of popularity. In the midst of it all, Friedrich Wilhelm IV appointed him his General Music Director.

Not until Verdi arrived in the 1850s did anyone come close to challenging Meyerbeer on the all-of-Europe scene. The fact that most of the better classical composers of his time didn't think much of his work had little impact on the public. His case is the flip side of that of Berlioz, who was highly admired by a select number of the better composers and virtually ignored by the public.

Just for fun, let's consider the Royal Opera House, Covent Garden, London, for the century-long period from the mid-1800s to mid-1900s. *Les Huguenots* was the sixth most frequently performed work—397 presentations of *Faust*, 374 of *Carmen*, 329 of *Aida*, 292 of *Rigoletto*, 292 of *La Bohème*, and 249 of *Les Huguenots*. Meyerbeer's *Le prophète* was in twenty-eighth place with 113 performances and his *L'Africaine* in thirty-second with 88.

There are many vocal parts in Meyerbeer's opera, but they are not the long ones of the Italian bel canto composers. He has heroes aplenty, but he did not worry about using music to depict their character as the Austrian Mozart did. He was composing in Paris, so sometimes he threw in a ballet. And he sought never, never, never to bore the public.

To devotees of the bel canto composers, the ones most taken by the human voice, Meyerbeer decimated vocalism with his spectacle, Wagner decimated it with his music drama, and Verdi at times came close to decimating it with his red-blooded melodrama.

But, as we have seen, vocalism isn't *all* of opera. Three quarters of a century ago, musicologist Paul Bekker wrote: "His [Meyerbeer's] treatment of the orchestra reveals him to be an instrumental composer ranking with Berliozian skill, while his wealth of melody shows an inventiveness equal to the Italians."

Canopied Cardinals

Hector Berlioz, who loved everything supersized himself, describes Meyerbeer operas, perhaps with a touch of envy. They consisted, Berlioz wrote, of "high C's from every type of chest, bass drums, snare drums, organs, military bands, antique trumpets, tubas as big as locomotive smokestacks, bells, cannon, horses, cardinals under a canopy, orgies of priests and naked women . . . the rocking of the heavens and the end of the world interspersed with a few dull cavatinas and a large claque thrown in."

Perhaps you share my special interest in the composers beloved by the public but slighted by the experts. Obviously these artists have *something* that captured the operagoers of their own and/or subsequent times. One cannot become King of European Opera on pure smoke and mirrors. Franz Liszt—true, a showman's showman, who knew a good deal about smoke and mirrors but also was probably *the* virtuoso pianist of all time—said nice things about Meyerbeer, crediting him with inaugurating a new epoch in operatic writing. But Liszt was an inordinate flatterer who said nice things about almost all his fellow composers.

KEYNOTE

The most popular opera by the King of Grand Opera. Spectacle, melodrama, and bloody religious uprisings. Listen for the Act IV love duet.

PLOT

August 1572, Touraine and Paris. Originally in five acts, the opera often has been given in three. Huguenots were French Protestants, persecuted by the Catholics during the religious wars of the sixteenth and seventeenth centuries. On August 24, 1572, the night of St. Bartholomew's in Paris, there was a massacre of the Huguenots by the Catholics.

Raoul de Nangis (tenor), a Huguenot nobleman, has rescued a lady who was being molested by students and fallen in love with her, although he doesn't know her name. She is Valentine (soprano), daughter of the Count de St. Bris (bass), a great Catholic leader. Queen Marguerite de Valois of Navarré (soprano), the betrothed of Henry IV, knows of the rescue and has decided that Huguenot Raoul should marry Catholic Valentine as a step toward religious peace. Having seen Valentine in the garden with Count de Nevers (baritone), however, Raoul believes that the two have been intimate and refuses to marry her. This upsets her father and his men, and swords are drawn, but the Queen intervenes to prevent bloodshed.

When Raoul later challenges St. Bris to a duel, St. Bris's Catholic followers conspire to ambush and kill him. Valentine has married Nevers by this time, but she still loves Raoul, overhears the plotters, and wants to warn him. For his part, Raoul discovers that a Catholic plot is brewing to massacre the Huguenots in cold blood, but he is unable to prevent it.

Meanwhile, Nevers has been killed in battle and Valentine, now a widow, is free to marry Raoul. But they can't marry unless he gives up his religion, which he won't do. She then decides to abandon Catholicism, become a Huguenot, and stay with him. Without knowing Valentine and Raoul are together, St. Bris and his followers fire a broadside at Raoul. This volley kills both of the lovers—the count unwittingly murders his own daughter.

HIGHLIGHTS

The Overture includes the Lutheran hymn "Ein' feste Burg."

Act I: Raoul's romance, "Plus blanche que la blanche hermine." The page Urbáin's mezzo-soprano salute to Raoul, "Nobles seigneurs, salut."

Act II: Marguerite's "O beau pays de la Touraine," praising Touraine. The chorus of the bathing girls, an example of Meyerbeer's skills at orchestration.

Act III: The battle song of the Huguenot soldiers, "Rataplan."

Act IV: The most famous number is the love duet for Valentine and Raoul, "O ciel! où courez-vous," which some consider Meyerbeer's most beautiful. Earlier in the act, Valentine's "Parmi les pleurs."

Family Values

Librettist Scribe, grand opera specialist, had a thing about close relatives. In Halévy's *La Juive*, the heroine is thrown into a cauldron of boiling water just as her true father is learning she is his daughter. In *Les Huguenots*, too, the father inadvertently orders the killing of his own daughter. In *Le prophète*, the hero blows up a palace and burns both his mother and himself. It was not good to be part of a loving family in a Scribe text.

COMMENTARY

The temper of the times was critical to the success of Meyerbeer's work. Evidence of this comes from the high praise for this German-born composer's Parisian opera from Italy's great patriot/revolutionist, Alessandro Manzoni. Few felt more strongly than he that the world must be made anew. After becoming familiar with *Les Huguenots*, Manzoni had found his kind of man. He wrote:

"That opera stands alone, a beacon to indicate to future composers the course through which Music may be directed toward a high social aim . . . The sense of a guiding Providence pervades the whole work. The sublime inspiration of faith and duty is the soul of the magnificent chorale with which the opera opens, and which throughout the piece re-echoes from time to time upon our hearts, holy as the chant of angels, yet stern and solemn as a passing bell; it finds its human expression in the austere, insistent, severe yet loving musical individuality of Marcel, in whom the rugged invincible earnestness of the believer ever rises above and dominates alike the lightest and most brilliant, or gloomiest and most bigoted, scenes of the Catholic world by which he is surrounded; so that his very presence on the stage arouses in the heart of the spectator the sense of a providential influence, a work to bring about the triumph of good through human suffering, sacrifice and love."

Manzoni wasn't a music critic, but his extravagant view of Meyerbeer helps explain the enormous popularity of a composer who in today's environment is most often portrayed as a crowd-pleasing fashioner of spectacles—of "operatic dinosaurs."

Among many reasons why *Les Huguenots* is performed only occasionally these days is that it requires seven top main singers. The nights it was given at the Metropolitan back in 1894 were known as "the nights of the seven stars." They were Lillian Nordica, American soprano, whose range was such that she could sing Wagnerian roles one night and Violetta from *La traviata* the next; Nellie Melba, Australian soprano who has given her name both to Melba toast and peach Melba; Sofia Scalchi, Italian mezzo-soprano; Jean and Edouard de Reszke, spectacular Polish tenor and bass; Victor Maurel, French baritone known for his dramatic ability; and Pol Plançon, famous French bass.

Australian soprano Joan Sutherland chose it for her last operatic role in Sydney before she retired.

MET PERFORMANCES
One hundred and twenty-nine performances over eighteen seasons, from 1884 to 1930.

RECORDING
CD—Decca/London 430 549-2 (4). Joan Sutherland, Martina Arroyo, Huguette Tourangeau, Anastasios Vrenios, Gabriel Bacquier, Dominic Cossa, Nicola Ghiuselev. Ambrosian Opera Chorus. New Philharmonia Orchestra. Richard Bonynge. 1969.

VIDEO
Sutherland, Thane, Austin. Australian Opera. French; English subtitles. Bonynge, conductor. 1990. HOME VISION.

∾

Number 54. *La fanciulla del West*
(The Girl of the Golden West)
by Giacomo Puccini
December 22, 1858–November 29, 1924

Premiere at the Metropolitan Opera, New York, 1910. Text by Guelfo Civinini and Carlo Zangarini from David Belasco's 1905 play, The Girl of the Golden West. *Three acts.*

One critic said after a 1970s production of this opera that it was the best thing since Gary Cooper in *High Noon*.

Puccini had used exotic Japan for *Madama Butterfly* and was to use exotic China for *Turandot*, so it wasn't far-fetched to consider exotic California. It's a little difficult to see this urbane Italian bellying up to the bar with John Wayne, but he gets high marks for courage.

The notion came after he visited New York City in 1907 to see the Met premiers of *Manon Lescaut* and *Madama Butterfly*. This is one of the few sound reasons to be in New York; if you haven't composed an opera, I recommend against the trip. But if one must be there, one of the things one does is go to the theater, and Puccini took in three Broadway shows, including David Belasco's *Girl of the Golden West*, a melodrama about a California gold-mining camp. Seven years earlier in London he had seen Belasco's *Madame Butterfly*, which had sparked that opera, and after reading an Italian translation of this California story he decided to adapt it.

In a preface to the score, in an effort to orient the operagoers of the world, Puccini quotes a description of this foreign land: "In those strange days, people coming from God knows where joined forces in that far Western land, and, according to the rude custom of the camp, their very names were soon lost and unrecorded, and here they struggled, laughed, gambled, cursed, killed, loved and worked out their strange destinies in a manner incredible to us today. Of one thing only we are sure—they lived."

Word from the Composer

In midcomposition, Puccini wrote: "We are getting on. The girl promises to become a second *Bohème*, but more vigorous, more daring and on an altogether larger scale."

Larger scale indeed. Frail Mimi wouldn't have lasted long in Minnie's rough-and-tough gold-mining camp.

For the American opera world, it was a real turn-on. The world premiere at the Met was the first ever held there, and the world-famous Puccini crossed the ocean for the occasion. Enrico Caruso and Emmy Destinn sang—the best. Arturo Toscanini conducted. Puccini had fifty-two or fifty-five curtain calls, depending on your source. The Vanderbilts threw a postopera reception. The Metropolitan presented it nine times in Manhattan that winter and gave performances in Philadelphia and Brooklyn. A Chicago-Philadelphia company introduced it in Chicago and also performed it in Baltimore, Philadelphia, and St. Louis. The Opera Company of Boston staged it seven times. Never before had American audiences been so involved in a big composer's newest opera, although the critics generally were not enthusiastic.

KEYNOTE

Meet the gold miners, the sheriff, Wells Fargo, the Pony Express, Mexicans, and Red Indians. In The Collection we've had singing contests for a lady's hand and several heroines who have offered themselves to other men to save the lives of their lovers, but this is the only opera in which a squeaky-clean lady who's never been kissed bets her body against her man's freedom in a poker game . . . and cheats . . . and wins.

*Benito di Bella, Maurice Stern, Anne Marie Antoine in a 1985 Spoleto Festival
production of* La fanciulla del West

PLOT

A gold-mining camp, California in 1848–49. Minnie (soprano), owner of the Polka Saloon, virgin, and friend of the entire camp, meets and falls in love with a stranger from Sacramento who calls himself Dick Johnson (tenor). Sheriff Jack Rance (baritone), is in love with Minnie and is pursuing her, but she has told herself that she'll commit to no man until she finds someone with whom she could be as happy as her parents were with each other. Minnie invites Johnson to her cabin for dinner, they talk, she falls in love, it's snowing and cold outside, and Minnie offers to put him up for the night, but not in her bed.

When the sheriff arrives, Minnie hides Johnson behind a curtain and then learns that he's really Ramerrez, a notorious bandit. After the law leaves, Minnie accosts Johnson, who tells her the sad story of his background. His father was a bandit who died leaving nothing for his wife and children. Help came only from his gang of thieves, which Johnson joined. True, he had come to the town to steal the miner's gold, but he had changed his mind as soon as he saw Minnie.

He leaves the cabin but returns immediately, shot and wounded by Rance. Minnie hides him in her cabin loft when the sheriff returns, but drops of blood from the ceiling disclose he's there. Minnie, knowing Rance is a big gambler, offers a deal: They will play three hands of poker. If she wins, Johnson goes free. If he wins, he gets both her and Johnson. They split the first two hands. On the third, Minnie holds weak cards and Rance has three kings, but when he gets up to get her a drink of water she pulls out cards she has hidden in her stocking and substitutes them for the hand she has been dealt. Her full house, aces high, is the winner. (Whatever has happened to Jack Armstrong and "Cheaters never win"?)

The sheriff leaves, but later Ramerrez is captured and taken to the gallows. As a last request, he asks that the miners tell Minnie that he's gone free so that she'll never know of his ignominious death. In response, Rance hits him in the face. But Minnie rides up before the hanging and pleads for his life and freedom. She has helped all the miners and their families for years, never asking anything for herself. Will they not grant her this one thing? The townspeople do, and the lovers walk off into the sunset together, singing "Good-bye, sweet country, good-bye, lovely snows and mountains."

HIGHLIGHTS

Act III: The opera's best-known aria is Johnson's when he is about to be hung: "Ch'ella mi creda libero e lontano": "I ask a favor for the woman you all love. Let her believe I'm free and far away and on my way to redemption." It was adopted by Italian soldiers as a countersong to England's "It's a Long Way to Tipperary."

COMMENTARY

Many musicians say this is a good opera that deserves a better fate than it has received, and one opera authority friend insists that it's a glorious and great one. But, although revived from time to time, and performed frequently enough to make The Collection, it has never been a big winner. Minnie, a tough lady of the American West, is different from other Puccini heroines. Armed and independent, prim but ready to cheat for her man, you'd not find her dying in despair on a Louisiana desert like his Manon Lescaut.

Puccini to Caruso

Tenor great Enrico Caruso created the role of Dick Johnson in *The Girl of the Golden West*, one of more than six hundred performances he gave at the Metropolitan between 1903 and 1920. At one point Puccini wrote him: "Tell me how *Fanciulla* is doing, and if the crowds are flocking to it, and if it is paying me well . . . I salute you, O singer of many notes."

Puccini first met Caruso when he was composing *Tosca*. After reluctantly granting the unknown singer an audition, he exclaimed: "Who has sent you to me? God?"

Analysts in *The Viking Opera Guide* observe: "Like *Tosca*—and perhaps even more so—the opera needs singing actors of the first quality in order to succeed on stage. What is undeniable is that *Fanciulla* is harmonically and orchestrally one of Puccini's most innovative scores, and in these two areas represents a high point in experimentation and musical daring. For this, and for many other reasons, it deserves a better relative placing in the Puccinian canon than it today enjoys."

Other analysts agree with *Viking* that Puccini does more with the orchestra here than in any of his operas except *Turandot*, his last.

You can hear several American-sounding themes, tunes, and folk dances and an Indian chant (not, sadly, "Hail to the Redskins"). Puccini worked them in as he did Japanese-sounding music in *Madama Butterfly* and Chinese-sounding music in *Turandot*.

Although it lacks the long, wondrous, gripping melodies found in Verdi's more popular operas, there's Puccini melody aplenty, beginning with the chorus of the homesick miners as the opera gets under way.

MET PERFORMANCES
Ninety-four performances over twelve seasons, from 1910 to 1993.

RECORDING
CD—Deutsche Grammophon 419 640-2 (2). Carol Neblett, Plácido Domingo, Sherrill Milnes, Gwynne Howell. Chorus and Opera of the Royal Opera House, Covent Garden. Zubin Mehta. 1977.

VIDEO

Daniels, Domingo, Milnes. Metropolitan Opera. Italian; English subtitles. Slatkin, conductor. 1992. PGD.

∿

Number 55. *Simon Boccanegra*
by Giuseppe Verdi
October 10, 1813–January 27, 1901

Premiere at the Teatro la Fenice, Venice, 1857. Text by Francesco Maria Piave from a play by Antonio García Gutierrez. Text for 1881 revision by Arrigo Boito. An opera in a prologue and three acts.

When first performed in Venice, *Simon Boccanegra*, especially its libretto, was assailed by the critics. A premiere at La Scala two years later was a disaster. Verdi himself called it "monotonous and cold." Although despondent about its reception, by this time he had the Big Three behind him and was secure enough so that he could afford to be self-critical.

"Self-critical" is the appropriate phrase, inasmuch as the initial libretto was as much Verdi's as it was librettist Francesco Maria Piave's. The composer had sent his own rough draft in prose to Piave and directed him to turn it into poetry. Several reviewers said the libretto was one of the least intelligible ever written.

Twenty-odd years later, Verdi asked Arrigo Boito, his magnificent future collaborator on *Otello*, to help him revise *Simon*. That version is the one we see today, although the plot still is so tangled that we don't see it as often as we might. Indeed, even now, libretto in hand at home, playing and rewinding on videotape, it's difficult to keep it all straight. Still, the Met revived it in the fall of 1995 and, with Texaco's radio and television help, gave it to the world.

For further discussion, see the Verdi Warhorses.

KEY

Meet Simon, Verdi's greatest statesman and possibly his strongest baritone personality. Two powerful father-daughter relationships dominate a plot that overflows with secrets, hidden identities, and political intrigues. Man of the sea, loving father, and wise ruler seeks political and family peace. Hear "Sia maledetto!" ("He is accursed!") in one of opera's best scenes.

PLOT

Genoa, fourteenth century, when Genoa was an independent republic. Simon Boccanegra (baritone) is a respected sailor who has cleared the seas of non-European pirates. He has had a secret love affair with Maria (soprano), the daughter of a nobleman names Fiesco (bass), has fathered her child, and wants to marry her. The child disappeared when very young. Two politicians, Paolo (baritone) and Pietro (bass), persuade him to run for Doge of Genoa. Since he would have the rank of a prince if elected, and then would be in a position to marry Maria, he agrees—and is elected. Fiesco is falsely suspected of keeping a secret mistress in his house, but in fact the girl is his daughter, Maria. She dies a natural death, and Boccanegra, searching through the palace, is stunned to come upon her corpse. Fiesco tells Boccanegra that there never can be peace between them until his grandchild, daughter of Simon and Maria, is found.

Comings and Goings

Plácido Domingo, in his autobiography: "There are indeed works that suffer periods of neglect for decades and then, for one reason or another, seem to be reborn. Look at Verdi's *Simon Boccanegra*, a rarity for decades and now so often revived—probably as a direct result of the extraordinary Abbado-Strehler production at La Scala" (Claudio Abbado, conductor, and Giorgio Strehler, stage director).

Twenty-five years later Fiesco, disguised and under the assumed name of Andrea, is still plotting against the Doge Boccanegra, aided by Gabriele Adorno (tenor), who is in love with Fiesco's orphan ward, Amelia. Though no one knows it, she really is his missing granddaughter, the long-lost illegitimate child of Boccanegra and Maria. Fiesco/Andrea blesses the marriage plans of Maria and his associate, Gabriele. When Boccanegra visits Andrea's palace, he and Amelia learn that they are father and daughter, but decide to keep the secret for now. Boccanegra had planned to arrange the political marriage of Amelia and Paolo, the leader of the plebeian party who had helped make him Doge, but he changes his mind after learning that Amelia is his daughter and that she loves someone else. Meantime Gabriele, unaware of the father-daughter relationship, believes his Amelia is Boccanegra's mistress.

Political and romantic plots are interwoven. The courage, sensitivity, and wisdom of the Doge are exhibited in a "Council Chamber Scene" in which he opens the gates to the commoners who are shouting for his death, takes on both the commoners and the patricians, reminds both that they share a brutal past, demands peace, and shows leadership qualities unsurpassed in opera: "To you I cry out peace, to you I cry out love."

Many turns of the wheel later, Gabriele abandons the plotters and joins the Doge against them, even though the Doge had once ordered the execution of his father. But he doesn't change sides in time to stop fellow political plotter Paolo from poisoning the Doge's wine. Meanwhile, Andrea has been captured for his part in the plot. When he and the dying Boccanegra meet, Andrea proudly reveals his true identity as Fiesco, father of Maria. They are reconciled when the Doge discloses that Amelia is the granddaughter for whom Fiesco has longed. Now there can be peace between them. Dying, Boccanegra pardons Fiesco and proclaims Gabriele the new Doge.

HIGHLIGHTS

Prologue: As Fiesco curses his daughter's seducer and prays before a statue of the Virgin, "Il lacerato spirito": "The mind of a distraught father was tortured by shame and grief. . . . Rise, Maria, and pray for me."

Act I: Amelia's aria as she looks over the sea and sky and thinks of her childhood and her lover, "Come in questa'ora bruna": "Now I live in a noble palace, but I have not forgotten my humble cottage." The Amelia-Gabriele love duet. The father-daughter recognition duet: "Daughter! The very word fills me with joy. Your loving father will open paradises for you . . . Your devoted daughter always will be beside you, drying your tears in times of sorrow." Then the entire finale, added by Boito, that features a sextet of the major characters and the chorus in a stormy scene in the Council Chamber. It is the opera's best scene. Analysts consider it one of Verdi's best scenes. Verdians think of it as one of opera's best scenes.

Act III: The bass-baritone duet between Fiesco and Boccanegra, in which the Doge announces there now can be peace between them. The quartet in the final scene with Amelia, Gabriele, Boccanegra, Fiesco, and chorus.

COMMENTARY

Despite the help of master librettist Boito the tortuous story line obviously was not sufficiently simplified by his revisions. Verdi loved Genoa, and the professionals advise us that this love comes through in the music, although it's uncertain that the Unwashed or the mildly Washed can sense this. What we can sense is the power of the music and the strong, statesmanlike quality of the Doge, a quality to be wished for in a New Hampshire primary. He, not the tenor Adorno, controls the opera and makes it work, despite the story's complications.

Reduced to the core, it's a story of a wise ruler at a time of political unrest who dies at the hands of a villain. Verdians say it's a testament to the composer's lifelong hunt for peace and universal brotherhood and see Boccanegra as one of the composer's most forceful characters, one who uses power wisely, not to empower himself but to achieve unity.

This is a Verdian big canvas creation, the sort of opera that is in a different world from Puccini's *Bohème*, *Madama Butterfly*, *Manon Lescaut*, or *Tosca*. Puccini had neither the capability nor the desire to conjure up a character as consistently strong as the Doge nor to concern himself with this kind of statesmanship. Now, if you want to talk long, flowing, wonderful melody . . .

Lawrence Tibbett, who starred as Boccanegra at the Metropolitan in the 1930s, is credited with doing more than anyone to keep the opera alive in this country. The father-daughter recognition scene and the "Council Chamber

Scene" should be enough to help it survive indefinitely. This is another opera that must be seen to be appreciated; compact discs don't do the job unless the listener is intimately familiar with the opera and can mentally redraw the scenes.

MET PERFORMANCES

One hundred and sixteen performances over fifteen seasons, from 1932 to 1995.

RECORDING

CD—Deutsche Grammophon. 415 692-2 (2). Mirella Freni, José Carreras, Piero Cappuccilli, Nicolai Ghiaurov, José van Dam. La Scala Chorus and Orchestra. Claudio Abbado. 1977.

VIDEO

Milnes, Tomowa-Sintow, Moldoveanu. Metropolitan Opera. Italian; English subtitles. Levine, conductor. 1984. PAR.

∾

Number 56. *Don Pasquale*
by Gaetano Donizetti
November 29, 1797–April 8, 1848

Premiere at the Théâtre des Italiens, Paris, 1843. Text by Donizetti and Giovanni Ruffini from Angelo Anelli's libretto for Stefano Pavosi's Ser Marcantonio *on the same subject. Opera buffa in three acts.*

This is an interesting masterpiece.

Although filled with sparkling music, unlike Donizetti's other three Collection operas it doesn't have a single big smash hit number—no Sextet as in *Lucia di Lammermoor*, no "Una furtiva lagrima" as in *The Elixir of Love*, no Salute to France as in *The Daughter of the Regiment*.

But it is a happy, charming, fun-filled work with a host of supporters among musicologists who insist that it's a better comic opera than *Elixir*, a significantly stronger work than *The Daughter of the Regiment*, and even a finer opera overall than *Lucia*, the other three most successful of the sixty-five to seventy operas Donizetti wrote.

It doesn't matter. See which one you like best. All are must-see (at least on videotape)-to-appreciate works.

Don Pasquale is a genuine example of the "old" Italian opera buffa, although it was composed close to the middle of the nineteenth century, near the end of the opera buffa era. As noted in the *Elixir* piece (Number 35), some musicologists call it the last true opera buffa to remain in the international repertory. That depends on what labels are put on Verdi's *Falstaff* and Puccini's *Gianni Schicchi*, which were still to come.

Four Effective Curses from The Collection

SIMON BOCCANEGRA—Boccanegra is Doge of Genoa. He orders his courtier, Paolo, to find the unknown person who has kidnapped his daughter, but meanwhile to curse him, whoever he may be. *Sia maledetto! et tu ripeti il giuro.* Let him be accursed. In fact, Paolo is the guilty one, and though terrified to curse himself, he has no choice but to repeat the oath. The curse works; Paolo loses his political standing and is scorned by the people. For revenge, he poisons the Doge's water carafe. The Doge drinks the water, but before he dies Paolo confesses to the abduction and the poisoning, and is taken off to be executed.

DAS RHEINGOLD—When Wotan takes from the Nibelung Alberich the ring Alberich has forged from gold he stole from the Rhinemaidens, Alberich lays a curse on it: *Wir durch Fluch er mir geriet.* It will bring death to any owner. Soon afterward, Wotan gives the ring to the giants Fasolt and Fafner as partial payment for building Valhalla. They immediately start bickering, and within moments Fafner kills his brother. It is opera's fastest-working curse.

RIGOLETTO—The Duke of Mantua has seduced the daughter of old Count Monterone, and she has died, apparently of shame. When Monterone accuses the Duke, both he and his jester Rigoletto make fun of him. When Monterone vows that his daughter will be avenged, the Duke has him arrested and he curses both the Duke and Rigoletto, *sii Maledetto,* for mocking a father's agony. The Duke shrugs it off, but Rigoletto, with a daughter of his own, is horrified. Although Monterone thinks the curse has been in vain, the Duke seduces Rigoletto's daughter and the jester then swears to kill him and get vengeance for both Monterone and himself. When Rigoletto finds his dying daughter tied in a sack, he recalls Monterone's curse one last time: *ah, la maledizione.*

THE FLYING DUTCHMAN—Long before the opera begins, the Dutchman, a sea captain, has sworn to round the stormy Cape of Good Hope if it takes until Judgment Day. He swears by all the devils, which offends Satan, who curses the captain and condemns him to stay at sea forever. An intervening angel rules that the Dutchman can land once every seven years to look for a wife who will be true. If he finds her, he'll be redeemed. The opera opens as he drops anchor in a cove in Norway, taking his once-every-seven-year shot, searching for the woman who might save him.

Assessments of Donizetti have shifted so much over the years that it may be worthwhile to look at the judgment of professionals today.

Some of his serious operas, including *Anna Bolena*, *Maria Stuarda*, and *Lucrezia Borgia*, have again become familiar. He's no longer almost ridiculed as he was for a half century, but neither are his weaknesses glossed over as they were for a few decades. He was a man of the theater, he knew how to choose his subjects, he wasn't afraid to experiment with his music, and he liked and understood people. He often wrote more quickly than he should have—and his heart was almost always in the right place.

"Skillful hand and generous heart conspire," wrote Andrew Porter in *The New Yorker* a dozen years ago, "but sometimes haste of execution takes its toll."

See *Lucia di Lammermoor*, the Donizetti Warhorse, Number 15, for more background.

Donizetti's Sixty-fourth

Don Pasquale is Donizetti's sixty-fourth opera and the third from his last. He called it a drama buffo; we call it a comic opera. His remaining two are *Maria di Rohan*, a tragedy, and *Dom Sébastien, roi de Portugal*, a huge five-act grand opera that took him six months to write.

KEYNOTE

The last-written of the Donizetti works in The Collection. Another fat old bachelor who wants to marry a pretty young thing. Another ending where he blesses the union of the young thing with the handsome tenor. Another delightful evening at the opera for all the young at heart.

PLOT

Early nineteenth century, Rome. Don Pasquale (bass) is a wealthy old bachelor who is upset with his nephew Ernesto's (tenor) stubborn refusal to marry the woman Pasquale has chosen for him. He also is looking for a wife for himself. Ernesto, who lives in Pasquale's house, is in love with a charming, young, poor widow named Norina (soprano), whom Pasquale considers beneath the family. Malatesta (baritone) is Pasquale's doctor and thus a confidante, but he is also Ernesto's closest friend. He tells Pasquale he has a sister, Sofronia, who has been in a convent and is the perfect woman for him. He'll introduce them. Pasquale is jubilant and informs a shocked Ernesto of his decision to marry. He also reprimands Ernesto for being too stubborn and tells him he's being thrown out of the house and disinherited.

Ernesto's world has fallen apart, but Malatesta tells Norina not to be alarmed since he really has no marriageable sister, and this is all a plot against Pasquale. It will work this way: Pasquale has never met Norina, so she will appear as Sofronia, the perfect sister Malatesta has described. A fake notary will be employed. Pasquale and Norina will undergo a mock marriage. Norina then will behave in such an outrageous way that Pasquale will regret ever having met her. He will "divorce" her, and this will clear the way for Norina and Ernesto to marry.

Just before the "marriage," Ernesto arrives. Unaware of the plot, he tries to stop the proceedings but is restrained by Malatesta. After the fake wedding ceremony, Norina/Sofronia changes from a shy, domestic little thing to an extravagant bride who instantly begins making expensive and luxurious plans for the future, staying out late, doing her own thing, and making life miserable for Pasquale. She even slaps his face when he tries to control her. Confused and infuriated, Pasquale is aghast over what he has gotten himself into. Ernesto, still ignorant of the plan, is also beside himself. After other escapades, the two young people meet in Pasquale's garden, where Ernesto sings of his love. When Malatesta announces that the real Norina will be coming to live in the Pasquale house, Norina/Sofronia says she never will put up with such an imposition and under these circumstances would leave at once. Ready to accept any solution just so he can shed his impossible bride, Pasquale welcomes the marriage of Ernesto and the unseen Norina. The hoax is revealed, and Pasquale learns that his bride, Sofronia, and Norina are the same person, but by now he's so relieved to get rid of her that he gives his blessing to the real marriage of the two lovers.

911

The little Neapolitan music company was in trouble. "If only you could give us something new, our fortunes could be made," said one singer to Donizetti, who promised an operetta within a week.

He recalled a short vaudeville piece he had seen in Paris, took that for his subject, and in nine days the libretto was written, the music composed, the parts learned, the operetta performed, and the theater saved.

The work was called *"Il campanello di notte"*; the time was 1836, a year after *Lucia di Lammermoor*.

HIGHLIGHTS

Act I: Malatesta's description of the woman the Don is looking for, "Bella siccome un angelo": "Fair as an angel, a pilgrim on earth, fresh as a lily that opens in the morning."

Norina's "Quel guardo, il cavaliere," sung as she reads a novel's love scene: "That look stabbed the cavalier in his heart." This leads into her "So anch'io la virtù magica" ("I too know all the tricks"), which is heard in the overture. The duet at the end of the act between Malatesta and Norina.

Act II: Ernesto's aria, "Cercherò lontana terra," as he declares he will go into exile, thinking he is losing both his love and his home.

Act III: A famous comic duet between Malatesta and Pasquale, "Cheti, cheti." Ernesto's serenade, "Com' è gentil," the opera's catchiest and loveliest aria, heard first in the overture, now again as he sings in the garden about his passion: "How tender is the spring night. The sky has no clouds, the moon is bright. Everything breathes the spirit of love. Why do you not belong to me?" The love duet between Ernesto and Norina, "Tornami a dir che m'ami": "Tell me again that you love me."

COMMENTARY

One critical assessment: In lightness of touch, frothy humor, sprightliness, and pace it remains a model of what true opera buffa should be. Donizetti, master crowd pleaser, set out here to write another entertaining opera . . . and succeeded.

The three works generally put forward as *the* masterpieces of comic opera are Mozart's *Marriage of Figaro*, Verdi's *Falstaff*, and Wagner's *Meistersinger*. Volumes of expert analysis have been written about them. Less profound are this work, Donizetti's *Elixir*, Rossini's *Barber of Seville*, and Puccini's *Gianni Schicchi*. Few look for hidden meanings or social commentary in them.

Some analysts characterize Norina, Rosina in *The Barber of Seville*, and Adele in *Die Fledermaus* as no-strain cream-puff roles for singers. Among famous Norinas are Joan Sutherland (who gets high marks for her comic gifts in Donizetti operas), Ileana Cotrubas, Lucia Popp, Kathleen Battle, and Mirella Freni. The role was Beverly Sills's last at the Metropolitan, in January 1979. Featured with her was a wonderful Don Pasquale, sung by French baritone Gabriel Bacquier. The two played off each other so beautifully and successfully that they scarcely needed to sing.

MET PERFORMANCES

One hundred and fifteen performances over twenty seasons, from 1899 to 1980.

RECORDING

CD—Angel/EMI Dig. CDCB 47068-2 (2). Mirella Freni, Gösta Winbergh, Leo Nucci, Sesto Bruscantini. Ambrosian Opera Chorus. Philharmonia Orchestra. 1982.

VIDEO

Mariotti, Rigacci, Matteuzzi. Italian; Japanese subtitles. Pido, conductor. JPN-SKL. (Japanese import).

∾

Number 57. *Le coq d'or (The Golden Cockerel)*
by Nikolai Rimsky-Korsakov
March 18, 1844–June 21, 1908

Premiere in Moscow, 1909. Text by Vladimir Byelsky from a fairy tale by Alexander Pushkin. Three acts.

Three of the concert hall's most popular orchestral pieces are George Gershwin's *Rhapsody in Blue*, Maurice Ravel's *Bolero*, and Nikolai Rimsky-Korsakov's *Scheherazade*.

When you hear *The Golden Cockerel* music, you hear *Scheherazade*, the familiar symphonic suite based on *A Thousand and One Nights*—fresh Russian melody and orchestral color.

Rimsky-Korsakov is one of Russia's top half-dozen classical music greats, a leading figure of his country's nineteenth-century nationalist music and the composer of several distinguished Russian operas. Nothing else he wrote, in opera or orchestral music, is as well-known as *Scheherazade*, although some critics feel his operatic music was his most original and imaginative. Others say those works become "monotonous and cloying" after several hearings. You decide.

The most familiar of Rimsky-Korsakov's other nonoperatic works include *Capriccio espagnol*, the *Russian Easter Festival* Overture, and the *Antar* Symphony. Of his fifteen operas, the best known include:

The Maid of Pskov, 1873, also known as *Ivan the Terrible*
May Night, 1880, a peasant-life comedy
Christmas Eve, 1895, also a rural village story
Sadko, 1898, from an eleventh-century legend
The Tsar's Bridge, 1899, a tragedy
The Tale of Tsar Saltan, 1900, a satirical fantasy
The Legend of the Invisible City of Kitezh, 1907, a criticism of government policies
The Golden Cockerel, his last, composed in 1907 but not performed until 1909,
    after his death

We have seen that Rimsky (along with Mussorgsky and Borodin) was one of the little group of nineteenth-century Russian composers called the "Mighty Five," who dedicated themselves to producing Russian music and in this relationship he undertook his comprehensive and controversial revisions of Mussorgsky's *Boris Godunov*.

It's not surprising that a famed orchestrator like Rimsky-Korsakov wrote works known more for their musical color than for their drama. Although his melodies sound as if they came right out of old Russia, the analysts say that they are distinctly original and that his harmonies are original, experimental, and brilliant.

Most successful opera writers like to play make-believe, and Rimsky loved the make-believe world. He wouldn't have fit comfortably into the late-nineteenth-century Italian verismo (truth/reality) school of Leoncavallo, Mascagni, and Giordano.

The audience is advised from the stage that *The Golden Cockerel* is only a fairy story. Censors, viewing it as an attack on government authority in general and a protest against the Russian war against Japan in particular, banned it until appropriate revisions were made. Although it's the Rimsky opera most frequently performed in the West, his *Sadko* is the one generally favored by the music profession.

Born in Tikhvin, Russia, in 1844, he trained for a naval career and studied a little music privately. A chance meeting with Mili Balakirev of the "Five" involved him seriously in music and, despite almost no formal training, he wrote a symphony during a two-and-a-half-year tour of sea duty (that included stops in the United States). He stepped up the pace of his composing on his return, and his first opera was so well received that, as a well-run government should, the government created a special job for him called Inspector of Naval Bands. Later he was a professor at the St. Petersburg Conservatory, a job he lost in 1905 for siding with his students, who were protesting against administrative and regulative practices. He was reinstated and died of a heart attack in 1908.

He was sixty-four when he wrote *The Golden Cockerel* and confessed to friends that he was well over the music hill.

Rimsky on Orchestration

Rimsky-Korsakov, Richard Strauss, and Hector Berlioz were among classical music's outstanding orchestrators. Rimsky wrote:

"It is a great error to say, 'Such and such a composer is a good orchestrator; such and such a work is very well instrumented.' For orchestration is one of the aspects of the very soul of the work. The work is thought orchestrally and from its very conception carries with it a certain orchestral coloring proper to it and to its author. Is it possible to separate Wagner's music from its actual orchestration? That would be tantamount to saying of a painting by a given master, 'What an admirable drawing with colors.' "

KEYNOTE

Orchestral color from a color magician. Not as bloody as it sounds. A fairy-tale political satire; a blend of humor, beauty, absurdity, wistfulness, and pathos. Hear some great tunes.

PLOT

The land of make-believe, in the past. King Dodon (bass) is confused by the conflicting opinions of his top aides. Like a recent U.S. First Lady, he sought help from the Astrologer (tenor), this one dressed in a blue robe with golden stars. Unlike the First Lady's astrologer, so far as we know, this one had a golden cockerel (soprano), which had a gift of prophecy. So long as it was perched with a clear view of the surrounding country, it would crow when the King was in danger. The cockerel does sound the alarm, and the King's sons rush out to fight the enemy. When the cockerel crows again, the King puts on a rusty suit of armor, which he has outgrown, and also goes to battle, carrying a sword that is too heavy.

After finding the bodies of his two sons, the King encounters the Queen of Shemakha (soprano), falls in love with her, and brings her home to the palace. When the Astrologer demands payment for services rendered by his golden cockerel, the King taps him on the head with his sword and kills him. This upsets the cockerel, who, anticipating Alfred Hitchcock, avenges his master's death by killing the King with a couple of pecks on his head. Darkness falls. When it is lifted, the Queen and the bird have disappeared.

HIGHLIGHTS

Act II: The Queen's "Hymn to the Sun," a famous operatic number.

Act III: The "Bridal Procession," the best known piece from any Rimsky-Korskov opera, except perhaps for the "Song of India" from *Sadko*.

COMMENTARY

This opera is vintage Rimsky-Korsakov; these are not sounds you would hear from Germany's Richard Wagner or France's Ambroise Thomas or Charles Gounod. Think legend, fairy tale, and mythology, especially those of Mother Russia. Think brilliant orchestral color, equaled by few other composers, in part because few composers had a more intimate knowledge of each musical instrument, each group of instruments, and how to wring the most from all groups in combination with all others.

In discussing jazz and the versatility of modern performers, American composer Virgil Thomson once pointed out that Rimsky-Korsakov knew all of the tricks of the trumpet that we now hear in a modern band—and more.

A 1945 Met production included Patrice Munsel, Norman Cordon, and Margaret Harshaw. Lily Pons and Ezio Pinza also did well by it. The analysts say it demands singers who can dance and dancers who can sing, although it has been given with singers seated at the sides of the stage while dancers pantomime the action. Vocal demands on the coloratura queen are great.

MET PERFORMANCES

Sixty-eight performances over eleven seasons, from 1918 to 1945.

Rosina Galli in The Golden Cockerel

RECORDING
    CD—MCA Classics AE02-10391 (2). Elena Brileva, Irena Udalova, Nina Gaponova, Oleg Biktimirov, Artur Eizen. Bolshoi Theater Chorus and Orchestra. Yevgeny Svetlanov. 1988.

∾

Number 58. *La sonnambula (The Sleepwalker)*
by Vincenzo Bellini
November 3, 1801–September 23, 1835

Premiere at the Teatro Carcano, Milan, 1831. Text by Felice Romani from Eugène Scribe's scenario for Jean-Pierre Aumer's ballet La sonnambula. *Two acts.*

Anna Bolena, an opera by Gaetano Donizetti, premiered at the Teatro Carcano in Milan in December of 1830. A historical opera about the trip to the scaffold of Henry VIII's wife, it was the work that established Donizetti as a first-rank composer.

That's relevant to our story because earlier that year Vincenzo Bellini was commissioned by Duke Pompeo Litta of Milan to produce an opera for the Teatro Carcano. His first choice was to do something based on Victor Hugo's *Hernani*—thirteen years before Giuseppe Verdi chose that work for his own.

But Donizetti was considerably better known in Italy, even if he was not yet famous throughout Europe, and Bellini decided it wouldn't be a good idea to take on such an established composer with another historical work. So he went in another direction into an interesting little story about a sleepwalking lady.

Too Soon

Bellini died less than two months shy of his thirty-fourth birthday. The official cause of death was an "acute inflammation of the large intestine, complicated by an abscess of the liver." He was buried in Paris in Père Lachaise cemetery, and years later his remains were returned to his birthplace in Catania, Sicily. On his tombstone is a line from *La sonnambula*:

"Ah, Non credea mirarti sì presto estinto, o fiore" ("Ah, I did not think to see you extinguished so soon, oh flower").

It's another melody opera, gentler than the more famous *Norma* (Number 48), which came later, and it remains popular despite a lack of tense dramatic situations.

Some current-day musicologists say flatly that Bellini was "the most lyrical opera composer who ever lived," the one whose work was most expressive of personal emotion and most suitable for singing. And other analysts say Bellini's harmonies are more interesting than either of the other two bel canto composers, Rossini and Donizetti. He loved the folk music of his native Sicily, some of which is heard in his tunes.

One friend who is an opera professional told me that the operas of Bellini and Donizetti truly excel only when the greatest singers are involved, that the works of Puccini can move an audience if the singers have average operatic abilities, and that Verdi still comes across as heavenly Verdi even if the voices are mediocre.

KEYNOTE

The first of Bellini's three big operas (*Norma* and non-Collection *I Puritani*). A soft melodrama: no blood, no violence, no deaths.

PLOT

A Swiss village, the nineteenth century. Amina (soprano), an orphan, and the fiancée of Elvino (tenor), a wealthy young landowner, walks in her sleep. One night she enters through the window into the room of a stranger who is spending the night at the neighborhood inn. He hears her talking of Elvino as she sleepwalks and, not wanting to embarrass her, leaves by the same window, softly closing it as she sinks down on the bed. She is found there by Elvino, who is understandably upset that his intended is in the bed of a stranger, even if the stranger is not sharing it at the time.

Convinced that she has been unfaithful, he becomes interested in Lisa (soprano), proprietess of the inn, and is ready to marry her. It turns out that the stranger whose room Amina had entered is Count Rodolfo (bass), the lord of the castle and the village. In order to persuade Elvino that he has accused Amina unjustly, the Count has him watch her on another sleepwalking expedition, this time across a dangerous bridge spanning the mill wheel. When she is awakened by Elvino, to her joy she finds him waiting for her with open arms.

The "Inas"

In *La sonnambula*, the heroine is "Amina." In Donizetti's *Elixir of Love*, she is "Adina." In his *Don Pasquale*, it is "Norina." One soprano summarized her bel canto career: "I do all the 'inas.'"

There's also Zerlina (*Don Giovanni*), Despina (*Così fan tutte*), and Rosina (*The Barber of Seville*). With the exception of Amina, a more lyric role, this is another way of referring to the light soprano, usually comical, "soubrette" repertoire.

HIGHLIGHTS

Act I: Amina's "Come per me sereno" ("How brightly things are shining for me"), as she is on top of her world. A duet for Amina and Elvino as he puts a ring on her finger, "Prendi, l'anel ti dono" ("Take this ring"). Another duet for the lovers, "Son geloso del zefiro errante," as they make up.

Act II: Amina's closing scene, starting with "Ah, non credea mirarti," when she thinks she has lost Elvino's love. This is perhaps second only to Norma's "Casta Diva" as an example of Bellini's long, flowing melodies. Then her joyous "Ah! non giunge," the most popular number from the opera, a favorite recording from it, and a tune familiar to many nonoperagoers.

COMMENTARY

La sonnambula was a smash hit from the start, then faded because it was too sweet, and now is again performed all over the world. Some experts consider it the first of Bellini's works to show that he was a truly creative fellow. It is a fine evening's entertainment, simple to understand, about the interesting phenomenon of sleepwalking.

By definition it's a "tragicomedy"—all of the "tragedy" coming from the painful misunderstanding between the two lovers. No babies are burned, no one commits suicide, there are neither stabbings nor deaths, and no one is tortured. It is tender and charming.

Amina is one of the most famous roles of the most famous Jenny Lind, who also starred in Donizetti's *Daughter of the Regiment*.

Bel canto opera was eligible for federal disaster relief in the mid-1900s. Luisa Tetrazzini had sung *La sonnambula* in London in 1910 and Lily Pons at the Met in 1932, but for a time there was little else except *Norma*, Rossini's *Barber of Seville*, and Donizetti's *Lucia di Lammermoor* and *The Elixir of Love*. The rest had been killed by Verdi, verismo, and Richard Wagner.

During these years it was overlooked that early bel canto had been sung by dramatic singer-actresses like Giuditta Pasta, Maria Malibran, and Giulia Grisi, not by the ultrahigh warblers. As noted earlier, Maria Callas was the prime mover in reminding the operatic world of the inherent drama brought out by those nineteenth-century superstars.

MET PERFORMANCES

Sixty-five performances over twelve seasons, from 1891 to 1972.

RECORDINGS

CD—Angel/EMI CDCB 47377 (2) (mono). Maria Callas, Nicola Monti, Nicola Zaccaria. La Scala Chorus and Orchestra. Antonino Votto. 1957.

or

—Decca/London 417 424-2 (2). Joan Sutherland, Luciano Pavarotti, Nicolai Ghiaurov. London Opera Chorus. National Philharmonic Orchestra. Richard Bonynge. 1980.

VIDEO

Ortis, Tamantini, Sinimberghi. Rome Opera. A film by Cesare Barlacchi. Italian; no subtitles. Mucci, conductor. 1949. VIEW (V.I.E.W. VIDEO).

Number 59. *Elektra*
by Richard Strauss
June 11, 1864–September 8, 1949

Premiere at the Dresden Opera, 1909. Text by Hugo von Hoffmannsthal from Sophocles' Greek tragedy. One act.

The early Richard Strauss was much a part of the avant-garde with his 1890s tone poems and his two bloody operas, *Salome* and *Elektra*, one featuring a lusty young girl kissing the bloody lips of the severed head of John the Baptist and the other about a woman's obsessive desire to kill her mother, both "decadent" in their stories, both built on strange-sounding dissonant music, both accused of using art for "shock" rather than "beauty."

This was the first collaboration between Strauss and Hugo von Hoffmannsthal, who were to work together for six operas. Hoffmannsthal, 1874–1929,

The American premiere of Elektra *at the Manhattan Opera House*

was an Austrian poet, dramatist, and librettist. He and Strauss met in Paris in 1900 when both were vacationing—or, in European fashion, on holiday.

The two remained together for *Der Rosenkavalier*, 1911; *Ariadne auf Naxos*, 1912, (revised in 1916;) *Die Frau ohne Schatten*, 1919; *Die aegyptische Helena*, 1928, and *Arabella*, 1933.

Elektra, daughter of Agamemnon and Clytemnestra in Greek mythology, is the main character in five classical tragedies—Aeschylus' *Libation Bearers*, Sophocles' *Electra*, Euripides' *Electra* and *Orestes*, and Seneca's *Agamemnon*. Strauss and Hoffmannsthal chose the Sophocles version.

KEYNOTE

Sordid, intense, savage, and mad. Bold experiment in atonal music blended with ancient Greek horror story. Hear the sister's screams of joy as brother kills mother.

No More Beauty

William J. Henderson, a distinguished critic, commented on *Salome* and *Elektra* in the *New York Sun* on Feb. 6, 1910:

"All you have to do when you go to hear *Elektra* is to take into consideration the patent fact that Strauss does not believe that melody and harmony of the old song style used by Mozart, Beethoven and many other masters can express with convincing eloquence the emotions which constitute the tragedy of such stories as *Salome* and this later work [*Elektra*].

"You can absorb yourself in listening to the amazing instrumental combinations. He demands of wind instruments technique such as the old masters never conceived . . .

"Those who can recall *Salome* will remember that the principal point at issue appeared to be the large proportion of ugliness in the score of the opera, but it can hardly be disputed that it contained much more music beautiful according to established standards than that of *Elektra*. Strauss has almost eliminated what we call beauty from *Elektra*. . . ."

PLOT

Antiquity, in Mycenae. Before the opera opens, much has happened. While King Agamemnon was off fighting the Trojan Wars, his wife, Clytemnestra, became involved with a lover, Aegisthus. When Agamemnon returned to Mycenae, the two lovers killed him and together ruled in his place. His daughters, Chrysothemis and Elektra, were kept almost as slaves after their brother, Orestes, fled to safety to escape the plotters. In the opera, Elektra (soprano) hopes Orestes (baritone) will return to avenge the murder of their father, but when a false rumor is spread that he has died she vows to take over the revenge herself. She plans to murder both mother Clytemnestra, (mezzosoprano) and her lover Aegisthus (tenor) with the same ax that killed Agamemnon, but Orestes returns in time to do the job on mother. Madly, gleefully, Elektra then lights the way for oblivious Aegisthus to enter the castle, where he, too, is killed. Elektra dances in demented ecstasy until she falls dead.

HIGHLIGHTS

More a symphonic than a lyrical opera. No famous set arias. One critic says it must be swallowed whole or it doesn't work. Watch for the "Recognition Scene," when Elektra identifies Orestes.

COMMENTARY

Although kissing the bloody lips of the severed head of John the Baptist presents a reasonably unpleasant scene, for demented horror *Salome* may not stand up to *Elektra*. Consider a daughter screaming "Stab her once more" as her brother is killing their mother. That's strong and repulsive enough without the musical and poetic artistry of Strauss and Hoffmannsthal. Descriptive phrases used about the opera include "two tortured women," "whipped into pathological frenzy," "ranting, moaning, shrieking and screeching." Professor Paul Henry Lang calls it the "unsurpassed final orgiastic opera issuing from the Wagnerian heritage," adding: "The great recognition scene dwarfs everything in its incestuous erotic intensity."

Musicologists describe *Elektra* as one of the seminal works of Expressionism, in which the music is designed to express the innermost feelings of the composer and/or his characters. Distortion and exaggeration are used consciously to picture a kind of inner reality.

One general tip from an expert advisor for almost any Strauss opera: "Turn to the last fifteen or twenty minutes. Usually, although not always, these are monologues for the leading soprano and they contain the opera's most sumptuous sweep-you-off-your-feet music. *Salome*, *Elektra*, *Der Rosenkavalier*, *Arabella*, *Daphne*, and *Capriccio* all have outstanding final scenes."

MET PERFORMANCES

Eighty-four performances over fifteen seasons, from 1932 to 1994.

RECORDING

CD—Decca/London 417 345-2 (2). Birgit Nilsson, Marie Collier, Regina Resnik, Gerhard Stolze, Tom Krause. Vienna State Opera Chorus. Vienna Philharmonic Orchestra. Georg Solti. 1966.

A Set of Madwomen

The original Clytemnestra was Madame Ernestine Schumann-Heink, famous Austrian mezzo-soprano and Wagnerian singer who became an American citizen. *Kobbé* quotes her own reaction to the first production: "I will never sing the role again. It was frightful. We were a set of madwomen . . . There is nothing beyond *Elektra*. We have lived and reached the furthest boundaries in dramatic writing for the voice with Wagner. But Richard Strauss goes beyond him. His singing voices are lost. We have come to a full stop. I believe Strauss himself sees it."

VIDEO

Nilsson, Rysanek, Dunn, Nagy, McIntyre. Metropolitan Opera. German; English subtitles. Levine, conductor. 1980. PAR.

❧

Number 60. *Lakmé*
by Léo Delibes
February 21, 1836–January 16, 1891

Premiere at the Opéra-Comique, Paris, 1883. Text by Edmond Gondinet and Philippe Gille from Pierre Loti's 1880 novel Le mariage de Loti. *A lyric opera in three acts.*

Peter Il'yich Tchaikovsky preferred Léo Delibes to both Richard Wagner and Johannes Brahms. The significance of that information is uncertain, but it gives some counterbalance to the critics who characterize *Lakmé* as a work that pales alongside its contemporary *Carmen*.

Most operas pale alongside *Carmen*, so the comparison is misleading. Harry Truman pales alongside Thomas Jefferson but looks pretty good alongside a couple of dozen other presidents.

Tchaikovsky and Truman notwithstanding, *Lakmé* mostly is a nice bouquet. A serious opera, but a bouquet. The Great Opera Czar in the Sky doesn't forbid nice bouquets.

Delibes was a Frenchman, born in St. Germain-du-Val, a master craftsman of ballets and a composer of more operettas than opera. But he wrote three operas for Paris's Opéra-Comique, of which *Lakmé* is the main survivor.

The mysterious East was a favorite of late-nineteenth-century Romantic poets and composers. This is a story, set in India, about an English army lieutenant and an Indian girl. It is a "tragedy"; the heroine poisons herself in her lover's arms. But she knows she is being transported to eternal life, so we don't feel too bad about it all.

The King in Iowa

Delibes's first opera was a comedy, *Le roi l'a dit* (*The King Says So*), which premiered in Paris at the Opéra-Comique in May 1873. It had its United States premiere ninety-four years later in April 1967 at the University of Iowa, which is an interesting example of the diversity of opera production in twentieth-century America. The Met isn't everything, or even close to everything.

Lakmé is a French lyric opera, one of several Collection works of a type that appeared in France in the latter part of the nineteenth century as Meyerbeer's spectacular grand operas were disappearing. The term "lyric" is a cloudy one, but it is applied loosely to such French Collection operas as these:

Gounod's *Faust*, 1859; *Roméo et Juliette*, 1867
Thomas's *Mignon*, 1866
Bizet's *Carmen*, 1875 (although *Carmen* stands alone)
Massenet's *Manon*, 1884; *Werther*, 1892
Charpentier's *Louise*, 1900 (although this is sterner stuff)

To set the time clock, across the hills in Italy, Verdi's *Aida* was premiered in 1871, his late-in-life *Otello* in 1887, and his final *Falstaff* in 1893. Puccini's big operas came in the early 1900s.

The roots of French lyric opera are in the Italian bel canto operas of Donizetti, Rossini, and other Italian composers that were performed in Paris. Musicologists say lyric opera inevitably also was influenced by—even if it is less grand and spectacular than—Meyerbeer's *Les Huguenots*, 1836, and other extravagant works.

In general, the lyric operas also fit into the opéra comique category. We have seen that one big difference between grand opera and opéra comique is that the former was sung throughout and the latter used spoken dialogue. And we have seen that although these spoken-dialogue works began as comic opera, the form branched out to include lightish serious opera with happy endings and, finally, true tragedy with tragic endings.

Aside from *Lakmé*, Delibes is best known for his ballet music. It is no surprise that ballet genius Tchaikovsky was taken by him and influenced by him; Delibes's *Coppelia* and *Sylvia* are put by the musicologists in the very top ballet

LAKMÉ

drawer. One French critic wrote: "In a class of composition which until then had been neglected, he brought an elevation and vigor of style, a fullness of forms and a richness of instrumentation unknown before him . . . He introduced symphonic music into the ballet, at the same time remaining truly French and preserving in choreographic music that nimble elegance, that caressing grace, that spiritual vivacity, which are like wings of the dance."

"Elegance" and "grace," in ballet as in *Lakmé*.

Delibes studied at the Paris Conservatory and later became choirmaster at the Paris Opéra, where he established his reputation in ballet. He became a member of the Institut in 1884, was a professor at the Conservatory, and died in Paris in 1891.

Suicide Watch

Although a few operas in The Collection are deathless, not too many are. Here are some in which leading characters kill themselves.

Liu, by knife, to teach Turandot love.
Aida, buried alive in a crypt, to die with her man.
Ernani, by dagger, to honor contract with Silva.
Senta, by leaping into the sea for being falsely accused.
La Gioconda, by dagger, to escape sex with Barnaba.
Lakmé, by nibbling a poisoned leaf, to pacify gods and save her lover.
Edgardo, by dagger, on a guilt trip.
Cio-Cio-San, by father's dagger, of grief at losing husband and son.
Norma, on a funeral pyre, for vow violation, and Pollione, to join her.
Peter, at sea, hounded by villagers.
Lisa, by drowning in a canal, doubting Hermann, and Hermann, by
    stabbing, from guilt.
Brünnhilde, by immolation, with poor faithful Grane.
Narraboth, by sword, driven by teenager's lascivious conduct.
Samson, crushed by the temple to conquer his enemy.
Tosca, by a leap from Castel Sant'Angelo, as her lover is dead and to
    avoid execution.
Leonora, by poison, to save herself from bargain struck with Luna.
Dido, of grief at Aeneas's departure for Rome.
Werther, by borrowed pistol, love unfulfilled, to preserve his honor.
Romeo and Juliette, he by poison, thinking her dead, she by dagger,
    seeing him dying.
Atys, but attempt failed. Turned into a tree.
Otello, by hidden dagger, heart broken by tragic error.

KEYNOTE

Take a trip to the Orient. Absorb the Oriental atmosphere. Hear the famous "Bell Song." Don't eat the plants. If you don't like opera, try *Lakmé* music anyhow.

PLOT

India, the nineteenth century. Lakmé (soprano) is the attractive daughter of a Brahmin high priest named Nilakantha (bass-baritone), a man who hates the English invaders, in part because they won't let him practice his religion. She falls in love with Gérald (tenor), a British soldier, who is trespassing on the holy temple grounds, a crime for which the penalty is death. He returns her love, although he's engaged to an English woman called Ellen (soprano). Lakmé's father becomes aware of the trespassing when he sees Gérald's footprints, and when Lakmé refuses to identify the intruder, he tries trickery to learn who it is. He instructs Lakmé to sing the "Bell Song" at a religious festival attended by the soldiers, convinced that her unknown lover will react when he hears her perform. Gérald doesn't give himself away, but Lakmé does, fainting when she sees him.

Nilakantha stabs Gérald in the back, but the wound isn't serious and Lakmé hides him in the woods, where she treats him with herbs. Swearing eternal love to one another, they plan to drink to their pact with a love potion. While Lakmé is drawing it from a spring, Gérald's friend Frédéric (baritone) appears to advise him he is wanted at once by his regiment. Gérald is willing to give up Ellen for Lakmé, but he hears the marching footsteps and can't turn his back on his duty. Heartsick at this decision, Lakmé nibbles a poisonous leaf. Her father and his followers rush in to find them in one another's arms. Gérald begs Nilakantha to kill him, but Nilakantha pauses as Lakmé tells him Gérald has drunk from the sacred cup. She dies in her father's arms as he ecstatically sings that she's gone on to eternal life and Gérald cries out in anguish.

HIGHLIGHTS

Act I: The opening music, followed by the "Flower Duet" between Lakmé and her slave, Mallika (mezzo-soprano), "Dôme épais le jasmin." Gérald's famous "Fantaisie aux divins mensonges" ("Divinely fabricated fantasy"). Lakmé's aria, "Pourquoi dans les grands bois" ("Why in the deep forest?"). The duet between Lakmé and Gérald, "C'est le dieu de la jeunesse" ("The god of youth, of springtime").

Act II: Lakmé's "Bell Song," "Où va la jeune Hindoue?"—one of the most famous coloratura arias in all opera and largely responsible for *Lakmé*'s success and survival: "Where does the young Indian go when the moonlight plays in the tall mimosas? The wild beasts roar for joy, and the young girl defies them. She holds a rod where a small bell tinkles . . . Since that day, in the deep forest, the traveler sometimes hears the light sound of the tinkling bell." The love duet between Lakmé and Gérald, followed by her "Dans la forêt près de nous." Also, as expected from a master of ballet, the dance music from this act.

Act III: Gérald's "Ah! viens dans la forêt profonde," as he awakens in the forest and expresses his happiness.

COMMENTARY

It is sensuous, charming, elegant, Oriental, graceful, and colorful—not powerful, forceful, frightening, and dramatically intense.

The ending is similar to that of Meyerbeer's earlier *L'Africaine* and also suggests the final scene in Puccini's *Madama Butterfly*, which comes twenty-one years later.

Lakmé is a singers' opera to be enjoyed, not a psychological drama with a message. It's the type of French opera that took the middle ground between Offenbach's Parisian counterpart of Broadway musicals on the one hand and Meyerbeer's grand opera spectacle on the other.

By and large it is owned by well-known coloratura sopranos. New productions were put together for Australian soprano Joan Sutherland in Philadelphia in 1964, Seattle in 1967, and Sydney in 1976. Earlier great singers who made the role famous include Luisa Tetrazzini, Amelita Galli-Curci, Marcella Sembrich, and Lily Pons.

MET PERFORMANCES

Sixty-three productions over fifteen seasons, from 1892 to 1946.

RECORDING

CD—Decca/London 425 485 (2). Joan Sutherland, Alain Vanzo, Gabriel Bacquier, Jane Berbié. Monte Carlo Opera Chorus and Orchestra. Richard Bonynge. 1970.

VIDEO

Sutherland, Tourangeau, Wilden, Grant. Australian Opera. French; no subtitles but libretto included. Bonynge, conductor. 1976. HOME VISION.

Number 61. *La fille du régiment*
(The Daughter of the Regiment)
by Gaetano Donizetti
November 29, 1797–April 8, 1848

Premiere at the Opéra-Comique, Paris, 1840. Text by J. H. Vernoy de Saint-Georges and Jean-François Bayard. Two acts.

This is yet another type of Donizetti opera, his first one in French, written for the Opéra-Comique in Paris. It was astonishingly successful, with forty-four performances in 1840, more than six hundred in Paris alone by 1875, and more than one thousand by 1914. It is still staged today, quite frequently in Paris but not nearly so often elsewhere.

Initially intended for a premiere in Naples, *The Daughter of the Regiment* was turned down there because of political implications. But it's a fun-and-games opera, with good contrasts between polite society and life in the army.

The first U.S. performance was in New Orleans in 1843, only three years after the Paris premiere. Many French operas—and this was not only written in French but employed French-style spoken dialogue rather than Italian song-like recitative—went to New Orleans for their first U.S. performances.

Donizetti later prepared an Italian opera buffa version, cutting some numbers, adding others, and replacing the spoken dialogue with recitative.

For a fuller Donizetti background, see *Lucia di Lammermoor*, the Donizetti Warhorse, Number 15, and his other two Collection operas, *The Elixir of Love*, Number 35, and *Don Pasquale*, Number 56.

KEYNOTE

A light, graceful comedy of manners, light years from the tragic *Lucia di Lammermoor*. The army takes care of its own. Military tunes, sentiment and pathos.

PLOT

The mountains of the Swiss Tyrol, 1815. Marie (soprano), an orphan girl, has been found and adopted by a regiment of Napoleon's soldiers quartered in Switzerland. She is brought up by the regiment in general and in particular by a gruff but kind sergeant named Sulpice (bass). She falls in love with a Tyrolean peasant called Tonio (tenor), who saved her life when she nearly fell off a cliff. The regiment is willing to approve their marriage if Tonio joins their French army, which he does. Before the ceremony takes place, however, word arrives that Marie is not a homeless waif but the niece of the Marquise of Berkenfeld (mezzo-soprano), who orders her to leave the unstable environmental life with a regiment of soldiers and come home.

She dutifully does so, even though her heart is broken by leaving Tonio and her mind preoccupied by the love she has left behind. With the Marquise, she's being taught to sing classical music, which turns her off. Nevertheless, in the midst of it she and Sulpice, who has come to see her, burst into the "Song of the Regiment," the Twenty-First Regiment of Grenadiers. Now that's music. The Marquise is working to arrange a proper marriage for her with a fatuous young duke when Tonio arrives. Through bravery on the battlefield he has been promoted to captain, status enough so that he believes he can make a strong case for Marie's hand.

They decide to elope, but when the Marquise discloses that Marie really is not her niece but her illegitimate daughter, Marie can't go against her mother's wishes. Preparations go forward for her marriage to the duke, but when the wedding guests arrive, she sings of her life in the regiment, scandalizing the proper people of the proper court. This puts a damper on the upper crust wedding, but the Marquise, touched by what she has heard, saves the situation by agreeing to the marriage of Marie and Tonio. The opera ends with the chorus singing a patriotic salute to France.

Little Orphan Beverly

A strong case can be made that Beverly Sills was *the* Daughter of the Regiment. She writes of the role in *Beverly*, one of her two autobiographies:

"The *Daughter of the Regiment* that I did in Boston was vintage Sarah Caldwell, which is to say it was brilliant. Before my career was over, I'm sure I sang the role of Marie at least a hundred times, often in productions that cost a fortune, but none touched hers. The *Daughter of the Regiment* that we did in 1970 was the most spectacularly imaginative production of that opera I've ever seen . . .

"The *Daughter of the Regiment* is unlike most bel canto operas I sang. The soprano doesn't go mad. No heads are chopped off. No one commits suicide or murder or expires at the end. It's a very cheery piece.

"I decided to take the gaiety one step further: I played Marie as a lovable klutz, and I got away with it. The first time the audience saw me, my uniform was buttoned all wrong, my sleeves were two inches too short, I wore the ugliest knee-length boots you've ever seen—black with horrible gold buttons—and I had my hair frizzed out like Little Orphan Annie's."

HIGHLIGHTS

Act I: Tonio's "Ah! mes amis" with nine high C's and chorus. The best-known number is the "Song of the Regiment," "Chacun le sait, chacun le dit," first sung by Marie. At the close of the act, Marie's farewell to the camp, "Il faut partir," "I have to leave."

Act II: The ensemble at the end of the opera, the salute to France, "Salut à la France," another sterling piece.

COMMENTARY

The Daughter of the Regiment is sometimes presented as a farce, to the distress of Donizettians, who insist that it was written as a charming and elegant comedy of manners. Composer/critic Virgil Thomson had this to say in a review of a 1940 Met performance with Lily Pons: "It has gaiety and melodic eloquence. It is good Donizetti all right. Only it isn't the best Donizetti. It lacks occasions for the grander flights of feeling; and most especially for those magnificently theatrical and expressive concerted numbers (arranged in parts) that he could write as no other composer ever did, except Mozart."

Thomson isn't the only one to praise Donizetti's skill in writing for ensemble, a group of three or more, with or without choral backing. Other professionals also put him well above Bellini and at or near the level of Rossini in his ensemble mastery—a direct heir of Mozart and a foreshadower of Verdi.

Marie was a favorite role of Beverly Sills, who sang her more than one hundred times. The first Marquise de Berkenfeld in 1840 was Marie Julie Boulanger, who was to become the grandmother of Nadia Boulanger, French conductor, teacher, and friend of Stravinsky and Fauré, whose scores of gifted students included Aaron Copland and several other Americans. Other famous Maries include Marcella Sembrich, Jenny Lind, Adelina Patti, Luisa Tetrazzini, Lily Pons, and Joan Sutherland.

MET PERFORMANCES

Eighty-one performance in twelve different seasons, from 1902 to 1995.

RECORDING

CD—Decca/London 414 520-2 (2). Joan Sutherland, Luciano Pavarotti, Spiro Malas. Chorus and Orchestra of the Royal Opera House, Covent Garden. Richard Bonynge. 1967.

VIDEO

Sills, McDonald, Malas, Costa-Greenspon. Wolf-Trap Festival. English; no subtitles. Wendelken-Wilson, conductor. 1974. VAI (Video Artists International).

❧

Number 62. Ernani
by Giuseppe Verdi
October 10, 1813–January 27, 1901

Premiere at Teatro la Fenice, Venice, 1844. Text by Francesco Maria Piave, from Victor Hugo's 1830 tragedy Hernani. *Four acts.*

None of Verdi's four previous operas did as much as this one for his reputation.

But the man who made it possible didn't like the final product at all. Victor Hugo was a leader of the Romantic movement in France, arguably *the* leader, and he protested that his play's wonderful prose was lost in the opera's extravagance.

And his play, indeed, was first-rate, a mainstay of the repertory of the magnificent Sarah Bernhardt, first lady of the theater, and one she featured when she was touring America.

This raises some interesting questions about operas and the works from which they are drawn.

A great drama for the legitimate stage can be downgraded into an excessive melodrama for the operatic stage. But the melodrama then can become great art of a different nature when it's enhanced by music. So sometimes it's a toss-up.

William Shakespeare, Friedrich von Schiller, and Victor Hugo have been identified as Verdi's three favorite authors. In addition to *Ernani* from *Hernani*, Verdi drew *Rigoletto* from Hugo's *Le roi s'amuse*. (Another Hugo play, *Angelo, tyran de Padoue*, was the basis for Collection composer Ponchielli's *La Gioconda*.)

This fifth opera was Verdi's best so far, the first to win him fans outside Italy on the Continent, and the first to cross the English Channel into Britain. He called it a lyrical drama in four parts. It also was the first collaboration between Verdi and Francesco Maria Piave, a respectable librettist, although one not considered the equal of Arrigo Boito—not surprising, since few librettists are regarded as Boito's equal.

Piave (1810–76) and Verdi worked together closely to develop their characters, and he was Verdi's librettist of choice for many years. The composer was rough on nearly all his collaborators, once writing Piave: "There is no effect unless there is action, and so let's have as few words as possible." And again: "Brevity is never a fault." (Would that Richard Wagner, for all his musical genius, had been bitten by the same brevity bug.) Verdi received twelve thousand Italian lire for *Ernani*, out of which he had to pay Piave. There were no royalties nor any payment to the composer after the initial one.

See the Verdi Warhorses for more discussion.

KEYNOTE

Verdi's first big romantic drama and his most successful opera before the Big Three. He was thirty-one. Critics found it brutal, but customers like the costumes and color. Look for a grim avenger with his horn of death.

PLOT

Spain, 1519. Elvira (soprano), a highborn lady, is about to marry her elderly kinsman and guardian, Don Ruy Gomez de Silva (bass). Wedding plans are going forward, although actually she's in love with a chief of rebel bandit mountaineers named Ernani (tenor). He really isn't Ernani at all but rather Don

Juan de Aragon, who was exiled by the King of Castile, Don Carlos (baritone), after Carlos ordered the death of his father, the Duke of Segovia. Ernani's primary goal is to avenge that death. The King also is violently in love with Elvira, so this is more of a quadrangle than a triangle: Elvira and Ernani love one another, King Don Carlos loves Elvira, Silva loves Elvira, and she is about to marry him.

In Silva's castle, Elvira sings of her unhappiness. The King arrives, in disguise, and speaks of his love. He is interrupted by Ernani, and then by Silva, who is dismayed and outraged at finding two suitors in his castle wooing his fiancée. When the King identifies himself, Silva asks forgiveness for showing his anger, which the King grants because he's running for Holy Roman Emperor and looking for support.

In the next scene, the King's troops are pursuing Ernani, who comes to Silva's castle for refuge, disguised as a hooded pilgrim monk. When Silva introduces him to Elvira and he learns this is their wedding day and he has lost her, Ernani throws off his disguise, speaks of the high price on his head, and offers himself to Silva to be turned over to the King. Having guaranteed him the safety of his castle, Silva refuses. His honor is at stake, the guest here is the master, he never will surrender a guest. He leaves to post guards and returns to find Ernani and Elvira in each other's arms. Silva denounces Ernani's vile treachery and contemptible abuse of hospitality and vows to cut out his treacherous heart, but he still won't give him to the King—in part because of the sanctuary of his castle and in part because he wants a more personal revenge.

When the King arrives to demand Ernani, Silva resists, saying he will die first. When the King declares that he will have either Ernani or Elvira, Silva still refuses to violate his hospitality, and the King leaves with Elvira. Silva brings Ernani out of hiding and demands a duel, but Ernani won't fight so old a man. Despite their hatred for one another, the two agree to join forces against the King. But Silva won't abandon his revenge. As part of the deal, Ernani gives Silva a hunting horn and promises to kill himself if Silva ever sounds it. "Whenever you want Ernani dead, sound this horn. Ernani will die at once."

In the next act, the King reviews his misspent youth and tells himself he will do better if he's elected Emperor. Three cannon shots signal that he has won that crown and become the world's most powerful man. He orders life imprisonment for the commoners who have been conspiring against him and death for the nobles. But Elvira persuades him to be a statesman and, emulating the wisdom of the great Charlemagne, he forgives all the conspirators and even agrees to the marriage of Ernani and Elvira.

Their wedding celebration is under way and they are singing of their happiness when they hear the sound of the hunting horn. Silva appears to claim the life that is owed him. Elvira and Ernani ask for mercy, but Silva is relentless. "Whenever you want Ernani dead, sound the horn. Ernani will die at once," he quotes. Like any good Spanish nobleman who has doubled as a bandit chief, Ernani sticks to his word, stabs himself with a dagger, and dies in Elvira's arms.

HIGHLIGHTS

Act I: The opera's most famous aria, "Ernani! involami" ("Ernani, fly with me"), sung by Elvira. Although plans have been made for her to marry her guardian, she's in love with Ernani: "Ernani, take me away from this dreadful embrace. I will follow you to caves and moors and hostile shores." Also Silva's fine bass solo "Infelice! e tu credevi" ("Unhappy me; I believed you"): "She is as pure as a lily. Dishonor falls on my gray head. At my age, why does a young heart beat in my breast?"

Act II: A passionate duet between Ernani and Elvira, when he finds her about to be wed: "Ah, morir potessi adesso" ("Ah, it would be a blessing to die"): "Unfaithful woman, how dare you look at me . . . I still am true to you; I thought you had perished."

Act III: A soliloquy by Carlos as he ponders life, "Oh, de' verd'anni miei" ("Oh, for my youthful years again"). The closing finale, "O sommo Carlo" ("Oh noble Charles").

Act IV: Ernani's "Solingo, errante misero," a Pavarotti TV favorite, in which he sings about his sad life and chooses a dagger over a cup of poison. This leads into a final trio for Ernani, Silva, and Elvira.

COMMENTARY

At this time in his young career Verdi was turning out a lot of operas. The musicologists advise us that he was making no giant musical breakthroughs in any single one but was experimenting a little more with each and learning from each. In *Ernani*, he is credited with giving a new and expanded role to the chorus, making it one of the protagonists instead of a background bystander. And although musicologists complain that only the King is a well-developed, individual dramatic character, they say Verdi nonetheless is already showing improved dramatic insight overall.

Few say many very good things about the libretto, but the lovely thing is that it doesn't make a lot of difference. Watch a videotape of *Ernani*, and listen to the chorus and the duets, trios, and quartets. Lap up the easy-to-enjoy melody. You'll get caught up in the silly plot, even if you become a little confused by just what Silva might do next, and why he destroys Elvira's happiness if he really loves her (and doesn't have long to live anyhow), and why the bold and strong Ernani tries to weasel out of the deal near the end when push comes to shove, and why he never avenges the death of his father, even though that is one of his prime objectives throughout the opera.

The three men who desire the same woman do so in three different voices. Ernani is a tenor, Don Carlos a baritone, and Silva a bass.

MET PERFORMANCES
Eighty-one performances over eleven seasons, from 1903 to 1985.

RECORDING
CD—Angel/EMI CDC 47082 (3). Mirella Freni, Plácido Domingo, Renato Bruson, Nicolai Ghiaurov. La Scala Chorus and Orchestra. Riccardo Muti. 1982.

VIDEO
Pavarotti, Mitchell, Milnes. Metropolitan Opera. Italian; English subtitles. Levine, conductor. 1983. PAR.

Verდi's Tinto Variation

Verdi spoke often of the "tinto" of a particular piece, meaning the sound color but also extendable to the dramatic atmosphere—the unique "taste" of a work, the thing that makes one piece stick in the memory as different from any other.

One professional source has given me the following "tinto variations," for each of a dozen or so leading composers, including Massenet. It's a four-point scale, with 1 as high and 4 as low.

Alphabetically:

Bellini—3
Britten—2
Donizetti—4
Gluck—3
Handel—3
Janáček—2
Massenet—4
Monteverdi—2
Mozart—1
Puccini—2/3
Rossini—4
R. Strauss—2
Verdi—1/2
Wagner—1

Although this deals with "tinto" and is not meant to be good-better-best ranking of opera composers, a good case can be made that it comes out pretty close.

∾

Number 63. *The Bartered Bride*
by Bedřich Smetana
March 2, 1824–May 12, 1884

Premiere at the National Theatre, Prague, 1866. Text by Karel Sabina. Three acts.
Now this one is fun.

It's the most fun when seen in Prague, where it's a national institution and appears almost as frequently as the "NBC Nightly News" in the United States.

Granted, Prague isn't convenient for opera lovers in Salt Lake City.

The Bartered Bride, or *Prodaná nevěsta*, is the most famous Czech opera and one of the finest folk operas from any country. It has comedy, color, sentiment, and gaiety. It gives pleasure. It has spirited polkas and choruses singing the praises of beer. The music is engaging and delightful. You have to be a real grinch not to like it.

In Prague and elsewhere in the Czech Republic, Bedřich Smetana is the hero of the people. He's the founder of modern Czech music, the first major nationalist composer of Bohemia, and the leading nineteenth-century figure of Czech opera. In Bohemia, as elsewhere in mid-nineteenth-century Europe, opera expressed the nationalism of the people. His operas reflected and cultivated that spirit.

Smetana was a generation older than Antonín Dvořák (*Rusalka*, 1901, see the Twentieth-century European Package) and thirty years older than Leoš Janáček (*Jenůfa*, 1904, Number 78).

Like both of those artists, Smetana was an all-around classical composer, not an opera specialist. Many readers will be familiar with the music of his *Moldau*, one of six tone poems that make up a piece called *Má Vlast* (*My Fatherland*), even if they don't recognize it by title and composer. The Moldau is a translation of "Vltava," the river that runs through Prague. A string quartet, *Out of My Life*, and two duets for violin and piano called *From My Homeland* also are frequently heard on classical radio. There is no easier-to-hear classical music.

Smetana was born in 1824 in Litomyšl, Bohemia, the son of a brewmaster. A child prodigy, he played both piano and violin in public concerts at five years old and was composing at eleven. After education in Prague and Pilsen, he began serious composition. In a few years he became concertmaster of an orchestra belonging to ex-Emperor Ferdinand I of Austria. He sympathized with the patriots in the abortive 1848 revolution in Prague and migrated to Sweden, where he worked as teacher, conductor, and composer.

In 1862 he returned home and became involved with the Prague Provisional Theatre, which was opened that year as a home for Bohemian music. Smetana's first opera for it was *The Brandenburgers in Bohemia* and the second, in 1866, was *The Bartered Bride*, which became popular gradually and has remained popular ever since. Although Smetana did not begin writing operas until late in his career, he completed eight in all.

A Mere Trifle

At a banquet celebrating the one hundredth performance of *The Bartered Bride*, Smetana said: "Actually, [it is] a mere trifle. I composed it not from ambition but from defiance, because after *The Brandenburgers* [*of Bohemia*] people declared I was a Wagnerite and couldn't do anything in the lighter, national style."

The one thousandth performance in Prague was in 1927.

I can't recommend a trip to New York for this opera since my declared position is that the only just cause for visiting that wasteland is to see a grandchild, and only that on rare occasions. But do yourself a favor for which you will be forever grateful. Go to Prague, watch the dusk fall on the castle across the Moldau, and see *The Bartered Bride*. If you hurry, the upper balcony still will cost only three or four dollars.

Suffering from syphilis and other ailments, Smetana grew deaf as he aged, became mentally ill, and lost both his memory and his speech. Like classical great Robert Schumann, he spent his last years in an asylum, where he died in 1884.

The Bartered Bride was first presented in the United States at the Metropolitan in 1909, in German, conducted by another classical great, Gustav Mahler.

KEYNOTE

The Czechs' favorite opera and their only one before Leoš Janáček to win international recognition. Melody, rhythm, comedy, and the dance music of the people. Plan a vacation to Prague.

PLOT

Bohemia, the late nineteenth century. Vašek (tenor) is the silly, not-too-bright son of a wealthy landowner named Mícha (bass). Mařenka (soprano) is a local young woman who is in love with a stranger in the village named Jeník (tenor), who has no money and an unexplained background. Mařenka's parents plan for her to marry Vašek because they are obligated to Mícha. To help consummate the deal and pick up his fee, Kečal (bass), the overly enthusiastic marriage broker, offers Jeník a bribe of three hundred gulden to renounce Mařenka. Jeník accepts the money but insists that their contract specify that he will retire from the field only if Mařenka marries a son of Mícha.

Bedřich Smetana

Everyone rejoices except Mařenka, who's considerably put out by Jeník's apparent desertion of her. But the opera ends happily when all learn that Jeník is a long-lost son of Mícha by a first marriage and thus qualifies for Mařenka's hand. He gets Mařenka, Mařenka gets him, and together they get the three hundred gulden. No one dies, no one murders his or her mother, and it's okay in Prague to come back tomorrow night, pay another three or four dollars, and see it again.

HIGHLIGHTS

The Overture, well known, which often is played as a concert piece.

Act I: The duet between Mařenka and Jeník, "Jako matka," in which they exchange pledges of eternal love. The spirited and eye-catching polka danced by the villagers at the act's close.

Act II: The peasant dance (a "furiant") as the villagers enter the inn.

Act III: The dance of the comedians when the circus troupe appears to entertain the villagers. A slow sextet, "Rozmysli si, Mařenko," which sings of Mařenka, her predicament and her choice of a husband.

COMMENTARY

This opera is alluringly fresh, warm, frank, and genially humorous. It is Czech from beginning to end. Some of the dances are polka-fast, others typical of Czech slow dances. In productions in the Czech Republic, special attention is paid to the authenticity of scenery and costumes.

Analysts note that other Smetana operas have more complicated music, with roots more distant from a folk base, but even in these he is never far from home.

A biographer, Paul Stefan, catches the flavor. He writes that Smetana's music sings of the Bohemia of old—its woods, plains, villages, romantic hills, and old legends, its great past and even its future. He adds: "It is all one great pageant of song and dance—dancing to native rhythms of astounding variety, singing to melodies of unique beauty, such as his homeland had never achieved before."

The opera was first shown in this country in Chicago, in Czech, in 1893.

Be neither Borrower nor Lender

When is folk music original and when is it stolen from the folk? British composer Ralph Vaughan Williams, a master of English folk music who sometimes was accused of leaning too heavily on tunes from the past, spoke to that point:

"Smetana's debt to his own national music was one of the best kind: unconscious. He did not, indeed, 'borrow'; he carried on an age-long tradition, not of set purpose, but because he could no more avoid speaking his own musical language than he could help breathing his native air."

RECORDING

CD—Suphraphon Dig. 10 3511-2 (3). Gabriela Beňačková, Jana Jonášová, Marie Veselá-Kabeláčová, Marie Mrázová, Peter Dvorsky, Miroslav Kopp, Alfred Hampel, Jindřich Jindrák, Richard Novák, Jaroslav Horáček, Karel Hanuš. Czech Philharmonic Chorus and Orchestra. Zdeněk Košler. (1980–1981).

MET PERFORMANCES

Seventy-five performances over fourteen seasons, from 1909 to 1978. Eight performances are scheduled for the 1996–97 season.

∾

Number 64. *Macbeth*
by Giuseppe Verdi
October 10, 1813–January 27, 1901

Premiere at the Teatro alla Pergola, Florence, 1847. Text by Francesco Maria Piave from William Shakespeare's 1606 drama. Four acts.

The composer nearly went ape. "No, by heavens, no!"

It wasn't just that *Macbeth* didn't do well during his lifetime. After uneven performances in New York in 1850 and Dublin in 1859, and a revision for a Paris opening in 1865, critics were still cool. The problem, some said, was that Verdi neither knew nor understood Shakespeare.

That was like saying John and Bobby Kennedy didn't know or understand politics.

"I may not have rendered *Macbeth* well," Verdi wrote angrily, "but that I do not know, do not understand and feel Shakespeare, no, by heavens, no! He is one of my very special poets, and I have had him in my hands from my earliest youth, and I read and re-read him continually."

This early Verdi opera was his first based on Shakespeare and came many years before his two Shakespearean triumphs, *Otello* and *Falstaff*.

Critics, then as now, differed. Some saw *Macbeth* as representing the end of the bel canto period, the end of the focus on set arias and ensembles, the end of an era, the end of what they cherished as "real" opera—the important entertainment that Italy loved most. Others thought the end came two years later with another of the best of Verdi's earlier operas, *Luisa Miller*, one of his three works based on the literature of German poet, playwright, and critic Friedrich von Schiller.

It's not surprising that different analysts choose different operas from this period of Verdi's life as the ones most illustrating him moving away from the conventional opera of the past. Logically, he advanced gradually as he became more experienced and more successful.

The important point is that from the late 1840s on he steadily paid more and more attention to drama and to his characters' psychological aspects. Earlier, most had been larger-than-life; now they were to become more human-sized.

See the Verdi Warhorses for more about his work.

KEYNOTE

The last Collection work before the Big Three, favored more by Verdi than by critics or public. Still: Verdi theater, Verdi character portrayal, Verdi patriotism.

Beauty Need Not Apply

Verdi comments to Salvatore Cammararo, who was producing *Macbeth* in Naples, on the singer chosen for the role of Lady Macbeth:

"I am astonished that she should have undertaken the part . . . I must say her qualities are too fine for this role. This may sound absurd, but Madame Tadolini is a handsome woman with a beautiful face, and I want Lady Macbeth to be ugly and evil. Madame Tadolini sings to perfection, and I don't want Lady Macbeth to sing at all. Madame Tadolini has a wonderful voice, clear, flexible and strong, while Lady Macbeth's voice should be hard, stifled and dark."

This rebellion against the Italian bel canto approach to opera upset not only some critics but also some of the public.

PLOT

Set in Scotland, chiefly in Macbeth's castle. Macbeth (baritone) and Banquo (bass) are generals in the army of Duncan, King of Scotland (silent). As they return home from battle they run into a coven of witches who predict that Macbeth will be king and Banquo the father of future kings. Home in the castle, when Lady Macbeth (soprano) reads a letter telling her of the prophecy, she decides it's unlikely to come true unless she helps it. Finding that Duncan will be coming home with Macbeth, she feels the time for her to prompt Macbeth is now. She persuades him that Duncan must be killed, and that night the vision of a bloody dagger helps lead Macbeth to do the deed. He's conscience-stricken; Macduff (tenor), a Scottish nobleman, and Banquo discover the body.

Macbeth now is king, Duncan's son Malcolm (tenor) has fled to England, and Macbeth and his wife decide Banquo's son, Fleance (silent), must be killed to stop the rest of the witches' prophecy from coming true. Their assassins kill Banquo, but Fleance escapes. In the banquet hall, Macbeth is advised of the assassination, but Banquo's ghost appears to take his place at the table. Distraught, Macbeth flees the castle. Later he joins the witches in their cavern, where they are brewing potions and casting spells. He's told to beware of Macduff but also to fear no man born of woman. He won't be harmed unless Birnam Wood "moves against him." But he sees apparitions of eight kings and decides that to be safe he must kill Macduff and his family.

Act IV takes place in a wild area, Birnam Wood, on the border of England and Scotland. Scots bewail what has happened to their country under Macbeth, and Macduff bewails the deaths of his wife and children, murdered by Macbeth's minions. Back in the castle, a sleepwalking Lady Macbeth talks about all the murders. Later, Macbeth hears that his wife has died and that an army is approaching from Birnam Wood. It's led by Macduff, who then discloses that he was taken prematurely from his mother's womb and thus was not "born of woman." Macbeth acknowledges defeat, is killed, and Malcolm is crowned king.

HIGHLIGHTS

Macbeth has been called an "instrumental" opera rather than a "singer's opera," but keep your ears open for the witches. Two scenes stand out, both also important in Shakespeare:

Act I: The deed-is-done scene, including the duet between Macbeth and Lady Macbeth as he appears from Duncan's chamber holding a dagger.

Act IV: The sleepwalking scene, with Lady Macbeth murmuring "Una macchia" (a spot) against a mood-setting orchestra. A melancholy and despairing Macbeth prepares to meet his enemies: "Pietà, rispetto, amore." He fears he will die without pity, respect, or love but will instead be cursed and hated.

COMMENTARY

Dramatically, Verdi and Piave made Lady Macbeth the central figure, more important than Macbeth and the witches. The role of Malcolm is cut way back from the play and the part of Macduff reduced somewhat. But Verdi had ordered Piave to keep as much as possible of the tone of Shakespeare's work, and he involved himself deeply in writing the text—more deeply, biographers say, than in any prior work.

In *The Experience of Opera*, Professor Paul Henry Lang writes that the Florence opera house where *Macbeth* was premiered had never before been confronted with the musical, technical, and dramatic demands now made upon it. "For this is real music drama," he writes. "One admires the assured competence with which the young composer, whose operas immediately preceding this Shakespearean essay were quite conventional, is able to fill his hearers' minds with an eerie, strongly charged atmosphere of psychologically penetrating drama. And there are elements in *Macbeth* that become of decisive influence for the future."

Another critical assessment holds that *Macbeth* was a monumental step forward musically but still quite "uneven" as dramatic art. Even "uneven" Verdi still turns out to be middling good opera.

MET PERFORMANCES

Eighty-one performances over nine seasons, from 1959 to 1988.

RECORDING

CD—Angel/EMI CMS7 64339-2 (2). Fiorenza Cossotto, José Carreras, Sherrill Milnes, Ruggero Raimondi. Ambrosian Opera Chorus. New Philharmonia Orchestra. Riccardo Muti. 1976.

VIDEO

Paskalis, Barstow, Morris. Glyndebourne Festival Opera. Pritchard, conductor. 1972. VAI.

❧

Number 65. *Eugene Onegin*
Peter Il'yich Tchaikovsky
May 7, 1840–November 6, 1893

Premiere in Moscow, 1879. Text by K. S. Shilovsky and the composer from Alexander Pushkin's 1831 poem. Three acts.

Peter Il'yich Tchaikovsky is Russia's greatest classical composer.

He is best known for three ballets, *Sleeping Beauty*, *Swan Lake*, and *The Nutcracker*, and for three symphonies, Nos. 4 in F Minor, 5 in E Minor, and especially 6 in B Minor, the *Pathétique*.

Keyboard devotees would single out a piano concerto you would recognize by sound, No. 1 in B flat minor. Or does his fame come from the Violin Concerto in D, one of music's most successful?

For all of these things, he is among classical music's top geniuses. Not Bach, Mozart, or Beethoven, but close.

He admired Mozart and many other Western European composers, and was influenced by them. In general, this made him more supple than many other Russians. He is not Mussorgsky, and his operas don't sound like *Boris Godunov*.

Although Tchaikovsky is less recognized for opera than for other music, the truth is that he spent a good part of his career writing operas, composing more of them than the combined total of the three ballets, the three famous symphonies, the piano and violin concertos—and the cannon-sounding *1812 Overture* thrown in for good measure.

He wrote ten in all, two of which are in The Collection:

Eugene Onegin (Number 65), his masterpiece
Pique Dame (The Queen of Spades) (Number 66), also still in today's repertory
    more than one hundred years after its premiere

Outside Russia, these works aren't considered the equal of Verdi, Wagner, or Mozart. Nor are they as popular as Puccini and the best of Richard Strauss or Bizet. Both works, in fact, were failures when first produced, and for years most books on classical composers paid little attention to them. On my desk is a twelve-page essay on Tchaikovsky written only fifty years ago which devotes one sentence to his work in this field: "Of the operas, we have to discard nearly all but *Eugene Onegin* and perhaps *Pique Dame*." That's it. Some other mid-twentieth-century excellent volumes on classical music don't mention them at all.

> ### *Moscow's Favorite*
>
> From available figures, the most popular opera in Moscow is *Eugene Onegin*. Two Western operas, Verdi's *La traviata* and *Rigoletto*, come next, followed by *Prince Igor*, *The Queen of Spades*, and Bizet's *Carmen*, and then other Russian works. In St. Petersburg, *La traviata*, *The Barber of Seville*, *Rigoletto*, *Madama Butterfly*, and *Tosca* all are in the Top 10.

The problem, not exclusively Tchaikovsky's, is that the operas of some classical music masters are overwhelmed by the success and popularity of their nonoperatic works. Except for opera bugs, few music lovers outside of Russia pay attention to *Eugene Onegin* when the *Pathétique* Symphony and the piano concerto are out there, both near the top of the charts. Similarly, everyone has heard of Beethoven, but how many have heard of *Fidelio*?

Tchaikovsky's first completed opera was *The Voyevoda*, 1869, later abandoned, although parts were used elsewhere. He then wrote *Undine* but destroyed it after it was rejected by the St. Petersburg Imperial Theatre. His first surviving complete opera is *The Oprichnik*, 1874, which contains a good bit of music from *The Voyevoda*.

Always a traveling man, Tchaikovsky heard *Carmen* in Paris in 1876 and then attended the opening of Wagner's Bayreuth Festival in Germany. He came home to write *Kuznets Vakula (Vakula the Smith)* recognized today as a fresh and delightful work, if considerably shy of a masterpiece.

What *is* called a masterpiece, despite its dramatic flaws, is his next work, *Eugene Onegin*, which premiered in 1879. In describing it, the professionals use words like "subtle" and "sensitive." It was drawn from a poem by Alexander Pushkin, 1799–1837, famous Russian Romantic revolutionary poet whose works also include *The Queen of Spades* and the basis for Mussorgsky's mighty *Boris Godunov*.

Tchaikovsky next turned away from Russian subjects for *The Maid of Orleans (Joan of Arc)*, 1881, a grand opera in the Meyerbeerian Parisian mold. He went back to Russian themes with *Mazeppa*, which he followed in 1887 with *The Sorceress* and in 1890 by *The Queen of Spades*. His last opera was the one-act *Yolanta* in 1892, a year before he died at only fifty-three.

His brother, Modest, described how the composer felt about opera when he was a young man: "Peter Il'yich at that time preferred operatic music to symphonic and not only took little interest in the latter but even regarded it somewhat disdainfully."

The problem that some critics find with Tchaikovsky—symphony, concerto, or opera—is that he wrote too much from his heart and not enough from his head. No dummy, he anticipated this criticism long before it was voiced. In an assessment of his own work, he said: "Medieval dukes and knights and ladies capture my imagination but not my heart, and where the heart is not touched there can't be any music." He did, however, identify strongly with the heroine of *Eugene Onegin*, a drama of unfulfilled love.

The intellectuals are critical because he is not cerebral enough and wrote too much from the heart. The composer and his vast public want it that way. The intellectuals say it makes his compositions too sentimental, too emotional, too mushy. The public says Right On.

Nowadays, as opposed to fifty or seventy-five years ago, some of the elitist critics—faced on the one hand by the musicians who love to perform his work and on the other by the adoring public that loves to hear it—have moved far enough so that they only deny that he was among the "supremely great" composers of instrumental music.

Weeping Willow

The famous Polish harpsichordist Wanda Landowska on Tchaikovsky: "He cries louder than any suffering could justify."

But she was not much kinder to Stravinsky, at the other end of the spectrum, characterizing his work as "an air-conditioned room compared to the normal temperature of the street." And also: "The sumptuousness of Stravinsky dazzles me, but rarely gives me happiness."

Born in 1840, Tchaikovsky was the son of a foundry director in Votkinsk. It was not a musical family, and he showed no early signs that he was to become Russia's first internationally acclaimed composer. The family moved to St. Petersburg when he was ten. Later he took up law, and at nineteen he entered the Ministry of Justice as a clerk. He had taken piano lessons for several years and played competently but without great talent.

At twenty-one, however, bored at his job (the Ministry of Justice in 1860 Russia could be fun?), he began seriously studying musical theory. Two years later, his father dead and the family broke, he entered the Russian Musical Society (which was to become the St. Petersburg Conservatory), where he encountered Anton Rubinstein, famed pianist and composer, and his brother Nicholas. Through Nicholas, he got a job teaching harmony at the Moscow Conservatory, where he remained for eleven years.

Meanwhile, of course, he was composing.

Many describe him as a sensitive poet who spoke from the heart. He was melancholy, tormented by doubts of his own ability, nervous, diffident—rarely a Happy Camper. He once wrote a friend: "There was a time when I was so possessed by the fear of mankind that I became almost insane." He had a tragic short marriage, entered into despite his awareness of his own homosexuality, after which he attempted suicide by throwing himself into a cold river so as to catch pneumonia. Tragic though his action was, one can't deny that it was bizarre. Death-by-self-inflicted-pneumonia would not be the personal choice of many of us.

His biographers, however, emphasize that for the most part he lived a reasonably normal life despite his abundant sensitivity—taking long constitutional walks, growing his flowers, composing his music, conducting, and teaching. One musicologist put it neatly: "Tchaikovsky, the so-called neurotic, was by no means unacquainted with peace."

The other Collection Russian operas are Mussorgsky's *Boris Godunov*, Rimsky-Korsakov's *The Golden Cockerel*, and Borodin's *Prince Igor*. Sergei Prokofiev, Dmitri Shostakovich, and Igor Stravinsky are represented in the Twentieth-century European Package. Mikhail Glinka, introduced in Chapter Five, was the first prominent Russian opera composer.

KEYNOTE

The Tchaikovsky theatrical masterwork. A story of tragic humanitarianism and frustrated love. Russian folk music and Russian life, city and country. Sad, emotional, lyrical Tchaikovsky, dealing here with characters as well as instruments.

PLOT

A country estate near St. Petersburg, eighteenth century. Tatiana (or Tatyana) (soprano) is the young and impressionable daughter of Madame Larina (mezzo-soprano) who falls in love with Onegin (baritone), a friend of her sister Olga's (contralto) fiancée, Lenski (tenor). In the "Letter Scene," one of the opera's most famous moments, Tatiana spends a long night writing Onegin a passionate letter about her feelings. In the garden the next day, he calmly advises her that she shouldn't think of romance and marriage. He regards her as a sister, no more. She is humiliated.

In the next scene, Tatiana's birthday is being celebrated at a party. A well-known waltz is played. Onegin and Lenski quarrel when Onegin flirts with Olga. The next morning they duel and Lenski is killed.

Six years pass. Onegin, who has been abroad, returns to St. Petersburg and attends a party being held at the palace of Prince Gremin (bass), who has married Tatiana. There Onegin sees Tatiana, speaks with her, and now realizes that he's in love with her. After he writes, asking to see her, they meet in her boudoir and he begs her to leave with him. Although passionate and tempted, she reminds him of her duty to her husband, orders him to leave, and rushes from the room. He has lost her forever and is in anguish.

Tchaikovsky on Pushkin

Tchaikovsky was a great admirer of the poet Alexander Pushkin, whose works he used for three operas, including *Eugene Onegin* and *The Queen of Spades*.

"By the power of his genius," Tchaikovsky wrote, "[Pushkin] very often breaks out of the narrow sphere of poetry into the infinite space of music. His words are more than mere words. Over and above his literal meaning, the verse itself possesses something that pierces to the depths of one's soul. And that something is Music."

HIGHLIGHTS

Act I: Lenski's aria and the interwoven duets between the two couples. The "Letter Scene," from which much of the opera's music develops.

Act II: The famous waltz scene and its ability to "zoom in" on one small group and then another within the whole. Lenski's farewell-to-life aria, considered by some the greatest tenor scene in Russian opera.

Act III: The polonaise, for the ballet at the ball (often played in concert halls). Onegin's repeat of the song Tatiana sings in the "Letter Scene."

Act III Ball of Eugene Onegin, *presented by the Bolshoi Opera at the Metropolitan Opera, 1991*

COMMENTARY

Keep your eye on Tatiana, the seventeen-year-old heroine who captured Tchaikovsky's heart.

Although the characterization of her is Tchaikovsky's best, some analysts complain that she still isn't defined sharply enough. So the opera's popularity outside Russia has been held down, though it's in the international repertories and, indeed, in the 1996–97 Metropolitan Opera season.

Tchaikovsky was aware of its flaws. "It is true that the work is deficient in theatrical opportunities," he said, "but the wealth of poetry, the humanity and the simplicity of the story . . . will compensate for what is lacking in other respects."

One problem was that Pushkin's work was a poem, not a play, and thus a work that was itself not theatrically dramatic.

Analysts have the following negative comments about Tchaikovsky's operas in general, although they say all observations apply less to *Eugene Onegin* (and to *Pique Dame*) than to the others:

- "Insufficient musical characterization." When the individual characters are presented, the music only partially portrays their suffering, love, jealousy, and defeat or triumph. (Tchaikovsky, typically emotional, told us where he stood with his characters: "Tatiana had become for me a living person in living surroundings. I loved Tatiana, and was terribly indignant with Onegin, who seemed to me a cold heartless coxcomb.")
- "Dominance of orchestra over voice." The orchestra says too much; not enough is left for the singers. Some critics blame Wagner's influence.
- "Dramatic effect lost to lyrical melody." Tchaikovsky—like Gounod in *Faust*—is charged with failing to make the most of the potential drama. Even in *Eugene Onegin*, his best work, some analysts complain that he does not make enough of the big emotional scenes, in part because he couldn't sympathize with Onegin, who comes across as a dandified cold fish incapable of returning Tatiana's passion.

But those are the blemishes. Tchaikovsky remains the preeminent Russian operatic composer and his technical virtuosity was supreme, even if some Westerners have problems with his Russian realism. Defenders note that Onegin's dull character is inherent in the Pushkin poem, and some commend the composer, especially in *Eugene Onegin*, for being less emotional than he was in many of his orchestral works. And everyone points to his graceful melodies and imaginative orchestration.

My recommendation: Say to yourself, "This drama is flawed" . . . and then just listen to the magnificent, colorful music.

One of the most famous Tatianas was Galina Vishnevskaya, wife of Mstislav Rostropovich, great cellist and former longtime conductor of the National Symphony Orchestra. He conducted the Bolshoi Theatre Chorus and

Orchestra in a production recorded in 1970, and Boris Khaikin directed a 1956 production in which she was featured.

MET PERFORMANCES
One hundred and three performances in eleven seasons, from 1920 to 1993. Nine performances are scheduled for the 1996–97 season.

RECORDING
CD—Deutsche Grammophon 423 959-2 (2). Mirella Freni, Anne Sofie von Otter, Neil Shicoff, Thomas Allen, Paata Burchuladze. Leipzig Radio Chorus and Dresden State Orchestra. James Levine. 1987.

VIDEO
Leiferkus, Novikova, Marusin. Kirov Opera. Russian; English subtitles. Temirkanov, conductor. 1984. KULTUR.

Number 66. *Pique Dame (The Queen of Spades)*
by Peter Il'yich Tchaikovsky
May 7, 1840–November 6, 1893

Premiere at the Maryinsky Theatre, St. Petersburg, 1890. Text by the composer's brother, Modest Tchaikovsky, from Alexander Pushkin's 1833 story. Three acts.

If you're looking for tunes to sing in the shower, this is not your opera. But if you can feel for a man obsessed, empathize with a deranged hero, and relate to an atmosphere of hallucination, it's worth a shot.

A drama about love gone wrong and the secret of three cards, *The Queen of Spades* was written in 126 days. It is Tchaikovsky's most popular opera except for *Eugene Onegin* and regarded generally as his best except for that more famous work (with some writers rating this one technically superior).

It is one of my second-tier favorites, although not many in the Western world seem to have taken it to their hearts as they do Verdi and Puccini.

A good place to look for the great Russian composer's approach to opera is in his own writings. For many years he carried on a strange relationship in a long exchange of letters with a wealthy Russian aristocrat named Nadezhda von Meck, a widow with eleven children and music lover extraordinaire. She subsidized him for life on the condition that they never meet. It worked for both of them: He had no worries about money; she had her private channel to a great composer. Although the letters are sometimes personal, nowhere in them does Tchaikovsky mention his homosexuality, although in those days homosexuality was readily tolerated in aristocratic circles. They are recommended reading for all who are uncouth enough to love Tchaikovsky's music, which is "too lush" and "too emotional" for some critics.

He wrote in 1879: "In composing an opera, the author must constantly think of the stage, i.e., not forget that the theatre needs not only melodies and harmonies but action to hold the attention of the theatre goer who has come to hear *and* see—finally, that the style of theatre music must correspond to the style of scene-painting: simple, clear and colorful. Just as a picture by Meissonier [French painter, 1815–1891] would lose all its charm if it were put on the stage, so would rich music, full of harmonic subtleties, lose a great deal in the theatre, for there the listener needs sharply drawn melodies against a transparent harmonic background. In my *Voyevoda* [an early opera], however, I was mainly concerned with filigree work and quite forgot the stage."

He continued, discussing pluses and minuses of opera versus instrumental composition: "The stage often paralyzes the composer's musical inspiration, so that symphonic and chamber music stand far higher than operatic music. A symphony or sonata imposes on me no limitations; on the other hand opera possesses the advantage that it gives the possibility to speak in the musical language of the masses. An opera may be given forty times in one season; a symphony perhaps once in ten years."

Tchaikovsky on Opera

Tchaikovsky's words five years before *The Queen of Spades* on the hold opera had on him: "To refrain from writing operas is, in its way, heroism. I don't possess this heroism and the stage with all its tawdry brilliance none the less attracts me."

In another assessment of opera's weaknesses and strengths, he told Madame Von Meck: "I am pleased by your supercilious attitude to opera, you are right in disapproving this really *false type of art*. But there is something irrepressible that attracts all composers to opera; it is that it alone gives you the means to communicate with the masses of the public ... It isn't just a matter of pursuing external effects, but of choosing subjects of artistic value, interesting, and touching the quick."

In this country, and in these times, we scarcely think of opera as a medium of mass communication, but if one goes back one hundred years to czarist Russia the concept makes good sense. It also is interesting to read that Tchaikovsky, unlike several gifted twentieth-century composers, was concerned with what interested the theatergoer.

The Met gave five performances in 1996, its first since 1972.

KEYNOTE

The most dramatic of Tchaikovsky's operas and the best balanced between music and drama. His own favorite. Learn the secret of the three cards at your own risk.

Menotti on Tchaikovsky

Gian Carlo Menotti, Italian-American composer and stage director, on *The Queen of Spades*: "The most difficult thing for a composer is to write an opera in which the music maintains its lyrical importance without stopping the action. Tchaikovsky comes very near it. He produced some of the most dramatic music that the opera literature has."

PLOT

St. Petersburg, end of the eighteenth century. In the park, children play and boys pretend they are soldiers. Two officers of the guard, Tchekalinsky (tenor) and Sourin (bass), discuss the peculiar demeanor and the gambling habits of their friend Hermann (tenor). He enters and advises his friend Count Tomsky (baritone) that he has fallen in love with a woman—an angel from heaven—even though he hasn't met her, doesn't know her name, and doesn't want to know it for fear he'll find she's already taken. When she enters the park he is distraught to learn that she is Lisa (soprano), fiancée of Prince Yeletsky (baritone) and granddaughter of the Countess (mezzo-soprano). Lisa has seen him before and is affected by seeing him again; the Countess says his looks scare her.

Tomsky tells the others that the Countess was once a famously successful card player, obsessed with gambling, to whom a male admirer in Paris had taught the secret of the "three cards" as a reward for one rendezvous in bed with her. Thereafter she was known as the Queen of Spades. She had passed on the secret to her husband and to one other lover, but had been told by a ghost that she would die if she revealed it to a third man. Alone in a thunderstorm, Hermann vows never to give up hope. He will have Lisa or die, and he also will have the secret of the three cards.

In her bedroom, Lisa longs for Hermann, though they never have met. Hermann visits her, hides when the Countess enters, and then declares his love. She surrenders to him as the curtain falls.

In Act II, after a masked ball, Lisa slips Hermann a key to her apartment, telling him to come through her grandmother's bedroom and then through a secret door behind a portrait of the Countess. In the next scene Hermann enters the Countess's bedroom, his mind set on discovering the secret of the three cards. He hides when she and her maids appear, not showing himself until she is alone. He tells her not to be frightened and begs for the secret of the three cards. She attempts to confront him but dies of shock when he draws his pistol to threaten her. Obsessed by love though he is, Hermann's first thought is that the secret of the cards has died with her. Hearing the noise, Lisa enters. After listening to Hermann, she protests that he has come not to see her but to pry the secret from her grandmother. Crying that she is ruined, she orders him from the house.

Hermann and Lisa are later reconciled, and the Countess's ghost appears before Hermann to tell him the secret of the three cards. The winning sequence is: Three . . . Seven . . . Ace. He leaves Lisa only long enough to go to the casino and use the secret to win money for them, but she misunderstands his motives, thinks he has gone mad, again decides that he's using her, and, in despair, throws herself to her death in the canal. Meanwhile, Hermann is in the casino, playing for huge stakes. He wins with the three and then again with the seven. Prince Yeletsky bets against him, and, without looking at it, Hermann proclaims the next card to be an ace. Instead it's the queen of spades, and he loses everything. When the Countess's ghost reappears, Hermann is so tortured, frightened, and distraught that he stabs himself, begging the Prince for forgiveness as he dies.

HIGHLIGHTS

Act I: Hermann's aria about Lisa, as he declares his love in her room, and the following duet.

Act II: The dramatic scene in the Countess's bedroom.

Act III: Lisa's aria at the canal as she waits for Hermann, the highest drama of the opera. Also Hermann's aria to Lisa here, singing of their future together.

COMMENTARY

Although *Eugene Onegin* is better known, some professionals believe *Pique Dame* is more tightly written and does a better job of portraying drama, in the critical bedroom scene with the Countess and particularly in the intense finale. It is not Italian melody, but it is Russian drama in music, even if Tchaikovsky is not credited with capturing it all as the critics think he should have.

Some purists attack it because it is quite different from Pushkin's original, although such variations were no less common in opera one hundred years ago than book-movie differences are today. Pushkin makes Hermann a cold-blooded villain who is interested only in money, whereas Tchaikovsky turns him into an obsessive gambler consumed by the secret but also an impassioned lover who wants the money chiefly so he'll be worthy of Lisa.

MET PERFORMANCES

Forty-two performances in five seasons, from 1910 to 1996.

RECORDING

CD—Deutsche Grammophon. Galina Vishnevskaya, Regina Resnik, Hanna Schwarz, Peter Gougalov, Bernd Weikl, Dan Iordachescu. Tchaikovsky Chorus. French Radio Women's Chorus. National Orchestra of France. Mstislav Rostropovich. 1977.

VIDEO

Grigorian, Guleghina, Borodina, Leiferkus. A film. Kirov Opera. Russian; English subtitles. Gergiev, conductor. 1992. PGD. Philips.

∾

Number 67. *Peter Grimes*
by Benjamin Britten
November 22, 1913–December 4, 1976

Premiere at Sadler's Wells, London, 1945. Text by Montagu Slater from George Crabbe's 1810 poem The Borough. *An opera in a Prologue and three acts.*

It often is said that Puccini's *Turandot* is the last opera that the opera-going public loves without hesitancy or reservation. Not the last great one, nor the one from the last great composer, but the last one the opera public indisputably loves.

What's going on here? *Turandot* appeared in 1926, seventy years ago.

Besides *Turandot* there are only three post–World War I operas in The Collection, all from men who are among the century's leading classical composers:

Jenůfa, 1904 (Number 78), Janáček
Wozzeck, 1925 (Number 76), Berg
Peter Grimes, 1945 (Number 67), Britten

Peter Grimes is a special favorite of the critics and musicologists, and although not a box-office smasheroo it has won a steadily increasing place in the repertories of the world's great opera houses after a couple of decades of the usual neglect of new works.

It is a Thinking Person's opera, dealing with the tragic fate of a man who is unjustly condemned by his neighbors for the death of a fishing apprentice even though he has been acquitted in an inquest. He is a social outcast, fiercely independent and equally insecure. The libretto is based on a poem . . . and Britten had the soul of a poet.

It is severe drama. So are *Jenůfa* and *Wozzeck*. Twentieth-century operas in The Collection, once the world had experienced World War I, are not happy ones.

My first book on music was based on fifty great classical composers. Before publication, one internationally famous conductor graciously went over a draft list of the fifty. One of his reactions was that Bach, Mozart, Beethoven, Haydn, and Schubert belong in one category of masters and all other composers belong in another. A second was: "It is inconceivable that you left out Benjamin Britten."

It would be even more inconceivable to leave him out of an opera book.

Britten wrote many operas after *Peter Grimes*, including *The Rape of Lucretia* in 1946, *Albert Herring* in 1947, *The Little Sweep* in 1949, *Billy Budd* in 1951, *Gloriana* in 1953, *The Turn of the Screw* in 1954, *Noye's Fludde* in 1958, *A Midsummer Night's Dream* in 1960, *Owen Wingrave* in 1971, and *Death in Venice* in 1973.

They come in a variety of shapes and sizes. *Peter Grimes*, *Billy Budd*, and *Gloriana* are traditional. *Lucretia*, *Albert Herring*, and *The Turn of the Screw* are chamber operas for a small theater, with an orchestra of thirteen, no chorus, and a small cast. *The Little Sweep* and *Noye's Fludde* are children's operas, the latter designed to be performed in a church. *A Midsummer Night's Dream* and *Death in Venice* are neither fish nor fowl, neither traditional nor chamber in form, and have been performed both at the Metropolitan and in small houses. *Owen Wingrave* was written for television.

Good Company

Peter Grimes first appeared in London at Sadler's Wells in June, 1945, shortly after the end of the European part of World War II. Critic Edmund Wilson wrote then that Britten was one of the few composers who had a natural gift for the theater, along with "Mozart, Mussorgsky, Verdi, Wagner and the Bizet of *Carmen*."

A strong case can be made—and Brittenians don't hesitate to make it, as you'll discover if you encounter one over lunch—that Britten is the principal opera composer of the twentieth century. Of the works mentioned, special attention is given the following:

Albert Herring. The twentieth-century rendition of Italian opera buffa, played out in terms of English society character types (the same tradition that gave us Monty Python).

Billy Budd. An all-male opera, based on Herman Melville's novella with a text by E. M. Forster and Eric Crozier.

The Turn of the Screw. A unique, uncanny psychodrama, based on Henry James. A ghost story in which the real ghosts may be inside out (see the Twentieth-century European Package).

A *Midsummer Night's Dream*. Brittenians insist that this is the only Shakespearean opera fit to stand alongside Verdi's *Otello* and *Falstaff*.

Death in Venice. Britten's last operatic testament and the only one in which he openly addresses the subject of homosexuality. There have been two Metropolitan productions of it.

Britten's first stage work, in 1941, was a "choral operetta" called *Paul Bunyan*. It was an experiment that didn't work, and a failure. He immediately withdrew it but brought it back to life in the mid-1970s after becoming world-famous.

Although many of his operas are performed, none has equaled the success of *Peter Grimes*, which has been described this way by opera scholars Harold Rosenthal and John Warrack: "With his first major work, *Peter Grimes*, he established himself as an opera composer of the first importance. Rooted in tradition, it is entirely original in its sharpness of invention and in the conception of the hero as what was to be the first of a series of 'outsider' figures in his art; and it reveals the deep sympathy for the victims of misunderstanding, horror of the destruction of innocence, and attachment to the native Suffolk seaboard that have always marked his work."

In addition to opera Britten wrote a large amount of respected chamber, choral, and orchestral music. Several works were composed for particular performers—the dramatic works for his lifetime companion, Peter Pears, and instrumental works, including a sonata, three solo suites, and a cello concerto for the famed cellist and conductor Mstislav Rostropovich.

The pride of postwar England, and a well-known conductor as well as a major classical composer, Britten was to become Lord Britten of Aldeburgh. He was born in Lowestoft, England, in 1913, studied at the Royal College of Music, and began a lifetime of composing immediately upon graduating in 1934. He was for many years closely associated with England's famous Aldeburgh Festival, which he, Peter Pears, and Eric Crozier founded in 1948 in the Suffolk town in which they lived. He died in Aldeburgh in 1976.

Britten flirted briefly with Berg-like twelve-tone music in *The Turn of the Screw* (and in several earlier instrumental works), but the musicologists say this was chiefly as an organizing scheme for that opera's many short scenes, which themselves are tonal. Unlike some twentieth-century experimenters who are content to have the audience stay home, Britten was not at all wary of meeting it halfway.

Some critics have said that Britten's music, although more modern than that of fellow Englishman Ralph Vaughan Williams, is not modern enough. His defenders agree that he was not avant-garde, but insist that he was continuously inventive and pushed the boundaries further in almost every work.

Unlike most composers, Britten rarely dealt in romantic love. He focused on the position of the outcast in society, the misfit, the dreamer, all themes possibly influenced by his own outsider status as a homosexual in mid-twentieth-century England. This common misfit/dreamer thread does alienate some operagoers, but clearly appeals to others.

Peter Grimes is drawn from an 1810 poem by George Crabbe called *The Borough*, which tells of fishermen from England's seacoast. In the poem, set in Aldeburgh, Peter is a sadist, a psychopathic fisherman who actually was responsible for the deaths of his father and three apprentices. Although the village gets low marks for handling the situation, he is a hateful fellow. Britten skips the father and one apprentice, makes Peter a misunderstood misfit instead of a proper sadist, and draws the unsympathetic village as the villain.

KEYNOTE

The first of Britten's eleven operas, still the first choice of public and critic. Like many twentieth-century operas, filled with social and psychological conflict. Beautiful and powerful music. Hear the haunting choruses.

PLOT

Around 1830 in the Borough, a fishing village on England's east coast. Peter Grimes (tenor), a fisherman, was blown off course while at sea and ran out of drinking water. His helper, an apprentice boy, died of thirst and exposure and for three days Peter went through the horrible experience of sailing with the corpse. When he returns to port, an inquest is held. Peter is acquitted but also advised formally to hire an older man rather than take on another apprentice. Despite the verdict, the villagers blame Peter for the boy's death, and their feeling against him runs high. Only the widowed schoolmistress, Ellen Orford (soprano),

Jon Vickers in the title role of Peter Grimes

stands by him. Since he needs a hand on the boat and can't afford to hire an older man, Ellen helps him get another apprentice from the workhouse. After she and Peter quarrel over the boy, Peter takes him to his clifftop hut. When the townspeople learn about the quarrel with Ellen, the whole village sets out for the hut.

Hearing the mob coming, Peter and the boy try to take another route down the cliff, but the boy falls to his death. Balstrode (baritone), a retired sea captain, advises Peter that now he's in such trouble that his only choice is sui-cide, sinking at sea with his boat. Peter follows Balstrode's advice. The coast guard reports to the villagers that a boat has been lost. For them, however, that was yesterday's problem. An ordinary new day has dawned, they shrug off the human tragedy in which they have been involved, and start out their day unconcerned by it.

HIGHLIGHTS

Six orchestral interludes: "Dawn" before Act I, "Storm" after the first scene, "Sunday Morning" before Act II, "Passacaglia" after the first Act II scene, "Moonlight" before Act III, and a final one after the first Act III scene. Some critics call that last one the most imaginative music in the opera.

Act I: Grimes's aria "What harbour shelters peace?" and his famous "Now the Great Bear and the Pleiades." Better yet, the entire first scene, from the "Dawn" interlude through the storm. Brittenians challenge you to leave the opera at that point.

Act II: Ellen's "Glitter of waves," heard first from the strings.

Act III: Ellen's solo "Embroidery in childhood," another of the opera's big arias.

COMMENTARY

Musically, *Peter Grimes* has a bit of English folksong (though it is far from a folk opera), intermingled with Britten's own original color, rhythm, and har-mony. A few themes keep coming back to help set the atmosphere. Orchestral interludes link the separate songs.

The musicologists say *Peter Grimes*, a dark character study, was the first British opera to deal so heavily with the psychological aspect of man. Dorothy Samachson, in an essay reprinted in *The Lyric Opera Companion*, writes: "In his first major work for the lyric theater, Britten demonstrated a genius for deline-ating character and plot musically, for presenting social and psychological con-flicts with originality and dramatic assurance, and for the shattering power and beauty of the score."

Canadian dramatic tenor Jon Vickers, a fine actor, who was successful for Tristan, Sigmund and Otello, also became known for sterling performances in the title role of *Peter Grimes*—*the* more recent great Peter Grimes. For many years that honor was given Peter Pears, for whom the role was written. Britte-nians point out that Pears was a lyric tenor and Vickers a heroic tenor, able to do big roles that Pears never would have attempted. When Vickers came on the scene, popular wisdom saw his kind of voice as the best possible approach to the role, especially in a big house. But the opera was written for a much smaller house, which made it just right for Pears.

Three in One

The New Yorker's respected Andrew Porter wrote of a 1983 Met revival: "Jon Vickers in the title role was inspired. Grimes comprises within himself three men—victim, destroyer and poetic dreamer—who in *Billy Budd* are separate."

MET PERFORMANCES
Fifty-nine performances over eight seasons, from 1948 to 1996.

RECORDING
CD—Decca/London 414 577-2 (3). Claire Watson, Lauris Elms, Jean Watson, Peter Pears, James Pease. Chorus and Orchestra of the Royal Opera House, Covent Garden. Benjamin Britten. 1958.

VIDEO
Vickers, Harper, Bailey. Royal Opera House, Covent Garden. English; no subtitles. Davis. 1981. HBO.

∾

Number 68. *Der Freischütz*
by Carl Maria von Weber
November 18, 1786–June 5, 1826

Premiere at the Schauspielhaus, Berlin, 1821. Text by Friedrich Kind. From German folk stories in Gespensterbuch *by Johann August Apel and Friedrich Laun. Three acts.*

- If you like history:

    Carl Maria von Weber is the first true Romantic classical composer, following the Classical era led by Haydn, Mozart, and Beethoven. The whole Romantic movement of Schumann, Chopin, Berlioz, and all the others was soon to follow. With *Der Freischütz*, Weber founded German Romantic opera.

- If you're into influence peddling:

     No single operatic composer had more influence on Richard Wagner, Weber's most zealous disciple and one of the Opera Giants.
- If you're blasé about music history and/or what one composer bequeathed to another and are simply looking for an opera of "intelligence, imagination and genius," of "fresh" melody and "striking" rhythm, of "irreproachable" score:

     Der Freischütz may be your choice, and you could do a whole lot worse.

It is still hanging around, 175 years after its birth, only in part because of its place in music history. The Metropolitan performed it as early as 1884 and as late as 1971. Much more recently it has been on national television.

Although many critics didn't like it at its 1821 premiere, the public did, and it was performed more than fifty times in less than eighteen months in Berlin alone.

Carl Maria von Weber frequently is called "the founder of German opera," which is a little puzzling at first hearing inasmuch as Mozart's *Magic Flute* was in 1791 and Beethoven's *Fidelio* in 1805. But though the language of both was German, *Der Freischütz* was the first to put together a surviving opera rooted in German sounds, the German people, and German folklore.

There is no good translation for a Freischütz, or "free-shooter." Man-in-the-woods-with-a-gun-who-knows-how-to-use-it may suffice. It is a love story in a wonderful forest with a terrifying scene in spooky Wolf's Glen, magic bullets, and a dramatic triumph of Good over Evil.

In the midst of the first-year audience frenzy, Weber wrote in his diary: "Greater enthusiasm there cannot be, and I tremble to think of the future, for it is scarcely possible to rise higher than this."

And he did not, in two later operas: *Euryanthe* in 1823 and *Oberon* in 1826, though each is respected.

Der Freischütz was an outgrowth of the earlier German works called Singspiel—light fare, as we have seen, with these general characteristics: a heroine who is saved, a hero who almost is not, the supernatural, nature, a foiled villain, a friendly village, and a benevolent nobleman whose final sensitive decisions make for a happy ending. *Der Freischütz* is a much more substantial work.

Musically, the overture remains a classic that is frequently heard on classical radio. In the opera proper, there are peasant dances and songs, good choruses, waltzes, a march, and solo songs. Professor Donald Jay Grout has written: "in *Der Freischütz*, Weber succeeds as no other composer had done in raising the music of the folk to the dignity of serious opera and combining it skillfully with more pretentious elements."

Weber was one of the finest musicians of his time. He was a child prodigy, a virtuoso pianist, a famed conductor, and a boundary mover. As the music people like to say, he "anticipated" Wagner in several ways—with strange new harmonies, with repetitive musical themes related to specific characters or situations, with the concept that the conductor is the dictator, with great emphasis on symphonic music in opera, with some deemphasis of arias, and with the desire to make opera a unity of all relevant elements of art: voice, orchestra, poetry of text, drama, and more.

Wagner's Good Deed

The body of Carl Maria von Weber was in England for eighteen years after his early death. Through the efforts of Richard Wagner, it was brought back to Germany for burial there. Wagner is not known for his generosity of spirit or as a vocal champion of other composers, but Weber was one whom he admired greatly.

He was born in Eutin, Oldenburg, in 1786, the son of a former soldier, court official, and musician who had become an actor. Parents and children appear to have been something like the George M. Cohan family, drifting through Germany as a theatrical troupe. His father had hopes that the talented Carl was another Mozart, which, of course, no one ever has been. When he was a little older Carl studied music in Salzburg with Michael Haydn, Genius Joseph's brother, and later in Munich and Vienna. After working in Breslau, Württemberg, and Stuttgart he served as Opera Director in Prague between 1813 and 1816. But his ideas of opera reform were too much for his constituency and he moved to Dresden as Royal Saxon Kapellmeister in 1817. There he wrote *Der Freischütz*, presented first in Berlin.

Weber had everything to make him a father figure for the nineteenth century Romantic period. In wanting to express his emotions, he was the essence of Romanticism. Like nearly all good Romantics, he was into nature, he loved the piano, and he sponged up poetry, fine novels, and all things literary.

He died young, at thirty-nine, his deteriorating health weakened by a trip to London to produce *Oberon* at Covent Garden. Although best known for *Der Freischütz*, he was not an opera specialist. He favored the clarinet and produced two famous clarinet concertos, a concertino for clarinet and orchestra, and a well-known clarinet quintet. His most famous piece of orchestral music, along with the overtures to the three operas is "Invitation to the Dance," originally written for the piano, and orchestrated by Berlioz.

KEYNOTE

The first German Romantic opera. Germany breaks from Italian convention. Delightful blend of meaningful and approachable music. The natural and the supernatural. See and hear the magic of the Wolf's Glen.

PLOT

Bohemia, middle of the seventeenth century. Max (tenor), a forester, loves Agathe (soprano), the daughter of Cuno (bass), the head ranger. Max wants Cuno's consent for the marriage and also hopes to get Cuno's job when he retires. To accomplish both objectives he must win a shoot-out to be held the next day before Prince Ottokar (baritone). His friends are concerned, however, since—shockingly, for a forester—he has just lost a shooting match to Kilian (tenor), a rich peasant. A sinister wild huntsman named Samiel (speaking part) hovers in the background, unseen.

When the others have gone, Caspar (bass), another forester, approaches Max, hands him a gun, and tells him to fire at an eagle circling high above. The eagle falls dead. Caspar explains that the bullet was charmed and that such bullets will always hit what the marksman wills them to hit. Caspar entices Max to meet him at midnight at the Wolf's Glen, the magic forest, where they will mold bullets for Max to use in the contest. Caspar has bargained his soul to the Devil, who is Samiel, and will be lost unless he finds Samiel some substitute. He has chosen Max as his replacement.

Debussy on Weber

Claude Debussy once described Richard Wagner's music as "beautiful, singular, impure, seductive." He called Wagner the "master symbolist," detested Wagner's leitmotifs, and at one time even said Wagner "was never of service to music." But throughout his life Debussy admired Wagner's precursor in German opera, one of Wagner's favorite composers, Carl Maria von Weber.

"His work had a sort of dreamy melancholy, characteristic of his time," Debussy wrote—but it was never marred by "the crude German moonshine in which nearly all his contemporaries were bathed."

Debussy said Weber was "perhaps the first to face the problems of establishing the due relationship of the infinite spirit of Nature to the finite spirit of the individual."

Acknowledging that Weber had a weakness for ostentation and florid arias, Debussy noted that there were extenuating circumstances: "He married a singer."

At the Wolf's Glen, seven magic bullets are forged, six to hit any target at which the shooter is aiming. But the seventh, once fired, can be guided by Samiel's powers to the target of his choice. The ghost of Max's mother tries to warn him away, but without success.

At the shooting range, Max wins the contest using the six magic bullets, but the Prince requests one more shot. Max fires at a flying dove, despite a too late warning from Agathe that the dove is herself. As she faints, everyone thinks she has been struck and killed by the bullet. Indeed, the sinister Samiel has directed it toward her, but it has been deflected by a magic leaf and strikes Caspar instead.

It's explained that Caspar's replacement for Samiel could not have been Max in any case, because according to the rules of the game he had not come to the Wolf's Glen of his own free will but only after being tempted by Caspar. This left Caspar as the Designated Victim. When Max confesses that he has been shooting magic bullets, he is banished by Prince Ottokar. But after his case is pled by an old hermit, (bass) a holy man respected by the whole village, the Prince relents, leaving Max and Agathe free to marry.

HIGHLIGHTS

The Overture: This is familiar music, regardless of one's familiarity with opera, and is one of the first opera overtures to preview full tunes from the opera proper.

Act I: Max's "Durch die Wälder, durch die Auen," as he thinks about his losing position: "No, I can no longer bear the loss of all hope! Must fate reign blindly? Is there no God alive?"

Act II: Agathe's aria "Leise, leise, fromme Weisse," one of the most famous soprano arias in opera: "Softly, softly, pious melody, rise up and float to heaven." Also the famous Wolf's Glen scene.

Act III: Agathe, in her room, praying for a happy outcome, "Und ob die Wolke": "And though it is hidden by the clouds, the sun remains, there reigns a hallowed will. The world does not serve blind chance." The ending, with one of the well-known tunes from the overture.

COMMENTARY

In its day, the Wolf's Glen, Samiel's home, in which the magic bullets are forged, was one of the spookiest places in all opera, the site of a frightening incantation scene. The ghost of Max's mother appears. Cadaverous animal things crawl from the rocks and spit flames and sparks. A Devil's workshop, it always has been a bonanza for the special effects people.

One top-level composer/commentator who later was particularly supportive was Hector Berlioz, whose tongue was often sharp: "It is difficult to find, in searching the new or old school, a score as irreproachable as *Der Freischütz*, as constantly interesting from beginning to end; whose melody has more freshness in the various shapes it assumes, whose rhythms are more striking, whose harmonic invention is more varied, more forcible, whose use of massed voices and instruments is more energetic without effort, more suave without affectation. From the beginning of the overture to the last chord of the final chorus, it is impossible for me to find a bar the omission or the change of which I would consider desirable. Intelligence, imagination, genius shine everywhere with a radiance the force of which might dazzle any but eagle eyes if a sensitiveness, inexhaustible as well as restrained, did not soften its glare, covering the listener with the gentle folds of its veil."

That's about as positive as a Frenchman can be about a German. Especially from Berlioz, sort of the Sam Donaldson of observers.

You owe it to yourself to try to see one performance of *Der Freischütz* in an opera house that has the resources to do it justice. This is a difficult opera to dislike.

Opera Tags from The Collection

If Oscars were awarded to operas:

Most spectacular—*Aida*
Most romantic—*La Bohème*
Sexiest—*Carmen* and *Salome*
Saddest—*Madama Butterfly* and *La traviata*
Most melodramatic—*Pagliacci*
Longest on-going lovemaking—*Tristan und Isolde*
Most dysfunctional family—*Die Walküre* and *Siegfried*
Most tuneful—*Carmen*, *Faust*, and *Il trovatore*
Most unfathomable—*The Magic Flute*
Most cataclysmic climax—*Götterdämmerung* and *Samson et Dalila*
Most oblique—*Pelléas et Mélisande*
Most mayhem—*La Gioconda*
Flimsiest male bonding—*The Force of Destiny*
Most sexist title—*Così fan tutte*
Most vengeful—*Elektra* and *The Force of Destiny*
Folksiest—*The Bartered Bride*
Spookiest—*Der Freischütz*
Best example of a deal is a deal—*Ernani*

MET PERFORMANCE
Thirty performances in seven seasons, from 1884 to 1971.

RECORDING
CD—Angel/EMI CMS7 69342-2 (2). Elisabeth Grümmer, Lisa Otto, Rudolf Schock, Hermann Prey, Karl Christian Kohn, Gottlob Frick. Chorus of the Deutsche Opera Berlin Philharmonic Orchestra. Joseph Keilberth. 1959.

VIDEO

Goldberg, Smitková, Ihle, Ketelsen, Adam, Wlaschihn. Semper Oper, Dresden. German; Japanese subtitles. Hauschild, conductor. 1985. JPN-COLO. Japanese import.

∾

Number 69. *L'Italiana in Algeri*
(The Italian Girl in Algiers)
by Gioacchino Rossini
February 29, 1792–November 13, 1868

Premiere at the Teatro San Benedetto, Venice, 1813. Text by Angelo Anelli for an 1808 opera by Luigi Mosca. An opera buffa in two acts.

A good fellow to keep in mind if you get into opera and stay for a while is Gioacchino Rossini.

We've already encountered his Warhorse, *The Barber of Seville*, a "comedy of character," which is in a class by itself. But the kind of composer who can produce a *Barber of Seville* is inherently capable of producing a good many other works worth seeing and hearing.

He wrote other comic operas that still are characterized as the crème de la crème of that eighteenth-century opera buffa format and he wrote serious operas that nineteenth-century composers copied in approach and style.

His career was meteoric. After a half-dozen one-act opera buffa works, he was barely out of his teens when in one year he composed two operas that were to sweep quickly across Europe and establish his reputation.

The first, based on a tragedy by Voltaire, was a serious melodrama, *Tancredi*, that premiered in Venice in February, 1813, when Rossini was twenty-one. The other was his first comic masterwork, *The Italian Girl in Algiers*, staged first at a different theater in Venice in May the same year. Composing it took him eighteen or twenty-seven days, depending on your biographer of choice.

The incomparable *Barber of Seville* was not to come until later, in Rome in 1816, when Rossini was just about to turn twenty-four.

A good many musicologists call him a born master of the operatic stage. He was a little senior to the other two bel canto composers—five years older than Donizetti and nine years older than Bellini. At the pace he and Donizetti moved, this was a near lifetime.

For more on Rossini, see his Warhorse, *The Barber of Seville*, Number 19.

KEYNOTE

Keep your eye on Isabella, a lady who knows what it's all about from start to finish. Sparkling, melodious tunes, catchy rhythms, big crescendos. Opera for fun. The message to men: You can't beat them, so get smart and enjoy them.

PLOT

A palace of Mustafà, the Bey of Algiers. Mustafà (bass) no longer loves his wife, Elvira (soprano), and gives his favorite slave, Haly (bass), six days to find an Italian woman to take her place. Elsewhere in the palace is an Italian man named Lindoro (tenor), recently captured and enslaved. To rid himself of Elvira, Mustafà tells Lindoro he must marry her. Offshore a storm causes a shipwreck and among prisoners taken is Isabella (contralto), who has sailed the seven seas in search of her lover, who, of course, is Lindoro. She is accompanied by a suitor, Taddeo (baritone).

It does not take long for Mustafà to fall in love with her. After many complications, he is being initiated into a secret society for husbands called "Pappatacci" ("Eat and be silent"), the most important rituals of which are for the members, as model husbands, to eat and to sleep soundly—and thus allow their women to do anything they please. While these rites are taking place, Isabella and Lindoro escape and are set to sail away. Mustafà eventually recognizes that he has been hoodwinked, but the entire experience leads him to renounce all Italian women and to beg Elvira to forgive him. The moral of the story is declared by the ensemble finale: A good woman is going to have her way, so don't fight it.

Another Italian Girl

Two brothers, Giuseppe and Luigi Mosca, composed fifty-seven operas between them in the late eighteenth and early nineteenth centuries. One of Luigi's seventeen was an earlier rendition of *L'Italiana in Algeri*, which premiered in Milan in 1808, five years before Rossini's effort.

HIGHLIGHTS

The Overture: It is one of Rossini's most famous, often played in the concert hall. The music is not repeated in the opera proper, although the right tone is set.

Act I: Isabella's "Cruda sorte!" ("Cruel fate!"), as she is shipwrecked on the shores of Algeria. A stupendous ensemble finale.

Act II: Isabella dressing in front of her looking glass and watched by three men as she sings "Per lui, che adoro." The trio for Lindoro, Mustafà, and Taddeo after Mustafà consents to join the "Pappatacci." Isabella's patriotic "Pensa alla patria," the only really dramatic aria in the opera, a challenge to mezzo-sopranos and famous in their "literature."

COMMENTARY

A fun-and-games opera. No other work in The Collection came from a composer as young as twenty one. The music is sparkling and witty, and so is the libretto. The analysts say that Isabella typifies the Rossini heroine—independent, bright, strong-willed, in control, and played best by a singer with a magnificent and agile voice.

This is one of the rare surviving operas written for a contralto as heroine, although in this century it has become customary for a mezzo-soprano to play the role. In the seventeenth century, the contralto usually was a nurse or a maid. In the early eighteenth, she was often a comic crone. Handel then had several contraltos as important characters, including Cornelia in *Julius Caesar*. Among major contralto roles in the nineteenth century were Fidès, the mother of the hero in Meyerbeer's *Le prophète*. In general, however, the contralto is regarded as a not-very-romantic voice—even less so than the male bass.

It takes little time for the audience to recognize that Isabella is the character in charge. By twisting the three men who want her around her little finger, she accomplishes all of her objectives: to capture Lindoro, to free all Italian prisoners, and to reunite Mustafà and his wife. Mustafà, who has had absolute power over all women in his life, is reduced to pablum by her sexuality and cleverness.

Marilyn Horne starred in a 1974 Met production and, with Kathleen Battle and Samuel Ramey, in a 1980 recording. A 1981 Met production featured Marilyn Horne, Rockwell Blake, Sesto Bruscantini, Ara Berberian, and Kathleen Battle.

MET PERFORMANCE

Fifty-one performances over five seasons, from 1919 to 1986.

RECORDING

CD—Deutsche Grammophon 427 331-2 (2). Patrizia Pace, Agnes Baltsa, Frank Lopardo, Ruggero Raimondi, Enzo Dara. Vienna State Opera Chorus. Vienna Philharmonic Orchestra. Claudio Abbado. 1987.

VIDEO

Soffel, Gambill, Von Kannen, Focile. Sudfunks Stuttgart. Weikert, conductor. Italian; English subtitles. 1987. BMG.

❧

Number 70. *Ariadne auf Naxos*
by Richard Strauss
June 11, 1864–September 8, 1949

Premiere at the Hoftheatre, Stuttgart, 1912; revised with premiere at the Hofoper, Vienna, 1916. Libretto by Hugo von Hofmannsthal from classical mythology. An opera in a Prologue and one act.

After the two Richard Strauss stunners earlier in his career and earlier in The Collection, *Salome* and *Elektra*, he and Hugo von Hofmannsthal decided to shift to a kinder, gentler "Mozart style." Their first effort was the Warhorse *Der Rosenkavalier*. This was the next.

Ariadne auf Naxos is a different and strange twentieth-century opera, as far from Verdi melodrama as opera might be, a blend of farce in seventeenth-century Vienna and high Greek tragedy, with the one invading the other. It also is considerably more intimate than Strauss's other three Collection works and much more conservative musically than *Salome* and *Elektra*.

The background is a little complicated. Max Reinhardt, who had produced *Der Rosenkavalier* in Dresden, had adapted for the stage a comedy by Molière called *Le bourgeois gentilhomme*. In the original Molière comedy, a wealthy man trying to climb the social ladder invites guests to dinner and entertains them with a Turkish ballet. As their thanks to Reinhardt for having produced *Der Rosenkavalier*, Strauss and Hofmannsthal agreed to write a short thirty-minute opera for him to use in the play in place of the ballet that was in Molière's original drama.

It sounded like a reasonable idea, but it didn't work, in part because Reinhardt had to hire two casts, one for their basic comedy and one for the opera insert, and in part because that insert from Strauss and Hofmannsthal ran ninety minutes instead of the projected thirty.

But the composer and his librettist had become caught up by the idea and fashioned a brand-new opera of their own, also in two parts. The first part, the Prologue, is an adaptation of the original Molière comedy. The second part, the entertainment that the wealthy host from the comedy is presenting for his guests, is a one-act opera, developed from the ancient Greek myth about Ariadne. The host and his guests watch it from onstage.

In the Prologue the prima donna rehearses for the role of Ariadne that she will be playing in the entertainment, and once the Prologue has ended we see her in that role, on the island of Naxos. Other characters in the Prologue, including a comedy team who are to be another part of the host's entertainment, also cross over into the "opera," confronting Ariadne on Naxos as she never was confronted in the ancient Greek story.

Many playwrights, including Shakespeare, have made effective use of a play within a play. Strauss and Hofmannsthal here concocted an opera within an opera.

In the Ariadne story in Greek mythology, Theseus, King of Athens, killed the Minotaur (half man, half bull) with the assistance of Princess Ariadne of Crete, who gave him a thread that helped him navigate a labyrinth. They fell in love, and Theseus carried her away, later abandoning her on the island of Naxos.

The myth has been a favorite plot for opera composers since Monteverdi and nearly fifty works on the Ariadne story survive (in print). Handel composed one in 1734, and French composer Darius Milhaud one in 1928, but the best-known today is Strauss's.

See *Der Rosenkavalier*, the Strauss Warhorse, Number 20, for more background on the composer and his works. See also *Salome* and *Elektra*, Numbers 42 and 59.

KEYNOTE

The fourth and last Strauss opera in The Collection. Keep your eye on sexy, zesty Zerbinetta, who links the two parts of the work and gets the best music. Listen also for the trio of the three nymphs.

PLOT

Nineteenth-century Vienna. In the Prologue, an opera company prepares for a performance in the private theater of a wealthy patron. It is to be an opera seria called *Ariadne auf Naxos*. But the fickle patron then directs that a comic play must be put on by another cast once the opera has been completed, a request that inevitably shakes up the opera company, especially the Music Master (baritone), who doesn't want his artistic serious opera followed by vulgar buffoonery. Zerbinetta (soprano), the leader of the comic group, has four followers: Harlequin (baritone), Scaramuccio (tenor), Truffaldino (bass), and Brighella (tenor). Matters worsen when the Major-domo (speaking role) advises both opera company and comedy company that the patron now wants the two entertainments performed simultaneously. As the Prologue ends, the Composer of the serious opera (trouser role, soprano), runs off in despair.

Now for the opera seria on which the opera company is working in the Prologue. When it begins, Ariadne is languishing on Naxos, where she is cared for by three "elementary beings," Naiad (soprano), Dryad (contralto), and Echo (soprano). Abandoned by Theseus, and disconsolate and lonely, she yearns for Death, and is not pleased to be interrupted by a comical, lusty woman named Zerbinetta and her male friends, all crossovers from the Prologue. Zerbinetta's philosophy is to love one man at a time but always to be ready for the next, who surely will come along. To prove her point, she flirts openly with three of the four men, ultimately taking up with the fourth. When a stranger arrives, Ariadne falls in love with him. At first she welcomes him as a messenger of Death, the Lord of the Dark Ship, for which she has longed, but in fact he turns out to

be Bacchus, god of wine and youth, representing not Death but Life. Her longing for Death becomes longing for Love. They retire together into a cave—or
into the sky, depending on the production. (In mythology, eventually they're
married, but the opera doesn't take them that far.)

Composer to Librettist: No More Wagner

Strauss wrote Hofmannsthal about *Ariadne*: "Your cry of pain has
pushed open the door to a whole new landscape in which, led by *Ariadne*, especially the new Prologue, I hope to make my way along the
path of an entirely un-Wagnerian opera of action, mood and humanity.
I now see the way clearly before me, and thank you for opening my
eyes . . . I promise you, that I have now cast off the whole musical
armour of Wagner forever."

HIGHLIGHTS

Prologue: The Composer's duet with Zerbinetta and her act-ending aria
praising the power and art of music. A recent Met production featured Jessye
Norman as the prima donna/Ariadne, Kathleen Battle as the high coloratura
Zerbinetta, and Tatiana Troyanos as the Composer.

Act I: Ariadne's "Es gibt ein Reich" (Everything is pure only in death).
Zerbinetta's entire big scene, in which she sings about how much she loves life,
with her recitative, "Grossmächtige Prinzessin" ("Gracious princess"). This is
considered one of the most difficult coloratura soprano scenes in opera. "I often
had two lovers at the same time, though always by compulsion and never by
caprice . . . If the Good Lord wanted us to resist men's advances, why did He
create so many varieties?"

COMMENTARY

The notion of blending comedy, even farce, with serious opera was not a
new one. Lully ballets often were plunked down inside a comedy.

An intimate opera in Mozart style, *Ariadne* is scored for a chamber orchestra of only thirty-nine musicians. Some analysts say it completes Strauss's tran-
sition from Wagnerian music drama to anti-Wagnerian opera—putting him
right back where his anti-Wagner father was in the beginning. Wagnerians
concede that there are many wonderful Mozartian elements in the work, but
note that the two trios for the nymphs in the "opera proper" are right out of the
Ring's Rhinemaidens scene. Further, they argue with some vigor, the final half
hour of the opera is more Wagnerian than anything in the operatic literature
since *Siegfried*—with the roles in the two operas often sung by the same singers.

Beverly Sills, in her discussions of three different types of coloratura singing, groups Zerbinetta with the Queen of the Night in *The Magic Flute* and Olympia in *The Tales of Hoffmann* in a category in which the singer mechanically belts out the high notes. One Strauss devotee I interviewed strenuously dissented. He agreed that Olympia is entirely mechanical and that the Queen of the Night can be, but argued that Zerbinetta requires a warm, full, lyric voice. But then, perhaps Ms. Sills could deliver a warm, full, lyric voice even when being mechanical.

MET PERFORMANCES
Sixty-two performances over nine seasons, from 1962 to 1994.

RECORDING
CD—EMI/Angel CDMB 69296 (2) (mono). Elisabeth Schwarzkopf, Rita Streich, Irmgard Seefried, Rudolf Schock, Hermann Prey, Karl Dönch. Philharmonic Orchestra. Herbert von Karajan. 1954.

VIDEO
Norman, Battle, Troyanos, Metropolitan Opera. German; English subtitles. Levine, conductor. 1988. PGD. London.

∿

Number 71. *Martha*
by Friedrich von Flotow
April 27, 1812–January 24, 1883

Premiere at the Karntthnerthor Theatre in Vienna, 1847. Text by Friedrich Wilhelm Riese from Vernoy de Saint-Georges' French ballet-pantomime, Lady Henriette, ou La Servante de Greenwich, *for which Flotow wrote one act. Four acts.*

This is a good example of a work that's opera, not operetta, but opera of a feathery nature—close to a borderline case. It's a light romantic comedy with airy, graceful, charming music. No deep emotions are stirred by music or plot: Two young ladies from the court, disguised as country maids, meet two young, handsome farmers and in due time everyone lives happily ever after.

Friedrich von Flotow is an opera specialist, not known for instrumental classical music. He wrote a good many other operas but none close to equaling *Martha* in popularity.

Historically, Flotow is part of a group of composers who were influenced by French opéra comique, which in the mid-1800s actually was comedy. Later, as we have seen, anything produced at the Opéra-Comique might be called opéra comique, no matter how serious and/or tragic it was. The French do that sort of thing from time to time.

Musicologists at one time considered *Martha* part of the French opera repertory, despite Flotow's nationality, chiefly because on stylistic grounds it seemed more French than German. Flotow's musical training was French, and the original story came from a French source. The current custom, however, is to group it with German operas of the period.

Another Collection opera to come, Otto Nicolai's *Merry Wives of Windsor*, 1849 (Number 79), is in a similar category. A third, somewhat later, in post-Wagner Germany, is Engelbert Humperdinck's *Hänsel und Gretel*, 1893 (Number 31). All three were very popular in their day, both in Germany and in this country, but *Hänsel und Gretel* has had the most staying power—and probably deserves it.

Flotow was born in Teutendorf, Germany, in 1812, studied in Paris, and soon began writing operettas. His first opera was performed with some success in 1835. *Martha*, his most popular work, came twelve years later, developed from the seeds of one act he wrote for an earlier ballet-pantomime. Within some thirty-five years it had more than five hundred performances in Vienna alone.

Hot in Hamburg

Flotow had other successful works besides *Martha*, the most popular, a three-act romantic opera called *Alessandro Stradella* that premiered in Hamburg in 1844. Statistics from Hamburg illustrate the popularity of both works. By 1932 *Alessandro Stradella* had been staged 212 times there and by 1955 *Martha* had been given 440 times. Nine other Flotow operas were also performed in Hamburg.

The late 1900s haven't been *Martha*'s best years, and it's one of a half-dozen operas in The Collection that professionals would be inclined to weed out if we weren't relying on total performance statistics.

KEYNOTE

A sentimental, old-fashioned opera with longtime staying power. Experts dismiss it and its popularity has faded, but it hangs on. Hear a very familiar song.

PLOT

Near Richmond, England, about 1710. Lady Harriet (soprano) is the maid of honor to Queen Anne. Weary of court life, she and her maid, Nancy (contralto), disguise themselves as peasant girls under the names of Martha and Julia. They go to the county fair, where they are hired as servants by two young farmers, Plunkett (bass) and his foster brother, Lionel (tenor). It's suspected that Lionel is "of gentler birth," but we're not sure. The men fall in love with

Martha *at the Metropolitan Opera*

the ladies, Lionel offering to marry Martha and thus elevate her to his good solid station of peasant.

When Lady Harriet/Martha tires of the game, she returns to court life, only to realize there that she's in love with Lionel. Nancy and Plunkett connive to bring about a meeting of the other two in the gardens of Queen Anne's palace, where they are happily united. Better than that, Lionel turns out to be the son of an earl, making him eminently worthy of Lady Harriet's love.

HIGHLIGHTS

Act II: Martha's main aria, "Die letze Rose" ("The Last Rose of Summer"). It's not original with Flotow, who borrowed it from an old Irish melody called "The Groves of Blarney."

Act III: Lionel's famous "Ach, so fromm," known to Italian audiences as "M'appari" and to English ones as "Martha" or "How so fair." One of opera's best-known arias. Flotow stole it from himself; it originated in his earlier opera, *L'âme en peine*, 1846.

COMMENTARY

The story of *Martha* (subtitled *The Market at Richmond*) is neither deep nor original; both story and music are simply graceful, gay, melodious, and provincial.

Nor are the singing parts strenuous. Enrico Caruso once suggested: "I keep my voices in sort of a drawer . . . An artist does not sing Vasco de Gama's music in *L'Africaine* with the same weight of tone he uses for that of Lionel in *Martha*. He approaches a song that is not operatic with consideration of the style demanded; and he suits his tones to fit. To adopt one weight and general color of voice for every piece of music is to be mechanical, inartistic and vocally limited."

MET PERFORMANCES
One hundred and sixteen performances over twenty-one seasons, from 1884 to 1961.

RECORDING
CD—Eurodisc 352 878 (2). Lucia Popp, Doris Soffel, Siegfried Jerusalem, Karl Ridderbusch, Siegmund Nimsgern. Chorus of the Bavarian Radio. Munich Radio Orchestra. Heinz Wallberg. 1977.

∽

Number 72. *Mignon*
by Ambroise Thomas
August 5, 1811–February 12, 1896

Premiere at the Opéra-Comique, Paris, 1866. Text by Jules Barbier and Michel Carré from Goethe's 1796 novel Wilhelm Meister's Lehrjahre. *A lyric opera in three acts.*

The first thing to remember about Ambroise Thomas is that he *is* French. It is Toe-mahs, not Thomas. No one will ask you back for tea if you say Thomas, as in Socialist Norman or in a Becket.

Another point is that he was a respected professor at the Paris Conservatory. As such, his music was respectably professorial: clear, correct, and melodious.

Thomas composed *Mignon* in 1866, when he was in his mid-fifties. The opera world loved it, and before the turn of the century it had been performed more than one thousand times in Paris alone. The sixteen hundredth staging at the Opéra-Comique came in 1927. We are now long past two thousand. Not all opera houses, including especially the Paris Opéra, are cooperative about providing data, and complete figures often aren't available (in part because of records lost by fires, war, and other tragedies). It was the fifth opera presented at the Metropolitan in New York—on October 31, 1883, nine days after the Met opened.

What is certain is that *Mignon* is considerably less popular now than it was a half century ago, although it's still performed both in Europe and the United States.

If you want the originality of Debussy, the power of Wagner, or the death of heroine by fire, *Mignon* is not the opera for you. If you want laughter, easy tears, sincere emotion, and professional musical depiction of character, it's a good one to try.

Doubting Thomas

Goethe's *Wilhelm Meister* was a tragic novel and as philosophical as one would expect from Goethe. Mignon dies. *Mignon*, though an opera, is operetta-light and doesn't know philosophy from philology. Thomas didn't think it was going to work. But it became one of France's most popular operas, along with *Carmen* and *Faust*. Some musicologists call it an outright imitation of the latter, but that's never bothered the public.

Thomas was present at the Opéra-Comique at the one thousandth performance of *Mignon* in 1894. Typical of opéra comique, the original version employed spoken dialogue. In order for it to be accepted in many other opera houses, including the Drury Lane in London, Thomas composed the recitative that was preferred in theaters outside Paris.

One of the many works that Thomas wrote for the Opéra-Comique, *Mignon* is an illustration of the kind of opéra comique that is more serious than comic, even if not tragic. Charles Gounod's "more robust" (the music people like that word) *Faust* is another example, and both Massenet and Delibes contributed others. These are mid-channel lyric operas, stronger than the charming and masterful Offenbach Parisian operettas but lighter and less pretentious than Meyerbeer's Parisian grand operas.

Born in Metz in 1811, Thomas attended the Paris conservatory, won the Prix de Rome, returned to Paris, and began composing operas. Several operettas and grand operas came before *Mignon*, his personal masterpiece. Although he tried his hand at Shakespeare's *Hamlet*, the professional judgment, then and now, is that he was not gifted enough for that heavy tragedy.

He was a favorite of Napoleon III and in later life was named director of the Paris Conservatory.

He became self-centered and something of a recluse the last third of his life, brooding over death. Twenty-five years before he died he purchased a granite tomb for himself on a small island off the French coast. But he did not fade away quietly. *Mignon* was as successful as ever when he died in 1896, and had a big public funeral at Montmartre in Paris, with Collection composer Massenet leading the orations.

KEYNOTE

Graceful and charming. Thomas's best opera. Still frequently performed, although long past its peak. Some good tunes. Unhappy Goethe ending changed so you can go home smiling.

PLOT

The late eighteenth century, Germany and Italy. A wandering minstrel named Lothario (bass) has lost his memory and also lost his daughter, who presumably is drowned. Mignon (mezzo-soprano) has become a gypsy who is mistreated by the chief of her gypsy band, Jarno (bass). Wilhelm Meister (tenor), a student who is traveling in the area, buys her and takes her home to be a servant in the castle in which he lives. After Mignon falls in love with him and then learns that he's in love with Philine (soprano), an actress, she considers drowning herself in the castle lake.

Lothario is attracted to Mignon and hears her say it would be a good thing if the castle theater, in which Philine is performing, were to be struck by lightning and destroyed by fire. Obedient to her jealous thought, he disappears to do the job, and before long flames are leaping up from the theater. Mignon and Wilhelm are happily united. But Lothario has goofed; when he regains his memory he finds that he's really the Marquis Cypriani and that he has burned down his own property.

It's also established, however, that his daughter had not drowned but had been abducted by the gypsies—and, of course, that she really is Mignon. The opera ends with a trio for Mignon, Wilhelm, and Lothario. No deaths, no suicides, and no real damage except for one replaceable castle.

HIGHLIGHTS

The Overture, built around two popular airs in the opera, often is heard on classical radio.

Act I: One of the popular airs heard in the overture is Mignon's "Connais-tu le pays?" as she tells Wilhelm of her past: "Do you know the country where the orange tree and crimson roses bloom. That is where I would want to live, love and die." Also a duet between Mignon and Lothario, "Légères hirondelles" ("Gliding swallows").

Act II: The "Styrienne," "Je connais un pauvre enfant," sung by Mignon. Wilhelm's aria "Adieu, Mignon, courage," as he says good-bye to her.

Another popular air is the "Polonaise," Philine's "Je suis Titania," a favorite of coloratura sopranos.

Act III: The closing trio with Mignon, Wilhelm, and Lothario, in which the music of "Connais-tu le pays?" is again heard.

COMMENTARY

Classical composer Robert Schumann described Thomas's music this way: "It is not heavy, not light, not classic, not romantic, not deep, not sickly, but always euphonious and in some places rich in fine melodies."

A somewhat similar evaluation of Mignon came from Eduard Hanslick (friend of Brahms, foe of Wagner), Vienna's best-known late nineteenth-century music critic. He considered the opera neither powerfully striking nor the work of an original genius, but nonetheless the product of a sensitive and refined artist. If the music was occasionally somewhat meager and tawdry, it was mostly spirited and graceful—not deep, but true and warm.

Monsieur Thomas was not obligated to write *Boris Godunov*. "Sensitive," "refined," and "of a master hand" are noteworthy. Still, Thomas did choose to draw his heroine from the great master Goethe and is commended by musicologists for portraying musically all the complex human emotions that Goethe gave her—love, affection, and loyalty as well as jealousy. He is recognized today as one of the leading nineteenth-century French opera composers. Not the most important, but one worthy of attention.

MET PERFORMANCES
One hundred and ten performances over twenty-two seasons, from 1883 to 1948.

∾

Number 73. *Mefistofele*
by Arrigo Boito
February 24, 1842–June 10, 1918

Premiere at La Scala, Milan, 1868. Text by the composer from Goethe's Faust. *After revisions, an opera with a Prologue, four acts, and an Epilogue.*

Arrigo Boito and Bill Clinton have a good bit in common.

Boito's first big chance, the premiere of his *Mefistofele* before an all-important La Scala audience in 1868, lasted six hours and was a terrible flop. Clinton's first big chance, a major speech at the Michael Dukakis Democratic convention in 1988, seemed to last longer and was even more of a flop.

Boito was stepping out of his role; he was a fine poet and Europe's most famous librettist trying to be a composer. Clinton was stepping out of his; he was a young governor of a political nonstate with no previous national exposure.

In time, both redid their acts and achieved reasonable success—in Boito's case, success enough so that *Mefistofele* has become part of the international repertory, and recent performances include several in 1996 by the Washington Opera.

The son of a Polish countess and an Italian painter, Boito was an intellectual who traveled widely in Europe and was held in high regard for his literary and critical works. He also was a composer, and *Mefistofele*, drawn from Goethe's *Faust* nine years after Gounod's opera from the same source was premiered, seemed an ideal blend of his music and literary interests. It was Boito's only completed opera and the first one ever presented at La Scala for which the composer was his own librettist.

After its first unqualified failure, Boito spent seven years in massive revisions, and its second appearance in Bologna in 1875 came off well. It has remained very popular in Italy and, interestingly, in South America, and has done reasonably well elsewhere. The first performances in the United States were in 1880 in Boston and New York.

Boito believed that Italian opera had become stilted and stereotyped. He wanted to reform it, to marry drama and music as no prior Italian had done. In *Mefistofele* he undertook the formidable task of not only putting into music the serious philosophy and symbolism of Goethe, but also of portraying the innermost thoughts and broodings of the characters. He was less concerned than many composers about how his audience might react—and, analysts say, this lack of concern shows in the final product.

The music is powerful, the atmosphere is mystical, and the spectacle is enjoyable if not in the grand opera category, but it's not easy to find a singable melody, and little of it really tingles the spine. Analysts question whether the beautiful music adequately portrays the serious drama. Still, if you watch Samuel Ramey's *Mefistofele* on videotape with the San Francisco Opera, it's a pleasant way to spend the evening.

The Establishment, which so often longs for cerebral activity and experimentation, views it as a stronger interpretation of Goethe than Gounod's *Faust* and a work of considerably more intellectual merit—and keeps hoping its popularity will rise.

Best Little Whorehouse in Italy

Boito had a longtime friend named Franco Faccio, whose first opera premiered in Milan in 1863. At a celebration dinner, Boito, then twenty-one, a poet as well as a composer and librettist, praised Faccio's work by attacking Italian opera in general, poetically comparing it to the splattered walls of a house of prostitution. This did not endear him to the Establishment, nor to Verdi, with whom Boito later worked extremely closely.

But *Faust* has buckets and buckets of tunes, and Boito's name today is best known as the peerless librettist for the two Verdi operas the Establishment likes best, both from Shakespeare—the tragic *Otello* and the comic *Falstaff*. He also helped Verdi revise *Simon Boccanegra*.

A second Boito opera, *Nerone*, set in Rome in Nero's time, premiered at

La Scala in 1924. It was completed by Toscanini and others after the composer's death.

KEYNOTE

A celebrated wager for the soul of Faust. Italian poet breaks tradition by writing lengthy opera from German literary masterpiece. Excellent drama and fine music, but not a powerful marriage of the two.

PLOT

Germany and Ancient Greece in the Middle Ages and Heaven at the same time. In the Prologue, Mefistofele, the Devil (bass), wagers with God over the soul of Faust (tenor), an aged German philosopher, and prepares to descend to earth to capture it. In Act I, in Faust's study in Frankfurt-on-Main, Mefistofele first is disguised as a hooded gray friar but then reveals himself and announces that his goal is to have destruction reign over the sun and the earth. He declares that he thrives on what men call Sin and Evil. As a philosopher, Faust is not overly concerned about the afterlife. His objective is to regain his youth and to experience one fleeting perfect moment in this life. Then let him die and, should it happen, let Hell's depths engulf his soul. This suits Mefistofele perfectly. He spreads his cloak, and off they fly.

In a garden scene, Faust (now rejuvenated as young Henry) wins the love of Margherita (soprano). After their time together, he leaves her and accompanies Mefistofele to the top of a mountain to attend the Witches' Sabbath. There is a wild witch dance and Faust sees a vision of Margherita with a blood-red necklace around her throat. Act III begins in a prison cell, where Margherita, now insane, has been incarcerated for having drowned her nameless illegitimate child and poisoned her mother after Faust deserted her. Calling upon God to forgive her, she rejects her former lover and dies. But just when Mefistofele thinks he has won her soul for Hell an angelic choir takes her in hand.

Act IV is on the banks of a Grecian river where Faust and Elena (Helen of Troy) (soprano) make love and she sees visions of the fall of Troy. This scene deals with Part II of Goethe's poem and symbolizes the union of Greek and German ideals. In the Epilogue, a remorseful Faust reads from his Bible, considers joining Mefistofele and his voluptuous sirens, prays, rejects Mefistofele and the women, and dies. To the distress of Mefistofele, his soul also is saved by a choir of angels.

HIGHLIGHTS

The spectacle of the Prologue.

Act I: Faust's aria "Dai campi, dai prati": "Through the fields and the meadows, in the dark of the night, I made my way home. Here I found peace."

Act II: The garden scene quartet, with Mefistofele, Margherita's friend Marta (contralto), Margherita, and Faust. See the lovemaking begin.

Act III: Margherita's aria "L'altra notte in fondo al mare" ("To the sea, one night of sadness"). The prison duet for Faust and Margherita, "Lontano, lontano" ("Far away, far away"). Also Margherita's death scene as voices from heaven advise that she is saved from the Devil.

Act IV: The spectacle of the Witches' Sabbath.

Epilogue: Faust's aria "Giunto sul passo estremo" ("Nearing the far limits"), as he sees peace, wisdom, and justice, seeks forgiveness . . . and receives it. "I have enjoyed the love of a woman and a goddess. In my old age I dream of my soul as ruler of a tranquil world giving life to a fruitful people."

COMMENTARY

Charles Gounod limited his opera to the first part of Goethe's *Faust*, the story of Faust and Marguerite. Boito tackles both parts of Goethe, a much more difficult task dramatically. Boito is more profound; Gounod much more of a crowd pleaser.

Boito often is praised for his selflessness in having served Verdi rather than spending more time on his own composing, but the professional consensus is that his choice was a wise one, proof that he really was as bright and analytical as reported. His literary gifts far surpassed his musical ones. One writer complained that in *Mefistofele* he polished a musical phrase until it had lost not only its bloom but also its connections with neighboring phrases on either side.

Musicologist Gerald Abraham, generally quite gracious, writes that the music "fails miserably to rise to crucial passages." That's not to say much of it isn't beautiful music.

Boito wrote in the preface of the final edition of the work: "*Mefistofele* is the embodiment of the eternal No addressed to the True, the Beautiful and the Good. Mefistofele is as old as the Bible and Aeschylus. Mefistofele is the serpent in the Garden of Eden; he is the vulture of Prometheus. Mefistofele is the doubt that generates learning and the evil that generates good. Wherever the spirit of negation is found, there is Mefistofele."

The last Met productions featured Feodor Chaliapin, Russia's most famous bass, and Italian tenor Beniamino Gigli, who had one of the most beautiful voices of the century.

MET PERFORMANCES

Fifty-four performances over eleven seasons, from 1883 to 1925.

RECORDING

CD—Angel/EMI CDCB 49522 (2). Montserrat Caballé, Josella Ligi, Plácido Domingo, Norman Treigle. Ambrosian Opera Chorus. London Symphony Orchestra. Julius Rudel. 1973.

VIDEO

Ramey, Beňačková, O'Neill. San Francisco Opera. Italian; English subtitles. Arena conductor. 1989. HOME VISION.

∾

Number 74. *Prince Igor*
by Alexander Borodin
November 12, 1833–February 27, 1887

Premiere at the Maryinsky Theatre, St. Petersburg, 1890. Text by the composer from a play by Vladimir Vasilevich Stasov, drawn from a medieval poem. An opera in a prologue and four acts.

It is unlikely that you have read a doctoral thesis entitled "On the Analogy of Arsenical with Phosphoric Acid."

Neither, it is safe to say, had the American musical team of George Forrest and Robert Wright, which, in 1953, agreed that it would be a good thing to make a New York musical out of the dances and arias from an opera called *Prince Igor.*

It was, indeed, a good thing. The musical was called *Kismet,* and it was a smash hit, both on Broadway and on many other stages across the United States and Europe. One of its hit tunes was "A Stranger in Paradise," a song familiar today to millions who were not yet born when the musical premiered. Another was "This Is My Beloved," borrowed from one of the same composer's string quartets.

The nineteenth-century St. Petersburg author of the doctoral thesis dealing with phosphoric acid and the composer of *Prince Igor* are, of course, the same man—a full-time research chemist and part-time weekend musician named Alexander Borodin.

One colorful music writer says Borodin was the first to furrow the musical fields of Western Europe with a Russian plough and to embed in it seeds that would blossom forth in a triumph of Russian national music. Well, he did something like that, something like impressing Western Europe with great Russian nationalist sounds.

Borodin was born in St. Petersburg, the illegitimate son of a prince and the wife of a court physician. Princes were like that. His father saw that he was well educated. He had a governess and special tutors, received the proper music lessons, attended orchestral concerts, and was launched on the serious career of research chemistry. At graduate school in Heidelberg, he met and married a fine pianist named Ekaterina Protopopova. Years later he dedicated his String Quartet No. 2 to her—the music from which Broadway stole the tune "This Is My Beloved."

He died of an aneurism during a carnival dance in 1887, at only fifty-three, just before his opera was finished. It was completed and orchestrated by Alexander Glazunov and Borodin's colleague in the Russian "Mighty Five," Rimsky-Korsakov (*The Golden Cockerel*). Recall that besides Borodin and Rimsky the other members of the "Five" were Mussorgsky (*Boris Godunov*), César

Cui, and Mily Alexeyevitch Balakirev. (Cui has no opera in The Collection and Balakirev wrote none). The small group was dedicated to establishing a distinctly nationalist Russian school of music,

Prince Igor is the work on which Borodin's reputation rests, although it was not his only dramatic piece and Borodin was by no means exclusively an opera composer. His best-known other classical pieces include *In the Steppes of Central Asia*, a tone poem; a colorful symphony, No. 2 in B Minor; and the second string quartet.

Borodin is not Russia's greatest composer, and *Prince Igor* is not Russia's greatest opera. *The* Russian tragedy and the most powerful Russian opera is Mussorgsky's *Boris Godunov*. But *Igor* is an epic in its own right, packed with historical splendor, Russian patriotism, and outpourings of lyrical music. And outside of Russia, it has survived very well for an opera from a fellow who basically was a highly respected medical research scientist, for years a professor/lecturer at the Medico-Surgical Academy in St. Petersburg.

He did not give up his scientific career for music; composition simply—or not so simply—was done on the side.

Praise from The Mighty Five

Borodin left this note about the reaction to *Boris Godunov* from his colleagues of the "Mighty Five": "It is curious to see how all the members of our set agree in praise of my work. While controversy rages amongst us on every other subject, all, so far, are pleased with *Igor*—Mussorgsky, the ultra-realist; the innovating lyrico-dramatist, Cui; our master, Balakirev, so severe as regards form and tradition, and Vladimir Stasov himself, our valiant champion of everything that bears the stamp of novelty or greatness."

When he was a student, one chemistry professor warned him against combining his two interests. "You make a mistake," the professor wrote, "hunting two hares at once." Fortunately, it was advice that Borodin didn't follow, but he did write slowly and tried not to let music interfere with his profession. It took him seventeen years, composing only when he could steal the time, to produce *Prince Igor*.

Musing on his two careers, he once wrote: "In winter, I can compose only when I am too ill to give my lectures. So my friends, reversing the usual custom, never say to me, 'I hope you are well,' but 'I do hope you are ill.' "

Vladimir Stasov, who wrote the play on which the opera is based, combined at least three talents: music criticism, archeology, and library science.

Although not formally a member of the "Five," he coined the name and was an honorary adjunct, and the opera—which took seventeen years to write—was his idea.

Borodin described his epic work this way: "*Prince Igor* is essentially a nationalist opera which can be of interest only to us Russians who like to refresh ourselves at the fountainhead of our history, and to see the origins of our nationality revived upon the stage."

Wrong. It has been of interest to many others and it survives today in this country, even if not nearly as popular as *Boris*—especially at the Met, whose statistics are useful albeit far from conclusive. It has been performed ten times there, compared with 230 for Mussorgsky's mighty work.

Now if you amble over to Broadway and enter *Kismet* in the race, the figures change significantly.

At the Bolshoi Theatre in Moscow, *Prince Igor* was the fifth most popular opera over three quarters of a century, topped only by Tchaikovsky's *Eugene Onegin*, Glinka's *A Life for the Czar*, and Verdi's *La traviata* and *Rigoletto*.

Stagings outside Russia include, but are not limited to, Berlin in 1930, Covent Garden in 1935, La Scala in 1940, Vienna in 1947, La Scala in 1964, Montreal (Expo) in 1967, the New York City Opera in 1969 and 1994, Opera North in 1982, and San Francisco in 1996.

KEYNOTE

Borodin's only opera. Unfinished and dramatically diffuse. Rich Russian music. See the slaves do the "Polovtsian Dances." Hear the Broadway tunes.

PLOT

The town of Poutivl, the Polovtsian camp, 1185. The opera is the story of the capture of Prince Igor (baritone) and his son Vladimir (tenor) by the Polovtsians, a Tartar race in Central Asia led by Khan Kontchak (bass). Being a captive isn't all that terrible, though. The Khan entertains Igor royally, among other things inviting him to special exhibitions by the Polovtsian dancers. He offers to let Igor go free if he promises never to fight again, but the Prince refuses. Later, however, he escapes and rejoins his wife, Yaroslavna (soprano), who has been under the care of her brother Prince Galitzky (bass).

Meanwhile, son Vladimir has fallen in love with the Khan's daughter, Kontchakovna (mezzo-soprano), and chooses to remain behind in the Polovtsian camp. The Khan, not a bad fellow although his forces devastated Poutivl, gives his permission for them to marry.

HIGHLIGHTS

The melody-filled overture.

Act I: Prince Galitzky's aria in which he brags that he is a man to be reckoned with. Also Yaroslavna's short song telling of her loneliness.

Act II: Vladimir's lovely aria about his love for the Khan's daughter,

"Slowly the daylight is fading away." Igor's longing for his homeland, "No sleep or rest," from the overture. The "Polovtsian Dances," also called the "Dances of the Polovtsian Maidens," often performed separately by ballet companies, the most popular part of the opera. *Kobbé* writes of them: "In scope they range from soft enticing melody to harsh vigour, with more than a touch of the barbaric in it . . . In context, they make a thrilling finale to an act whose varied musical splendours constitute perhaps Borodin's most enduring memorial."

COMMENTARY

Prince Igor is an epic poem, exuding folklore and East Russian color, serious, but not tragic. In it you should expect:

- Rich individual arias
- Splendid choral scenes
- A powerful Russian atmosphere
- The famous "Polovtsian Dances," Oriental in nature, played separately in concert halls everywhere, heard frequently on classical radio—and containing the music of "A Stranger in Paradise"
- A so-so libretto, Borodin's own, although based on Stasov
- A good bit of rambling, in part because Borodin was not a trained composer and in part because two other artists worked on the opera after his death.

There are two main deep bass roles. One artist who has sung both in the same performance is Bulgarian Boris Christoff, who was also a celebrated Boris in *Boris Godunov*. Among other basses known in this work were the Polish Adam Didur and the Russian Ivan Petrov.

MET PERFORMANCES

Ten performances over three seasons: 1915, 1916, and 1917.

RECORDING

CD—Sony Dig. S3K 44878 (3). Stefka Evstatieva, Alexandrina Milcheva-Nonova, Kaludi Kaludov, Boris Martinovich, Nikola Ghiuselev, Nicolai Ghiaurov. Sofia National Opera Chorus and Festival Orchestra. Emil Tchakarov. 1990.

VIDEO

Kinyaev, Milashkina, Nesterenko. A film with Kirov Opera. Russian; English subtitles. Provatorov, conductor. 1969. KULTUR.

Gustave Charpentier

Number 75. *Louise*
by Gustave Charpentier
June 25, 1860–February 18, 1956

Premiere at the Opéra-Comique, Paris, 1900. Text by the composer. A "Roman musical" in four acts (five tableaux).

It is not a well-known fact that Gloria Steinem and I won a dancing contest together.

The time was a distant New Year's Eve, the place the suburban Washington home of a mutual friend, and the judge the friend's small daughter. The party was small; only three other couples participated in the contest. A paper star was the prize.

Another suitable prize for Ms. Steinem would have been a recording of Gustave Charpentier's *Louise*, famous not only for its music but because it was the first important Women's Lib opera.

Louise, produced first in 1900, is a little difficult to categorize. It belongs partly to the lyric opera that was performed at Paris's Opéra-Comique in the second half of the nineteenth century—such operas as Gounod's *Faust* in 1859, Thomas's *Mignon* in 1866, Bizet's *Carmen* in 1875; Delibes's *Lakmé* in 1883, and Massenet's *Manon* in 1884. But it also belongs partly to the naturalism/realism/verismo school, initiated by *Carmen*, epitomized by Mascagni's *Cavalleria rusticana* of 1890 and Leoncavallo's *Pagliacci* of 1892 and seen somewhat in Puccini's *La Bohème* in 1896.

Charpentier was a socialist, and this one work for which he is remembered is known for its liberal social views—from free love to graphic pictures of the miseries of poverty. Set totally in the composer's beloved Paris, it startled and frightened middle-class Paris with its revolutionary view that a woman has the right to live her own life.

The staid Paris Opéra, stunned by the realism, the contemporary setting, and the real-life costumes, would have no part of the work. But the Opéra-Comique accepted it, after some hemming and hawing. The audience cheered at the premiere after each act and, contemporary critics said, gave it a "thunderous" demonstration of appreciation at the end.

Charpentier is known best for this one work, but he also wrote songs, a little orchestral music, and another opera that had a tad of success, *Julian*, 1913, a sequel to *Louise*.

Born in Dieuze, Lorraine, in 1860, he studied under Massenet at the Paris Conservatory, where he won the Prix de Rome. Returning to Paris, he lived in Bohemian Montmartre, contemptuous of authority, concerned with social justice, a defender of the working class in his writings, and a coworker on several humanitarian projects.

The Elbow Nudge

No one does a better job of finding wonderful quotations than Harold C. Schonberg, longtime *New York Times* music critic. For Charpentier he looks into the diary of Alma (Mrs. Gustav) Mahler, writing about a Charpentier visit to Vienna: "Spits under the table, chews his nails, draws your attention by the pressure of a knee or a nudge of his elbow. Trod on my foot last night to call attention to the beauty of *Tristan* . . . He's a socialist and wants to convert me."

Charpentier is not Bizet, and *Louise* is not *Carmen*. But it is a good opera to think about if you have a chance to drift around Montmartre in the cold rain some spring Parisian day, sampling wine and looking for a windmill to paint.

KEYNOTE

A blend of realism, socialism, sentiment, and symbolism. A seamstress is the heroine and Paris the hero. A portrait of a city and the start of a century.

PLOT

Contemporary Paris. Julien (tenor), a young artist, is in love with Louise (soprano), a dressmaker. Her father (bass) is suspicious of artists—and of all others who live Bohemian lives. Because she loves her parents and doesn't want to part on bad terms, Louise has Julien write a letter asking permission for the two to marry. When her father won't give his blessing, they go off to live together in the Paris Bohemian area of Montmartre. Derelict citizens of Paris are selling milk and picking rags on the streets.

Although Julien is displeased that Louise needs and wants parental consent, they are in love and have each other. Her fellow workers don't care about her, she has been scolded and beaten by her mother, and her father has treated her like a child, but she and Julien are together and free. She thinks of the current beauty of her life, happy since the day she gave herself to him.

However, when her mother, the one most opposed to the match, brings word that her father is dying, Louise rushes to his bedside. He tries to talk her into staying home, but she needs and wants Julien and hears the city calling her back to freedom. As she leaves, her father shakes his fist at the evil city that has disrupted his life and unsettled his home. His final words: "O Paris."

HIGHLIGHTS

Act II: Julien's serenade to Louise, "Dans la cité lointaine" ("In the distant city").

Act III: Louise's lyric soprano "Depuis le jour," remembering when they first made love, much the best-known aria of the opera. "Since the day when I gave myself to you, my future has blossomed. What a beautiful life . . . Ah I am happy and I tremble at the memory of the first day of our love."

COMMENTARY

Louise has lasted for the same reasons all operas last: because the public likes the music. But the most "different" thing about it, for a 1900 opera, is the plot. Louise loves her father deeply, she is tender with him, she understands his concerns, but she is going to be free and do her own thing and she will not have her parents dictate her actions.

Her father always treated her like a little girl; even when grown she sat on his lap. Her mother beat and scolded her; in one aria proclaiming, "He whom you love, you chastise." Psychologists today would find much wrong with Louise's home environment.

It is a sentimental work flavored with a good bit of symbolism, personified in a tenor identified as a "Night Prowler," who represents the "pleasures of

Paris." Musically, there are songs, spoken and sung passages, and continuous orchestral music.

Debussy: "More Silly than Harmful"

One contemporary composer who was not enthralled by *Louise* was Claude Debussy. In a letter to a friend he wrote: "It seems to me that this work had to be. It supplies only too well the need for that cheap and idiotic art that has such appeal."

Debussy complained that Charpentier had taken "the cries of [Paris] which are so delightfully human and picturesque" and turned them into "sickly, parasitic" harmonies. "It is so silly that it is pitiful . . . more silly than harmful."

If this is what was to be called Life, he said, he would prefer to die then and there.

A woman named Marthe Rioton created the role of Louise. Her understudy, who had never sung before an audience, was a young singer named Mary Garden. When Rioton became ill during a performance, Garden stepped in, was a sensational hit, and sang the role more than two hundred times at the Opéra-Comique over the next several years. Born in Aberdeen, Scotland, Garden became one of the most glamorous opera singers of the twentieth century. Later she was to create the role of Mélisande in Debussy's *Pelléas et Mélisande*, which also premiered at the Opéra-Comique. She ended her career with the Chicago Opera, where, in 1919, she became the first woman to direct a major opera company. Although she failed financially as a manager, she remained with the company as a singer until 1931.

MET PERFORMANCE
Fifty-two performances over nine seasons, from 1921 to 1948.

RECORDING
CD—CBS/Sony S3K 46429 (3). Ileana Cotrubas, Jane Berbié, Plácido Domingo, Michel Sénéchal, Gabriel Bacquier. Ambrosian Singers. New Philharmonia Orchestra. Georges Prêtre. 1976.

VIDEO
Grace Moore, Thill, Pernet. A film in black and white by Abel Gance, French; no subtitles. 1938. BCS (Bel Canto Society).

❦

Number 76. *Wozzeck*
by Alban Berg
February 9, 1885–December 24, 1935

Premiere at the Berlin Staatsoper, 1925. Text by the composer from Georg Büchner's 1837 play Woyzeck. *An opera in three acts, five scenes in each act. Performed without intermission.*

"You see, Doctor, sometimes people have a character of a certain kind, but with nature it's quite different . . . You see, with nature, it is . . . what should I say . . . for example . . . when nature is at an end, when the world becomes so dark that you have to grope around it with your hands, until you feel that it's disintegrating like spiders' webs, or when things are and yet aren't! Oh! Oh! Marie, when everything is dark, and all that's left is a red glow in the west, as from a furnace, what can you hold on to?"

The speaker is Wozzeck, a bewildered soldier, the hero (or nonhero) of *Wozzeck*, a vastly different piece of work from most operas in (or out of) The Collection. Though powerful, compassionate, and humanitarian, clearly it isn't for everyone.

Some contemporary critics say *Wozzeck* is the twentieth century's best opera. But earlier on a few considered it a squalid tragedy that failed to meet the mark.

Why is it different? In parts the music is atonal. The construction deals with specific musical forms used by composers, like symphonies, marches, and fugues, and weaves them into the dramatic action. The plot is concerned chiefly with inner feelings rather than action and a story line.

Low Hopes

Alban Berg, responding to an interviewer: "You want my opinion on the following questions: What I require of the modern opera house . . . and also, what I hope for and expect, as a composer, from opera managers? As to the first, I want the classical operas produced as if they were modern, and vice versa. And as the composer of *Wozzeck*, I naturally hope that this opera of mine will be produced . . . but I do not expect it."

Assessments today are rarely, if ever, as negative as some that came immediately after its premiere nearly seventy-five years ago. One critic then wrote that he felt he had been in an insane asylum. Another said he thought the walls of the opera house were crashing down on him.

The reviews were so excessive that the publisher had them printed in a little booklet. A year after the Berlin premiere a production in Prague caused a riot. Interestingly, the next production was in Leningrad. The work made Berg famous; within ten years it had more than 150 performances in 25 cities and towns. Sir Adrian Boult conducted a broadcast in New York in 1934, and Leopold Stokowski performed it in New York.

The Soviets, and later, the Nazis, were not impressed. The Nazis included Berg among their list of degenerate artists who purveyed cultural Bolshevism. The Soviets found a different set of problems with the opera:

One—It revealed the helplessness of the Western European petty bourgeois intelligentsia before oncoming fascistization.

Two—It demonstrated the existing crisis not only in the individual consciousness of the bourgeois Western European composer, but in all Western European musical culture as well.

Professor Joseph Machlis, in "Introduction to Contemporary Music," wrote: "Like *Carmen* and *Boris Godunov*, *Pelleas*, and *Salome*, *Wozzeck* creates an atmosphere all its own. It envelops the listener in a hallucinated world in which the hunters are as driven as the hunted. *Wozzeck* could have come only out of central Europe in the Twenties. But its characters reach out beyond time and place to become eternal symbols of the human condition."

We have gone through the drill of diatonic and chromatic scales, of tonality and atonality. At the end of the nineteenth century, some composers began to get away from music that was strictly tonal, built around a specific key. Two Collection composers who made significant moves in this direction were Wagner and Debussy. Arnold Schoenberg (see the Twentieth-century European Package) then composed in twelve-tone serial music, with no one note or chord as a tonal center. This made dissonant music that sounds unlike Bach, Beethoven, Schubert, and Verdi.

Schoenberg's two chief disciples were Anton Webern and Alban Berg. Berg's best-known work is *Wozzeck*, based on a play by Georg Büchner. In *Wozzeck*, although the music is atonal it's not composed strictly according to Schoenberg's twelve-tone method. Berg's second opera, *Lulu*, 1937, which he didn't finish, *is* a twelve-tone work (see the Twentieth-century European Package).

But *Wozzeck's* novelty wasn't only in its musical language. It came also from the opera's message. Berg was an expressionistic composer.

The term "expressionistic" is borrowed from painting to describe certain kinds of twentieth-century music written to "express" the composer's innermost feelings. Like expressionist paintings, which use distortion and exaggeration to try to duplicate a sort of inner reality, expressionist music is harsh and discordant as well as emotional and dramatic. In an expressionistic opera, the action taking place on stage isn't important compared with the psychology of the characters.

One message Berg is expressing in *Wozzeck* is that life is a tragedy for any human being who feels. When that cynical message is exaggerated, the result can be shocking.

For many opera houses in the late 1920s, the issue was not so much whether the management "liked" *Wozzeck* but whether the audiences would come to see such a strange work. One observer applauded its excellence but still described it as nightmare music from a nightmare world.

The negative critics called the atonal music "chaotic" and the plot "degenerate and psychosexually sordid" because it expressed the hopelessness in the life of the downtrodden Wozzeck, a simple soldier. He is a symbol of the oppressed—a symbol of all men and women who are humiliated and overcome by a world too big for them to handle.

Berg's strong and compassionate social statement about the downtrodden drew the reaction one would expect from the self-defined German Nazi supermen thugs who were controlling his Austria in the 1930s.

But his problems weren't limited to Germany. In an open letter written in 1951 to protest the failure of the Metropolitan Opera to produce *Wozzeck*, Pulitzer Prize–winning composer Virgil Thomson, critic for the *New York Herald-Tribune*, addressed Metropolitan general manager Rudolf Bing:

"You know perfectly well," he said, "that it [*Wozzeck*] was removed from the German and Austrian theaters in the 1930s both for its political content and for its composer's religion. You also know that both its political content and its musical style place it out of bounds today everywhere behind the Iron Curtain. Also that last summer's production in Salzburg, which you mention as selling less well than Verdi's *Otello* [hardly surprising] had to run against the opposition of the powerful Austrian clergy, determined to remove it from the repertory on theological grounds. You know too that Switzerland and Italy have seen the work revived since the war and that Paris will see the Vienna Opera Company's production next spring. Nobody ever suggested to you that it probably would be a draw at the Metropolitan like *Cav* and *Pag*, though it would probably do as well in any season as *Parsifal*. It has merely been pointed out that if the Met is looking for twentieth-century works of unquestioned musical 'importance' and tested appeal, *Wozzeck* is up near the top of the list. And if the Met is afraid of attempts at political or religious censorship, then I am ashamed of it."

That was twenty-six years after its Berlin premiere. And it was another eight years before *Wozzeck* finally did make it to the Met.

Professor Paul Henry Lang calls *Wozzeck* a "convincing masterpiece" but also points out that no one with the exception of Britten in *The Turn of the Screw* has as yet successfully duplicated Berg's type of musical and dramatic approach.

KEYNOTE

Banned by the Nazis and long ignored by the Met. One of the big twentieth-century psychological operas. Different themes and different sounds from a first-level talent.

PLOT

The plot is disjointed. Berg emphasized that the important thing was the idea of the opera, not the fate of the characters. Germany, about 1830. Wozzeck (baritone) is a fumbling ordinary soldier who is despised by—and consistently put down by—his captain (tenor). While cutting sticks with his friend Andres (tenor), he hears strange sounds, sees visions, and senses mysterious forces. He thinks the red sunset is the world on fire. Marie (soprano), his mistress, and the mother of his child, flirts from her window with a passing Drum Major (tenor) and later lets him into the house to make love to her.

Wozzeck is examined by a half-crazy doctor (bass) who is using him in food experiments the soldier doesn't begin to understand. After the doctor and the captain torment him about Marie's infidelity, he questions her in a vague way and she more or less denies it, but later he must listen to the drunken Drum Major boast of the conquest.

The Drum Major further humiliates him by knocking him down when Wozzeck refuses to drink with him. Marie reads in the Bible about the sin of adultery, repents, and asks the Lord to have mercy on her. When Wozzeck comes to see her, the two go walking in the moonlight, and as they walk past a pond he cuts her throat with a knife. Later, in a tavern, he sees blood on his hands, rushes back to the pond to find the knife, throws it into the water . . . and is drowned as he's trying to wash off the blood. Their little boy, now an orphan, is playing with his hobby horse with other children when he hears that Marie's body has been found. But he doesn't understand what has happened and follows the others when they all run off.

HIGHLIGHTS

Act III: The "interlude" that is the climax of the opera, extraordinary music depicting extraordinary compassion.

COMMENTARY

Seventy years after the premiere, many people still are uncertain quite what to make of *Wozzeck*. Unquestionably it is a powerful drama. Atonal music no longer is strange to any professional ears, and, although Dvořák and Tchaikovsky remain far more popular with most nonprofessional classical music lovers, fewer and fewer listeners today are shocked by "modern" (the early-century term) musical sounds.

While most of *Wozzeck* is atonal, not all of it is "harsh" atonality. Here in the mid-1900s, some of the orchestral music is not at all difficult to take. (But some is, for my ears, though I've just listened to the full opera four times on earphones while doing my daily two-mile walks. Maybe it will soften up on the fifth hearing.) The music people today describe it as one of the few really successful operas "in a fully modern style."

Vocally, the opera is a stew: singing melody, which sounds peculiar because of the atonality; straight speech; rhythmic speech; and half-song half-speech. It is continuous music, without conventional set arias.

Instrumentally, there also is a smorgasbord: a military band, a restaurant orchestra, high-pitched violins, an accordion, an out-of-tune upright piano, a tuba brass band, and a chamber orchestra.

Structurally, it is unique. Each of three acts has five scenes. Act I has a suite, a rhapsody, a military march, a lullaby, a passacaglia (a dance form), and a rondo. Act II's scenes are constructed like five movements of a symphony. Act III's scenes are a series of musical "inventions": "variations" on a theme, on a tone, on a rhythm, on a chord, and on a tonality (central note). But we amateur listeners don't recognize all of this unless we are tracking a libretto that describes it.

Even if you never see *Wozzeck*, you owe it to yourself to hear the Act III interlude between scenes four and five. Berg here does use a key, D minor, and the music fraternity has come to call it "the great D minor interlude." (In opera, an interlude is an orchestral piece that comes between two vocal sections.)

The Critic and the Composer

Not surprisingly, the old-line music critics in the mid-1920s were shocked by the different sounds of Berg's *Wozzeck*. One wrote: "The listener attains an hypnotic state in which he believes the walls of the theater are about to crash down on him."

And another: "As I was leaving the State Opera, I had the sensation of having been not in a public theater but in an insane asylum. On the stage, in the orchestra, in the stalls—pure madmen . . . We deal here, from a musical viewpoint, with a capital offense."

The composer described his own thoughts: "I never contemplated the reform of opera through the composition of *Wozzeck* . . . Aside from the desire to create good music . . . I intended nothing more than to bring to the theater that which by right belongs to the theater.

"I wanted to create music at every moment conscious of its responsibility to the drama—yes, even more, drawing from within itself those elements necessary for the transposition of drama into reality; an achievement that demands of the composer the resolution of all essential tasks of stage direction. This was to be done without violating the autonomy of the music . . .

"No matter how well one may be acquainted with the musical forms to be found in this opera, with its stringent and logical construction, with the artistic skill exhibited in its details, I demand that from the moment the curtain rises till the moment it falls, no one in the audience shall be conscious of this diversity of fugues, inventions, suite forms, and sonata forms, variations, and passacaglias—no one, I repeat, be filled with anything but the *idea* of the opera, which far transcends the individual fortunes of *Wozzeck*."

Singer Snippets: The role of Marie was created by Sigrid Johanson in Berlin in 1925. A famous concert performance in Chicago in 1984 starred Benjamin Luxon as Wozzeck and Hildegard Behrens as Marie. Conducted by Claudio Abbado, it had full costumes but no scenery. Behrens sang the role of Marie in many productions. A 1959 Met staging featured American soprano Eleanor Steber as Marie and the German bass-baritone Hermann Uhde, a famous Wagner Dutchman, as Wozzeck. Karl Böhm conducted.

MET PERFORMANCES

Forty-four performances over eight seasons from 1959 to 1990. Five performances are scheduled for the 1996–97 season.

RECORDING

CD—Decca/London 417 348–2 (2). Anja Silja, Hermann Winkler, Horst Laubenthal, Heinz Zednik, Eberhard Wächter, Alexander Malta. Vienna State Opera Chorus. Vienna Philharmonic Orchestra. Christoph von Dohnanyi. 1979.

VIDEO

Behrens, Grundheber. Vienna State Opera. German; English subtitles. Abbado, conductor. 1989. HOME VISION.

Murder and Manslaughter

How good can an opera be if it doesn't give the audience at least one violent death? I asked criminal lawyers and former prosecutors for criminal law findings that might be expected today in the following operas. Penal law differs in various states and this is a blend of East and West Coast opinion.

AIDA—After disclosing the Egyptian line-of-march to Aida, and thus to the enemy, Radames is sentenced to be buried alive in a crypt. Finding: Radames is innocent of treason because of lack of intent. He is guilty of unauthorized release of classified information.

ANDREA CHÉNIER—After Gerard signs the indictment, Chénier is sentenced to be executed as a counter-revolutionary. Madeleine joins him in the death cell. Finding: Gerard is guilty of malicious pros-ecution and, since he knew the accusation was false, of murder. No liability can be placed for the execution of Madeleine, who has joined Chénier of her own volition.

BORIS GODUNOV—Young Dmitri, half-brother to the Tsar and his heir, is killed by Boris's order. Boris's sole objective is to seize power. Finding: Boris is guilty of aiding and abetting murder, and of conspiring to commit murder.

CAVALLERIA RUSTICANA—Alfio, jealous husband, kills Turiddu in a duel. Finding: Duelling is a crime: the fighting of two persons, one against the other, at an appointed time and place, upon a precedent quarrel. Both men are guilty of it. Alfio also is guilty of involuntary manslaughter.

THE GOLDEN COCKEREL—In a dispute over payment of a reward, King Dodon kills the Astrologer with his sceptre. The cockerel pecks Dodon to death. Finding: Dodon is guilty of murder. The King has sover-eign immunity for civil liability but not for the criminal act of murder. The cockerel may be seized by order of the court, but trouble may be ex-pected from animal rights groups if an attempt is made to put it to death.

DON CARLOS—By order of King Philip, Rodrigo is killed by an assassin while visiting Carlos in prison. Finding: The King is guilty of murder for hiring the killer, that is, for soliciting, requesting, com-manding, or importuning the commission of a homicidal act.

DON GIOVANNI—Don Giovanni kills the Commendatore as he reluctantly defends himself in a duel after the Commendatore has come to his daughter's room to help her. Finding: Don Giovanni is guilty of burglary in the first degree, entry for the purpose of commit-ting a felony, if it can be established that his intent was to rape Donna Anna. In that event, he knowingly entered a dwelling to commit a crime therein, was armed with a deadly weapon, and subsequently caused physical injury (death) to another person therein, the Commendatore. Seduction is not a crime. Giovanni is also indicted for murder, although his attorneys will argue self-defense in that the force he employed against the Commendatore was used to resist an attack upon his person.

ELEKTRA—Orestes kills his mother, Clytemnestra, and his stepfather, Aegisthus, at Elektra's urging. Finding: Orestes is guilty of a double murder. Elektra, his sister, is guilty of two counts of solicitation to murder. The murder finding is of the first degree or second degree, depending upon the locality. In some states murder in the first degree is reserved for such homicides as causing the death of a police officer, peace officer, corrections officer, or a witness to a crime.

EUGENE ONEGIN—Lenski considers his friend Onegin to be overly flirtatious, challenges him to a duel, and is killed. Finding: Duelling is a crime, as noted. Onegin is guilty of voluntary manslaughter.

THE FORCE OF DESTINY—Leonora's father dies when Alvaro's pistol is accidentally discharged after the father finds him in Leonora's bedroom. Later, in a duel he tries to avoid, Alvaro mortally wounds her brother, Carlo. Before he dies, Carlo stabs Leonora. Finding: Though dead, Carlo technically is guilty of battery for striking Alvaro in the face. He is not guilty of assault, in that his slap was not executed with intent to cause bodily harm. Both men are guilty of duelling. Alvaro is guilty of voluntary manslaughter for the death of Carlo and Carlo of murder for the death of Leonora. It is unlikely that Alvaro would be indicted for murder or manslaughter in the death of Leonora's father, in that he had not committed burglary to gain entrance to the dwelling, and because he attempted to avoid harming him.

DER FREISCHÜTZ—Caspar is killed by a magic bullet that has been fired by Max at a dove but is guided by the devil to hit Caspar. Finding: If the forest is in an incorporated city, Max may be guilty of possession of a gun or discharging a gun. He is not guilty of murder. The killing was accidental, with no intent, and caused by an intervening force over which he had no control.

LA GIOCONDA—Barnaba throws La Cieca, blind mother of Gioconda, into the canal, to drown. Finding: Murder.

HANSEL AND GRETEL—The bad witch plans to bake the children in her oven and eat them. They push her into the oven and she is made into a gingerbread cake. Finding: No crime. Justifiable homicide. Self-defense.

LES HUGUENOTS—Count de St. Bris, a Catholic, orders his men to fire on Raoul and Marcel, two Huguenots. They do so, killing both men. Their shots also accidentally kill Valentine, the Count's daughter.

Finding: St. Bris is guilty of three murders. Crimes against humanity. In the case of his daughter, he showed an indifference to human life in recklessly engaging in conduct that created a grave risk of death.

JENŮFA—Kostelnicka drowns the illegitimate daughter of her stepdaughter, Jenifer, to protect Jenifer from shame and to preserve her forthcoming marriage to Laca. Finding: No justification. Murder.

LOHENGRIN—Frederic and four followers crash into the bridal chamber intending to kill Lohengrin, but he kills Frederic with one swipe of his sword. Finding: No crime. Self-defense. Justifiable homicide.

LUCIA DI LAMMERMOOR—After being tricked into thinking Edgardo has deserted her, Lucia is forced by her brother, Henry, to marry Lord Arthur Bucklaw. When she and Bucklaw retire to their chambers, she goes crazy with despair and stabs him. She dies of grief and Edgardo, on a guilt trip, stabs himself. Finding: Lucia is not guilty by reason of insanity. Suicide is a crime and Edgardo is guilty of it.

MACBETH—Macbeth murders Duncan, King of Scotland, with a dagger. He also sends assassins to murder Banquo. Macbeth has been egged on throughout by Lady Macbeth. Finding: Macbeth is guilty of murder and solicitation to murder. She is guilty of solicitation or conspiracy in the first degree.

A MASKED BALL—Renato joins an assassination plot to shoot and kill his friend and superior, Riccardo, the Governor of Boston, who is in love with Renato's wife. Finding: Murder. Given Riccardo's official position, murder in the first degree.

OTELLO—Driven by Iago's villainous treachery, Governor/ General Otello smothers his wife, Desdemona, in her bed, and stabs himself. Finding: Murder. The fact that the homicide was committed under the influence of extreme emotional disturbance constitutes a mitigating circumstance. Suicide also is a crime.

PAGLIACCI—Canio, a suspicious husband, chases and stabs to death his wife, Nedda. When her lover, Silvio, tries to help her, Canio also kills him. Finding: Not premeditated, in either case. In some localities, manslaughter in the first degree, causing the death of another person with the intention of causing grave physical injury, or with the intent to cause death. In other localities, second degree murder.

PELLÉAS ET MÉLISANDE—Golaud finds Mélisande with his half-brother, Pelléas, and kills Pelléas with his sword. Finding: Second degree murder or manslaughter, finding his wife with another man. No premeditation or malice, but acting with intent to cause serious physical injury or death. In some localities, manslaughter in the second degree if Golaud recklessly caused the death of another person, and manslaughter in the first degree if he intended to cause the death.

RIGOLETTO—Rigoletto hires an assassin to kill the Duke. When his daughter, Gilda, substitutes herself for the Duke, the assassin kills her and stuffs her in a sack. Finding: Rigoletto is guilty of murder solicitation. The doctrine of transferred intent makes it irrelevant that the wrong victim was killed.

SALOME—Herod, in disgust, orders his soldiers to crush Salome with their shields after she has kissed the lips of the severed head of John the Baptist and danced the Dance of the Seven Veils. Finding: Herod is guilty of murder solicitation. It is not relevant that he is king. Salome is guilty of conspiracy in the first degree in that she conspired with Herod with intent that conduct constituting a Class A-1 felony (the murder of John the Baptist) be performed.

SAMSON ET DALILA—Samson, a prisoner of war, kills himself, Dalila, and a whole mob of Philistines by pulling down a temple on them all. Finding: Presumably self-defense. In any event, since Samson died there is no reason to decide whether this was murder and suicide, or a self-defense killing and accidental death.

THE RING—*Das Rheingold*: The giant Fafner kills his brother Fasolt with one strong blow as they argue over money. Finding: Voluntary manslaughter. *Die Walküre*: Hunding, husband of Sieglinde, kills Siegmund with his sword in a duel after Siegmund has run off with, and impregnated, Hunding's wife. Finding: Voluntary manslaughter. Killing in a sudden quarrel or heat of passion. *Siegfried*: Siegfried kills and stabs Fafner-as-a-dragon. Siegfried also kills his foster father, the little sneak Mime, when he learns Mime is planning to poison him. Finding: No charge for killing a dragon. Siegfried will plead self-defense for wiping out Mime, but is unlikely to prevail. *Gotterdämmerüng*: Hagen thrusts his spear into Siegfried's back, killing him. Hagen also stabs and kills his half-brother, Gunther. Finding: Two counts of murder.

TOSCA—Tosca murders the villainous Scarpia with a fruit knife, as he lusts for her and is torturing her lover, Cavaradossi. Finding: Tosca is not guilty of murder, which is an unjustified, intentional, premeditated killing. Guilty of justifiable homicide on the grounds of self-defense and defense of another.

TRISTAN UND ISOLDE—While King Mark is away, Melot finds Tristan and Isolde together. In a sword fight, Tristan kills Melot, is wounded, and flees. Finding: No crime. Self-defense.

WOZZECK—As the moon rises, Wozzeck, tormented, jealous, and confused, stabs and kills Marie, the woman he loves. Finding: Either not guilty by reason of insanity or, depending on the locality, second degree murder or manslaughter in the first degree. In either event, emotional instability, meaning the lack of capacity to premeditate.

~

Number 77. *Werther*
by Jules Massenet
May 12, 1842–August 13, 1912

Premiere in a German version at the Hofoper, Vienna, 1892. First performed in Paris at the Opéra-Comique in 1893. Text by Edouard Blau, Paul Milliet, and Georges Hartmann from Goethe's 1774 novel, Die Leiden des jungen Werthers. *Four acts.*

Here's a challenge. Listen to the last fifteen minutes of Act I of this romantic tragedy and the first fifteen minutes of Act III. My guess is that will cause you to start wondering whether *Manon* really is Jules Massenet's best opera and also lead you to challenge the comment sometimes made that everything Massenet wrote except *Manon* is now out of date.

So maybe these thirty minutes won't grab you as Puccini does, but five will get you ten that you'll like the music, that you'll be glad you listened, and that the music will stay with you. And probably you'll decide that both *Manon*, Number 29, and *Werther* are splendid operas.

Manon was written in 1884 and *Werther* in 1892. Some scholars make the case that Massenet matured during those years and refined his technique, particularly his orchestration. (Though he was over fifty even for *Manon*).

The reasons for Massenet's choice of a work by the great German Goethe are as tantalizing as Gounod's selection of one Goethe work and one of Shakespeare's. Both composers are known more for French grace and charm than heavy drama. Also, Massenet usually went for heroines as central figures, not suicidal males: Manon in one opera, Thais in another, Cinderella in a third.

Suicide Starter

Massenet's *Werther* came almost 120 years after a partly autobiographical novel by Goethe. Very popular in its day, the novel began a craze of suicide among depressed literary-minded young men. Several operas were written from it before Massenet's, including one in 1792 and another in 1802.

Massenet's was a "middle period" work, like Wagner's *Lohengrin* and Verdi's *La traviata*. It took him seven years to compose, much longer than his usual time. Although technically a number opera, with arias, duets, and choruses connected by recitative, few numbers are emphasized and there is a sense in it of Wagner's "continuous melody."

This Goethe work, however, is hyper-romantic and not in the *Faust* category Gounod selected.

If you have flown into Germany, odds are you've flown into Frankfurt. Thirty-three miles away is the town of Wetzlar, the setting for Goethe's novel. Massenet and his publisher visited the town on a journey to Richard Wagner's Bayreuth, a trip taken because the French composer was captured by Wagner's music. There, according to an account by James Harding, who wrote a biography of Massenet in 1970, Massenet was inspired to take on *Werther*:

"Hartmann [Massenet's publisher] produced a copy of the book and told him to read it. They went to a nearby tavern filled with noisy students, and over a couple of bocks, Massenet immersed himself in the letters which tell of the unhappy romance between Werther and Charlotte. At first he was but mildly interested. Then, as he read on, his feelings were aroused by the lovers' fugitive happiness, Charlotte's marriage with Albert, her betrothed, and Werther's despairing suicide. Forgetful of the reek of beer and pipe smoke, he gave in wholeheartedly to the charm of a love story that had entranced generations of romantically minded readers.

" 'Such rapturous and ecstatic passion brought tears to my eyes,' Massenet exclaimed. 'What moving scenes, what thrilling moments it could all give rise to! *Werther* it was'!"

Well, one is wise to be suspicious of stories and quotes like these. In one distant life I kept a file of "quotes printed but never uttered," and some musicologists suggest the opera was already under way when this reported conversation took place. But it doesn't matter. Six months later, it was completed.

KEYNOTE

Intimacy. Lovers by moonlight. Sentiment. Wisps of music here and other wisps there. More sentiment. *Werther* is Massenet's most melodic opera and his second most popular, having been performed more than 1300 times in Paris alone.

Professional Praise

The 1954 *Grove Dictionary of Opera* said of Massenet that "to have heard *Manon* is to have heard the whole of him." When he was with *The New Yorker*, critic Andrew Porter dissented. He would rephrase to say, "To have heard *Manon* and *Werther* is to have heard the best of him."

PLOT

About 1780. Near Frankfurt, Germany. Werther (tenor), a melancholy young poet and dreamer, and Charlotte (mezzo-soprano) are in love, although

Charlotte is engaged to Werther's more practical friend, Albert (baritone), the man her dying mother made her promise to marry. When Charlotte says she must keep her promise, Werther leaves in despair. Three months later he returns to find her married and apparently happy. Had he won her, his life would have been heaven. After Werther and Albert talk, Werther decides he should leave again. But the proximity to Charlotte is too much for him, and before going he reveals that he still loves her. After considering suicide, he does leave, planning not to return.

Not until he's gone does Charlotte realize that she still returns his love. She is so distraught that Albert recognizes for the first time that she and Werther care for one another. Another three months later, on Christmas Eve, when Charlotte is sitting alone, rereading letters he has sent her, Werther appears in the doorway, and before long they are in each other's arms. Filled with guilt and remorse, she rushes away and locks herself in her room.

Deciding that his death is the only honorable answer, Werther borrows a set of pistols from Albert and shoots himself. Charlotte finds him with the pistols at his side, attempts to revive him, confesses she loves him, and they kiss for the first time. Werther dies, hearing children singing "Noël" and imagining he's hearing angels promising that he has been forgiven.

HIGHLIGHTS

Act I: The magical "Moonlight Sonata"—"Clair de Lune"—interlude and the duet between Werther and Charlotte that follows.

Act II: Werther's "Un autre est son époux" and "J'aurais sur ma poitrine," as he knows he can never marry Charlotte, a favorite aria of French tenors.

Act III: Charlotte's "Letter Scene," which opens the act, as she rereads the letters Werther sent her: "Werther, Werther, Who would have told me of the place he holds in my heart today!"

This is followed by her prayer for aid, "Va, laisse couler mes larmes": "Please, let my tears flow—they do me good. The tears we don't shed all fall back into our soul."

Also Werther's "Pourquoi me réveiller?" ("Why awaken me?"), as he sings of his tragic love.

COMMENTARY

The biggest letter scene in opera belongs to Tatiana in *Eugene Onegin*. Another big one is Charlotte's, also powerful and convincing. Here she turns from an unattractive, standoffish person into flesh and blood.

Negative critics find it too sugary. I hope you don't and offer condolences if you do.

MET PERFORMANCE

Sixty performances over nine seasons, from 1894 to 1989.

A Domingo Favorite

In his autobiography, Plácido Domingo calls *Werther* "an opera I love" and writes of his debut in it in Munich: "The sets were stark and extremely effective, and the production by Kurt Horres was outstanding, as was the conducting of López-Cobos ... A little over a year later I recorded the work with a different company at studios in Bayer-Leverkusen, just outside of Cologne. Bayer aspirin is produced there, and it occurred to me during those sessions that poor Werther would have done much better to resolve his problems with aspirin than through the more drastic means he eventually resorted to."

RECORDING

CD—Phillips 416 654-2 (2). Isobel Buchanan, Frederica von Stade, José Carreras, Thomas Allen. Orchestra of the Royal Opera, Covent Garden. Colin Davis. 1980.

VIDEO

Dvorsky, Fassbaender, Vasary. A film by Petr Weigl. French; English subtitles. 1984. West German Television.

∾

Number 78. *Jenůfa*
by Leoš Janáček
July 3, 1854—August 12, 1928

Premiere at the National Theatre, Brno, Moravia, 1904. Text by Janáček from Gabriela Preissova's 1890 play, Her Foster Daughter. Three acts.

This is a grim opera of suffering, tragedy, and love.

Leoš Janáček was an operatic master. He also was deeply entranced by language. Some people collect stamps, some copper pots, some decoy ducks, some baseball trading cards. One Canadian acquaintance, who rarely misses an auction on either side of the New York–Quebec border, collects gentlemen's canes.

Janáček collected Moravian peasant language sounds.

At an early age he began traveling through Moravia, meeting with choirmasters, talking with peasants, and gathering samples of the language, studying the rhythms, the inflections, and the melodies. He was convinced that different people in different conditions of life and different moods speak differently, and his goal was to translate the language sounds he captured into musical expression, not only for his operas but for his instrumental music, which is shot through with Czech speech rhythms and is unlike the rhythms of any other composer.

Jenůfa, built around Moravian peasant life but not a folk opera, is one of his earlier operas and his best-known one. It took him twenty-seven years to write it.

Chronologically, Janáček was the most recent of the three leading Czech composers of classical music, after Bedřich Smetana (*The Bartered Bride*, Number 63) and the great Antonín Dvořák (*Rusalka*, see the Twentieth-century European Package).

The Bartered Bride is a Czech institution. But *Jenůfa* also is a national favorite and Janáček's international status with both the professionals and the public has grown each year since the end of World War II. He combines great talent with rare originality, and two prominent musicologists—who privately break the rules of The Club and admit to order-ranking talent and genius—advise me that they would include Janáček on any list of opera's all-time top ten composers.

If a single word were picked to characterize his music it might be "bleak." His works don't have the soft, sweet flowing melodies of Smetana and Dvořák. And—unlike many composers who mellowed out—the older he grew, the more dissonant and progressive he became.

Four of his other operas, all different in style and all performed today in the United States, are:

Kátă Kabanová, 1921, which combines Romantic and twentieth-century music into a strong drama

The Cunning Little Vixen, 1924, a fantasy of animals and humans, his least dissonant opera

The Makropoulos Case, 1926, drawn from a 1922 play by Karel Čapek, with a 337-year-old heroine

From the House of the Dead, 1930, based on Dostoevsky's 1862 account of his prison life in Siberia. It's an opera without drama or even story but with strong characters. Characters are important to Janáček. His ability to depict them in music is part of what lifts him into the upper levels of opera composers.

See the Twentieth-century European Package for more on Janáček, especially on *The Cunning Little Vixen*. He, Britten, Berg and Richard Strauss are the four twentieth-century composers who are in both The Collection and that package.

Janáček was the ninth of thirteen children, born in Hukvaldy, northern Moravia (now part of the Czech Republic), not far from Poland, in 1854. His father was the village schoolmaster and the founder of a local singing society. After studying music in Brno and later in Prague, young Janáček returned to Brno to help found an organ school with which he was associated for forty years as it grew into a conservatory. He died in Brno in 1928.

Suffering Keenly Shared

Writing in *The New Yorker* in September 1980, music critic Andrew Porter said this about Janáček's masterpiece: "*Jenůfa*—does it still need saying?—is one of the great operas of our century. Suffering and despair have not been more keenly shared. Attending it is a searing experience. Poor little Butterfly draws easy, enjoyable tears; *Jenůfa* is drama and music on another level. It would be unbearable but for the composer's tenderness and compassion. Out of the tragedy and the horror, understanding and love are born."

Most of his best works were written in his later years. The first production of *Jenůfa* was in Brno in 1904, when he was fifty. Although it had local success, it was not until a dozen years later that an interested friend helped arrange for a performance in more sophisticated Prague. Prague—a favorite city of Mozart's and the one in which his *Don Giovanni* premiered—was one of the longtime musical centers of Central Europe. The *Jenůfa* production there established Janáček's name in the regional music world, and international fame began eighteen months later when a German translation was performed in Vienna.

Janáček began writing it in 1875 when he was traveling around rural Moravia but didn't finish it until twenty-seven years later. After a Berlin production in 1924 it was quickly staged in a dozen German cities. The first American showing was at the Metropolitan Opera in New York in 1924. Although very popular through Central Europe, Germany, and especially England (England seems to have a thing about Janáček), it never has established itself as a fixture in the United States, despite high praise from many in the professional Music Establishment.

Because of the composer's preoccupation with the Czech language, Janáček operas are most enjoyed when heard in that language rather than in German or English translations.

In the instrumental field, his best-known classical works include Sinfonietta, a suite in five movements; *Taras Bulba*, a tone poem; the *Kreutzer* String Quartet, and the *Glagolitic Mass*.

Jon Vickers as Laca and Teresa Kubick in the title role of Jenůfa,
a Metropolitan Opera production

KEYNOTE

Grim peasant opera of raw tragedy, passion, and compassion. Folk-style melodies. One of the top twentieth-century opera composers with one of the century's top operas.

PLOT

A village in Moravia in the nineteenth century. Števa (tenor) is a ne'er-do-well mill owner who has slept with his cousin Jenůfa (soprano) and made her pregnant. His half brother, Laca (tenor), a farm hand, also is in love with Jenůfa, who is the stepdaughter of the female sexton, known as the Kostelnička (soprano). Jenůfa waits to see whether Števa will be drafted or will stay home and thus be free to marry her. Although he's not drafted, he comes home drunk and the Kostelnička rules that he must go for a year without a drink to prove he's worthy of Jenůfa.

Meanwhile, when Jenůfa won't let Laca kiss her, he angrily slashes her face with a knife.

By the time Jenůfa has borne Števa's illegitimate son, he's now in love with Karolka (mezzo-soprano), the mayor's daughter, and Laca has apologized to Jenůfa and asked her to marry him. To conceal Jenůfa's indiscretion and avoid family disgrace, the Kostelnička gives her a sleeping potion, takes her baby, drowns it in the icy water of the brook, and later tells Jenůfa it has died of a fever.

As a double marriage is about to take place of Jenůfa-Laca and Števa-Karolka, word is brought that a baby has been found under the ice. Jenůfa admits it's hers and to save her from murder charges the Kostelnička admits her guilt. She hears Jenůfa forgive her as the authorities lead her away. Jenůfa offers to free Laca from his marriage commitment now that he knows about her affair and the baby, but he stands by her, pleads for her love, and receives it as the curtain falls.

HIGHLIGHTS

By design, there are no big show-stopper arias. The best-known numbers are several choral pieces, especially in the folk scenes of Act I.

COMMENTARY

Jenůfa is a tragedy of love, life, death, and moral principle. Like all of Janáček's works, it is in the Czech language. And, like all, it shows his mastery of the theater.

Musically, it has set numbers, especially choruses and ensembles, based on Janáček's speech-melody concept. Dramatically, it is powerful. The critics use words like "savage intensity" and "barbaric strength."

The greatest early triumph of *Jenůfa* was in Berlin, six years after its 1918 German language premiere in Vienna, led by Erich Kleiber, one of the top conductors of the time, who had studied in Prague and was sympathetic to the opera. During the dress rehearsal, the composer whispered to a friend, "That it was given to me to live to witness that."

After the performance, Janáček wrote Kleiber a thank-you note, saying in part: "I am still thinking of you. You turned my work into a string of delightful sun-drenched peaks. The Recruits' song and Jenůfa's song had always come off as a hacking military march. You breathed the life of hot young hearts into it. . . . Yours is the first well conceived *Jenůfa*, not the Prague or the Vienna one. If I might ask anything at all of you it would be (1) the introduction to Act I a little faster, to give it a suggestion of unrest. And put the xylophone on stage, near that mill wheel. That will muffle its icy sound. That's all."

Swedish soprano Elisabeth Söderström, born in 1927, performed *The Makropoulos Case*, *Kátă Kabanová*, and *Jenůfa*, working frequently with the acknowledged Janáček authority among contemporary conductors, Sir Charles Mackerras.

MET PERFORMANCES

Thirty-one performances over five seasons, 1924, fifty years later in 1974, and then in the 1985–86 season, and in 1993.

RECORDING

CD—Decca/London 414 483-2 (2). Elisabeth Söderström, Eva Randová, Wieslaw Ochman, Peter Dvorsky. Vienna State Opera Chorus. Vienna Philharmonic Orchestra. Charles Mackerras. 1982.

VIDEO

Alexander, Silja, Langridge. Glyndebourne Festival Opera. Czech; English subtitles. Davis, conductor. 1989. HOME VISION.

&

Number 79. *Die Lustigen Weiber von Windsor* *(The Merry Wives of Windsor)*
by Otto Nicolai
June 9, 1810–May 11, 1849

Premiere at the Berlin Hofoper, 1849. Text by Hermann von Mosenthal, from Shakespeare's 1600–01 play, The Merry Wives of Windsor. Three acts.

The Merry Wives of Windsor is light fare—airy-hearted, witty, and gay. It remains a tremendous favorite in Germany, having been performed more than four hundred times at the Staatsoper in Hamburg alone. Although this is less than half as often as Mozart's big operas are given there, all comparisons with Mozart are meaningless and it's a noteworthy record.

Otto Nicolai was a melody-maker and Merry Wives (Die Lustigen Weiber von Windsor) is a melodic comic opera. Be not misled, however; although not one of music's demigods Nicolai was a serious and talented musician and composer—he was principal conductor of the Vienna Hofoper for several years, founder of the Vienna Philharmonic Orchestra, and Kapellmeister and director of the Royal Opera in Berlin. He died the very day that he was appointed a member of the Berlin Academy of Arts.

As the Hofoper's conductor, he was the first to introduce Beethoven's Léonore No. 3 overture as something played between the acts of Fidelio, a custom that has endured, although with less and less frequency.

On the one hand, the professionals say he belongs in the second rank, while on the other they hold him considerably higher than a fellow German also in The Collection, Friedrich von Flotow (Martha). Let's just say that this is a fun work, a good example of German Romantic comic opera, well worth seeing and hearing—enjoyable, even if not in the league with Verdi's Falstaff on the same subject.

Nicolai was a man who enjoyed his job. "My new opera," he wrote, "has in its composition made me very happy. The happiest hours of an artist are those which he spends in creation."

German time check: This was midcentury, a time in Germany between Carl Maria von Weber and the full development of Richard Wagner. The major operas were:

Beethoven's powerful *Fidelio*, 1805–1814
Weber's German Romantic *Freischütz*, 1821
Wagner's *Flying Dutchman*, 1843; *Lohengrin*, 1850; more Wagner in the 1860s.
Flotow's melodic *Martha*, 1847
Nicolai's light *Merry Wives*, 1849
Humperdinck's fairy tale *Hänsel und Gretel*, 1893

The real operatic challenge to Wagner as a great master came not from fellow Germans such as Flotow, Nicolai, or Humperdinck but from composers in other European countries.

The Merry Wives is an example of several operas that are popular in Europe and included in The Collection even though they're not often seen in the United States. It's also good to have it in The Collection as evidence that artists who aren't Mozart-Verdi-Wagner giants can produce fine and enduring works.

KEYNOTE

Nicolai's masterpiece. German wit and fresh melody applied with German musical skill to an immortal English comedy.

PLOT

Windsor, England, during the reign of Henry IV. The plot is much the same as Verdi's *Falstaff*, but has some different characters. Two English ladies, Mistress Ford (Frau Fluth) (soprano) and Mistress Page (Frau Reich) (mezzo-soprano), decide to punish the sometimes oafish Sir John Falstaff (bass) for his arrogance and for writing them both love letters. Mistress Ford especially is furious at all men.

Sir John is trying to woo her at the Ford house when Mr. Ford (Herr Reich) (baritone), always suspicious of his wife, returns with friends, hoping to catch her with another man. Sir John hides in a basket full of laundry, which is carried out by two servants. Mistress Ford scolds her husband for his unjustified doubts about her.

At the Garter Inn, Sir John boasts of his success with Mistress Ford. He returns to her house to try again. Mistress Page appears to announce that Mr. Ford is again coming home, and this time they disguise Sir John as an old woman. Mr. Ford and his wife confront one another while Sir John is smuggled out.

At the Page home, the two wives explain to their husbands that they have joined forces to embarrass Sir John, and Mr. Ford apologizes for his suspicions. Later, in Windsor Park, the two women again flirt with Sir John, leading him on as though they were attracted to him, though the village knows he is a victim of his own arrogance. A subplot throughout concerns Mistress Page's attempt to marry her daughter Anne (Anna) (soprano) to the wealthy Dr. Caius (bass), although she is in love with Fenton (tenor), a poet. Anne and Fenton elope, her parents accept their marriage, and all three Windsor wives are merry.

HIGHLIGHTS

The Overture, heard in the concert hall and on classical radio. Perhaps the opera's best-known tune.

The opening duet between the two wives.

Act I: The opening duet between the two wives. Mrs. Ford's plan, "Nun eilt herbei": Nothing is too wicked that punishes menfolk without mercy. Men are so bad that one cannot torture them enough. Above all that fat glutton who wants to seduce us!"

Act II: "Als Büblein klein," Flastaff's drinking song at the beginning. The comic duet between Falstaff and Ford. The aria for Fenton, "Horch, die Lerche singt im Hain."

Act III: Anne Page's aria, the opera's top soprano aria.

COMMENTARY

The analysts say this is the first German opera featuring ensembles since Mozart's *Marriage of Figaro*. The only one of several Nicolai operas still performed, it blends Italian voice characteristics—in Italy, always the voice—with German craftsmanship.

Right On

"German operatic music," said Otto Nicolai, "contains enough philosophy but not enough music."

A pair of German singers are perhaps the most famous in the leading roles: tenor Fritz Wunderlich as Fenton and bass Gottlob Frick as Falstaff. German-then-American soprano Lotte Lehmann was known as a hard-to-beat Frau Fluth.

MET PERFORMANCES

One performance in 1900. It was produced in Philadelphia in 1863, in London in 1864, 1878, 1907, and 1943, and at the New York City Opera in 1980 under Beverly Sills.

RECORDING 69348-2 (2).

EMI/ANGEL Ruth-Margret Pütz, Edith Mathis, Fritz Wunderlich, Gottlob Frick. Bavarian State Opera Chorus and Orchestra. Robert Heger. 1963.

❧

Number 80. *Duke Bluebeard's Castle*
by Béla Bartók
March 25, 1881–September 26, 1945

Premiere at the Budapest Opera, 1918. Text by Béla Balázs, from Maurice Maeterlinck's play based on an old Bluebeard legend. An opera in a Prologue and one act.

Béla Bartók's only opera is one of the strangest in The Collection, challenged chiefly by *Wozzeck*. It is a grim psychological mood piece overflowing with symbolism, a powerful drama about human isolation that some critics said was influenced by Claude Debussy, Arnold Schoenberg, and Sigmund Freud.

That combination of mentors is unlikely to produce gay, light, airy, easy-to-handle stuff. A word the music people like to use is "accessible." A lot is not accessible about impressionist Debussy and even less about atonal Arnold Schoenberg . . . and for Freud it's every mother-loving son for himself.

The composer himself denied Schoenberg's influence, insisting that the roots of his compositions came from peasant music alone.

Hungary's Béla Bartók, like Russia's Mussorgsky, was a nationalist composer, one of music's greatest collectors of folk music and *the* outstanding expert on Hungarian folk works. His one opera, written at age thirty, has not begun to win the same general acclaim as Mussorgsky's *Boris Godunov*. However, together with Igor Stravinsky . . . and some say Arnold Schoenberg . . . and some say Benjamin Britten . . . and some say Leoš Janáček, he is one of the twentieth century's leading composers.

Bartók was one of the early-twentieth-century masters who was not captivated by melody and who experimented with his own different harmonies. "Harsh" and "slashing" are the kinds of words used in describing his work, although as music has changed during the twentieth century it comes across as a good bit less "harsh" and "slashing" today than when his compositions were first published.

"It may sound odd," he wrote, "but I do not hesitate to say that the simpler the melody, the more complex and strange may be the harmonizations and accompaniments that go with it."

Bartók was born in Nagyszentmiklós, Hungary, the son of an agricultural school director and a piano teacher. He studied at Budapest at the Royal Academy of Music. His interest in Hungarian folk music began when he was still young, and over time he published some two thousand folk tunes, from Hungary, Romania, and other countries in Eastern Europe. A valid research scientist, he wrote five books and many articles on folk music.

He also insisted, and proved his point, that folk music—or at least the folk music of Hungary and other Central European countries—was not made up of simple little folksy tunes.

In 1939, after his mother died, he left Hungary because of the Nazis and moved to the United States, where he had financial problems and suffered from leukemia. A stubborn, shy "I'm-all right-Jack" individualist, he refused offers of help from friends, although some got around this by silently securing commissions for him. One of these resulted in his most famous instrumental work, the *Concerto for Orchestra*, commissioned by Serge Koussevitzky, successful Russian-born conductor.

Yes!

If *Duke Bluebeard's Castle* is not your thing, stick with other Bartók music, just for his love of freedom. In 1938 he wrote a friend: "There is imminent danger that Hungary will also surrender to this [German Nazi] system of robbery and murder. How I could then continue to live or—which amounts to the same thing—work in such a country is quite inconceivable."

Harold C. Schonberg shares with us this paragraph from a will Bartók wrote before leaving Hungary for the United States: "If after my death they want to name a street after me, or to erect a memorial tablet to me in a public place, then my desire is this: as long as what were formerly Oktogon-ter and Korond in Budapest are named after those men for whom they are at present named (Hitler and Mussolini), and further, as long as there is in Hungary any square or street, or is to be, named for those two men, then neither square nor street nor public building in Hungary is to be named for me, and no memorial tablet is to be erected, in a public place."

Bartók and *Bluebeard* belong in The Collection on their record and merit, but I would include the man who produced a will such as that, just for the honor of it.

Bartók's reputation as a classical composer has grown gradually but consistently since his death in New York near the end of World War II. A ballet, *The Miraculous Mandarin*, has had more success than this one opera, and a suite from it is often performed. His other best-known classical works include *Music for Strings, Percussion and Celesta*, his second violin concerto, several string quartets, and Hungarian folk and peasant songs.

A Met-Texaco joint venture on radio and television in 1989 gave the opera enormous exposure. Stick with it; it sounds a little less "slashing" with each hearing.

KEYNOTE

Hungarian opera's greatest masterpiece, a haunting journey into the mysteries of the subconscious. Hungarian folk melody married to twentieth-century irregular rhythm. Be prepared: A totally different kind of opera with its symbolic castle.

PLOT

A Gothic castle. In the Prologue, a bard appears onstage to ask the audience to reflect on whether the play takes place in the world outside or the world within—on the stage or in the mind. The hall of the old castle—or mind or skull if you will—is without windows but has seven doors. Bluebeard (baritone/bass) arrives with his new wife, Judith (soprano), whose family has opposed their marriage. She declines his offer to leave but wants light in the gloomy place and, seeing no windows, decides to open some of the doors. He prefers not to give her a key but does so reluctantly after she explains that she loves him and wants to know all about him. The first door leads to a torture chamber, in which the walls are wet with blood. Surprisingly, Judith is not intimidated. She moves on, asking for the key to the second, which opens into an arsenal for war. The third shows a treasure room, a treasury of riches, but they also are smeared with blood.

Three doors down and four to go. Ignoring Bluebeard's concerns, Judith presses ahead, obsessed with learning everything about him and his life. The next door shows a garden, filled with bloodstained flowers, and the fifth brings in dazzling, blinding white sunlight. Bluebeard takes her in his arms, but she sees blood-colored clouds forming. Still acting against Bluebeard's counsel, she opens the sixth door, and finds water. Bluebeard explains that it comes from human tears. She asks about other women in his life before her, but he avoids a direct answer, urging her to love him without question. He is reluctant to give her the final key, but she insists upon having it, now believing he's keeping it from her because the rumors are true that he has murdered his previous wives. He advises her that behind this door are all his former wives. Three pale but lovely women come out—the bride of the morning of his existence, of his midday, and of his evening. One by one they then disappear back through the door.

Judith is the bride of the night; Bluebeard says she is the most beautiful of all. She must take her place with the others. He fetches a crown, a robe, and jewels from the treasury room. As if in a dream, she follows the other three women back through Door Number Seven, which shuts after her. Bluebeard is alone; the stage is dark; there is only night.

HIGHLIGHTS

This has been characterized as a cross between a long tone poem and an opera, more like a one-act Wagner music drama than a Verdi-type composition. It has a striking Wagner-like orchestral "blood motif" that is repeated as different doors open, but no big aria. Bluebeard's last long farewell is one of the most striking scenes.

COMMENTARY

One message of *Duke Bluebeard's Castle* is this: Man is essentially lonely; woman is too often incapable of penetrating that loneliness.

All or Nothing

Belá Bartók was unhappy with the treatment given one of his works by The Budapest Philharmonic Society. He wrote the director:

"I did not wish to be a kill-joy and so did not speak up against the barbarity of your performing my 1st Suite in a mutilated way at your gala concert in Vienna. Now that this has been done once more in Budapest . . . I am obliged to protest against your procedure. It is the common consensus that works of the sonata or symphony type ought not and cannot be performed with movements omitted, at serious concerts . . .

"I must, under the circumstances, declare that I should be extremely grateful to you if you would never again perform any of my works."

Never apt to win over the general public because it is so unconventional, ambiguous and expressionistic, *Bluebeard* is one of those works which turn on many professionals. After a 1986 concert performance by the Philadelphia Orchestra in Carnegie Hall, critic Andrew Porter wrote "*Bluebeard* can be overwhelming in the theater but is scarcely less impressive when the orchestra alone depicts the gloomy, menacing castle hall, the shafts of light streaming in as each door is opened, the scenes revealed behind them . . . Some performances of *Bluebeard* use the score for a display of high-powered orchestral virtuosity. The Philadelphia performance, played with great warmth and beauty of tone, was subtle and moving. The emotions of the drama and its mysterious psychological symbolism took first place."

"Mysterious" and "symbolic" are the key words. If the text is enigmatic, like Debussy's *Pelléas et Mélisande*, the ambiguous music seems to fit the enigmatic text. Some sounds are shadowy and impressionistic, and some sounds are like Hungarian folksong. The sung phrases have a hypnotic effect as they follow the rhythms of the Hungarian language, somewhat as the Czech composer Janáček did. There are no breaks for breath or applause. It is not easy music in which to find melody, but the orchestration, totally different with the opening of each door, is regarded as masterly.

Desmond Shawe-Taylor wrote in London's Sunday *Times* a quarter of a century ago: "Bartók, whose own need for inner solitude was imperious, and whose remoteness could be frightening, threw himself into the subject with an intensity which grips the listener."

With only two characters and little action, this is one of the best nominees in The Collection to try on compact disc, heard but unseen. Several performances are available.

Bass Samuel Ramey in the title role and Eva Marton as Judith are one combination the critics like. Ramey's "dark" voice is considered ideal for the character. Other Bluebeards have included Dietrich Fischer-Dieskau, one of the great baritone singers of the century, (and a noted interpreter of lieder), and Austrian bass-baritone Walter Berry, with Romanian Julia Varady and Germany's Christa Ludwig as their mezzo-soprano Judiths.

MET PERFORMANCES

Twenty-two performances in three seasons from 1973 to 1989.

RECORDING

CD—CBS/Sony Dig. MK 44523 (1). Eva Marton, Samuel Ramey. Hungarian State Orchestra. Adám Fischer. 1987. In Hungarian.

VIDEO

Kovats, Sass. A film. Hungarian; English subtitles. Solti, conductor. 1981. PGD.

❧

Number 81. *Orfeo*
by Claudio Monteverdi
May 15, 1567–November 29, 1643

Premiere at the Palazzo Ducale in Mantua, 1607. Text by Alessandro Striggio after Ottavio Rinuccini's libretto, based on the Orpheus legend, for Jacopo Peri's 1600 opera Euridice. *Musical fable in a Prologue and five acts.*

Orfeo is the first of the five Golden Oldies, which will be given in chronological order as the last five Collection operas.

This is a biggie. The Italian hand stretched out here by Claudio Monteverdi was grasped centuries later by Giuseppe Verdi. If there were to be a World Opera Day, it should be May 15, Monteverdi's birthday.

Monteverdi is one of the giant figures of music—not only the first great composer of opera nearly four hundred years ago but also one of music's finest and most original all-around classical geniuses.

And herein lies a minor structural problem for this section. *Orfeo or The Fable of Orfeo*, is the first great opera, demands the major share of historical attention, and must be part of The Collection. But despite its fame, Monteverdi's own greater masterwork was *L'incoronazione di Poppea*, his last opera, which came thirty-five years later at the end of his life.

Many musicologists' comments here about Monteverdi apply more to *Poppea* than to *Orfeo*. *Poppea* is not in The Collection but receives special Honorable Mention attention at the end of this section.

Before getting into opera, Monteverdi created masses, motets, requiems, and madrigals with enormous talent and recognition. It is not difficult today to find musicologists who say unequivocally that he was the most distinguished pioneer in the whole history of music. Fortunately for opera lovers and opera development, he combined a deep feeling for drama with these immense musical gifts.

One doesn't talk of a Meyerbeer, a Massenet, or a Donizetti—and, indeed, many analysts would include a Puccini—in the same breath as a Monteverdi, however many operas those meritorious composers might have contributed to a Collection of 85.

Passionate Winds?

When associates were urging him to compose one opera, Monteverdi wrote this rejection: "How can I imitate the language of the winds, which cannot speak, and move hearts through their mouths. Ariadne was moving because she was a woman, and Orpheus because he was a man, not a wind. These mythological personifications, these Tritons, these Sirens, are not capable of interesting and moving the spectator."

He wrote *Orfeo* the year that Jamestown was founded, 1607. It isn't permitted to become even mildly involved with opera without at least watching and enjoying a videotape of it. Honor will be done your name if you see and hear *Poppea* as well.

Monteverdi's story of Orpheus (English translation), like Christoph Gluck's *Orfeo ed Euridice*, Number 52, is based on the Greek legend of the poet who tried to rescue his beloved from Hell. Monteverdi is true to the legend; in his opera the rescue attempt fails. Other settings, including Gluck's, have a happier ending. Scores of other composers have used the same story, among them Franz Joseph Haydn and Johann Christian Bach, son of Big Time J. Sebastian.

Legend has it that Orpheus, their hero, had such a magnificent voice that beasts of the jungle followed after his song and trees uprooted themselves to chase after him. Today an opera about an Orpheus would demand an Environmental Impact Statement.

Monteverdi was born in Cremona, Italy, in 1567. That was more than one hundred years before Bach and Handel, both born in 1685, and nearly two hundred years before Mozart's birth. His first work was a book of madrigals, published in 1583. Shortly thereafter he was appointed violist in the Duke of Mantua's court orchestra and the two became close associates for a number of years. In 1613, after getting into opera and when left unemployed by the Duke's death, he moved from Mantua to become music director at the famous St. Mark's Cathedral in Venice. He died in Venice in 1643.

For its first thirty years, *Orfeo* was produced privately by musical societies and court theaters. But it also was presented outside Mantua, as part of a move toward public opera and a departure from the tradition that opera should only be for a particular wedding or other court celebration.

Orfeo took a while to reach America. Although performed in concert form at the Metropolitan in 1912, its first American stage performance was in 1929 in Northampton, Massachusetts, under the auspices of Smith College. It has been revived at the New York City Center in 1960, the Sadler's Wells Opera in London in 1965, the Edinburgh Festival in 1978, and the English National Opera under John Eliot Gardiner in 1981. Like many operas in the second half of the twentieth century, its greatest audiences have come from U. S. television.

Unlike the Florentine Camerata, Monteverdi was not concerned with going back to the ancient Greeks. His interest was in producing music drama—theatrical works that had both musical and dramatic truth. Musically, he used solo arias, recitative, duets, choruses, and orchestral pieces.

Musicians' Union Needed

The Duke of Mantua was a person of enormous importance to Monteverdi. But the good duke was one who expected more than a full day's work for a full day's pay, genius or no genius. At one point when he was ill and felt the workload to be a little excessive, the composer wrote his employer this plaintive note:

"I do most heartily pray your most Serene Highness, for the love of God, no longer to put so much work upon me; and to give me more time, for my great desire to serve you, and the excess of my fatigue, will not fail to shorten my life; and if I live longer, I may yet be of service to your Serene Highness, and of use to my poor children."

Professor Donald Jay Grout advises us that the orchestra Monteverdi used to characterize the dramatic situations was made up of the following instruments, although not all were used at the same time (note that he did not use percussion instruments):

Chord-playing Instruments

Two clavicembalos, one double harp, two chitarrones, two bass citterns, three bass gambas, two organs with wood (flute) pipes, one organ with reed pipes.

Stringed Instruments

Two small violins, a ten-string ensemble (possibly four violins, four violas, and two cellos), two contrabass viols.

Winds

Four trombones, two cornettes, one high recorder, one high trumpet, three soft trumpets.

Some musicologists today call Monteverdi the first great expert in instrumentation. Translation: He knew the capabilities of his instruments and used them skillfully to show changes in mood as the drama unfolded. He also is credited with improving the type of recitative that was used in early opera. Writing nearly a century ago, musicologist William Foster Apthorp said that

*Ronald Raines, in the title role of Monteverdi's Orfeo
at the Julliard American Opera Center*

Monteverdi changed the ponderous, leaden musical accompaniment of the Camerata into a vivacious, passionate, excited accompaniment that took its own rhythm, "thus establishing the basis for nearly all modern writing for a voice . . . with instrumental accompaniment."

Comparing Monteverdi opera with the early Camerata works, the music people say:

- His harmony is incomparably richer
- His recitative, as noted, is much more melodic and expressive
- He gave a much larger support role to a much bigger orchestra
- He introduced the first operatic overture, in the form of an introductory "toccata" (a keyboard composition).

Founder Score Card

Thirty-second time-out here to help keep opera founders, initial masters, and early reformers in perspective:

Italy: Monteverdi, 1567–1643. *Orfeo*, 1607. The father of opera.

France: Lully, born in Italy in 1632 and died in Paris in 1687. *Atys*, 1676. The father of French opera.

England: Purcell, 1659–1695. *Dido and Aeneas*, 1689. The father of English opera.

Germany: Handel, born in Germany in 1685 and died in his adopted England in 1729. *Julius Caesar*, 1724. A pre-Mozart giant.

France: Rameau, 1683–1764. *Castor et Pollux*, 1737. Major French figure between Lully and Gluck.

Plus the other old-timer introduced earlier in The Collection:

France: Gluck, German Bohemian who captured Paris and lived from 1714 to 1787. *Orfeo ed Euridice*, 1762. The great reformer.

KEYNOTE

The first great opera.

PLOT

In Greek mythology, Orpheus (English) was the poet and singer who could charm wild animals with his voice. When his wife, Eurydice (English), died, he followed her to Hades and won her back with his singing, on the condition that he couldn't turn to look at her until they had left the Underworld. At the last moment, worried about her, he couldn't help himself. When he turned to see if she was all right, she was snatched back to Hades. His grief turned him against all women, and he was torn to pieces in Thrace. The Muses collected fragments of his body and buried them at the foot of Mount Olympus.

In Monteverdi's opera (using Italian names), Orfeo (soprano or tenor [written for castrato]) is to be married to Euridice (soprano) and sings a hymn of rejoicing, joined by nymphs and shepherds. Then word is heard that she has died of a snakebite. Orfeo is led to the gates of Hades by Hope (soprano), who must leave him there. (In Dante's words, "All abandon hope, ye who enter here.") At first the boatman, Charon (bass), won't let him pass, but eventually Orfeo lulls him to sleep with his music and rows himself across the River Styx.

Prodded by his wife, Proserpina (soprano), Pluto (bass), King of the Underworld, authorizes Euridice's return to earth, but only under the don't-look-back condition. When Orfeo is unable to stick to the rules and does glance back, she slowly disappears. Orfeo returns to earth alone, having conquered Hades but failing to control his own emotions. In the fields of Thrace, he laments his loss and is renouncing all women when the heavens open and his father, Apollo (tenor or baritone), appears in a chariot.

After Apollo consoles his son, they both return to heaven, where Orfeo will see his Euridice in the stars.

HIGHLIGHTS

Act I: The first of Orfeo's big solos, a hymn to Euridice, "Rosa del ciel."

Act II: "Ecco pur ch'a voi ritorno," the pastoral episode opening the act. Then the solo by the Messenger, "Ahi caso acerbo," when he brings word of Euridice's death, and the accompanying scene in which Orfeo, the shepherds, and the chorus react to this news.

Act III, IV, V: Assorted Orfeo solos.

COMMENTARY

A key to the success of *Orfeo* is the singer playing the main part, who is onstage almost continuously from Act II on. This usually is a tenor.

MET PERFORMANCES

One appearance in 1912, in concert form.

RECORDING

CD—Deutsche Grammophon Dig. 419 250-2 (2). Julianne Baird, Lynne Dawson, Diana Montague, Anne Sofie von Otter, Mary Nichols, Anthony Rolfe Johnson, Nigel Robson, Willard White, John Tomlinson. Monteverdi Choir. English Baroque Soloists. His Majesty's Sackbutts and Cornetts. John Eliot Gardiner. 1985.

VIDEO

Huttenlocher, Turban, Schmidt. Zurich Opera House. Italian; English subtitles. Harnoncourt. 1978. PGD.

Honorable Mention: *L'incoronazione di Poppea*

Premiere at the Teatro di Santi Giovanni e Paolo in Venice, 1642. Text by Giovanni Francesco Busenello based on Roman works of Tacitus and others. An opera in a Prologue and three acts.

The Coronation of Poppea was Monteverdi's last opera, written when he was seventy-five. It demands attention on the grounds that the music reaches sublime heights, that it's possibly the most erotic opera ever written, and that it defines one ideal of musical drama in a way that *Orfeo* doesn't begin to.

Music Versus Poetry

Although he was a magnificent master of music, Monteverdi's mission was to use it to express the essence of the poetry for which it was composed.

"The text should be the master of the music," he wrote, "not the servant."

It's rarely wrong to think in terms of William Shakespeare. One of my preferred experts argues that the balance of seriousness and comedy in *Poppea* directly follows Shakespeare and sets the stage for Mozart. There is, he contends, nothing of significance in this genre in between the two.

A side issue is that there's been some debate in recent years whether Monteverdi was the only composer of *Poppea*, but we'll stick with the conventional thinking.

Poppea is about lust and ambition. It is the story of the love of the Roman emperor Nerone (Nero) for Poppea, the wife of one of his generals, Ottone. To get Poppea, Nerone banishes Ottone and divorces his own wife, Ottavia.

Professor Grout writes: "This rather sordid subject is handled by the poet with consistency, good taste and dramatic insight . . . The composer's greatness lies in his power of interpreting human character and passions—a power which ranks him among the foremost musical dramatists of all times."

There it is again: the ability of an opera composer to use music to portray the emotions, fears, and desires of his characters—bold music for this one, hesitant music for that one, and lyrical music for the next.

Poppea is much more solidly in the international repertory than *Orfeo*, despite the historical attention given the latter. Musicologists say that Giovanni Francesco Busenello (1598–1659) was the first great librettist. He was a poet, lawyer, and ambassador.

∾

Number 82. *Atys*
by Jean-Baptiste Lully
November 28, 1632–March 27 1687

Premiere in Paris, 1676. Text by Philippe Quinault, from Book IV of Ovid's Fasti. *A tragédie en musique in a Prologue and five acts.*

Jean-Baptiste Lully was an unlikely fellow to be the founder of French national opera.

He was born Italian, a comedian, a ballet dancer, and a violinist, with little formal training in music. In his early years he was known for writing scurrilous songs.

But he also had lived in Paris since age fourteen, had developed into a reasonably skilled composer, and was a strong conductor. He changed the spelling of his name from the Italian Lulli to the French Lully and became a naturalized Frenchman. Even then, at first he was not interested in opera for France, but later he changed his mind.

Of primary significance to the success of his career was the support of the King of France, and Lully bore the title of "maître de la musique de la famille royale." If you want to found French opera, that's a good job to have: Music Boss for the Royal Family. Lully knew how to bow low before King Louis XIV, but he also was a ruthless decision maker and a born monpolist capable of keeping a foot on the throat of the opposition.

Had there been a "maître de anti-trust de la famille royale," Jean-Baptiste Lully would have been in deep yogurt. But there wasn't, and he maintained control by conning the King into going along with him. For instance:

- He had an order approved forbidding any theater other than his own to use more than six violins.
- No theater other than his own was permitted to employ more than twelve musicians.
- None of his actors could work in any theater other than his own.

The opposition did not melt rapidly. Rick's twentieth-century Casablanca was no match for Paris in the 1600s as a city of intrigue, and before long there was the Affair Guichard, which went something like this:

Monsieur Guichard was an opera manager, frustrated by the Lully edicts and scorned by Lully as a librettist. Guichard's good friend was Sebastian Aubry, and

Aubry's sister, Marie, was Guichard's mistress. In front of them both, Guichard spoke about poisoning Lully's tobacco. But then he left Marie for another mistress. This was not wise. Annoyed, she ran to Lully himself and reported the plot. Lully demanded, and obtained, Guichard's arrest. It took three years for the dust to settle, and in the end the courts were as confused as the populace. The first verdict was for Guichard to pay all costs, but on appeal this was reversed and Lully was ordered to pay. In any event, it was a lovely scandal.

Thievery

Lully was one of several composers from whom the great Handel stole. The Abbé Prévost wrote in 1733: "Some critics, however, accuse him [Handel] of having the matter of many beautiful things from Lully, especially from our French cantatas, which he has the skill, so they say, to disguise in the Italian style."

Lully died in action. While conducting a Te Deum for the King, who was ill and not expected to live long, he struck himself in the foot with his long baton. This caused an abscess that led to medical advice to amputate the toe, later the foot, and finally the leg. Lully stubbornly refused and died on March 22, 1687, after writing one will to disinherit his son Louis, known as both libertine and scoundrel, and then, under the influence of his wife, another to bring Louis back in again.

(As a time check, both Bach and Handel were born in 1685, two years after his death. Mozart was seventy years away.)

He was a stormy fellow who led a stormy life.

His renowned librettist, Philippe Quinault, influenced him enormously. A successful playwright, Quinault helped see to it that Lully's operas followed the form and dramatic structure of the strong dramatic tragedies for which the French were famous.

But a dramatic tragedy on the stage is worthless unless the audience hears the words. In opera it is recitative that moves the plot along, that keeps the story going, that sets the stage for the arias, duets, and ensemble numbers in which characters express their emotions and reactions. Without comprehensible recitative, there can be no operatic drama. Yet a lot of Frenchmen—and no doubt some Frenchwomen as well—believed that the French language was not suitable for recitative. The presumed problem chiefly had to do with accent. To improve his knowledge of the flow of the language in order to make opera more attractive to the ear, Lully listened for hours and hours to tragedies at the Académie Française.

"We Parisians have the world's finest drama," the French said in effect, "and the world's finest ballet. Let the Italian canaries do their thing in opera."

With the support of Louis XIV, however, and after seizing control of the Académie Royale de Musique, Lully produced an opera nearly every year from 1673 until his death in 1687.

His kind of opera, called tragédie-lyrique, was to last in that general form for one hundred years or more, through the life of Jean-Philippe Rameau (*Castor et Pollux*, Number 85) and even the reforms of Gluck (*Orfeo ed Euridice*, Number 52).

Lully's works include *Cadmus et Hermione*, 1673; *Alceste*, 1674; *Thésée*, 1675; *Atys*, 1676; *Isis*, 1677; *Psyché*, 1678; *Bellérophon*, 1679; *Proserpine*, 1680; *Phaëton*, 1683; *Amadis*, 1684; *Roland*, 1685, and *Acis et Galathée*, 1686.

Productions of these operas lasted until the middle of the eighteenth century or so. *Thésée* (*Theseus*) and *Amadis* were revived later in France. Workshops today produce others. Recorded excerpts from some are on and off the market—and so is an occasional complete performance. And Lully's ballet-plays sometimes are performed.

A Musician of Property

It is a good thing to be in high favor with the court. At his death, Lully left four houses, all in the better quarters of Paris, plus securities and other possessions amounting to a considerable fortune. His was known as a parsimonious family.

But his wife and six children erected to his memory a splendid monument, surmounted by his bust, in the left-hand chapel of the church of the Petits Pères in Paris.

The selection here of *Atys* is an arbitrary one, made in part because as this is written one can find it on compact disc and cassette tape. The purpose is chiefly to offer a taste of Lully; we cannot ignore the founder of French opera. *Thésée* remained in the international repertory longer than any of his other operas, and it may return to the record shelves. It isn't easy to see a live Lully opera today, but it shows a little couth to know about him. And there was a 1989 performance of *Atys* at the Brooklyn Academy of Music by Les Arts Florissants, an important early opera revival group.

KEYNOTE

A representative opera of the founding father of French opera. Please the King, and the show goes on. See the hero turned into a pine tree.

PLOT

In mythology, Atys is the Phrygian counterpart of the Greek Adonis. He was loved by Cybèle, the mother of the gods, who drove him mad out of jealousy. He castrated himself, died as a pine tree, and violets sprang from his blood. Gaius Valerius Catullus, Roman lyric poet, wrote a poem on the subject.

Characters in a fifteen-minute Prologue include the God of Time (baritone); the Hours of the Day and Night (chorus); Zephyr (haute-contre [the highest male voice in classical French opera]); four small Zephyrs; Melpomene, the Muse of Tragedy (soprano); Flora, Goddess of Spring (soprano); a batch of hero dancers, including Castor, Pollux, and Hercules, and assorted others. Not for a moment is it forgotten that King Louis XIV is the only audience that counts. "Nothing can stop him when glory calls," it is sung of the King. "The greatest of heroes," it is proclaimed. And much more. Flora and Time vie with one another to pay him homage.

The opera proper deals with Cybèle, a goddess queen (soprano); King Celenus of Phrygia (baritone), and Sangaride (soprano), a nymph. Celenus and Sangaride are to marry, but she loves Atys (haute-contre). He also falls in love with her, even though this makes him disloyal to his friend, Celenus. Goddess Queen Cybèle at first helps Sangaride and Atys, although she loves Atys herself and later tries to get him. After great confusion, Atys falls under a spell cast by Cybèle, is blinded, thinks Sangaride is a monster, stabs her, tries to commit suicide, and is turned into a pine tree by Cybèle. Now that she has lost him forever, she laments him.

HIGHLIGHTS

The Overture.
Act III: The orchestral interlude sleep scene.

COMMENTARY

Thanks to his homework and skill, Lully shaped a style of recitative, accompanied by instruments, that accommodated the accent and flow of the language. Future musicologists were to call it Lully's "exemplary" French recitative. It was devised to satisfy the drama-oriented French who wanted to hear the words.

Among the leading characteristics of *Atys* and other Lully operas were these:

- Larger choruses with bigger roles.
- Obligatory—not optional—ballet.
- A formal two-part overture.
- Small set arias only and those assigned only to some characters. Also, less of a distinction between arias and recitative than in Italian opera.
- No comic figures, unlike Italian opera seria.

- Five acts.
- Always—always, always—a prologue glorifying the King.
- Less coloratura ornamentation than in the Italian operas and a narrower vocal range, to preserve dramatic intensity. In the highest ranges, Italian castrati and sopranos were difficult to understand. To the voice-oriented Italians, the exact words were not so essential, but the drama-oriented French wanted to hear and understand every word. Lully soprano roles could be sung by the deeper-voiced mezzo-sopranos, tenor roles by high baritones.

None of this meant "freedom" for the composer. Rigidity, formality, and strict adherence to the Lully rules were the orders of the day. The King was the main spectator, the King's pleasure was to be met, and that which was put before the King was not to be prepared in a frivolous manner. This was Louis XIV, the Sun King, and one did not casually make the Sun King stormy.

The music was conventional, without startling chords or adventurous shifts from one key to another. Moderation was the thing. Violence was not good. Undue passion was not good. It was dignified but often stereotyped.

But because of Lully, inspired by the great spoken drama of his time, it *was* French opera.

MET PERFORMANCES
No performances of Lully operas. In 1912 there was one performance of a dance work, *La Danse*, along with the works of several other composers.

RECORDING
CD—Harmonia Mundi Dig. HMC 901257/9 (3). Agnès Mellon, Guy De Mey, François Semellaz, Guillemette Laurens, Noémi Rime, Jean-François Gardeil. Les Arts Florissasnts Chorus and Orchestra. William Christie. 1987.

Number 83. *Dido and Aeneas*
by Henry Purcell
c. 1659–November 20, 1695

Premiere at the Josias Priest School for Girls in London, about 1689. Revived by the Royal College of Music in London, 1895. Text by Nahum Tate from Book IV of Virgil's Aeneid. An opera in a Prologue and three acts.

The Josias Priest School for Girls is an unlikely place for the premiere of England's greatest opera, and the seventeenth century is an unlikely time for it.

Nonetheless, even considering twentieth-century Benjamin Britten, and his works, *Dido and Aeneas* arguably is England's finest operatic work and Henry Purcell its leading operatic composer.

Praise from Handel

Musicologist R.J.S. Stevens in 1775 recorded the following anecdote about Handel and Purcell: "When Handel was blind and attending a performance of the Oratorio of *Jephtha*, Mr. [William] Savage, my master, who sat next him, said, 'This movement, sir, reminds me of old Purcell's music.' 'O got te tettel,' said Handel. 'If Purcell had lived he would have composed better music than this.' "

To reach this judgment we must stipulate that Handel, however great during his life in England, was really German and that Gilbert and Sullivan, however marvelous in their music, are not truly operatic.

Brittenians, of course, would protest, and we can't really be resolute in our analysis because Purcell died young, without a chance to compose more works in the same form.

His *Dido*, a love story from Virgil's *Aeneid*, written three hundred years ago, is a masterpiece, with magnificent music, potent drama, and deep human understanding. It is a landmark Golden Oldie.

Here is a ready challenge: Kirsten Flagstad was the greatest Wagnerian soprano of her day. Purcell's seventeenth-century music is a mighty distance from Wagner. But get a recording of Kirsten Flagstad singing Dido's "Lament," or "Farewell to Life." Listen to it in front of a living-room fire, preferably with someone you love. Then claim (a) you don't like opera and (b) you have heard music that is more beautiful. If you can make both of those statements, take two aspirin and call me in the morning. You are not well.

The fashionable things to see and hear in seventeenth-century England were extravagant stage spectacles. Italians were into opera and so were the French, but the English were frying other fish. Their theater was in a state of disarray.

Example: In 1672, a new theater was opened in London. It specialized in elaborate musical productions, such as a souped-up version of Shakespeare's *Macbeth* with appropriate instrumental music. Some characters from the original Shakespearean drama were cut, others were added. New scenes were inserted to provide magic and mystery. Dances were tossed in. This was what the Londoners wanted, not something of the caliber of *Dido and Aeneas*.

Most Americans who spent time in England in World War II have never given up their love affair with the English people. One hopes that the England we knew would not have chosen souped-up Shakespeare over Maestro Purcell (although, in truth, Purcell had his hand in the same kind of thing with his own version of *The Tempest*).

Purcell wrote a great deal of vocal music, and a considerable amount has been recorded: things like songs, odes, hymns, and elegies. For the stage he wrote overtures and music for plays and pieces called "masques" and "interludes." But his only dramatic work that is sung throughout, and the only one regarded as an opera today, is *Dido and Aeneas*.

Purcell was born in a house on St. Ann's Lane, Old Pye Street, Westminster, in London, probably in 1659. His father was a professional musician. Among the posts the senior Purcell held was "Gentleman of the Chapel Royal." Who but England would have a Gentleman of the Chapel Royal? He also was a member of the Royal Band and sang at Westminster Abbey. Young Purcell also became a member-chorister of the Chapel Royal and studied music under Matthew Locke and Captain Henry Cooke, who was Master of Children. Captain Henry Cooke earned his title in the English Civil War and is not related to Captain James Cook, mariner and explorer of Alaska and Hawaii.

For a period of years Purcell was employed by the Crown as "keeper, maker, mender, repayrer, and tuner of the regalls, organs, virginalls, flutes and recorders and all other kind of wind instruments whatsoever, in ordinary, without fee, to his Majesty." For these duties he received "[pounds] 30 a year together with fine holland, handkerchiefs and a felt hat."

Locked Doors

This was Purcell's will: "I William Purcell of the City of Westminster, gent., being dangerously ill as to the constitution of my body but in good and perfect mind and memory (thanks be to God) do by these presents publish and declare this to be my last Will and Testament And i do hereby give and bequeath unto my loving wife Frances Purcell all my estate both reall and personall of what nature & kind and to her Assignes forever And I doe hereby constitute and appoint my said loving wife my sole Executrix of this my last Will and Testament revoking all former Will or Wills."

This was good news for Mrs. Purcell. William was not without fondness for alcoholic spirits and, according to Sir John Hawkins, old English historian, on one night "heated with wine from the tavern at an hour later than prescribed him," he found that she had locked the doors of his house against him.

In 1689 *Dido and Aeneas* premiered at a girl's boarding school in Liza Minnelli's Chelsea. Josias Priest, the owner, was a famous dancer and choreographer. His daughter had played the part of Adonis in an earlier work staged there. The original copy of the libretto has this inscription: "An Opera performed at Mr. Josias Priest's Boarding school at Chelsey, by young gentlewomen, the words by Mr. Nat Tate. The Musick composed by Mr. Henry Purcell." Musicologists are uncertain whether *Dido* was written for the girls or composed for court performance and adapted for the young ladies.

Purcell had a distinguished career in Musick. In time he succeeded composer John Blow as copyist at Westminster Abbey and then as organist at the Abbey. In 1682 he became organist at the Chapel Royal and in 1688 he played the organ as William and Mary were crowned at the Abbey. He died in Westminster of tuberculosis in 1695.

KEYNOTE

England's first opera. If not England's best, it's close enough, coming from the seventeenth century. You must hear Dido's "Lament."

PLOT

Dido (soprano), Queen of Carthage, and Aeneas (tenor or high baritone), famed Trojan prince, are in love. But a Sorceress (mezzo-soprano or, rarely, bass-baritone), who is an enemy of Dido's, is plotting the destruction of both Dido and the city of Carthage. The sorceress has her trusted elf (alto), disguised as the god Mercury, appear before Aeneas to command him to leave Carthage at once to found the new Troy (Rome) on Latin soil. Aeneas feels he has no choice but to obey the gods. When he tells Dido what he intends to do, she at first compares him to the deceitful crocodile that lives in the Nile. This causes Aeneas to start to waver, but the damage is done so far as Dido is concerned. She says she wants no part of a lover who would even think of leaving her. At the same time, she knows within herself that once he is gone there is nothing for her but death. As Aeneas and his fleet sail away, she dies of a broken heart.

HIGHLIGHTS

Act III: Dido's "Lament," one of the most moving expressions of sorrow in all opera.

COMMENTARY

Purcell was a superstar. The thing he did best was write for the voice. He composed fine music for several plays, but only *Dido* is characterized as an opera. Lord Harewood, cousin to the Queen, editor of the revised *Kobbé's Complete Opera Book*, and former director of both the Royal Opera House at Covent Garden and the English National Opera, writes:

"His great mastery is universally admitted, and many of the most gifted of contemporary English composers are glad to acknowledge their indebtedness to him not only for his inspiration and example but also for the practical lessons they have learned from his music. It is opera's eternal loss that *Dido* should be the only true opera he has left behind him; the feeling for dramatic expression, which it shows to have been his, only emphasizes what was removed by his death at less than forty years of age."

Dido often is considered an opera for the principal soprano. Dame Janet Baker's 1961 recording is credited with helping establish her as a top-drawer talent. Kirsten Flagstad, although technically a Wagnerian with a voice that presumably was too powerful for the role, also was a magnificent Dido. Evelyn Lear was featured at the Met in 1973.

MET PERFORMANCES

Thirteen performances in one season in 1973. The first American performance was at the Plaza Hotel in New York in 1923.

RECORDING

CD—Decca/London 425 720-2; 425 720-4 (1). Janet Baker, Patricia Clark, Monica Sinclair, Raimund Herincx. St. Anthony Singers. English Chamber Orchestra. Anthony Lewis. 1961. From an LP by L'Oiseau-Lyre. (At this writing, the EMI recording with Kirsten Flagstad has been withdrawn.)

∾

Number 84. *Julius Caesar (Giulio Cesare)*
by George Frideric Handel
February 23, 1685–April 14, 1759

Premiere at the King's Theatre, Haymarket, in London, 1724. Text by Nicola Francesco Haym from Giacomo Francesco Bussani's libretto for Giulio Cesare in Egitho, Antonio Sartorio's 1676 opera. First performed in the United States in Northampton, Massachusetts, at Smith College in 1927. An opera in three acts.

It is sort of shocking to realize that the composer of the sacred Heaven-touching *Messiah* was, in fact, pretty much of a lusty old goat.

An oratorio, not an opera, the *Messiah* is not on our agenda. But George Frideric Handel is, one of early opera's most powerful figures and an unchallenged master in musical history. Opinions differ on the label of "genius" for many opera composers in The Collection. Some, like Verdi or Wagner, qualify for it. Others, like Boito or Nicolai, are described more appropriately as "gifted artists."

Handel's genius is set in stone.

In his lifetime, not even Mozart—born shortly before Handel died—packed in theatrical audiences the way Handel did. He produced not only forty operas over thirty years but also an incredible amount of famous concert and chamber music and a long string of celebrated oratorios.

Yet Mozart's operatic popularity is as strong as ever while Handel, until just a few years ago, had for two centuries been emptying both theater and concert halls. Some of the reasons for his decline may be due to opera conventions during his lifetime, which included:

- The aria was all-important, particularly the A-B-A "da capo" aria in which the third part repeated the first, word for word. This practice was expected by the audience and desired by the singer, but it didn't do much for dramatic impact.
- The singer exited after each aria, a custom which also sometimes detracted from the drama.
- There were few choruses and no large ensemble numbers, and thus no bang-up conclusions that would send the onlookers home talking.
- The castrati got the big roles. Voices they had, but analysts today advise us that their ability to portray dramatic heroes convincingly was often weak.

His Sire, the Sun

Charles Burney was one of two great historians of eighteenth-century music (Sir John Hawkins was the other). Here is one Burney description of Handel:

"He was impetuous, rough and peremptory in his manners and conversation, but totally devoid of ill-nature or malevolence; indeed, there was an original humor and pleasantness in his most lively sallies of anger or impatience, which, with his broken English, were extremely risible. His natural propensity to wit and humor, and happy method of relating common occurrences, in an uncommon way, enabled him to throw persons and things into very ridiculous attitudes... Handel's general look was somewhat heavy and sour, but when he did smile, it was his sire, the sun, bursting out of a black cloud. There was a sudden flash of intelligence, wit, and good humor, beaming in his countenance, which I hardly ever saw in any other."

Although he was involved with the London opera scene for some thirty years, music historians say that no Handel operas were performed outside Germany and England between 1754 and 1920. Then a significant revival began, first in Germany and more recently elsewhere. In fact, early in the 1900s Handel supporters forecast that before the century ended his humane wisdom and profound art would win over both producers and the public.

One big opera singer who profited by the end of the famine—and, indeed, contributed to that end—was Beverly Sills. By her own account, she stormed her way into the New York City Opera's production of Julius Caesar by threatening to resign when the manager was reaching outside the City Opera stable for a Cleopatra. Sills had her way, and writes about what it meant to her: "The next morning I took the shuttle back to Boston . . . I read the New York papers on the plane, and I'd gotten sensational reviews. There was no question that my performance in *Julius Caesar* was going to change my life. I'd finally been in the right place at the right time. At the age of thirty-seven, I became an 'overnight' star."

If Handel changed the public image of Sills, the *Messiah* set the after-death public image of Handel himself. A biographer calls him a "prince of public entertainers," a "pantheist and hedonist who loved to depict the sensual pleasures, not least when they transgressed the stricter ethical principles, and who was repelled by the barren negativity of the Puritan." By a single irony—the production of the *Messiah*—he transformed himself into a monument of respectability who stood alongside the angels.

Both Germany and England claim him as their own and both with justification. He was born German, in Halle, Saxony, a central German province, the son of a barber-surgeon. The year was 1685, also the birth year of Johann Sebastian Bach (who wrote no opera). Most of his creative work was done in England, he died in London, and he is buried in the Poets' Corner of Westminster Abbey, next to Charles Dickens. Being buried alongside Charles Dickens in Westminster Abbey is about as British as a body can be.

The Music Establishment has long regarded him as England's only great opera composer between Henry Purcell and Benjamin Britten, the only other two Englishmen in The Collection. Handel and Purcell never met, as Purcell died in 1695 when Handel was only ten. (Nor did Handel and Bach ever meet.)

Haydn on Handel

Handel died in 1759 and the great classical composer Franz Joseph Haydn lived from 1732 to 1809, so their lives overlapped. Haydn's assessment of Handel: "He is the master of us all."

The opera side of Handel began when he was still in his teens. His first, *Almira*, was composed when he was a violinist in the Hamburg opera orchestra. This was followed by three other operas and a passion oratorio. His Hamburg associates later described him as "skilled at counterpoint" but "knowing little of melody." (Counterpoint, as we have seen, is the musical science of combining two or more simultaneous melodic lines, as opposed to one single melody supported by chords.)

From 1707 to 1710, he lived in Florence, Rome, Venice, and Naples, swimming in Italian opera, rubbing shoulders with the reigning masters, including Alessandro Scarlatti, absorbing the eighteenth-century Italian style of opera seria, and marrying it to the German theory he had learned.

The last and best of his early operas was *Agrippina*, presented in Venice in

1709 when he was twenty-four and his fans were shouting "Long live the Dear Saxon." Not only was it a security blanket, it also set the style for all Handel operas to come.

From Italy, he went back to Germany to be Kapellmeister in Hamburg. But after an eight-month visit to England the next year, and a revisit in 1712, he moved to London, anglicized his name, and settled in for life as composer, entrepreneur, and longtime earthy man-about-town.

Julius Caesar, 1724, the only Handel opera in The Collection, is one of his three "heroic" operas that are accepted today as masterpieces. The others are *Tamerlano* and *Rodelinda*. In all three, the music people say, plot, characters, and music are beautifully matched.

Among other works particularly successful in his day were some so-called magic operas, which are filled with sorcery, witchcraft, and such—*Orlando* and *Alcina*, generally considered the two best, and *Rinaldo*, *Teseo*, and *Amadigi*.

All of his operas were Italian opera seria, in the dominating style of his times. Many now seem stilted, stultifying, and monotonous. Castrato (male sopranos), for which parts were written, are gone. Never an innovator—like Wagner, nor a reformer, like Gluck, the great reformer—he took opera as he found it, working with the forms that already were made. Oratorio was his thing, the form in which his genius appeared "in all its majesty and richness."

But don't tell that to Beverly Sills or to Dame Janet Baker. Handel's genius overrides statistics and demands a place for him in The Collection.

Thieves, Bawds, and Pickpockets

Handel shifted from opera to oratorio in part because his career was being torpedoed by *The Beggar's Opera*, written by John Gay with music arranged by John Christopher Pepusch. First performed in London in 1728, it was a "ballad opera," something that borrowed from existing music and instituted a national British comic opera.

The characters are convicts, pickpockets, bawds, and other colorful people on the street, the language is low and racy, the satire ridicules both formal Italian opera seria and the politicians of the day, and the result made for a right pleasant evening.

KEYNOTE

Every contemporary opera repertory should have something from music's Baroque period. Handel is the certain nominee and *Julius Caesar* has been his most popular twentieth-century opera.

PLOT

Egypt. Pompey had fled to Egypt after his defeat by Caesar in 48 B.C., with Caesar in pursuit. Handel and his librettist didn't pay a lot of attention to historical accuracy. On a plain by the Nile, Caesar (castrato, now a contralto) is celebrating his victory. Pompey's widow, Cornelia (contralto), and her son, Sesto (tenor), ask for clemency but are interrupted by Achilla (bass), general and counselor to King Ptolemy of Egypt (castrato, now contralto), who brings in Pompey's severed head. Caesar is infuriated by Ptolemy's action.

In Ptolemy's palace, Cleopatra (soprano), Queen of Egypt and joint ruler with her brother, Ptolemy, decides to seek an alliance with Caesar against her brother. Achilla tells Ptolemy of Caesar's anger and offers to kill him to stabilize the situation if Ptolemy wil give him Cornelia as a reward. Ptolemy agrees.

When Cleopatra arranges to seduce Caesar to facilitate an alliance with him against her brother, they fall in love. Sesto, who is determined to avenge his father's death, tries to stab Ptolemy but Achilla stops him. Achilla announces that Caesar has jumped from the palace window to defend himself against attacking soldiers and presumably has drowned. Meanwhile, Ptolemy has fallen in love with Cornelia and refuses to give her to Achilla, despite his promise. As a result, Achilla prepares to defect to Caesar's side.

Reports of Caesar's death have been premature. Achilla is mortally wounded in battle. Sesto and Caesar join forces. Ptolemy tries to win Cornelia, but she threatens him with a dagger and Sesto arrives to kill him in a duel. At the harbor in Alexandria, Caesar and Cleopatra rejoice in their love and in peace.

HIGHLIGHTS

Act I: Caesar exulting in Egypt now that he is world conqueror, "Presti omai."

Act II: Cleopatra's love song, "V'adoro pupille," one of Handel's greatest melodies.

Act III: Cleopatra's lament after being put in chains, "Piangerò la sorte mia." Caesar's "Aure, deh, per pietà," as he prays for help and news of Cleopatra.

COMMENTARY

One professional I interviewed told me this story: "I once edited *Giulio Cesare* for a production, trying to cut a four-hour opera to under three hours. You can't imagine how hard this was to do without disturbing the balance of the whole, upsetting the psychology, or leaving out something essential to the plot. *That* is a sign of his genius."

Irving Kolodin, respected critic and musicologist, also commented on the merit of the opera in a piece he wrote twenty-five years ago: "Within that spacious realm [of Handel works], *Julius Caesar* stands out for vitality of dramatic content and richness of musical fulfillment, not to mention proven theatrical worth. Now that it has been demonstrated that name singers of other standard operatic matter (Beverly Sills and Maureen Forrester, as the most prominent) can readily adapt themselves to Handel's requirements, there is no valid reason why others cannot conform."

A Devil at the Keyboard

Composer Domenico Scarlatti was the most famous harpsichord player of his day. The German-born Handel was a huge success in Italy with his new operas. The two had not met. At an Italian ball, Handel stayed masked while taking a turn at the harpsichord. Scarletti listened in astonishment and exclaimed: "Why, it's the devil, or else that Saxon everyone is talking about."

When Handel's operas first were revived, the castrato part of Caesar was transposed down and given to baritones and basses. In one version, Tatiana Troyanos was Cleopatra and baritone Dietrich Fischer-Dieskau was Caesar. More recently, Caesar was transposed for women to play that original castrato part. Among Caesars have been Dame Janet Baker, first in London in 1979 and then in San Francisco in 1982, Joan Sutherland, and, in the 1990s, Jennifer Larmore.

But different productions go different ways. One which worked had six mezzo-sopranos for the major roles, even one for Cleopatra.

MET PERFORMANCES

Despite success elsewhere, there were no Met performances of *Julius Caesar* until nine in 1989, followed by three in 1990 and three in the 1992–93 season. Handel's *Rinaldo* had twenty-one performances in 1984.

RECORDING

CD—Harmonia Mundi Dig. HMC 901385/7. Barbara Schlick, Marianne Rørholm, Jennifer Larmore, Bernarda Fink, Derek Lee Ragin, Furio Zanasi. Concerto Koln. René Jacobs. 1991.

VIDEO

Baker, Masterson, Jones. English National Opera. English; no subtitles. Mackerras, conductor. 1984. HBO.

cv

Number 85. *Castor et Pollux*
by Jean-Philippe Rameau
September 25, 1683–September 12, 1764

Premiere at the Paris Opéra, 1737. Text by Pierre-Joseph Justin Bernard from Greek legend. A tragédie en musique in five acts and a Prologue.

In appearance Jean-Philippe Rameau was not unlike Ichabod Crane—a tall, gaunt, long-legged chap who wore skimpy clothes that didn't quite fit. But he was a class musician of integrity and talent, and when he died his mourning colleagues described him as the God of Harmony.

Lully, fifty years his senior, was the founder and first master of French opera, but Rameau was the first French-born master.

He was a late bloomer, still having a tough time of it in his early forties. Although a topflight organist, he had been turned down for the big Paris church appointment he most wanted, little attention had been paid to his compositions of harpsichord music, and a published volume on composition theory had been ignored by most and attacked by some. He was still single, he wasn't making much money teaching, and he didn't write his first opera until he was fifty.

Voltaire On Rameau

"Jean-Baptiste Lully, who was born in Florence in 1632 and was brought to France in his fourteenth year, as yet knowing only the violin, was the true father of music in France. He accommodated his art to the genius of the language . . . After Lully all other [French] musicians . . . simply imitated him until Rameau came, when by the depth of his harmony he surpassed them and made of music a new art."

But today a good many experts call him France's greatest musical dramatist. Despite relative anonymity with the music public outside of France, the Establishment holds him dear (but, my favorite analyst says, not so dear that it listens to him much!). Composers and musicologists describe him as one of classical music's most respected early theorists on harmony and composition. In the In-Group, his keyboard music is universally admired. The operas that came late in life are hailed by scholars, and he belongs on France's all-time Top Classical Composer list, along with Berlioz, Debussy, François Couperin, and one or two others.

Hear Claude Debussy, in the early 1900s: "And what has become of the subtly flowing syllables of our language? We will find them again in [Rameau's] *Hippolyte et Aricie*, the opera of 1733 that the [Paris] Opéra is going to revive, now in 1908 . . . We can be sure that the feeling of the opera has been preserved intact, although perhaps the setting, and something of the pomp of the music, have faded a little. It could never seem 'out of place,' for it is one of those beautiful things that will remain forever so, and despite the neglect of mankind, will never completely die."

And hear Professor Paul Henry Lang in the late 1900s: Rameau was "the one and only French musician to excel in all fields cherished by French thought—a profound and keen thinker, a great composer, and a superb performer—a man whose theoretical writings became the foundation of modern musical theory, whose works are filled with a wealth of invention seemingly inexhaustible, a born dramatist of the first order, and an artist in whose works nothing is left to the hazards of inspiration. This greatest and most French of composers remains a man frequently mentioned as a great thinker, occasionally played as a spirited harpsichord composer, and totally ignored as one of the greatest creative artists of the eighteenth century."

It is unlikely that his best-known opera, *Castor et Pollux*, 1737, is going to show up at your local opera house next season—unless you plan to spend that season in Paris. Maybe it will be aired on public television as an example of early-eighteenth-century work. It is more stilted, formal, and ornate than any Warhorse, but that doesn't put it out of bounds. Literature of the 1700s is a little different, too.

The French still like it, but, of course, Monsieur Rameau is their fellow. As noted earlier, European opera companies today do a good job in their yearly programs of blending splendid less-seen older operas with the standard fare.

Lully is the founder of French opera; Rameau is the major immediate successor to whom the torch was passed and is now regarded as the main opera reformer between Monteverdi and Gluck.

Rameau is best known today for his keyboard music, heard reasonably often on classical music radio stations. But he also wrote some thirty-odd works for the theater, including operas and opera-ballets.

Born in Dijon in 1683, he studied at a Jesuit school there, continued his education in Italy, and later, for six years, played the organ at the cathedral in Clermont-Ferrand. After other organ posts and years of teaching, his first dramatic success was with an opera-ballet, *Les Indes galantes*, in 1735. Among his many operas and opera-ballets were *Hippolyte et Aricie*, 1733; *Dardanus*, 1739; *Platée*, 1745; *Pigmalion*, 1748; and *Zoroastre*, 1749.

Castor et Pollux was so successful when first introduced in Paris that it had seventeen performances in succession and a total of 254 between 1737 and 1785. One visiting Englishman wrote that while all the critics were abusing it none of the public could buy a ticket. There has been a significant twentieth-century revival in France.

Statuary Esteem for Foreigners

Evidence of foreigners' contribution to French opera: Native French-man Rameau is honored along with Bohemian-Austrian Gluck and Italian-born Lully by the statues in the magnificent hall of the beautiful old Paris Opéra house that now presents ballet and drama but not opera.

KEYNOTE

Rameau's masterpiece. Dated but downright dramatic. Superhit in its day. Some eighteenth-century passion and a happy (mostly) ending.

PLOT

In Greek mythology, the stories of Castor and Polydeuces are told in many versions. In some both are mortal sons of Tyndareus, in some immortal sons of Zeus, and in some Castor is mortal and his brother immortal. In late myths, they were identified as the constellation Gemini. In Rome, Polydeuces was known as Pollux.

In Rameau's opera version, Pollux (bass) is the son of Jupiter (bass) and is immortal. His twin brother, Castor (haute-contre [highest French male voice in classical French opera]), the son of Tyndareus, is mortal. Both are in love with Télaïre (soprano), daughter of the Sun. After Castor has been killed in combat, Pollux offers himself to Télaïre in Castor's place, but she insists that Jupiter must be persuaded to restore Castor to life. Jupiter consents, but only if Pollux renounces his immortality and takes Castor's place in Hades. Selflessly, out of love for his brother, Pollux agrees.

At the gates of Hades, Pollux is met by Phébe (soprano), a Spartan princess who loves him and tries to turn him back as Télaïre is pushing him on. With the help of Mercury, who descends from above, he enters Hades. Twin brother Castor agrees to return to earth temporarily, but only to tell Télaïre he can't accept Pollux's sacrifice. At this point Jupiter moves into the action and rules that both Castor and Pollux should be taken up to Olympus, with Télaïre to follow. This is great for those three, but leaves Phébe behind, without her love, so she kills herself.

HIGHLIGHTS

Act I: The mourning chorus opening, "Que tout gémisse," cited by analysts as an outstanding example of using the chorus for dramatic purposes. Also Télaïre's aria "Tristes apprêts."

The choruses, ballet scenes, and orchestral interludes throughout the opera. Also the "Funeral Music" and Castor's soliloquy, "Séjour de l'éternelle paix."

His and Her Corners

Rameau was a leading participant in the Guerre des Bouffons, a musical war between forces on one side who liked his kind of French serious opera and people on the other who went for a new style of Italian comic opera called the "intermezzo," a forerunner of Italian opera buffa.

The "war" was a two-year affair, with King Louis XV and Madame Pompadour, his DM (Designated Mistress), the court, and the aristocracy on one side and the Queen (natch, given the DM) and most intellectuals on the other.

Another name for the fight was the War of the Corners. Advocates of French serious opera gathered around the King's box in one corner of the hall and supporters of the Italian style around the Queen's box in another.

COMMENTARY

Castor et Pollux and his other works basically follow the same patterns as Founding Father Lully's, but Rameau was a finer all-around musician, even if a less dominant figure on the Paris scene. Like Lully, he wrote about mythological or legendary subjects and, like Lully, he liked big chorus and ballet scenes. Today it takes a lot of money to produce a Rameau opera as it was intended to be done.

Although still formal, Rameau was looser and more flexible than Lully and considerably more advanced in his use of instrumental music. The musicologists tell us that there were about fifty players in the Paris Opéra orchestra in the mid-1700s, including two flutes, four oboes, five bassoons, one trumpet, and percussion instruments in addition to the strings. When clarinets and horns were needed, extra players were hired.

Musicologists describe Rameau as:

- A master of the capabilities of different instruments, he was the first "modern" colorist.
- A master of harmonic theory, he brought to music expressive sounds that the Italians had not made.
- A master of the theater (of his time), he (like Lully before him) emphasized the dramatic side of the music/drama formula.

RECORDING

CD—Teldec/Warner 2292 42510-2 (3). Zeger Vandersteene, Gérard Souzay, Norma Lerer, Jeanette Scovotti, Märta Scheele, Rolf Leanderson, Jacques Villisech. Stockholm Chamber Chorus. Vienna Concentus Musicus. Nikolaus Harnoncourt. 1972.

A Hit Parade from Collection Operas
(Top Forty)

1. *Aida*, Celeste Aida
2. *La traviata*, E strano . . . Ah, fors' è lui . . . Sempre libera
3. *La traviata*, Libiamo ne'lieti calici
4. *Rigoletto*, Caro nome
5. *Rigoletto*, La donna è mobile
6. *Il trovatore*, The Anvil Chorus
7. *Il trovatore*, Di quella pira
8. *Madama Butterfly*, Un bel dì
9. *Tosca*, E lucevan le stelle
10. *Tosca*, Vissi d'arte
11. *Tosca*, Recondita armonia
12. *La Bohème*, Mi chiamano Mimi
13. *La Bohème*, Che gelida manina
14. *Turandot*, Nessun dorma
15. *Gianni Schicchi*, O mio babbino caro
16. *The Magic Flute*, O zittre nicht
17. *The Marriage of Figaro*, Voi che sapete
18. *Don Giovanni*, Madamina! il catalogo è questo
19. *Tristan und Isolde*, Mild und leise (Liebestod)
20. *Die Walküre*, Winterstürme
21. *Die Meistersinger*, Prize Song
22. *Tannhäuser*, Ode to the Evening Star
23. *Carmen*, Habanera
24. *Carmen*, Séguedilla
25. *Carmen*, Toreador's Song
26. *Faust*, Jewel Song
27. *Faust*, Soldiers' Chorus
28. *Faust*, Valetin's aria, Avant de quitter ces lieux
29. *Samson et Dalila*, Mon coeur s'ouvre à ta voix
30. *Pagliacci*, Vesti la giubba
31. *Martha*, M'appari
32. *The Barber of Seville*, Largo al factotum
33. *The Barber of Seville*, Una voce poco fa
34. *The Tales of Hoffmann*, Barcarolle
35. *The Elixir of Love*, Una furtiva lagrima
36. *Louise*, Depuis le jour
37. *Orfeo ed Euridice*, Che faro senza Euridice
38. *Dido and Aeneas*, Dido's Lament
39. *Lakmé*, Bell Song
40. *Norma*, Casta diva

Chapter 7

THE TWENTIETH-CENTURY EUROPEAN PACKAGE

❧

Prepare for a radical change. Twentieth-century opera will not necessarily be beautiful. That isn't to say it won't be moving, emotional, and powerful. But to be captured by some of the best of it, you may need to abandon orthodox beauty.

With many composers, of course, it still *will* be beautiful in the traditional sense—as well as tuneful. And, not surprisingly, the twentieth-century works that have been most successful with the general opera-going public are the ones that most closely follow the conventions.

Sixteen operas from this century are in The Collection, but that leaves out a great many others worth exploring—or, at the minimum, worth knowing about for future exploration.

Here, we've hand-picked additional European operas without reference to how often they are performed. Each has been selected on its own merits, after lengthy counseling with opera professionals who have become friends. The result is a smorgasbord.

Some have become and/or are becoming hits, others have gained high critical esteem but haven't made it with the ticket buyers, and still others have been chosen because they show something special.

Nineteen "new" composers are in this package plus four who also are in The Collection: Richard Strauss, Leoš Janáček, Alban Berg, and Benjamin Britten. A few men have two works each here, so there are twenty-nine operas in this chapter.

Ten of the composers here were born German or Austrian: Franz Lehár,

Arnold Schoenberg, Erich Korngold, Paul Hindemith, Ernst Krenek, Kurt Weill, Hans Werner Henze, Bernd Alois Zimmermann—and Strauss and Berg.

Five are English: Gustav Holst, Ralph Vaughan Williams, Michael Tippett, Peter Maxwell Davies—and Britten.

Three were born Russian: Igor Stravinsky, Serge Prokofiev, and Dmitri Shostakovich.

Two are French: Maurice Ravel and Francis Poulenc. Two are Czech: Antonín Dvořák—and Janáček. One is Polish: Krzysztof Penderecki.

Some of them have experimented radically both with the text/poetry/libretto side of opera and with the music. As a result, their ultimate product is often significantly different from Giuseppe Verdi or Gaetano Donizetti. Some are more conventional.

The concept of Expressionism, the technique of twelve-tone composition, and the trend toward atonality get a lot of attention in this Twentieth-century European Package, and we'll return to them in a moment, but those scarcely fully reflect the century or the package.

Tragedy and comedy are represented in these operas. So are satire, symbolism, morality, philosophy, Sigmund Freud, and the dominance of the subconcious over the conscious.

Underlying all twentieth-century compositions are the changes in the world, cited in chapter five—the two world wars, the Nazi and Communist dictatorships, the exploration into psychoanalysis and the subconscious, the nuclear phenomenon, the focus on the heroism of one man or woman when millions die on the battlefields or in the concentration camps, as well as the assassination of leaders and all the other happenings of these one hundred years.

Though labels oversimplify, they are useful, in this case to help show the diversity of operatic activity in this century and in this chapter. This package includes these types of works from the composers in it:

Expressionist: Berg's *Lulu* and Davies's *Taverner*.
Antiopera: Weill's antiopera cabaret and dance-hall works, *The Threepenny Opera*, and his ultracynical *Rise and Fall of the City of Mahagonny*.
Jazz: Krenek's *Jonny spielt auf*, the first big operatic use of the jazz idiom.
Serial: Berg's *Lulu* and Schoenberg's *Moses und Aron*. Krenek, Weill, and Hindemith are others who sometimes used the serialist technique.
Nineteenth-century traditional: Vaughan Williams's *Riders to the Sea*.
Fantasy: Prokofiev's *Love for Three Oranges* and Ravel's *L'enfant et les sortilèges*.
Epic: Prokofiev's *War and Peace*.
Allegory: Tippett's *Midsummer Marriage*.
Political satire: Henze's *Der junge Lord*.
Subconscious: Britten's *Turn of the Screw*.
Chamber opera: Holst's *Sàvitri*.
Fairy tale: Dvořák's *Rusalka*.

Pluralism: Zimmermann's *Die Soldaten*.
Operetta: Lehár's *Merry Widow*.

In the nineteenth century, the "dramatic" and "different" included bel canto opera, Meyberbeer's spectacle grand opera, Italian verismo, and Wagner's music drama. None of these, nor all combined, constituted the whole, yet each merited special attention.

Similarly, in the twentieth century, Expressionism and the twelve-tone technique are only one part of opera but also deserve special focus as elements that have been "dramatic" and "different" in opera production these last several decades.

Expressionism is a word pilfered from the visual arts, especially from a school of German painters who worked in Munich, Berlin, Vienna, and other German and Austrian centers from about 1905 to 1930. The end of the experiment coincided with the beginnings of Nazism, whose leaders called it "perverted art." Expressionist painters went beyond a visual appearance to depict the artist's subjective interpretation of reality, using distortion, exaggeration, and symbolism. In music, the term "Expressionism" is used broadly for work written in a deeply subjective and introspective style.

Composers most often identified as "Expressionist" are German or Austrian: Schoenberg, Berg, and, in some of their works, Krenek and Hindemith. One of many Expressionist composers from other nationalities is England's Peter Maxwell Davies.

For the composers, an Expressionist approach that enabled them to interpret reality in their own way offered obvious freedoms and advantages. The case has been made that Expressionism is an extreme extension of nineteenth-century subjective Romanticism.

For the opera audience, the potential ramifications are also apparent. One professional opera friend shared these thoughts with me: "I think of Expressionism, in painting or in music, as a use of the medium to pre-empt the reactions of the beholder/listener. Verdi presents his dying Violetta in *La traviata* in a way that is natural and deeply moving. We feel for her situation and make it our own. One could imagine the same thing in a play or a painting.

"But if the music gets to us *first*, before we can really get inside this woman, we feel her pain before we know *why* we feel it. As in Schoenberg's *Erwartung*, pain becomes a thing in itself, divorced from character or even situation. Although only the early twentieth-century artists used it as an artistic philosophy, the temptation to resort to Expressionism in this sense has been with us forever after."

On the composition side, a major development—again originating in Germany and Austria—was twelve-tone music.

Arnold Schoenberg, as noted earlier, is *the* twelve-tone composer, the man who devised a new method of composition that used in turn all twelve tones of the chromatic scale—all twelve white and black notes in an octave on the piano—in any order the composer chooses. No one tone may be repeated before the other eleven have appeared, and the order remains basically unchanged throughout the composition.

Thus traditional rules and conventions governing all aspects of music, including tonality, melody, harmony and rhythm, are discarded and replaced with new rules and principles.

Tonality is replaced by atonality—pleasant "concordant" music by often harsh "discordant" music (although a composer can select a tone row to produce quite mellifluous combinations). In any event, it's a matter of habit. Ears that never heard anything but twelve-tone serial music would find Mozart's music strange. Well, maybe they would, although that's a little hard to contemplate.

Musicologists note that in some extreme twelve-tone works melody was eradicated, harmony ignored, and national characteristics obliterated as one work seemed to sound much like another.

Not all twelve-toners, or serialists, however, are tarred with the same brush. Berg was Schoenberg's leading disciple. Some composers in this package, like Krenek and Hindemith, dabbled with serialism but didn't go all out for it. Among orthodox avant-garde serialists are Henze in Germany, Penderecki in Poland, and Davies, leader of a strong British school. Britten worked with serialism, but with a soft glove, keeping tonal elements.

Twentieth-century atonality is a part of opera that never before existed, although tonality began to break down in the works of Wagner, Debussy, and Richard Strauss, who were not twelve-tone composers.

Many twentieth-century composers continued the deliberate disintegration of tonality, but by no means did all of them. Tonality made a marked comeback with Stravinsky, Britten, and Henze, and again in the past few years.

A case can be made that antiheroism and a preoccupation with the new-found ills of society go hand in hand with Expressionism and that it goes hand in hand with the employment of twelve-note serial music and its offshoots.

Composers who experienced the intensity of the twentieth-century world found themselves turning to distortion and exaggeration as an outlet for their emotions. But how to convey the Expressionist theme in music? "Traditional" music, tonal music, is consonant and agreeable. Tensions are created . . . and released. The Expressionist composer, however, demanded peak tension and had no desire to slacken it. Professor Joseph Machlis in *The Enjoyment of Music* notes that Expressionist music was inevitably impelled to push on to atonality.

Thus Schoenberg, Berg, Krenek, Hindemith, Davies, and others in this package were both Expressionistic in their approach and twelve-tone in their technique. And they challenged the conventional musical language of several hundred years.

But right alongside their twentieth-century works is Igor Stravinsky's *Rake's Progress*, which ignored both atonalism and serialism and went back to the number opera of the eighteenth century with set arias accompanied by the orchestra.

The most recent opera in the package is Davies's *Taverner*, first performed in 1972. But we do not mean to denigrate aleatory opera, which involves elements of chance in composition or performance, or rock opera, or minimalist opera, or opera that features taped synthesized sounds—some of which are in the American chapter.

Two last thoughts:

Be cautious about operatic pigeonholes, in the twentieth century or any other. Richard Strauss composed fifteen operas, all but one in this century. Four are in The Collection, and a fifth is in this package. His operas include an early Wagnerian piece set in medieval Germany; the two "new music" erotic shockers, *Salome* from an Oscar Wilde play and *Elektra* from Greek mythology; the lovely romantic back-to-Mozart *Der Rosenkavalier* with its Viennese waltzes; an experimental play-and-opera merger in *Ariadne auf Naxos*, and the allegorical *Die Frau ohne Schatten*. Later Strauss works are based on Greek myths, politics and the military, materialism, man-and-nature, and the relationship of words and music in opera.

Finally, lest we forget, most of Giacomo Puccini's Collection operas are from the twentieth century. So are George Gershwin's *Porgy and Bess*, the works of Gian Carlo Menotti, whose stated aim has been to entertain; and many other successful "conventional" operas discussed in the American chapter.

∾

TWENTIETH-CENTURY EUROPEAN OPERAS
Rusalka
by Antonín Dvořák
September 8, 1841–May 1, 1904

Premiere at the National Theatre, Prague, 1901. Text by Jaroslav Kvapil from Friedrich de la Motte Fouqué's tale Undine. *Three acts. Setting: A fairy-tale world of a forest with a lake and a palace.*

This is a twentieth-century opera, barely coming in under the wire, but after listening for two minutes you'll know it's a hangover from the past, not a new "modern" thing. Antonín Dvořák is a lyrical, melodious Romantic composer, infected neither by the anti-Romantic virus nor the new century's Expressionist concentration on the artist's self.

It helps to keep straight the Czech generations. The father of Bohemian classical music is Bedřich Smetana, 1824–1884, whose *Bartered Bride* is high in The Collection. The leader of the next generation, who gave Czech classical music *international* popularity, is Dvořák, 1841–1904. And the master who followed him is Leoš Janáček, 1854–1928, who has one opera in The Collection and a second in this package.

Rusalka, a charming, sad, and fanciful fairy tale, perfect for Dvořák's lyrical powers, is one of two twentieth-century operas by the man who for a century has been considered the greatest Czech classical composer. Outside of the Czech Republic, Dvořák is best known for his instrumental music, which included one of music's most popular symphonies, *From the New World*, completed in 1893. Other famous pieces include a cello, a violin, and a piano concerto, the *Carnival* Overture, *Slavonic Dances*, and his *American* string quartet.

Much less is known in America of his ten operas, of which *Rusalka* is the most successful. In The Collection we encountered the most popular Czech opera by far, *The Bartered Bride*. Today, however, one school of analysts holds that neither Dvořák nor Smetana but rather Leoš Janáček is the one to include among history's dozen greatest opera composers.

Lucky Prague.

Many in the music world are upset by any attempt to "rate" composers, as though all were equally gifted or the differences in their talent should be overlooked. I believe the exercise is a useful one if it helps lead the Unwashed to the top composers and their works. In another field, we know that the Joes Namath and Montana were both superb, and both more talented than most of their counterparts. The same is true of Messrs. Bach and Beethoven. (For the uninitiated, Namath and Montana are fourteenth-century lutists, both with strong legions of supporters, who never faced one another in a head-to-head lute-off.)

"Lyric" is the main word for Dvořák music. Dvořákians often say "inspired lyricism." In my book on classical music, I cite Ethan Mordden's quotation about Dvořák's masterworks: "How can anything that catchy be any good?"

Self-Assessment

Antonín Dvořák today is recognized as one of the great Czech nationalist composers but is known primarily for his instrumental works. Yet in an interview shortly before his death in 1904, he said: "I proved many years ago that my main inclination was towards dramatic creation."

With ten operas, he was, indeed, one of the most prolific Czech opera composers. *Rusalka* is the most frequently performed Czech opera, except for Smetana's *Bartered Bride*. But, except for *Rusalka*, there are few performances of his dramatic works outside the Czech region.

Listening to Dvořák, it isn't surprising to learn that his favorite Wagner opera was The Collection's *Tannhäuser*, which with *Lohengrin* is one of the German's two most melodious works.

Dvořák, a symphonist, was a magnificent orchestrator. *Rusalka* came toward the end of his life, but he was only sixty and was at his peak maturity. (A strong case can be made that maturity doesn't begin to peak until fifteen years later, but that's a self-serving statement, even if one with which Verdi would agree.) We know that opera is a play in music; in Dvořák's case, as we might suspect, the emphasis is more on the music than on the drama.

Dvořák's other twentieth-century opera is *Armida*, written in 1902–03, which has not caught on. Earlier nineteenth-century works include *Alfred*, 1870; *The King and the Charcoal Burner*, 1871, revised 1874; *The Stubborn Lovers*, 1874; *Vanda*, 1876; *The Cunning Peasant*, 1877; *Dimitrij*, 1881, with later revisions; *The Jacobin*, 1887–88, revised 1897; and *The Devil and Kate*, 1898–99.

The Opera

In Russian and Czech mythology, a "rusalka" is a water sprite, usually looking for vengeance since she once was a mortal who drowned herself out of betrayed love. In his opera, Dvořák combines several different rusalka myths.

The water sprite Rusalka (soprano) falls in love with a Prince (tenor) but can't marry him because she isn't mortal. She sings of her feelings in "Hymn to the Moon," the opera's best-known music and for many years the only part of it known outside Bohemia. Try it; you're bound to like it (and possibly already have liked it in Disney's *Little Mermaid*). She seeks help from the witch Ježibaba (mezzo-soprano), and a deal is struck. Ježibaba will turn her into a human, but under several conditions. One is that she'll no longer be able to speak and another that the Prince must never deceive her. If he does, both will be damned forever. The Water Gnome, the Spirit of the Lakes (bass), water guru and Rusalka's father, despairs at the deal, but it is irrevocable.

Even before marriage, the Prince is unfaithful, dallying with a Foreign Princess (soprano). Rusalka wants to kill herself, but the witch reminds her that if she does she'll be cursed through eternity unless the Prince also kills himself. At the end, the Prince appears to ask her to return with him. She tells him that her fate is sealed and that a kiss now would kill him. He begs for such peace, she does kiss him, and he dies. Rusalka asks for mercy on his soul and disappears into the lake, beneath the moonlit waters. In some productions the Spirit of the Lake doesn't permit her to live without the Prince, but they come together in death. Or, in a sadder ending, she isn't permitted to join him and is forced to live on indefinitely in sprite form.

There is a video of the English National Opera production, a superb Freudian-tinted transference of this story to an Edwardian nursery.

Some elitists don't take kindly to the lovely sounds produced by Dvořák. In a 1993 review in *The Wall Street Journal*, a well-known music critic shared with us a classic comment to him from a fellow critic. "Strip away the beauty," said the colleague, "and what's left?"

I suppose one can make the same comment about *Winged Victory*, the *Mona Lisa*, Fred Astaire, and the swing of Arnold Palmer.

෨

Die lustige Witwe
The Merry Widow
by Franz Lehár
April 30, 1870–October 24, 1948

Premiere at the Theatre an der Wien, Vienna, 1905. Text by Viktor Léon and Leo Stein from Henri Meilhac's 1861 comedy L'attaché d'ambassade. An operetta in three acts. Setting: Paris at the turn of the century.

So maybe we cheat a little, but Johann Strauss's *Fledermaus* is in The Collection and some musical theater that may offend opera purists is included in the Twentieth-century American Opera group, in chapter seven.

If *Die Fledermaus* is an opera, Franz Lehár's *Merry Widow* (*Die lustige Witwe*) is probably the greatest of all European operettas. If *Die Fledermaus* is an operetta, *The Merry Widow* probably is the second greatest. Either way, it deserves attention for its excellence and its fresh, wonderful melodies.

Lehár tried a few operas, but none came close to the success of this light, gay, frivolous, marvelous work. In 1993 it became the only operetta ever performed by England's Glyndebourne Opera Festival. It's often described as history's most frequently performed operetta, but no one really knows.

One of the distinguishing features between opera and operetta, as noted earlier, is the depth of the characters. Lehár's are on the lightweight side, but the atmosphere and the music are delightful, and so is the triumph of young love. A German version has been conducted by Herbert von Karajan with the Berlin Philharmonic and an English-language version by Richard Bonynge with the National Philharmonic Orchestra. That's respectable stuff.

Unprecedented Success

Franz Lehár was the twentieth century's top operetta composer and *The Merry Widow*, launched in 1905, became the most successful in operetta history. It also was the work that kept Beverly Sills eating in 1954 when she found work singing in it for Cleveland's summer Musicarnival, then the largest tent theater in the country. Sills, who sang it later elsewhere after she became famous and brought it to the New York City Opera, calls it "almost foolproof."

The operetta was one of Adolf Hitler's favorites, which helped keep Lehár safe in Vienna and Bad Ischl during the 1930s and war years, even though his wife was Jewish.

Lehár, who lived for years in Bad Ischl, Austria, one of Europe's most picturesque regions, was the leading composer of Viennese twentieth-century operetta. (The next time you go to Salzburg, spend a few days in this neighboring lake country and visit his museum in Bad Ischl.) Of Czech and Hungarian descent, Lehár studied at the Prague Conservatory and in his early career was a military band leader. One work, *Kukuschka*, was produced in 1896 in Leipzig. Others include:

Der Graf von Luxemburg (The Count of Luxembourg), an operetta in three acts, 1909.
Zigeunerliebe (Gypsy Love), an opera in three acts, 1910.
Paganini, an operetta in three acts, 1925.
Das Land des Lächelns (The Land of Smiles), a romantic operetta in three acts, 1929.

The Operetta

The merry widow is Hanna Glawari (soprano), who was friends with Count Danilo (tenor) before she married a wealthy chap named Glawari. When the two old friends meet in Paris, Danilo hesitates to pursue her because he doesn't want her to think he's just after her money. Meanwhile, Camille de Rosillon (tenor) has an improper eye on Valencienne (soprano), wife of Baron Zeta (baritone). A secret rendezvous is arranged and there are other goings-on, but in the end Hanna announces that she'll lose her fortune if she remarries, thus clearing the way for Danilo to propose.

The hit number is Hanna's act-two recounting of a national folk tale about a maid of the woods and a hunter's unrequited love, "Vilja."

If you don't want operetta mixed up with your opera, just pass this up, pack a lunch, and sit through *Parsifal* again. But do so knowing that this one is performed in opera houses all over the world.

Sàvitri
by Gustav Holst
September 21, 1874–May 25, 1934

Premiere at Wellington Hall, London, 1916. U.S. premiere at the Palmer House, Chicago, 1934. Text by the composer based on the Mahabharata, *one of the two great epics of ancient India. A one-act chamber opera. Setting: A wood in India in the evening.*

This little jewel from a trombone player is regarded by some musicologists as the first important English opera since Henry Purcell's Collection *Dido and Aeneas*, written more than two hundred years earlier.

Gustav Holst was born in Cheltenham, England, of Swedish origin. Much of his career was spent teaching, chiefly at St. Paul's Girls' School, Hammersmith. A "modernist" classical composer, he was well known in the early part of the century, although today little is heard of his music except *The Planets*, a big seven-section orchestral work first performed in 1918 and still a favorite of classical radio stations. Professional analysts find in it "echoes" of Debussy, Stravinsky, Mahler, and Schoenberg. (The music people like the words "echoes" and "anticipates.")

He had a deep interest in Hindu literature and philosophy, although not specifically in Indian music, and learned Sanskrit in order to read the Hindu scriptures.

Among a dozen other Holst operas are:

The Perfect Fool, 1923, an opera in one act
At the Boar's Head, 1925, a musical interlude in one act
The Wandering Scholar, 1934, revised in 1951, a chamber opera in one act

His choral music includes *Hymn of Jesus*, 1917, and *Choral Fantasia*, 1930.

The Opera

Sàvitri (soprano) is the wife of Satyavān (tenor), a woodcutter. She is alone in their home when Death (bass) arrives in the person of a stranger and announces that he has come for her husband, even though he's young and strong. She hears Satyavān singing and serenading her beauty as he is coming home. When he arrives, he tries to face Death with his ax, but Death causes him to drop to the ground and the ax falls from his hand. He is dying. After persuasion by Sāvitri, however, Death promises to grant her any one request, so long as it's not the life of her husband. Her request is that she shall be given her own life. But, Death notes, she already has her life. No, she says. "If thou are not a blind spirit, thou must understand that, for a woman, Life means stalwart sons and bright-eyed daughters; life is a communion and eternal." Outwitted, Death grants her wish, since if Satyavān dies she will only be "an image floating on the waters of memory." Death retreats and the couple lives happily.

The music is a haunting mixture of Indian-sounding music and English folksong. One dramatic moment is the opening, when Death's voice is heard without accompaniment. A sparse, austere work, it sometimes is paired in production with Ralph Vaughan Williams's *Riders to the Sea*.

Holst described the setting for *Sàvitri* in this note on the score: "The piece is intended for performance in the open air or in a small building. When performed out of doors there should be a long avenue or path through a wood in the center of the scene. When a curtain is used, it should be raised before the voice of Death is heard. No curtain, however, is necessary. The orchestra consists of two string quartets, a contra-bass, two flutes and an English horn. There is also a hidden chorus of female voices."

❦

L'heure espagnol
L'enfant et les sortilèges
by Maurice Ravel
March 7, 1875–December 28, 1937

L'heure espagnol (Spanish Time, or The Spanish Hour). *Premiere at the Opéra-Comique, Paris, 1911. Text by Franc-Nohain from his own comedy. Comic opera in one act. Setting: Toledo, Spain, in the eighteenth century.*

L'enfant et les sortilèges (The Child and the Spells). *Premiere at the Monte Carlo Opera, 1925. Text by Colette. Fantasy opera in two parts. Setting: A Norman country house and its garden.*

These are two brilliantly orchestrated and highly theatrical works from the early part of the century, not nearly eligible for The Collection on the basis of frequency of performance but eminently worthy of inclusion in a hand-picked treasury of twentieth-century opera.

Both, especially *L'enfant*, use jazz idioms.

Both have been staged at the Metropolitan—*L'heure espagnole* for seven performances back in 1925 and *L'enfant et les sortilèges*, a work still gradually growing in popularity, for sixteen performances much more recently, in 1981 and 1982. It was revived by Baltimore's Peabody Conservatory in 1996, an excellent example of the opera work done today in workshops, universities, and conservatories.

Maurice Ravel was born in Ciboure, in the Basses-Pyrénées, and lived his life in or around Paris. His name and music often are linked with those of Claude Debussy—Debussy as the founder of "Impressionism" in music, a characterization Debussy personally rejected, and Ravel as a Debussy copycat, a description Ravel violently and justifiably opposed. Both men were taken by the writings of Stéphane Mallarmé, the French poet who was the leader of the French literary movement called Symbolism (not the painting movement, Impressionism).

One of France's all-time top classical composers, Ravel is better known for several ballets, especially *Daphnis et Chloé*, than for either of these operas—and, indeed, perhaps better known also to the general classical public for a string of instrumental works. One of the most celebrated of these is the *Boléro*, a seventeen-minute piece built upon a single motif and its counter-theme and popularized in the 1980s by the English world-class ice-skating team of Torvil and Dean and by the movie *10*.

Ravel liked things Spanish. Among his applauded instrumental works are

Rapsodie espagnole and *Alborada del gracioso*, both in the Spanish style. Other known instrumental works include *La valse* and *Valses nobles et sentimentales*. He also was taken by fantasy, including the fantasy of animals and children, as found in some of his orchestral works, including *Ma mère l'oye* (*Mother Goose Suite*).

One of music's masters of orchestral color, Ravel orchestrated the popular classical piece *Pictures at an Exhibition*, which had been composed for the piano by Modest Mussorgsky. As to his general approach to composition, he said: "I did my work slowly, drop by drop. I tore it out of me by pieces." He said he had never felt the need to formulate the principles of his aesthetic, but basically identified himself with Mozart's simple pronouncements on the subject—that there is nothing music cannot undertake to do, or dare, or portray, provided it always remains music and continues to charm the listener.

"Great music," he said at another time, "must always come from the heart. Any music created by technique and brains alone is not worth the paper it is written on. A composer should feel intensely what he is producing."

In the early 1930s, somewhat depressed, he wrote: "I have failed in my life. I am not one of the great composers. All the great ones produced enormously. But I have written relatively very little, and with a great deal of hardship. And now I cannot do any more, and it does not give me pleasure."

L'heure espagnole

L'heure espagnole, the first of Ravel's two complete operas, is a light comedy, a work considered delicate, tactful, witty, refined ... and oh so French. (An earlier unfinished opera was *Shéhérezade*, for which only the overture survives.)

The heroine is Concepción (soprano), flirtatious wife of an absent-minded clockmaker, Torquemada (tenor), and a woman with a string of lovers. When Torquemada isn't home, one innocent muleteer (baritone) who initially is just trying to have his watch fixed winds up in Concepión's bed while two of her regular lovers (tenor and bass), who arrive separately in search of sex, are hidden by her in different grandfather clocks. In the end, when Torquemada comes home and discovers them there, the fate they suffer, as any Frenchman would know, is that each must buy the expensive clock he has occupied. And the final French touch is an opera-ending quintet, sung in friendship by husband, wife, and her three lovers.

Ravel said he wrote it to breathe new life into Italian opera buffa.

L'enfant et les sortilèges

L'enfant et les sortilèges, Ravel's second opera, which took him five years to write, is a sophisticated one-act work, sometimes called an opera-pantomime. Charming, light, and lyrical, a miniature masterpiece, it was a big hit in Paris in 1926. It is the story of a naughty Child (mezzo-soprano) of six or seven who throws a fit, is punished, and regains his innocence. In a scene of destruction, he smashes a Teacup (light soprano), pokes a pen into pet Squirrel (mezzo-soprano), pulls the Cat's (mezzo-soprano) tail, pours the contents of the Tea Kettle (tenor) into the fireplace, breaks a Grandfather Clock (baritone), tears up his books, and carries on in other awful ways. Many of us had six-year-olds who did most of those things, albeit not all at the same time (one of my five came reasonably close). Then a magic spell begins as everything he has mistreated comes to life. In the end he binds the Squirrel's paw with a ribbon, proves himself to be good and kind at heart, and is encouraged by the animals as he holds out his arms for his mother.

Stage directors say it is challenging to stage. The Child always must be played by an adult, and the furniture and furnishings must be moved skillfully by wires in order for them to be properly enchanted.

Maurice Ravel was a cat man, a cat fancier. He owned many, he liked to play with them, and he liked to talk to them in cat language. Indeed, *L'enfant et les sortilèges* includes a cat duet between a black tomcat in the house and his white mate in a moonlit garden. It is in cat language, not the language of two-foots, which no self-respecting cat would use.

Don't miss a wonderful bilingual number between a Cockney black Wedgwood Teapot and a Chinese Teacup. The teapot speaks ragtime, with piano, sliding trombone, xylophone, woodblock, and cheese grater. It is one of opera's great dialogues.

∾

Die Frau ohne Schatten
by Richard Strauss
June 11, 1864–September 8, 1949

Premiere at the Staatsoper, Vienna, 1919. Text by Hugo von Hofmannsthal. Three acts. Setting: A legendary empire in the South Eastern Islands.

Question: What feature of opera do operagoers like most?

Answer: Spectacle. Visual, orchestral, and vocal spectacle.

In a good production, with an excellent cast, *Die Frau ohne Schatten* (*The Woman Without a Shadow*) provides spectacle with the best of them. Well, almost with the best of them.

It is a fairy tale, but not a simple one, wholly unlike a *Hänsel und Gretel*. It overflows with symbolism, certainly more than we need worry about, but also offers the rich orchestral music for which Richard Strauss was famous and superb vocal parts for several of its many characters.

Perhaps it's the symbolism—often compared with that in Mozart's *Magic*

Flute—that has kept it from being performed more regularly today or from becoming as popular with operagoers as the four more straightforward Strauss works in The Collection. Usually—not always—the public likes the composer to tell it like it is. Still, anyone can admire this opera's beautiful melodies and fine orchestration without worrying whether it is a profound statement about life and humanity—man, woman, the union of the two and a higher principle.

It's a long work. Each act takes more than an hour, even when the third act is cut, as it is in some productions.

The Opera

The Emperor of the South Eastern Islands (tenor) has been hunting. He was about to kill a gazelle when it turned into its real form as the daughter (soprano) of Keikobad, leader of the spirit world. The Emperor loved her and married her, but they had no children and she remained part human, part spirit, and unable to cast a shadow. The opera opens at the waning of the twelfth moon as Keikobad's messenger (baritone) arrives to say that the Emperor will be turned into stone and the Empress returned to her father if she doesn't become pregnant—and thus cast a shadow—within three days.

The Empress instructs the Nurse (mezzo-soprano) to buy a shadow from a human. Since Barak the Dyer (baritone) wants children, the Nurse decides to purchase one from his Wife (soprano), promising her a life of luxury in return.

Like Richard Wagner's *Ring*, the opera is organized into various levels of existence. One is the spirit world, occupied by its ruler, Keikobad, and his falcon (soprano), another a plain, ordinary world of the Dyer and his Wife, and a third a middle world of the human Emperor and his spirit Empress.

The opera concerns the relationships between individuals in each world and among the different worlds as the Empress seeks her shadow. The Emperor finally is turned to stone, but by this time the Empress refuses to save him or herself by claiming the Wife's shadow because she knows that Barak and his Wife will be parted forever if she does. She has changed from a creature of the spirit world to someone with human emotions, so Keikobad forgives her for having married a mortal and restores the Emperor to life.

The music for the Dyer and his Wife is warm and emotionally direct; the music of the spirit world is more complex, and the music around the Empress moves from one form to the other.

Author's recommendation: Read carefully a detailed account of the complex and symbolic plot, and then find the recording with the Vienna Philharmonic Orchestra conducted by Georg Solti and starring Plácido Domingo and Hildegard Behrens, and just listen to Strauss's sensual music. Better, if you ever get the chance—and the chance doesn't come very often—just see it. You may decide this one rates some special attention.

Strauss's four Collection works are *Der Rosenkavalier*, 1911, *Elektra*, 1909, *Salome*, 1905, and *Ariadne auf Naxos*, 1912.

Chinese or Berliners: All the Same

Richard Strauss lived to be eighty-five, long after the premiere of *Die Frau ohne Schatten*. During the Hitler regime, he was appointed President of the Reichsmusikkammer (Reich Chamber of Music) and replaced Bruno Walter and Arturo Toscanini as conductor both in Berlin and Bayreuth after they had refused to deal with Hitler's Third Reich. In a 1935 letter to a friend, Strauss showed his nonconcern with "political" matters:

"For me there are only two types of person, those that have talent and those that have not, and a people only exists when it becomes an audience. Whether this consists of Chinese, Upper Bavarians, New Zealanders or Berliners is all the same to me."

The letter displeased the Hitlerites, and Strauss was forced to quit as president of the Reichsmusikkammer. He continued to live and work in Germany, criticized from abroad for tolerating the Hitler regime and out of favor at home for his political indifference.

∾

Die Tote Stadt
(The Dead City)
by Erich Wolfgang Korngold
1897–1957

Premiere in 1920 simultaneously in Hamburg and Cologne. An opera in three acts. Libretto by Paul Schott, a pseudonym for Erich Korngold and his father, Julius. From a novel by Georges Rodenbuch, Bruges-la-morte. Time: Bruges, at the end of the nineteenth century.

Q: What do Errol Flynn and Erich Korngold have in common?

A: "Captain Blood," 1935 Hollywood movie. Flynn was the sword-slashing hero; Korngold wrote the musical score. He composed seventeen more film scores over the next twelve years, including two for which he won Oscars: *Anthony Adverse* and *Robin Hood*.

Not today a familiar name in most households, fifty to seventy-five years ago Erich Korngold was probably *the* child-and-juvenile-prodigy composer of the twentieth century. Born in Moravia and brought up in Vienna, the son of a well-known music critic, he became internationally famous during and immediately after World War I for two operas, *Violanta* in 1916 and *Die Tote Stadt* in 1920. He wrote the first at seventeen, the second at twenty-three.

Several years earlier, at eleven, he had composed a ballet, *Der Scheemann*, which was produced in Vienna when he was thirteen. Among those who proclaimed him a genius was Gustav Mahler. Inevitably, some established critics and musicologists called him another Mozart. Not hardly, but this was a gifted kid.

Die Tote Stadt is a symbolistic dream story about death and decay. It is mildly Expressionist, but melody-filled with the kind of familiar-to-the-ear orchestration you might expect from one who would become a very successful Hollywood film score writer. It was the first German opera to appear at the Metropolitan after World War I, with twelve performances there in 1921 and 1922. *Violanta* had five performances at the Met in 1927. Neither work has been back since, but *Die Tote Stadt* lingers on international stages.

Korngold kept composing during World War I as music director of his regiment. Although he worked in Vienna during the twenties, he and his family were Jewish, and the authorities wouldn't permit his works to be staged. In 1934 he left Vienna for Hollywood to begin that long career there. After World War II he also turned to orchestral and chamber works, including a symphony and a violin concerto.

He is one of several composers who have been called the last of the Romantics, or one of the "late Romantics." The music of *Die Tote Stadt* is lush and lusciously orchestrated, not lean and "Twentieth-Century Modern." Some musicologists hear Puccini and Richard Strauss in it—one reason, perhaps, for its extraordinary popularity for a number of years.

The dead city is Bruges, with its empty canals, crumbling old buildings, and medieval atmosphere, but the dead person is Marie, young wife of Paul (tenor). The opera is the story of Paul, who can't get over the loss of Marie and sees her in the person of a dancer. In a nightmare, he finds his Marie being unfaithful to him with his friend Frank (baritone), and strangles her with a braid of her own hair. When he wakes up he realizes he must leave Bruges . . . leaving behind all memories of her.

If you come across a recording, listen for a glorious love duet in Act I, "Gluck, das mir verlieb." One of my opera friends insists that it is as gorgeous a tune as anything of Puccini. Listen also for the haunting "Mein Sehnen, mein Wahnen" in Act II.

The Love for Three Oranges
War and Peace
by Serge Prokofiev
April 23, 1891–March 5, 1953

The Love for Three Oranges. *Premiere at the Auditorium, Chicago, 1921. Text by the composer from Carlo Gozzi's 1761 comedy. An opera in a prologue and four acts. Setting: A mythical land.*

War and Peace. Premiere in Moscow, 1945. Text by the composer and Mira Mendelson from Tolstoy's 1863–69 novel. An opera in thirteen scenes and a choral prelude. Setting: Russia in 1806–12.

Sergei Prokofiev belongs in the top echelon of anyone's classical composer list for his instrumental concert music, but the historians tell us that deep down inside his first love was opera. Regrettably, he had little good fortune with most of the seven he completed.

These two represent two poles of Prokofiev's seven operas. The first is a comic, ironic, fairy-tale fantasy, interesting and appealing, lyrical, and romantic, filled with "theater," and in the composer's lifetime the most frequently performed of his operas. The second is an epic, considered by some analysts to be the only masterpiece opera from twentieth-century Russia—but one that doesn't compete with Puccini for opera audiences.

Of course, neither does Tolstoy's novel compete with Tom Clancy for buyers in the bookstores.

Prokofiev's standing as a virtuoso pianist and composer of classical music is unquestioned. He wrote symphonies, piano and violin concertos, film music, ballets, chamber music, and the short piece that should be in the home of every child, *Peter and the Wolf.*

His life was a strange one. By his own choice, he left Russia after the 1917 Revolution, stayed away until 1936, and then returned to Soviet control and communism for the rest of his life, a time of severe government repression of artistic experimentation, imagination, and initiative. He wasn't very successful while outside the Soviet Union, but he lived comfortably once he returned, with production of his instrumental works and audiences assured so long as he followed the Kremlin's rules.

Tolstoy's epic novel deals with the Russian people's struggle against Napoleon's invasion in 1812. Prokofiev chose this work over other projects he was considering because of the German invasion of Russia during World War II. His final version (of many) is in two huge parts, with seven scenes in Part I and six in Part II. The opera begins on a moonlit night in the house and garden of the Rostov estate of Otradnoye and ends after the Battle of Borodino in a savage blizzard as the battered French army is retreating. A cast of almost thousands includes Napoleon as well as the families and lovers from the novel.

Significant praise comes for *War and Peace* from the opera professionals. Gerald Abraham, noted author and musicologist, says the music is by turns lyric, dramatic, and epic. He suggests it is the most worthy of all Russian operas, including the great nineteenth-century masterpieces. Professor Donald Jay Grout writes: "More than any of his other works for the theater, *War and Peace* places Prokofiev in the great tradition of Russian opera: profoundly national in inspiration and musical style but also profoundly human and therefore transcending national limitations."

The Love for Three Oranges is an entirely different kind of composition, a fantasy packed with ridiculous action and ludicrous characters, including a

King of Clubs (bass), a Prince (tenor) who will die unless he laughs, a group of little devils, a treacherous Prime Minister costumed as a King of Spades (baritone), a bad witch named Fata Morgana (soprano), a wicked niece named Clarissa (contralto), a good sorcerer named Tchelio (bass), and three oranges containing people. It has no big arias, choruses, or set numbers (it does have a popular march), but the audience gets a lot of theater in an opera in which the hero is turned into a rat and the Princesses live inside the oranges.

States of mind of different groups are presented: highbrows, wits, romantics, and lowbrows. Prokofiev wrote in his autobiography: "Some critics tried to guess whom I was making fun of—the audience, Gozzi [author of the comedy from which it was taken], the operatic form or those who do not know how to laugh."

Revivals of *Three Oranges* keep popping up in the international repertory, usually with considerable success. Prokofiev experimented a good bit with dissonances and rhythms but not with wildly atonal music. An orchestral suite based on the opera is one of his popular compositions.

Of his seven operas, only four were produced during his life. Works seen today include *The Fiery Angel*, *Bethrothal in a Monastery* and *The Gambler*. He is one of three Russians in the Twentieth-century European Package, along with Dmitri Shostakovich and naturalized American Igor Stravinsky.

&

The Cunning Little Vixen
by Leoš Janáček
July 3, 1854–August 12, 1928

Premiere at the National Theatre, Brno, 1924. Text by the composer from Rudolf Těsnohlidék's 1921 novel Příhody Lišky Bystrouška. Three acts. Setting: A Moravian village and surrounding woods.

Leoš Janáček is a hot item in the mid-1990s, applauded as original, substantial, and appealing, and this is one of his most lyrical and successful works.

In my first weeks as a young reporter in Cleveland immediately after World War II, I made the mistake of interviewing two dogs who were looking for homes. City editor James W. Collins would have none of it. "In this newspaper, Goulding, animals never, never, never speak. Not dogs, not cows, not horses, not any."

Well, Janáček's animals talk up a storm in *The Cunning Little Vixen* (and Wagner's birds talk in *Siegfried*, although in that case they talk bird language). Speaking and singing animals include a Vixen, a Fox, a Dachshund, a Cock, a Hen, a Badger, a Screech Owl, a Woodpecker, and a half-dozen two-footed humans.

Janáček's Collection *Jenůfa*, his third opera, was written at age fifty. *Vixen* is one of four outstanding others composed after his sixty-fifth birthday, follow-

511

ing *Kátă Kabanová*, 1921, and preceding *The Makropulos Case, 1926;* and *From the House of the Dead*, 1930.

The *Vixen* story is an old Czech rustic fable in which animals and humans are laced together. Sharp Ears, the Vixen (child soprano as a cub, soprano as a young woman), is caught by the Forester (baritone) and kept as a pet until he escapes and is shot by a poacher. When the aging Forester comes across a fox cub that looks exactly like her dead mother, he realizes that nature always renews itself and is content. Some analysts use phrases like the wondrous continuity of the natural world, which is one way of putting it.

Blooming Late

If you are over fifty and feel you haven't accomplished much, take heart. Janáček's most famous opera, The Collection's *Jenůfa*, came in his fiftieth year. Four operas that the critics like best, and presumably his "greatest," were written when he was past sixty-five. So were his best-known instrumental works, including two string quartets, his Sinfonietta (more than twenty minutes long, in five movements, dedicated to the Czech armed forces), and a powerful piece called the *Glagolitic* (or *Slavonic) Mass.* Sample it for the best sense of Leóš Janáček.

But the Vixen also is meant to be symbolic of femaleness and sexuality. At one point she and a male Fox (soprano) discuss their sexual inexperience and enjoy ecstatic premarital sex. She becomes pregnant. In the morning, they look for the Woodpecker (contralto) to marry them. During one of the interludes between the many scenes, a beautiful girl, representing the essence of the female, emerges from the sleeping vixen and returns into it at dawn.

The size of Janáček's animals is generally equated with the pitch of the voices, with the Fox as soprano, the Dachshund as mezzo-soprano, and the big Badger as bass.

Several Janáček operas are performed reasonably frequently today. My age group likes the idea of the aging Forester dreaming of the spring of his life and finding peace in the new life of the forest. Janáček wrote this one just before he turned seventy, a relatively youthful time of life. It is his happiest work musically, with ballets helping portray his animal kingdom.

Janáček's research into Czech speech patterns led to a musical style built of short phrases which sort of drop away. Don't look in his works for the long-spanned, flowing melody characteristic of Italian composers. But the atmosphere is strong, aided by the offstage chorus voice from the forest. He liked offstage choruses and used them in several operas.

Suggestion: The easy way is to listen first to his magnificent twenty-minute orchestral suite drawn from the opera.

∾

Cardillac
Mathis der Maler
by Paul Hindemith
November 16, 1895–December 28, 1963

Cardillac. *Premiere at the Staatsoper, Dresden, 1926. Text by Ferdinand Lion from E.T.A. Hoffmann's 1819 story "Das Fraulein von Scuderi." Three acts. Setting: Paris in the late seventeenth century.*

Mathis der Maler (Mathias the Painter). *Premiere at the Stadt Theatre in Zurich, 1938. Text by the composer. An opera in seven scenes. Setting: Mainz, 1524.*

Both of these works deal with the relationship of the artist to the society in which he lives, a dominant theme of many twentieth-century operas.

Paul Hindemith had an outstanding career in Germany in the 1930s, but his wife was Jewish, he had Jewish friends, and he even used Jewish musicians in his orchestra! When he fled Germany in 1940 after Hitler invaded Poland, he found refuge as a music instructor at the University of Buffalo. To his regret, he also found snow—and, as he wrote his family, "black snow." We don't have black snow on the east side of the state on Chateaugay Lake, ten miles from the Canadian border.

Hindemith left Buffalo in 1940 to teach music at Yale. He became an American citizen but returned to Europe after World War II to live the rest of his life in Switzerland.

Composer, conductor, and virutoso performer on viola and violin, he was a musician's musician, perhaps the most technically gifted of any twentieth-century composer. He wrote symphonies, other concert music, chamber music, ballets, vocal music, and sonatas for every instrument from tuba to bassoon.

His other operas include:

Mörder, Hoffnung der Frauen, one act, 1921
Das Nusch-Nuschi, one act operetta for marionettes, 1921
Sancta Susanna, opera in one act, 1922
Hin und zuruck, sketch in one act, 1927
Neues vom Tage, opera in three parts, 1929
Die Harmonie der Welt, opera in five acts, 1957
The Long Christmas Dinner, his last opera, a one-act work, 1961

Caught in the Switches

Paul Hindemith in his early years of composition was a passionate model railroader. He owned nine hundred yards of model railway track and the most sophisticated electrical equipment, with remote-control points and signals.

Politically, he walked a difficult track between two friends and collaborators—the poet Gottfried Benn, a right-winger, and Bertolt Brecht (librettist for Kurt Weill for *Rise and Fall of the City of Mahagonny* and *The Threepenny Opera*), a communist.

But *Mathis der Maler*, Hindemith's opera about an independent artist, was too strong a statement in support of the autonomy of art for the Hitlerites to swallow. When Wilhelm Furtwängler was prohibited from conducting it at the Berlin State Opera and instead performed Hindemith's symphony of the same name, the Nazis were not pleased. They said: "Furtwängler has committed a regrettable blunder . . . The case of Hindemith does not differ from that of . . . various artists, who for fourteen years have carried the flag of the old system and who now are being foisted upon us as revolutionary supporters of the state."

Furtwängler replied: "What would be the result if unrestricted political denunciations were applied to the arts?"

The bottom line: Furtwängler was forced to resign from all of his music positions, and all of Hindemith's works were banned. Furtwängler later refused to conduct in Nazi-occupied countries.

(After the war, the Jewish community was divided about Furtwängler's decision to stay in Germany during most of the Nazi period. His defenders said he was an unworldly artist, concerned primarily with his music and not with the world around him—precisely the theme of both *Cardillac* and *Mathis der Maler*: an artist's relationship to the society in which he lives and works.)

Like Krenek, Weill, and Schoenberg—other German/Austrian composers in the Twentieth-century European Package who emigrated to the United States between the wars—Hindemith was a twelve-tone composer, if only for a time. But, like Alban Berg, he used more of a gloved hand than Schoenberg. He went through various musical phases, experimenting with everything from jazz to Bach-like counterpoint. (Other important emigrants from Europe include Béla Bartók from The Collection, Igor Stravinsky from this section, and French composer Darius Milhaud.)

Cardillac, Hindemith's fifth opera and his first full-length one, is an example of the opera experimentation that took place in the 1920s in Germany,

France, and England (but much less so in Italy, opera's traditional home). It's also indicative of the reaction of the general operagoer to the "new" and the "modern" of this century as opposed to the more conventional. *Cardillac* premiered at about the same time as Puccini's *Turandot. Turandot* thrives; *Cardillac*, an outstanding musical effort by an extremely talented composer of classical music, barely survives.

Cardillac tells the story of a master goldsmith who is so taken by his own works that he murders the customers who buy them so he can steal them back. This rise in the murder rate understandably upsets the people of Paris. At the end, when his workshop is about to be torn apart by an angry mob, Cardillac confesses his crimes in order to save his artistic works from being destroyed. He is then torn apart by the citizens. In the middle, there's the high drama of a suspense thriller as a lady awaits her lover in her bedroom. He arrives, bringing with him a fine golden belt, but as the two start to make love they're joined by a cloaked and masked figure, Cardillac, who stabs the man to death and retrieves the belt. The lady's screams will stick with you through the night.

German opera had been dominated for years by the two Richards, Wagner and Strauss. Structurally, Hindemith stepped away from their through-composed ("continuous music") works to create an opera in the older musical form, reemphasizing traditional arias and duets. To the astonishment—and disappointment—of some critics and musicologists, Hindemith revised the whole work in 1952, almost twenty years after its first performance. He rewrote the text, making the hero more human, and changed the order of some of the musical numbers. Today the initial version seems to be the preferred one.

Mathis der Maler is Hindemith's masterpiece, his eighth opera, written in the early days of the Nazi takeover of Germany. Like Wagner's *Die Meistersinger* from The Collection, it's dedicated to the glory of national art. Mathias Grünewald was an actual sixteenth-century painter who worked in the service of the Archbishop of Mainz. In the opera, the artist leads the Peasants' War against their overlords and the church, then becomes disillusioned with that cause and eventually renounces the outside world.

Needless to say, the Nazis weren't turned on. They attacked both music and plot as "cultural Bolshevism" and banned a scheduled 1934 premiere in Berlin.

Jonny spielt auf
by Ernst Krenek
August 23, 1900–December 23, 1991

Premiere at the Stadttheatre in Leipzig, 1927. U.S. premiere at the Metropolitan Opera, New York, 1929. Text by the composer. An opera in two parts, eleven scenes. Time: The 1920s.

Think jazz—and overwhelming short-term prosperity.

Ernst Krenek was a composer who reacted against nineteenth-century romanticism by writing contemporary opera in a modern way. That way included jazz, even if the jazz was used satirically and not, as George Gershwin was to use it, as the natural expression of his characters.

Krenek was only twenty-seven when he produced this smash hit, the most successful opera from Germany between the wars and for a short time the biggest thing that twentieth-century European opera had experienced. Its first year it scored a record number of performances in Germany, and for the next two years it filled the opera houses in twenty-odd European cities.

It also went to the Metropolitan for seven performances in one season, although never to return. With the Depression and World War II, its sudden, almost unprecedented, popularity faded just as quickly as it had come. Revivals since have been infrequent.

Born and reared in Vienna, Krenek followed his music instructor to Berlin in his early twenties, worked in Kassel, and returned to Vienna before emigrating to the United States in 1938 when Adolf Hitler and his Nazi thugs were eying Austria and preparing for war. He made America his home for the rest of his life, had a distinguished teaching career, and died in Palm Springs, California.

In all he wrote twenty-one operas, eleven in Europe before the war and ten later in the United States. During several musical periods, his works varied from "legitimate" opera to "popular" music, and some that were in between.

Unfriendly Critic

Ernst Krenek had written two previous operas before *Jonny spielt auf*, which premiered at the Leipzig Opera House when he was only twenty-seven. Although it was a sensational success, not all opening-night critics were captivated. One wrote:

"The art that Schubert extols in song as holy has been debased and prostituted."

After *Jonny*, he turned first to less adventuresome-sounding music and then moved on to the twelve-tone technique initiated by Arnold Schoenberg. He used that style in 1931–33 for *Karl V*, an opera about an individual's conflict between devotion to God and allegiance to the state. But the Vienna censors, already reactionary even before the fascists took over, would have none of it and its premiere was not until five years later in Prague. In later writings, Krenek called it "explicitly anti-Nazi, pro-Austrian and pro-Catholic."

Here in the United States, Krenek wrote several chamber operas and, in

1955, *Pallas Athene weint*, about the loss of democracy in ancient Athens and how to defend freedom without yielding to tyranny. Other works in the twelve-tone technique include *The Bell Tower*, 1957, and *The Golden Ram*, 1964.

Jonny presents different kinds of music, each symbolic of something. Max (tenor), an intellectual opera composer, meets Anita (soprano), an opera singer, on top of a glacier. They fall in love. Later she is seduced by Daniello (baritone), a womanizing virtuoso violinist. Yvonne (soprano), a hotel chambermaid, is in love with Jonny (baritone), a black jazz band saxophonist. When he comes to see her as she is cleaning Daniello's room, he is taken by Daniello's beautiful violin. He steals it and becomes the toast of Europe. After many goings on, including Daniello's being crushed under a train, Max and Anita are reunited and leave on a boat train bound for America. Jonny stays behind, playing his new jazz music on an Old World violin while straddling a globe on the station clock, and the townspeople dance the Charleston.

Musically, the work is a blend of catchy jazz tunes and animated rhythms, dissonant but not excessively so. Although it has a lot of jazz and is commonly called a jazz opera, the jazz actually is simply part of the plot. Dramatically, *Jonny* is part realism and part fantasy, and packed with ambiguous symbolism. Jonny is presumably the symbol of the new man, free from inhibitions, musical and sexual. Although many audiences took it as a comedy, it was not designed as one. Krenek's stated objective was to make a connection between the rejuvenation of the European people and the revitalization of European music by American jazz.

Late in life, he spoke of the two conflicting forces that face many composers: "Early in my career I was attracted by the idea of pure, uncompromising creation, independent of the fashions of the day, and even explicitly opposed to them. At the same time, I always felt the temptation to achieve practical results 'in this world.' "

Orpheus After World War I

We have met *Orfeo ed Euridice*, Number 52 in The Collection, by Gluck the great reformer, and Monteverdi's *Orfeo*, Number 81. Krenek adds *Orpheus und Eurydike*, a German version, a three-act work from a play by Oskar Kokoschka, who experienced and was influenced by World War I. It premiered in Kassel in 1926 and deals with the two lovers in a twentieth-century Expressionistic way. The music is atonal. Its text is about male-female connections and man-God-nature relationships. The Spirit of Hades—who has impregnated Eurydice—appears as a sailor, soldier, drunk, and dolt. It is a long way from Monteverdi . . . but perhaps no farther than 1926 is from 1607.

❧

The Threepenny Opera
The Rise and Fall of the City of Mahagonny
by Kurt Weill
March 2, 1900–April 3, 1950

Die Dreigroschenoper (The Threepenny Opera). *Premiere at the Theatre am Schiffbauerdamm, Berlin, 1928. U.S. premiere at the Empire Theatre, New York, 1933. Text by Bertolt Brecht, a revision of John Gay's 1728* The Beggar's Opera. *A play with music in three acts. Setting: Soho, London.*

Aufstieg und Fall der Stadt Mahagonny (Rise and Fall of the City of Mahagonny). *Premiere at the Neves Theatre, Leipzig, 1930. Text by Bertolt Brecht. Three acts. Setting: The present, in the imaginary city of Mahagonny, on a desert in America.*

Kurt Weill and his collaborator Bertolt Brecht were two gentlemen who were not captivated by the capitalist system.

"Mack the Knife," the most popular tune ever heard in a Kurt Weill opera, is known to the least soaped of the Unwashed. Its formal name is "Die Morität von Mackie Messer," and it's the opening ballad of the work that first made Weill famous, *Die Dreigroschenoper*, a play with music that updated Englishman John Gay's *Beggar's Opera*.

Weill had two careers, one in Europe and a second in the United States. He settled in the United States in 1935 and became an American citizen in 1943.

His librettist for several works was the German playwright Bertolt Brecht, a man dedicated to ultraliberal causes who eventually converted to out-and-out communism. Brecht considered the capitalist system to be corrupting a society that, in his opinion, wasn't worth much in any case. Weill was not a Marxist and broke with him at that time, but remained a left-wing radical, a "militant humanist" if you will, opposed to the intolerance and prejudice he found in a capitalist society.

The son of the chief cantor of the Dessau synagogue, Weill initially wrote some low-key "modern" music that didn't cause much of a stir, but then he teamed up with Brecht to produce *The Threepenny Opera*. It came shortly after Ernst Krenek's jazzy *Jonny spielt auf* and was almost eclipsed by *Jonny's* incredible popularity. *Jonny* quickly faded away, however, whereas *The Threepenny Opera* grew stronger as the years passed. Today Krenek is virtually gone but Weill is still very much with us, performed in large and small houses and a favorite of cabaret-type performances in this country.

The Threepenny Opera is the story of Macheath (tenor), Mac the Knife, head of a band of street robbers, who marries Polly Peachum (soprano), daughter of Jonathan Jeremiah Peachum (baritone), the head of a band of beggars.

Peachum thinks that the loss of his daughter is going to ruin his beggar business and tries to turn Mac over to the police, but Mac leaves his new wife and flees. The whores with whom he has been friendly betray him, and he is captured and about to be hanged. When his friends gather at the gallows to say good-bye, he asks them to forgive him for the trouble he has caused. But the ending is happy, as he is saved at the last moment by a messenger from the King. Peachum explains to the audience that Mac really should have been hanged, but reminds it that mercy tempers justice.

It is another twentieth-century political and social work, blending cabaret music, jazz, folk music, ballads, dance rhythms, and melodrama. Whatever the design of the composer and librettist in the late 1920s, today it's known and appreciated more for its music than its outdated text.

Enfant terrible

When he was twenty-seven, American composer Aaron Copland saw *Mahagonny* at a music festival in Baden-Baden. Acknowledging that Weill was the new "enfant terrible" of Germany, Copland was unimpressed. He said Weill was not without musical talent but too often sacrificed those musical gifts for questionable dramatic effectiveness.

In 1933, after collaborating with Brecht on other works, including a ballet-song composition called *Die sieben Todsünden*, or *The Seven Deadly Sins*, Weill left Germany for France and then the United States, where he wrote many musical pieces for Broadway, and also worked unhappily in Hollywood. He composed two American operas, *Street Scene* in 1946, which has an occasional revival, and *Down in the Valley* in 1948, which is sometimes put on by colleges and was given in 1995 by the Lyric Opera of Kansas City. Though these two works had some success, they didn't work nearly as well for Weill as *The Threepenny Opera*, which never pretended to be an opera anyhow.

But the 1930 *Rise and Fall of the City of Mahagonny* was a full-length one that was by far the most ambitious work of the Weill-Brecht collaboration.

Mahagonny is an imaginary city somewhere west of Chicago, built by a truckload of fugitives who have been convicted of white slaving and fraud. It is a city of material things and pleasure, life elsewhere not being worth living. The opera is a direct assault on the capitalist society and the capitalist value system, which becomes apparent when Jim Mahoney (tenor), who has bought Jenny Smith (soprano) for thirty dollars, is sentenced to two days for indirect murder and sentenced to death for not paying his bar bill.

Leipzig Cheers and Jeers

The first performance of *Mahagonny* was at the Neves Theatre in March 1930. Composer/author H. H. Stuckenschmidt, who studied with Arnold Schoenberg, describes the reaction: "The Leipzig audience reacted with an uproar which ruined the end of the performance. Jeers and cheers vied with each other for fifteen minutes; finally the applause triumphed. The political implications of the reception were obvious. The protestors belonged to the right, to a section of the middle class that had already accepted fascist ideas and reacted accordingly.

"Berlin proved itself to be less politically contaminated. When *Mahagonny* was performed in the Theatre am Kurfürstendamm in 1932 with a cast of actors and singers conducted by Alexander von Zemlinsky, it was a great success."

Weill was blacklisted after Hitler came to power and arrived in New York in 1935 after two years in Paris and Scandinavia.

There is little warm and fuzzy in any of the collaborative works of Weill and Brecht, which are sound examples of the type of twentieth-century opera that was designed primarily to communicate a social message. *Mahagonny* has been described by critics as rabble-rousing art, but Weill also has been called a genius of the concert hall and Brecht a genius of the stage. Their design was to talk about the evils of a capitalistic society, and their message comes through loud and clear. No interpreters of symbolism are required.

But there also is music, of course, not only raucous dance-hall music but also rich and melodious music. Weill's tunes can stand beside those of many happier composers. *Mahagonny* is not challenging *La traviata* in any opera house of the world, but after nearly seventy years neither has it gone away.

Moses und Aron
by Arnold Schoenberg
September 13, 1874–July 13, 1951

Premiere in Zurich, 1957. Written in 1932. First performed in Berlin in 1959, at Covent Garden in London in 1966, in the United States in Boston, staged by Sarah Caldwell, in 1966, and in Paris in 1979. Text by Schoenberg from the Book of Exodus in the Bible. An opera in two acts; a third act was begun but not completed. Time: Biblical.

Arnold Schoenberg was born Jewish, abandoned his faith, was baptized a Lutheran, returned to Judaism, taught at the Prussian Academy of Arts, and wrote this major opera, about Mount Sinai and the voice of God in a burning bush.

His name has surfaced frequently in this book as a musical master, one of the leading classical composers of the twentieth century, some argue the most important one by dint of the influence of his twelve-tone music.

He started work on *Moses und Aron* in 1927 and in 1932 completed the second act, but it still was unfinished when he died in Los Angeles in 1951. He had said he was hung up in part on reconciling some of the "almost incomprehensible contradictions in the Bible."

Schoenberg was an acquired taste during his lifetime, and he still is an acquired taste today. At the outset, his twelve-tone system shocked half of the music world and alienated the other half, with both halves agreeing that what they heard was unique. Although his work now is heard more often than it was earlier, the kindest way to measure him is by historical influence rather than public acceptance.

With the possible exception of *Verklärte Nacht*, a sextet later redone for chamber orchestra, no Schoenberg works really have entered the popular classical repertoire, important though they are. And *Verklärte Nacht*, characterized as late Romantic, was written when he was greatly under the influence of Richard Wagner and before he got into twelve-tone composition.

Other instrumental works include *Pierrot Lunaire*, a big dramatic song cycle for soprano; six pieces for the piano; five pieces for orchestra; and the String Quartet No. 3.

He wrote three operas in addition to *Moses und Aron*:

Erwartung (Expectation), 1909, a monodrama in one act
Von Heute auf Morgen (From One Day to the Next), 1930, the first twelve-tone opera
Die glückliche Hand (The Fateful Hand), 1913, produced 1924

A combination of things makes Schoenberg's operas less approachable (a kind way of saying lots of people don't come to see them) than, say, Puccini's. As noted in the introduction to this section, he was an Expressionist, concerned chiefly with externalizing his characters' feelings and subconscious. Expressionism entered European opera through Richard Strauss in *Salome* and *Elektra* before bursting into full bloom with Schoenberg and Alban Berg. Schoenberg's challenge was to fashion a musical language that would convey the Expressionism of the text, and he did so by using atonal twelve-tone composition. The result does not remind listeners of the music of *La Bohème*.

In the opera, Moses (a semispeaking role uttered in "Sprechgesang," or "Sprechstimme," which is an intermediate step between speech and song) hears as a chorus the voice of God in the burning bush: He must lead the Israelites out of Egypt. Moses replies that he doesn't have the eloquence and the required communication skills to undertake this mission, but God tells him his brother Aaron (English spelling) (a lyric tenor), does and that Aaron will be His spokesman. So they bring God's message to the Israelites in different ways. Moses accepts an unknowable, invisible, infinite God: no graven images. Aaron believes the people need concrete manifestations of God in order to gain the strength to free themselves from Pharaoh.

In an effort to convince the people, Aaron performs miracles. He changes Moses' staff into a writhing serpent, and he turns Moses' hand leprous and then cures it. Moses believes that the people in the desert will live on pure contemplation, but Aaron promises them that God will provide for them by turning sand into fruit. While Moses is on Mount Sinai for forty days hearing about the Ten Commandments, the people get restless and angry, and threaten to kill their leaders unless their old gods are brought back.

Aaron promises a comprehensible form for God and asks for gold to be brought. A golden calf is cast. The "Dance before the Golden Calf" is the high point of the opera; it's a tumultuous mob scene involving suicide, drunkenness, dancing, and sexual and religious orgies. Old men sacrifice themselves in front of the calf, a youth dies amidst rape and destruction, and four naked virgins are embraced by priests and stabbed before the scene ends from exhaustion. Moses comes down from the mountain. The Israelites follow a pillar of fire across the stage. Moses is left alone.

The text of the third act—chiefly a dialogue between Moses and Aaron—was finished, but the music was not.

Counterattack

Hans Keller was a respected musicologist and critic in London. Composer Arnold Schoenberg sought his assistance in replying to another critic who had not been friendly. On January 10, 1951, Schoenberg wrote Keller: "Enclosed you find a very unpleasant review, written by one of these non-musicians, who look in my music only for the twelve notes—not realizing in the least its musical contents, expression and merits. He is very stupid and insolent and would deserve a treatment like that you can give him. I hope you are interested! Now, sharpen your pen."

That the opera isn't in the standard international repertory is not surprising given that the music is atonal and the drama is a conflict between the thinker and the man of action. Schoenberg knew he was writing "unapproachable" music but believed that in time history would justify his work. The public jury is still out. It is an opera that attracts the most radical stage directors, and at least three productions, one in Covent Garden, one by the New York City Opera and another in Vienna, were hot-ticket sell-outs, either for the graphic nature of the golden-calf scene or the strong political subtext. Schoenbergians regard it as a great masterpiece, fight for tickets whenever it is staged, and continue to hope that a wide audience is around the corner for the next production. Their consolation is in the knowledge of the enormous avant-garde influence of Schoenberg on other composers. Obviously no one knows today where the opera or his influence will be fifty years hence.

But, like the credit card, you can't leave opera without him—or at least knowledge of him.

∾

Lady Macbeth of the Mtsensk District
by Dmitri Shostakovich
September 25, 1906–August 9, 1975

Premiere at the Maly Opera, Leningrad, 1934. U.S. premiere in Cleveland, 1935. Libretto by the composer and Alexander Preis from Nicolai Leskov's 1865 short story. Four acts. Setting: Karsh Gurbenia, 1865.

It wouldn't be friendly for the President of the United States to walk out of your first serious opera in a huff and blast you in *The Washington Post* as a composer of "degenerate" music.

But it would be great for ticket sales, and the opposition in Congress would attack the President for his boorishness, and your publisher would fax you a "Right on!"

Not so in Russia in the mid-1930s. Not if Joseph Stalin came to see a two-year-old work that had enjoyed big success with two hundred performances at home and abroad, was infuriated by what he saw, and ordered *Pravda* to lay down the law.

"Muddle without music," *Pravda* declared. "Is its success abroad not explained by the fact that it tickles the perverted bourgeois taste with its fidgety, screaming, neurotic music?"

That's what happened to Dmitri Shostakovich with *Lady Macbeth*. A major composer of classical music and a major symphonist, he never wrote another serious opera. If he displeased the Kremlin, he knew he would lose his job, his home, his other perks . . . and, not inconceivably, his freedom and his life. He was a talented dramatic composer, however, and produced an operetta, a comic opera, several ballets, and some film scores.

It was another dozen years after *Pravda*'s comments before the dictatorial communist government declared war on all Soviet composers who didn't toe the line. The orders were clear: The theme must be socialist; the music must be "realistic," without harsh tonalities, and must be based on Russian folksong; the plot must be "positive," and the ending must be a state-praising happy one.

Lady Macbeth was revised years later and circulated as *Katerina Ismailova*, although the original version also was approved for production.

The earliest showing in the United States was in the winter of 1935 in Cleveland, Ohio, where the sun sometimes shines between October and March. It was produced at Severance Hall by the Cleveland Orchestra just a year after its debut in Russia. Herbert Elwell, critic of the Cleveland *Plain Dealer*, a gentle and soft-spoken composer who befriended me as a young *Plain Dealer* reporter twelve years later, said in his review that it was a blend of realism and satire without a single dull moment.

After two Cleveland performances, it moved to New York for one day at the Met.

Quacks, Grunts, and Growls

Pravda, the mouthpiece organ of the Soviet government, blasted Shostakovich and his *Lady Macbeth of the District of Mtsensk* in a January 28, 1936, editorial entitled "Confusion Instead of Music." It said, in part:

"The author of *Lady Macbeth* was forced to borrow from jazz its nervous, convulsive, and spasmodic music in order to lend 'passion' to his characters . . . [This is] the coarsest kind of naturalism. He reveals the merchants and the people monotonously and bestially. The predatory merchant woman who scrambles into possession of wealth through murder is pictured as some kind of 'victim' of bourgeois society. . . .

"And all of this is coarse, primitive, and vulgar. The music quacks, grunts, and growls, and suffocates itself, in order to express the amatory scenes as naturalistically as possible. And 'love' is smeared all over the opera in the most vulgar manner. The merchant's double bed occupies the central position on the stage. On it all 'problems' are solved . . .

"The composer apparently never considered the problem of what the Soviet audience expects and looks for in music."

Analysts today describe it as a mixture of parody, satire, modernism, and realism . . . and as a contemporary masterpiece. The music is brilliant and the arias melodious by twentieth-century standards. Big choruses are employed. The scenes are linked by orchestral interludes that no longer sound "different" to our twentieth-century ears. Many composers outside Russia, of course, disagreed with *Pravda*'s position. In his biography of Bejamin Britten, Humphrey Carpenter reports Britten's remarks after attending a 1936 concert performance: "Of course, it is idle to pretend that this is great music throughout—it is stage music, and as such must be considered. There is some terrific music in the entre'acts. But I will defend it through thick and thin against these charges of 'lack of style' . . . The satire is biting and brilliant. It is never boring for a second—even in this [concert] form."

In truth, old Uncle Joe Stalin, as President Truman used to call him, did watch a downright depressing opera. The Lady Macbeth involved is Katerina (soprano), wife of Zinovy (tenor), a merchant. Bored with her marriage, she has an affair in his absence with Sergei (tenor), a servant in their home. When her father-in-law, Boris (high bass), learns of it and has Sergei flogged, Katerina poisons Boris. When Zinovy returns, Sergei talks her into murdering him. After his body is discovered during their wedding celebration, both Katerina and Sergei are sent off to Siberia. En route, Sergei seduces another convict, Sonyetka (contralto), by buying her with Katerina's stockings. Shattered, Katerina throws herself into a raging river, but not without dragging Sonyetka in with her.

Analysts today characterize it as a domestic drama that deals with the issue of passion and eroticism and as a critique of socialism and of the terrible boredom in the huge Russian society, especially the boredom of a woman caught in a hopeless marriage. Some note that it deals also with a more universal theme: What can cause a perfectly normal woman to commit murder? What kinds of lust and love bring out this dark side of a human being? Which of us, under dehumanizing circumstances, has no murder in his—or her—makeup?

Musically, *Lady Macbeth* is more tonal, "more accessible," than Shostakovich's earlier works. The scenes within each act are connected with instrumental interludes. The analysts say he was naturally gifted as a theatrical composer, and the musicologists deplore the fact that Soviet repression took him out of the opera business.

Mass murderer that he was, Stalin didn't want it on the stage in front of him. The Met did, again in the 1994–95 season.

Riders to the Sea
by Ralph Vaughan Williams
October 12, 1872–August 26, 1958

Premiere at the Royal College of Music, London, 1937. The text follows almost word for word the text of J. M. Synge's 1902 tragedy of the same name. A thirty-five minute opera in one act. Setting: The island of Aran, off the west coast of Ireland.

Ralph Vaughan Williams leads you to think of fish-and-chips, Big Ben, and the dartboard in the King's Arms. He was one of his country's most respected classical composers, determined not to be overly influenced by the style of music crossing the Channel from Continental Europe, even though he did commit to three months of intensive study under Maurice Ravel.

He loved England and all things English, including especially Elizabethan and Tudor folk music, and sounds akin to those past eras are heard in his work.

He and Gustav Holst from this Twentieth-century European Package were the two top British composers in the early years of the century, and both made solid contributions to opera, although Vaughan Williams is remembered today chiefly for nine symphonies, an orchestral *Fantasia on Greensleeves*, several choral works, and—a must-hear—the very short *The Lark Ascending*, a romance for violin and orchestra. The best-known work of his vocal music is *On Wenlock Edge*, a cycle of six songs.

Brünnhilde as Love Potion

Ralph Vaughan Williams was so taken by Richard Wagner as a young man that he spent his honeymoon in Berlin so that he and his bride could attend the *Ring* cycle. Available sources do not advise of the reaction of the new Mrs. Vaughan Williams.

Of six dramatic works, written between 1910 and 1932, *Riders to the Sea* is his masterpiece and the only one that has kept a place in the international repertory. Understandably, given his symphonic success, his operas are praised more for orchestra and melody than for theater and drama. But musicologists credit Vaughan Williams and Holst for reestablishing English opera in the first third of the century and thus clearing the way for Benjamin Britten and the opera revival he launched after World War II with *Peter Grimes*.

Riders to the Sea is a man-against-nature (or woman-against-nature) opera, a theme Vaughan Williams liked and one he developed in his instrumental works, including *The Pastoral* Symphony and *Sinfonia Anartica (sic)*. The story is moving, with a haunting atmosphere and Celtic inevitability and fatalism. Maurya (contralto), an old woman who is the widow of a fisherman, had six sons. Before the opera opens, four of them and her husband had drowned and the fifth is missing. When her two daughters (soprano) discover his clothes, taken off his corpse, they hide them in a loft so she won't see them. With his brother gone, the last son, Bartley (baritone) now must take both horses to the Galway Fair. In crossing open water, he is knocked into the sea by his brother's pony and drowned. Maurya is resigned at the news, almost relieved, and finally at peace. Blessing the living and the dead, she sings: "No man at all can be living forever, and we must be satisfied."

One source describes this as Vaughan Williams's most primal opera, a "superbly reticent" setting of J. M. Synge's tragedy.

ɔ

Lulu
by Alban Berg
February 9, 1885–December 24, 1935

Premiere of Acts I and II in Zurich, 1937. Premiere of the three-act version at the Opéra, Paris, 1979. Text by the composer, adapted from Frank Wedekind's 1895 Erdgeist (Earth Spirit) and 1903 Die Büchse der Pandora (Pandora's Box). An opera in three acts, finished after Berg's death by Friedrich Cerha. Setting: Prague, late in the nineteenth century.

Alban Berg was only fifteen when the new century began and obviously was tempered intellectually, artistically, and musically by it. The plot of *Lulu* is cloudy, the title character is an amoral temptress, the work is Expressionistic, the composition is twelve-tone, and the sum is an opera that is both musically and dramatically complex.

Berg is much more a product of the twentieth century than such composers in this package as Vaughan Williams and Dvořák, the environment that shaped him a far cry from theirs, and *Lulu* a far cry from *Riders to the Sea* and *Rusalka*. Many have considered it a degenerate work. A case can be made that it is a little on the sordid side since Lulu destroys all the men who love her, sleeps with the son of one husband she had shot, is loved by a lesbian countess, becomes a prostitute, and is murdered in an attic.

Few newcomers to music will know that Berg is using twelve-tone techniques, but anyone can hear that this music is different. Berg, however, handles the technique in a way that is considerably more lyrical than the raw, atonal compositions of his mentor, Arnold Schoenberg.

We have met Berg in The Collection with *Wozzeck*, Number 76. After fourteen years of stop-and-go work on *Lulu*, he had finished two acts and sketched in most of the rest before he died. The first complete production was not until 1979, in Paris.

Lulu is the story of the adventures of Lulu (soprano) as she copes, or tries to cope, with all manner of men. Her first husband has a heart attack when he finds her with a portrait painter (lyric tenor), her second (the painter) cuts his throat because she is having an affair, she shoots and kills her third as he is trying to force her to shoot herself, a Marquis (buffo tenor) in her life in Paris threatens to sell her to a Cairo brothel, and she ends up as a London prostitute. Her first—and last—three clients are a professor (high baritone), a black man (lyric tenor) who clubs to death her onetime stepson with whom she had slept, and Jack the Ripper (heroic tenor), who murders her in her attic room and then stabs to death the countess (mezzo-soprano) as she rushes to help her.

Composer Erwin Stein, who made the piano score of the first two acts and prepared one version of Act III (restructured by Friedrich Cerha), commented

Dietrich Fisher Diskau in Lulu

about Berg and twelve-tone music: "The music itself shows Berg at the height of his musical achievement. It enriches the picture we had already gained of the composer through his original and important achievements and is another confirmation of the fact that twelve-tone compositions are capable of the greatest variety of expression.

Schoenberg's Pupil

Young Berg became a private pupil of Arnold Schoenberg in Vienna after his brother had shown the master some lieder Alban had written. Nearly fifty years later Schoenberg recalled their time together:

"When Alban Berg came to me in 1904 he was a terribly shy young lad, but when I looked through the things he had written I realized immediately that here was real talent. As a result I accepted him as a pupil even though he was not in a position to pay the tuition fees. Later his mother came into a large inheritance and told Alban . . . that he could go on to the Conservatory. I was told that he burst into tears and could not be pacified until his mother agreed that he should carry on studying with me."

"The lyrical passages . . . are some of the most beautiful things Berg wrote . . . The music surrounds every figure with a special atmosphere, showing up the features and giving weight to their miming and gestures. The comic element . . . is also depicted with incisive humor. Yet the whole is enveloped in sound of a unique character. And in spite of occasional powerful *crescendos*, the orchestration of *Lulu* shows a preference for the delicate, gracious colours befitting the heroine."

Lulu has been overshadowed by the better-known *Wozzeck*, but today Berg is both highly respected by the professionals and increasingly popular with the public and *Lulu* is earning its own place despite a libretto that may not be your personal favorite—one that Schoenberg characterized as immoral. Bergians note that the opera is not at all realistic but rather lavishly Expressionistic, which makes everything okay.

∾

The Rake's Progress
by Igor Stravinsky
June 17, 1882–April 6, 1971

Premiere at La Fenice, Venice, 1951. Text by W. H. Auden and Chester Kallman after eight engravings by William Hogarth from 1735. An opera in three acts and an Epilogue. Setting: England in the eighteenth century.

"A year and a day have passed away
   Since first to you I came . . .

" 'Tis not your money but your soul
   Which I this night require."

If one of your ancestors had walked into William Hogarth's London engraving shop in 1735, he would have admired two sets of plates, *The Rake's Progress* and *The Harlot's Progress*.

More than two hundred years later Igor Stravinsky and two poets, one the celebrated W. H. Auden, collaborated to construct an opera inspired by Hogarth's artistry.

Stravinsky is one of the most influential classical composers of the twentieth century. From him came the most celebrated "new music" of the early 1900s—the new rhythms, harmonies, and melodies that shocked the ears of the music public, were likened by critics to grunts and growls, and caused riots in the theater (even though they were less "different" than the twelve-tone sounds of Arnold Schoenberg). The works that created the most fuss then and that remain his best-known compositions are three great ballets: *The Firebird*, *Petrushka*, and the strikingly discordant, for its time, *Rite of Spring*.

Peak Audience

The Rake's Progress has not disappeared from sight. On the contrary, the largest single audience ever to see and hear it was on the night of January 3, 1996, when it was shown in the United States on "Great Performances" on the Public Broadcasting System.

Although the opera was written in English, the filmed television production originated in Sweden rather than any English-speaking country. Well-known conductor Essa-Pekka Salonen led the Swedish Radio Symphony Orchestra.

The Rake's Progress was produced in 1951, late in Stravinsky's life, more than forty years after spectators watching *The Rite of Spring* had slapped one another's faces and stormed out into the night. In the interim, although rhythm rather than melody and song always was his main interest, Stravinsky had returned to a much more melodious and approachable style. This is his only full-length opera, serious (although also witty) and moral-driven. It tells the story of a young man's deterioration through sex, drink, gambling, and other activities common to full-blooded rakes (and a good many kids who turn out quite well). It doesn't make The Collection on a statistical basis, but it demands special attention for its powerful rhythms, its captivating (if still somewhat dissonant) music, and its strong, imaginative libretto.

Analysts call it one of the best modern examples of a work that goes back to the classics, with separate solo and ensemble numbers accompanied by a small orchestra. The recitative is supported by a harpsichord. And, like Mozart's *Don Giovanni*, there is a closing moral.

Stravinsky also produced a two-act opera-oratorio, *Oedipus Rex*, 1927, in which the singers are masked and the text is in Latin. Two other still-performed stage works are *L'histoire du soldat*, or *The Soldier's Tale*, 1918, which has speech, acting, and music but no singing, and *Les Noces*, or *The Wedding*, 1914–17, a ballet with songs and chorus. Aside from the ballets, his best-known orchestral works include his *Symphony of Psalms*, the Symphony in C, and the Symphony in Three Movements.

Born in 1882 in Oranienbaum, Russia, Igor Stravinsky was the son of a bass singer at the St. Petersburg Opera. When still young, he attracted the interest of the great Russian ballet master Sergei Diaghilev, impresario of the Ballets Russes. Out of this association came the three ballet masterpieces that made him one of the most controversial and publicized composers in the music world. He left Russia permanently before the communist takeover, lived in both Switzerland and France, and settled in 1940 in the United States.

In his youth he went through a nationalist phase that reflected Russian culture, background, and folklore. Then for many years he was a neoclassicist, looking to the past for musical models and philosophy. Late in life he worked with the twelve-tone serial music of Schoenberg and Berg, whose approach he previously had rejected. He died in New York in 1971, having been a big part of the American musical scene. He loved jazz, owned a house in Hollywood, became an American citizen, wrote a polka for circus elephants to dance, and even produced a new arrangement of "The Star-Spangled Banner."

Sensible Singing

W. H. Auden, Stravinsky's librettist, offered his rebuttal to all who condemn opera texts for not being sensible. "A good libretto plot," he said, "is a melodrama in both the strict and the conventional sense of the word; it offers as many opportunities as possible for the characters to be swept off their feet by placing them in situations which are too tragic or too fantastic for 'words.' No good opera plot can be sensible, for people do not sing when they are feeling sensible."

The Opera

Tom Rakewell (tenor) is in love with Anne Trulove (soprano), whose father (bass) considers him lazy and a bad match. Nick Shadow (baritone) appears with good news: A rich uncle has died in London and left Tom a lot of money. Tom and Nick go off together, Nick acting as a servant and Tom promising to reckon with him after a year and a day. Nick advises the audience: "The progress of a rake begins." Among other things, Nick takes Tom to Mother Goose's (mezzo-soprano) brothel. He also tempts him to marry the fantastic bearded lady of the circus, Baba the Turk (mezzo-soprano), and then to invest in a fake machine for turning stones into bread. Tom goes bankrupt. At the end of a year and a day, Nick reveals himself as the Devil and claims Tom's soul. When he also suggests a card game as a gamble for the soul, Tom agrees . . . and wins. The Devil, however, is not easily had, and as Devil/Nick sinks into the ground he condemns Tom to insanity. The final scene finds Tom in the asylum of Bedlam, thinking he's the Greek hero Adonis, and Anne saying her last good-bye to him. In the Epilogue, the characters sing this moral: "For idle hearts and hands and minds the Devil finds a work to do."

∾

The Turn of the Screw
by Benjamin Britten
November 22, 1913–November 4, 1976

Premiere at La Fenice, commissioned for the Venice Biennale, 1954. Text by My-fanwy Piper from Henry James's 1898 novella. Chamber opera in a Prologue and two acts, with an orchestra of thirteen players. Setting: An isolated country house in England in the nineteenth century.

This is perhaps the greatest chamber opera ever written. It is not a simple work, or a painless one, in plot or in music. It's a wonderful example of twentieth-century music that sounds different, albeit not all that different.

Benjamin Britten, in The Collection with *Peter Grimes*, Number 67, is the master of twentieth-century opera written in English, perhaps the century's leading opera composer, and arguably among history's top dozen. Like Berg, Janáček, and Richard Strauss from The Collection, he rates additional recognition in this Twentieth-century European Package.

Progress

When Benjamin Britten was seventeen he was taught at the Royal College of Music by British composer John Ireland, then in his early fifties. After his first full-length lesson with Ireland, Britten wrote in his diary: "He is *terribly* critical and enough to take the heart out of any one."

Twenty-four years later, in the fall of 1954, Ireland wrote a friend: "I have listened twice to Britten's new opera, *The Turn of the Screw*. I am no judge of opera as such, but this contains the most remarkable and original music I have ever heard from the pen of a British composer—and it is on a firmly diatonic and tonal basic. Also, what he has accomplished in sound by the use of only thirteen instruments was, to me, inexplicable, almost miraculous. This is not to say I *liked* the music, but it is gripping, vital and often terrifying. I am now (perhaps *reluctantly*) compelled to regard Britten as possessing ten times the musical talent, intuition and ability of all other living British composers put together."

While the international avant-garde in the twentieth century was doing its thing, Britten in England (and Dmitri Shostakovich in the Soviet Union, perhaps for different reasons) wrote in a more conventional way. The avant-garde made the headlines, but by and large the people came to see and hear operas with music that sounded not too unlike what they were used to.

The Turn of the Screw is almost entirely tonal. However, accepting some aspects of Schoenberg's twelve-note approach, Britten chose as his organizing principle a series of variations on a theme that, like the "screw" of the title, spirals through all twelve notes of the keyboard. Successive scenes are based on successive notes of this theme, each in a different key and moving farther and farther away from home base as the powers of evil take hold.

That's the way the analysts describe it. We amateur listeners need not know how the composer is achieving this effect in order to recognize that Evil is present.

There are sixteen scenes, with an orchestral interlude between each. Each scene is almost entirely within its own key, and therefore this is not serial music at all. Professor Roger Brunyate characterizes it this way: "It is a masterly use of a technique associated with the most academic of highbrow composers in the service of theater which is direct, powerful, and hauntingly melodic."

Britten found in Henry James's *Turn of the Screw* the same concentration on guileless, guiltless, and defenseless misfits that he found in George Crabbe's poem *The Borough*, the basis for *Peter Grimes*.

The Turn of the Screw is the aching story of two orphans, brother and sister, Miles (treble) and Flora (soprano), who live in an English country house that's also occupied by unspeakable evil and the ghosts of former inhabitants—Peter Quint (tenor), a valet/manservant, and a governess he seduced, Miss Jessel (soprano). Their objective is to control and destroy the children. A new Governess (soprano) sees and hears the ghosts. Though indecisive and ineffective, she tries to cope with them and to protect the children. Flora is taken away to safety by Mrs. Grose (soprano), the housekeeper, but little Miles dies in the new Governess's arms, shouting the name of Peter Quint.

Britten loved children and was preoccupied with the corruption of innocence. In this opera, as in several others, he deals with both themes.

Here's a challenge. Borrow a recording or a videotape and listen to the glorious warm summer's evening music of the governess's aira in Act I, Scene 3, or the haunting ghost music that opens Act II. Then see if you can avoid listening to the whole thing.

❧

The Midsummer Marriage
King Priam
by Michael Tippett
Born January 2, 1905

The Midsummer Marriage. *Premiere at Covent Garden, London, 1955. Text by Tippett. Three acts. Time: The present.*

King Priam. *Premiere at the Coventry Theatre (Covent Garden Theatre), Coventry, 1962. Text by Tippet. Three acts. Setting: Troy, in antiquity.*

Sir Michael Tippett, in his nineties at this writing, has composed symphonies, concertos, sonatas, quartets, and much more. He is best known now for a few symphonies, a big choral work, and five mature operas. His admirers grow weary of hearing that Collection composers Henry Purcell from the seventeenth century and Benjamin Britten from the twentieth are England's only two truly great opera composers.

The Midsummer Marriage, his first opera, wasn't well received in 1955, in part because its symbolism made it incomprehensible to the public. But today it is regarded as a masterpiece, just as Tippett is now acknowledged as a master composer. *King Priam* was his next opera, and while it tells a simple and familiar story from the Greek legend, it is also extremely symbolic.

Interestingly, while Britten was alive, Tippett was considered quite secondary—an eye-catching composer but an enigmatic one. In the last two decades his popularity has increased enormously as more people seem willing to endure his complexities—his symbolism, allegory, fantasies, dreams, and myths. Some analyst experts in English opera suggest that his critical esteem might one day eclipse Britten's, although that hasn't happened yet.

Tippett was greatly influenced by the theoretical writings of T. S. Eliot, the great poet, critic, and dramatist, who created new poetic forms and, indeed, a whole new poetic language and who for many years was a leader of the literary avant-garde. As public-pleasers, T. S. Eliot and Giacomo Puccini have little in common.

Tippett is a man of letters, of deep compassion and humanity, of youth and culture, and of intelligence and insight. My several opera-friend professional advisors, who to my distress and consternation frequently disagree, do concur here that his works are among the most original and important of the twentieth century. But he is deeply interested in symbolism and allegory, in fantasies and dreams and myths, and in how—if possible—to reconcile the perplexities of human beings.

Tippett has always been a man of conviction. In the early years of World War II, he made a strong political gesture with an oratorio, *A Child of Our*

Time, and later chose prison as a conscientious objector over military service. It was a forthright and honorable choice; he didn't run away or play draft-dodging games with his government.

His other operas are:

The Knot Garden, 1970
The Ice Break, 1977
New Year, 1989

The Midsummer Marriage is a comedy, described by Tippett as one concerned "with the unexpected hindrances to an eventual marriage." One of them is as simple as parental opposition; the more complex ones include what he defined as our ignorance and illusion about ourselves. It's a story of the inner development of both Mark (tenor), the man, and Jennifer (soprano), his fiancée, and the trials that make them understand their true selves. They come together through mutual sacrifice. Tippett has said that he was strongly influenced by Mozart's *Magic Flute*.

If you see or hear it, look and listen for the "Ritual Dances" from Act II, which often are excerpted as an orchestral suite.

Negative critics at the premiere felt the whole thing to be too obscure; defenders then and now have spoken of its singable melody, its lyricism, and its musical power. It's an undeniable classic, Tippettians say; that will live a long, long time—long after many Collection favorites have fallen away. Composed between 1946 and 1952, with its world premiere in England in 1955, it was not until 1983 (in San Francisco) that it was first shown in America. But that gap, in today's entertainment-filled world, is not extraordinary.

The New World

Michael Tippett, born in 1905, did not visit the United States until 1965. That visit triggered his fourth opera, *The Ice Break*, about racial conflicts, and led eventually to his fifth, *New Year*, staged first in Houston in 1989 and commissioned jointly by the Houston Grand Opera and Glyndebourne Festival in England.

Tippett was influenced by Swiss psychologist Carl Gustav Jung, so it's not surprising that he dealt in dreams, fantasies, mythologies, and the unconscious. A few ounces of T. S. Eliot and a few ounces of Jung blend into a potion that takes a bit of sipping.

But then there's that singable melody and that strong musical construction. And it gained many supporters after a 1963 BBC broadcast.

Tippett began to write *King Priam* six years after he completed *The Midsummer Marriage*. It is a work about the Trojan War, with Priam (bass–baritone), King of Troy; Hecuba (soprano), his wife; Hector (baritone), their oldest son; Paris (treble as a boy, tenor as a man), their younger son; Andromache (soprano), Hector's wife; the great Greek Achilles (tenor); and their friends and companions. The story is fairly straight out of Homer. Paris is born, Hecuba dreams that he will cause the death of his father, and Priam orders him killed but changes his mind and gives him to a shepherd. When Paris is grown he and Priam meet, and Priam takes him to Troy. There Paris falls in love with Helen, abducts her, and starts the Trojan War. Before it ends Paris kills Achilles, whose son then kills Priam, fulfilling the prophecy. Tippett said at its first performance that it's about "choice"; it also is about human suffering, courage, and ordeal. The premiere was successful. The verdict today: offbeat but musically and dramatically powerful.

∾

Dialogues of the Carmelites
by Francis Poulenc
January 7, 1899–January 30, 1963

Premiere at La Scala, Milan, 1957. U.S. premiere at the San Francisco Opera, 1957. Text by Emmet Lavery after Georges Bernanos's 1948 drama, which was based on Gertrude von le Fort's 1931 novel, Die letze am Schafott. *Three acts. Setting: The Carmelite Convent at Compiègne; Paris, between 1789 and 1792.*

Francis Poulenc barely missed being born in the twentieth century. *Dialogues des Carmélites* is much more in step with the century he left behind than the one in which it was produced. It's out of step, almost hopelessly so, with many of the dominant twentieth-century trends.

It's tonal, it's sentimental, and it's most decidedly emotional. It breaks no new ground in theme, musical idiom, or form. The music is not twelve-tone serialism. The approach is not Expressionistic. There is no left-wing radicalism, no jazz undertone, no political doctrine, no social protest.

Right on, say the traditionalists. No wonder it has gained and kept international recognition. Give it a few more years and it may make a most-frequently-performed collection. On the negative side, maybe it won't. There are few take-home tunes, the gray convent walls make it colorless, and the men's roles are minor. Also, as the title suggests, it is composed largely of conversations rather than action.

Still, it is the most successful post–World War II French opera, the one that has achieved the greatest international status. The composer said it was about the psychology of fear, the conquering of fear through divine grace. An entire colony of Carmelite nuns, caught in the religious persecutions under the

Reign of Terror during the French Revolution, goes to the guillotine rather than deny its faith.

If the final scene is not the most emotional in all French opera, it's close enough, as they used to say, for government work. (That cliché is dreadfully unfair to some civil servants I knew who worked seventy-hour weeks.) A primary challenger would be *Carmen*.

Poulenc was one of Les Six, a Parisian group of classical composers led by Erik Satie that included two other major opera figures, Darius Milhaud (1892–1974), the most prolific twentieth-century French composer, and Arthur Honegger (1892–1955), a Swiss. Poulenc wrote only two other operas, one a satirical surrealist comedy, *Les mamelles de Tirésias* (*The Breasts of Tirésias*), 1947, that uses wrong notes, barroom songs, and parodies of sentimental songs, and *La voix humaine*, 1959, a one-act lyrical tragedy.

Dialogues is one of the few operas in this package that is making it with the Metropolitan—first in 1977, then in 1978 and 1980, next as one of several contemporary operas chosen by the Met for its 1983 centenary season (along with Britten's *Peter Grimes* and *Billy Budd*), and, most recently, in the 1993–94 season. It has been sung there both in French and English.

Poulenc's Will

Under the terms of Poulenc's will, *Dialogues of the Carmelites* may be performed only with the full orchestra that is called for by the score. This rules out performances in smaller theaters with small orchestra pits. When the Summer Opera Theater Company of Washington, D.C., wanted to stage the opera in 1994, it received permission from Ricordi, the publishers, to use only keyboard instruments and onstage percussion. An organ console was put several feet above stage level. With this arrangement, five performances were given to standing-room-only audiences in a six-hundred-seat theater.

Its cast is almost all women. With two dramatic exceptions—the death of the Old Prioress and the final scene—the actual violence of the French Revolution is offstage. The "dialogue" has to do with the different reactions to the certainty of death after the nuns vote, with only one dissent, to take a vow of martyrdom in order to save the order from harm. After being taken from their convent to the prison, they mount a scaffold one at a time, and with each drop of the guillotine one less voice is heard from their chorus. As the last nun left on the scaffold is about to die, she sees among the spectators the face of the one who had fled from the convent after casting the only vote against martyrdom.

That lone dissenter takes up the chant, steps forward from the crowd, and follows her sisters to the scaffold.

Poulenc dedicated *Dialogues* to the four opera composers he most respected: two Italians, Monteverdi, and Verdi; a fellow Frenchman, Debussy; and a Russian, Mussorgsky, all Collection composers. And he had no apology for defying the music trends of his time. My nuns, he said, can sing only tonal music. You must forgive them.

∾

Der Prinz von Homburg
Der junge Lord
by Hans Werner Henze
Born July 1, 1926

Der Prinz von Homburg. *Premiere at the Staatsoper, Hamburg, 1960. Text by Ingeborg Bachmann from Heinrich von Kleist's 1811 drama. Three acts. Setting: Fehrbellin, Germany, 1675.*

Der junge Lord (The Young Lord). *Premiere at the Deutsche Oper, in Berlin, 1965. U.S. premiere at the Civic Theater, San Diego, 1967. Text by Ingeborg Bachmann from Wilhelm Hauff's 1826 parable* Der Scheik von Alessandria und seine Sklaven. *A comic opera in two acts. Setting: The German town of Hülsdorf-Gotha, 1830.*

Der Prince von Homburg deals with a poet's conflict with the military; *Der junge Lord* is a dark comedy.

The composer was a Marxist and a big fan of Fidel Castro's.

Years after Hans Werner Henze served in the Nazi military (and was an English prisoner of war) he dedicated an oratorio to Che Guevara and conducted the premiere of his Sixth Symphony and its revolutionary songs in Castro's Cuba.

Born between the wars, he became one of the leading and most prolific composers of the post–World War II period. In addition to thirteen operas and musical dramas, his works include seven ballets, seven symphonies, piano and violin concertos, choral works of all sizes, several string quartets, other chamber pieces, and film music.

We've met Arnold Schoenberg, Alban Berg, and other twelve-tone and serial composers and are about to meet Bernd Zimmermann and Peter Maxwell Davies. Henze was a particular student of René Leibowitz (1913–72), a Parisian Pole and a twelve-tone devotee who spearheaded a post–World War II center for avant-garde music in Darmstadt, Germany. Not surprisingly, German composers were looking for ways to get away from the kinds of rules the Nazis had imposed on their work.

Like most of the others, Henze didn't immerse himself fully in serialism but rather borrowed from it as he saw fit, composing during his life in a whole range of styles. Like Igor Stravinsky in this package, at one point he adopted neoclassicism. His pieces for music theater have as wide a range as virtually any composer's in history. *El Cimarrón*, 1970, is for baritone and three players. *We Come to the River*, 1976, for 111 singers and three orchestras, is an antiwar and class-conflict work. The music is atonal; the text blasts capitalism and what Henze viewed as its militaristic values.

His works are more concerned with the psychology of the characters and their innermost feelings than with the outside events of the plots. Others in this package with similar concerns include Schoenberg, Berg, and Davies.

After being a solid part of the post–war Music Establishment in Germany, Henze moved permanently to Italy in 1953. By the end of the 1950s, he was an outspoken supporter of of "revolutionary socialism," twin of out-and-out Marxism, and an outspoken foe of fascism and "capitalist militarism." The oratorio dedicated to Che Guevara came in 1968 and his visits to Cuba in 1969 and 1970.

Der Prinz, an opera that deals with understanding and forgiveness, is based on a dramatic masterpiece by Heinrich von Kleist about a romantic, poetic soldier, lost in his own dreams, trying to cope on a battlefield. Henze was no more fond of German military values than of capitalistic military values. One wonders how he felt about Cuba's militaristic values when it armed itself with nuclear-tipped missiles.

Henze did not turn his back on melody or on the musical genius of the operatic giants of the past, which was important for his success with the public. He said he had modeled *Der Prinz* after Verdi and that he had been influenced by the "angelic melody of Bellini," the "sparkling brio of Rossini," the "passionate intensity of Donizetti," and the rhythms, the "hard orchestral colors," and the "unforgettable melodic lines" of Verdi.

Henze Makes It Work

Not only did Hans Werner Henze model some of his operas on Italian nineteenth-century works, he also approached Arnold Schoenberg's serialism with a soft glove. Author Gerald Abraham writes: "The only twelve-tone composer to achieve repeated success is Henze, and he has been exceptionally free-and-easy in his attitude to twelve-tone composition, putting sensuous effect before orthodoxy."

Der junge Lord is Henze's fifth full-length opera and his first alleged comic one, but it isn't an ordinary opera buffa of earlier centuries, filled with fun and building to a happy ending. It's bitter, even cruel, satire. Sir Edgar (silent role), a rich English lord, arrives in a small German town, but doesn't show himself except to attend the performance of a touring circus. Luise (soprano), wealthy ward of the Baroness (mezzo-soprano), and Wilhelm (tenor), a student, are in love. The Baroness prefers a better match for Luise and favors young Lord Barrat (tenor), who has come to visit his uncle. Lord Barrat is elegantly dressed at a reception given by his uncle. His behavior is a little odd, but Luise is attracted to him, and other guests, impressed by his aristocratic blood, fawn upon him and try to imitate him. Finally, he becomes involved in such frenzied dancing that he tears off his gloves and clothes, swings from the chandelier, and is recognized as a plain, ordinary performing ape.

No Henze opera has made the Metropolitan, although *Der junge Lord* was staged by the New York City Opera in 1973. In April 1986, there was a whole Henze week at the Manhattan School of Music. Critics commented on the "musical manner" in which Henze linked his lyrical, sensuous music to his Marxist thinking.

❧

Die Soldaten
by Bernd Alois Zimmermann
March 20, 1918–August 10, 1970

Premiere at the Cologne Opera House, 1965. American premiere by the Opera Company of Boston, 1982. Text by the composer from Jakob Michael Reinhold Lenz's 1776 play. Four acts. Setting: Flanders, 1776.

This is the twentieth century in full multimedia bloom. By his own description, in *Die Soldaten* Bernd Zimmermann employed speech, singing, screaming, whispering, jazz, Gregorian chant, dance, film, and other modern techniques, all to serve the idea of the pluralistic form of musical drama.

This second-half-of-the-twentieth-century composer perceived opera as "total" theater, which meant using architecture, sculpture, painting, musical theater, spoken theater, ballet, film, microphone, television, tape and sound techniques, electronic music, concrete music, a circus, and all forms of motion.

Not only is this far from Rossini, Verdi, and Puccini, it's also far from such fellow twentieth-century composers as Ralph Vaughan Williams, Francis Poulenc, Erich Korngold, and Benjamin Britten.

But *Die Soldaten* has been one of the most frequently performed operas in Germany—East and West, when they were divided—and is viewed by some analysts as the most significant German opera since Alban Berg's *Lulu*.

Zimmermann, born near Cologne, lived his life in Germany in times of technical discoveries unknown to a Handel, a Mozart, or a Wagner. It is scarcely surprising that he wanted to use and coordinate those discoveries.

My guess is that for the Unwashed the name of Zimmermann is one of the two or three least known in this twentieth-century group. He is a serialist, another one influenced by Arnold Schoenberg. Musicologists advise us that early in his career he first brought together the neoclassicism of Igor Stravinsky and the twelve-tone serialism of Schoenberg, then concentrated chiefly on serialism, and finally wound up in a kinder, gentler, more tonal style.

Die Soldaten was his only opera. He also wrote concertos, other orchestral works, chamber music, and a big Requiem.

Commentary on the art of postwar Germany—opera, classical music, literature—inevitably focuses on the unstable psychological underpinning for composers, painters, and writers who were brought up under Nazism and then lived in a defeated and divided nation that had torn asunder much of the world while also imposing on human history the indescribable horrors of the Holocaust. One wonders how any could cope, and, indeed, Zimmermann ended his own life in August 1970.

The Viking Opera Guide, like Kobbé and the four-volume New Grove Dictionary of Opera, a source of consistent research assistance for this book, notes that Die Soldaten is "one of the most characteristic products of early 1960s Germany, with its desperate need to reject its own intellectual and military history while rummaging in that history for causes, explanations and scapegoats."

Twentieth-century Opera

Zimmermann lectured in music at Cologne University from 1950 to 1952, and from 1957 until his death he taught at the Cologne Musikhochschule—professor of composition and of radio, film, and stage music. No composer was more independent. His approach was indeed strange: He frequently used quotations from both European and non-European music as part of his pluralism, has tubas and trombones accompany a Bach chorale, and consciously mixed past and present. His one opera is filled with compassion and humanity, and some critics insist he was Germany's finest composer since Alban Berg.

Die Soldaten is a stage director's nightmare—or, perhaps depending on his or her creativity, imagination, and budget, a stage director's ultimate dream. Zimmermann's original idea was for several scenes to be played simultaneously, on as many as twelve separate stages, each with its own orchestra, all on the perimeter of a circle, with the audience sitting in the center on chairs that swiveled.

Why not? This is, after all, the end of the twentieth century. No law says a Zimmermann must design a Handel opera. What does the music sound like . . . and are the characters real human beings . . . and does the work have compassion and humanity? On these scales, musicologists give Die Soldaten pretty high marks.

Zimmermann's concept was rejected at first by the Cologne Opera as being too demanding technically. A "simplified" version still requires several acting levels and huge projection screens to convey simultaneous action.

Die Soldaten's story is along somewhat the same lines as Alban Berg's Collection *Wozzeck*. It tells of a girl named Marie (very dramatic coloratura soprano) who is engaged to a soldier called Stolzius (high baritone). After she's seduced by Baron Desportes (high tenor), a young high-ranking officer, her reputation is doomed and her downfall assured. Later, homeless and terrified, she is raped by a gamekeeper and becomes a prostitute. Stolzius poisons Desportes's soup and then kills himself.

It is a work worth knowing about even if few opera apprentices may want to rush out to buy it. And there's an interesting link between it and *Wozzeck*. *Wozzeck* was from a play by Georg Büchner, an author who earlier had written a novel about Jakob Michael Reinhold Lenz, whose 1776 play was the basis for *Die Soldaten*.

❦

The Devils of Loudun
by Krzysztof Penderecki
Born November 23, 1933

Premiere at the Staatsoper, Hamburg, 1969. Text by the composer from John Whiting's 1961 drama The Devils, *based on Aldous Huxley's 1952 novel* The Devils of Loudun. *Three acts. Setting: Loudun, near Poitiers, 1634.*

Krzysztof Penderecki once bawled out a musicologist friend of mine for mispronouncing his name.

His displeasure was understandable, perhaps, because he's a man of considerable consequence—the first post–World War II Polish composer to establish an international reputation, the acknowledged leader of music's avant-garde in Poland thirty years ago, and one of the century's top composers. *The Devils of Loudun* not only has been more successful in the world's opera houses than any other Polish work but is important when considered with most operatic competition.

No one confuses Penderecki with TV's Mr. Rogers. He deals in the grotesque, in torture and intrigue, in fanaticism and death, in conflicts between good and evil.

Penderecki is another of the scores of 1950s avant-garde composers who either were full-fledged serialists or who used serialist ingredients in their works. Sometimes it's tough for a composer to win. He handled his avant-gardism in a way that was approachable enough for audiences to like it—and thus he was criticized by the Club for catering to the ticket buyer.

His international fame began in 1960, before he turned to opera, with a big work for fifty-two strings, *Threnody for the Victims of Hiroshima*. (A threnody is a poem or musical lament expressing grief for the dead.) Another of his major works was the *St. Luke Passion*, 1965. And he has written dozens of film scores.

The Devils of Loudun is the story of Father Grandier (baritone), the handsome vicar of St. Peter's Church in Loudun, who was falsely accused of being in league with the Devil. His chief accuser was the prioress of St. Ursuline's Convent, Mother Jeanne (dramatic soprano), who had sexual visions involving him and who told people how he forced her and other nuns to engage in a sexual orgy in the chapel. When he refused to sign a confession, he was burned at the stake in 1634.

Masterly Color

The Earl of Harewood, who edited and revised *Kobbé's Opera Book*, was present at the Hamburg premiere. He later wrote: Penderecki's "use of musical colour, whether individual instruments or combinations, the not so common moments of full orchestra or the frequently added chorus (live or amplified) struck me as masterly and hard to parallel on such a scale in any opera I have ever heard."

One analyst said in an interview: "Penderecki is interesting for the effects he gets with blocks of sound, in which precise notes are not given, but singers and orchestra play anything within a given range and volume. It is very powerful stuff."

The first U.S. performance was in Santa Fe in 1969. There was also a film, *The Devils*, by the well-known British film and stage director Ken Russell, who is always deliberately provocative and controversial in his work.

As to pronunciation: Classical music stations use an "s," "Pendereski," but I don't guarantee it. Another friend, who has met him, argues for "ts," as in Penderetski.

Taverner
by Peter Maxwell Davies
Born September 8, 1934

Premiere at Covent Garden in London, 1972. American premiere by the Opera Company of Boston, 1986. Text by the composer from sixteenth-century sources. Two acts. Setting: The sixteenth century, during the lifetime of English composer John Taverner.

This is still another twentieth-century opera about the role of creative artists in society and whether, in conscience, they can work in isolation from the oppressions, tyrannies, and anguishes of that society.

Fascinating individuals have always interested Peter Maxwell Davies, who was born in Manchester, England, and has lived since 1970 in Orkney. Take Miss Donnithorne, the subject of his 1974 music theater piece, *Miss Donnithorne's Maggot*. After being stood up on her wedding day, she spends the next thirty years wearing her wedding dress, the wedding breakfast uncleared from her tables.

In one of his works, King George III talks and sings to the birds, and in another the soprano wears a scarlet nun's habit and shouts through a megaphone.

No one in his generation has composed more for the theater than Davies, a post–World War II composer who was knighted in 1987 in recognition of his work. Much of his music is highly dramatic. His scores of works include several symphonies, operas, ensemble pieces, piano sonatas, and film scores, written in different styles at different periods.

In *The Lives of the Great Composers*, Harold Schonberg calls Davies the "complete eclectic," a composer who in one piece mingled old plain chant, new serialism, jazz, Renaissance polyphony, and Broadway musical. And he has been into electronic music.

His works in the 1960s and 1970s, when he produced *Taverner*, his first opera, were Expressionist, exaggerating feelings beyond normal levels, portraying not what one perceived from without, but what one felt from within. *Taverner*, in fact, is characterized as not merely Expressionistic but as "fiercely" Expressionistic. (Major Expressionist artists included Norwegian painter Edvard Munch, German sculptor Ernst Barlach, Austrian poet Franz Werfel, and German playwright Bertolt Brecht, librettist for Kurt Weill.)

In 1967, Davies and English composer Harrison Birtwistle founded a performing ensemble group in London called the Pierrot Players. Later Davies re-formed it as the Fires of London, a traveling music-theater ensemble that toured several countries, including the United States. He composed many chamber works for it.

Over the last two decades his operas and their kin have included:

The Martyrdom of St. Magnus, a chamber opera in nine scenes, premiere at St. Magnus's Cathedral on Orkney in 1977 and at the Aspen Music Festival in Aspen, Colorado, in 1978.

Le jongleur de Notre-Dame, a music theater piece, premiere at Orkney in 1978.

The Lighthouse, a one-act chamber opera, premiere in 1980 in Edinburgh and in 1983 by the Boston Shakespeare Company. Other performances in this country include those in Philadelphia and San Diego.

Resurrection, a one-act opera, premiere in 1988 in Darmstadt, Germany.

Even some of the most esteemed Washed acknowledge that Davies's music often challenges their understanding, although this is not an assessment meant by the esteemed Washed to be negative. His best-known earlier compositions are *Eight Songs for a Mad King*, 1969, probably the best short introduction to his Expressionist bent, and *Miss Donnithorne's Maggot*, 1974, for solo voice and small instrumental ensemble. Both feature a crazed person.

Sir Peter of Princeton

Peter Maxwell Davies, knighted in 1987 and now Sir Peter, is one of Britain's leading post-World War II composers. *Taverner*, his first and most successful opera, was started in the early 1960s during two years Davies spent in the United States at Princeton on a fellowship. He finished it in England in 1968, but the manuscript was destroyed by fire and he had to rewrite it in 1970.

The Opera

John Taverner (c. 1490–1545) was an English composer of masses and motets, one of the leading musicians of his day, who became entangled with the church over whether he had accepted heathen Lutheran views, which were contrary to Catholic doctrine. Davies's opera is about the difficulty Taverner has in reconciling religious faith and artistic freedom. In a nutshell, he turns his back on music, loses his identity, and seeks a way to save his soul.

Taverner (tenor) is tried by the White Abbot (baritone) for Protestant heresy but at the last minute is pardoned by the Cardinal (tenor) because of the contribution his music has made. In a switch, Taverner then prosecutes the White Abbot for heresy. In Act II, after the Reformation, the White Abbot is presumably burned at the stake, but the man whose creative life really is destroyed is Taverner, who rejects his own musical past and confesses that he was part of the corrupt old order. Hysterical goings-on include Death spinning a wheel of fortune. Musically, Davies quotes from actual masses composed by the Tudor Taverner and uses Renaissance instruments such as viols and lutes to create the atmosphere of sixteenth-century England.

Chapter 8

OPERA IN AMERICA AND AMERICAN OPERA

~

Here's a test for your mildly Washed dinner guests. Ask them to name five American operas. Most will fail, unless they cross the line into American musical theater.

For a companion test, ask them for five twentieth-century European opera composers other than Puccini. Most likely they won't do much better.

That game confirms that Collection operas from earlier centuries still dominate the commercial American opera scene, including what is heard on radio, seen on television, or even worked into movies as background music.

Odds are that your dinner party test will trigger a discussion over the definition of opera, what it is, what it isn't, and how opera is faring today in the United States, and just who are the top American opera composers and what are the names of their operas.

This chapter discusses those questions. The short answers are that opera in America is doing better today than ever before and that opera by American composers is making a reasonable showing, if not a spectacular one.

One word in advance. Some cynics say that American opera is an oxymoron. This is nonsense. There's a great deal of excellent American opera. Check the Dream Season at the end of this chapter. Several American composers are every bit as worthy as 95 percent of the Europeans cited in the previous chapter. Among several "standard" American operas performed in a given season these days may be Carlisle Floyd's *Susannah*, 1955; Robert Ward's *The Crucible*, 1961; Douglas Moore's *The Ballad of Baby Doe*, 1956; Dominick Argento's *Postcard from Morocco*, 1971—and, invariably, George Gershwin's *Porgy and Bess*, 1935.

Here, as in Europe, we have had conservative and adventurous opera, folk and satirical jazz opera, experimental opera, and opera that dealt with national scenes and subjects. Some American composers adopted variations of the twelve-tone technique just as some European composers did, and some wrote harshly atonal avant-garde creations. Works by American composers, like works by colleagues in Europe, have dealt with political and social issues, from war to entrepreneurial capitalism.

You'll hear that the best European opera is "simply better" than the best American. Of course it is. The best European opera is "simply better" than any other opera from any other place, Europe included. When you've said Verdi, Wagner, and Mozart, you've said the best. The twentieth-century composer born in Vincennes, Indiana, doesn't measure up to those giants and neither does the twentieth-century composer born in Verona, Italy; Vienna, Austria; or Vinnytsya, Ukraine.

There's some relatively recent good news about the future of American opera. For decades many composers in the United States wrote for themselves and their peers. More recently most appear to have moved back to writing for audiences, using attractive melodies and harmonies and seeking emotional responses from the people in the seats. And despite the dominance of Collection operas, perhaps the most significant trend in the last ten years has been increased management interest in new works.

We look first at opera in America and then at twentieth-century opera by American composers.

OPERA IN AMERICA

Opera is the only performing fine art to show growth in the recession-marked years of the 1980s and early 1990s. Box-office receipts at major opera companies in the United States totaled $174 million in 1992, compared with $135 million in 1988. Attendance has risen 30 percent since 1980. Opera in America is alive—and financially healthier than it once was, although making ends meet is still difficult.

And it's everywhere—in the cities, in the suburbs, and sometimes even in the boondocks.

Let's talk first about the commercial opera houses, especially the major ones, and then about the productions of the many workshops and universities, where much more American opera is found.

During the last thirty years the numbers of companies with annual budgets of $100,000 or more increased nearly tenfold, from 27 to 209. By the beginning of the 1990s, six opera companies had annual budgets of more than $10 million:

Metropolitan Opera
San Francisco Opera

New York City Opera
Lyric Opera of Chicago
Houston Grand Opera
The Los Angeles Music Center Opera

Rounding out the top ten are the Washington Opera in the District of Columbia and the Seattle, Dallas, and Santa Fe operas.

All produce some new works, and several stage quite a few new or older-but-less popular works. Some American companies aim each year for a world premiere of an American opera. But let's not kid ourselves. Despite an enormous amount of activity by American composers and an increased willingness to experiment by opera executives, the operas staged by commercial houses still are basically older European masterpieces. American works are junior partners at best.

The masterpieces sell better, a critical point inasmuch as American companies, much more than their European counterparts, rely on private rather than public support. One survey a decade ago showed that 56.4 percent of their money came from earned income, 37.9 percent from private support (corporations, foundations, guilds, gifts), and 5.7 percent from local, state, and federal governments.

American opera has a trade association in Washington, D.C., called Opera America. It describes itself as a not-for-profit service organization that offers a variety of informational, artistic, and administrative services to professional opera companies in North America. Its member companies are in the United States and Canada. From its statistics come these two relevant facts about old and new opera:

Fact: The ten most frequently produced operas in a recent season were these:

La traviata	19 productions
Carmen	18
The Marriage of Figaro	14
Don Giovanni	13
Rigoletto	12
Madama Butterfly	12
La Bohème	12
The Barber of Seville	11
Lucia di Lammermoor	9
Die Fledermaus	9

These ten familiar works accounted for nearly one third of all productions staged by the companies that belong to Opera America. All are Warhorses and other top Collection operas.

Second fact: Eighteen of the twenty-three productions in the 1994–95

Metropolitan Opera season were Collection operas, and three others were by Collection composers. Most were Warhorses. The other two were *Lady Macbeth of Mtsensk* from the Twentieth-century European Package and American John Corigliano's *Ghosts of Versailles*, discussed in this chapter. (Even these figures suggest that the Met is experimenting more than it used to.)

But there also is happy news for the pro-American claque. In recent years there has been a huge increase in the number of professional opera companies in the United States—those substantial enough to be part of Opera America.

At mid-century, there were only nineteen. The Lyric Opera of Chicago then was formed to make it twenty. Today there are more than one hundred in the United States and another ten in Canada. In the last decade alone, the number of productions by companies belonging to Opera America has increased by more than 33 percent and the number of performances has gone up by 75 percent.

"Finally," said Ardis Krainik, general director of the Lyric Opera of Chicago, "opera in North America is coming into its own."

Beverly Sills writes that when she first started singing in the mid-fifties the opera scene was pretty much restricted to New York, San Francisco, and Chicago, with occasional performances in Baltimore, Philadelphia, and New Orleans. But by the start of the 1970s, in Texas alone she had sung in Austin, Dallas, Forth Worth, Houston, Laredo, McAllen, San Antonio, Waco—and more.

In her delightful customary down-to-earth approach, Sills writes in her autobiography, *Beverly*:

"Opera became popular in Texas the same way it did in a lot of previously isolated regions of the nation. It started with money. In the case of Texas, it was oil money, and it made a lot of people very rich, very fast. That kind of money creates a following for the arts, because after using it to buy houses, private planes, cars and jewelry, people have to spend it on other things. And for other purposes, such as creating a social hierarchy . . .

On ne parle pas francais ici

For twenty-one years the Opera Theater of St. Louis has performed opera only in English. It operates in Webster College's 950-seat theater where the stage is flanked on three sides by audience seats, and presents four new productions each spring. In 1996 they were Mozart's *La Clemenza di Tito*, Puccini's *La Rondine*, Rossini's *Barber of Seville*, and Britten's *The Rape of Lucretia*.

"Small groups of wealthy people began plunking down hard cash to pay for visits by leading opera stars. During those visits, the donors would put on lavish parties because they wanted to show off their wealth and fancy clothes. Musicians steeped in opera, many of them World War II refugees from Europe, were hired to teach, direct, and produce operas. That's how opera companies sprang up all over the country. This is a good old American tradition, and it works, and I'm not ridiculing it, either."

Some of today's companies are national and some regional. Some present only opera, and some present opera, operetta, and musical comedy. Some specialize in producing operas in English, or are committed to premieres, or feature American artists exclusively—and some do none of these things.

Consider, as one of dozens of examples, Houston Grand Opera, which in January of 1995 premiered *Harvey Milk*, a three-act opera by composer Stewart Wallace and librettist Michael Korie. A joint venture, commissioned by Houston, New York City Opera, and San Francisco, and offering a drag-queen chorus line, it deals with the 1978 murder of Milk, the openly gay member of the San Francisco board of supervisors.

Houston Grand Opera, which has developed an outstanding reputation over the last two and a half decades, has commissioned more American operas than any other company, including John Adams's *Nixon in China* and Leonard Bernstein's *A Quiet Place*. In 1994, the acclaimed twenty-six-year-old mezzo Cecilia Bartoli, one of the hottest new singers around, chose Houston for her U.S. debut, as Rosina in *The Barber of Seville*.

An example of a different type of innovative company that operates on a smaller scale is Virginia Opera, which in 1995 staged the world premiere of Thea Musgrave's *Simón Bolívar*, a three-hour work about the life of the nineteenth-century Latin American liberator. Musgrave, born in Scotland and an established composer of symphonic and operatic music, is not new to success; back in 1977 the New York City Opera, another bold company, produced her work, *The Voice of Ariadne*. It was the first opera by a woman to be performed by a major U.S. company since the Met staged Ethel Smyth's *Der Wald* in 1902.

Aside from the Met, no American company is better known than the New York City Opera, which celebrated its fiftieth birthday in 1993. Despite its reputation and fame, it almost always has financial problems, which leads to the typical opera company predicament—the *Carmen* or perish syndrome. Can it afford to present American operas, or new operas, or experimental productions . . . or must it stick to the Warhorses and other dependable works that sell the most tickets?

Auditoriums of American companies vary from big halls seating 3,800 to intimate theaters seating 200. Some are high school auditoriums, and some are glorious converted old movie theaters. Many companies perform outdoors.

You name it, you can have it, from Anchorage to Tucson, from Baton Rouge to Salt Lake City, from Durham to Syracuse. In Charlottesville audiences pay eight to twelve dollars to see Mozart or Donizetti, in Augusta ten to thirty-four dollars for Puccini or Rodgers and Hammerstein's *South Pacific*, in Toledo five to forty-one dollars for Gounod or *Porgy and Bess*.

This Old House

The Washington Opera, which now performs at the Kennedy Center, is moving to downtown Washington to an old building that housed the Woodward & Lothrop department store. Conversion costs, to turn the old structure into a world-class opera house, are an estimated $105 million. Construction is planned to start in 1997. Placído Domingo is Washington Opera's artistic director. Among future plans: Washington Opera's first production of Wagner's four-opera *Ring* cycle, which every five years will be repeated three times over a three-week period.

No company is more colorful than Central City Opera in Central City, Colorado. The tiny opera house there has stood on a narrow, winding street for 114 years and operas have been performed there since 1932.

The diversity of opera in America is typically American. Sometimes joint ventures are executed, chiefly for financial reasons. For example, Leonard Bernstein's *A Quiet Place* was jointly commissioned by Houston Grand Opera, La Scala in Milan, and the Kennedy Center for the Performing Arts in Washington, D.C. For the most part, however, commercial opera in America is a slew of individual companies doing their own thing.

And despite the unquestioned domination by Collection operas, production of other works is significant and substantial.

Nineteen world premieres were presented in a recent season by the companies that belong to Opera America—up nearly 50 percent from the previous season. Not surprisingly, these works haven't yet become household words. We'll know more about that some years hence. But, as examples:

The Aspern Papers by Dominick Argento, presented by the Dallas Opera.
Charlotte's Web by Charles Strouse and Joseph Robinette, presented by Opera Delaware in Wilmington.
Dangerous Glee Club by Steve Elsón and Charles Moulton, presented by the Music-Theater Group in New York City.
Empty Places by Laurie Anderson, presented by Spoleto Festival U.S.A. in Charleston, South Carolina.

In addition to these world premieres in our sample season, eight U.S. premieres also were staged. Some American companies are reaching back for nearly forgotten works of the Great Greats of yesteryear, such as Handel and Purcell. Others find lesser-known works of an early-nineteenth-century Rossini or a first-half-of-the-twentieth century European composer like Francis Poulenc.

Important point: The work of commercial opera companies is only one part of opera in America today. The four-volume *New Grove Dictionary of Opera*, an opera bible, reports that more than a thousand organizations in the United States are presenting opera in one form or another.

An incredible amount of action is taking place in colleges, workshops, and conservatories. One expert source estimates that in a recent year some three hundred such operatic groups gave about two thousand performances of the standard repertory and another two hundred modern works. Many American operas owe their world premieres to these student, apprentice, and semiprofessional operations.

Here are a half-dozen examples of university opera:

Amahl and the Night Visitors by Gian Carlo Menotti, Indiana University, 1951, first staged production
The Bell Tower by Ernst Krenek, University of Illinois, first produced in 1964
Billy Budd by Benjamin Britten, Indiana University, 1952, first American production
Carry Nation by Douglas Moore, University of Kansas, first produced in 1966
The Jumping Frog of Calaveras County by Lukas Foss, Indiana University, first produced in 1950
The Medium by Menotti, Columbia University, first produced in 1946

Universities also are responsible for reviving many operas that had not been staged for years—or even centuries. Among dozens of examples:

The Cooper by Thomas Arne (1710–1788), Southern Oregon Stage College
L'Erismena by Pier Francesco Cavalli (1602–76), University of California at Berkeley
Orontea by Pietro Antonio Cesti (1623–69), Cornell University
Il trionfo di Camilla by Giovanni Battista Bonocini (1670–1747), Peabody Institute, in Baltimore

So the opera sun in the United States doesn't rise and set on the stage of the Metropolitan in New York—or a half-dozen other major houses—however powerful and important the Met and a few others are. It's just as foolish to ignore what is happening in the fifty states as to dismiss the critical role of the Metropolitan.

Opera was not new to the United States at the beginning of the twentieth century. The Metropolitan opened on October 22, 1883. Within ten years it had become the most important theater in the world for vocal performance. In Martin Mayer's *One Hundred Years of the Met*, he writes:

"Paris was the capital for art, London for theater, Vienna for instrumental music, St. Petersburg for ballet. The best opera, vocally if not dramatically, very nearly year-in and year-out, was to be found in New York."

Let's look back to the turn of the century, at the Met season in 1900–01:

L'Africaine (by Meyerbeer)
Aida
La Bohème
Carmen
Cavalleria rusticana
Le Cid (by Massenet)
Don Giovanni
Faust
Fidelio
Der fliegende Holländer
Götterdämmerung
Les Huguenots
Lohengrin
Lucia di Lammermoor
Mefistofele
Die Meistersinger
Pagliacci
Das Rheingold
Rigoletto
Roméo et Juliette
Salammbô (by Ernest Reyer)
Siegfried
Tannhäuser
Tosca
La traviata
Tristan and Isolde
Il trovatore
Die Walküre

You have met all but three in The Collection, and only *Salammbô* is by a non-Collection composer.

But opera in America didn't start with the Met. In its opening season, all but one of the eighteen operas (*La Gioconda*) already had been performed in the United States. As early as the 1840s opera was appearing at the 1,800-seat Astor Theatre and at other New York theaters including Niblo's Gardens, Castle Garden in the Battery, and the Broadway Theater. The Academy of Music, on Fourteenth Street near Union Square, opened in 1854 and was the leading opera house in the city until the Metropolitan.

You have to look hard, however, for *American* works early in the twentieth century, even in New York and Chicago, where they were most apt to be performed. Musicologist Charles Hamm made a search and found the following in those two cities:

1913—*Cyrano de Bergerac*, Walter Damrosch
1914—*Madeleine*, Victor Herbert
1917—*Azora*, Henry Hadley
1917—*The Canterbury Pilgrims*, Reginald De Koven
1918—*A Daughter of the Forest*, Ethelbert Nevin
1918—*Shanewis*, Charles Wakefield Cadman
1919—*The Legend*, Joseph Breil
1919—*The Temple Dancer*, John Adam Hugo
1920—*Rip Van Winkle*, Reginald De Koven
1920—*Cleopatra's Night*, Henry Hadley

"The problem," writes Hamm in his informative book *Music in the New World*, "is that none of these works enjoyed a lengthy run, none was performed by an operatic company other than the one responsible for the premiere, none was revived, almost none appeared in print."

Despite the activity in American universities, workshops, and conservatories, during the twentieth century new opera has been more apt to appear in Europe than in the United States. Europe has the opera tradition—Italy, France, and Germany and, later, Bohemia and Russia. The United States—and England—don't. Opera on the Continent played a central part of life for years; opera here and in England has been on the fringe.

Throughout the century, the most important distribution of opera came from radio and, later, television. The first broadcasts from the Met were in 1910. Texaco's broadcasts not only brought opera into millions of homes but also motivated many American composers to begin writing radio opera. Much more recently, the success of English subtitles on televised operas inspired major opera houses to use English subtitles. A great victory for the Unwashed.

AMERICAN COMPOSERS

The Collection illustrates that European opera from the time of Monteverdi came both from opera specialists like Verdi and Wagner and all-purpose classical composers like Mozart and Tchaikovsky. After all, opera doesn't exist in a musical void.

In America, however, many of the finest twentieth-century classical composers weren't into opera, though their music influenced those who were and should be noted here. Before focusing on the opera writers, let's look briefly at those other composers.

Charles Ives (1874–1954) and Roy Harris (1898–1979) specialized in nationalist music; Howard Hanson (1896–1981) and Walter Piston (1894–1976) were traditional in their approach; Milton Babbitt (b. 1916) is a modernist; Charles Griffes (1884–1920) and David Diamond (b. 1915) neo-Romantics; Edgard Varèse (1883–1965), Henry Cowell (1897–1965), Carl Ruggles (1876–1971), and John Cage (1912–92) experimentalists; and Steve Reich (b. 1936) and Terry Riley (b. 1935) minimalists.

Recall that at the turn of the century European composers like Richard Strauss and Claude Debussy did some adventurous things with their composition—some "daring" things, for those days, that made their music sound different. Their work was known as "new" or "modern" music, a term still in use today even though it was first used one hundred years ago. After Strauss and Debussy came Stravinsky, Bartók, and Paul Hindemith, and also some artists who took the process farther out, such as Arnold Schoenberg and his disciple Alban Berg. Most of those European, sometimes atonal, composers wrote operas, which was a good way of becoming famous and making money.

Many American classical composers borrowed from Schoenberg's technique. As we have seen, his music, however respected by critics, composers, and musicologists, was not accepted warmly by general audiences while he was alive and today, nearly fifty years after his death, fares only little better with the public. Other Americans stuck more to the nineteenth-century Romantic style. And some specialized in nationalist music, while others paid little or no conscious attention to their American heritage.

In this country, after the early century "new" music composers came the more radical experimentalists—men like Varèse, Cowell, and Cage—who investigated not only electronic music but also captured the sounds of honking horns and cement mixers. Like the "new" music composers, they also represented a break with the past, but this time of an entirely different nature. Opera could be fashioned of the Schoenberg–Berg music, even if the sounds were unusual and the audiences initially perplexed, but to fashion opera out of these experimental sounds was another matter entirely.

In The Collection we found that at the time of Louis XIV, the Sun King, the musicians worked not to satisfy the general public but to please the King. That was mandatory, or they were out of business. No one else mattered, neither audiences nor performers.

Some of the more radical twentieth-century classical composers were similarly elitist. They wrote for themselves, or for each other, not for a broad audience. Even modernists such as Babbitt—let alone experimentalists such as Varèse—were not primarily concerned with whether a public liked or understood their work. Nor did they gear it to nonprofessional musicians. Their audience consisted chiefly of themselves and their peers.

These classical composers were among America's best—serious, educated, and trained, doing serious work. And they were not working alone, ignored, and hungry in cold attic rooms. They won the fellowships, the grants, the prizes, the critical praise, the respect of their colleagues—and the jobs in universities and schools of music. They were, in fact, the backbone of American classical composition.

America is too young to enjoy a stable of classical composers from earlier centuries. And given that many American twentieth-century composers weren't concerned about meeting an audience even one third of the way, it's understandable that as late as the 1990s the classical composers to whom American audiences still react most favorably are not homeboys Piston, Babbitt, and Cage but earlier foreigners Tchaikovsky, Schubert, Chopin, Mozart, and Mahler. Audiences fifty years from now may make other choices.

Some musicologists make the case that this same indifference to the public also kept many twentieth-century American classical composers away from opera. Although there are exceptions, most successful opera composers have been men dedicated to the theater and to creating a product that the public would enjoy. After all, that's the way they were making their living, not with fellowships, grants, university posts, and the plaudits of their colleagues. Also, even the composer who was prepared to woo an opera audience has had to work against significantly more competition in the entertainment arena (movies, radio, TV, VCR) than existed one hundred years ago.

With that background on other American classical composers, let's begin to look at American opera.

We found in the previous chapter that most twentieth-century opera is significantly different from most opera of the past. Much of it is less melodious. Following Richard Wagner's lead, the arias in many cases are more woven into the whole of the music and there are fewer star spots for star aria singers. By and large, twentieth-century opera—American or European—doesn't have built-in places for audience applause while the conductor stops the action. In these operas, the set arias are less spectacular than their earlier counterparts.

Remember also a gut fact from the last chapter: Twentieth-century opera is not necessarily beautiful. But no law rules out beauty, and, as you might expect, the public is inclined to like it better that way.

TWENTIETH-CENTURY AMERICAN OPERAS

The Collection is based on statistical frequency of performance. The Twentieth-century European Package was hand-picked for excellence, uniqueness, onetime popularity, and/or importance to opera development.

This American anthology borrows from each of those approaches. Most of the operas were the best known of their day. But this section is not an equal-time undertaking. Considerably more attention is given some composers than others—more to a George Gershwin than a Louis Gruenberg.

No American operas from before World War I have enough individuality to survive, and only a handful from before World War II are on my list.

But first, some intriguing findings:

- The most successful American opera composer of the twentieth century is scarcely American at all.
- The most beloved American classical composer of the century wrote hardly any opera at all.
- The most famous music drama from the most famous American composer/conductor/musician of the century wasn't opera at all.
- The new breed of twentieth-century "opera" Americans loved best wasn't opera at all.
- And finally, astonishingly, the greatest American opera of this or any other century came from a composer who wasn't a classical musician at all.

The 1920s

The King's Henchman
1927, by Deems Taylor (1885–1966)

KEYNOTE: The first really successful opera by an American composer. The first to receive international attention. Musically conservative; late European Romantic in style.

1990s STANDING: Dead in the water.

This was one of the leading operas of the twenties, with a libretto by Edna St. Vincent Millay and a plot from a tenth-century Saxon story that is akin to Wagner's *Tristan und Isolde*. Commissioned by the Met, it had seventeen performances there in the late twenties. Its success led the Met to commission a second opera by Taylor, *Peter Ibbetson*, which premiered in 1931 and was staged sixteen times in four seasons. Taylor's third opera, *Ramuntcho*, was produced by the Philadelphia Opera Company in 1942, and his last, *The Dragon*, a fantasy based on a play by Lady Gregory, was introduced in New York in 1958.

Taylor was well known as a New York music critic and broadcaster. His operas had more Met appearances than those of any other American composer, evidence in itself that they were in the European tradition. The melodies are pleasing, the harmonies don't disturb, and the works were what most of the operagoing public of his day wanted.

Show Boat
1927, by Jerome Kern (1885–1945) and
Oscar Hammerstein II (1895–1960)

KEYNOTE: Exciting. The start of a whole new breed of music theater. Not quite a folk opera but almost. Not quite as much an opera as early French opéra comique but almost. Arguably an operetta and arguably America's greatest. Strong song from a songwriter but theatrically serious.

1990s STANDING: As hot as ever.

The major event of the 1920s in the field of drama-in-music was the premiere of a composition about a boat named the *Cotton Blossom*, skippered by a man named Captain Andy and featuring a gambler named Gaylord Ravenal.

The year was 1927, the date November 15, the place Washington, D.C., en route to the Ziegfeld Theatre in New York.

It is the story of the love and marriage of Captain Andy's daughter, Magnolia, and Ravenal. They join the show-boat cast when the boat's leading actors, Julie and Steve, are forced to leave because Julie is discovered to be part black. Ravenal eventually leaves Magnolia and their daughter in Chicago, and Magnolia becomes a singer.

Early programs spoke of a chorus of ninety-six that included thirty-six white chorus girls, sixteen white chorus boys, sixteen black male singers, sixteen black female singers, and twelve black girl dancers. In those days it was known as *Ziegfeld's Show Boat*, with little credit given Kern.

Not until 1954 was it presented by a major opera company—the New York City Opera, an organization that has produced a good many things that are commonly accepted as "operettas" or "musical comedies." It has been consistently revived by Dallas Summer Musicals, Los Angeles Light Opera, St. Louis Opera, and on Broadway.

Everyone is familiar with its songs.

"Ol' Man River" has been labeled the first "popular" racial protest song, an "incredibly daring" one for 1927. It was accepted for decades as a modern black spiritual, with the tragic overtones of a folksong. The love music includes "Make Believe," "Can't Help Lovin' Dat Man," "Why Do I Love You?," and "Bill." Song was the core: lyrical song to carry on the story line, lyrical song to develop the character of the characters.

Show Boat was a bridge between traditional European operetta and a new kind of American musical theater, arguably operetta, even if different from European operetta, and arguably "folk opera," though there's no single universally accepted definition of a "folk opera." The American music world decided in the late 1920s that the term "operetta" wasn't stylish in this country and that the genre that had come from Europe's Johann Strauss, Franz Lehár, Jacques Offenbach, and Gilbert and Sullivan should be known as "musical plays."

The analysts' assessment of *Show Boat*: Like a good play, it has dramatic truth, sharp characterizations, effective background and atmosphere, and a logical story line. It has social consciousness. The music is an integral part of the whole, not something tacked on. Like an opera, it is more a play *in* music than a play *with* music. No chorus girls, no synthetic humor. And, though less than "opera," it's much, much more than eye-filling and ear-pleasing entertainment.

It was based on the 1926 best-selling novel by Edna Ferber and adapted by Oscar Hammerstein II, who also wrote the lyrics. For two years and 575 performances it grossed an average of $50,000 a week in New York. After a faltering Depression-time start on the road, it played always to sold-out houses. Over the years it has been revived in every part of the country. Later the international dam burst. There have been adaptions for three motion pictures. In 1952, twenty-seven years after its premiere, a new concert version was given at the

Lewisohn Stadium in New York. Only some computer somewhere knows how many opera houses it has been in since.

No one knows what might have happened if Kern, who died at sixty, had crossed the border and said to himself: "Now I will write a 'real' opera."

But he didn't.

Grumpy Old Men

Show Boat opened on Broadway on December 27, 1927, but it was not until January 8, 1928, that the noted Brooks Atkinson of *The New York Times* got around to commenting on it: "Shortly after the opening . . . the henchmen of the press were privately and publicly acclaiming it as 'the best musical show ever written' . . . *Show Boat* becomes one of those epochal works about which garrulous old men gabble for twenty-five years after the scenery has rattled off to the storehouse."

Hal Prince's recent revival opened at the Gershwin Theatre on Broadway in October 1994. A *Washington Post* review by Lloyd Rose put it in historical perspective: "With its strong story, operatic sweep, high sentiment, social consciousness, regional flavor and heady combining of musical styles, *Show Boat* started a whole new tradition. It's the fountainhead of what we know today—from Rodgers and Hammerstein to Sondheim—as the American musical."

Jerome Kern was born in New York on January 27, 1885, and died there November 11, 1945. From 1939 on he lived and worked in Hollywood. He was a songwriter; by the beginning of World War I he had written more than one hundred for some thirty shows: "The Last Time I Saw Paris," "The Way You Look Tonight," too many to count.

If you don't like Jerome Kern, may the smoke always be in your eyes.

The 1930s

Transatlantic
1930, by George Antheil (1900–59)

KEYNOTE: Story of corrupt presidential campaign from experimentalist composer. His first opera. A hit when premiered in Germany by the Frankfurt Opera.

1990s STANDING: Rarely, if ever, produced.

George Antheil (born in Trenton, New Jersey) toured Europe as a performing pianist in the early 1920s, settled and studied in Paris with the avant-garde, and became an enfant terrible of music. Commenting on his music in those days, analysts use words like "violent" and "dissonant." The best known of his early works is the "Ballet mécanique," in which he used motors, sirens, and other nonmusical sounds. He characterized his own compositions at that time as "anti-expressive, anti-romantic and coldly mechanical."

His words about one of his pieces summarize his approach: "It was conceived in a new form, that form specifically being the filling out of a certain time canvas with musical abstraction and sound material composed and contrasted against one another with the thought of time values rather than tonal values. I used time as Picasso might have used the blank spaces of his canvas. I did not hesitate, for instance, to repeat one measure one hundred times."

After Paris and several years in Berlin, he returned to the United States in the early 1930s and wrote an unsuccessful opera, *Helen Retires*, which was performed at the Juilliard School of Music in 1934. Then he moved to Hollywood for the rest of his life and concentrated on film music. In the 1950s he went back to opera, now much more conservative, trying consciously to write works that the public could understand and enjoy:

Volpone, introduced at the University of Southern California in 1953, a long
    work, his best known, but one that is rarely performed today
The Brothers, which premiered in Denver in 1954
The Wish, commissioned by a Rockefeller Foundation grant, first given in
    Louisville, Kentucky, in 1955

The Emperor Jones
1933, by Louis Gruenberg (1884–1964)

KEYNOTE: No arias. Big success in its day. Pullman porter rules Caribbean island.

1990s STANDING: Almost none.

This is based on a Eugene O'Neill play about an escaped slave who became a railroad porter, murdered a man in a dice game, and fled to become an island emperor. In the end he kills himself with a silver bullet. It premiered at the Met, where it had fifteen performances over two seasons, 1933 and 1934.

After opening night, which featured the great baritone Lawrence Tibbett, *The New York Times* had this headline on its review: "*The Emperor Jones* Triumphs as Opera." But it never returned to the Met over the following sixty years, although it was made into a movie.

Gruenberg, a pianist who was into jazz at an early time, wrote several other operas and some operettas.

Four Saints in Three Acts
1934, by Virgil Thomson (1896–1989)

KEYNOTE: One of two intriguing operas by a Pulitzer Prize winner. *The Mother of Us All*, 1947, is the other. Creative, imaginative, non-European,

America's first four-star opera. Provocative, with Gertrude Stein libretto and an all African-American cast at its premiere. Gregorian chant to gospel tunes.

1990s STANDING: Class composer. Highly respected, but his operas now are produced only occasionally.

Thomson was a classical artist of considerably greater talent (and ego) than Gruenberg, a gifted composer, and a longtime outspoken music critic. Born in Kansas City, Missouri, he studied at Harvard and with Nadia Boulanger in Paris. His first major work, *Four Saints* was a tantalizing opera with a libretto by the abstract verbalist intellectual Gertrude Stein. It is often called a "nonnarrative" work, a reasonable description, Stein being Stein.

It was introduced with an all-black cast in Hartford, Connecticut, by an organization with the magnificent title of the Society of Friends and Enemies of Modern Music. Although it didn't make the Metropolitan that year or for many years to come, it was revived in 1973 for twelve Met performances.

Thomson paid his full dues as a classical composer, and *Four Saints* today is considered an important American opera. In 1952 it was presented by a black company in Paris during the Festival of Twentieth-Century Art. And it was produced in Houston in 1996. The songs are melodic but not easy to sing.

The choral overture is in these Gertrude Stein words:

"To know to know to love her so.
Four saints prepare for Saints,
Four saints make it well fish.
Four saints prepare for saints it makes it well fish
    it makes it well fish prepare for saints."

A side exercise for skeptics: Read that aloud four or five times, and you risk being captured by it.

Another opera with an all African-American cast is Gershwin's *Porgy and Bess*. Professor Donald Jay Grout comments on the differences: "Gershwin's *Porgy and Bess* is true folk opera, the vernacular of the black culture skillfully communicated in sung recitative and spirituals. The hymn-like dignity and tuneful simplicity of Thomson's *Four Saints in Three Acts* glimpses a vernacular of a different hue. Gertrude Stein's text, written expressly for Thomson, represents an abstract threading together of words, out of which evolves a plotless libretto in praise of Spanish saints in general and of Saint Teresa of Avila in particular. Stein viewed words as independent entities, divorced from contextual association, mere sounds which, when placed in proper sequential configurations, would evoke meaningful interpretations. The following line from *Four Saints in Three Acts* is indicative of her style of writing: 'Saint Therese [sic] in a storm in Avila there can be rain and warm snow and warm that is the water is warm the river is not warm the sun is not warm and if to stay to cry.' Why, one might rightfully query, did Thomson use an all-black cast for an opera about

Catholic saints and the Counter-Reformation? The composer provided this answer: 'Blacks sing so beautifully and they look so beautiful.' "

In 1940, Thomson succeeded Lawrence Gilman as music critic of the *New York Herald Tribune*, a job he held until 1954. His score for the movie *The Louisiana Story* won him a Pulitzer Prize in 1949.

Another important Thomson opera is *The Mother of Us All*, 1947, a work about Susan B. Anthony, women's suffrage leader and other characters from American life, from Daniel Webster to Lillian Russell, all talking among themselves. Gertrude Stein again was the librettist. Based on American speech rhythms, it had gospel hymns, marches, sentimental ballads, and intoned sermons. It was very popular for a time, running up more than one thousand performances across the United States.

Although still held important by the professionals, it's not often performed today except at colleges and conservatories, in part because it is more intellectual than emotional. Not many of us go to opera for intellectual enlightenment. We have television for that.

The language is more specific than that of *Four Saints*, but Stein is still Stein. At the end, a marble statue of Susan B. Anthony says: "But do I want what we have got, has it not gone, what made it live, has it not gone because now it is had, in my long life in my long life. Life is strife, I was a martyr all my life. Not to what I won but to what was done. Do you know because I tell you so, or do you know, do you know. My long life, my long life."

A third interesting Thomson opera was *Lord Byron*, 1972.

Merry Mount
1934, by Howard Hanson (1896–1981)

KEYNOTE: Only opera by a renowned conductor and composer, a big champion of American composers and American music.

1990s STANDING: Overtaken by time.

Hanson was born in Wahoo, Nebraska. How could anyone born in Wahoo not be a champion of American music? His five-act opera, *Merry Mount*, was introduced at the Metropolitan in 1934 and had nine performances that season, but never has returned. It is based on Nathaniel Hawthorne's short story "The Maypole of Merry Mount," a story of witchcraft and sexual fixation among Puritan settlers in seventeenth-century New England. The opera's main character is a fanatical clergyman obsessed by demonic dreams. He and his lover are burned to death when his church catches on fire. Hanson uses a large orchestra, an elaborate ballet, and wind machines. An orchestral suite from the work is sometimes heard on classical radio.

Hanson was one of America's most prestigious composers and classical teachers, for forty years director of the Eastman School of Music in Rochester, New York. His instrumental works, largely in the nineteenth-century Romantic tradition, include seven symphonies, some symphonic poems, and chamber and piano music.

Porgy and Bess
1934, by George Gershwin (1898–1937)

KEYNOTE: America's greatest opera.
1990s STANDING: Still at the top.

This is the Big One. *The* Great American Opera. Porgy, Bess, Sportin' Life, and a Charleston waterfront courtyard called Catfish Row.

To get there, we must turn back the clock to the 1920s, after World War I, before the Great Depression, when a young composer named George Gershwin wrote a piece of music that was greeted in these words by the respected *New York Herald Tribune*: "This music is only half alive. Its gorgeous vitality of rhythm and of instrumental color is impaired by melodic and harmonic anemia of the most pernicious sort. How trite and feeble and conventional the tunes are, how sentimental and vapid the harmonic treatment, under the disguise of fussy and futile counterpoint."

The *Trib* was not alone. Later, from an earlier edition of *The New Grove Dictionary of Music and Musicians*—a bible of record—came this assessment: "Gershwin has only limited experience in developing musical material and . . . his serious works are structurally defective."

The half-alive music, as you may have guessed, was from a piece called *Rhapsody in Blue*—then pernicious, then trite and sentimental, now the American instrumental music most frequently played in world concert halls. Aaron Copland aside, or perhaps Aaron Copland included, no more American-sounding concert music has come from the twentieth century—chiefly, the analysts say, because it was the most successful blending of traditional classical music and American jazz.

True, Gershwin lacked formal training in counterpoint, composition, and orchestration. True, he had to bring in composer/arranger Ferde Grofé to complete the scoring. True, he had not studied in Paris under Nadia Boulanger. True, he had attended no conservatory. True, he had not been influenced by Arnold Schoenberg (but he had been by Igor Stravinsky).

Surely this composer, untrained in classical theory, would not attempt an opera. Not a fully developed opera.

Not the grandson of Yakov Gershovitz, who served in the Czar's army, not the son of Morris Gershvin who lived above Simpson's Pawn Shop at the corner of Hester and Eldridge Streets on New York's Lower East Side.

Not a fellow who learned to play keyboard on a player piano.

But, gauche though it was, he did attempt an opera, completing it a decade after *Rhapsody in Blue*—and shortly after a Piano Concerto and another instrumental piece called *An American in Paris*. It was his last serious work before an early death, this full-length opera, set in what then was called the Negro tenement district of Charleston, South Carolina, this masterpiece called *Porgy and Bess*.

It is drawn from DuBose Heyward's novel *Porgy*, which he and his wife, Dorothy, turned into a play. The action takes place in the early twentieth century in Charleston, South Carolina. The black characters these white southerners created include Porgy, a beggar with a disability ("cripple" was the term used in those days) who can't stand upright and gets about in a goat-cart; a tough, mean-tempered stevedore named Crown; Bess, Crown's girlfriend whom Porgy loves; and Sportin' Life, a New York gambler who uses "happy dust."

In a crap game, Crown kills one of the players with a cotton hook and flees, leaving Bess to take care of herself. Porgy takes her in and finds his first happiness. At a picnic on Kittiwah Island, Crown reappears and persuades Bess to come back to him. Eventually, Porgy stabs and throttles him. No one will tell the police Porgy has done it, but they take him off to identify the body. While he is gone, with the help of "happy dust," Sportin' Life talks Bess into returning to New York with him. Porgy comes back home, finds her missing, and sets off to find her as the opera ends.

From the opera came many famous songs, including "I Got Plenty o' Nuttin'," "It Ain't Necessarily So," and "Summertime." Today these are familiar opera arias, sung in concert, by opera singers. Later, Leonard Bernstein, in *West Side Story*, was to give us "Maria," "Tonight," and "I Feel Pretty."

Not Tosca's "Vissi d'arte" or Radames's "Celeste Aida." But how far from Carmen's "Habanera"? And then, Puccini and Verdi weren't Gershwin, Kern, or Bernstein.

Some call *Porgy and Bess* grand opera, others call it folk opera, or folk grand opera, or American grand opera. Gershwin preferred "folk opera" because, he said, it was a folk tale in which the people naturally would sing folk music.

In the beginning, a *New York Post* critic denigrated it as a "hybrid." Another distinguished writer said it was "an aggrandized musical show." Much later, critic/composer Virgil Thomson, never a nonelitist, wrote that America's up-to-date composers such as Copland, Harris, Cowell—and himself—never could "compete with Gershwin for distribution, nor he with us for intellectual prestige."

Oh dear.

Thomson, who enjoyed the formal classical music training that Gershwin never had, wrote that Gershwin's "lack of understanding of all the major problems of form, of continuity, and of straightforward musical expression, is not surprising in view of the impurity of his musical sources and his frank acceptance of them."

Either you were trained in the conservatory, and then preferably in Germany or France, or you didn't count as a serious classical musician.

Thomson later was to say; "Gershwin does not even know what an opera is . . . and yet *Porgy and Bess is* an opera and it has power and it has vigor."

Although most of the criticism was negative, not all of it was. After the Boston opening, conductor Serge Koussevitzky declared that *Porgy and Bess* constituted "a great advance in American opera." The *Boston Evening Transcript* acknowledged that Gershwin "has traveled a long way from Tin Pan Alley" and "must now be accepted as a serious composer." The *New York Herald Tribune*, which had been so sour on *Rhapsody in Blue*, found that *Porgy* was "a notable achievement in a new field," adding: "It tells of unusually effective craftsmanship; it reflects a marked advance in Mr. Gershwin's progress."

Prediction

One of the least prescient observers was Frederick Jacobi, a composer and faculty member of the Juilliard School of Music, who predicted that *An American in Paris* would live longer than either the *Rhapsody in Blue*, or the Piano Concerto, and that of the four *Porgy and Bess* would be "the first to go."

Well, maybe it will. We now are sixty to seventy years later, two of the four are still as solid as Mount Rushmore, *An American in Paris* is not doing badly, and the Concerto is still in evidence. Don't bet the farm that *Porgy* will be the first to go.

Suffering in part from the critical New York reviews, at first *Porgy and Bess* didn't do well. But in time it became a smashing popular success. It has toured the nation and the world; it was the first opera by a natural American to be heard at La Scala. It rolled on through the forties, fifties, and sixties. Like Mussorgsky's *Boris Godunov*, it was revised and "improved" in various productions. The money was earned on the commercial theater stage, not the opera stage, and for many years it was pushed in that dollar-oriented direction. Then, in 1976, the innovative and challenging Houston Grand Opera staged it with the original score and orchestration. Houston revived it in 1987 and, in 1995, celebrated its own fortieth anniversary with an expensive spanking-new production with an African-American director.

The Met presented it in 1985 for the first time, and has since revived it, and it was a triumph in England at Glyndebourne the next summer.

Why do we call this Gershovitz piece an opera? The answer: Because it is an opera:

- It has recitative and arias.
- It has descriptive orchestral music.
- It has dramatically cogent scenes and large-scale production numbers.
- It has duets and superb choral writing.
- It has real-life characters who show real-life emotions.
- It has, writer David Ewen points out, humor, tragedy, penetrating characterizations, dramatic power, and sympathy.
- It is, musicologist Charles Hamm says, the greatest nationalist opera of the century, not only of America but of the world.

One treasure of opera literature, *The Viking Opera Guide*, published in 1993, concludes its Gershwin section with these comments:

"As representative examples of resourcefulness in making the most of the libretto's potential, one might mention the powerful succession of recitative, arioso, and duet that comprises the scene between Bess and Crown . . . the six simultaneous unmeasured prayers of the hurricane scene, the rhythmic and vocal contrasts that shape 'My Man's Gone Now.' Indeed, the entire scene containing this impassioned solo shows Gershwin's genius at achieving overall unity through variety: linked choral passages, expressive recitative, one section of spoken dialogue, and two arias (with chorus) combine to create a uniquely varied pictured of grief. Even with its minor imperfections and infelicities acknowledged, *Porgy* stands as the most vital and completely successful of American operas. One of the great might-have-beens of 20th-century music is the thought of the scores that Gershwin could have gone on to write if he had lived beyond the age of 38."

Although Gershwin was a close friend of twelve-tone Arnold Schoenberg, the analysts say nothing in *Porgy* has European roots. Gershwin, however, had set goals by European standards. He said in advance that he wanted the charm of Bizet's *Carmen* and the depth of Wagner's *Die Meistersinger*.

Some have attacked the opera for having too many "songs" instead of extended arias. The composer met this criticism—and others—head on. He said he wanted his opera to be entertaining and to include all elements of entertainment. He wanted it to have both light and serious music, to handle humor as well as tragedy. He wanted an American opera based on American material. He said he was not ashamed of writing songs for an opera as long as they were good songs. He knew he was writing an opera for the theater, and without songs, he thought, it could be neither for the theater nor entertaining. Besides, he said, songs were entirely in the operatic tradition and the most successful operas of the past had had songs, including nearly all of Verdi's operas and most certainly *Carmen*, almost a collection of song hits. And, he asked, what about "The Last Rose of Summer," perhaps one of the most widely known songs of the generation? How many of those who sing it know that it is from an opera?

But he also emphasized that the songs were only part of the whole. He made the recitatives as close to the "Negro" inflection in speech as possible. He believed his songwriting apprenticeship had served him invaluably in that respect because the songwriters of America had the best conception of how to set words to music so that the music gives added expression to the words. He said he had used sustained symphonic music to unify entire scenes and had prepared himself for that by further study in counterpoint and modern harmony.

English-speaking countries, by the terms of Gershwin's will and the rule of the Gershwin estate, may only produce the opera with black casts.

In more recent years, questions have been raised about the sociological side of *Porgy and Bess*. DuBose and Dorothy Heyward knew the Catfish Row scene well; it had been an elegant mansion before becoming a black tenement.

But they knew it from the outside, looking in. Heyward described his novel in these words: "My own white man's conception of a summer of aspiration, devotion, and heartbreak across the color wall." Andrew Porter spoke to the racial issue in a sensitive piece in *The New Yorker* in 1985, after the opera had finally made it to the Met.

"Heyward envies the Negroes," Porter wrote, "and he seems to envy their simplicity, naturalness, the ability to sing away their cares. Credulity, fecklessness, gullibility are found charming. *Porgy* is affectionate, and not patronizing by intention, but some things about it give one pause. From the start, Gershwin's opera has inevitably aroused a certain uneasiness in both blacks and whites—and in both performers and spectators. Duke Ellington scorned Gershwin's 'lampblack Negroisms.' Douglas Watt, reviewing the London album in these [*New Yorker*] columns, noted that it is 'hard to find trained black singers willing to immerse themselves with what must amount to almost atavistic abandon, in a white man's version of black folkways and characterizations from which their race has so painfully fought to escape.' It's a tricky matter. Maybe it is enough to conclude that when a black cast today is prepared to throw itself heart and soul into the work, white spectators should simply forget their scruples and enjoy the show. The Met has expunged the word 'nigger' from the libretto."

All of this, of course, causes a few to challenge whether *Porgy and Bess*, drawing on the Afro-American idiom in the way it does, is acceptable. Others find in it no hint of condescension or intolerance.

Still, without reference to intolerance, it is a curious and interesting case. It often is called a "nationalist" opera, but it is unlike most other nationalist operas. Customarily they are firsthand expressions of a majority people—*Boris Godunov* by the Russian Mussorgsky or *The Bartered Bride* by the Czech Smetana, for example. But *Porgy* is the expression of a particular deprived segment of a minority people at second hand, written by a trio of gentlemen who didn't belong to the race in question and were peering in from the outside.

I asked my house opera expert, Roger Brunyate, for an opinion on the issue of African-American casting. He is head of the opera department at the Peabody Institute of Music and has been identified with opera from La Scala to Glyndebourne. He replied:

"There is always something uncomfortable about attending a performance, leading to overcompensation on both sides of the curtain. *Porgy* is the only opera I know of which is restricted by contract to performance by members of a particular ethnic group. *Butterfly* can be performed by Caucasians, *Tosca* by African-Americans or Asians or anything you care to name, but *Porgy* can *only* be performed by black Americans. It can, therefore, never be done by most repertoire houses, except by furloughing most of the regular company and importing a new troupe.

"Does this matter? It should not, but I think it does. One minor point is that it puts the Met, or the Santa Fe Opera, or whatever, into a curious position, in that the Met production of *Porgy and Bess* comes down to a team of white guys conducting, directing, and generally moving around an imported team of black artists—a position which I find patronizing on the one hand and demeaning on the other. (There is no reason why they should be white guys, but the sad truth is that they usually are.)

"Second, with the copyright proviso, *Porgy* has become something of a staple of employment for many African-American singers—a situation which I find sad, and which further muddies the waters.

"Finally, and most importantly, if *Porgy* works with audiences of all races, it does so because it takes a particular human situation, lovingly described in great detail, and distills something *universal* out of them.

"I think it should become the property of world stages to play on their universal level by whatever means are appropriate, including, if necessary, changing the original locale, or representing the Charleston community by actors of any nationality—*not* in blackface, but openly, as black and Asian artists have been able to sing the full range of roles in the rest of opera literature for years now."

This is not a short opera. Some productions have run as long as four hours. Others over the years have been cut considerably—nothing new in opera; producers have been cutting long operas for centuries. Some critics, composers, and performers think it comes across best as a full-scale, all-out thing, and others prefer it whittled down to ballad-opera size.

The Cradle Will Rock
1937, by Marc Blitzstein (1905–64)

KEYNOTE: A far cry from Catfish Row. Controversial expose of steel industry violence. American blues and American jazz used to tell his social message. Another important Blitzstein opera was *Regina*.

1900s STANDING: Blitzstein's first, if not his best or most popular. Still respected, but somewhat dated and infrequently staged.

The Left Wing

American/composer/critic Virgil Thomson on *The Cradle Will Rock*, 1938: "The most appealing operatic socialism since *Louise*." (Charpentier's *Louise*, 1900, Number 75 in The Collection.)

Marc Blitzstein was born in Philadelphia to a wealthy banking family and studied at the Curtis Institute in Philadelphia and in Berlin with Arnold Schoenberg. This work, introduced in New York, is a controversial play-in-music in ten scenes about violence in the steel industry. It is a propaganda opera, pro-labor and pro-union, originally to be produced by the Federal Theatre Project. Before it opened, the nation experienced actual sit-down strikes and violence as unions tried to organize the automobile and steel industries. With the country on edge, the Roosevelt administration, caught in the middle, postponed the opening in an effort to placate its opponents without losing its supporters. The administration closed the theater, seized the costumes and props, and forbid the federal company to perform it on any stage. Orson Welles and John Houseman then took it over as an independent production.

After receiving a Guggenheim Fellowship, Blitzstein completed a second social protest opera in 1941, *No for an Answer*. But a more important operatic success was *Regina*, based on Lillian Hellman's *The Little Foxes*, about a greedy post–Civil War family in the South. After an introduction at the Shubert Theater in New Haven, it was staged in New York in 1949 at the Forty-sixth Street Theater.

Regina, more of a traditional opera with less Broadway than *The Cradle Will Rock*, was revived in Houston in 1980, in Chicago and at Wolf Trap, Virginia, outside of Washington, in 1982, and by the Boston Lyric Opera and New York City Opera in the 1990s. It is on a far bigger scale than his earlier works—the music people say of "operatic" rather than "theater" size.

Blitzstein also made an English adaptation of Kurt Weill's *Threepenny Opera*. Today, his reputation rests chiefly on *The Cradle Will Rock*, *Regina*, and that translation.

Blitzstein had an interesting view of composers, quoted by biographer Eric A. Gordon. Not everyone, Blitzstein said, can be the "great American composer." "A cultural epoch," he wrote, "is made up not only of the perfect work of geniuses, but also of the combined efforts of lesser talents, a whole geological formation of them. With them wiped out, the genius exists without subsoil, becomes isolated, ingrown, 'eccentric.' "

Amelia Goes to the Ball
1937, by Gian Carlo Menotti (b. 1911)

KEYNOTE: The first of a long string of successful operas by a two-time Pulitzer Prize winner, America's most successful American opera composer, although he was born in Italy, kept Italian roots, and used Italian sounds. Check also *Amahl and the Night Visitors* and *The Saint of Bleecker Street*.

1990s STANDING: Strong. Although some analysts turn up their noses, his works still are produced in the United States and abroad.

A one-act work in the old Italian opera buffa style, *Amelia Goes to the Ball* was begun in Vienna while Menotti and American Samuel Barber were traveling together. Menotti was only twenty-three. It is the story of Amelia, her husband, her lover, and the police chief who takes her to a ball after she has hit her husband over the head with a vase. It went over so well after a premiere at the Curtis Institute in Philadelphia that the Metropolitan Opera combined it on a double bill with Richard Strauss's *Elektra*. The tunes are singable, the public relates to them, and it sounds like an opera.

No avant-garde stuff here. *The New York Times* at the time praised it highly, calling it "something that has not materialized so far from an American-born composer." After World War II it was staged at La Scala, and it remains one of Menotti's most popular works.

Pros and Cons

The Saint of Bleecker Street was attacked by many critics because of its religious implications and applauded by many others for its music and drama. Jay S. Harrison of the *New York Herald Tribune* wrote: "Whatever else one may think or say of Gian Carlo Menotti and his talent and skills, his ability to split the musical world cleanly down the middle is nothing short of phenomenal." Harrison's own view: "It is without any question his finest work to date."

Like Puccini, Menotti has been an opera specialist. He wrote his own librettos. For twenty-five years or more after World War II he was America's most successful and acclaimed opera composer, probably *the* most successful in our short history.

But he's not a nationalist American composer. In many operas, he is a blood-and-thunder melodrama fellow, an offshoot of the Italian verismo school—not right out of it, like Leoncavallo and Mascagni with their *Cav-Pag* doubleheader, but a nephew. Professor Donald Jay Grout describes him in his book as one of the very few serious opera composers on the American scene in the 1950s who thoroughly understood the requirements of the theater and made a consistent, sincere effort to reach the large operagoing public. Other analysts speak of his intuitive grasp of character and situation. His operas range from gripping tragedies to charming opera buffa. Among his many works are:

The Old Maid and the Thief, commissioned by NBC Radio, an opera in fourteen scenes about how a good woman can make a thief of an honest man
The Medium, 1946, a two-act tragic melodrama, a supernatural thriller
The Telephone, 1947, a twenty-two minute one-act comic chamber opera
The Consul, 1950, his first full-length, three-act opera, a sensitive tragedy of a homeless refugee that won him a Pulitzer Prize
Amahl and the Night Visitors, a one-act Christmastime classic produced first on television in 1951 and still repeated on TV during the holiday season
The Saint of Bleecker Street, 1954, another tragedy (in three acts) that brought him the Drama Critics' Circle Award, the New York Music Critics' Circle Award, and a second Pulitzer

He founded an annual festival of the arts in Spoleto, Italy, in 1958 and its twin in Charleston, South Carolina, in 1977. Both have continued to thrive, although he broke off connections with Charleston in 1994.

Menotti was born in Italy of Italian parents, studied in Milan and at the Curtis Institute, and from 1943 to 1973 lived in Mount Kisco, New York, with Samuel Barber. They sold their house and Menotti and his adopted son moved to Scotland. Probably more people have seen Menotti operas than those of any other American, even though there's nothing Yankee Doodle about him. Professor Lang advises us that an Italian writes Italian opera whatever the tale and the locale, for the simple reason that opera to the Italian is not an acquired medium but his natural mode of dramatic expression.

The 1940s and Musical Theater

Pal Joey
1940, by Richard Rodgers (1902–79)
and Lorenz Hart (1895–1943)

KEYNOTE: The beginning of a new made-in-America breed called "New York opera." Inserted in the lineup here as one Designated Hitter for all other "New York operas."

1990s STANDING: Solid.

Based on short stories by John O'Hara, Pal Joey is a throwback to John Gay's eighteenth-century Beggar's Opera. No dukes, lords, or their American equivalents here. It is the unsentimental and sordid story of a lowlife nightclub dancer operating in a world of greed, stupidity, and shabbiness. Joey lives on Chicago's South Side. He gives up the girl he loves for an older, hard-boiled, wealthy woman willing to pay for sex, tires of her, and winds up broke and alone.

Vienna to Broadway

Erich Korngold of the Twentieth-century European Package, authority back home in Vienna on Johann Strauss's Fledermaus (Number 49 in The Collection), conducted the orchestra for the 1942 Broadway presentation of the musical Rosalinde, an adaptation of Strauss's operetta. Another refugee was Oscar Karlweis, well-known comedian in Berlin and Vienna, who played Prince Orlofsky. Rosalinde was the hit of the season.

It was staged 374 times on Broadway, faded away during World War II, and returned more than a decade later for another five-hundred-odd performances. Although no one knew it at the time, it was the beginning of a Broadway musical genre that was something new, blending not just song and dance but song, dance, and drama.

It also was the last joint venture of Rodgers and Hart, who had been writing songs and musical shows together for years. Hart died and Rodgers found a new partner named Hammerstein.

Oklahoma!
1943, by Richard Rodgers and Oscar Hammerstein II

KEYNOTE: American musical. The first collaboration of this dynamite pair. Great show, great music. Another superb example of "New York opera."

1990s STANDING: Top-drawer. A classic.

Oklahoma! is a musical play in two acts, lasting two hours and forty-five minutes. Richard Rodgers composed the music for a small theater orchestra; Oscar Hammerstein II, who did most of the lyrics for *Show Boat*, wrote the lyrics. It is based on the play *Green Grow the Lilacs* by Lynn Riggs. The premiere was March 31, 1943, at the St. James Theater, New York. The setting is the Indian territory (present-day Oklahoma) in the early 1900s.

Hit tunes: "Oh, What a Beautiful Morning," "The Surrey with the Fringe on Top," "I Can't Say No," and "People Will Say We're in Love."

Even more than *Pal Joey*, *Oklahoma!* integrated song, dance, and drama into a new genre—and with unprecedented success. The Rodgers and Hammerstein combination produced thirty stage musicals and films. The professional assessment: On the minus side, it used the chorus in conventional ways and the main plot and subplot have little to do with one another. On the plus side, each song was a near perfect fit with the story line, not just a throw-in.

Unlike *Porgy and Bess*, *Oklahoma!* can't be called opera. Unlike *Show Boat*, it can't be slipped slyly into the folk opera tent. Unlike Leonard Bernstein's *West Side Story*, it isn't a ballet-with-songs. But you really can't leave American opera without it and the musical drama it represents. Give your neighbor Nicolai and Flotow from The Collection; you take Rodgers and Hammerstein.

Musical Theater: An Interlude

In the wake of *Pal Joey* and *Oklahoma!* came the big parade of familiar musicals, including three more winners from Rodgers and Hammerstein:

South Pacific, 1949
The King and I, 1951
The Sound of Music, 1959

Also:

Annie Get Your Gun, Irving Berlin, 1946
Kiss Me, Kate, Cole Porter, 1948
Brigadoon, Alan Jay Lerner and Frederick Loewe, 1947

Guys and Dolls, Frank Loesser, 1950
Paint Your Wagon, Lerner and Loewe, 1951
My Fair Lady, Lerner and Loewe, 1956
And from Leonard Bernstein: *On the Town*, 1944, and *Wonderful Town*, 1953.

During most of this period television didn't exist in a significant way, but radio, recordings, and the movies took the songs and the full productions all over the world. The companies went on the road, here in America and overseas.

Everyone agrees that these works form the backbone of American musical theater, that they're special, and that they aren't traditional opera. It's feasible to construct a diagram with a 1920s revue at one end and *Tristan und Isolde* at the other. But similar diagrams could have been created in the 1820s—or the 1720s. Indeed, debates continue today on the nonopera *Beggar's Opera* of John Gay back in Handel's time and on the Kurt Weill *Threepenny Opera* version two hundred years later.

As another example of blurred lines, consider Bedřich Smetana's *Bartered Bride*, Number 63 in The Collection. It began life as a two-act operetta, with spoken dialogue. In time, Smetana expanded it to three acts, added some arias and some now famous dances, composed recitative to replace the spoken dialogue, altered the plot to make it more of a mixture of comedy and serious emotion—and then no one questioned that it was, indeed, a proper opera.

Opera deals with classically defined voice categories—lyric soprano, dramatic soprano, mezzo-soprano, and so on—which will be discussed in a separate chapter and which help distinguish opera from operetta, light opera, and "New York opera." Does a particular work call for classical voice specialization? Irving Berlin's and Richard Rodgers's do not. George Gershwin's *Porgy and Bess* does.

A more recent contributor to "New York opera" who further confuses the lines is Stephen Sondheim, who wrote the lyrics for Bernstein's *West Side Story*, studied how-to-make-musicals under Hammerstein, and learned music theory from the abstract American serialist Milton Babbitt. His lyrics are sometimes simple and sometimes complex. Analysts say his music set new standards for Broadway, with extended ensembles, through-composed musical scenes, recitativelike passages, and catchy show tunes.

One professional friend advises me that Sondheim's level of musical complexity is greater than almost anybody else writing on or off Broadway. His interest lies in touching on genuinely new subjects and finding theatrical solutions to them that occur *in and through music*, not by some sort of aggregation of music and speech. Sondheim virtually reinvents the term "musical theater" with each new show.

From him have come:

A Funny Thing Happened on the Way to the Forum, 1962
Anyone Can Whistle, 1964
Company, 1970

Follies, 1971
A Little Night Music, 1973
Pacific Overtures, 1976
Sweeney Todd, the Demon Barber of Fleet Street, 1979
Merrily We Roll Along, 1981
Sunday in the Park with George, 1984
Into the Woods, 1987
Assassins, 1991
Passion, 1994

Whatever it is, America does "New York opera" better than anyone—and it represents the drama-with-music form that America does best.

Montezuma
composed 1941–63, premiere 1964,
by Roger Sessions (1896–1985)

KEYNOTE: The major operatic work of America's top classical composition teacher. An atonal avant-garde invective against the futility of conquest in war. A shorter work, *The Trial of Lucullus*, on the same theme, premiered almost a generation earlier.

1990s STANDING: Solid with the music world. Neither *Montezuma* nor *The Trial of Lucullus* ever caught on with the public.

A native of Brooklyn, Sessions earned a degree at Harvard at eighteen, studied at Yale and at the Cleveland Institute, spent several years in Italy and Germany, and established himself at Princeton University for a long career. He is one of the top classical composers of his time, characterized by the analysts as more daring than Hanson, Piston, Barber, and Menotti. Critics often like daring; the public generally does not—at least not at first.

Sessions's major operatic work is his avant-garde second opera, the three-act *Montezuma*, on which he worked for twelve years. First performed in West Berlin in 1964, it was staged twelve years later by Sarah Caldwell's Opera Company of Boston. Described as a "monumental atonal score" and "a stunning achievement," it concerns the futility of conquest, in this case the sixteenth-century Spanish conquest of Mexico. Montezuma, the Mexican leader, is taken prisoner and eventually stoned by the people for whom he has been fighting.

Sessions's earlier opera, *The Trial of Lucullus*, which also deals with military authority and the philosophical issues of war, premiered in 1947, the same year as Menotti's *The Telephone*. A short atonal work, it was written in three months to fill out a doubleheader with Stravinsky's *The Soldier's Tale* for performance by students at the University of California. Nineteen years passed before its New York premiere. It features the Roman general Lucullus, who has died and is facing a jury of ordinary people in the afterworld. The witnesses tell of the cities he has conquered and ruined and the treasures he has stolen.

Neither work has been warmly welcomed by the public. In some of his comments on opera, Sessions sounds not unlike The Collection's old Christoph Willibald Gluck, the great reformer. He wrote that opera could again become a vital dramatic medium, with music and drama welded together into an ensemble "in which neither is subservient to the other." Musicologists say that his operas had little impact on other artists but that many young musicians were influenced by his teachings and writings.

After an early period in which he was influenced by Stravinsky, Sessions began doing his own composition thing. Most of his music was sharply dissonant, atonal, and not easy to understand. His works include nine symphonies, a Concerto for Violin, another for Violin, Cello and Orchestra, and another for Orchestra. One of his best-known compositions is a cantata, *When Lilacs Last in the Dooryard Bloom'd*. A meticulous craftsman, he was about as nationalistic as an outer-space alien—and proud of it. One short quotation summarizes his response to those who argued for "American" music. Mankind must be one, he said, adding: "Americanism is by its very definition inclusive, all-inclusive, not in the smallest degree exclusive, and . . . loyalty to America means nothing less than a consistent devotion to the human principle in that inclusive sense."

Those of you who are still here in fifty years may find Roger Sessions here with you.

INTERMISSION

Before entering the 1950s it's prudent to pause. Something important is happening to opera in America—with where it is performed and under what sponsorship and for what kinds of audiences.

The King's Henchman and *The Emperor Jones* premiered in New York at the Metropolitan Opera House. That's normal; operas were supposed to premier in opera houses. That's the tradition of several centuries.

But:

Porgy and Bess opened in Boston and moved to New York for a run at the Alvin Theatre on Broadway, *Four Saints in Three Acts* opened in Hartford and moved to Broadway, *The Cradle Will Rock* was sponsored by the Federal Theatre Project, and *Amelia Goes to the Ball* opened in Philadelphia and moved to the New Amsterdam Theatre in New York.

The venue for these operas was not the opera house. Either it was Broadway, where you make or lose a buck, or it was subsidized theater departments in universities. During the 1930s and 1940s, Copland's *The Second Hurricane*, 1937, premiered at the Henry Street Settlement Music School in New York; Moore's *The Devil and Daniel Webster*, 1939, at the American Lyric Theatre in New York; Menotti's *The Medium*, 1946, at Columbia University; *The Tele-*

phone, 1947, at the Heckschner Theatre in New York; and *The Consul,* 1950, in Philadelphia.

Also: The leading opera composers of the 1930s and 1940s, that is to say the ones the public liked best—Gershwin, Menotti, Thomson, Gruenberg, and Moore—all had two important things in common:

In their own vastly different ways, each—like Mozart, Donizetti, Verdi, and Puccini—made a musical effort to reach the audience. With rare exceptions, that has been the road taken through operatic history by all successful opera composers.

In all cases, the voice, not the orchestra, was central. In that sense, American opera has been more like Italian opera than German.

But when we get to the 1950s and beyond, America is no longer the same country. It had been through the Great Depression and a long, difficult, incredibly costly world war. The Holocaust had touched all civilized people everywhere. Atomic bombs had been dropped. Thermonuclear war was on the horizon and at one point in the early 1960s was frighteningly closer than any American knew at the time. The world was vastly changed and, inevitably, composers writing in the postwar years were tempered by the changes.

In America, as in Europe, the opera composer and the operagoer were disconnected. As Charles Hamm pointed out in 1983, most composers were no longer concerned with finding a common ground with their audiences. This applied to both music and text. "It is a matter of historical record," Hamm said, "that no American opera of the past quarter-century has made a substantial impact on our audiences."

And it's a matter of common sense that the opera that doesn't seek an audience is unlikely to get one. The off opera that did seek an audience was "New York opera."

The 1950s

The Tender Land
1954, by Aaron Copland (1900–90)

KEYNOTE: Copland's only big opera. An American work about ordinary American people by the American public's favorite classical composer.

1990s STANDING: Rarely produced, except by colleges and workshops.

Aaron Copland is the most loved American classical composer. He's the quintessential American classical composer. By overwhelming popular vote (and with strong, albeit not unanimous, support from the music world), he is *the* Great American Composer. If the world worked properly, he should have written *the* Great American Opera.

But he didn't. If he weren't Aaron Copland, we almost could stop there and move on. But he is, so we can't.

His first opera, *The Second Hurricane*, 1937, was a "play opera for high school performance." Six children, helping in a flood, are themselves marooned—and, before rescue, learn how to support one another. Today the professionals find the libretto to be nicely sentimental but not mawkish and the score to be "beautifully spare."

His only other opera, *The Tender Land*, 1954, was commissioned by Rodgers and Hammerstein to celebrate the thirtieth anniversary of the American League of Composers. It is a warm and gentle drama about a 1930s Midwest farming family that hires two drifters at harvesttime. When introduced by the New York City Opera at the New York City Center in 1954, critics found it "uninspired." The music is tonal, like his much more familiar ballet music. A revised version was given at Oberlin College in 1955.

Today, looking back, musicologists describe the reception as "uneasy," which, if it weren't Copland, would translate as "lousy." One source says it's as "guileless" as an opera can be. But it's not quite kept in the closet like Great Uncle Fred or most Presidential brothers. It also has strong defenders. One opera source told me in an interview:

"It is a beautifully crafted opera, still done a lot in colleges and workshops. The trouble is that it lacks scale. Its cost is small, the milieu is very downhome, and the emotions entirely normal and touching. Thus it's devoid of blood, grub, decadence, and perversion. It is a great work, a whole opera made out of *Appalachian Spring*, which is another great work. But it's not what the public wants in opera."

Copland's fame came much more from his early instrumental music and through his work as a lecturer, teacher, writer, and promoter of modern music.

After World War II, except for *The Tender Land*, he turned more to European-type composition, including twelve-tone serial music. His Piano Quartet, 1950, was a twelve-tone piece; his *Piano Fantasy*, 1957; and *Connotations for Orchestra*, 1962, also were in a Schoenbergian serial style. Although that is the Copland many in the music world prefer, it isn't the one that has grabbed the general public. The public hears and admires the following:

First, a trio of ballets, each with a subsequent orchestral suite:

Billy the Kid, 1938
Rodeo, 1942
Appalachian Spring, 1944

Plus

El Salón México, 1936, orchestral suite
An Outdoor Overture, 1938
The Quiet City, 1939 (incidental music, arranged for small orchestra)
Our Town, film score, 1940 (arranged as orchestral suite)

A *Lincoln Portrait*, 1942, for speaker and orchestra
Fanfare for the Common Man, 1943
The Red Pony, film score, 1948 (arranged as orchestral suite)

Susannah
1955, by Carlisle Floyd (b. 1926)

KEYNOTE: Homespun. A major folk opera about mountain valley intolerance. Traditional pre-Schoenberg sounds. Successful from the start, with imitations of Appalachian square dances, folksongs, and revival hymns.

1990s STANDING: Still often performed; far and away the most frequently staged American opera. High ratings.

After a premiere at Florida State University (note: not at a major opera house in New York, Milan, or Paris), it made Floyd the top American opera composer of his generation (almost a generation younger than Menotti). In 1956, Erich Leinsdorf conducted it at the New York City Opera. Critic Winthrop Sargeant once wrote that it was "probably the most moving and impressive opera to have been written in America—or anywhere else, as far as I am aware—since Gershwin's *Porgy and Bess*."

A musical drama in two acts, *Susannah* is about a Tennessee mountain girl who is caught bathing in a creek used for baptisms. Denounced and seduced by Olin Blitch, a revivalist pastor, she is threatened and rejected by the townspeople despite her innocence. It is, like Handel's oratorio *Susanna*, from the Old Testament.

Susannah, which won a New York Music Critics' Circle Award, is Floyd's best-known work. Hear hymns, square-dance melodies, folk-type tunes, and exceptional melody. The New York City opera revived it successfully in 1982 with the great bass Samuel Ramey as Olin Blitch.

Floyd studied at Syracuse University, was on the faculty at Florida State University, and became a professor at the University of Houston. Among his other works on Americana themes:

Wuthering Heights, 1958
The Passion of Jonathan Wade, 1962, revised for Houston Grand Opera, 1991
Of Mice and Men, 1970
Willie Stark, 1981

The Ballad of Baby Doe
1956, by Douglas Moore (1893–1969)

KEYNOTE: One of America's best operas, pleasant and homespun, far from the avant-garde. The rise and fall of a Colorado silver baron. Another fine Moore folk opera, *The Devil and Daniel Webster*, came earlier, in 1939.

1990s STANDING: Both are firmly in the U.S. repertory, with *Baby Doe* produced more often.

Douglas Moore studied at Yale, in Paris with Vincent D'Indy and Nadia

Boulanger, and in Cleveland with Swiss-born Ernest Bloch. From 1926 to 1962 he taught at Barnard College in New York.

Moore is one of the few American classical composers whose most important works are operas. Others include Dominick Argento, Robert Ward, Carlisle Floyd, and Gian Carlo Menotti, all of whom, like Moore, were musically conservative.

He draws on folk music and usually deals with rural or pioneer life. His most successful work is *The Ballad of Baby Doe*, 1956, a Beverly Sills favorite, which she says is one of the best operas she ever did. "It was the first major triumph of my career," she writes in her autobiography, *Beverly*, "and for a long time I thought it might be the only one. Although people began paying attention to me after *Baby Doe*, a full eight years passed before I experienced the same combination of artistic accomplishment and recognition."

Set in Washington, D.C., California, and, especially, Colorado, it is the story of the rise and fall of Horace Tabor, a silver baron, who leaves his wife, Augusta, for Baby Doe, who has a husband in Central City. The basic story is true: Their love affair caused a big scandal, and Tabor died bankrupt in Baby Doe's arms, after giving her the Matchless Mine and making her promise never to sell it. In 1935, she was found frozen to death at the abandoned mine's entrance. If you ever get to Aspen, Colorado, close your eyes and drive over the Hill—outsiders call it the Independence Pass, but in my old Aspen time it was the Hill—to Leadville, which still has a silver-mine flavor. Don't drive home to Aspen if you have had a beer.

Baby Doe gets many professional—and many amateur—votes as one of America's best operas. Check it out for easy listening pleasure. It is scheduled to be produced in the 1996–97 season by the Washington Opera. The simple plot is perfect for an opera. The dialogue is down-home. The arias are beautiful—and at the end of them Moore allows pauses for opera-style applause. The folk tunes, although all original Moore creations, have the sound of real American folk music. In opera—rarely Broadway—style, Moore gives different kinds of arias to different types of characters. Wife Augusta gets one type; Baby Doe another much less formal one with her coloratura color and trills; Tabor a third.

In true opera fashion, Moore has different groups all singing together: dandies, cronies, and women. His characters speak fluent "American," not "English."

Moore was a traditional composer, distant from the cutting edge of the "modern" music of an Alban Berg, even though *Baby Doe* came a generation after Berg's *Wozzeck* and at the same time that Igor Stravinsky finally was experimenting with twelve-tone music.

The Devil and Daniel Webster, with a libretto by Stephen Vincent Benét, is one act, a blend of folksong, spoken dialogue, and hymns. It is about Jabez Stone, who has sold his soul to the devil. When the time comes, his case is argued by Daniel Webster before a devil-oriented judge and jury. Webster wins for Stone by pleading in the name of liberty, freedom, and individuality.

In 1961, Moore's *Wings of a Dove*, based on the Henry James novel, had its world premiere at the New York City Opera, but—despite some pleasant music—it wasn't well received, perhaps because of its unfavorable comparison to *Baby Doe*. His final work, *Carry Nation*, 1966, is based on the life of the advocate of women's suffrage.

West Side Story
1957, by Leonard Bernstein (1918–90)

KEYNOTE: The most popular and successful composition of theater music by one of America's most versatile musical greats.

1990s STANDING: High.

Here, as the least Washed know, is a different kind of player in twentieth-century American music.

When *West Side Story* was first produced in 1957, associate justice of the Supreme Court Felix Frankfurter declared: "The history of America is now changed."

Dealing with this history-changer, one must separate Bernstein the all-around musical genius from Bernstein the composer. His closest friends said Bernstein himself never knew who or what he was. Do you want pianist? Conductor? Television personality? He-who-mixes-with-beautiful-people? Educator? Or composer?

If the choice is composer, then, if feasible, we need to separate the many phases of Bernstein's composition. Do you want popular? Serious? Opera? Various levels in between? Ballet? Song?

Zero in on stage works. *The Norton/Grove Concise Encyclopedia of Music* puts them in these groups:

Operas: *Trouble in Tahiti*, 1952; *A Quiet Place*, 1983
Musicals: *On the Town*, 1944; *Wonderful Town*, 1953; *Candide*, 1956; and *West Side Story*, 1957
Other dramatic works: *Fancy Free*, ballet, 1944; *Facsimile*, ballet, 1946; *On the Waterfront*, film score, 1954; *Mass*, theater piece, 1971; *Dybbuk*, ballet, 1974.

Although Bernstein's operas were not unsuccessful, they worked less well for him than most of the things he undertook in his unrestrained, extroverted life. *Trouble in Tahiti* is a small opera with a life of its own, a one-act creation in seven scenes, first presented in 1952 as part of a doubleheader with Marc Blitzstein's translation of Weill's *Threepenny Opera*. It has nothing to do with Tahiti; rather, it is an attack on complacency in the American suburbs: love, alienation, and poor family communication. It is part humor, part sadness, part classical composition, part popular song—and it appeared on national television. More than thirty years later it was incorporated into a revision of Bernstein's second opera—and his first big one—*A Quiet Place*.

Commissioned by Houston Grand Opera, the Kennedy Center, and La

Scala, *A Quiet Place* is a three-act sequel involving the family he introduced in *Tahiti*. Among major characters are Junior, his sister Dede, and her husband, François, who formerly was Junior's lover. All of this is difficult for Widower Sam, father of Junior and Dede, but in time he accepts François, some reconciliation is reached, and the family has a new sense of unity.

After the Houston premiere, a revised version was presented at La Scala. It is long and serious, and some professionals say it lacks the irreverence that gives *Tahiti* its punch. The Vienna State Opera produced it in 1985.

Bernstein also composed genuine musical comedies, including *On the Town*, which was suggested by his ballet *Fancy Free* and premiered at the Adelphi Theatre in New York in 1944, and *Wonderful Town*, from the play *My Sister Eileen*, which premiered at the Winter Garden in New York in 1953. The first is a lighthearted show about three sailors on twenty-four-hour shore leave in New York City; the second tells of two Ohio sisters who look for love and success in Greenwich Village.

But the acknowledged Bernstein masterpiece, the drama-in-music for which he is most remembered, is *West Side Story*, a piece about two gangs on New York's West Side in the 1950s, one Puerto Rican and one Anglo. It is a Romeo and Juliet love story involving Tony, an Anglo, and Maria, Puerto Rican. Tony is killed by the Puerto Rican gang, and only Maria's intervention stops further bloodshed.

So how is it different from musical comedies?

- It isn't light, frivolous, and happy.
- It isn't a comedy. It is drama, the story of the turbulent, poverty-stricken life of New York street gangs.
- The chief male character dies a violent death, rare for musicals.
- It reaches much deeper into the gut than the usual Broadway musical.
- It gives artistic dance a major place, indeed, a central and essential place.
- The songs are top-level, and they require vocal talent, not just charm. "Tonight," "I Feel Pretty," and "Maria" all are worthy of high-caliber operatic voices. This has been proven many times—by high-caliber operatic voices. One available recording features Kiri te Kanawa, José Carreras, Tatiana Troyanos, and the offstage voice of Marilyn Horne. You don't get much higher caliber operatic than that.

It also had 732 performances on Broadway and became one of Hollywood's most successful musicals.

The music professionals have trouble deciding exactly how to categorize *West Side Story*. It is something less than an opera . . . but something more than a Broadway musical. It hasn't made the Met, nor was it intended to. Most books about American opera that were written thirty years ago don't mention it. But it usually is included in more recent literature, sometimes without explanation or apology but often with the one-word description: "musical."

A strong case can be made that an unequivocal distinction between first-level Broadway musical and opera has had its day. In fact, until the late nineteenth and early twentieth centuries, the so-called popular connection always has been a staple of opera: major works of Monteverdi, Gay, Mozart, Verdi, and just about everything else except dedicated Italian opera seria and the German music drama of Richard Wagner.

Whatever label is given *West Side Story*, there is less difficulty in tagging Bernstein's *Candide*, which has been staged both on Broadway and with great success by the Opera Theater of St. Louis and the Boston Lyric Opera. *Candide* is commonly called an operetta, and was described by the composer as a "comic operetta." Some critics hail it as Bernstein's best music for the stage.

Vanessa
1958, by Samuel Barber (1910–81)

KEYNOTE: Barber's first opera to be staged. A major hit from a major classical composer. Homespun, tuneful, and dramatic.

1990s STANDING: Continued respect and success.

Barber was a leading American composer whose instrumental works are performed worldwide. *Vanessa* premiered at the Metropolitan, a major news item in itself. It takes place in 1905 in a Scandinavian country house where Vanessa is waiting for her old lover and welcomes instead the son of that lover. The story is built around two women, the beautiful Vanessa and her beautiful young niece, Erika. You would recognize the melody of two arias, "Must the winter come so soon?" and "Under the willow tree."

In librettist Gian Carlo Menotti's words, *Vanessa* is about "the central dilemma which faces every human being: whether to fight for one's ideals to the point of shutting one's self off from reality, or compromise with what life has to offer, even lying to one's self for the mere sake of lying."

Vanessa is an opera that the Unwashed can embrace—not atonal, not ambiguous, not dissonant, not serial. The music is lyrical and the drama is powerful. One critic called it a near masterpiece. Paul Henry Lang said its impeccable vocal writing and sumptuous orchestration would be an eye-opener for Europeans. After the 1958 premiere, it returned to the Met in 1959 and again in 1965, for a total of eighteen performances. It was the first American opera ever performed at the Salzburg Festival and was a 1995 big hit for the Washington Opera.

Another of Barber's operas, *Antony and Cleopatra*, was commissioned for the opening of the Met's new home in Lincoln Center in 1966, but it did poorly and was withdrawn. Opera journalists from all over the world paid more attention to the new facility than to the opera. It reappears occasionally today.

Among Barber's classical compositions are *Adagio for Strings*, one of classical radio's often played pieces; the song cycle *Knoxville: Summer of 1915*; and *Dover Beach*, for voice and string quartet. Some of his works are conservative and in the Romantic tradition; later he experimented with twelve-tone serial music—but in sort of a conservative way. Barber studied music from an early age and then attended the Curtis Institute in Philadelphia. His many musical honors include two Pulitzer Prizes, the first for *Vanessa*, and the Prix de Rome, an award coveted by the music world.

Six Characters in Search of an Author 1959, by Hugo Weisgall (b. 1912)

KEYNOTE: Grand opera tradition with twentieth-century dissonant sounds by one of America's most respected opera composers.

1990s STANDING: Still applauded by the opera community and sometimes—but not often—performed.

Hugo Weisgall produced a string of music dramas over a long period beginning after World War II. Most are dissonant—and some exceedingly dissonant. The first was *The Tenor*, 1952, a one-act work about an opera singer with many female admirers, one of whom shoots herself when he breaks off their affair. This was followed, the same year, by *The Stronger*, another one-act opera set in a bar on the afternoon before Christmas. It is a monologue for a soprano who gets drunker and drunker talking to a friend she accuses of trying to steal her husband.

The Tenor has big orchestral numbers alternating with set arias; *The Stronger* features vivid mood shifts of the one singing character. *Six Characters in Search of an Author*, from a play by Luigi Pirandello, is Weisgall's best-known full-length opera. It is a play within a play in which six family characters tell their individual stories, each complaining that the author, the director, and the actors have misrepresented them. It was introduced successfully in the 1959 New York City Opera season but didn't have another professional production until it was brought back in 1990 by the Lyric Opera of Chicago's junior company, Lyric Opera Center for American Artists.

Other Weisgall works, most based on literary classics and dealing with twentieth-century philosophies and moral dilemmas, include:

Nine Rivers from Jordan, 1968
Jenny, or the Hundred Nights, 1976
Will You Marry Me?, 1989
The Gardens of Adonis, revised, 1992
Esther, 1992 (recently given by the New York City Opera)

Weisgall was born in Bohemia, emigrated to the United States with his parents in 1920, studied at the Peabody Conservatory in Baltimore for five years, and then worked with Roger Sessions and at the Curtis Institute in Philadelphia. In 1940 Johns Hopkins University awarded him a Ph.D. for his dissertation on primitivism in seventeenth-century German poetry. For some twenty years he taught at Johns Hopkins and the Juilliard School. *Grove* calls him one of America's most important opera composers.

The 1960s, 1970s, and 1980s

The Crucible
1961, by Robert Ward (b. 1917)

    KEYNOTE: Based on Arthur Miller's 1953 play condemning Joe McCarthy and witchcraft. Pulitzer Prize winner. Conservative music.

    1990s STANDING: Approachable opera. Commended by critics. Admired, but dated.

    The Crucible, commissioned by the Ford Foundation, premiered at the New York City Opera in 1961 and was revived for London's Abbey Opera in 1984 on June 6, forty years after the D-day invasion of World War II. An opera in four acts with a libretto by Bernard Stambler, it is the story of John Proctor, a good man in Salem, Massachusetts, in 1692, who is seduced by a seventeen-year-old girl, denounced for witchcraft by girls she has intimidated, and sentenced to be executed, a victim of hysteria and the system. It tracks an Arthur Miller play that draws parallels between the Senator Joseph McCarthy era of the 1950s and the Salem witchcraft trials.

    Ward was born in Cleveland and attended the Eastman School of Music, the Juilliard School, and the Berkshire Music Center. His first opera, *He Who Gets Slapped*, was introduced in New York in 1956. His texts are concerned with social and political issues; the music is conservative.

    Among his other operas:

The Lady from Colorado, which premiered in Central City, Colorado, in 1964
Claudia Legare, 1978
Abélard and Héloïse, 1981
Minutes Till Midnight, 1982

    His most acclaimed orchestral work is his Second Symphony.

Postcard from Morocco
1971, by Dominick Argento (b. 1927)

    KEYNOTE: One of the major American opera composers of the second part of the century. One reason: "I want my work to have emotional impact. I want it to communicate, not obfuscate."

    1990s STANDING: High.

    There's something in the blood. The most successful American opera composer in the middle of the century was Italian-born Gian Carlo Menotti. The most successful one in the second part of the century is Dominick Argento, born of Italian parents.

    Although they worked in vastly different ways, both have tried to reach the operagoing public—and neither is reluctant to say so.

    In 1947 Argento went to the respected Peabody Conservatory in Baltimore, something I intend to do in my next life when I come back as a conductor, in part because of the generous, talented artists associated with it and in part because of its picturesque environment.

Argento studied further at the Eastman School in Rochester, New York, and under several fine teachers, including Henry Cowell, Hugo Weisgall, Bernard Rogers, and Howard Hanson. In 1959 he went to the University of Minnesota, where he has spent his career and where he helped found Center Opera, which became the Minnesota Opera Company—an important cog in twentieth-century American opera and one that has commissioned many new works.

His early, short *Postcard from Morocco*, scored for only seven singers and eight instruments, is his most popular work. It takes place in a railroad station in Morocco in 1914—or it might be any railroad station in any exotic place. Stranded travelers bare their souls to strangers, puppets and people are intermingled, and so are fantasy and reality. It is tuneful and entertaining, although the audience is left with characters unable to resolve who they are.

A more recent work, *The Aspern Papers*, 1987, based on a novella by Henry James, was commissioned by the Dallas Opera and shown on national public television. Other works include:

The Boor, 1957
Colonel Jonathan the Saint, 1971
Christopher Sly, 1963
The Masque of Angels, 1964
The Shoemaker's Holiday, 1967
A Waterbird Talk, 1977
The Voyage of Edgar Allan Poe, 1976, his most ambitious work up to that time
Miss Havisham's Fire, 1971
Miss Havisham's Wedding Night, 1981
Casanova's Homecoming, 1985, a three-act work that was retitled *Casanova*
    when the New York City Opera staged it
The Dream of Valentino, 1994, which premiered at the Washington Opera.
    A story about a film star with great sex appeal who is destroyed by the intrigues and machinations of other people. Rated solid by the experts, although perhaps less so than *The Aspern Papers*. Appropriately, film clips are part of the production

Argento's works have not been seen extensively overseas. Although an opera specialist, in 1985 he introduced a song cycle, *Casa Guidi*, drawn from letters by Elizabeth Barrett Browning. Other song cycles are *Letters from Composers*, 1968, and *From the Diaries of Virginia Woolf*, 1975.

Einstein on the Beach
1976, by Philip Glass (b. 1937)
    KEYNOTE: Minimalist repetition.
    "Knock, knock."

"Who's there?"
"Knock, knock."
"Who's there?"
"Knock, knock."
"Who's there?"
"Philip Glass and John Adams."

1990s STANDING: Professional respect for both composers. Glass has made the Met and Adams the tube.

Repetition and a steady, pulsating beat are basic to minimalism, a composition concept developed in the 1960s in the United States by composers La Monte Young, Steve Reich, and Terry Riley. Some analysts say they have a hard time finding variations in texture, harmony, and, especially, rhythm. The idea is to pare down the music to its most basic elements; the roots of the style are in India rather than Western Europe. Most minimalist composers utilize synthesizers and other electronic instruments to help achieve their objectives.

Einstein on the Beach, Glass's first well-known work, is meant to deal not only with physicist Albert Einstein but also with all science, technology, and ecology. It was conceived by American designer, playwright, and director Robert Wilson, who is given much credit for its success. It's an opera in four acts, although its creators call it a "manifestation of the theater of images." Two other major Glass operas linked with it are *Satyagraha*, 1981, about Mahatma Gandhi's nonviolent activity in South Africa, and *Akhnaten*, 1984, about the Egyptian pharaoh. The three comprise a trio—music people say triptych—about men whose revolutionary ideas affected their world—Einstein, science and related fields; Gandhi, politics; and Akhnaten, religion.

Later works, which range from musical theater to chamber opera and to three-act opera, include:

The Civil Wars, 1984
The Making of the Representative for Planet 8, 1988
The Fall of the House of Usher, 1988
1,000 Airplanes on the Roof, 1988
Hydrogen Jukebox, 1990
The Voyage, 1992

Glass is the leading creator of minimalist opera and other minimalist stage works. In the late 1960s he wrote most of his compositions for an eight-piece ensemble he had founded, the Philip Glass Ensemble, consisting of amplified wind instruments and three electric keyboards: synthesizer, organ, and piano. In the mid-1970s he turned to opera. Several have been produced more than once, an uncommon event for today's living opera composers.

Two have been at the Metropolitan: *Einstein on the Beach*, which premiered at the Avignon Festival in France in mid-1976 and was seen at the Metropolitan

Opera house that November (although it was not a Met production), and *The Voyage*, 1992, in a prologue, three acts, and an epilogue, which was commissioned by the Met in commemoration of the five hundredth anniversary of Columbus's arrival in America. Typical of Glass, *The Voyage* deals more with how the mind works than how the ship navigates. Although ambiguous, it's considerably more conventional than the early three.

Glass was born in Baltimore. He studied with Nadia Boulanger in Paris and in India.

In discussing Glass and minimalism, Professor Donald Jay Grout suggests in his book that observers are unwise to compartmentalize: "Unfortunately, the terms 'minimalist' and 'maximalist' which are applied to Glass's manner of composing are far too restrictive to define a style of opera that is closely tied to the visual arts of stage design and governed by the textual sounds derived from archaic languages. Nor do these terms adequately describe a style of composition that seems to be in a constant state of development, for each of the operas marks a different plateau in Glass's career."

As the professor says, Glass's operas are not alike. *Einstein* is a four-act, five-hour abstract creation, without intermissions and without real characters. The music comes from a five-instrument ensemble that works with a violinist, a singer, and speakers. Both *Satyagraha* and *Akhnaten* are more like traditional operas, with singers, chorus, and orchestra (except that there are no violins in *Akhnaten*).

Nixon in China
1987, by John Adams (b. 1947)

KEYNOTE: The first opera of Adams, America's other big opera minimalist. Great exposure on national TV. Atypical in that it deals with current history.

1990s STANDING: Adams is one of the hot new guys.

John Adams was born in Worcester, Massachusetts, studied at Harvard, and began teaching in 1972 at the San Francisco Conservatory. He characterizes *Nixon in China* as a summary of his musical languages over ten years.

One source notes that it's in the tradition of old opera seria—dealing with quasi-heroic figures, demythologizing them, and simultaneously creating a new myth out of the ashes of a mixed career. *Nixon in China* is in three acts, two and a half hours long, drawn from the late president's actual 1972 trip to China but concentrating on what the characters are feeling rather than the actual events. Henry Kissinger is onstage the entire time without dominating the scene, proof that opera involves the suspension of disbelief.

Although he uses the minimalist technique, Adams doesn't stay with it throughout. If you hear or see *Nixon*, listen for some beautiful chorus work—and expect some synthesizer activity.

A later Adams opera, *The Death of Klinghoffer*, 1991, is from the 1985 news story of the kidnapping of the cruise liner *Achille Lauro*, and the murder by

Palestinian terrorists of a helpless old man in a wheelchair. It is unlike conventional opera, featuring big choruses and little action. A depiction of Arab-Jewish tensions, it caused protests in San Francisco and was canceled in Los Angeles.

In both works Adams collaborated with producer Peter Sellars, a controversial longtime wonder kid of late-twentieth-century opera direction and production.

The Ghosts of Versailles
1991, by John Corigliano (b. 1938)

KEYNOTE: His first full-scale opera. Picks up Figaro from where Rossini and Mozart left him.

1990s STANDING: Standing tall. Commissioned by the Met, it premiered there in 1991 and returned in 1995 with Teresa Stratas and Marilyn Horne. Standing ovations.

Corigliano was born in New York, the son of the concert master of the New York Philharmonic. This was his first full-scale opera, although he had written a good deal for films and won several awards. Described as a "grand opera buffa in two acts," it is based on the final part of the trilogy about Figaro by Pierre-Augustin Beaumarchais, *La mère coupable*, although it's not simply a setting of that text. A big two-act opera, to a libretto by William M. Hoffman, it was the first new opera given at the Met since 1967.

Mozart used the second part of the Beaumarchais piece for *The Marriage of Figaro*, Rossini later drew upon the first part for *The Barber of Seville*, and Corigliano quotes from both in his opera.

Hoffman has said *Ghosts* is primarily a love story but is also about the French Revolution, the nature of revolution in general, the nature of love, and the nature of time. One of the characters is Beaumarchais himself, one of several spirits that inhabit Versailles. He falls in love with Marie Antoinette and writes a new play in order to change history. The opera takes place in three worlds: one of the ghosts and spirits, one of history, and one of the theater.

SURFING 1990s OPERA IN AMERICA

Here are a few diverse samples of other 1990s American operas:

McTeague by William Bolcom, which had its world premiere at the Lyric Opera of Chicago in 1992. Bolcom, then fifty-four, was a professor of composition at the University of Michigan School of Music and a 1988 Pulitzer Prize winner. The libretto by Arnold Weinstein is from Frank Norris's 1899 novel about an alcoholic dentist who is driven by a greedy wife and a treacherous friend to abusing his wife, stealing her money, and killing her and her friend. He winds up in Death Valley handcuffed to the friend's corpse.

Marilyn, by Ezra Laderman, one of three new operas that premiered at New York City Opera in 1993. Laderman was born in Brooklyn in 1924 and has composed nine earlier operas, based on historical, biblical, and other themes. His best known is *Galileo Galilei*, which premiered in 1978.

Dangerous Liaisons, by Conrad Susa. The world premiere was in late 1994 by the San Francisco Opera. It is based on the novel, play, and film; the original source was an eighteenth-century French novel, *Les liaisons dangereuses*, by Pierre Chodleros de Laclos. It is a story about two lovers who try to manipulate each other by outperforming one another in sexual conquests. After the San Francisco opening it was shown on PBS, with Frederica von Stade and Thomas Hampson. Susa was born in 1935 in Springfield, Pennsylvania, and studied at the Juilliard School. In 1988 he joined the faculty of the San Francisco Conservatory of Music. He has written three other operas, many choral works, and scores of film and television scores.

Ligeia, a two-act work by Augusta Read Thomas, which premiered in 1994 at the Peabody Conservatory in Baltimore. The librettist is Leslie Dunton-Downer. Based loosely on the life of Edgar Allan Poe, it was commissioned by Galina Vishnevskaya, former Russian opera superstar, who is the wife of cellist/conductor Mstislav Rostropovich.

Brain Opera by Tod Machover, *Emmeline* by Tobias Picker, and *King of Hearts* by Michael Torke, good examples of the diversity of American contemporary opera in the 1990s, all had stage premieres within one week in midsummer, 1996. Machover was forty-two, Picker, forty-two, and Torke, thirty-five. *Brain Opera* was presented in New York at the Juilliard School as part of a Lincoln Center Festival, *Emmeline* at Santa Fe Opera in New Mexico, and *King of Hearts* at the Aspen Music Festival in Colorado. *Brain Opera* is an audience-participation opera, a total departure from the conventional; *Emmeline* is an evening-long, large-scale work involving traditional operatic voices and orchestra, based on a novel about a nineteenth-century teenage girl, and *King of Hearts* is a short chamber opera, involving rock and funk, commissioned by and made for television.

AN AMERICAN OPERA DREAM SEASON

Can we fashion an American repertory out of this twentieth-century American bouquet that combines opera, folk opera, operetta, musical, New York opera, combinations of the above, and none of the above?

Of course, even without defining a special cubicle for each work. Dozens of American opera houses in the fifty states put together all kinds of different seasons, blending Handel with Hammerstein to their heart's desire.

Everyone's Dream Season would be different. A good one follows, with a thumbnail rationale for each selection:

Show Boat, 1927, by Jerome Kern. Because it's close enough to folk opera and may be America's finest operetta, because it's fit for operatic voices, and because it would be outrageous to leave it out.

Four Saints in Three Acts, 1934, by Virgil Thomson. Because the composer is so talented and the joint venture with Gertrude Stein and an all-black-cast is too provocative to ignore. And because it also represents Thomson's *The Mother of Us All*.

Porgy and Bess, 1935, by George Gershwin. Because it is *the* American opera of this or any century.

Oklahoma!, 1943, by Richard Rodgers and Oscar Hammerstein II. Because it was their first collaboration, which opened the door to Broadway opera, and because it's the essence of America.

Regina, 1949, by Marc Blitzstein. Because it's an example of legitimate opera launched on Broadway and also is a proxy for Blitzstein's *The Cradle Will Rock*.

Amahl and the Night Visitors, 1951, by Gian Carlo Menotti. Because he's America's most successful opera composer and this is his best-known work.

Trouble in Tahiti, 1952, by Leonard Bernstein. Because it is the major opera of the all-around classical/popular music genius of twentieth-century America.

The Tender Land, 1954, Aaron Copland. Because he is Aaron Copland and this is his only real opera.

Susannah, 1955, by Carlisle Floyd. Because it's the most successful of a dozen works he wrote on American themes and one of America's most important mainstream operas.

The Ballad of Baby Doe, 1956, by Douglas Moore. Because it's another fine homespun American opera, because Leadville is the real world, and because Beverly Sills and the New York City Opera made it famous, or vice versa.

West Side Story, 1957, by Bernstein. Because it's his world-class composition with 732 performances on Broadway and a work of art in its own right, whatever it is.

Vanessa, 1958, by Samuel Barber. Because Barber, like Mozart, remembered not to ignore the Unwashed, and because it survives strongly in the 1990s on operatic stages as one of America's best operas after a strong performance record at the Met.

The Crucible, 1961, by Robert Ward. Because he was dedicated both to American opera and to accessible opera and because this enhanced the drama of Arthur Miller's book.

Postcard from Morocco, 1971, by Dominick Argento. Because here at the end of the twentieth century he has become one of the most versatile and prolific American opera composers and this early chamber-size work is one of his finest.

A Little Night Music, 1973, by Stephen Sondheim. Because this is a play in music not a play with music, because his lyrics are so good and his standards so high that they help erase the artificial Broadway–opera house demarcation line, and because it represents *Sweeney Todd* and other works.

Akhnaten, 1984, by Philip Glass. Because of his standing as a leading contemporary American composer and his minimalist contribution and because this also stands in for *Einstein on the Beach*, *Satyagraha* and his other major operas.

Nixon in China, 1987, by John Adams. Because he's the other minimalist drawing attention today and because my favorite experts have persuaded me that in fifty years *Porgy and Bess*, *The Ballad of Baby Doe*, *Show Boat*, and *Nixon in China* will still be around. If young enough, tune in then.

The Ghosts of Versailles, 1991, by John Corigliano. Because it's the most recent American opera to have premiered at the Met and because the Met brought it back in 1995, with no end of stagings in sight.

That's eighteen. If you're 100 percent purist, eliminate *Oklahoma!* and *A Little Night Music* and settle for sixteen. If you're 50 percent purist, delete *West Side Story* and *Show Boat*, and accept a season of fourteen. If you're truly wise, keep all eighteen, add *Pal Joey* and *Guys and Dolls*, and demand to know why Vienna's *Fledermaus* is in and these Broadway gems are out. In arguing your case, use phrases like "integrated and highly dramatic impact," "accomplished and effective orchestration," and "superior vocal potential."

Finally, if anyone says *Porgy* isn't real opera, show tolerance and compassion. Do not talk about reservoirs of melody in arias and choruses or recitative or dramatic truth or musical variety or the self-portraits of the residents of Catfish Row. Just say, "You're probably right," smile, and walk away. Or respond with a question: "What do you expect from a New York-based Jewish songwriter working with a southern white male novelist on a story about Carolina blacks? How could that be real opera?"

Opera for Hundreds of Millions

It would be unseemly and ludicrous to leave "Opera in America" without mentioning Texaco, Inc., and the Texaco–Metropolitan Opera International Radio Network. For the last three fifths of the century this joint venture has brought opera to audiences of sizes beyond the imagination of the Camerata, Mozart, or Richard Wagner.

It all began on a Saturday afternoon in 1940, with an estimated listening audience of 500,000 people in the United States. By the late 1980s, hundreds of radio stations across the United States and Canada reached tens of millions of listeners. Starting in 1990, Texaco went international with broadcasts into a dozen European countries and the Soviet Union.

It is by far the longest-running program on radio.

Fiftieth anniversary figures show that home listeners (and picnickers, boaters, automobile passengers, and joggers) had had the opportunity of hearing *La Bohème* thirty-six times, *Aida* thirty-three, *Carmen* thirty-one, *Tosca* and *La traviata* twenty-nine each, *Madama Butterfly* twenty-six, *Il trovatore* twenty-five, *Die Walküre* twenty-four, and all the rest, every Saturday afternoon for twenty weeks each year, live from the Met.

Since 1977, Texaco also has sponsored more than fifty televised Metropolitan performances. In 1990 these included telecasts of Wagner's *Ring* cycle over four successive nights. Texaco's total financial commitment to the Met has run over $100 million.

So, for opera fans, there is a free lunch after all.

Listeners get not only wonderful opera but insightful commentary, much of it geared to the Unwashed. Texaco, like Mozart's father, decided early on that it wouldn't talk only to the Scrubbed, although for them it programs an opera quiz and special features.

Nor has Texaco been alone. Other oil companies, businesses, and opera companies also have worked together to spread the opera couth. As one of many, many examples, over a few weeks in the spring of 1994 more than five hundred radio stations carried WFMT–Chicago Fine Arts Network's rebroadcasts of 1993–94 Chicago Lyric Opera first nights.

Chapter 9

VOICES, ROLES, AND SINGERS

Wchat is a tenore di grazia? Who is a tenore di grazia? Is he or it different from a hoher tenor? Where do I find either or both? Why isn't anyone speaking English?

Assistance from The Great Conductor in the Sky is needed for the Unwashed who want to forge links between the types of voices opera singers possess, the roles and arias friendly to those voice types, and superstars who have made the parts famous.

It would be nice to put every singer in a special niche. Each time a performer is catalogued and filed, however, he or she slithers away into another drawer. Sometimes another cabinet. Even another office.

Oh, there is faint hope. Some broad compartmentalizing is feasible. For example, four Big Time performers can be described this way:

Beverly Sills—lyric coloratura soprano, high, acrobatic voice
Leontyne Price—versatile lyric soprano, flexible; most of Verdi's later soprano
   roles are for her kind of voice
Birgit Nilsson—dramatic soprano, powerful but never agile, good for Wagnerian opera
Marilyn Horne—agile mezzo-soprano, a notch deeper than the heaviest soprano voice; needs her vocal agility for earlier Italian opera but not as much for Verdi opera

That's a start, but it also triggers a warning: this chapter will appeal only to those who stay loose. Or to those whose desks are untidy and who leave the cap off the toothpaste tube. It will frustrate people who enjoy making out their own income tax returns or who can program a VCR without the help of a twelve-year-old.

Ideally, one might lay out the characteristics of a "light tenor," and then determine that John Doe meets those qualifications, and then calculate that John's best roles, therefore, would be X, Y, and Z. And sometimes it does work reasonably well that way, but often it doesn't.

There are several reasons why not. The most important is that we're dealing with human beings. Every voice is unique—yours, mine, Jimmy Carter's, Enrico Caruso's, Ross Perot's, Luciano Pavarotti's, Michael Jordan's, and Rush Limbaugh's.

First, a little background. Back in the time of the old Gregorian chant in the eighth and ninth centuries, the range of all singers was about that of today's tenor. In the fifteenth century, music was separated into four distinct ranges, corresponding to today's bass, tenor, contralto, and mezzo-soprano, although almost all the music from this period was sacred and performed exclusively by males, with boys singing the higher parts. It was not until the rise of opera in the seventeenth century that serious attention was paid to the range of human voices and to the singer's mission of depicting human character by his or her voice.

The leading hero (primo uomo) of seventeenth-century opera was a castrato, the leading heroine (prima donna) a high soprano, the supporting male a bass, and the supporting female a contralto—high voices for the leads, low voices for the supporting cast. Musicologists note, however, that sometimes that pattern was modified—which is par for the course when you talk about voices.

Since then, the voice-role-singer equation has become much more complex.

In part this is because of the way basic voice types are defined. The President has issued no Executive Order setting the standard. One opera source might decide that all sopranos should fit into six categories . . . but the expert across the hall might put them all into only three or four categories. It can be done either way—and, in fact, we do it two ways in this chapter. One voice-sorter, for example, might classify all sopranos at the lighter end of the spectrum as "light," "light lyric," and "lyric," and another might place these upper-end singers into just two groups.

Also, countries classify their voice types differently, not only as to range but by other characteristics. And, again, some nations employ more divisions than others. A reader or listener comes across an Italian term, a German term, an English term: "Tenore di grazia," "hoher tenor," light lyric tenor. These can't be expected to match perfectly, and they don't.

Another complication in definitions is that many Collection composers wrote operas with particular performers in mind, just as Hollywood writers still write film scripts with major box-office stars in mind. In these cases, the composer knew the precise capabilities of his superstar singer. Perhaps the voice demands of Act III are vastly different from the demands of Act I. That worked ideally for the composer's chosen singer, but not so well for other star singers that came along. That's not to say the original singers were "better"; they simply were more suited for the part that had been composed for them.

Musicologists advise us, for example, that Violetta in Verdi's *La traviata* is mostly for a "normal" lyric voice—but that the finale to Act I demands special acrobatic trills and roodle doodles beyond the scope of many "normal" lyric sopranos.

Giovanni Battista Rubini was a great early-nineteenth-century Italian tenor. His range was astonishingly high; his style extremely individualistic. He was a smash hit in a Rossini opera, and Donizetti and Bellini each wrote roles especially for him. He defined a distinct bel canto style. But the same composers also wrote operas for other special tenors with lower voices, and for all-purpose tenors with all-purpose voices. So we can't safely settle rigidly even on a "typical bel canto tenor," let alone equate one precisely with French or German or English terminology.

Time out for some background points:

- Most opera is sung in the language in which it was written. Traditionally, in Germany and Italy the home language was more apt to be used, but that's becoming less common. So most successful opera singers have to have good enunciation in several languages, even if they aren't linguists. Some are linguists.
- In general, German composers and most French composers are less concerned with vocal athletics than most Italian composers.
- The inflection of the voice is important to a singer's acting ability.
- Style and "musicianship" are noted. The tasteless show-off more concerned with exhibiting his or her voice than communicating the meaning of the aria is not welcome.

Roles and voices are classified by several characteristics, among them:

- Range—how low and how high the singers can go. The entire series of notes they can reach.
- Size—the ability to cut through an orchestra's sound.
- Tessitura—where a vocal part "sits" or "lies, whether high or low in its average pitch. From the singer's standpoint, where *most* of that singer's notes lie. It differs from range in that it excludes the few isolated highest and lowest notes.

A good example of two types of singers and voices: Léonore is the soprano heroine of Beethoven's *Fidelio* and Zerlinia is the intriguing peasant soprano in Mozart's *Don Giovanni*. Léonore sings a magnificent aria known to all the Washed. She is a real heroine, ready to give up her life to rescue the husband she loves. She must come across as noble, generous, courageous, and human. Her part is for a majestic soprano voice—not at all the same kind as Zerlina's, who is a resourceful and flirtatious peasant bride.

As evident in the Sills-Price-Nilsson data above, within such basic ranges as soprano are several different categories. One, as we'll soon see, is the "lyric soprano." Perhaps a particular lyric soprano is most comfortable as Mimi in Puccini's *La Bohème* or Micaela in Bizet's *Carmen*. But possibly she's versatile enough to sing successfully the airier role of Mozart's Susanna in *The Marriage of Figaro*, a role usually taken by a "light" soprano, and/or to move in the other direction for the "darker" and more "dramatic" role of Puccini's *Tosca*.

Or consider two imaginary singers, Max Schlepperman and Kevin O'Donnell. Both are baritones, but their voices are different. O'Donnell's is deeper and darker; Schlepperman's is higher. Although they share many roles, when both appear in Leoncavallo's *Pagliacci*, an opera with two main baritone parts, O'Donnell always plays Tonio, the hunchback, and Schlepperman, son of a Brooklyn cantor, sings Silvio, the lover. This isn't because either the composer or the conductor is pro-Semitic or an Irish-hating Brit. It's because Tonio calls for a dramatic baritone, a darker voice, and Silvio demands the more lyric voice of a baritone lover. It has to do with the timbre of their voices.

Songs versus Arias

I asked my favorite analyst to talk about songs and arias:

His response: "In opera, songs are distinct from arias, and even classical operas can have both. In *Figaro*, Cherubino's 'Voi che sapete' is a song; his 'Non so pi'u' is an aria. Carmen's solo music is almost all song, but Micaëla and Don José in *Carmen* have arias. 'Musicals' tend to have all songs and few, if any, arias. Indeed, the song/aria ratio is perhaps the most valuable touchstone of the distinction between an opera and a musical.

"An aria is an extended song, a solo vocal piece with instrumental accompaniment. Traditionally, it is in various sections, according to strict rules of form, especially in serious opera. The rules changed at different periods of history."

Some singers are more able than others to reach up to lighter roles and down to darker ones. Some unwittingly ruin their voices when they overreach. And others stretch beyond themselves even though they are aware of potential consequences, drawing everything possible from their voices at the price of a shorter career. Maybe they're bright enough to want to spend more time with their spouse and children, or maybe they want to manage a major opera company while at the peak of their energy, or maybe they just want to fish.

This chapter is salted with illustrations of various voices, roles, and famous singers. The first section defines key types of voices and gives a few examples of the roles for each type, all from Collection composers. The second section ties one hundred opera arias to different voice types. The third gives snapshots of a few dozen opera stars and superstars, most from this century, and identifies their favorite roles.

We'll treat the female voice first.

Stay loose.

DIFFERENT VOICE CATEGORIES
Female Voices

Highest: soprano
Middle: mezzo-soprano
Lowest: contralto, a voice seldom heard these days

Sopranos

In this section the soprano field is handled in four basic categories, from the top down: light, lyric, lyric-dramatic, and heroic. In the next section, sopranos in the one hundred selected arias are divided into coloratura, soubrette, light lyric (not soubrette), full lyric, spinto, and dramatic. Some explanation between now and then will help bridge the differences in terminology, but it's never going to come out even, so don't worry about it.

LIGHT SOPRANO

These roles call for the highest soprano voices, or at least one type of those voices. Often, but not always, the light soprano is for comic parts:

Adina, from Donizetti's *Elixir of Love*
Ännchen, from Weber's *Der Freischütz*
Despina, from Mozart's *Così fan tutte*
Norina, from Donizetti's *Don Pasquale*
Pagagena, from Mozart's *The Magic Flute*
Susanna, from Mozart's *The Marriage of Figaro*
Zerlina, from Mozart's *Don Giovanni*

The analysts advise us that with a relatively small amount of downward stretching, the light soprano who's comfortable as a Norina or Susanna also can handle Gounod's Juliette in *Roméo et Juliette*. A little more pushing takes her down to Charpentier's *Louise*, and, depending on the depth of the tessitura, maybe to Mélisande in Debussy's *Pelléas et Mélisande*.

Maria Callas

That doesn't mean that every good Susanna also can excel at Mélisande. Some can, some can't.

We have spoken of coloratura, an Italian word which applies usually to a vocal passage that contains rapid runs, trills, and other virtuoso-like ornamentation. Many eighteenth- and nineteenth-century operas, particularly Italian, or those written in the Italian style, have these kinds of arias, which are extremely difficult to sing. The term coloratura is used also for a virtuoso singer, usually but not always soprano, who is able handle such passages.

In his book *Voices, Singers & Critics*, John B. Steane writes that at one time there was no more loathed term in the whole music glossary than "coloratura soprano." He quotes the local music critic of his evening paper in the mid-1940s as saying that the pyrotechnics and shrill of this kind of aria had "absolutely nothing" to do with the art of music. In those years, Steane writes, it seemed that the coloratura was a threatened species.

But no longer. The "Jewel Song" from Gounod's *Faust* is a good example of this kind of vocal fireworks. So is the "Bell Song" from Delibes's *Lakmé*, and so are the arias of the Queen of the Night in Mozart's *The Magic Flute*. Other examples are among the one hundred arias in the next section.

Maria Callas and Joan Sutherland took coloratura to great heights. More recent known coloraturas include June Anderson and Edita Gruberova. Among others in the past are Adelina Patti, Nellie Melba, Luisa Tetrazzini, Amelita Galli-Curci, and Lily Pons.

Another term associated with light soprano is "soubrette." Definitions differ somewhat, so we turn to Webster: "A coquettish maid or frivolous young woman in comedies; an actress who plays such a part; a soprano who sings supporting roles in comic opera." Examples are such cunning servant girls as Adele in Johann Strauss's *Die Fledermaus*, Susanna in Mozart's *The Marriage of Figaro*, and the peasant girl Zerlina in Mozart's *Don Giovanni*. Other examples are in the one-hundred arias section.

Steane describes a soubrette as the sweet little seventeen-year-old in the pink embroidered apron who is a light soprano with a voice that is bright in tone color but without great reserves of power.

Wearing the Red Trunks: Rudolf Bing

Met boss Rudolf Bing canceled Maria Callas's Met contract when she would not agree to the performance schedule he had proposed. She complained of his "Prussian tactics," telling the press: "I cannot switch my voices. My voice is not like an elevator, going up and down . . . So Mr. Bing cancels a twenty-six-performance contract for three *Traviatas*.

"When I think of those lousy *Traviatas* he made me sing without rehearsals, without even knowing my partners . . . Is that Art? . . . And other times, all those performances with a different tenor or a different baritone every time . . . Is that Art?"

Bing was never one to remain silent long. He said in a press statement: "I do not propose to enter into a public feud with Madame Callas since I am well aware that she has considerably greater competence and experience at that kind of thing than I have."

Despite his comments, Bing was a worthy opponent. Callas biographer Arianna Stassinopoulos reports that he once responded to criticism by the French press of a Met singer with this statement: "Miss Peters may have had a bad night but the Paris Opéra has had a bad century."

Needless to say, not all soubrettes stay soubrettes forever. Seventeen-year-olds grow, aprons shrink, and voices develop. Also, Mozart's Susanna winds up pretty much running the whole show and doesn't at all fit the sweet little frivolous part of the definition. Barbara Bonney, Kathleen Battle, and Barbara Hendricks have sung many soubrette roles, but didn't confine themselves to these parts. Many voices are suitable for both light soubrette and lyric roles.

LYRIC SOPRANO

This is the next weight step. The music people use words that remind us of the language of the wine people—a little fuller than the light soprano, a little more ample, but still usually graceful and charming. Nothing, of course, prevents a particular singer from having a voice that is in between the two and being able to reach in both directions. And there is considerable variety within the central lyric soprano roles. Here are a few examples:

Liù, in Puccini's *Turandot*
Marguerite, in Gounod's *Faust*
Mimi, in Puccini's *La Bohème*
Pamina, in Mozart's *The Magic Flute*
Micaëla, in Bizet's *Carmen*
Gilda in Verdi's *Rigoletto*

Within stretched lyric boundaries, add:

Donna Elvira in Mozart's *Don Giovanni*
Tatiana, in Tchaikovsky's *Eugene Onegin*
Desdemona, in Verdi's *Otello*
Amelia, in Verdi's *Simon Boccanegra*

Like most singers, the lyric soprano has her eye on other roles. If she has agility, only a small amount of movement toward the dramatic end takes her to Elvira in Bellini's *I Puritani*. Considerably more movement, the professionals advise, is needed for three big, big title roles which normally are sung best by a dramatic soprano, or at least a lyric-dramatic one: first to Puccini's *Tosca* and *Butterfly* and then on to Verdi's *Aida*.

Among better-known lyric sopranos of past and present are Licia Albanese, Frances Alda, Victoria de los Angeles, Emma Eames, Geraldine Farrar, Mirella Freni, Dorothy Kirsten, Elisabeth Rethberg, Renata Scotto, and Teresa Stratas.

DRAMATIC—AND LYRIC-DRAMATIC—SOPRANO

The term "dramatic" encompasses a wide variety of voices. How wide depends on the user. Some use it to mean any soprano voice the deeper side of "lyric," even including a heavy-voiced, "heroic" Isolde in Wagner's *Tristan und Isolde*. Indeed, that's the use in the one hundred-aria section that comes next in this chapter. In this section we have a separate box for heroic sopranos, but combine into one the sopranos which fall between "lyric" and "heroic"—both "lyric-dramatic" and, a step deeper, "dramatic."

A little normal voice dust still exists, however, in part because the Italian term "spinto" is also employed for some of these same roles. One radio commentator might call Leonora in *Il trovatore* a "Verdi lyric-dramatic soprano" and another might call her a "spinto," (or "lirico spinto," which is the same thing). Spinto, which is translated as "pushed," is heard more often to describe a type of tenor voice that is less weighty than a big heroic tenor, but more dramatically exciting than a pure lyric tenor. Sometimes, however, it is applied to sopranos.

Verdi especially liked the lyric-dramatic soprano, who needs a flexible, dramatic and powerful voice, and the ability to sing soaring notes. The group above includes as *lyric* sopranos his Gilda from *Rigoletto* and, with a stretch, Amelia from *Simon Boccanegra*. Violetta from *La traviata* is perhaps a little weightier than Amelia and fits between Amelia and Verdi's "true" lyric-dramatic heroines, of whom the four best known are:

Aida, the title role. In the Italian categories, Violetta is called "lirico" and
   Aida "spinto" or "lirico spinto."
Elisabeth de Valois, the wife of King Philip in *Don Carlos*.
Two Leonoras, one from *The Force of Destiny* and the other from *Il trovatore*.

Lyric-dramatic roles from other Collection operas include:

Valentin, from Meyerbeer's *Les Huguenots*
Santuzza, from Mascagni's *Cavalleria rusticana*
Tosca, the Puccini title role.

Another notch down are:

Salome, from her opera by Richard Strauss
Sieglinde, sister/lover of Siegmund in Wagner's *Die Walküre*

As noted earlier, many composers wrote roles with specific singers in mind and tailored their work to those singers' capabilities. Others simply wrote for the voices of multipurpose sopranos. Some even created an especially difficult role to spite producers who were forcing an inept sister-in-law upon them. It is said that any good *lyric* soprano can sing the songs given Tosca in Acts I and III but that the Tosca in Act II demands a heavier voice, at the *dramatic* soprano level. The issue isn't whether the lyric soprano can sing Act II, but how well she can sing it. Some lyric sopranos who are perfect for frail, dying Mimi in *La Bohème* also have the voice and temperament to handle the volatile lyric-dramatic Tosca and others don't.

Olive Fremstad as Sieglinde in Die Walküre

Heroic Sopranos

Think Brünnhilde. The heroic soprano is the end of the soprano line and a jumping-off place for sopranos who venture into mezzo-soprano roles. Other than Brünnhilde, examples of "true" heroic soprano parts include:

Armide, the queen title role from Gluck's *Armide* (non-Collection)
Rezia, in Weber's *Oberon* (non-Collection)

Among famous Wagnerian sopranos are Lilli Lehmann, Lillian Nordica, Olive Fremstad, Kirsten Flagstad, the top Brünnhilde of this century who died in 1962, and Birgit Nilsson, born in 1918, her successor.

Mezzo-Sopranos

It has been said that mezzo-sopranos play only witches, bitches, and boys.

Technically the central ground between the high and low female voices, the mezzo-soprano (often shortened to mezzo) is rich and mature, not fresh and girlish. Normally she isn't a wealthy, temperamental superstar like the soprano, although there are exceptions. In general, if you want to get rich, throw fits, and live like a spoiled princess—albeit a talented and hardworking princess—be a soprano. Or else be one of the world's best mezzo-sopranos.

In most operas, the female lead is a soprano. The mightiest exception is Bizet's Carmen and another good one is Dalila in Saint-Saëns's *Samson et Dalila*. Verdi's Azucena, a major role in *Il trovatore*, also is a mezzo, although technically she's not the lead.

Among well-known mezzo-soprano roles:

Lyric and light lyric mezzo—Dorabella in Mozart's *Così fan tutte*, Charlotte in
   Massenet's *Werther*, and Mignon in Thomas's *Mignon*
Lyric mezzo plus coloratura—most of the Rossini heroines
Trouser roles—Cherubino in Mozart's *The Marriage of Figaro*, Octavian in Richard
   Strauss's *Der Rosenkavalier*, and the Composer in Strauss's *Ariadne auf Naxos*
Verdi mezzo—Azucena in *Il trovatore*, Eboli in *Don Carlos*, and Amneris in *Aida*
German dramatic mezzo—Fricka in Wagner's *Ring* and Ortrud in his *Lohengrin*,
   Herodias in Richard Strauss's *Salome*, and Clytemnestra in his *Elektra*

The lines, as always in opera, are blurred. In Bellini's *Norma*, Adalgisa is written for a heavier soprano voice than Norma and often she's played by a "light" mezzo; indeed, a light mezzo Adalgisa might reappear another time as Norma herself. Santuzza in Mascagni's *Cavalleria rusticana* is sung by a soprano or a mezzo-soprano. Kundry in Wagner's *Parsifal* and Venus in *Tannhäuser*, both good "heavy" parts, also are tackled by either weighty soprano or normal mezzo-soprano.

Famous mezzo-sopranos include Teresa Berganza, a fairly light mezzo voice; Frederica von Stade, a medium one, and Marilyn Horne, a heavier one.

In *Carmen*, Micaëla is written for a soprano and Carmen for a mezzo. But Carmen has been sung by all manner of singers, mezzos and sopranos, including Agnes Baltsa, Marilyn Horne, Leontyne Price, Tatiana Troyanos, Teresa Berganza, Victoria de los Angeles, Maria Callas, Grace Bumbry, Jessye Norman, and Regina Resnik.

Not all operas have a mezzo-soprano role. Among famous ones that don't are Beethoven's *Fidelio* and Puccini's *Tosca* and *La Bohème*.

Contralto

The contralto is the lowest female voice and one that has almost become an endangered species. Like all other voice categories, it encompasses a set range that then is extended by individual singers. Madame Ernestine Schumann-Heink is quoted as saying back in 1928: "I am looking for the contralto singer who will be my successor. She must be *the* contralto."

Schumann-Heink was one of the last, probably the greatest, and certainly the most agile of the contraltos. *The* contralto to succeed her hasn't appeared.

Examples of important true contralto roles in operas performed frequently today include:

Erda in Wagner's *Das Rheingold* and *Siegfried*
Ulrica in Verdi's *Masked Ball*
La Cieca in Ponchielli's *La Gioconda*

Some legitimate contraltos are able to reach up for some great mezzo roles, such as Azucena in *Il trovatore* and Amneris in *Aida*. In the other direction, the Met's famous Regina Resnik sang soprano roles for years before burrowing down through mezzo-soprano all the way to contralto. A great contralto was the British singer Kathleen Ferrier, who died in 1953. She was spectacular in the title role in Britten's *Rape of Lucretia*, which was written for a contralto. An earlier singer with a deep, rich voice who sang contralto roles was Maria Olczewska, although technically she was a mezzo-soprano.

MALE VOICES

Highest: Countertenor
High: Tenor
Middle: Baritone
Lowest: Bass

Tenor

Any baritone will tell you that the tenor makes all the money, has all the good songs, and gets the girl.

As noted, countries subdivide tenors according to their own traditions and language, and the categories don't match perfectly inasmuch as each country sets its own definitions of range and other characteristics.

Let's begin with four Italian terms: the ultra high and lyrical "tenore di grazia," or graceful tenor, with his bright, flowing voice; the more dramatic "tenore di forza," with a sturdier voice; the "tenore spinto," with a fuller, still more dramatic sound with ringing tones, and the "tenore robusto," or heroic tenor, the heaviest of all for Italian opera. Some examples:

Tenore di grazia—Alfredo in *La traviata*. A special Italian category of lyric tenor for a high voice able to handle some Verdi and the serious bel canto operas of Rossini, Donizetti, and Bellini.

Tenore di forza—Cavaradossi in Puccini's *Tosca*, Don Carlos in Verdi's *Don Carlos*, and tenors in some of Donizetti's more dramatic roles. In German opera, perhaps the title role in Wagner's *Lohengrin*, but "tenore di forza" is an Italian term and that is a German opera, so there is no specific match. In English terms, roughly lyric-dramatic.

Tenore spinto—(also called lirico spinto). Ernani in Verdi's *Ernani*, Don Alvaro in Verdi's *Force of Destiny*, and Dick Johnson in Puccini's *Girl of the Golden West*. Not as heavy as a full heroic tenor, but more dramatically exciting than a pure lyric role.

Tenore robusto, for the heaviest tenor roles—Verdi's *Otello*, and Wagner's *Siegfried* and *Tristan*.

In German terminology and German opera, from the top down:

Hoher tenor: The Italian Singer in Strauss's *Der Rosenkavalier*
Spieltenor: David, Hans Sach's apprentice in Wagner's *Die Meistersinger*
Lyrischer tenor: Max the huntsman in Weber's *Der Freischütz*
Heldentenor, or Wagner heldentenor: Siegfried in the *Ring* cycle

But most tenors worth their high pay can handle three of the Italian or German categories, so don't agonize over the terminology. In the simplest terms, light equals "lyric," heavier equals "lyric-dramatic," still heavier equals "dramatic," and heaviest equals "heroic."

However, even the plain, ordinary "lyric" tenor tent is a large one of circus size, not a pup tent for the backyard. Among the better-known performers who have occupied it are Enrico Caruso, Tito Schipa, Jussi Bjorling, Alfredo Kraus, Beniamino Gigli—and the TV Three, José Carreras, Luciano Pavarotti, and Plácido Domingo. An enormous amount of variety is at play there.

The leading tenore di grazia of his generation and an excellent example of one type of *lyric* tenor was Tito Schipa, who had a magnificent light voice with no trace of baritonal quality. He concentrated a lifetime on a few of the lighter and most graceful major roles, of which ten from Collection operas are good examples of this voice type:

Don Ottavio in Mozart's *Don Giovanni*
Almaviva in Rossini's *Barber of Seville*
Elvino in Bellini's *La sonnambula*
Nemorino in Donizetti's *Elixir of Love*
Ernesto in Donizetti's *Don Pasquale*
Edgardo in Donizetti's *Lucia di Lammermoor*
The Duke of Mantua in Verdi's *Rigoletto*
Alfredo in Verdi's *La traviata*
Wilhelm Meister in Thomas's *Mignon*
Des Grieux in Massenet's *Manon*

Note that eight of these are Italian and two French.

All of these are said to make moderate demands on the vocal range. The lyric tenor is the sort of fellow who is young, handsome, and in love, and plays opposite the lyric soprano. Alfredo Kraus, the leading light lyric tenor of his generation and regarded by many as second only to Schipa in this range, sings the same kinds of roles (but also others that Schipa didn't attempt).

The voice of the Italian "spinto" tenor is essentially lyrical, but it has a heavier, fuller quality than Schipa's.

Deeper in range is the "robusto," or "heroic," tenor. Examples of his roles are:

Manrico in Verdi's *Il trovatore*
Radames, in Verdi's *Aida*, somewhat heavier than Manrico
Canio in Leoncavallo's *Pagliacci*
Otello and Siegfried. These are far limits in Italian and German opera for a
    lyric tenor.

We move to German opera for the heldentenor, presumably the heaviest tenor. But one size doesn't fit all here either. The heldentenor voice required for Wagner's Tristan is so heavy that it makes most other heldentenor roles seem almost lyric by comparison. Wagner's Lohengrin is lighter than his Tannhäuser and his Tannhäuser is lighter than his Siegfried, and his Siegfried is lighter than his Tristan (although more strenuous). Thus some gifted general-purpose tenors can cope with certain heldentenor parts but not with others.

Again, it isn't strictly a matter of "weight" or "depth" but also of how the voice comes across to the audience. Tenor Jon Vickers sounded like big John Wayne leading the cavalry. Tenor Plácido Domingo, who began as a baritone, fits generally into the heroic tenor category and is strong enough to be an Otello but nonetheless sounds more like a lover than a doughty warrior governor.

But be relaxed. The objective is simply to get a general sense of things, to recognize that although Domingo and Pavarotti may sing some of the same songs on television, and may perform some of the same roles in the opera house, there are many operatic parts that one sings and the other doesn't. Some of you can tell this quickly just by listening to their voices. Others of us have less-trained ears.

Finally: The record suggests that big-voiced tenors can make it with voice alone, even if their acting is second-rate, but that smaller-voiced tenors, like thirty-five-year-old fireball baseball pitchers or thirty-eight-year-old boxers, usually need to compensate with other skills: musical knowledge, control, finesse, dramatic intensity, tone color, taste, style, and all-around technique. In short, they need to be Tito Schipa.

Baritone

The baritone is the normal speaking voice for a man, as a mezzo-soprano is the average speaking voice for a woman. Baritones can be regarded as light or dramatic, but generally they don't seem put into classifications as well defined as tenors (even if those tenor classifications don't seem all that well defined). In most Italian operas the hero and heroine are sung by tenor and soprano, but in Verdi's operas a baritone usually has a strong part and in four—*Nabucco, Rigoletto, Simon Boccanegra,* and *Falstaff*—he is the lead. Other major baritone roles include:

Iago in Verdi's *Otello*
Scarpia in Puccini's *Tosca* (written for a high baritone)
Sheriff Jack Rance in Puccini's *Girl of the Golden West*
Renato in Verdi's *Masked Ball*
Rodrigo in Verdi's *Don Carlos*
Barnaba in Ponchielli's *La Gioconda*

Typical of a lighter lyric baritone of a type that Verdi favored especially is the senior Germont in *La traviata*, and a good example of an aria for this kind of baritone is Germont's "Di Provenza." Handel, Rossini, and Donizetti also have many light baritone roles. In the French repertory, a lightish baritone part is Pelléas in Debussy's *Pelléas et Mélisande*, a role light enough so that it is often sung by a tenor. In the same opera, Golaud (Pelléas's older brother) is a darker bass-baritone and old King Arkel is a bass.

Kings almost always are basses. You don't see many tenor kings.

The deepest baritone voices straddle the bass and baritone ranges. One example is the Wagnerian bass-baritone. Not many singers can handle these Wagner roles excellently, but if one can, his career is made. It isn't easy. One reason is that Wagner's orchestra is so dominant that it's difficult for a singer's voice to be heard, and another is that Wagner's operas are so long that the singer's voice tires. Act III of *Die Meistersinger* for example, is as long as all of Puccini's *La Bohème*. Hans Sachs in *Die Meistersinger*, a wonderful role, is too deep for a normal baritone but, the analysts say, doesn't sound right when a true bass tries to reach up to it. Other Wagner bass-baritones include Wotan and Alberich in *The Ring* and the Dutchman in *The Flying Dutchman*.

Mussorgsky's *Boris Godunov* is a special case—no headline news, inasmuch as almost everything in this chapter is a special case. It would seem that the big Russian Boris should be a big Russian bass with a big Russian bass voice. A bass-baritone voice, however, is said to be better suited for the role.

Puccini's most evil villain, Scarpia in *Tosca*, was written for a high baritone, but a versatile bass-baritone can handle it. Mozart's Don Giovanni, Wozzeck in Berg's *Wozzeck* and Porgy in Gershwin's *Porgy and Bess* also are usually sung by bass-baritones, although the official characterization of the three roles is "baritone."

Unwritten rule: When baritones turn to tenor parts they often turn to Otello, which is at the far deep end of the tenor repertory.

Two major baritones who span the last two thirds of the twentieth century are Lawrence Tibbett, who died in 1960, and Sherrill Milnes born in 1935. Other big baritone names, all Italian, from different time periods, are Titta Ruffo, Antonio Scotti, Giuseppe De Luca, Tito Gobbi, who died in 1984, and, Piero Cappuccilli, born in 1929.

Bass

Not all full-blooded basses are the equivalent of a tuba. That tuba kind of "black" (no relation to skin color) or "dark" bass—very deep, with great volume—is heard in Wagner's *Ring*—the giant Fafner in *Siegfried*, Fasolt in *Das Rheingold*, and Hagen in *Götterdämmerung*—and as the Grand Inquisitor in Verdi's *Don Carlos*.

Let's look at both Italian and German categories. First, the Italian, from high bass down:

Basso cantate (or singing bass)—light bass, with a pleasant style. Padre
   Guardiano, the abbot in *The Force of Destiny*.
Basso comico or basso buffo—Agile bass with a talent for comedy. Bartolo in
   The Marriage of Figaro.
Basso profundo—low range, powerful voice, solemn character. Ramfis, the
   High Priest in *Aida*.

The Germans use:

Hoher bass, Caspar, the evil huntsman in *Der Freischütz*
Bass buffo or komischer bass, Osmin, the overseer in Mozart's non-Collection
   Abduction from the Seraglio
Tiefer bass, Sarastro in Mozart's *Magic Flute*

Other examples of the (relatively) lightish "basso cantate" include Silva in Verdi's *Ernani*, King Philip in *Don Carlos* (a lighter tone than the deep, deep

Inquisitor in the same opera), King Henry in Wagner's *Lohengrin*, and the Landgrave in his *Tannhäuser*.

But don't forget to stay loose and avoid little compartments. Sometimes in *Don Carlos* the basses who have played King Philip and the Inquisitor in one production swap places for another production. This works if both men occupy middle bass ground.

Opera's most famous bass is Russia's Feodor Chaliapin (1873–1938), by near unanimous agreement *the* Boris Godunov from Mussorgsky's epic opera. A marvelous actor, his voice was so flexible that he also sang many baritone roles. Others with top international reputations include the six-foot-six Luigi Lablache and Karl Formes in the last century (1815–89); Edouard De Reszke and Pol Plançon, who straddle centuries, and Alexander Kipnis, Gottlob Frick and Boris Christoff in this century.

Frick is an example of what the music people call a large-voiced "black" bass. His roles included Hagen, Fafner, and Hunding from the *Ring* operas.

Castrato

If you were a young boy in Italy in the seventeenth and eighteenth centuries, and if you had a truly promising voice, and if you hadn't reached puberty, and if your parents wanted financial security, and if you yearned for fame and fortune, and if you were really lucky, you stood a chance of being castrated.

Some musicologists say the practice of castration for musical purposes originated in Spain, and the records show it was practiced a little in southern Germany, but basically it was an Italian thing that began long before opera. Most castratos were primarily singers in the Catholic church, although some also performed for the nobility. The custom began, in part, because in Italy women's voices were not allowed in the church and boys' voices changed shortly after they were trained for the higher parts. The apparently obvious solution was a good honorable castration.

The New Grove Dictionary of Opera reports that there is evidence to suggest that in the seventeenth century the practice was considered a contribution toward celibacy for those joining monastic orders. Even in the late eighteenth century castrations were carried out with only a hint of concealment, although by this time the procedure was less accepted.

Baroque opera can't be accurately reproduced today, castratos being relatively hard to find. Christoph Willibald Gluck, the great reformer, wrote the title role of *Orfeo ed Euridice* for a castrato but later, in his French-language revision, adapted it for tenor. Although that's one option, tenors generally can't sing the castrato repertoire unless it's transposed (rewritten at a different pitch). Baritones are sometimes chosen, although one of my mentors says that using baritones that way changes the clarion trumpet sound the composer intended into a murky trombone.

The most frequent solution is to use a mezzo-soprano or contralto in a so-called pants role or trouser role, and, indeed, most of the recordings of *Orfeo* do employ a mezzo. In one production of Handel's *Julius Caesar*, six mezzos were featured in a cast of seven, with only one of those roles having been written for a genuine female.

Another solution to the castrato problem has been the use of countertenors in the roles. Countertenors are intact males who have never felt the surgeon's knife and whose natural voices would be in the baritone range but who have specially developed their upper falsetto register (the one men talk in when they try to imitate a woman) until it has the resonance and power of a regular singing voice. Even so, the most stalwart of countertenors can't match the trumpet tones of the great castrati, so this solution works best in music where the orchestration is comparatively light, in small houses, or on recordings.

In a performance today of Monteverdi's *Coronation of Poppea*, it's a toss-up whether the leading role of Nerone is sung by a tenor, a countertenor, or a mezzo-soprano. Since this opera is about sex and includes a scene with a man and a woman in bed, the choice must be made between the two voices moving around each other at the same pitch, as Monteverdi wrote them, or the visual impact of who's in bed with whom.

ONE HUNDRED ARIAS BY VOICE CATEGORY

Another way to understand the voice types is to look at selected famous arias. I needed professional help beyond my own research for this and am especially indebted to Roger Brunyate, opera chieftain of the Peabody Conservatory in Baltimore. He chose the arias and provided the analysis, most of which remains in his own words, although I've fussed a little with the language and Anglicized some of the titles. All but five of the one hundred arias are from Collection operas. Three are from a non-Collection Mozart opera, *The Abduction from the Seraglio*, and two from the Twentieth-century European package.

These arias are arranged by voice type. Note that distinctions are sometimes made between the voice category of the aria and that of the role itself. Professor Brunyate has coded them as follows:

A Includes significant acting content
C Comic (buffo) aria
D Dramatically intense
E High-energy aria, mostly fast
H Heartbreak aria, with much pathos
M Melting marshmallow, guaranteed irresistible
S Simple, songlike, easy to absorb at first hearing
V Virtuoso displays
X Extended number with several sections

Sopranos

Divisions used are coloratura, soubrette, light lyric (not soubrette), full lyric, spinto, and dramatic.

Coloratura soprano

1. Marie in *The Daughter of the Regiment* (Donizetti): "Ah, Chacun le sait." Simple military march turned into a display piece. **S**

2. Olympia in *The Tales of Hoffmann* (Offenbach): "Les oiseaux dans la charmille." Song for a mechanical doll, virtuoso. **CV**

3. Lakmé in *Lakmé* (Delibes): "Où va la Jeune Hindoue?" The celebrated "Bell Song," very high, virtuoso. **V**

4. Oscar in *A Masked Ball* (Verdi): "Volta la terrea." Rare example of soprano (not mezzo) pants role, with coloratura. **S**

5. Lucia in *Lucia di Lammermoor* (Donizetti): "Regnava nel silenzio." Lyric coloratura, on the borders of dramatic, followed by a sparkling "Quando rapita in estasi." The Act III mad scene goes even further. **AX**

6. Konstanze in *The Abduction from the Seraglio* (Mozart): "Martern aller Arten." Dramatic coloratura—a supremely difficult aria. **EV**

7. Queen of the Night in *The Magic Flute* (Mozart): "O zittre nicht." Shows both the lyrical and dramatic sides of this larger-than-life character. Her second aria, "Der Hölle Rache," is even more dramatic. **AVX**

8. Norma in *Norma* (Bellini): "Casta diva." Although containing neither passion nor fireworks, the aria is the prime example of Bellini's long, long melodies, in a role sung only by the largest coloratura voices. **M**

9. Zerbinetta in *Ariadne auf Naxos* (Richard Strauss): "Grossmächtige Prinzessin." Zerbinetta's celebrated fifteen-minute aria, Mount Everest for coloraturas. **AVX**

Soubrette

10. Blonde in *The Abduction from the Seraglio* (Mozart): "Durch Zärtlichkeit und Schmeicheln." Tuneful, soubrette with a lot of coloratura. **CS**

11. Zerlina in *Don Giovanni* (Mozart): "Batti, batti, o bel Masetto." Zerlina seduces Masetto into accepting her apology. For added fun, note the solo cello in the orchestra. **AM**

12. Susanna in *The Marriage of Figaro* (Mozart): "Deh vieni, non tardar." Although Susanna is a soubrette role, this lovely aria is entirely lyric. **M**

13. Norina in *Don Pasquale* (Donizetti): "Quel guardo il cavaliere." Typical soubrette theme of cataloguing her feminine wiles, some coloratura. **CV**

14. Adèle in *Die Fledermaus* (Johann Strauss): "Mein Herr Marquis." The famous "Laughing Song," very tuneful. **ACS**

15. Musetta in *La Bohème* (Puccini): "Quando me'n vo' soletta." Musetta's famous waltz song as she languidly flaunts her sexuality. **AMS**

Light lyric soprano (not soubrette)

16. Pamina in *The Magic Flute* (Mozart): "Ach, ich fühl's." Heartbreaking aria in which Pamina reacts to Tamino's refusal to talk.　　**H**

17. Nannetta in *Falstaff* (Verdi): "Sul fil d'un soffio etesio." Nannetta's magically floating aria as Queen of the Fairies.　　**M**

18. Lauretta in *Gianni Schicchi* (Puccini): "O mio babbino caro." One of the simplest and most effective heart tugs in all opera.　　**HMS**

19. Gilda in *Rigoletto* (Verdi): "Caro nome." A coloratura aria in a non-coloratura role.　　**V**

20. Cleopatra in *Julius Caesar* (Handel): "V'adoro, pupille" or "Piangerò la sorte mia." "V'adoro" is seductively simple, "Piangerò" another heartbreaker, with a dramatic middle section.　　**SH**

21. Marguerite in *Faust* (Gounod): "Ah, je ris." Marguerite's song on seeing Faust's gift of jewels, another aria that is lighter than the role as a whole.　　**E**

Full lyric soprano

22. Countess in *The Marriage of Figaro* (Mozart): "Dove sono." Extended *scena* (a scene, longer and usually more dramatic than an aria) in which she comes to grips with her husband's neglect and decides to turn the situation around.　　**AHX**

23. Violetta in *La traviata* (Verdi): "Addio del passato." Coming to terms with her approaching death. (The Act I *scena*, "Ah, fors' è lui . . . Sempre libera" is, like Gilda's aria "Caro noma" in *Rigoletto*, a famous but atypical example of a coloratura aria in what is essentially a lyric role.)　　**H**

24. Micaëla in *Carmen* (Bizet): "Je dis que rien ne m'épouvante." Micaëla's prayer in the smugglers' lair, a perfect example of the "suffering-determination" mixture that is typical of lyric roles.　　**H**

25. Rosalinda in *Die Fledermaus* (Johann Strauss): "Klänge der Heimat." This is Rosalinda's mock-Hungarian czardas; compare the much lighter Adèle aria above.　　**ACX**

26. Nedda in *Pagliacci* (Leoncavallo): "Qual fiamma avea nel guardo." This is the *scena* culminating in the famous "Ballatella."　　**AX**

27. Mimi in *La Bohème* (Puccini): "Mi chiamano Mimí." Mimí's self-introduction. This is virtually the defining aria for the lyric voice.　　**M**

28. Manon in *Manon* (Massenet): "Adieu, nôtre petite table." Manon's farewell prior to leaving her true love, very simple and poignant.　　**HS**

29. Louise in *Louise* (Charpentier): "Depuis le jour." Sung as she basks in requited love.　　**M**

30. Anne Truelove in *The Rake's Progress* (Stravinsky): "No word from Tom." Anne's *scena* that ends Act I (and takes the experts back to the old cavatina-cabaletta convention of earlier operatic years. A cavatina is a short solo, simpler than the conventional aria and without the repetition; a cabaletta is the caboose that comes next, usually in more rapid tempo). From the Twentieth-century European Package.　　**EVX**

Spinto *soprano*

31. Léonore in *Fidelio* (Beethoven): "Abscheulicher!" Léonore's impassioned denunciation of the evil Pizarro, very demanding for the singer. **ADV**

32. Leonora in *Il trovatore* (Verdi): "Tacea la notte placida." Another cavatina-cabaletta combination, not dissimilar to Lucia's "Regnava nel silenzio" (see above) but requiring an even more dramatic voice. **X**

33. Aida in *Aida* (Verdi): "Ritorna vincitor!" Aida's *scena* that ends the opening scene, dramatic in its middle sections but ending with the ethereal prayer "Numi, pietà." **MX**

34. Santuzza in *Cavalleria rusticana* (Mascagni): "Voi lo sapete, o mamma." Santuzza's account of her betrayal by Turiddu. **AD**

35. Tosca in *Tosca* (Puccini): "Vissi d'arte." Tosca's query to God about why such terrible events have happened to her, deceptively simple but requiring great control. **DHS**

36. Butterfly in *Madama Butterfly* (Puccini): "Un bel dì vedremo." Butterfly's aria of belief that Pinkerton will return. A justifiably celebrated heartbreaker. **HM**

Dramatic *soprano*

37. Elsa in *Lohengrin* (Wagner): "Einsam in trüben Tagen." Elsa's dream. Requires power for the climax, but Elsa is more lyric than the later Wagner heroines. **X**

38. Ariadne in *Ariadne auf Naxos* (Richard Strauss): "Es gibt ein Reich." Ariadne's dream of the arrival of the god of death, Wagnerian but much more vocal. **M**

39. Salome in *Salome* (Richard Strauss): Final scene. Perverted, sensuous, and decadent—but irresistible music. **AMX**

40. Isolde in *Tristan und Isolde* (Wagner): "Mild und leise." Isolde's "Liebestod," summing up the emotion of the entire opera. **M**

41. Brünnhilde in *Götterdämmerung* (Wagner): "Starke Scheite." Brünnhilde's "Immolation Scene," the twenty-minute finale to the entire *Ring*. The singer first must pull together all the threads of the whole cycle and then back off and have the orchestra take over completely. **ADX**

Mezzo-Soprano

Divisions used are light lyric, lyric, and character and dramatic.

Light lyric mezzo

42. Rosina in *The Barber of Seville* (Rossini): "Una voce poco fa." Although sometimes sung by sopranos, the aria is typical of the coloratura mezzo voice-type that Rossini used for virtually all his heroines. **CEV**

43. Cherubino in *The Marriage of Figaro* (Mozart): "Voi che sapete." Song

sung by Cherubino, the prototype of the so-called pants roles or trouser roles, that are bread and butter for those mezzos with the figure for them. **S**

44. Dorabella in *Così fan tutte* (Mozart): "Ah, scostati . . . Smanie implacabili." A parody of opera seria. **CE**

45. Siébel in *Faust* (Gounod): "Faites-lui mes aveux." Another pants role, a lively and effective aria. **ES**

46. Orlovsky in *Die Fledermaus* (Johann Strauss): "Chacun à son goût." Still another pants role. Prince Orlovsky's party-invitation aria, generally sung with a Russian accent. **AS**

Lyric mezzo

47. Dido in *Dido and Aeneas* (Purcell): "When I am laid in earth." Dido's "Lament," sung over a regularly repeating bass line. Sometimes sung by sopranos. **H**

48. Orfeo in *Orfeo ed Euridice* (Gluck): "J'ai perdu mon Euridice" ("Che fàro senza Euridice"). Orfeo's celebrated lament at the second loss of Euridice. Another pants role but one requiring a more mature voice than most. **H**

49. Carmen in *Carmen* (Bizet): "L'amour est un oiseau rebelle." The famous Habanera, in which Carmen taunts Don José. **S**

50. Dalila in *Samson et Dalila* (Saint-Saëns): "Mon coeur s'ouvre à ta voix." The most sensuous of Dalila's three arias. **M**

51. Charlotte in *Werther* (Massenet): "Werther . . . Werther." Charlotte's "Letter Scene," in which she reads Werther's letters and gets the first premonition of his suicide. Lyric, with dramatic overtones. (Another aria, "Va, laisse couler mes larmes," later in the act, is shorter and even more poignant.) **AHX**

52. Composer in *Ariadne auf Naxos* (Richard Strauss): "Sein wir wieder gut!" Another pants role (based on Mozart himself and on Cherubino in *The Marriage of Figaro*) but one requiring power to carry the huge climax over the orchestra. Magnificently lyric and exuberant. **EM**

Character and dramatic mezzos

53. Witch in *Hänsel und Gretel* (Humperdinck): "Hurr, hopp, hopp, hopp!" The Witch's broomstick dance, anticipating her triumph. A character role, sometimes taken by a tenor. **CE**

54. Azucena in *Il trovatore* (Verdi): "Stride la vampa." Azucena's aria describing how she burned her own child. Her second aria, "Condotta ell'era in ceppi," is even more obviously dramatic, though less tuneful and less often found in excerpts on recordings. Verdi's mezzo-sopranos virtually own the dramatic mezzo territory. **ADES**

55. Erda in *Das Rheingold* (Wagner): "Weiche, Wotan, weiche." Included as an example of the rare dramatic contralto voice. **D**

Tenors

Divisions used are light lyric, lyric, spinto, and dramatic.

Light lyric tenor

56. Almaviva in *The Barber of Seville* (Rossini): "Ecco ridente in cielo." Almaviva's aubade: high, light, and graceful, typifying the coloratura agility required of Rossini tenors. **EV**

57. Tonio in *The Daughter of the Regiment* (Donizetti): "Ah, mes amis." Another light, agile role, noted for its nine high C's. **SV**

58. Don Ottavio in *Don Giovanni* (Mozart): "Il mio tesoro." Although by no means merely a coloratura role, Roger Brunyate advises that this aria requires immense breath control in the passagework. **V**

59. Tamino in *The Magic Flute* (Mozart): "Dies Bildnis ist bezaubernd schön." Truly a light lyric role, with almost no coloratura.

60. Nemorino in *The Elixir of Love* (Donizetti): "Una furtiva lagrima." A famous sentimental aria, showing no sign of the comedy of the role as a whole but included in nearly all highlight selections of the opera. **HS**

61. Fenton in *Falstaff* (Verdi): "Dall'labbro il canto." Fenton's tender arietta at the start of the last scene. This shows a hint of Puccini composition. **M**

62. Tom Rakewell in *The Rake's Progress* (Stravinsky): "Here I stand." This is another example of Stravinsky looking back to Handel in this twentieth-century opera. A particularly exciting climax. **E**

63. Frantz in *The Tales of Hoffmann* (Offenbach): "Jour et nuit." Included as an example of the many supporting roles for comic character tenors. **AC**

Lyric tenor

64. The Duke in *Rigoletto* (Verdi): "La donna è mobile." Verdi's most famous tenor aria, requiring a solid voice with a youthful swagger. **S**

65. Des Grieux in *Manon* (Massenet): "En fermant les yeux." The famous "Dream Aria," sung almost entirely softly, in half voice, or mezza voce. **M**

66. Rodolfo in *La Bohème* (Puccini): "Che gelida manina." Requires a youthful-looking singer with a fresh lyric voice. The high C sung by lyric tenors is not written in the score. **M**

67. Faust in *Faust* (Gounod): "Salut! demeure chaste et pure." A fine poetic aria, with a ringing high C. **C**

68. Cavaradossi in *Tosca* (Puccini): "Recondita armonia." Although this particular aria is lyrical, the role as a whole stretches the boundaries of the lyric category.

Spinto tenor

69. Manrico in *Il trovatore* (Verdi): "Di quella pira." Although short (technically a cabaletta) this is one of the most exciting of all arias. **DEV**

70. Radames in *Aida* (Verdi): "Celeste Aida." A short, popular aria at the start of a huge and demanding role.   **S**

71. Don José in *Carmen* (Bizet): "La fleur que tu m'avais jetée." The "Flower Song."   **M**

72. Canio in *Pagliacci* (Leoncavallo): "Vesti la giubba." Everyone has heard this. The clown's lament that he must laugh with grief in his heart.   **H**

73. Calaf in *Turandot* (Puccini): "Nessun dorma." A short and immensely effective declamatory aria.   **D**

Dramatic tenor

74. Florestan in *Fidelio* (Beethoven): "Gott! welch' Dunkel hier!" The big scene in the dungeon, long and difficult.   **DX**

75. Walther in *Die Meistersinger* (Wagner): "Morgenlich leuchtend." Walther's "Prize Song," which wins him the lady. Walther is perhaps the most lyrical of the major Wagner tenor roles.   **MS**

76. Siegmund in *Die Walküre* (Wagner): "Winterstürme wichen dem Wonnemond." A glorious tune, the most "lyrical" moment in what is generally a "heroic" role.   **MS**

77. Siegfried in *Götterdämmerung* (Wagner): "Mime hiess ein mürrischer Zwerg." Siegfried's long narration after he regains his memory, recalling the highlights of his life.   **AHX**

Baritones

Divisions used are lyric and dramatic.

Lyric baritone

78. Papageno in *The Magic Flute* (Mozart): "Der Vogelfänger bin ich ja." Papageno's entrance aria, in popular style. He accompanies himself on his panpipes.   **CS**

79. Don Giovanni in *Don Giovanni* (Mozart): "Finch'han dal vino." This is known as the "Champagne Aria," perhaps because of its fizz. Don Giovanni's Act II serenade, "Deh vieni alla finestra," shows a completely different side of him.   **E**

80. Figaro in *The Barber of Seville* (Rossini): "Largo al factotum." Figaro's high-energy entrance aria; vocally, he is everywhere at once.   **CEV**

81. Dr. Malatesta in *Don Pasquale* (Donizetti): "Bella siccome un angelo." Simple-sounding but difficult to sing.   **S**

82. The Count in *The Marriage of Figaro* (Mozart): "Hai gia vinta la causa." An intense aria of jealousy and frustration, though still for a lyric baritone voice.

83. Valentin in *Faust* (Gounod): "Avant de quitter ces lieux." Valentin's prayer for the safety of his sister; substantial lyric.   **H**

84. Fritz (Pierrot) in *Die Tote Stadt* (Korngold): "Mein Sehnen, mein Wähnen." From the Twentieth-century European Package, included here because of its nostalgic beauty. A real winner.   **HM**

Dramatic baritone

85. Count Di Luna in *Il trovatore* (Verdi): "Il balen del suo sorriso." One of the great baritone arias, a lyric oasis in a generally more dramatic role.   **S**

86. Renato in *A Masked Ball* (Verdi): "Eri tu." Renato's vengeance aria, showing both the dramatic and lyric sides of the characteristic Verdi baritone.   **D**

87. Tonio in *Pagliacci* (Leoncavallo): "Si può?" Tonio's prologue, sung in front of the stage curtain.   **AX**

Bass and Bass-Baritone

Divisions used are buffo bass, bass-baritone, and "Other bass arias."

Buffo bass

88. Osmin in *The Abduction from the Seraglio* (Mozart): "Ha, wie will ich triumphieren!" Osmin's aria of triumph, comically excessive and very difficult.   **CEV**

89. Leporello in *Don Giovanni* (Mozart): "Madamina, il catalogo è questo." Leporello's catalogue aria, first enumerating, then acting out his master's sexual conquests.   **AC**

90. Don Basilio in *The Barber of Seville* (Rossini): "La calunnia." Basilio's aria on the power of rumor, a perfect example of Rossini's use of crescendo. Rossini was known in his time as Signor Crescendo.   **ACV**

91. Dr. Dulcamara in *The Elixir of Love* (Donizetti): "Udite." The quack Dr. Dulcamara's sales pitch, full of typical buffo patter.   **CE**

Bass-baritone

92. Figaro in *The Marriage of Figaro* (Mozart): "Non più andrai." Figaro teasing Cherubino on his induction into the army.   **ACS**

93. Dapertutto in *The Tales of Hoffmann* (Offenbach): "Scintille diamant." A lyric moment for one of the opera's four villains.   **S**

94. Escamillo in *Carmen* (Bizet): "Votre toast." The "Toreador Song," famous from the overture and numerous parodies.   **ASX**

95. Wotan in *Die Walküre* (Wagner): "Leb wohl, du kühnes, herrliches Kind." Wotan's farewell to Brünnhilde and the "Magic Fire Music," the final twenty minutes of the opera, drawing all the strands into one in this second opera in the cycle. Brünnhilde does a similar thing at the end of the entire *Ring* (see No. 41 above).   **AMX**

Other Bass Arias

96. Sarastro in *The Magic Flute* (Mozart): "O Isis und Osiris." The high priest Sarastro's invocation; solemn, melodious, and low. George Bernard Shaw wrote that this music came from the mouth of God.   **S**

97. Count Rodolfo in *La sonnambula* (Bellini): "Vi ravviso, o luoghi ameni." An excellent example of a lyric aria for a basso cantante, or "singing bass."   **H**

98. King Philip in *Don Carlos* (Verdi): "Ella giammai m'amò." The king's *scena*, meditating on old age and his wife's alleged infidelity. **AHX**

99. Colline in *La Bohème* (Puccini): "Vecchia zimarra." Although a character role, Colline has this pathos-laden arietta (miniaria) before he sells his coat to buy medicine for Mimi. **H**

100. Hagen in *Götterdämmerung* (Wagner): "Hier sitz' ich zur Wacht." An example of Wagner's music for "black" bass villains. **DAX**

FAMOUS OPERA SINGERS

Female Singers

AGNES BALTSA (b. 1944). Greek mezzo-soprano who has sung in Europe and America. Powerful, dramatic voice.

KATHLEEN BATTLE (b. 1948). American soprano. Prima donna fired in 1994 by the Met for acting like a prima donna while preparing for the role of Marie in *The Daughter of the Regiment*. She came to the Met in 1977 and had 118 performances through 1985. Talk of her "lively temperament" turned out to be an understatement. Among her other roles were the "inas"—Rosina in *The Barber of Seville*, Zerlina in *Don Giovanni*, Despina in *Così fan tutte*, Adina in *The Elixir of Love*. The statement from Met general manager Joseph Volpe was terse: "Kathleen Battle's unprofessional actions during rehearsals for the revival of *La fille du régiment* were profoundly detrimental to the artistic collaboration among all the cast members, which is such an essential component of the rehearsal process. I could not allow the quality of the performance to be jeopardized."

HILDEGARD BEHRENS (b. 1937). German dramatic soprano who became known internationally after singing Léonore in Beethoven's *Fidelio* in 1975. Specialized in the dramatic soprano repertory, including Agathe in *Der Freischütz*, the Countess in *The Marriage of Figaro*, Elsa in *Lohengrin*, and the title role in *Salome*. One of opera's top acting singers. Her first Met performance was in 1976 and over the next several years she sang Donna Anna in *Don Giovanni*, Leonore, Elettra in Mozart's *Idomeneo*, Giorgetta in Puccini's *Il tabarro*, Tosca, Marie in Berg's *Wozzeck*, and several heavy Wagner roles including Isolde, Brünnhilde, and Sieglinde.

LUCREZIA BORI (1887–1960). Spanish lyric soprano. Debut in Rome in 1908 as Micaëla in *Carmen*, one of her best roles. Other favorite parts were Mimi in *La Bohème*, Manon in *Manon Lescaut* and Juliette in Gounod's *Roméo et Juliette*. Her Met career began in 1912 as Manon Lescaut. She suffered throat problems, returned to the Met in 1921 and remained there until 1936. Clear, modest-sized voice.

GRACE BUMBRY (b. 1937). American mezzo-soprano, then soprano, who spent eighteen seasons at the Met between 1965 and 1985. Among her roles: Santuzza in *Cavalleria rusticana*, Carmen, Eboli in *Don Carlos*, and Azucena in *Il trovatore*. Warm voice and strong stage presence.

MONTSERRAT CABALLE (b. 1933). Spanish lyric soprano, weak actress, known for her lovely soft high notes and versatility. Debut in Basel in 1956 as Mimi in *La Bohème*. Helped revive bel canto opera after winning an international reputation singing Donizetti's *Lucrezia Borgia* in New York in 1965. She began with Italian roles, including Tosca, and then reached out to some Wagner and much Richard Strauss. Later settled more on the Bellini-Donizetti repertory, but with a lighter voice than Joan Sutherland.

Early Callas

Maria Callas was a featured star of the opera in Athens but was unknown in the United States in 1945. After listening to her audition, the great tenor Giovanni Martinelli, who had been with the Met more than thirty years, told her: "You have a good voice, but you need many more lessons." Callas was crushed.

A little later she sang for Gaetano Merola, impresario of the San Francisco Opera.

"You are young, Maria," he told her. "Go and make your career in Italy and then I'll sign you up."

According to Arianna Stassinopoulos in her biography *Maria Callas*, Callas replied: "Thank you, but once I have made my career in Italy I will no longer need you."

MARIA CALLAS (1923–77). American soprano of Greek ancestry. The best-known—and most controversial—female opera singer of the second half of the century, perhaps the all-time best known to the general public, in part because of her offstage personal life. Musicologists say her range, technique, and style made her the first soprano since Lilli Lehmann to handle such different roles as Wagner's Isolde and Brünnhilde, Donizetti's Lucia, and Verdi's Violetta. Known for her dramatic intensity, diction, highly individual voice, and unusual personality. Arguably no soprano since Melba and Tetrazzini could trill as Callas did. Although Joan Sutherland (and later Beverly Sills, Marilyn Horne, Teresa Berganza, and Montserrat Caballé) were to follow, she was the primary mover in reviving the bel canto operas of Bellini, Donizetti, and Rossini. Bellini's Norma and Donizetti's Lucia had been perceived as vocal display roles; she changed them into true drama. Her career was short, peaking in the 1950s and early 1960s, although she continued to make recordings. When looking for Callas records, look for the earlier years.

EMMA CALVÉ (1858–1942). French dramatic soprano. Debut in Brussels in 1882. One of the great dramatic sopranos of the French repertory, and

Geraldine Farrar as Tosca

the best-known Carmen of her time. She was with the Manhattan Opera in 1907–09 and sang for 261 performances over six seasons at the Met, between 1893 and 1904. This included 137 Carmens. Impulsive stage personality.

MARIA CANIGLIA (1905–79). Italian soprano, Milan's leading lyric-dramatic soprano of the 1930s. Warm and human personality who sang most of Verdi's lyric-dramatic soprano roles.

ANGELICA CATALANI (1780–1849). Italian soprano. Mozart specialist, the great prima donna of the early nineteenth century, and one of opera history's highest-paid prima donnas. Beautiful woman with superb voice. Fine but sometimes uncontrolled acting.

FIORENZA COSSOTTO (b. 1935). Italian mezzo-soprano who sang chiefly in Milan but joined the Met for twelve seasons between 1968 and 1984. Among her roles there: Santuzza in *Cavalleria rusticana* and Azucena in *Il trovatore*. Forceful temperament for forceful roles.

RÉGINE CRESPIN (b. 1927). French soprano turned mezzo. Debut in Mulhouse, France, in 1950 as Elsa in *Lohengrin*. Better known for Wagnerian than French roles. Sang Kundry in Wagner's *Parsifal* at Bayreuth in the late 1950s and was a well-known Marschallin in *Der Rosenkavalier*. Elegance, eloquence, fine diction, and fine acting.

VICTORIA DE LOS ANGELES (b. 1923). Spanish soprano who formally retired from the opera stage in the late 1960s but returned occasionally and continued on the concert stage for many years. Met debut was as Marguerite in *Faust* in 1951. Sang Verdi, Puccini, Wagner, Massenet, Debussy— and more. Great personal and vocal charm.

EMMY DESTINN (1878–1930). Czech dramatic soprano, the main rival of Geraldine Farrar. Better actress than Farrar but with a less beautiful voice. She created Minnie at the Met's 1910 world premiere of *Girl of the Golden West*. Her best roles were the more dramatic Italian ones: Santuzza in *Cavalleria rusticana* and Madama Butterfly. One of the top sopranos of her time.

EMMA EAMES (1865–1952). An American beauty, a great lyric soprano, and a more versatile singer than her rival, Nellie Melba. Roles included Marguerite in *Faust*, Elsa in *Lohengrin*, and Micaëla in *Carmen*. Pure technique.

GERALDINE FARRAR (1882–1967). American soprano. Beautiful, enormously popular and one of America's most famous sopranos. The French and Italian repertory was her specialty. She sang the title role at the 1906 U.S. premiere of *Madama Butterfly* and was known especially as Tosca and Carmen. With the Met from 1906 until her 1922 retirement.

KIRSTEN FLAGSTAD (1895–1962). Norwegian-born but perhaps the most beautifully-toned Wagnerian soprano of opera history. *The* Wagnerian soprano from the mid-1930s to the early 1950s. Teamed often with Lauritz Melchior. Particularly famous for Sieglinde, the three Brünnhildes of the *Ring* cycle, and Kundry in *Parsifal*. She continued to record after retiring from live performances in 1954. Some call her the savior of the Metropolitan Opera house. After her first Met appearance, as Sieglinde, at age thirty-nine in 1935,

Amelita Galli-Curci as Gilda in Rigoletto

she gave 261 performances over nine seasons, until 1952. Headed Wagnerian casts with such stalwart Wagnerians as Melchior, Lotte Lehmann, Helen Traubel, and Elisabeth Rethberg. Other Wagnerian heroine voices are more dramatic, but none more beautiful.

OLIVE FREMSTAD (1871–1951). Swedish-born Wagnerian dramatic soprano and actress, reared in Minnesota. She sang the challenging title role of Richard Strauss's *Salome* at its New York premiere in 1907, after which it was withdrawn as morally indecent. Among famous roles: Brünnhilde and Sieglinde in *The Ring*, Isolde in *Tristan und Isolde*, and Kundry in *Parsifal*. She was at the Met for eleven straight seasons, singing soprano and mezzo roles.

MIRELLA FRENI (b. 1935). Italian lyric and then dramatic soprano, and a top Italian soprano voice in the century's second half. Fine actress with great personal charm. Debut in Modena, Italy, in 1955. She began by specializing in soubrette roles, especially Adina in *The Elixir of Love*, Susanna in *The Marriage of Figaro*, Zerlina in *Don Giovanni*, and Nannetta in *Falstaff*. When her voice thickened she moved to darker, more dramatic Italian soprano roles, including Elisabetta in *Don Carlos*, Desdemona in *Otello*, and the title roles in *Aida*, *Madama Butterfly*, and *Tosca*. Also sings Tatyana in Tchaikovsky's *Eugene Onegin*. Married to bass Nicolai Ghiaurov.

AMELITA GALLI-CURCI (1882–1963). Coloratura soprano, one of opera's most acrobatic, with a voice described as thin, agile, and sharp. Her finest roles were the leading coloratura ones, including Lucia in Donizetti's *Lucia di Lammermoor* and Elvira in Bellini's *I Puritani*. Known also for Gilda in *Rigoletto* and Violetta in *La traviata*. Her voice was more charming and graceful than intensely dramatic.

MARY GARDEN (1874–1967). Singing actress, Scottish-born American soprano, essentially lyric. Debut in Paris in 1900 in the title role of Charpentier's *Louise*. Voice small but acting magnificent. Specialized in the French repertory, including *Louise*, Massenet's *Manon* and *Thaïs*, and Debussy's *Pelléas et Mélisande*. Created Mélisande in 1902. She spent the 1921–22 season running the Chicago Opera, but lacked the managerial talents Beverly Sills was to show a half century later at the New York City Opera. After a disastrous season of overspending, she returned to singing for another decade. Her last U.S. operatic appearance was as Carmen in Cleveland in 1932. Never sang at the Met.

GIULIA GRISI (1811–69). Italian soprano. Created Bellini's Elvira in *I Puritani* and Norina in Donizetti's *Don Pasquale*. Versatile, rich voice that could handle lyric and dramatic roles, from the lighter Rossini and Donizetti to the heavier Verdi and Meyerbeer. Impressive actress.

FRIEDA HEMPEL (1885–1955). The great German soprano of her generation, although not for Wagner's *Ring* or *Parsifal*. The Marschallin in *Der Rosenkavalier* was her most famous role. Among other favorites: the Queen of the Night in *The Magic Flute*, Violetta in *La traviata*, and Eva in *Die Meistersinger*. During seven years at the Met she was regarded as the successor to the great Marcella Sembrich. Naturalized American.

MARILYN HORNE (b. 1934). Versatile American coloratura mezzo-soprano, the leading one after World War II. Her voice is both big and lovely, both high and low. She has sung such comedy roles as Rosina in *The Barber of Seville* and Isabella in *The Italian Girl in Algiers*, and such serious bel canto roles as Adalgisa in *Norma*. Teamed beautifully with soprano Joan Sutherland in *Norma*.

MARIA JERITZA (1887–1982). Czech dramatic soprano, later naturalized American. Beautiful, a fine actress, and the opera star of Vienna between the two wars. Strauss chose her to create the title role of *Ariadne auf Naxos*. Selected for the Vienna premieres of many Puccini and Strauss operas.

LILLI LEHMANN (1848–1929). German soprano, debuted in Prague in 1865. Another Wagnerian, but a diverse one, both a top German "heavyish" soprano and a lyric singer who enjoyed coloratura roles. She specialized in Isolde, Brünnhilde and Sieglinde in *The Ring*, Elisabeth in *Tannhäuser*, Elsa in *Lohengrin*, and Kundry in *Parsifal*. But she also sang Carmen (who didn't?) and Verdi's Violetta in *La traviata*.

LOTTE LEHMANN (1888–1976). German-born American and a leading Wagnerian and dramatic soprano between the wars. Wagnerian roles included Elsa in *Lohengrin*, Eva in *Die Meistersinger* and Sieglinde in *Die Walküre*. Also a famous Marschallin in *Der Rosenkavalier*. Lovely voice and strong personality. After World War II she continued as a German lied singer.

JENNY LIND (1820–87). Swedish soprano. Publicized by P. T. Barnum to become the most famous soprano of her generation. Debut in Sweden in 1838. Her specialty was German and Italian opera, including Alice in Meyerbeer's *Robert le Diable* and Bellini's Norma. The first singer whose name became a household word in the United States, thanks to her own gifts and the unabashed showmanship of Barnum, who made her the "Swedish Nightingale."

MARIA MALIBRAN (1808–36). Spanish mezzo-soprano with extraordinary range and flexibility. Fine actress. Concentrated on Rossini, Mozart, and Bellini's *Norma*. Her father was Manuel García, the Spanish tenor who was among the first to bring opera to America. Died young after a riding accident while she was pregnant.

EVA MARTON (b. 1943). Hungarian. Dramatic soprano (or mezzo-soprano) with a big powerful voice. Another fine actress in both German and Italian operas. Among German roles: Elsa and Ortrud in Wagner's *Lohengrin*, Sieglinde and Brünnhilde in *The Ring*, Elisabeth in *Tannhäuser*, and the Empress in Strauss's *Die Frau ohne Schatten*. Italian parts include the title roles in Puccini's *Turandot* and Ponchielli's *La Gioconda*. First Met appearance was in 1976 as Eva in Wagner's *Meistersinger*.

AMALIE MATERNA (1844–1918). Austrian. The first great Wagnerian soprano. Created Brünnhilde in *Siegfried* and *Götterdämmerung* and Kundry in *Parsifal*. A bright and powerful voice, ideal for Brünnhilde. The first Brünnhilde in America, at the Met in 1885. Her acting ability was not praised.

MARGARETE MATZENAUER (1881–1963). American contralto (technically), born in Hungary of German parents. Her voice was so wideranging that she sang mezzo-soprano and soprano roles. As a soprano she was known for Wagner's Brünnhilde, Kundry, and Isolde. Her mezzo roles included Ortrud in *Lohengrin* and Venus in *Tannhäuser*. Among Met performances: Ortrud, Brünnhilde in *Die Walküre*, Kundry in *Parsifal*, and Dalila in Saint-Saëns's *Samson et Dalila*.

NELLIE MELBA (1861–1931). Australian soprano of Scottish descent. Super superstar—*the* opera soprano after Adelina Patti. Large in size and weak in acting. A versatile lyric soprano, famous first in coloratura roles and later in heavier Wagner parts. Debut in Brussels in 1887 as Gilda in Verdi's *Rigoletto*. Other special roles: Lucia in *Lucia di Lammermoor*, Rosina in *The Barber of Seville*, Violetta in *La traviata*, Juliette in Gounod's *Roméo et Juliette*, and, particularly, Mimi in *La Bohème*. Later: Elsa in *Lohengrin* and the two big Italian dramatic soprano roles, Aida, and Desdemona in *Otello*. She and Emma Eames were bitter rivals, and she almost ruined her voice competing with Lillian Nordica as Brünnhilde in a single performance of *Siegfried*. She left the Met temporarily in 1906 to sing at Hammerstein's Manhattan Opera and later returned, but considered London's Covent Garden her operatic home. Sang until 1926, but her most famous years were in and around 1900. Peach Melba and Melba toast were named after her.

ZINKA MILANOV (1906–89). Croatian lyric-dramatic soprano who sang between the wars and immediately after World War II. Specialized in Italian dramatic soprano works, including Aida, the Leonoras in *The Force of Destiny* and *Il trovatore*, Ponchielli's *La Gioconda*, and Bellini's Norma. Sang more than 350 performances in Zagreb in the late twenties and early thirties. In 1937 she began an association with the Met that lasted nearly thirty years.

CLAUDIA MUZIO (1889–1936). Italian soprano. Best-known roles included Violetta in *La traviata*, Desdemona in *Otello*, and all other leading Verdi and Puccini heroines. A big repertory included Maddalena de Coigny, the heroine of Giordano's *Andrea Chénier*. Powerfully dramatic.

BIRGIT NILSSON (b. 1918). Swedish soprano. Often called the finest Wagnerian soprano of her day. She spent her early career with the Royal Opera in Stockholm, was associated with Bayreuth from 1954 to 1970, and sang both at Covent Garden and the Met. A distinguished Elektra and Turandot, but most famous in Wagner roles. Her voice was described as bright and powerful, with perfect intonation. Retired in 1984.

LILLIAN NORDICA (1857–1914). American soprano who dazzled the operatic world by singing Brünnhilde one night and Violetta in *La traviata* the next. A big woman physically, with an ultrapowerful voice, who excelled in florid singing. Among her roles: Elsa in *Lohengrin*, Aida, Leonora in *Il trovatore*, and Brünnhilde in *Die Walküre*. Tangled frequently with her main competition, Emma Eames and Nellie Melba.

JESSYE NORMAN (b. 1945). American lyric and dramatic soprano. Versatile, with powerful, beautiful, noble-sounding voice. Debut in Berlin in 1969 as Elisabeth in Wagner's *Tannhäuser*. Among her roles: Cassandra and Dido in Berlioz's *Les Troyens*, Verdi's Aida, the Countess in Mozart's *The Marriage of Figaro*, Wagner's Sieglinde in *Die Walküre*, and Ariadne in Strauss's *Ariadne auf Naxos*. Her debut at the Met was in 1983 as Cassandra. And she has sung Carmen. Studied at Howard University, the Peabody Conservatory in Baltimore, and the University of Michigan.

ELENA OBRAZTSOVA (b. 1939). Russian mezzo-soprano who sang in French, Italian and Russian opera. Among roles at the Met: Amneris in *Aida*,

Carmen, Adalgisa in *Norma*, Dalila in *Samson et Dalila*, and Charlotte in *Werther*. Fine actress with a particularly flexible voice.

MARIA OLCZEWSKA   (1892–1969). German mezzo-soprano, known for acting and singing. Began in operetta and sang through the 1920s and 1930s. In three Met seasons, from 1933 to 1935, she had fifty-seven performances, including nine as Brangäne in *Tristan und Isolde* and eight as Amneris in *Aida*.

SIGRID ONÉGIN   (1889–1943). Born in Sweden of French and German parents. A contralto with the upper extension of a mezzo. Extremely powerful voice. Among her most famous roles: Lady Macbeth in *Macbeth*, Eboli in *Don Carlos*, and Fricka in *The Ring*. Excellent in concerts. Some say her voice was the finest of its kind since Schumann-Heink.

GIUDITTA PASTA   (1798–1865). Italian soprano. Bellini wrote Norma and Amina in *La sonnambula* for her and Donizetti Anna Bolena. A nineteenth-century legendary diva, with Paris successes as Desdemona in Rossini's *Otello* and Donna Anna in *Don Giovanni*. Considered the greatest soprano in Europe before her voice wore out.

ADELINA PATTI   (1843–1919). Spanish lyric soprano, possibly opera history's greatest. After a strong London debut in 1861, she was the dominant female opera voice for the rest of the nineteenth century. Admirers said her pure, flexible voice was "flawless." The queen in a golden age of singers that included Nellie Melba, the De Reszke brothers, Emma Eames, Marcella Sembrich, Pol Plançon, Victor Maurel, Francesco Tamagno, and Christine Nilsson. Her last performance was at Covent Garden in 1903 as Violetta in *La traviata*.

LILY PONS   (1898–1976). American soprano of French birth. After singing in Europe, her Met debut was in 1931 as Lucia in *Lucia di Lammermoor*. She stayed at the Met for twenty-eight seasons, ending as Lucia in 1958. She also appeared in films. Very high coloratura voice.

Sing For Free

Rosa Ponselle discloses in her autobiography that she ended her nineteen-season career with the Metropolitan during the 1937–38 season because she wanted to sing *Adriana Lecouvreur*, an opera by Francesco Cilèa, when the Met management refused to revive it. Ponselle writes that she offered to sing the first twelve performances without receiving a salary, but management didn't budge.

ROSA PONSELLE   (1897–1981). American lyric-dramatic soprano. The leading Verdi soprano of the years between the wars, one of the top singers of this century, perhaps vocally the greatest dramatic soprano of all time and the most beautiful voice of the century. She sang at the Met for nineteen seasons after a debut with Enrico Caruso in 1918 as Leonora in *The Force of Destiny*. Other favorite Verdi roles included Violetta in *La traviata* and Aida. The Met revived Spontini's *La vestale*, Bellini's *Norma*, and Ponchielli's *La Gioconda* for her.

LEONTYNE PRICE (b. 1927). American lyric soprano and the first black soprano to win international attention. *The* Verdi soprano of the 1960s, 1970s, and into the 1980s. Among her greatest roles: the two Verdi Leonoras (*Il trovatore* and *The Force of Destiny*), Aida, and Amelia in *A Masked Ball*. Also famous for Puccini roles, including Liù in *Turandot* and Tosca. Her voice was vigorous, rich and beautiful; her acting suspect, but few cared. Her Met debut was in 1961 as Leonora in *Il trovatore* and her Met retirement in 1985 as Aida.

REGINA RESNIK (b. 1922). American dramatic soprano, later mezzo. Met debut in 1944 as Leonora in *Il trovatore* and she performed at the Met until 1974. She sang more than four hundred Carmens all over the world and performed as Dame Quickly in Verdi's *Falstaff* with a dozen of opera's great baritones. Nominated for a Tony for *Cabaret*. An intelligent singing actress.

ELISABETH RETHBERG (1894–1976). German (later American) lyric-dramatic soprano who sang both the German and Italian repertory. Among major roles: Desdemona in *Otello*, Sieglinde in *Die Walküre*, Elsa in *Lohengrin*, and Elisabeth in *Tannhäuser*. Most of her career was between the two World Wars. She has been called both the "greatest living soprano" and "the most perfect of women singers." Leading Met soprano for twenty-one consecutive years, beginning with *Aida* in 1922.

Rysanek's Swan Song

Leonie Rysanek returned to the Met at age sixty-nine in January 1996 to make her last U.S. operatic appearance. She was cast as the Countess in Tchaikovsky's *Queen of Spades* and received a twenty-three-minute standing-and-shouting good-bye ovation.

LEONIE RYSANEK (b. 1926). Austrian dramatic soprano. Splendid actress who specialized in dramatic soprano roles, particularly in German opera. Her rich voice and fiery onstage temperament were just right for such Strauss roles as Ariadne in *Ariadne auf Naxos*, Salome, the Marschallin in *Der Rosenkavalier*, and the Empress in *Die Frau ohne Schatten*. Among her Wagnerian roles: Senta in *The Flying Dutchman*, Sieglinde in *Die Walküre*, Elsa in *Lohengrin* and Elisabeth in *Tannhäuser*. Versatile enough to reach out to Kundry in *Parsifal*, more often a mezzo-soprano role. Her Met debut was not until 1959,

Ernestine Schumann-Heink as Ortrud in Lohengrin

when she replaced Maria Callas in the dramatic role of Verdi's Lady Macbeth. She had a long career at the Met and also sang in Munich, Vienna, London, and San Francisco. In 1988 she went back to the Met for Ortrud in *Lohengrin*, and in 1996, at age sixty-nine, gave her last performance there as the Countess in Tchaikovsky's *Queen of Spades*.

ERNESTINE SCHUMANN-HEINK   (1861–1936). Austrian contralto superstar and mezzo-soprano who became an American citizen. For the first third of this century she was opera's top singer in her range. Known as the last of the great contraltos. Among her leading roles: Azucena in *Il trovatore* and Erda, Fricka, and Waltraute in *The Ring*. She also created Klytemnestra in *Elektra*. Centered on Wagner, but had a repertory of 150 roles, and sang on Broadway.

ELISABETH SCHWARZKOPF   (b. 1915). German soprano and the leading Mozart and Strauss opera singer of her time, most famous as the Marschallin in *Der Rosenkavalier*. She began as a coloratura, singing such roles as Zerbinetta in *Ariadne auf Naxos*, but later undertook lyric soprano parts in Strauss and Mozart operas, including the Countess in *The Marriage of Figaro* and Donna Elvira in *Don Giovanni*. The top female lied singer of her time. Retired from the stage in 1972.

Schwarzkopf on Innovative Productions

The great soprano Elisabeth Schwarzkopf, an autocratic perfectionist, turned eighty in December 1995. There has been no more famous Marschallin for Richard Strauss's *Der Rosenkavalier*. In a birthday interview she expressed her dislike of "conceptual" opera productions.

"What does innovation have to do with Beethoven or Mozart," she said. "Or even Richard Strauss, for that matter."

RENATA SCOTTO   (b. 1934). Italian lyric coloratura soprano. Debut at La Scala in Milan in 1954 as Violetta in *La traviata*. Like Callas, her fame came more from her acting and ability to pull maximum drama from her roles rather than the sheer beauty of her voice, agile and powerful though that voice was. A 1976 triumph at the Met singing Cio-Cio-San in *Madama Butterfly*. Among others of her great roles: the leads in *Tosca*, *Lucia di Lammermoor*, *La Bohème*, and *Don Carlos*. Sang at London's Covent Garden from 1962 to 1971 and at the Met between 1965 and 1987.

MARCELLA SEMBRICH   (1858–1935). Polish lyric coloratura soprano, one of the great coloratura singers at the turn of the century. Naturalized American. Debut in Athens in 1877 as Elvira in Bellini's *I Puritani*. Among her coloratura roles: Lucia in *Lucia di Lammermoor* (on the Met's second night in 1883), Marguerite de Valois in Meyerbeer's *Les Huguenots*, and Rosina in *The*

Barber of Seville. After retiring in 1909 she taught voice in New York City. One of the dozens of great singers whose careers soared after joining the Met.

BEVERLY SILLS (b. 1929). Brooklyn-born American coloratura soprano and opera general director. After years of little attention, she became famous overnight in 1966 when she sang Cleopatra in Handel's *Julius Caesar* at the New York City Opera. She combined a fine voice with some of the best acting on the operatic stage, outstanding dramatic diction, a wonderful vocal technique, and a superb stage personality. Few singers in history established a warmer relationship with the audience. Among her best-known roles: Lucia in *Lucia di Lammermoor*, the three Queens in Donizetti operas set in Tudor England—*Roberto Devereux*, *Maria Stuarda*, and *Anna Bolena*, the title roles in Massenet's *Manon* and *Thaïs*, and all three soprano roles in *Tales of Hoffmann*. Many television appearances as head of the New York City Opera and as a general representative of opera in America. Despite international fame, her Met career came late: debut in 1975 as Palmira in Rossini's *Siege of Corinth*. In 1980 she was awarded the Presidential Medal of Freedom. Most important, a first-class human being.

GIULIETTA SIMIONATO (b. 1910). Italian mezzo-soprano. Agile coloratura mezzo who also sang such dramatic roles as Amneris in *Aida* and Azucena in *Il trovatore*. Four Met seasons, between 1959 and 1965. Retired in 1966. Outstanding stage presence for comedy and tragedy.

JOAN SUTHERLAND (b. 1926). Australian lyric-dramatic coloratura soprano. One of the great sopranos of her time, with a beautiful voice of wide range, brilliant tone, and awesome power. Still referred to as La Stupenda. Began as a dramatic soprano but shifted to a lyric coloratura. Her agility was characterized as "almost unprecedented" for such a powerful voice. International success came at London's Covent Garden in 1959 as Lucia in *Lucia di Lammermoor*, also her 1961 Met debut role. She was a famous Norma, effective especially when teamed with Marilyn Horne as Adalgisa, and she became Callas's big rival as a bel canto stylist. Among other famous bel canto revivals: Rossini's *Semiramide* and Donizetti's *Daughter of the Regiment* and *Anna Bolena*. Also helped revive Handel's *Alcina* and *Rodelinda*. Her final operatic performance was in Sydney in 1990 as Marguerite de Valois in Meyerbeer's *Les Huguenots*.

RENATA TEBALDI (b. 1922). Italian lyric-dramatic soprano. Twelve years older than the other Renata (Scotto), Tebaldi sang from the mid-1940s to the early 1970s. Her voice has been characterized as one of the most beautiful Italian voices of the century but her acting was not strong. She and Callas were rivals, although as a lyric-spinto soprano she sang almost none of the coloratura roles that Callas did. Among her favorite heroines: Mimi in *La Bohème*, *Madama Butterfly*, *Tosca*, Elisabetta in *Don Carlos* and Aida. She joined the Met in 1955, and was there for seventeen seasons.

KIRI TE KANAWA (b. 1944). Creamy-voiced New Zealand lyric soprano who first went to London's Covent Garden in 1970. Among her major roles there: the Countess in *The Marriage of Figaro*, Desdemona in *Otello*, Amelia in *Simon Boccanegra*, Marguerite in *Faust*, Micaëla in *Carmen*, and

Fiordiligi in *Così fan tutte*. She came to the Met in 1974 and has been featured there as Fiordiligi, Violetta in *La traviata*, the *Figaro* Countess and Donna Elvira in *Don Giovanni*. Mellow and warm voice. She has sung everywhere.

A Rose Opens

Kiri Te Kanawa, New Zealand soprano, began her career at the Metropolitan in 1974 in a broadcast of *Otello*. *Opera News* noted that only a few in the audience had heard of her when she was called in with only three hours' notice to sing Desdemona opposite Jon Vickers and Thomas Stewart. *The New York Times* described her voice as one that could "open like a luscious rose."

LUISA TETRAZZINI (1871–1940). Italian coloratura soprano, one of the most famous of all. Her career was from 1890 to 1934. She stuck close to the acrobatic roodle-doodle repertory, was a physically large woman who didn't concern herself too much with acting, and had the voice to get away with it. The main rival for a time of Queen Nellie Melba. Among her best-known roles: Lucia in *Lucia di Lammermoor*, Violetta in *La traviata*, Rosina in *The Barber of Seville*, Norina in *Don Pasquale*, and Adina in *The Elixir of Love*—three of the "ina" roles. Sang in New York with the Manhattan Opera from 1908 to 1910 and at the Met in 1911–12. Technically superb. Chicken Tetrazzini was named after her.

EVA TURNER (1892–1990). English dramatic soprano. Very pure and very powerful voice. Considered by some as England's all-time "perfect" Turandot. Famous also for the dramatic soprano roles in Wagner and Verdi.

SHIRLEY VERRETT (b. 1931). American mezzo-soprano, later soprano. Fine physical presence. Wide range. Met debut in 1968 and longtime member of the Met company. Among her most frequent Met roles: Tosca, Cassandre in Berlioz's *Les Troyens*, Azucena in *Il trovatore*, Eboli in *Don Carlos*, and Lidoine in Poulenc's *Dialogues des Carmélites*.

PAULINE VIARDOT-GARCÍA (1821–1910). French mezzo-soprano of Spanish origin. Daughter of Manuel García and sister of Maria Malibran. She was born in Paris and most of her roles were in French operas, including Euridice in a revival of Gluck's *Orfeo ed Euridice* and his *Alceste*. Known especially for big dramatic parts. She also taught music and composed operettas.

FREDERICA VON STADE (b. 1945). American mezzo-soprano. Attractive woman with a very clear voice. Her Met debut was in 1970. Among Met roles: Rosina in *The Barber of Seville*, Siébel in *Faust*, Zerlina in *Don Giovanni*, Cherubino in *The Marriage of Figaro* and Mélisande in Debussy's *Pelleas et Mélisande*. A high mezzo-soprano voice, gracious charm, and fine dramatic talent.

EDYTH WALKER   (1867–1950). American mezzo-soprano who sang chiefly in Europe, specializing in German opera. Debuted at the Met in 1903 as Amneris in *Aida* and was a member of the Met until 1906. Among roles there: Ortrud in *Lohengrin* and Kundy in *Parsifal*. She retired in 1918 after several seasons in the Munich festivals.

LJUBA WELITSCH   (b. 1913). Austrian soprano born in Bulgaria. Salome was her most famous role. Among others: Tosca, Aida, and Musetta in *La Bohème*. Highly temperamental and dramatic with one of the most interesting voices of the immediate post-World War II years.

GERTRUD WETTERGREN   (b. 1897). Swedish contralto, one of the leading singers of her country in the 1920s and 1930s. Among her roles: Amneris in *Aida*, Carmen, Dalila in *Samson et Dalila*, Venus in *Tannhäuser*, and Brangäne in *Tristan und Isolde*. One of the few true contralto voices. Strong personality.

A Twentieth-century Hall of Fame
Female Singers

Maria Callas—The century's greatest singing actress
Geraldine Farrar—Public favorite and beautiful singing actress
Kirsten Flagstad—The Wagnerian heroine of the century
Marilyn Horne—A leading American mezzo-soprano
Lotte Lehmann—*The* singing/acting Strauss Marschallin soprano
Nellie Melba—Spanned the centuries as the Soprano Queen
Birgit Nilsson—Heiress to Flagstad as the top Wagnerian soprano
Lily Pons—The century's glass-breaking high coloratura
Rosa Ponselle—One of opera's greatest dramatic sopranos
Leontyne Price—Met mainstay and outstanding spinto soprano
Ernestine Schumann-Heink—The legendary contralto
Beverly Sills—Renowned soprano and administrator, Presidential Medal of Freedom winner, and leading opera spokesperson
Joan Sutherland—A major rescuer of the Italian opera repertory
Renata Tebaldi—One of the century's most beautiful Italian voices
Luisa Tetrazzini—Bridged the centuries as major coloratura soprano

---

Male

Castrati

Most of the best-known singers of the seventeenth and eighteenth centuries were castrati. These included Antonio Bernacchi, Caffarelli, Giovanni Carestini, occasionally referred to as Cusanino, and Carlo Broschi, better known as Farinelli, the biggest name of them all. Also Baldassare Ferri, Gaetano Guadagni, and Gasparo Pacchiarotti, one of the last of the truly great.

Tenors, Baritones, and Basses

CARLO BERGONZI (b. 1924). Italian tenor, briefly a baritone in his early years. Known for his beautiful voice and elegant singing. After performing in Italy and London, he joined the Met in 1956 and was there for twenty-three seasons through 1981. Among frequent roles: fifty-seven as Radames in *Aida*, thirty-three as Riccardo in *A Masked Ball*, and twenty-nine as Canio in *Pagliacci*.

JUSSI BJOERLING (1911–60). Superstar. Magnificent lyric-dramatic Swedish tenor who sang mostly the Italian and French repertory. Recognized around the world for his outstanding voice, technique, personality, and thoughtful, talented work. A glorious member of the Met company from 1938 to 1959, except for the war years. Among his Met roles: Manrico in *Il trovatore*, Cavaradossi in *Tosca*, and Rodolfo in *La Bohème*.

JOSÉ CARRERAS (b. 1946). Spanish lyric tenor. His American debut was in 1972, and he later sang at London's Covent Garden, at the Met, and in many other leading opera houses. In 1987, at the peak of his career, he became ill with leukemia. After extensive treatment, he returned to operatic roles and appearances for charity. Before his illness he had one of the most naturally beautiful tenor voices of the time and was one of the most popular lyric tenors. Most recently known for the international "Three Tenor" telecasts made with Plácido Domingo and Luciano Pavarotti. His most frequent role while at the Met for seven seasons, beginning in 1974, was Rodolfo in *La Bohème*.

ENRICO CARUSO (1873–1921). Italian tenor. The most famous and colorful tenor in history and the richest of his time. No one ever has approached him in worldwide fame, postwar television notwithstanding. The first male to challenge sopranos for popularity, both with operagoers and the general public. He fits on the lyrical rungs of the tenor ladder for the earlier part of his career and on the dramatic/heroic rungs later—but never on the far Wagner edge. Of some sixty operas in his repertory he sang more than half at the Met between 1903 and 1920. His recordings did much to bring opera to the Unwashed of his day—and of later days.

FEODOR CHALIAPIN (1873–1938). Born the same year as Caruso. The best-known Russian bass of his time—and probably of any time. Most famous for the title role in Mussorgsky's *Boris Godunov* but also for Méphistophélès in Gounod's *Faust* and in Boito's *Mefistofele*. A fine actor with a voice so flexible that he also could fill baritone roles. Films and many recordings.

FRANCO CORELLI (b. 1923). Italian spinto or dramatic tenor, especially known as Manrico in *Il trovatore*, Ernani, Radames in *Aida*, Calaf in *Turandot* and other parts in the Italian spinto tenor repertory. Fifteen seasons and 365 performances at the Met, between 1961 and 1975. Excellent stage presence.

Enrico Caruso as Enzo in La Gioconda

MARIO DEL MONACO (1915–1982). Italian dramatic tenor, with a very powerful voice. A leading dramatic tenor for Italian operas in the 1940s and 1950s, most famous for *Otello*. Other roles included Don José in *Carmen*, Canio in *Pagliacci*, and Samson in *Samson et Dalila*. A top Met star through the 1950s.

GIUSEPPE DE LUCA (1876–1950). Italian lighter baritone, one of the top bel canto singers of the twentieth century but also at home with Verdi, Puccini, and other composers. A long Met career began in 1915 and ended in 1946. He slowly took on all the leading baritone roles in the Met's Italian opera.

EDOUARD DE RESZKE (1853–1917). Polish bass, brother of tenor Jean, and a man of huge voice and stature. Ideal for many Wagnerian roles. Retired in 1903 after stellar twenty-seven-year career.

JEAN DE RESZKE (1850–1925). Polish tenor who began life as a baritone. Edouard's brother. Jean sang the Don in *Don Giovanni* before shifting to tenor. A famous Faust in Gounod's opera before moving down to heldentenor/heroic roles: Wagner's Lohengrin, Tristan, and Siegfried, and Walther in *Die Meistersinger*. In seven Met seasons, he performed seventy-one times as Faust, fifty-four as Lohengrin, and forty-three as Raoul in *Les Huguenots*. Handsome man with a beautiful, flexible voice.

PLÁCIDO DOMINGO (b. 1941). Spanish tenor superstar. Opera's leading lyric-dramatic tenor since the death of Jussi Bjoerling, with a more robust voice than Pavarotti's. Early in his career he sang three hundred performances of twelve operas with the Hebrew National Opera, most of them in Hebrew. Most opera singers learn fifteen to twenty roles; he has learned more than eighty to become history's busiest singer. Lacks the on (and off) stage personality of Caruso and Pavarotti. His Metropolitan debut was in 1966, as Turiddu in *Cavalleria rusticana*. Among his most frequent roles: Cavaradossi in *Tosca*, Manrico in *Il trovatore*, Hoffmann in *The Tales of Hoffmann*, and Don José in *Carmen*. But he has sung many others, most of them in Italian opera, a few in French works, and several in German, including Wagner's Lohengrin, Parsifal, and Siegmund. Astonishing versatility proven in singing Hoffmann, Lohengrin, and Otello. Many consider him history's finest Otello. Named artistic director of the Washington Opera in 1995.

GERAINT EVANS (b. 1922) Welsh lyric baritone. A leading British baritone of his time before retiring in 1984. His voice was warm and trained, although not large, and his acting exceptional. Known especially, but not exclusively, for comic roles, including Beckmesser in *Die Meistersinger* and Papageno in *The Magic Flute*. Other favorites included Falstaff and Balstrode in *Peter Grimes*.

DIETRICH FISCHER-DIESKAU (b. 1925). German baritone. One of the century's finest singers, at home in opera and acclaimed around the world for German lieder. His career has centered in Berlin. Featured often as Hans Sachs in *Die Meistersinger*. Sings many Italian roles, from Falstaff to Rigoletto, but is most at home in German opera.

GAETANO FRASCHINI (1816–87). Italian tenor and fine actor, greatly admired by Verdi. Created the roles in several Verdi operas, including *A Masked Ball*. The opera house Teatro Fraschini in Pavia is named after him.

MANUEL GARCÍA (1775–1832). Spanish tenor, composer, and singing teacher. Founder of an opera company that in 1826 gave the first performance in America of *Don Giovanni*. The cast included him, his wife, a son, and a daughter. Four of his children became singers. Central figure in opera's history.

NICOLAI GEDDA (b. 1925). Swedish tenor, perhaps the leading tenor of French opera in the 1960s, 1970s, and beyond. An accomplished linguist who sang in seven languages, and a cultured artist. His Met career began in 1957 when he sang Faust in Gounod's opera. In 1958 created the role of Anatol in Barber's *Vanessa*. In twenty-four Met seasons, other frequent roles included Don José in *Carmen*, Hoffmann in *The Tales of Hoffmann*, Don Ottavio in *Don Giovanni*, and Lensky in *Eugene Onegin*.

NICOLAI GHIAUROV (b. 1929). Bulgarian bass, one of the best since Pinza for his type of bass voice. Known as Méphistophélés in Gounod's *Faust* and in Verdi operas, particularly as Philip II in *Don Carlos*. Critics' analysis: rich voice, confident technique, emotional interpretations and sound characterization. Married to soprano Mirella Freni.

BENIAMINO GIGLI (1890–1957). Superstar Italian tenor who specialized in the central lyric tenor parts: *La Bohème*, *La Gioconda*, *Andrea Chénier*, *Mefistofele*. By the 1920s the heir to Caruso for lyric roles at the Met, where he was the principal tenor throughout the 1920s. He left the Met in 1932 in protest against salary cuts. After performing brilliantly through the 1930s in Italy, elsewhere in Europe and in South America, he returned to the Met in 1938–39.

TITO GOBBI (1913–84). Italian baritone. Another superb superstar. One of the great Italian baritones of the twentieth century, magnificent in both comic and tragic roles. Excellent voice and excellent acting. His repertory ran to some one hundred operas, and he made many films. Among his favorite roles: Falstaff, Rigoletto, Iago in *Otello*, and Scarpia in *Tosca*.

HANS HOTTER (b. 1909). German bass-baritone. A top Wagnerian singer and the Wotan in the *Ring* cycle at Bayreuth after World War II. Other roles included the Grand Inquisitor in *Don Carlos*, Orestes in *Elektra*, the Dutchman in *The Flying Dutchman*, Pogner in *Die Meistersinger*, Amfortas in *Parsifal*, and Jokanaan in *Salome*. His last major operatic role was in 1972, but he still was singing on stage twenty years later.

ALEXANDER KIPNIS (1891–1978). Russian bass who left Germany for the United States in the 1930s and became an American citizen. Known for Russian, Italian, and German opera. Sang at the Met from 1940 to 1946. Refined and flexible voice.

ALFREDO KRAUS (b. 1927). Spanish tenor of Austrian descent. Highly respected tenore di grazia. Warm voice. Debut at Met in 1966 as the Duke in *Rigoletto*. Considered the best light lyric tenor of his generation. Handsome man with elegant presence on the stage. Still performing at the Met.

Among many frequent roles: Ernesto in *Don Pasquale*, Tonio in *The Daughter of the Regiment*, Des Grieux in Massenet's *Manon*, Werther, and Hoffmann in *The Tales of Hoffmann*.

GIACOMO LAURI-VOLPI (1892–1979). Italian tenor, one of the most applauded lyric-dramatic tenors of his day. At the Met between 1923 and 1933. Roles included: the Duke in *Rigoletto*, Alfredo in *La traviata*, Calaf in *Turandot*, and Radames in *Aida*. He sang in public until the late 1950s.

CORNELL MACNEIL (b. 1922). American baritone. A mainstay baritone at the Met and a favorite there for more than twenty-five years beginning in 1959. Among more than six hundred Met performances: Seventy-three as Scarpia in *Tosca*, sixty-three as Amonasro in *Aida*, sixty-two as Tonio in *Pagliacci*, and thirty as Alfio in *Cavalleria rusticana*. Tonio and Alfio came after a career centering on Verdi. His last Met role was in 1987.

GIOVANNI MARTINELLI (1885–1969). Italian tenor superstar. Thirty-one consecutive seasons at the Met, beginning in 1913, with scattered performances even later. *The Caruso successor for dramatic and heroic tenor roles*, including Manrico in *Il trovatore*, Radames in *Aida*, and Otello. Enormously popular with operagoers in the United States and Europe, and acclaimed by critics. Sensitive perfectionist.

VICTOR MAUREL (1848–1923). French baritone, outstanding singing actor, and author of books on singing. He performed at the New York Academy of Music in 1873 and at the Met in 1894–96 and 1898–99. In 1893, the first Falstaff in Verdi's opera. Dramatic interpretations of his characters.

JOHN McCORMACK (1884–1945). Irish tenor. Spectacular voice. Gave up opera in midcareer in part because of weak acting. Sang with the Boston, Manhattan, and Philadelphia–Chicago opera companies (Philadelphia and Chicago had a joint venture, organized by Oscar Hammerstein I), and with the Met in 1910, 1917, and 1918. Among his Met roles: Rodolfo in *La Bohème*, Pinkerton in *Madama Butterfly*, Cavaradossi in *Tosca*, and Alfredo in *La traviata*. Became an American citizen in 1919.

LAURITZ MELCHIOR (1890–1973). Danish tenor, the Great Dane, the greatest Wagnerian tenor of this century—and possibly of all time—and the singing partner of Kirsten Flagstad. Melchior and Flagstad were the biggest team in American opera after Caruso and Farrar. Melchior sang at the Royal Opera in Copenhagen beginning in 1913, first as a baritone. One of the Met's all-time top attractions from 1926 to 1950. Among his roles there: Siegfried in the *Ring* operas, Lohengrin, Parsifal, Tannhäuser, and Tristan. Became an American citizen in 1947.

ROBERT MERRILL (b. 1917). American baritone. He made his Met debut in 1945, as Germont in *La traviata*, was fired by general manager Rudolf Bing in 1951, and returned to be featured through 1984 for a total of thirty-two Met seasons. Among his most frequent roles: Germont in *La traviata*, Rigoletto, Renato in *A Masked Ball*, and Figaro in *The Barber of Seville*. Respected more for fine singing than dramatic acting.

A Twentieth-century Hall of Fame
Male Singers

Jussi Bjoerling—The greatest lyric tenor of his generation
Enrico Caruso—The century's most beautiful tenor voice
Feodor Chaliapin—A colossal bass of incredible talent
Plácido Domingo—The top lyrical-dramatic tenor
Nicolai Gedda—Outstanding, beautifully toned, linguist tenor
Beniamino Gigli—Heir to Caruso as lyrical romantic tenor
Tito Gobbi—A top Italian baritone of the century
Hans Hotter—The renowned Wagner baritone
Giovanni Martinelli—Heir to Caruso as heroic dramatic tenor
Lauritz Melchior—The century's greatest heldentenor
Ezio Pinza—The best-known bass, from stage and screen
Luciano Pavarotti—The most famous tenor since Caruso
Tito Schipa—A gracious and elegant tenore di grazia
Lawrence Tibbett—The quintessential American baritone

SHERRILL MILNES (b. 1935). American baritone, one of the best after World War II. Specialized in Italian opera, especially Verdi. Regarded as Leonard Warren's successor as a Verdi baritone at the Metropolitan, although his voice was somewhat thinner. At the Met for more than thirty seasons, beginning in 1965. Among the most frequent of twenty-odd Met roles: Iago in *Otello*, Don Giovanni, and Tonio in *Pagliacci*. At his peak, mentioned with Tibbett, Warren, and Merrill.

JAMES MORRIS (b. 1947). American bass-baritone who specialized for years in lyric Italian roles, including Banquo in *Macbeth*, sang at his British debut at Glyndebourne. Often sings Wotan in the *Ring* cycle but doesn't consider himself a "Wagner singer." Debut at the Met in 1971 as the King in *Aida*. Striking presence to accompany a striking voice.

TANCREDI PASERO (1893–1983). Italian bass, the leading bass at La Scala in Milan for twenty-five years before, during, and after World War II. Sang Italian, French, German, and Russian roles, including those in Verdi operas, Boris in *Boris Godunov*, and Mefistofele in Boito's *Mefistofele*. Warm and wide-ranging voice rather than a spectacularly beautiful one.

LUCIANO PAVAROTTI (b. 1935). Italian tenor. Ah, Pavarotti. *The* showman of late-twentieth-century opera, probably surpassing Maria Callas (because of longevity and television) as *the* opera show person. Many analysts say he has provided the most beautiful lyric sound since Beniamino Gigli. He made his debut at La Scala in 1965, San Francisco in 1967, and the Met in 1968. Aside from Pavarotti and Domingo (and Carreras because of the "Three

Tenors" television productions), most major singers today are anonymous outside the opera world. An interesting minipart of Pavarotti's fame comes from the way he could handle the nine high C's in the second act of *The Daughter of the Regiment*. Some analysts say he could have made the same beautiful sounds for years if he had stuck to the true lyric roles as Tito Schipa did, but he started to sing parts that some analysts regarded as unsuitable for his light, lyric voice. Even so, his voice changed little in his fifties. His most frequent roles at the Met have been Rodolfo in *La Bohème*, Riccardo in *A Masked Ball* and Nemorino in *The Elixir of Love*. The whole football (soccer) world became familiar with his singing of "Nessun dorma" from *Turandot* in connection with the World Cup in 1990. If you are buying only one opera recording, you could do worse than Bellini's *Norma* featuring Pavarotti, Joan Sutherland, Marilyn Horne, and Samuel Ramey. Or Donizetti's *Daughter of the Regiment* with Sutherland. Or Puccini's *La Bohème* with Mirella Freni.

EZIO PINZA   (1892–1957). Italian bass, best known to the general public from the 1949 Broadway musical *South Pacific* and several Hollywood films, but earlier the top Italian bass for most of the between-the-wars years. Cultivated voice, handsome presence, and engaging personality. Although a Verdi specialist, his many other roles included the Don in *Don Giovanni* and Figaro in *The Marriage of Figaro*. A leading bass at the Met from 1926 to 1948.

RUGGERO RAIMONDI   (b. 1941). Italian bass who studied and sang in Europe and then debuted at the Met in the early 1970s as Silva in Verdi's *Ernani*. Among Met roles: Banquo in *Macbeth*, Silva in *Ernani*, and Don Giovanni. One of the top lighter basses in the later 1900s.

SAMUEL RAMEY   (b. 1940). American bass, the most acclaimed one in recent decades. His first season at the Met was in 1984, when he sang Argante in Handel's *Rinaldo*. He made his early reputation in Handel and Rossini but then greatly widened his repertoire. A master "basso cantante," a lighter voice than the "basso profondo." Singing and acting talents have made him a spectacular Mefistofele in Boito's opera. Magnificent stage presence.

TITO SCHIPA   (1889–1965). A super superstar. Renowned Italian tenor, stylish, aristocratic, and superb. The outstanding *tenore di grazia* or lyric tenor of his generation. His voice was at its peak in the 1920s and early 1930s. Few tenors have been more admired by their fellow singers. He concentrated on twelve operas: *Don Giovanni, The Barber of Seville, La Sonnambula, The Elixir of Love, Don Pasquale, Lucia di Lammermoor, Rigoletto, La traviata, Martha, Lakmé, Mignon*, and *Manon*. Featured with the Lyric Opera of Chicago from 1919 to 1932 and at La Scala during the 1930s. Met debut as Nemorino in *The Elixir of Love* in 1932.

FRIEDRICH SCHORR   (1888–1953). Large-voiced Hungarian (later naturalized American) bass-baritone, recognized as the leading Wagnerian bass–baritone for much of the first half of the century. Settled in the United States in 1931. Rarely sang anything but Wagner, and is known especially for Wotan in *The Ring* and Hans Sachs in *Die Meistersinger*.

Antonio Scotti as Don Giovanni

ANTONIO SCOTTI (1866–1936). Italian baritone, one of Puccini's favorites, and major Met figure. Starting in 1899, he performed for thirty-five seasons at the Met, where he sang many of opera's great baritone roles, including two hundred seventeen Scarpias and one hundred forty-three Marcellos in *La Bohème*. Dramatic power and vocal agility. Friend of Caruso; couldn't read music.

LEO SLEZAK (1873–1946). Austrian tenor with a powerful voice, perfect for such roles as Otello, Radames in *Aida*, and Lohengrin. The all-star Otello of the first quarter of the century and the leading Wagnerian tenor before Lauritz Melchior. Known for a wonderful sense of humor as well as a magnificent voice. Sang in *Lohengrin*, *Tannhäuser* and *Die Meistersinger* at the Met, but not in *Parsifal*, *Tristan and Isolde*, or *The Ring*. His son, Walter, New York and Hollywood actor, wrote a book about him called *What Time's the Next Swan?*, the title taken from a stage whisper when Lohengrin's swan-boat began to move off before he was aboard.

MARIANO STABILE (1888–1968). Italian baritone, perhaps the greatest Falstaff who ever sang the role. Performed for years at La Scala in Milan and frequently in London. Beginning at La Scala in 1921, he sang Falstaff nearly 1,200 times over more than forty years.

FRANCESCO TAMAGNO (1850–1905). Italian dramatic tenor, one of opera's greatest, an acclaimed interpreter of Verdi's dramatic parts, including Radames in *Aida*, Riccardo in *A Masked Ball*, and Adorno in *Simon Boccanegra*. The title role in *Otello* was written for him, and he was the original Otello at La Scala, in 1887. One of the strongest-voiced and best-paid tenors in opera history.

RICHARD TAUBER (1891–1948). Austrian tenor who became a British citizen in 1940. One of the top Mozart tenors of this century, most active between the two world wars at the Munich and Salzburg festivals. Sang operetta and in concert and made many recordings. Known especially to the general public for Franz Lehár's most popular song, "Dein ist mein ganzes Herz" ("You are my heart's delight").

LAWRENCE TIBBETT (1896–1960). Quintessential American baritone. Superstar. Fine actor and a handsome man. For years one of opera's best-known names, appearing on Broadway, in films, and often on the radio. Particularly famous for opera's two supreme villains, Verdi's Iago and Puccini's Scarpia. Succeeded Antonio Scotti as the baritone mainstay at the Met and stayed for twenty-seven seasons, until 1950. Among many other roles: Germont in *La traviata*, Rigoletto, Tonio in *Pagliacci* and Ford in *Falstaff*.

GIORGIO TOZZI (b. 1923) American bass-baritone. Intelligent and versatile. Sang in Salzburg, San Francisco, Frankfurt, Munich, and Lisbon. Twenty-one seasons at the Met beginning in 1955. Among frequent performances there: Ramfis in *Aida*, Colline in *La Bohème*, Basilio in *The Barber of Seville*, and Pogner in *Die Meistersinger*.

RICHARD TUCKER (1913–75). American lyric and dramatic tenor from the late 1940s through the early 1970s. A cornerstone of the Met for three decades with more than 600 performances. He had a beautiful large voice and was energetic in his acting, which didn't always please the critics. Specialized in Italian roles but also sang several French operas. Among the most frequent of his thirty roles at the Met: Don José in *Carmen*, Rodolfo in *La Bohème*, the Duke in *Rigoletto*, and Cavaradossi in *Tosca*.

GIUSEPPE VALDENGO   (b. 1914). Italian baritone. After years in Milan, he came to New York and the Met in 1947. Performances during seven years there included Figaro in *The Barber of Seville*, Marcello in *La Bohème*, and Tonio in *Pagliacci*. Well known for recordings from NBC Toscanini broadcasts.

JON VICKERS   (b. 1926). Canadian-born tenor, one of the great post–World War II English-language heroic tenors. Domingo is a "lighter" lyric-dramatic tenor and Pavarotti a still "lighter" lyric tenor. Vickers's voice is one of the most powerful tenor voices of the century, praised for its ringing tone and his excellent enunciation. He threw himself into all his roles. Another example of superstar versatility, illustrating the futility of being overly rigid in voice classification. As a top heroic tenor, he sang Wagner's Siegmund in *Die Walküre* and Parsifal, Britten's Peter Grimes (he succeeded Peter Pears as *the* Peter Grimes, although the role had been written for Pears's much lighter voice), Herman in Tchaikovsky's *Queen of Spades*, Florestan in *Fidelio*, and Aeneas in *Les Troyens*. But he also was comfortable as Don José in *Carmen*. He joined the Met in 1960 and sang there for twenty-five years.

Death at the Met

The first onstage death at the Metropolitan Opera resulted from baritone Leonard Warren's 1960 heart attack during a performance of Verdi's *Force of Destiny*. The second was January 5, 1996, when tenor Richard Versalle suffered a heart attack and fell ten feet from a ladder in the opening scene of Leoš Janáček's *Makropulos Case*. He was sixty-three. There was another death within Met walls in 1988 when a member of the audience committed suicide in a plunge from the upper balcony during an intermission of Verdi's *Macbeth*. In none of these cases did the performance continue.

RAMON VINAY   (1912–96). Chilean tenor, originally a baritone. Others who made this shift include Renato Zanelli, also from Chile, Giovanni Zenatello, Plácido Domingo, and Carlo Bergonzi. Vinay sang at the Met between 1946 and 1966. Among his most frequent roles: Don José in *Carmen*, Canio in *Pagliacci*, Tristan, Otello, and Samson in *Samson et Dalila*. Artistic singer and fine actor.

At the Met in the 1990s

For a glimpse of leading Metropolitan Opera singers in the 1990s, here are the featured performers in eight 1996 operas, including Warhorses, others from The Collection, and non-Collection works. I chose Texaco's Saturday afternoon broadcast operas, the ones most apt to reach a broad audience. The dates are for Met debuts of the star singers. It is an interesting blend of the famous veterans and the new—although "new" only to the Met.

THE BARBER OF SEVILLE—Soprano: American Ruth Ann Swenson, 1991. Tenor: Argentinian Raul Gimenez, debut season. Baritone: American Mark Oswald, 1991. Basses: American John Del Carlo, 1993, and Italian Simone Alaimo, 1992.

THE MAKROPULOS CASE—Sopranos: Americans Jessye Norman, 1983, and Marie Plette, 1993. Tenor: United Kingdom Graham Clark, 1985. Baritone: Swedish Hakan Hagegard, 1978. Bass-baritone: New Zealander Donald McIntyre, 1975.

SALOME—Soprano: American Catherine Malfitano, 1979. Mezzo-soprano: German Hanna Schwarz, 1988. Tenors: American Kenneth Riegel, 1973, and Mark Baker, 1986. Baritone: Austrian Bernd Weikl, 1977.

THE VOYAGE—(Philip Glass)—Soprano: American Patricia Schuman, 1990. Mezzo-soprano: South African Sally Burgess, 1995. Tenor: American Philip Creech, 1979. Baritone: American Timothy Noble, 1988.

AIDA—Soprano: Russian Nina Rautio, debut season. Mezzo-soprano: American Dolora Zajick, 1988. Tenor: American Michael Sylvester, 1991. Baritone: Spanish Juan Pons, 1983. Bass: American Paul Plishka, 1966.

MADAMA BUTTERFLY—Soprano: American Diana Soviero, 1986. Mezzo-soprano: American Wendy White, 1989. Tenors: American Richard Leech, 1989, and Canadian Bernard Fitch, 1989. Baritone: Pons.

ANDREA CHÉNIER—Soprano: American Aprile Millo, 1984. Mezzo-sopranos: American Wendy White and Russian Larissa Diadkova, debut season. Tenors: Italian Luciano Pavarotti, 1968, and French Michel Senechal, 1982. Baritone: Pons.

DIE WALKÜRIE—Sopranos: German Gabriele Schnaut, debut season, and American Deborah Voigt, 1991. Mezzo-soprano: German Hanna Schwarz. Tenor: Spanish Plácido Domingo, 1968. Basses: Americans John Macurdy, 1962, and Robert Hale, 1990.

LEONARD WARREN (1911–60) American baritone, the leading baritone of his day. Debuted at the Met in 1939 as Paolo in *Simon Boccanegra* and remained a member of the company until his onstage death there in 1960 during a performance of *The Force of Destiny*. In the post–World War II years the best-known singer of Verdi baritone roles, including Rigoletto, Germont in *La traviata*, Renato in *A Masked Ball*, and Di Luna in *Il travatore*.

WOLFGANG WINDGASSEN (1914–74). A leading German heldentenor after World War II. Known for musical knowledge and discipline rather than power and beauty. Most of his career was in Europe, but in 1957 at the Met he sang Siegmund *and* Siegfried in *The Ring*.

Chapter 10

BUILDING A COLLECTION: "THE TEN BEST OPERAS"

❧

I have exposed the Unwashed to an enormous number of operas in this book—eighty-five in The Collection, about thirty in the Twentieth-century European Package and twenty-five or so American works. These total more than 140 operas for the newcomer to absorb. That is cruel.

One original thought three years ago was to limit the book to the Twenty-Five Warhorses, and I walked that path for a few early months, but that left the Unwashed and the minimally Washed stranded in No Man's Land. It's nice to know about *Aida, Carmen* and *La traviata*, and eight or ten numbers from them make wonderful listening, but that shouldn't satisfy an amateur who is ready to discover and explore opera.

So The Collection became eighty-five instead of twenty-five, and that left out some wonderful twentieth-century European operas, and all of American opera was still ignored, and then the publishers and I agreed that we needed a short historical perspective, and then something had to be done about the different kinds of operatic voices, and even then we wanted to identify the most famous singers, and that's the way things happen.

I'm glad we did it as we did. One hundred and forty operas are far fewer than the thousand-odd that are performed today. That's significant progress; that gives the Unwashed something of a lifeline.

But if you want to build your own opera collection—cassette tapes or compact discs or videotapes—one hundred and forty is still undoubtedly excessive. The objective of this chapter is to whittle down the number.

In that regard, the three questions I was most frequently asked by non-opera people who knew I was writing this book were these:

"Which operas are your favorites?"

"What ten operas would I most enjoy seeing and hearing?"

"Which are the ten very best operas?"

I'll pass on the first since it really doesn't matter. The safe answer to the second is the obvious one. Pick the first ten Warhorses in The Collection. By definition, those are the ones the average operagoer has most enjoyed seeing, and without knowing your interests and personal taste, that's the best we can do for you.

But—as emphasized early and often in the book—the most popular and successful operas aren't necessarily the greatest ones.

That brings us to Question Number Three. It's a reasonable question, even if the answer must be subjective and even if it infuriates the elitists who think it is obscene to order-rank art. Their disdain, however noble, doesn't help the amateur a bit. The questioner isn't asking us to put our lives on the line; he or she is simply seeking a little helpful guidance.

It's worth a shot. I'd like to list the ten very best operas and would if I could. I've tried, first on my own and then after consultation with a dozen musicologists and opera experts who have become friends and allies as I've worked my way through the book. I had no trouble finding gifted professionals who were anxious to reach out to the Unwashed and help identify the ten or twenty All-Time Best.

We found it couldn't be done to our satisfaction. Our lists were hopelessly unbalanced and incomplete. Perhaps you'll see why as I retrace our steps.

We began by choosing the greatest half-dozen composers, with the view of then selecting their most outstanding works. Mozart, Verdi, and Wagner were unanimous choices at the top, as entrenched for opera as Mozart, Bach, and Beethoven are for classical music. Without trying to rank the others in any order, my professionals quickly added Richard Strauss and Puccini. The sixth choice became a battle between Monteverdi and Handel, with the expert consensus for Monteverdi on the grounds that his approach to music-drama is paradoxically the more "modern" of the two. But there also were holdouts and strong arguments in support of Handel.

The simple way to resolve that controversy was to take both.

The next step was to pick the top operas by our Chosen Seven composers. In an effort to keep this list short, at the outset we decided that Monteverdi, Puccini, Strauss, and Handel should be represented by only one opera each. On historical grounds, we selected *Orfeo* rather than *The Coronation of Poppea* for Monteverdi. We chose *La Bohème* for Puccini, and *Der Rosenkavalier* for Richard Strauss.

Handel, one of the greatest classical composers of all, was somewhat more difficult. How can one choose between one work and another since virtually none has established itself in the repertoire on an individual basis? We settled on *Julius Caesar*, considered by some to be the crown jewel of Handel's operas and by the group to be "representative."

Now we had four operas.

But the other three chosen composers—Mozart, Verdi, and Wagner—clearly require several operas apiece. Who can decide between Mozart's *Marriage of Figaro* and *Don Giovanni*—or ignore *Così fan tutte* for that matter? And then there's his utterly different, but equally great German opera *The Magic Flute*. We couldn't slight any of the four.

That gave us eight operas.

It seems generally agreed within the opera world that Verdi's crowning achievements are his last three works, *Aida*, *Otello*, and *Falstaff*, although the last two are something of an acquired taste. We need all three of these. But what about the Big Three of his middle period: *Rigoletto*, *La traviata*, and *Il trovatore*? Which of those public favorites do we select for a short list, and how do we defend bypassing the other two?

Impossible to discriminate. We can't rule out any of those six from Verdi if we want a solid collection for an Unwashed amateur. Now we're up to fourteen, and we haven't touched Richard Wagner.

For him, we must have *Tristan und Isolde*—all of my panel insisted on that—and at least one of the *Ring* operas. But which? *Die Walküre*, the most approachable for the Unwashed? Or *Götterdämmerung*, the most monumental? We couldn't agree, and took both. But then is it feasible—or desirable—to leave out the genial humanism of *Die Meistersinger von Nürnberg*?

Eighteen, and we are tentatively avoiding *Parsifal*, *Lohengrin*, *Tannhäuser*, and the other two *Ring* operas. Worse yet, far worse, we still haven't considered many other composers and several operas that must be near the top of anybody's list: Rossini's *Barber of Seville*, for instance, or Bizet's *Carmen*. What about those composers whose chief works are less popular but are undeniably important masterpieces: Mussorgsky's *Boris Godunov*, Debussy's *Pelléas et Mélisande*, or Berg's *Wozzeck*? Can we presume to ignore *Cav-Pag* or slight Mr. Beethoven and his *Fidelio*?

And dare we overlook the rest of the twentieth century? Benjamin Britten must be on our list, at least once and probably twice, and Leoš Janáček. Should we not have another Puccini opera such as *Madama Butterfly*, or *Tosca*, or his later *Turandot*, or one of the two explosive early Richard Strauss works, *Salome* or *Elektra*? Then we must look at composers like Donizetti and Massenet, who have made major and highly popular contributions to the repertoire but somehow fail to make the topmost rank.

If we include those, it would be hard not to make an even stronger case for still more operas by the Big Three: *The Abduction from the Seraglio* or *Idomeneo* by Mozart, *A Masked Ball* and *Don Carlos* by Verdi, and more Wagner. Are not some or all of those works "greater" than Massenet's *Werther*? And so it went. How do we accommodate Stravinsky's *Rake's Progress*, Schoenberg's *Moses und Aron*, and Rimsky-Korsakov's *Golden Cockerel*?

So, after a long caucus, the experts and I agreed that we faced two options. One was to give up completely, declare defeat, and leave the Unwashed with our 140-odd operas. The other was to hold to our objective but modify it by lengthening our list. After debate, we decided that the second option, less than perfect, would be more helpful to the Unwashed than the first.

Our end product was not ten or twenty operas but sixty by thirty-four composers. All but three of those composers are in The Collection, and the others are either in the Twentieth-century European Package or the American Dream Season. And all but two operas are from those sources. One intruder is Monteverdi's 1643 *Coronation of Poppea*, discussed earlier, which is simply too good to leave out. The other intruder is *Idomeneo*, still another Mozart opera, and Mozart never needs defense.

We didn't attempt to order-rank the operas, one through sixty, but for convenience of the Unwashed we did put them into groups of twelve. In forming those groups, we started with operas that are more approachable than others but also tried to maintain some kind of balance within most groups.

So Mozart's *Marriage of Figaro* and *Don Giovanni* are in the first set, but his *Magic Flute*, which I find more complicated (although my opera-expert friends don't), is postponed—not on grounds of excellence but on its accessibility for the Unwashed. Verdi is represented initially by *Rigoletto* and *Aida*, great works by any account, even if not as highly esteemed by musicologists as *Otello* and *Falstaff*, which are harder to get into and so are not included until later on.

Tristan und Isolde, arguably Wagner's most outstanding work, is also less accessible and thus similarly delayed until the second dozen. Its place in the first group is taken by *Die Meistersinger*, almost as great as *Tristan* (and even longer), but much more melodic in the conventional sense, more varied in mood and easier to enjoy.

We had to be sturdy. Donizetti is represented by only two operas and Rossini by only one. Schoenbergians will be aghast that we excluded *Moses und Aron*.

In general, the first two dozen build the basic repertoire of Mozart, Verdi, and Wagner and add a few individual works by other composers. As indicated, the first group tends to be lighter than the second. The third and fourth dozen attach a few more works by the Big Seven, but mainly introduce individual operas by other composers, aiming to give the beginner the greatest variety possible.

The role of the fifth dozen is to plug the gaps in order to make this handpicked offering for your own collection as complete as any sixty-opera compilation can be. So in it are four Golden Oldies from the time before Mozart, two one-of-a-kind works from the nineteenth century, and six major operas from the twentieth.

My professional friends suggested calling this a Starter Kit, but I think it's much too grand and complete for that. I regard it as an Opera Library, something one could spend many years collecting and something to be passed on to children and grandchildren.

How does our Library compare with The Collection?

The same composers dominate both. Seven of Verdi's twelve Collection operas are here, five of Wagner's ten and four of Puccini's seven. Richard Strauss has the same four in each. Mozart goes up one, from four in The Collection to five here. Those five powerhouse composers wrote twenty-five of these sixty operas.

Five other composers are represented here by two works. Massenet has the same two Collection operas and Donizetti two of his Collection four. Monteverdi has the Collection *Orfeo* plus *Poppea*, Britten's from The Collection, *Peter Grimes* plus *The Turn of the Screw*, and Janáček his Collection *Jenůfa* plus *The Cunning Little Vixen*.

Each of the other twenty-four operas here is from a different composer— twenty-one from The Collection, Ravel and Stravinsky from the Twentieth-century European Package, and Gershwin from American opera.

Core scenes and passages from these sixty operas are identified in the next chapter.

Operas in each group are listed in chronological order.

FIRST DOZEN

1. Mozart: *The Marriage of Figaro*, 1786
2. Mozart: *Don Giovanni*, 1787
3. Rossini: *The Barber of Seville*, 1816
4. Verdi: *Rigoletto*, 1851
5. Verdi: *La traviata*, 1853
6. Wagner: *Die Meistersinger von Nürnberg*, 1868
7. Wagner: *Die Walküre*, 1870
8. Verdi: *Aida*, 1871
9. Bizet: *Carmen*, 1875
10. Puccini: *La Bohème*, 1896
11. Richard Strauss: *Der Rosenkavalier*, 1911
12. Britten: *Peter Grimes*, 1945

SECOND DOZEN

13. Mozart: *Così fan tutte*, 1790
14. Mozart: *The Magic Flute*, 1791
15. Donizetti: *Lucia di Lammermoor*, 1835
16. Verdi: *Il trovatore*, 1853
17. Wagner: *Tristan und Isolde*, 1865
18. Johann Strauss: *Die Fledermaus*, 1874
19. Wagner: *Götterdämmerung*, 1876
20. Verdi: *Otello*, 1887
21. Massenet: *Werther*, 1892
22. Puccini: *Tosca*, 1900
23. Debussy: *Pelléas et Mélisande*, 1902
24. Richard Strauss: *Salome*, 1905

THIRD DOZEN

25. Handel: *Julius Caesar*, 1724
26. Bellini: *Norma*, 1831
27. Donizetti: *The Elixir of Love*, 1832
28. Wagner: *Lohengrin*, 1850
29. Gounod: *Faust*, 1859
30. Mussorgsky: *Boris Godunov*, 1868
31. Offenbach: *The Tales of Hoffmann*, 1881
32. Mascagni: *Cavalleria rusticana*, 1890
33. Leoncavallo: *Pagliacci*, 1892
34. Verdi: *Falstaff*, 1893
35. Puccini: *Madama Butterfly*, 1904
36. Richard Strauss: *Ariadne auf Naxos*, 1912

FOURTH DOZEN

37. Mozart: *Idomeneo*, 1781
38. Beethoven: *Fidelio*, 1805
39. Stravinsky: *The Rake's Progress*, 1951
40. Verdi: *A Masked Ball*, 1859
41. Smetana: *The Bartered Bride*, 1866
42. Saint-Saëns: *Samson et Dalila*, 1877
43. Massenet: *Manon*, 1884
44. Humperdinck: *Hänsel und Gretel*, 1893
45. Janáček: *Jenůfa*, 1904
46. Richard Strauss: *Elektra*, 1909
47. Berg: *Wozzeck*, 1925
48. Puccini: *Turandot*, 1926

FIFTH DOZEN

49. Monteverdi: *L'Orfeo*, 1607
50. Monteverdi: *The Coronation of Poppea*, 1642
51. Purcell: *Dido and Aeneas*, 1689
52. Gluck: *Orfeo ed Euridice*, 1762
53. Weber: *Der Freischütz*, 1821
54. Tchaikovsky: *Eugene Onegin*, 1879
55. Bartók: *Duke Bluebeard's Castle*, 1911
56. Janáček: *The Cunning Little Vixen*, 1924
57. Ravel: *L'enfant et les sortilèges*, 1925
58. Schoenberg: *Moses and Aron*, 1957
59. Gershwin: *Porgy and Bess*, 1935
60. Britten: *The Turn of the Screw*, 1954

Chapter 11

BLEEDING
HUNKS

❧

This final suggestion offers a handy shortcut into the guts of each of the sixty operas featured in the last chapter.

It is an excerpt approach, useful for anyone with access to a complete opera—live, on the radio, on television, or through audio or visual recording. Our focus, as always, is on the Unwashed, but in this case the material also should be interesting to the modestly Washed.

Every concertgoer—and every classical radio listener—has heard orchestral excerpts from Richard Wagner's operas. Critic Ernest Newman used to describe these excerpts as "bleeding hunks." This is because most parts of a Wagner opera flow continuously into one another and there is no good way of ending them short of rewriting the music. Inasmuch as comparatively little of Wagner's music is frequently excerpted as separate arias, the best way of tasting the flavor of his work is with these longer passages—ten, fifteen, or even twenty minutes in length. The same is true of Debussy and Richard Strauss and, indeed, for many composers of the twentieth century.

Even for other composers—the Puccinis, Verdis, Rossinis, and Mozarts, for example—the bleeding-hunk technique has many advantages. People often think of opera in terms of a collection of arias, and, indeed, we have highlighted arias for each Collection opera, singled out a Top Forty in a little sidebar insert, and identified one hundred representative ones in chapter nine.

Don't walk away from these famous tunes. Check them out, listen to them, come to recognize them, hum them, and anticipate them when hearing and/or seeing the complete opera from which they come.

Paradoxically, despite the high enjoyment they provide, arias are seldom typical of an opera as a whole. An aria generally takes time out from the main action; it is a static oasis in an otherwise dynamic form. Furthermore, the aria-based approach can turn all too easily into a personality cult, responding to the performer not the composer, the singer not the character, and the individual moment rather than the succession of such moments.

Maybe you just want to seize and treasure the moment and settle for opera music—a noble settlement—rather than get into opera as a whole.

But the mark of true *operatic* genius in a composer shows not in his ability to write arias but in his power to build a sequence of musical events into a coherent, dramatically compelling whole.

For those who also want to sample this dramatic whole, the bleeding-hunk approach is highly recommended. These shortish passages of continuous music are great things to listen to first, before plunging into a complete opera, to get the flavor of the whole. Where possible, passages have been chosen that can be enjoyed immediately in musical terms for their sound alone. But it's never a bad idea to get a general sense of the plot and setting before listening and some listeners also enjoy following along in a libretto. Others close their eyes and listen. You'll do it your way.

A few operas (*Otello* is a better example than any) start right off with a bang. Most don't, however, and by the time a beginner has gotten through all the necessary exposition he or she may have lost interest. The passages suggested here contain some of each opera's most splendid music in the most concentrated form.

Inevitably, the excerpts do include some arias. Consider them a bonus, received just for playing the game. The emphasis here is on what many experts regard as the quintessential opera medium: *ensemble singing*. This includes anything from duets to choruses. In most cases each of our excerpts contains several different types of ensemble.

Before we go on, I must take time out to credit Professor Roger Brunyate, head of the Opera Department at the Peabody Conservatory in Baltimore. The addition of the bleeding hunks to the book was his idea, one of the many substantial contributions he made after reading an early draft of the entire manuscript.

Not only did Professor Brunyate provide the idea and the selection, he also wrote the bleeding-hunk commentary. I have substituted a couple of operas and fussed with one percent of the language. So Roger Brunyate, to whom I owe so much, deserves all of the credit for what goes right in the bleeding hunks but none of the blame where I may have misinterpreted his meaning.

To locate a bleeding hunk on a recording is a cinch for anyone working with compact discs. The written material that accompanies most opera CDs will help a listener find each hunk within a few seconds, and he or she can zero in on it by pushing a couple of buttons on the CD player or the remote control. It doesn't take too much longer to arrive at a hunk by fast-forwarding a videotape. People using audio cassettes need considerably more patience. And if you are just listening on the radio, a libretto or detailed plot summary is almost mandatory to locate the excerpt.

Having collected a library of opera videotapes, my practice is to watch the bleeding hunks there, record them onto a blank cassette tape, and replay them in the car on our long drives between Washington, D.C., and the North Country Adirondacks.

The times cited are approximate, varying according to the specific productions:

THE HUNKS

1. *Mozart:* **The Marriage of Figaro.** *Act II finale.* **25 min**

This finale, considered one of Mozart's greatest contributions to opera, sets the pattern for what is called a "cumulative finale." It begins with two performers, the Count and the Countess, onstage. Moods change and tensions tighten with the entrance of each new character, until it ends with a fast-paced free-for-all septet. One option is just to sit back and listen to the glorious music. Another, which lets you appreciate the drama, is to follow the music with a libretto.

2. *Mozart:* **Don Giovanni.** *Act I opening.* **18 min**

This is another opera that sets the tone from the start. Gounod described this opening scene as "the greatest exposition of the lyric drama known to me." Start with the overture, and move without a break into the action: a courtyard by night; Don Giovanni inside intent on a conquest; his servant, Leporello, waiting disgruntledly outside; the entrance of the Don, pursued by his latest victim, Donna Anna; the fight with the Commendatore, Anna's father; his death; the stunned reaction to that death; a snatch of recitative—and then the return of Donna Anna with her fiancé, Don Ottavio; their discovery of the body, and her demand that Ottavio swear vengeance. Indeed, you might as well keep listening from there on, for the musical invention and violent changes of dramatic mood continue without a break until the end of the act.

3. *Rossini:* **The Barber of Seville.** *Act II finale.* **20 min**

A good example of the "cumulative finale" found in Rossini's comic operas, a technique he borrowed from Mozart's *The Marriage of Figaro*. Count Almaviva, hoping to get in to see his beloved Rosina, presents himself at her guardian's house disguised as a drunken soldier with billeting orders. Complication is added to complication; at the end the characters themselves say it is like being tossed in a storm at sea. Near the end there is "Freddo ed immobile," a slow ensemble of stunned amazement, a Rossini specialty.

4. Verôi: **Rigoletto.** *Act II, central portion.* **15–30 min**

This is the opera's second scene. In some productions it is Act II, in some Act I, Scene 2. Start with Gilda's entrance to buoyant music. Hear the great melody in her duets with Rigoletto and the disguised Duke. If you carry on to the end of the act you get Gilda's "Caro nome" (aria 19 in chapter 9), one of opera's most famous coloratura arias, and her abduction by the courtiers. If you start earlier, you hear the sinister interview between Rigoletto and the assassin Sparafucile, and Rigoletto's first big aria, "Pari siamo."

5. Verôi: **La traviata.** *Act II, opening.* **18 min**

Act II opens with Alfredo's aria "De' miei bollenti spiriti," in which he sings of his happiness with Violetta. The main part of this excerpt, however, is the long duet between Violetta and Alfredo's father, Germont, in which he persuades her to give Alfredo up for the sake of a younger sister who is about to get married. If you follow the scene in the text, you can make up your mind whether Germont is a manipulative hypocrite or a sympathetic man of feeling, but in either case the music presents a kaleidoscope of passion, desperation, tenderness, and pathos.

6. Wagner: **Die Meistersinger von Nürnberg.** *Act III, enô of Scene 1 anô start of Scene 2.* **25 min**

Start with Walther's entrance toward the end of the scene as he tells Sachs of the song that has come to him in a dream and sings two stanzas of his "Prize Song" (aria 75 in chapter 9), with which he hopes to win Eva's hand. After an emotional exchange between Eva and Hans Sachs (who has worked with Walther on the song), is a famous quintet in which the new song is baptized. Amid trumpet fanfares and excited music, the scene changes to the festival meadow outside the town. There the various guilds vie for prominence and the apprentices start a boisterous dance that is interrupted by the solemn procession of the Mastersingers themselves, ending the excerpt. Nowhere else in Wagner—and not many places in opera—are there passages that so delightfully combine solo and ensemble singing, choruses, dances, and orchestral music. Don't say you don't like Wagner until after sampling this twenty-five to thirty minutes of music.

7. Wagner: **Die Walküre.** *Act I, laôt portion.* **15–25 min**

Ideally, start this scene after the exit of Hunding, with Siegmund's meditation by the sinking fire, "Ein Schwert verhiess mir der Vater." Listen carefully and hear the orchestra hinting that the sword he seeks may not be far away. Indeed, it's in the tree right above his head. For a shorter hunk, begin with Siegmund's aria "Winterstürme wichen dem Wonnemond" (aria 76 in chapter 9) and the ecstatic reply from Sieglinde, "Du bist der Lenz." As the twins recognize one another, the music becomes more passionate. Siegmund withdraws the sword from the tree, takes his sister-bride, and flees with her into the night. It is one of the most exciting endings of an act in opera.

8. Verdi: Aida. *Act II, Scene 2.* 10–25 min

This is the famous "Triumphal Scene" in which the victorious Egyptians, commanded by Radames, lead in their Ethiopian captives, among whom is Aida's father, Amonasro. The mounting excitement of the choruses and the great march played by successive ranks of onstage trumpets make this the best known of all operatic spectacles (even without any elephants!). The mock-exotic ballet music that follows is less inspired, but the big ensemble in which Amonasro pleads for mercy for his men ("Ma tu, Re, tu signore possente") is absolutely beautiful, a prime example of what makes Verdi the greatest grand opera composer of all time.

9. Bizet: Carmen. *End of Act I.* 20 min

Almost any section of *Carmen* is chock-full of tunes, but this excerpt contains a bit of everything. Start with the charming duet between Don José and his hometown sweetheart, Micaëla, "Parle-moi de ma mère." After she has left, there's a disturbance at the cigarette factory and José is ordered to arrest Carmen, who with her famous sequidilla ("Près des remparts de Séville") seduces him into letting her go. The act ends with Carmen's escape amid mocking, triumphant music in the orchestra.

10. Puccini: La Bohème. *Act I love music.* 20 min

Start with Rodolfo alone once his companions have left. What follows is perhaps the greatest concentration of hit music in all opera. Mimi comes in, seeking a light for her candle; Rodolfo instead detains her by "accidentally" blowing his out. We then have his aria to her, "Che gelida manina" (aria 66 in Chapter 9), her reply telling about herself "Mi chiamano Mimi" (aria 27), and the closing duet that follows Rodolfo's "O soave fanciulla," as they go out together for Christmas Eve on the town.

11. Richard Strauss: Der Rosenkavalier. *Act II opening and Act III conclusion.* 10–25 min

Because it's difficult to select between them, two excerpts are chosen here. The first is the Presentation of the Rose, which opens Act II. Sophie tries to calm herself as her maid describes the arrival of the Rose Cavalier, Octavian. He arrives at the first big musical climax, Sophie falls to the ground in a deep curtsy, and the music perfectly captures the mood. The young people fall in love and, although they don't yet know it, the orchestra does. Stop when the big singing stops and the music changes to a gentle dancelike theme.

For the second excerpt, start either at Ochs's exit toward the end of Act

III or with the famous women's trio "Hab' mir's gelobt," in which Octavian's older lover, the Marschallin, gives him up to the younger woman. This, and the folksonglike duet that follows, are among opera's more captivating passages.

12. *Britten:* Peter Grimes. *Act I, second half.*   20 min

Start just before the end of the first scene with Peter's aria "What harbour shelters peace?" This leads into the terrifying 'Storm Interlude' and thence into the smoky warmth of the pub, where the villagers are gathered for shelter. Peter interrupts with his second aria, "Now the Great Bear and Pleiades," which brings into the room a chill that is then dispelled by a round, "Old Joe has gone fishing." At the climax, Ellen comes in with Peter's new apprentice, whom Peter immediately drags off into the night. The whole scene is tense, dramatic, and highly effective.—and, for some, made more so by following it with a libretto. (But not for everyone).

13. *Mozart:* Così fan tutte. *Act I, Scene 2.*   22 min

This is the scene in which Fernando and Guglielmo pretend to take leave of their fiancées, Fiordiligi and Dorabella, to go off to war. It consists almost entirely of ensembles, numbers involving more than one singer. There's an opening duet for the women, a mock-distraught entrance for Don Alfonso, a quintet that parodies the heroic style, the soldiers' chorus, a second quintet of tearful farewells (suddenly turning serious halfway through, in one of the emotional masterstrokes of this score), and a marvelous trio, "Soave sia il vento," as the women and Don Alfonso pray that their lovers will return safely from their voyage. The entire scene has a special atmosphere different from all other Mozart operas.

14. *Mozart:* The Magic Flute. *Opening scene.*   25 min

This is one of those rare operas that has some of the best music right at the start. It includes Tamino's entrance as he is chased by the serpent, the Three Ladies quarreling over who gets to stay with him, three great arias in succession for Papageno, Tamino, and the Queen of the Night (numbers 78, 59, and 7 in chapter 9), and the lovely quintet in which the Ladies give Tamino and Papageno the magic flute and the bells and send them off on their quest. Some dialogue is spoken between the numbers.

15. *Donizetti:* Lucia di Lammermoor. *Act II, Scene 2.*   15 min

This is the biggest ensemble scene in the opera, in which Lucia signs a contract to marry Arturo, believing her own lover, Edgardo, has been unfaithful. Edgardo's arrival at the height of the ceremonies triggers a famous sextet, "Chi mi frena in tal momento," a landmark among Italian opera ensembles, containing at least two of those tunes that just stick with you.

16. *Verди:* Il trovatore. *Act IV, Scene 1.*   20 min

Verdi spoke of the importance of establishing a characteristic "tinto," or dramatic sound color, for each of his operas. No scene captures the peculiar *Trovatore* atmosphere of dark deeds by night so much as this one, set outside the prison in which Manrico is condemned to die the next morning. Leonora, his lover, waits outside and sings "D'amor sull'ali rosee." Then Manrico's voice is heard from his cell, as the monks chant the "Miserere," followed by a short passage by Leonora. Now Manrico's enemy, the Count di Luna, comes in and, in a duet full of repressed sadism, offers Leonora Manrico's freedom in exchange for her body. Leonora accepts but secretly takes poison, leaving him nothing but a corpse. Melodrama of the highest order.

17. *Wagner:* Tristan und Isolde. *Act II love дuet.*   16 min

Start with the words "O sink' hernieder, Nacht der Liebe" and continue until the entrance of King Mark. The third voice heard, in addition to Tristan and Isolde, is the maid Brangäne, who is keeping watch from the tower, but the lovers are too involved in their passion to heed her warning. Many consider this the most sensuous music in all of opera. But the lovemaking is interrupted. The same music is not completed until Isolde's "Liebestod" (aria 40 in chapter 9) at the very end of the opera.

18. *Johann Strauss:* Die Fledermaus. *Act II, finale or complete.*   10–35 min

Some performances of this opera (and some recordings) insert "guest spots" and/or additional ballet music into the party that makes up the second act. Without them, however, the act is really quite compressed and filled to overflowing with the melodies for which Strauss is so well known. Among other things, the act contains Orlovsky's aria, Adèle's "Laughing Song" and Rosalinda's czardas (arias 46, 14, and 25 in chapter 9). For a short excerpt, start later in the act, but be sure to go through to the finale, with its snappy toast to champagne, followed shortly by the melting ensemble in praise of friendship, "Brüderlein und Schwesterlein."

19. *Wagner:* Götterdämmerung. *Act II, the summoning of the vassals.*   12+ min

This is the only chorus in *The Ring*. Start just after Siegfried's exit, at Hagen's words "Hoiho, ihr Gibichsmannen!" as he takes his cow horn and summons the vassals. Note how the barbaric music becomes civilized as the procession begins with Gunther leading in Brünnhilde and how the mood is quickly shattered when Brünnhilde recognizes Siegfried, who has unwittingly betrayed her. Stop at this point for a short excerpt or continue through the vengeance trio that ends the act. Alternatively (or additionally), turn to Act III and string together Siegfried's narration before his death (aria 77 in chapter 9), the great funeral march, and Brünnhilde's "Immolation Scene" (aria 41), a fitting forty-five-minute conclusion to the entire *Ring*.

20. Verði: Otello. *Opening scene or all of Act 1.*   *15–35 min*

The most arresting operatic opening of all time—play it loud! Find a friend with a laser disc player and play it again, loud. If now you don't like opera, dial 911 for the paramedics. A crowd gathered in the harbor at night watches Otello's ship being buffeted by a storm. Otello comes safely to land with news of a great victory, the storm subsides, and the people light a fire to celebrate. As the first stage in his plot, Iago sings a drinking song, enticing Rodrigo to get drunk. You may either fade out here, or continue for a further twenty minutes to the moonlight love duet that ends this act of sheer genius. Then start again from the beginning.

21. Maddenet: Werther. *Act I, near the end.*   *15 min*

Start with Albert's little aria, "Elle m'aime; elle pense à moi," which goes immediately into the magical moonlight orchestral interlude that is typical of Massenet's lucid style. Werther and Charlotte enter, realize they are very much in love, but the news of Albert's return reminds Charlotte of her deathbed promise to her mother that she would marry him, and this ends all possibility of happiness with Werther. For an alternative excerpt, start at the beginning of Act III, with Charlotte's two great arias (see aria 51 in chapter 9), her scene with her sister, Sophie, and at least the beginning of the duet with Werther.

22. Puccini: Tosca. *Opening scene.*   *20 min*

There is a bit of hole-in-the-corner music involving the escaped prisoner Angelotti, but the real musical meat begins with the entrance of the painter Cavaradossi and his "Recondita armonia" (aria 68 in chapter 9), which is interrupted by the grumbling comments of the Sacristan. Soon Tosca arrives, and her duet with Cavaradossi establishes a note of unclouded lyricism that will not be heard again in this opera. Listen especially for her little aria "Non la sospiri la nostra casetta," which leads into a great climax sung not by the soprano but by the tenor, one of many masterstrokes in *Tosca*.

23. Debuddy: Pelléas et Mélisande. *Act III, Scenes 1–3.*   *10–18 min*

The opening scene of the act, which begins with Mélisande combing her long hair at a window in a high tower, is one of the most lyrical in the opera, a love duet with interesting and curious innocence since neither Pelléas nor Mélisande is aware of their growing love. Roger Brunyate recommends going on to listen to one or more of the brief enigmatic scenes that follow, noting that the glory of the opera is in the constant changes of atmosphere and the marvelous orchestral transitions between scenes.

24. *Richard Strauss:* **Salome.** *Closing scene.*   20 min

Start at the point where Herod orders the execution of John the Baptist. There is a minute of eerie music as the deed is done offstage. Then a huge black arm appears out of a cistern with the prophet's head on a platter. From then on, the scene is entirely Salome's, as she sings an extended necrophiliac love song to the severed head. It is a perverted parody of the closing moments of *Tristan* or *The Ring* but gloriously vocal and sensuously rich in its orchestral color— simultaneously seductive and repelling. The scene ends with Salome being crushed to death under the soldiers' shields on Herod's command. (Brunyate sound bite: If you want to get to know an unfamiliar Strauss opera, look to see whether it ends with a monologue for the soprano. If it does, this is likely to be some of the best music in the work.)

25. *Handel:* **Julius Caesar.** *Act I, numbers 14–16.*   20 min

The bleeding hunks approach doesn't work for Handel since his operas are essentially arias. The last scene of Act I does, however, give a good sample of the style, and includes a rare duet. Start with Caesar's aria "Va tacito e nascosto," in which he describes his velvet-glove approach to his enemy Tolomeo in terms of a hunter stalking his prey. Hear the horn solo. The young Sesto challenges Tolomeo to a duel but is arrested with his mother, Cornelia. After the strong aria "Tu sei il cor di questo core," in which the general Achillas presses his attentions on Cornelia, mother and son prepare for imprisonment in a heartbreaking duet, "Son nata a lagrimar."

26. *Donizetti:* **The Elixir of Love.** *Act I, duet, trio, and finale.*   25 min

These three numbers make up a "cumulative finale" of the type found in Mozart or Rossini. Start after the exit of Dulcamara with Nemorino's line "Caro elisir, sei mio!" He drinks the potion (really cheap wine) that is supposed to make Adina fall in love with him within twenty-four hours. When she gets engaged to Sergeant Belcore to spite him, Nemorino at first just laughs it off. Learning that the soldiers must leave town, however, Adina moves the wedding to that very day, plunging Nemorino into despair. The ensuing ensemble, "Adina credimi," is one of the masterpieces of bel canto opera and a supreme example of the long liquid melodies for which Donizetti is famous.

27. *Bellini:* **Norma.** *Act I, Scene 2.*   15 min

This scene contains a recitative for Norma, the first of two duets with Adalgisa, and a dramatic trio with Pollione, as both women realize they love the same man. The second Norma-Adalgisa duet, in Act II, contains the even more beautiful passage "Mira, o Norma," but the earlier scene has greater variety.

28. *Wagner:* **Lohengrin.** *Act I, Lohengrin's arrival.*   16 min

Lohengrin arrives in his boat, drawn by a swan, to champion Elsa of Brabant, who has been falsely accused of murdering her brother. Begin with Elsa's aria "Einsam in trüben Tagen" (aria 37 in chapter 9), in which she recounts having seen a knight in shining armor in a dream. Then comes a triple summons of the herald and the astonishment of the chorus as Lohengrin appears. The excerpt ends with Lohengrin's short song thanking the swan. This is a young Wagner, composing in a much more ethereal mood than later.

29. *Gounod:* Faust. *Act III.   15–35 min*

The act ends with a lovely moonlit garden quartet in which Faust and Marguerite exchange vows while Méphistophélès keeps the widow neighbor Martha out of the way. Or you can start at the beginning of the act and hear Siebel's aria "Faites-lui mes aveux" (aria 45 in chapter 9) and Marguerite's back-to-back arias about the King of Thule and the jewels Faust left her (aria 21). But it is the quartet that contains the most rapturous, seductive (and occasionally funny) music.

30. *Mussorgsky:* Boris Godunov. *Prologue, Scenes 1 and 2.   18 min*

This excerpt shows why the opera is often described as being about the Russian people. In a strikingly realistic opening scene, a crowd huddled in a courtyard is manipulated into calling for Boris to accept the crown. The second scene is the coronation itself, filled with the sound of great church bells in huge clashing orchestral chords. Boris has an aria combining public modesty with secret guilt for the murder that won him the crown.

31. *Offenbach:* The Tales of Hoffmann. *Act II.   30 min*

This is the Venice act, which is sometimes played as Act III or even Act IV. It is framed by the celebrated Barcarolle, which the least Washed will recognize, and also contains a memorable bass aria "Scintille diamant" (aria 93 in chapter 9). Hoffmann pursues the beautiful courtesan Giulietta who, under the control of the magician Dapertutto, robs him of his reflection in the mirror (i.e., his soul) before floating away in a gondola with a dwarf.

32. *Mascagni:* Cavalleria rusticana. *Easter procession, aria, and duet.   26 min*

Start with the choral ensemble "Regina Coeli" about twenty-five minutes into the opera. It is Easter Day and the congregation inside the church is joined by a large crowd of worshipers in the town square as the Easter procession passes. Santuzza's voice rises above the others in a plea for the redemption she already knows is beyond her. Immediately after follows Santuzza's aria, "Voi lo sapete, o mamma," a celebrated verismo highlight in which she tells of her seduction by Turiddu. This leads into her duet with Turiddu, in which she pleads with him to return to her. The duet offers some of the most fervent music in the score, its dramatic intensity heightened by the interruption of Lola's innocent-sounding offstage ditty.

33. Leoncavallo: Pagliacci. *Nedda's scena and duets.* **16 min**

Start with Nedda's line "Qual fiamma avea nel guardo" (aria 26 in chapter 9) when she is left alone for the first time and the hot sun stirs desires within her that she can't even name. The scene continues with her "Stridono lassù," as she dreams of being able to fly with the birds. Two duets follow: one with the lovesick hunchback Tonio, the other a passionately lyrical exchange with Silvio, with whom she promises to elope that evening—very real feelings expressed in pure melody. Stop at Canio's entrance.

34. Verdi: Falstaff. *Act I, Scene 2.* **16 min**

Verdi's last opera—and his only successful comedy—is significantly different from all his other works. The music goes by so fast that it's impossible to catch it all at one hearing. It is continuous, light-footed movement, interrupted by the radiant duets of the young lovers, Nannetta and Fenton. The scene shows two separate groups making their plans for revenge on Falstaff: the four women, then the five men, then the women again, finally all combining into a grand conclusion, although neither group knows what the other is up to. The opera's final scene (Act III, scene 2) is also a good example of Verdi's late style.

35. Puccini: Madama Butterfly. *Act II, end of Scene 1.* **12 min**

Start with Goro's exit. Butterfly, still waiting for Pinkerton, says she would rather die than become a geisha again. The sound of the cannon announcing the arrival of his ship leads to a lovely duet between Butterfly and Suzuki as they decorate the house with flowers. The scene ends with a magical "Humming Chorus" as the women settle down to wait through the night.

36. Richard Strauss: Ariadne auf Naxos. *Act II, Adriadne's aria and commedia scene.* **30 min**

This long but very rich excerpt starts with Ariadne's magnificent aria "Es gibt ein Reich" (aria 38 in chapter 9), followed by virtually all the commedia dell'arte music from the opera proper. This consists of two quintets—playful music to accompany the comedians' dance routines—framing Zerbinetta's long aria, *Grössmachtige Prinzessin* (aria 9).

37. Mozart: Idomeneo. *Act II, Scene 2.* **15 min**

This is the greatest scene from Mozart's outstanding opera seria, which is not in The Collection but would be if we had cheated a little on statistics. It starts with the lovely barcarolle chorus "Placido è il mar," which frames Elettra's small aria "Soavi zeffiri." After a short recitative is the farewell trio with Elettra, Idamante, and Idomeneo. The mood is then suddenly broken by the appearance of a terrible sea monster, and the act ends with the chorus fleeing in all directions.

38. Beethoven: Fidelio. Act II, opening.   25 min

This is the dungeon scene, the musical and dramatic crux of the opera. It opens with Florestan lamenting his state and his dreams of lost happiness with Léonora (aria 74 in chapter 9). Léonora, still disguised as a man, first offers him food and then defies Pizarro, the prison governor who has come to murder him. The scene ends with a swift duet between the husband and wife, now reunited. Quintessential Beethoven at the height of his powers.

39. Stravinsky: The Rake's Progress. Act I, Scene I (end) and Scene 2.   18 min

Set back-to-back, these scenes show two different aspects of Stravinsky's response to the eighteenth century. Start with the little *duettino* "Farewell for now," which uses minuet music to evoke a pastoral Eden of another age. Then Tom is plunged into the London of Hogarth, with its raucous chorus of Roaring Boys and Whores, and the grotesque scene in the brothel of Mother Goose. The final chorus, "Lanter-loo," somehow combines the two elements, like the echoes of an almost-forgotten nursery song which, like childhood itself, is a thing of the past. Another entry from the Twentieth-century European Package.

40. Verdi: A Masked Ball. Act II, complete.   24–30 min

The act begins with Amelia by the gallows at midnight, but we might tune in with the entrance of the king, Riccardo, which triggers a magnificent love duet. This turns into a trio when Amelia's husband, Renato, enters to warn the King of the approaching conspirators. Renato at this time doesn't know that the woman with the King is Amelia. When she drops her mask in an effort to save him, everyone laughs at him for being part of his own wife's infidelity. The Verdi "tinto" here is passionate and grotesque at the same time, and this act contains an unbroken succession of brilliant music.

41. Smetana: The Bartered Bride. Act II, opening.   20 min

Almost any part of the tuneful *Bartered Bride* is introduction enough to the complete work. This excerpt has a drinking chorus, the famous "furiant" dance, Vašek's aria, and a duet between Vašek and Mařenka—a good cross section of a glorious opera.

42. Saint-Saëns: Samson et Dalila. Act II, Scene 3.   20 min

Dalila finally seduces Samson in the midst of a hot summer thunderstorm. The scene contains dramatic music for both voices and Dalila's main aria, "Mon coeur s'ouvre à ta voix" (aria 50 in chapter 9), one often found in recordings of opera's major mezzo arias.

43. Massenet: Manon. Act III, Scene 2.   20 min

In this church scene, Manon persuades Des Grieux to take her back and abandon his intention to take holy orders. After a chorus, the scene contains three fine arias, one for Des Grieux's father, one for Des Grieux, and one for Manon. These culminate in a long love duet between Des Grieux and Manon. *Manon* is one of several operas in which Massenet deals with the conflict between sex and religion, a theme that makes for powerful theater.

44. *Humperdinck:* **Hänsel und Gretel.** *Act III,* *opening.* *12 min*

An opera filled with delightful music, so there are many possible choices here. An especially lyric one is the opening of Act III. After the Dew Fairy's song, Gretel wakes up, sings happily to the birds, and awakens Hänsel by tickling him. As they talk they find they have dreamed the same thing. The scene changes magically, and the gingerbread house appears. The children love this and dance a joyous waltz. The Witch appears. The hunk can end here or continue to the end.

45. *Janáček:* **Jenůfa.** *Act I, central portion.* *12 min*

Start with the entrance of Števa and the army recruits. Števa, the good-for-nothing father of Jenůfa's unborn child, is drunk. The scene quickly works up to a raucous dance. In some ways it is similar to the dances in fellow Czech Smetana's *Bartered Bride*, but that is one of the happiest of operas and the music here is frenetic and ominous.

46. *Richard Strauss:* **Elektra.** *Final scene.* *20 min*

A good starting place is when Elektra recognizes her brother Orestes, crying "Orest! Orest!" Then fasten your seat belt. In rapid-fire order come the murder of their mother, Clytemnestra; the entrance of her husband, Aegisthus and his murder, and Elektra's wild dance of triumph—so wild that she drops dead at its end. In many ways the scene is similar to the finale of Strauss's *Salome*, although it is less sensuous (almost everything in opera is less sensuous than this) and requires bigger singing. *Salome* is more decadent in mood, *Elektra* more gut-check primitive.

47. *Berg:* **Wozzeck.** *Act III, Scene 4, Interlude, and Scene 5.* *12 min*

Wozzeck has stabbed his mistress, Marie, and is half crazed with guilt. He goes to find the murder weapon in the forest pool where he has thrown it. Seeing the moon rise red, he imagines himself covered with blood, enters the water to wash it off, and drowns. The Captain and the Doctor, passing by, think they hear someone calling for help but do nothing about it. There's then a huge orchestral interlude designed to release all the opera's pent-up passion. In the final scene, a group of children run off to see the body in the woods. Marie's child, not knowing what's going on, follows on his hobbyhorse. (Another good excerpt is Act I, Scene 3, where Marie first sees the Drum Major, who will seduce her, and then sings a lullaby to her child.)

48. *Puccini:* **Turandot.** *Act I, invocation to the moon.*   *10–30 min*

The chorus is the big star of the first act. For a longer excerpt, start at the beginning of the act; for a shorter one, at the famous invocation to the moon "Perchè tarda la luna?" as the crowd waits for the moon to rise in order to witness the execution of Turandot's latest suitor. The rest of the act deals with Calaf's determination to woo Turandot despite the taunts of a trio of courtiers, the arguments of his old father, and the prayers of Liù, his faithful maid servant. Liù's "Signore, ascolta" and Calaf's reply, "Non piangere, Liù," close the act with two hit arias.

49. *Monteverði:* **Orfeo.** *Act II, opening.*   *10+ min*

The act opens (much as does Purcell's *Dido and Aeneas,* below) with a succession of relatively brief solos, recitatives, and choruses leading up to an animated song for Orfeo, "Vi ricorda, e boschi ombrosi." The mood changes with the arrival of the Messenger, who delivers the news of Euridice's death in powerful recitative. This type of recitative was to become the mainstay of Monteverdi's *Coronation of Poppea,* written thirty-five years later. In *Orfeo* it's a sound idea to have a libretto on hand, especially from this point on.

50. *Monteverði:* **The Coronation of Poppea.** *The last four scenes.*   *20 min*

Although Monteverdi's *Orfeo* is in The Collection, his *Poppea*—written much later—is the favorite of the musicologists today. Begin the hunk with the entrance of Poppea after the exit of Ottone and Drusilla. Then comes a sensuous intertwining of several actions: Poppea's love duet with Nerone; Empress Ottavia's heartbreaking farewell to Rome, "Addio, Roma," after she has been banished, and the pageantry of the coronation scene itself, which ends with a second love duet, "Pur ti miro," which Professor Brunyate calls one of the most ravishing ever written.

51. *Purcell:* **Dido and Aeneas.** *Act I, complete.*   *20 min*

Dido is characterized by a pattern of short choruses, recitatives, arias, and dances. The scene begins with Belinda's attempt to console the melancholy Dido, who sings "Ah! Belinda, I am prest with torment," a preview of her showstopping and famous "Lament" that comes in the last act (aria 47 in chapter 9). The courtiers persuade her to accept the hand of Aeneas, who enters to a lively duet and chorus, "Fear no danger to ensue." The act ends with another chorus and another dance, this time one of rejoicing. Although this is a superb hunk, don't miss the Act III Lament.

52. *Gluck:* **Orfeo ed Euridice.** *Act III, complete.*   *25 min*

In this, the opera's main action, Orfeo leads Euridice out of Hades, only to give in to her pleading, turning to look at her, and so losing her once more. It includes Orfeo's great lament, "Che farò senza Euridice?," one of opera's most famous arias. This is followed by a final trio in which Amor brings off a happy ending. These numbers are linked by long but very expressive recitative.

53. *Weber:* **Der Freischütz.** *Act II, Scene 2.*   *15 min*

The pioneering German Romantic opera in which the yen for the supernatural is illustrated in the macabre Wolf's Glen scene in which Kaspar, aided by the devil Samiel, casts his seven magic bullets. This spectacular scene was the beginning of a century and a half of supernatural music. If you persist in not liking opera, this is another good one to avoid.

54. *Tchaikovsky:* **Eugene Onegin.** *Act I, Scene 1.*   *15–30 min*

This opening is chosen over other hunk candidates because it captures the atmosphere of Russian rural life. It consists of the prelude, a quartet for women, the chorus and dance of the reapers and an aria for Olga. The shorter fifteen-minute segment would omit these and start with the quartet that follows the entrance of Lensky and Onegin and the interwoven conversations (including a Lensky aria) as the two couples stroll around the garden. Roger Brunyate points out that this gives an effect of "cross-cutting" that anticipates the techniques of filmmaking. Other great hunks include Tatiana's great "Letter Scene" (Act I, Scene 2) and two ball scenes (Act II, Scene 1, and Act III, Scene 1).

55. *Bartók:* **Duke Bluebeard's Castle.**
The final part.   *12–25 min*

The action centers around the opening of the seven closed doors in the castle. The most beautiful music comes as the seventh door is opened, revealing Bluebeard's former wives, and his lament as his new bride goes in to join them and the door closes behind her. To set the scene for this, tune in earlier, perhaps with the fifth door, to get used to the rhythm of the Hungarian language that fascinated Bartók.

56. *Janáček:* **The Cunning Little Vixen.** *Act I.*   *25 min*

Another opera from the Twentieth-century European Package, supplementing Janáček's Collection *Jenůfa*. If it were less difficult to do, one might pluck out each of the orchestral interludes and string them together to get the best taste of Janáček. But a more feasible approach is to take on the entire first act. Begin with the prelude and the first scene, which establish the atmosphere of the forest. The scene ends with the Forester capturing the little Vixen and taking her home to his children, who appear after another orchestral interlude. The second scene, hard to follow, contains more action, but it has still another long orchestral interlude, perhaps the loveliest single passage in the opera.

57. *Ravel:* **L'enfant et les sortilèges.** *End of Scene 1.*   *20 min*

This is in the Twentieth-century European Package, although—as it is a one-act work, not regularly performed in the major houses—not in The

Collection. A starting point is the chorus of wallpaper shepherds and shepherdesses that the naughty Child has ripped from the wall. This is followed by a duet with the Princess from the storybook the Child has defaced; his lovely aria "Toi, le coeur de la rose," in which he becomes aware of his loss; a nightmare arithmetic lesson; and a love duet between the two cats.

58. *Schoenberg:* Moses und Aron. *Act I, scene 1.* 8 min; *scene 2.* 7 min. Act II. 9 min

Perhaps the best sense of the special flavor of "Moses und Aron" can be captured by listening to the first two scenes. In the opening, with Moses at the Burning Bush, the voice of God is depicted as a layered tissue of sound. Six solo voices sing the words slowly, creating a musical halo within which other voices sing the same phrases more quickly and still others speak or whisper the words. The musical layering continues into the next scene where Moses' strong patriarchal "Sprechstimme" (pitched speech) is contrasted with the elegant tenor lyricism of his brother Aaron. The great show-stopper, on stage or in a video, is the Worship of the Golden Calf in Act II—a solemn ritual of sacrificial slaughter that turns into a wild orgy of drunken sex. But the music is highly complex and emphasizes spiritual emptiness rather than carnal satisfaction. Listeners wanting a preview might pick up earlier at the sacrifice of the Four Naked Virgins (the score reads: "Naked to the extent that the rules and necessities of the stage allow and require") and carry on to the wrathful arrival of Moses.

59. *Gershwin:* Porgy and Bess. *Opening scene.* 14 min

Not in The Collection but the prime opera in the American twentieth-century anthology. Although the opening contains none of the high drama that will come later, it gives a masterly picture of life on Catfish Row. Three separate strands are introduced: Jasbo Brown's piano blues, the well-known "Summertime," and the men's crap game. All are then combined at the end of this lengthy introduction.

60. *Britten:* The Turn of the Screw. *Act I, Scenes 6–8.* 20 min

Based on a ghost story by Henry James, this work from the Twentieth-century European Package features a young Governess who comes to believe that her two charges, Miles and Flora, are under the control of the ghosts of the former valet and governess. Orchestral interludes separate all the scenes. Begin the excerpt with variation five—a fugue, in musical construction—and hear how a sinister atmosphere overtakes first Miles's schoolroom lessons and then Flora's games by the lake. In Scene 8, the ghosts make their appearance, first in eerie wordless incantations and then in cascades of glittering images that lead the children from their beds and out into the night.

INDEX

Pal Joey (Rodgers and Hart), 571–72, 591

Paris Opéra, 25, 42, 51, 60, 62, 109, 599

Parsifal (Wagner), 25, 62, 73, 133–34, 140, 146, 155–58, 250, 445, 603

Pasero, Tancredi, 638

passions, 20, 53

Pasta, Giuditta, 626

Patti, Adelina, 626

Pavarotti, Luciano, xx, 606–7, 638–39

Pears, Peter, 410, 412–13

Pêcheurs de perles, Les (The Pearl Fishers) (Bizet), 73, 110, 115

Pelléas et Mélisande (Debussy), xxiii–xxiv, 22, 31, 71–72, 239, 283–89, 442, 451, 467, 597, 607, 658

Penderecki, Krzysztof, 542–43

Peter Grimes (Britten), 71–72, 408–13, 532–33, 656

Piave, Francesco Maria, 245–46, 248, 361, 386–87, 395, 397

Picker, Tobias, 589

Pinza, Ezio, 639

Pique Dame (The Queen of Spades) (Tchaikovsky), 228, 398–99, 402–8, 627

polyphonic music, 35–36

polyphony, homophony vs., 35

Ponchielli, Amilcare, 16, 57, 98, 228, 274, 634

Collection opera of, 297–301

in history of opera, 54, 57

Verdi and, 387

violence in, 450

Pons, Lily, 385–86, 626

Ponselle, Rosa, 626–27

Porgy and Bess (Gershwin), xviii, 5, 478, 498, 561, 563–68, 572–73, 590–91, 666

Postcard from Morocco (Argento), 584–85, 590

Poulenc, Francis, xvii, 5, 73, 536–38, 540

preludes, 29

Price, Leontyne, 593, 596, 627

Prince Igor (Borodin), 69, 228, 401, 435–38

Prinz von Homburg, Der (Henze), 73, 538–39

Prokofiev, Serge, 509–11

prophète, Le (Meyerbeer), 60, 116, 352, 355, 421

Puccini, Giacomo, xviii, xxiii, 16, 22, 26–28, 93–108, 238, 363, 408, 469, 498, 509, 515, 520–21, 534, 540, 546, 570, 604–5, 620, 643, 646–47

arias of, xx, 97–100, 103–4, 106–7, 260–61, 304, 318, 359, 611–13, 615–16, 618

background of, 98

Bellini and, 374

Berlioz and, 341

bleeding hunks of, 655, 658, 661, 664

Britten and, 408

Charpentier and, 440

chronological order of operas of, 97–98

Collection operas of, 95–108, 258–62, 301–5, 316–19, 356–61

Donizetti and, 365, 368

in history of opera, 54–55, 57, 69–70, 72–73

Humperdinck and, 250

Leoncavallo and, 125–27, 258–59

Mascagni and, 174, 177, 258–59

Massenet and, 98, 241–42, 244–45, 258–59, 261

Mozart and, 95, 97–98, 189

Ponchielli and, 298–99

Rossini and, 214

Photo Credits

© Phillip Norton

About the Author

PHIL G. GOULDING was never professionally trained in classical music, which made him the perfect author for this book. He was a Washington newspaper reporter, an assistant secretary of defense, a petroleum industry executive, and the author of *Classical Music* and *Confirm or Deny*, a book about the Pentagon, the press, and the public.

Who are the ten most important classical composers?

Who in the world was Palestrina?

Why did Stravinsky's "Rite of Spring" cause a riot?

*Which five of each important composer's
works should you buy?*

What is a concerto and how does it differ from a sonata?

Discover the answers with this fun and informative
book by Phil G. Goulding

CLASSICAL MUSIC
The 50 Greatest Composers and
Their 1,000 Greatest Works

"Amusingly irreverent . . .
Goulding gets top marks for user-friendly style,
giving heavily anecdotal accounts of the composers' lives, lots of
fun trivia . . . and easy-access text."
—*The Seattle Times*

"This book uses every conceivable
gimmick to immerse readers in the richness of
classical music: lists, rankings, sidebars devoted to lively
anecdotes, and catchy leads."
—*The Washington Post*